lonely p

D0454068

Egypt
WITHDRAWN

Alexandria & the
Mediterranean Coast
p305

Cairo
Outskirts
& the Delta
p141

Suez
Canal
p340

Sinai
p373

Cairo
p54

Northern
Nile Valley
p182

Siwa Oasis &
the Western Desert
p266

Luxor p182

Red Sea
Coast
p350

Southern
Nile Valley
p229

Jessica Lee, Anthony Sattin

Contents

KITESURFING P354

BIBLIOTECA ALEXANDRINA
P314

4FR/GETTY IMAGES ©

REPINA VALERIYA/SHUTTERSTOCK ©

Contents

Welcome to Egypt

Egypt welcomes you with its mighty Nile and magnificent monuments, the beguiling desert and lush delta, and with its long past and welcoming, story-loving people.

Pyramids & More

With sand-covered tombs, austere pyramids and towering Pharaonic temples, Egypt brings out the explorer in all of us. Visit the Valley of the Kings in Luxor, where Tutankhamun's tomb was unearthed, and see the glittering finds in the Egyptian Museum in Cairo. Hop off a Nile boat to visit Dendara, Edfu or one of the other waterside temples, cross Lake Nasser to see Ramses II's masterpiece at Abu Simbel, or trek into the desert to find the traces of Roman trading outposts. You never know – your donkey might stumble across yet another find, for that is the way many previous discoveries were made.

Beaches & Beyond

That empty beach with nothing but a candle-lit cabin, and a teeming coral reef offshore: they're waiting for you in Egypt. The coast along the Red Sea has a rugged desert beauty above the waterline and a psychedelic vibrancy below – rewarding to explore on a multiday outing to one of the globe's great dives or on an afternoon's snorkelling jaunt along a coral wall. There is even more space and just as much beauty in Egypt's vast deserts. Whether you're watching the sun rise between the beautiful shapes of the White Desert or the shimmering horizon from the comfort of a hot spring in Siwa Oasis, Egypt's landscapes are endlessly fascinating.

Going with the Flow

The old saying that Egypt is the gift of the Nile still rings true: without the river there would be no fertile land, no food and a lot less electricity. Although people's lives are increasingly physically detached from the water, the Nile still exerts a uniquely powerful role. Luckily for visitors, the river is also the perfect place from which to see many of the most spectacular ancient monuments, which is one reason why a Nile cruise remains such a popular way to travel.

Two Religions

Egypt once ruled an empire from Al Qahira – Cairo, the City Victorious. The metropolis is packed with soaring minarets and medieval schools and mosques, some of the greatest architecture of medieval Islam. At the same time, Egypt's native Christians, the Copts, have carried on their traditions that in many respects – such as the church's liturgical language and the traditional calendar – link back to the time of the pharaohs. Tap into the history in Cairo's early churches and in remote desert monasteries.

Why I Love Egypt

By Anthony Sattin, Writer

Is it the way the glorious past casts long shadows over the present? Is it the way the lush Nile Valley gives way, from one footstep to another, to the harshness of the desert? Or is it the glint in the eye of someone telling me stories in a cafe? Depth of history, intensity of sunlight, love of life and sense of family: these are some of the many reasons I love this country. But there is also this fact: however much I see and hear and know, there is always more discover.

For more about our writers, see p512

Above: Valley of the Kings (p200)

Egypt

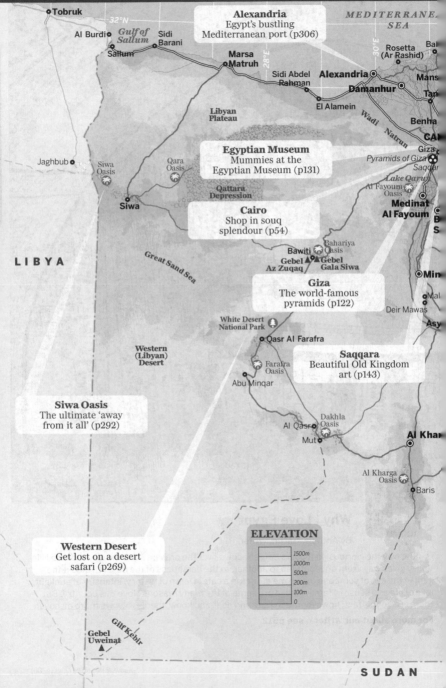

Alexandria
Egypt's bustling
Mediterranean port (p306)

Egyptian Museum
Mummies at the
Egyptian Museum (p131)

Cairo
Shop in souq
splendour (p54)

Giza
The world-famous
pyramids (p122)

Saqqara
Beautiful Old Kingdom
art (p143)

Siwa Oasis
The ultimate 'away
from it all' (p292)

Western Desert
Get lost on a desert
safari (p269)

MEDITERRANEAN
SEA

LIBYA

SUDAN

Gulf of
Sallum

Libyan
Plateau

Qattara
Depression

Great Sand Sea

Western
(Libyan)
Desert

White Desert
National Park

ELEVATION

1500m
1000m
500m
200m
100m
0

Tobruk
Al Burdi
Sidi
Barani
Sallum
Marsa
Matruh
Sidi Abdel
Rahman
El Alamein
Rosetta
(Ar Rashid)
Bal
Alexandria
Damanhur
Mans
Tan
Benha
CAI
Giza
Pyramids of Giza
Saqqar
Lake Qaru
Al Fayoum
Oasis
Medinat
Al Fayoum
C
B
S
Min
Mal
Deir Mawas
Asy
Al Khar
Baris

Jaghbub
Siwa
Oasis
Qara
Oasis
Siwa

Bawiti
Gebel
Az Zuqaq
Gebel
Gala Siwa
Bahariya
Oasis

Qasr Al Farafra
Farafra
Oasis
Abu Minqar

Al Qasr
Mut
Dakhla
Oasis

Al Kharga
Oasis

Gebel
Uweinat
Gilf Kebir

Wadi Natrun

32°N

28°E

30°E

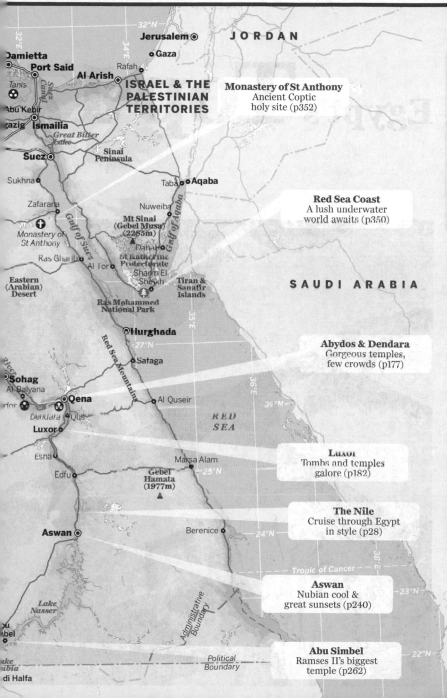

Monastery of St Anthony
Ancient Coptic
holy site (p352)

Red Sea Coast
A lush underwater
world awaits (p350)

Abydos & Dendara
Gorgeous temples,
few crowds (p177)

Luxor
Tombs and temples
galore (p182)

The Nile
Cruise through Egypt
in style (p28)

Aswan
Nubian cool &
great sunsets (p240)

Abu Simbel
Ramses II's biggest
temple (p262)

Egypt's Top 17

Luxor

1 With the greatest concentration of ancient monuments in Egypt, Luxor (p182) is somewhere you could spend weeks visiting, although most visitors stay for only a day or two. However long you have, be sure to walk through the columned halls of the great temple complexes of Luxor and Karnak on the east bank of the Nile, or climb into the tombs of pharaohs, queens, courtiers and workmen in the Theban hills on the west bank. Watching the sun rise over the Nile or set behind the Theban hills are some of Egypt's unforgettable moments. Below left: Karnak, Luxor (p185)

Pyramids of Giza

2 The Pyramids of Giza (p122) are at the top of most travel itineraries and for good reason. However familiar the image of the only surviving wonder of the ancient world, the pyramids remain both awesome to see and fascinating to visit. While archaeologists continue to debate exactly how and why the millions of blocks were hauled into place, visitors tend to marvel at the size of each block, which is only fully appreciated when you stand beside one. For a panoramic view of the three pyramids with all of Cairo as a background, head for the cliff beyond the third pyramid.

IFAKLISHAKGULIDZE/SHUTTERSTOCK ©

MKR-BRODKIN PHOTOGRAPHY/GETTY IMAGES ©

Cruising the Nile

3 The Nile (p28) is Egypt's lifeline, the artery that runs through the entire country, from south to north. Only by being adrift on it can you appreciate its importance and its beauty and, more practically, only by boat can you see some archaeological sites as they were meant to be seen. Sailing is by far the slowest and most relaxing way to go, especially on a dahabiyya (houseboat), but even from the deck of a multi-storey floating hotel you're likely to glimpse the magic.

Cairo's Quiet Mosques

4 The tranquil, shady arcades of a medieval mosque are perfect for taking a break from the modern world. Far from being sites places of worship, many mosques function as peaceful places in an increasingly noisy city as well as being prayer halls: many Cairenes drop in for a quiet chat or an afternoon nap. While some mosques bustle with theological students and others have become national monuments, the Mosque-Madrassa of Sultan Hassan (below; p82) is a medieval monument, working mosque and architectural wonder. Kick your shoes off, sit down and stay a while.

3

4

NICHOLAS PITT/GETTY IMAGES ©

NICHOLAS PITT/GETTY IMAGES ©

Abu Simbel

5 Ramses II built Abu Simbel (p263) a long way south of Aswan, along his furthest frontier and just beyond the Tropic of Cancer. But these two impressive temples are a marvel of modern engineering: in the 1960s they were relocated, block by block, to their current site to protect them from the flooding of Lake Nasser. To appreciate the isolation, spend the night at Abu Simbel, either on a boat on the lake or at Nubian cultural centre and ecolodge Eskaleh.

Red Sea Diving

6 Egypt's Red Sea coastlines (p350) are the doorstep to a wonderland that hides below the surface. Whether you're a seasoned diver or a first-timer, Egypt's underwater world of coral cliffs, colourful fish and spookily beautiful wrecks is just as staggeringly impressive as the sights above. Bring out your inner Jacques Cousteau by exploring the enigmatic wreck of WWII cargo ship the *Thistlegorm*, a fascinating museum spread across the sea bed. Even if diving isn't your thing, with a mask and snorkel it is still possible to see some of this beautiful underwater world.

Aswan Sunset

7 Watch the sun set over Aswan (p240), frontier of the ancient Egyptian empire and southernmost outpost for the Romans. It's still the gateway to Nubia, where cultures blend to create a laid-back place that values time to enjoy the view. There is something about the way the river is squeezed between rocks, the proximity of the desert, the lonely burial places of the Aga Khan and of forgotten ancient princes that makes the end of the day more poignant here than anywhere else along the Egyptian Nile.

SENDERISTAS/SHUTTERSTOCK ©

Coptic Sites

8 It was to the barren mountains and jagged cliffs of the sprawling desert that the first early ascetics came. Today Coptic monasteries such as those of St Anthony (above; p352) and St Paul (p353), where the tradition of Christian monasticism began, play an increasingly important role in the modern Coptic faith, especially with so much pressure on their communities along the Nile. Visit Wadi Natrun, or walk on the walls of St Anthony's, and ponder the impressive faith that took men away from the ease of the towns and into the wilderness.

Egyptian Museum

9 The scale of the Egyptian Museum (p131) is so overwhelming that, if you have the time, we recommend at least two visits. The vast rooms are packed to the rafters with some of the world's most fascinating treasures: glittering gold jewellery, King Tut's socks and mummies of the greatest pharaohs. After taking in the highlights, go back a second time and wander through the less-visited rooms, looking for alabaster offering tables, life-size wood statues, scale models of armies, farms and ships, and even mummified pets – everything the ancients hoped would accompany them to the second life.

Old Kingdom Art

10 The walls of the tombs around the Step Pyramid of Saqqara (p144) are adorned with some of the world's oldest art works. The exquisite painted reliefs in the Mastaba of Ti (p148) or the tomb of Kagemni (p148) give a subtle and most detailed account of daily life in the third millennium BC. The first rooms in the Egyptian Museum (p131) show the most brilliant Old Kingdom art. Looking at these masterpieces is essential to understand artistic development in the thousands of years that follow.

Siwa Oasis

11 The grandest and most remote of Egypt's Western Desert oases, Siwa (p292) on the edge of the Great Sand Sea offers the ultimate oasis experience. This is not only where Alexander the Great came to consult the oracle of the gods, it is also the perfect place to hang out and relax after travelling along the Nile. Cycle through huge palm groves, take a desert tour to hot and cold water springs and lakes, or slide down the inclines in the many dunes. Below top: Fatnas, Lake Siwa (p296)

Western Desert Safaris

12 You need only travel for a couple of hours into the desert, by 4WD, camel or foot, to be able to savour the simple beauty and sheer isolation of wildest Egypt. Highlights of an excursion into Egypt's Western Desert (p269) include camping under a star-studded sky among the surreal formations of the White Desert, heading into the mesmerising dunes of the Great Sand Sea, and deep desert excursions, such as living out *The English Patient* fantasies at the remote Gilf Kebir.

Alexandria

13 Flaunting the pedigree of Alexander the Great and powerful queen Cleopatra, Egypt's second-largest city (p306) is rich in history, both ancient and modern. Visit the Bibliotheca Alexandrina, the new incarnation of the ancient Great Library, or any number of great small museums around town. Walk the souqs of atmospheric Anfushi, the oldest part of the city, or hunt for dusty antiques in Attareen. Above all, be sure to stop on the corniche or head along the coast to feast on fresh seafood with a Mediterranean view. Below top: Fort Qaitbey, Alexandria (p313)

Souqs

14 The incessant salesmanship of Egyptians makes more sense when you see it at work in one of the country's many souqs. Here vendors are set up cheek by jowl, all hawking their wares in their set district, cajoling and haggling. Visit a centuries-old souq such as Khan Al Khalili (p70) first, and you'll see its pattern at work everywhere, even in ad hoc modern markets set up near the main tourist sights. Along the way, pick up rusty antiques, lovely Egyptian cotton, King Tut kitsch...or even a donkey.

AARSTUDIO/GETTY IMAGES ©

PAUL PRESCOTT/SHUTTERSTOCK ©

Abydos

15 Time is short and everyone wants to see the Pyramids, Tutankhamun's gold and the Valley of the Kings. But some of the most rewarding moments in Egypt are to be had away from the crowds at the less-visited monuments, where you can contemplate the ancients' legacy in peace. Nowhere is this more true than at Abydos (p177), an important place of pilgrimage for ancient Egyptians and home to some of the most beautiful wall carvings. It's north of Luxor – the opposite direction from the tour buses. Above left: Wall carvings, Temples of Ramses II, Abydos (p179)

Bahariya Oasis

16 It's impossible not to relax in an oasis: after all, this was what inspired the idea of paradise, something you will appreciate as, with the endless desert shimmering on the horizon, you float in hot springs or explore the remains of ancient Roman outposts and dusty villages. Even in Bahariya (p286), the most easily accessible oasis from Cairo, you can soak in hot or cold springs in the shade of lush date palms, drive out into the White Desert, or visit the museum to see the latest ancient finds: the golden mummies.

Ahwas

17 Though the *ahwa* gets its name from the Arabic word for coffee, *shai* (tea) is much more common at the traditional cafe that is a major centre of Egyptian social life. With your drink on a tiny tin-top table, a backgammon board in front of you and perhaps a bubbling shisha (water pipe) to one side, you'll slip right into the local groove. These days, *ahwas* can be a series of tables in old-city alleys, such as Fishawi's (p109) in Cairo, or a chic lounge serving a range of flavoured tobaccos.

Need to Know

For more information, see Survival Guide (p471)

Currency
Egyptian pound (LE)

Language
Arabic

Visas
Single-entry, 30-day tourist visas cost US$25. Egypt launched e-visas in 2017. Many nationalities can now purchase visas online at www.egyptvisa.com. Otherwise, available at the airport on arrival.

Money
ATMs are widely available. Credit cards are increasingly widely accepted. There is a major shortage of small change; large bills can be difficult to break.

Mobile Phones
Egypt's GSM network has thorough coverage. Bring your passport when purchasing a local SIM card (LE15). Pay-as-you-go data service costs about LE5 per day or LE50 per month.

Time
GMT/UTC plus two hours

When to Go

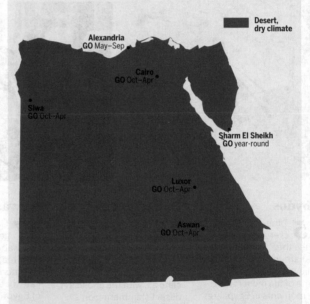

Desert, dry climate

Alexandria
GO May–Sep

Cairo
GO Oct–Apr

Siwa
GO Oct–Apr

Sharm El Sheikh
GO year-round

Luxor
GO Oct–Apr

Aswan
GO Oct–Apr

High Season
(Oct–Feb)

➡ Egypt's 'winter' is largely sunny and warm, with very occasional rain (more frequent on the Mediterranean).

➡ Be prepared for real chill in unheated hotels, especially in damp Alexandria.

Shoulder
(Mar & May, Sep & Oct)

➡ Spring brings occasional dust storms disrupting flights.

➡ Heat can extend into October, when crowds are lighter.

➡ Warm seas and no crowds at Mediterranean spots in autumn.

Low Season
(Jun–Aug)

➡ Scorching summer sun means only the hardiest sightseers visit Upper Egypt.

➡ Avoid the Western Desert.

➡ High season on the Mediterranean when the weather is cooler than elsewhere; the coast is crowded.

Useful Websites

Egypt Tourism (www.egypt. travel) Official tourism site with trip-planning tools.

Daily News Egypt (www.daily newsegypt.com) Independent English newspaper.

Mada Masr (www.madamasr. com) Independent, progressive online reporting in English.

Egypt Independent (www. egyptindependent.com) Respected online news.

Egyptian Streets (www.egypt ianstreets.com) Independent features.

Lonely Planet (www.lonely planet.com/egypt) Destination information, hotel bookings and traveller forum.

Important Numbers

Drop 0 from the area code when dialling from abroad.

Country code	☑20
International access code	☑00
Ambulance	☑123
Fire	☑180
Tourist police	☑126

Exchange Rates

Australia	A$1	LE13.64
Canada	C$1	LE13.74
Euro	€1	LE21.52
Israel & the Palestinian Territories	1NIS	LE5.08
Japan	¥100	LE16.55
Jordan	JD1	LE24.89
New Zealand	NZ$1	LE12.69
UK	£1	LE24.26
USA	US$1	LE17.65

For current exchange rates, see www.xe.com.

Daily Costs

Budget: Less than LE600

➡ Basic double room: LE170

➡ Falafel sandwich: LE2.50

➡ Cairo–Luxor 1st-class train ticket: LE113–203

Midrange: LE600–1800

➡ Midrange double air-con room: US$30

➡ Two sit-down meals: LE120

➡ Flight from Cairo to Luxor: from LE650

Top end: More than LE1800

➡ Luxury hotel room: US$150

➡ Two sit-down meals: LE300

➡ High-end Nile cruise: from US$175 per person per night

Opening Hours

The weekend is Friday and Saturday; some businesses close Sunday. During Ramadan, offices, museums and tourist sites keep shorter hours.

Banks 8.30am–2.30pm Sunday to Thursday

Bars and clubs Early evening until 3am, often later (particularly in Cairo)

Cafes 7am–1am

Government offices 8am–2pm Sunday to Thursday; tourist offices are generally open longer

Post offices 8.30am–2pm Saturday to Thursday

Private offices 10am–2pm and 4pm–9pm Saturday to Thursday

Restaurants Noon–midnight

Shops 9am–1pm and 5pm–10pm June to September, 10am–6pm October to May; in Cairo shops generally open 10am–11pm

Arriving in Egypt

Cairo International Airport Pre-arrange taxi pickup (around LE150) or bargain on arrival (LE120); 30 minutes to one hour to Downtown. Buses LE4; up to two hours to Downtown.

Hurghada Airport Pre-arranged pickup recommended. Hard bargaining required for airport taxi; ideally LE35 to central Sigala district.

Sharm El Sheikh Airport Taxi drivers will rarely drop below LE100 to Na'ama Bay. Pre-arranged pickup recommended.

Luxor Airport Most hotel airport transfers are preferable to having to haggle with taxi drivers at the airport.

Getting Around

Transport in Egypt is fairly efficient and very reasonably priced. Be aware that because of security concerns, some areas and transport modes are or may become off limits to foreign travellers.

Air Most domestic flights go through Cairo. When using EgyptAir's website, switch your home location to Egypt to get the cheapest domestic fares.

Train The most comfortable option for travelling to Alexandria, Luxor and Aswan. The two classes of trains – Spanish and the more expensive Special – both have air-con 1st and 2nd-class seats.

Bus There are frequent buses between Egyptian cities. Buses are comfortable and reliable. Book in advance.

Car Cars with driver are readily available and reasonably priced.

For much more on **getting around**, see p489

PLAN YOUR TRIP NEED TO KNOW

First Time Egypt

For more information, see Survival Guide (p471)

Checklist

➡ Ensure your passport is valid for a minimum of eight months.

➡ Check your country's foreign office advisory before booking your airline ticket.

➡ Organise travel insurance that includes medical cover.

➡ Inform your credit/debit card company of your travels before you leave home.

➡ Check if you can use your mobile abroad.

➡ Book accommodation and domestic flights.

What to Pack

➡ Hat, sunglasses and a good sunscreen

➡ Two-pin electrical adaptor to recharge gadgets

➡ Good mosquito protection

➡ A mobile phone compatible with an Egyptian SIM

➡ Patience to cope with a different concept of time

Top Tips for Your Trip

➡ Visit during the shoulder season (spring and autumn) when the weather is less extreme and there are fewer visitors around.

➡ Learn a few words in Arabic – greetings and 'thank you' are the obvious ones – and you'll get a laugh or a smile from the person you are talking to. One of the highlights of the trip is meeting good-humoured Egyptians.

➡ Keep small change to hand (LE5 and LE10 notes), as it is useful to give out as much needed baksheesh (tips) just about everywhere.

➡ Start your visits early in the morning to avoid the midday heat.

➡ Rent a car with a driver rather than driving yourself. Avoid travelling on roads outside cities and towns at night, which can be particularly dangerous.

What to Wear

Egypt is a conservative country, so modest attire is recommended. Out of resort towns, women will usually feel more comfortable wearing loose clothes. There are places (mosques and churches, for instance) where arms and legs should be covered. In resort towns the dress code is more relaxed. Cotton or linen clothing is recommended for the heat, and a fleece or wool sweater is needed for the cooler nights.

The dress code in most places is fairly casual, even at night, although Cairenes do dress up to go to the hip spots in town.

Sleeping

It's generally only necessary to book your accommodation in advance if you are planning to visit during the Christmas, Easter and half-term school holidays.

Hotels Range from dusty fleapits to deluxe accommodation in the larger cities and resorts. In smaller towns accommodation is mostly limited to basic options.

B&Bs Less common in Egypt, and places that call themselves B&Bs are often small family-run one- or two-star hotels.

Safety

Although the situation in Egypt has become increasingly unstable in recent years, most of the country is calm most of the time. In the current climate, it pays to be more than usually aware so check government travel advisories before leaving home, and stay up-to-date with the latest local news while on the road. See safe travel (p472) for more.

Bargaining

Bargaining is part of life when shopping in souqs and markets. It may seem an annoyance, but it pays to see it as a game. Just follow the basic rules:

➡ Shop around to get an idea of prices.

➡ Decide how much you want to pay, and then offer a lower price than that.

➡ Don't show any excitement.

➡ Walk away if you can't agree, and the vendor will follow you if your price was right.

Tipping

Always keep small change as baksheesh is expected everywhere. When in doubt, tip.

Cafes Leave LE5 to LE10.

Guards at tourist sites LE5 to LE20.

Metered taxis Round off the fare or offer around 5% extra, depending on the ride.

Mosque attendant Leave LE5 to LE10 for shoe covers, more if you climb a minaret or have some guiding.

Restaurants For good service leave 10%; in smart places leave 15%.

DANIEL REINER/SHUTTERSTOCK ©

Fresh hummus with chickpeas

Etiquette

Egypt is a mostly conservative country, so observing the following will avoid any awkward moments:

Sacred ground Remove your shoes before entering a mosque.

Touching Don't touch someone from the opposite sex in public.

Feet Don't show the soles of your feet; it's considered disrespectful.

Hands Eat with your right hand; the left hand is used for ablutions.

Ramadan Don't eat or drink in public during the fasting month of Ramadan.

Eating

Cairo, Alexandria, Luxor and the Red Sea resort towns have a wide variety of eating options (p460). Away from the main centres, choices are more limited.

Restaurants Range from smart and expensive hotel dining, where booking ahead is essential, to canteen-style budget restaurants typically serving Egyptian kebab and stew favourites. European-style dishes can be hit and miss at budget establishments and most don't serve alcohol.

Cafes Usually open for most of the day and night, and they only serve drinks and shisha, no food.

Street food A huge part of the Egyptian food scene. Fast and fresh staples at local prices.

If You Like...

Wildlife

Along the Nile, in the lush river delta and in sprawling salt lakes, bird life flourishes. Underwater coral reefs teem with colour. Even Egypt's arid deserts host a surprising array of plants and critters.

Aswan Get up before dawn to spot squacco herons, hoopoes and more with expert birders. (p247)

Wadi Rayyan This brackish lake, not far from where the ancients worshipped crocodiles, is a lifeline for migrating birds. (p153)

Shiatta Gazelles and flamingos frolic at this salt lake in the desert west of Siwa. (p297)

Lake Nasser Take a tour with African Angler to snare some fish for dinner – or just enjoy the view. (p262)

Marsa Alam Reefs off the coast here are home to mantas, spinner dolphins and even sharks. (p367)

Islamic Architecture

Bein Al Qasreen A string of the finest buildings from the Mamluk era, now restored as an open-air museum. (p71)

Mosque of Qaitbey Trek to Cairo's not-actually-that-spooky City of the Dead to admire the most beautiful stone dome in Cairo. (p85)

Al Qasr This oasis town was built in the Ottoman era, starting in the 16th century – check out the beautifully carved lintels over doorways. (p279)

Rosetta's Ottoman Houses Try to find the secret staircase to the women's gallery in one restored residential compound, and admire the millworks at another. (p331)

Al Quseir The old Hajj port is a tumble of Ottoman-era buildings that seem lost in time. (p365)

Deserts

Seeking blissful isolation? The desert landscape in Egypt is vast and surprisingly varied. And there's just as much variety in how you can explore it.

White Desert National Park For a truly mind-bending experience, schedule your overnight trip to this eerie landscape during the full moon. (p286)

Sinai Trail Trek Egypt's first long-distance trail through wadis and vast desert plains to the rugged mountain heartland surrounding St Katherine. (p402)

Monastery of St Simeon For desert beauty without the dayslong trek, visit this Coptic site in Aswan. (p245)

Eastern Desert Once crisscrossed by ancient trade routes, with rock inscriptions, gold mines and great landscapes, now only accessible with a guide. (p370)

Markets & Shopping

Whether you're just browsing or searching for gifts for everyone on your list, Egypt's souqs are the perfect destination, with as much entertainment as anything else – not to mention more offers of tea than you could ever drink.

Khan Al Khalili Cairo's medieval trading zone is still a commercial hub – the perfect place to polish your haggling skills. (p129)

Souq Al Gomaa Get in the scrum at this weekly Cairo junk swap, and you might come out with new clothes or old taxidermy. (p112)

Oum El Dounia One-stop shop in central Cairo for the best and most-stylish Egyptian crafts. (p112)

Attareen Antique Market An Alexandrian trove, where you

can find some mid-20th-century gems. (p329)

Habiba An excellent selection of the best of Egyptian crafts. (p225)

Ancient Traces

Given Egypt's Pharaonic riches, you could find something with a story thousands of years old in any destination. These are some of the more out-of-the-way sites to add to your itinerary.

Medinat Madi You need a 4WD to get here, but the sight of sphinxes half-buried in drifting sand is exactly what archaeology buffs come to Egypt for. (p154)

Red Pyramid At Dahshur, south of Cairo, you'll likely be the only visitor to this enormous monument, making the climb inside its tunnels all the more exciting. (p149)

Deir Al Muharraq In Egyptian terms, Christianity is relatively new history – but this Coptic monastery claims the world's oldest church, from AD 60. (p173)

Traditional Arts

Fair Trade Egypt A good starting point for finding traditional Egyptian crafts. (p112)

Makan An intimate space in Cairo hosting an intense Nubian musical ritual called a *zar*. (p110)

El Dammah Theatre This traditional music space sees regular shows by Suez Canal–area artists and others. (p110)

Eskaleh This Nubian cultural centre and hotel offers guests a chance to immerse in local food and music. (p265)

Top: Lanterns for sale in Khan Al Khalili, Cairo (p70)

Bottom: St Katherine's Monastery, Sinai (p402)

Month by Month

TOP EVENTS

D-CAF, March

3alganoob, April

Ramadan, May

Eid Al Adha, August

Siyaha, October

Cairo International Film Festival, November

January

In most of Egypt, winter means balmy days, perfect for sightseeing, but chilly nights, especially in unheated hotel rooms. Alexandria and the Mediterranean coast can be a bit rainy, but otherwise precipitation is rare.

🎇 Cairo International Book Fair

Held at Nasr City Fairgrounds in Heliopolis in the last week of January and the first of February, this is one of the city's major cultural events (www.cairobookfair.org.eg). Most of the lectures and other events (and the books themselves) are in Arabic only.

🏃 Egyptian Marathon

Endurance runners take to the west bank of the Nile near Luxor, starting from in front of the Temple of Hatshepsut. The race takes place in late January or early February, followed by a half-marathon in Sharm El Sheikh in March. See the website for dates.

February

The winter chill continues, though it's the perfect time of year in the south. Tourists think so too, and Aswan and Luxor are packed, as are the beaches.

◉ Ascension of Ramses II

Takes place on 22 February. One of the two dates each year (the other is in October) when the sun penetrates the inner sanctuary of the temple at Abu Simbel to illuminate the statues of the gods within. Draws a big crowd of theorists of all kinds.

🏃 International Fishing Tournament

Held at Hurghada on the Red Sea; attended by anglers from all over the world.

March

With warmer days come winds, especially the *khamsin,* a hot southerly current that causes periodic, intense sandstorms lasting a few hours and often grounding flights. Bear this in mind when booking trips through to early May.

🎇 D-CAF

Downtown Cairo's Contemporary Arts Festival is international, multidisciplinary and great fun. It's also a wonderful way to see the often dilapidated venues in the city centre.

April

The *khamsin* carries on, but on days when it's not blowing, the air is pleasantly fresh. This is the shoulder season for tourism, and archaeological sites begin to empty out.

🎇 3alganoob

This three-day live-music event in Tondoba Bay, outside Marsa Alam, has grown into Egypt's premier music festival with a range of artists playing funk, rock, disco and rap.

Top: *Mosaher* (wake-up man) calling Muslims to prayer during Ramadan.

Bottom: Pistachio and chocolate Egyptian pastries.

Shamm Al Nassim

The Monday after Coptic Easter (29 April 2019, 20 April 2020, 3 May 2021). Meaning 'sniffing the breeze', this spring ritual came from Pharaonic tradition via the Copts. It's celebrated by all Egyptians, who picnic in parks, on riverbanks and even on traffic islands.

Moulid of Abu Al Haggag

In the third week of the Islamic month of Sha'aban (approximately 20 April 2019, 8 April 2020, 28 March 2021), this Sufi festival in Luxor offers a taste of rural religious tradition. Some villages have *moulids* (religious festivals) around the same time.

May

Ramadan

The ninth month of the Islamic calendar is dedicated to fasting by day and feasting by night. Foodies will love a visit during this time; ambitious sightseers may be frustrated. Ramadan starts 5 May 2019, 23 April 2020, 12 April 2021.

June

Egypt lets out a collective sigh of relief after school is let out and the summer holidays begin. The heat is in full force by the end of the month.

Eid Al Fitr

The feast that marks the end of Ramadan lasts three

days and, if it's possible, involves even more food than the past month put together.

August

This is a major Egyptian vacation period. Expect beach zones, especially in the Mediterranean, to be thronged. Anywhere else is so hot you can feel your eyeballs burn. Life generally takes place after sundown.

✕ Eid Al Adha

For the Feast of the Sacrifice (11 August 2019, 30 July 2020, 19 July 2021), a four-day Islamic (and national) holiday, families slaughter sheep and goats at home, even in densest Cairo. There's literally blood in the streets, and the air smells of roasting meat. In short, not for vegetarians.

September

★ Citadel Festival

Ten days of classical, traditional and orchestral Arabic music held within the Citadel and the Cairo Opera House in either August or September. See www.cairo-opera.org for schedules.

October

As the summer heat finally breaks, students head back to school and the cultural calendar revs up again, especially in Cairo. An ideal time for travelling, with manageable weather and few other visitors.

◉ Birth of Ramses

The 22nd of October is the second date in the year when the sun's rays penetrate the temple at Abu Simbel.

★ International Festival for Experimental Theatre

A long-running event held at venues all over Cairo, from standard stages to antiques shops. Shows can be hit or miss, but many are very tourist-friendly as you don't have to speak Arabic to enjoy them. See www.cdf-eg.org for the line-up.

★🔔 Moulid of Sayyed Al Badawi

In the last week of October, close to a million pilgrims throng the city of Tanta in the Nile Delta, where a 13th-century mystic founded an important Sufi order. Part family fun fair, part intense ritual, it's worth a trip if you don't mind crowds.

★🔔 Siyaha

An oasis-wide celebration of the date harvest, Siwa's annual get-together takes place around the full moon this month. Much like a *moulid*, though not as raucous, there's Sufi chanting and plenty of food.

November

With a light chill in the air, restaurants start serving up heartier stews, while visitors start trickling in to enjoy ruins and beaches at a moderate temperature.

☆ Cairo International Film Festival

This prestigious festival, held in November/December, shows a vast range of Arab and international films. Unusually for Egypt, screenings are uncensored. Tickets to more controversial and risqué movies tend to sell out fastest. Schedules at www.ciff.org.eg.

★🔔 Moulid An Nabi

Prophet Mohammed's birthday is a nationwide celebration with sweets and new clothes for kids. In Cairo, the week before is an intense Sufi scene at Midan Al Hussein.

December

Not much is on the calendar in Egypt, but this is when winter tourism begins to peak, as visitors flood in for winter sun and sightseeing. There's a surprising amount of Santa Claus kitsch to be seen.

★🔔 International Cairo Biennale

This fairly conservative government-sponsored show (www.cairobiennale.gov.eg) doesn't fully reflect the contemporary Egyptian art scene, but it's worth checking out, although its future looks precarious. It should open late December.

Itineraries

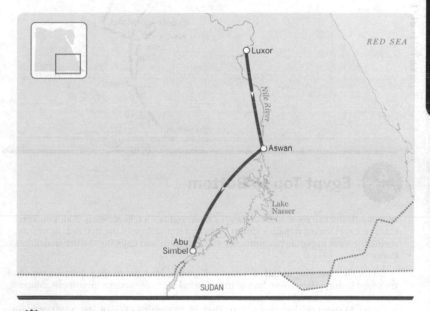

 **Treasures of the Nile**

Many visitors now skip Cairo and fly direct to Luxor, the world's largest open-air museum. There's plenty to keep you busy here before spending a few days cruising the Nile, which is definitely the most relaxed way to see Egypt.

In **Luxor** spend two days on the east bank visiting **Karnak** and **Luxor Temple** and the brilliant **Luxor Museum**, as well as strolling through the souq. The next few days cycle around the west bank of the Nile where the major sights include the **Valley of the Kings**, the **Ramesseum** and the **Memorial Temple of Hatshepsut**. Try to save some energy for less-visited sights, such as **Medinat Habu**, the **Tombs of the Nobles** and **Deir Al Medina**, which can be just as rewarding.

In the second week arrange four days sailing up the Nile to **Aswan** on a budget-friendly felucca or a luxurious dahabiyya; the shorter version is to find a taxi to take you there, stopping at the temples on the way. From Aswan you can visit the temples at **Abu Simbel**, perched on the edge of Lake Nasser.

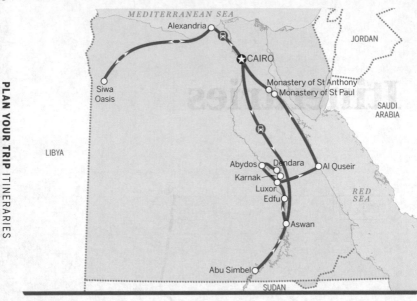

4 WEEKS Egypt Top to Bottom

In a month you can cover most of Egypt's main sights – a trip of nearly 2000km. This takes in Egypt's most romantic desert oasis and snorkelling in the Red Sea, as well as seeing the most important monuments along the Nile and enjoying the urban delights of Cairo.

On the first morning in **Cairo**, visit the Egyptian Museum to get a grasp on the country's long history. Have a few days of urban delights in the modern metropolis. Along with the top sites, make time to sit in one of the city's bustling *ahwas* (coffeehouses), wreathed in sweet shisha smoke. Next, visit the **Pyramids of Giza** and continue to the necropolis of **Saqqara**.

Head south from Cairo on the sleeper train to **Aswan**, where you can soak up Nubian culture and make the side trip for a day or two to the awesome temples of **Abu Simbel**. Sail back down the Nile from Aswan to **Edfu** on a felucca, or take a taxi stopping at various temples along the way, continuing on to **Luxor**. Visit the vast temple complex of **Karnak**, and Luxor Temple on the east bank, and then hang out on the west bank of the Nile for a few days – there is so much to see here. For a great day out of Luxor, take a boat or drive to the sacred site of **Abydos**, visiting the Ptolemaic temple at **Dendara** on the way.

When you've had your fill of ancient ruins, head from Luxor to **Al Quseir** for some days of snorkelling and relaxing on a Red Sea beach. When you're done head back to Cairo, and on the way stop in at the **Monastery of St Paul** and **Monastery of St Anthony**.

Return to Cairo and from there take the train to **Alexandria** and spend a couple of days in its wonderful cafes and museums. From there continue along the Mediterranean coast heading for **Siwa Oasis**, one of Egypt's most idyllic spots. This is the best spot for hanging out for a few days, cycling around the oasis and perhaps going on a desert safari.

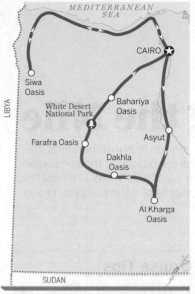

2 WEEKS Desert Escape

The Western Desert offers a wonderful mix of lush oasis gardens, stunning desert landscapes and ancient monuments. There's nowhere in Egypt as peaceful as the oases.

Begin a trip to the amazing Western Desert with a bus from Cairo or Asyut to **Al Kharga Oasis**, and explore the Al Kharga Museum of Antiquities as well as the Graeco-Roman temples and tombs.

From Al Kharga, head northwest to **Dakhla Oasis** to see the fascinating, hive-like mudbrick settlements of Balat and Al Qasr. Next, hop north to the small and quaint **Farafra Oasis**. From there you may be able to make a two- or three-day trip to camp in the stunning **White Desert National Park**, and then head for the closest oasis to Cairo, **Bahariya**.

The desert road from Bahariya to **Siwa Oasis** is currently closed, so you will have a long detour via Cairo to get there. Worth the trouble? Certainly. Perched on the edge of the Great Sand Sea, and surrounded by some staggeringly beautiful desert, Siwa is renowned for its dates as well as for being the place of the oracle where Alexander the Great was declared son of the god Amon.

1 WEEK Urban Jaunt

Get a taste of contemporary urban life in Egypt's two largest cities. The heaving metropolis of Cairo allows you to wander through time in its different quarters. In Alexandria, soak up cafe culture and catch a glimpse of the Graeco-Roman achievement

In **Cairo**, head to the Egyptian Museum to immerse yourself in Egypt's long history and then stroll through the faded elegance of Downtown. The next day visit the **Pyramids of Giza**, and continue to the necropolis of **Saqqara**. For contrast on your third day, take the metro to Coptic Cairo and visit the excellent Coptic Museum. Take a taxi to Al Azhar Park to enjoy lunch and great views over the city and then spend the afternoon in Islamic Cairo. On your last day, cafe-hop in leafy Zamalek, visit some art galleries and end atop the Cairo Tower for a final view.

The next morning, take an express train to **Alexandria**. Follow a morning in the stunning Bibliotheca Alexandrina with a visit to the excellent Alexandria National Museum. On your second day, indulge in nostalgia: ride the creaking streetcar and tour Pastroudis and other cafes where the city's literati once sipped coffee.

Plan Your Trip
Cruising the Nile

The world's longest river and its extraordinary monuments, the stunningly fertile valley and the barren beauty of the surrounding desert, the light and heat, and the joy of slow travel in a superfast world all add up to one of the highlights of a trip to Egypt, or anywhere in the world.

Key Cruises

Best for Adventure
A *felucca* is the most likely way to find adventure. An open-top sailing boat without cabins or facilities, it is best taken from south to north – if the wind fails, you can always float downriver.

Made for Romantics
Dahabiyyas – the name translates as 'the golden one' – will waft you back into the 19th century, when these large and luxurious sailing boats were the only viable form of transport for visitors.

Most Popular Route
The stretch between Luxor and Aswan is the most popular route and as a result busiest part of the river – you might find yourself in a long line of boats.

Far from the Crowds
Lake Nasser is the place to go if you would rather see empty landscapes and the odd wild animal than crowds of tourists.

Cruise Tips

When to travel Summer (June to August) can be extremely hot and is therefore the cheapest season to cruise. Christmas and Easter are usually the busiest and most expensive. Spring and autumn are ideal, with the light being particularly good in October and November.

Where to start Most cruises starting from Luxor are a day longer than those starting from Aswan, partly because they are going against the Nile's strong current. If you want to spend longer in Luxor or are concerned about cost, start from Aswan and head north.

Cabin choice On cruisers, try to avoid the lowest deck. Many boats have decent views from all cabins, but the banks of the Nile are high (and get higher as the river level drops) and you want to see as much as possible. Ask for a deck plan when booking.

Sailing time Many passengers on Nile cruisers are surprised by how little time is spent cruising – the boats' large engines cover distances relatively quickly, cruise times are often only four hours per day, and on some itineraries you only spend one night en route.

Itineraries & Sites

Large cruisers stick to rigid itineraries on the busy Luxor–Aswan stretch of the Nile. On these trips, generally lasting from three to six nights, days are spent visiting monuments and relaxing by the pool or on deck. By night there is a variety of entertainment: cocktails, dancing and fancy-dress parties – usually called a *galabeya* (man's robe) party, as passengers are encouraged to 'dress like an Egyptian' – are all part of the fun. Actual sailing time is minimal on most of these trips – often as little as four hours each day, depending on the itinerary.

Feluccas and dahabiyyas determine their own schedules and do not need special mooring spots, so can stop at small islands or antiquities sites often skipped by the big cruisers. But even these boats usually have preferred mooring places. Because they use sail power instead of large engines, a far greater proportion of time is spent in motion. Night-time entertainment is more likely to be stargazing, listening to the sounds of the river, and occasionally riverbank fireside music from the crew or villagers.

The stretch of the Nile between Luxor and Aswan has the greatest concentration of well-preserved monuments in the country, which is why it also has the greatest number of boats and tourists (sailing in both directions).

Feluccas and dahabiyyas rarely sail between Luxor and Esna because police permits are difficult to get and because of the issue of passing the Esna lock. Dahabiyya operators will bus passengers to Esna from Luxor. Felucca trips generally start in Aswan and end south of Esna; captains can arrange onward transport to Luxor, but this often costs extra.

Cairo to Luxor

This stretch of the river was removed from cruise itineraries after attacks on boats in the 1990s. The archaeological sites at Dendara and Abydos have been on some tour schedules for the past few years, however, and it is also possible to take a day cruise to Dendara from Luxor. Few boats cruise between Cairo and Luxor, and those that do can only travel at high water in the hottest summer months.

Luxor

The capital of Egypt's glorious New Kingdom pharaohs, home to Tutankhamun, Ramses II and many other famous names, Luxor is blessed with some of the world's

Cruising the Nile

most famous ancient monuments. Most cruises only cover the bare minimum, so if you are interested in seeing the sights, it pays to spend an extra day or two here away from the boat.

Highlights include the temples of Karnak, Luxor Temple, Luxor Museum, Valley of the Kings, Tombs of the Nobles, Deir Al Bahri and Medinat Habu.

Luxor to Aswan

This most famous stretch of the river is studded with stunning architecture and

---

THE BEST OF THE NILE

Close to the Nile in luxury Enjoying a private cruise on a grand dahabiyya such as the *Meroe*.

Economy cruise Taking a felucca trip from Aswan to Edfu.

Nubian adventure Safari to Abu Simbel on African Angler's *Ta Seti*.

Nostalgia trip Reliving Agatha Christie's Egypt, on the Nile's last steamer, the *Sudan*.

Five-star plutocracy Style and luxury on Oberoi's award-winning *Philae*.

---

varied scenes of great natural beauty. All cruisers stop to visit the Ptolemaic temples of Esna, Edfu and Kom Ombo. On the shorter cruises, all three sites are visited in a single day. While none of the sites is so large that this is unrealistic, exploring three great temples is a lot to jam into one day and the rushed visit means that you will be moored longer at Luxor or Aswan.

Dahabiyyas and feluccas take longer to cover the distance between the three temples, usually seeing only one a day. Most dahabiyyas (and some feluccas) also stop at the rarely visited and highly recommended sites of Al Kab (p233) and Gebel Silsila (p236). Cruisers do not have moorings here, so visitors may be limited to your fellow passengers, giving a taste of how it might have been for 19th-century travellers.

Aswan

The Nile is squeezed between rocks and a series of islands at Aswan, which makes it particularly picturesque, especially with the desert crowding in on both sides of the river. If you alight here you will probably spend only one night in town, but some cruisers stay moored for two nights. Most itineraries include a visit to Philae, site of the Temple of Isis (p257); the High Dam (p258); and the Northern Quarries, site of the Unfinished Obelisk (p242). Occasionally cruisers offer a felucca ride around Elephantine Island (p242) as an excursion; if not, it is worth organising your own. Some also offer an optional half-day tour (usually by plane) to Abu Simbel (p263).

Lake Nasser

The lake was created in the 1960s when the High Dam was built near Aswan, and now covers much of Egyptian Nubia, once home to hundreds of tombs, temples and churches. Some monuments were moved from their original sites before the building of the dam and are grouped together at four locations: Kalabsha (p260), Wadi As Subua (p261) (accessible only by boat), Amada (p262) (accessible only by boat) and, of course, the Temples of Abu Simbel (p263).

Because so few cruisers operate on Lake Nasser, moorings are never crowded and monuments – with the exception of the Temple of Ramses II at Abu Simbel – are not overrun. Itineraries are generally three nights/four days from Aswan to Abu Simbel, or four nights/five days from Abu Simbel to Aswan.

Sailing a Felucca

For many travellers, the only way to travel on the Nile is slowly, on board a traditional felucca (Egyptian sailing boat). Except for swimming, this is as close as you can get to the river. Read on to make sure that this is for you and that you avoid the pitfalls.

A Slow Journey

Most felucca trips begin at Aswan; the strong northward current means that boats are not marooned if the wind dies. Trips go to Kom Ombo (two days/one night), Edfu (three days/two nights – the most popular option) or Esna (four days/ three nights).

Feluccas are not allowed to sail after 8pm, so most stop at sunset and set up camp on the boat or on shore. Night-time entertainment ranges from stargazing and the crew singing to partying, depending on you and your fellow passengers.

Planning Your Felucca Trip

With so many feluccas (hundreds, thousands?), arranging a felucca trip can be daunting. Small hotels can be aggressive in trying to rope you in. To be sure of what you're getting, it's best to arrange things yourself.

Top: Felucca on the Nile

Bottom: Egyptian
breakfast aboard a
felucca

CHAMELEONSEYE/GETTY IMAGES ©

FELUCCA TIPS

➡ There are no onboard toilet facilities, so you will need to go to the toilet overboard or find somewhere private when you stop on shore. Some captains now travel with basic toilet tents – really no more than a screen and a hole in the sand.

➡ Check that the captain has what appears to be a decent, riverworthy boat, and the essential gear: blankets (it gets cold at night), cooking implements and a sunshade. If a different boat or captain is foisted on you at the last minute, be firm and refuse.

➡ Establish whether the price includes food; to be sure you're getting what you paid for, go with whoever does the shopping.

➡ Agree on the number of passengers beforehand and ask to meet fellow passengers – you're going to be sharing a small space, after all.

➡ Decide on the drop-off point before you set sail; many felucca captains stop 30km south of Edfu in Hammam, Faris or Ar Ramady.

➡ Don't hand over your passport. Captains can use a photocopy to arrange the permit.

➡ Bring comfort essentials. It can get bitterly cold at night, so bring a sleeping bag. Insect repellent is a good idea. A hat, sunscreen and plenty of bottled water are essential.

➡ Wherever you stop, be sure to clean up after yourself.

Many of the better felucca captains can be found having a drink in Nileside restaurants such as the Aswan Moon; Emy, near the Panorama restaurant in Aswan; or on Elephantine Island. Meet a few captains – and inspect their boat – before choosing one you get on well with. Women alone or in a group should try to team up with a few men if possible, as some women travellers have reported sailing with felucca captains who had groping hands and there have been some rare reports of more serious assault.

Officially, feluccas can carry a minimum of six passengers and a maximum of eight. Fares are open to negotiation and dictated by demand. Expect to pay at least LE150 per person per day, including food, for sharing a boat between six to eight people. On top of this you need to add LE5 to LE10 per person for the captain to arrange the police registration – this needs to be arranged the day before sailing. You might find boats for less, but take care; if it's much cheaper, you'll either have a resentful captain and crew, or you'll be eating little more than bread and *fuul* (fava bean paste) for three days. Do not hand out the whole agreed amount until you get to your destination because there have been several reports of trips being stopped prematurely for a so-called breakdown.

If you do have problems, the tourist police or the tourist office should be the first port of call.

Dahabiyyas, the Golden Boats

The 19th-century novelist Amelia Edwards likened travelling by sailing boat or steamer to the difference between horse-carriage and railway. She thought the former was slow and delightful, if expensive, while the latter was quick, cheap and without charm. When she travelled in the 1870s, package tours by steamer were already crowding dahabiyyas off the Nile. But they have made a comeback in the past few years and dozens of them are now afloat. *Nour el Nil, La Flâneuse du Nil, Lazuli* and *Nile Dahabiya* are all companies with boats that are beautifully appointed, with an antique feel, tasteful decor and double lateen sails. As they carry small numbers of passengers, this is the most luxurious way to see the monuments without crowds.

As most dahabiyyas have flexible itineraries and personalised service, it is also the best way to feel truly independent while still travelling in comfort, although often at considerably more expense than on feluccas or cruisers. Prices include all meals and usually also transfers to and from airports/train stations. Some include entrance to monuments and guide fees, but you should check when booking your trip. Trips are best arranged before you depart for Egypt.

Meroe (www.nourelnil.com; 5 nights per person from €1700) A replica of a 19th-century dahabiyya indistinguishable from the original, the beautifully finished Meroe is the best-run and coolest dahabiyya on the Nile. It is also rare for being owner-operated. It has room for 20 passengers in 10 comfortable, stylish white cabins with private bathroom, and large windows overlooking the Nile.

Because it is newly built, spaces have been thought through – there is ample storage for clothes and suitcases, for example – and plumbing and water filtration are good. During the day, when not visiting an ancient site or walking in the countryside, there is plenty of space on deck to read in your own corner, to watch the scenery or to dive off and swim in the strong current of the Nile. Food comes from farmers and markets on the way, and the chef produces delicious and copious meals with plenty of fresh vegetables, farm-bred chicken, duck and fish.

This tailor-made trip, with moorings at small islands and outside villages, is a unique way to see the Nile, reminiscent of another age. If there is no wind, the dahabiyya is towed by a motor boat. The same owners have three other boats, the eight-cabin Malouka, El Nil and Assouan, which are less expensive. All boats only run from Esna to Aswan (five nights).

Orient (www.nile-dahabiya.com; 3 nights from €525) With four double cabins and one suite, the well turned-out Orient is smaller than many dahabiyyas but none the worse for that. It's run by Egyptians who also own one of our favourite restaurants in Luxor (Sofra (p490)); this and its sister ships Zekrayaat and Loulia are good midrange choices.

La Flâneuse (www.la-flaneuse-du-nil.com; 2 nights per person from €900) is well fitted and well run. Like original dahabiyyas, it relies on sails (or tugs) to move, but it does have air-con in the seven cabins. Tours are shorter than some, taking four nights from Esna to Aswan and three nights from Aswan back to Esna.

Lazuli (☎0100 877 7115; www.lazulinil.com) There are now three Lazuli dahabiyyas on the Nile, one with five cabins and two with six. The long, elegant boats have spacious decks with deck chairs, cushions and a long table at which most meals are served. The cabins are comfortable with compact but modern private bathrooms and solar-power energy.

Cruisers

There were as many as 300 cruisers plying the waters between Aswan and Luxor until the tourism slump led to many being tied up. Like hotels, the ones still running range from slightly shabby to sumptuous, but almost all have some sort of pool, a large rooftop area for sunbathing and watching the scenery, a restaurant, a bar, air-con, TV, minibars and en-suite bathrooms.

A cruise remains the easiest way to see the Nile in comfort on a midrange budget and can be ideal for families with older children who want to splash in a pool between archaeological visits, or for people who want to combine sightseeing with relaxation. The downside is that monuments are almost always seen with large

---

TRAVEL ACCOUNTS ON THE NILE

A Thousand Miles Up the Nile (Amelia B Edwards) Edwards was so absorbed by the remains of ancient Egyptian civilisation she came across on her journey that she founded the London-based Egypt Exploration Fund, which still finances archaeological missions today.

The Histories by Herodotus Egyptian customs, curious manners, tall tales and a few facts from a curious Greek historian in the 5th century BC.

A Winter on the Nile (Anthony Sattin) How a 19th-century Nile journey helped form Florence Nightingale and Gustave Flaubert.

Old Serpent Nile: A Journey to the Source (Stanley Stewart) A view from the ground as Stewart travels from the Nile Delta to its source in the Mountains of the Moon, in Uganda, during the late 1980s.

NILE FACTS

As the world's longest river, the Nile cuts through 11 countries and an incredible 6680km of Africa as it winds its way north towards the Mediterranean Sea. It has two main sources: Lake Victoria in Uganda, out of which flows the White Nile; and Lake Tana in the Ethiopian highlands, from which the Blue Nile emerges. The two rivers meet at Khartoum in Sudan. Some 320km further north, they are joined by a single tributary, the Atbara. From here, the river flows northwards to its end without any other tributary and almost no rain adding to its waters.

groups and the itineraries are generally inflexible. Boats are almost always moored together, and the sheer volume of traffic means that generators and air-con units overwhelm the peace of the river. The consensus from our research is that scrimping on cruises means substandard hygiene, no pool, cubby-hole cabins and lots of hidden extras, which makes a felucca trip a far better option.

The only way around this is to book an all-inclusive package to Egypt. Not only are the prices usually lower but, in the case of cut-price cruises, the agency guarantees the reliability of the boat. The best deals are from Europe. Avoid booking through small hotels in Egypt: the hotels are not licensed as travel agencies so you will have no recourse if there are problems.

With the uncertain state of tourism at the time of writing, prices, which include all meals, entrance to monuments and guides, varied considerably; you should check prices with the company before you book.

Between Luxor & Aswan

M/S Sudan (www.steam-ship-sudan.com; 3 nights from €850) The *Sudan* was built as part of Thomas Cook's steamer fleet in 1885 and was once owned by King Fouad. It was also used as a set in the film *Death on the Nile*. It has been refurbished and offers 23 cabins, all with private bathroom, air-con and access to the deck. It's unusual in that it has no pool, but it's also unique because it has so much history and character, something sorely missing on most cruisers. Its configuration means it cannot moor to other cruisers, so night-time views are good. There is a choice of three- and four-night cruises. Note that the management does not accept children under seven.

M/S Philae (www.oberoihotels.com; cabins per night €425-1370) The award-winning *Philae* is the best of the modern cruisers currently operating on the Nile and has had a thorough refit. It is also one of the most expensive. It has 18 cabins and four suites, all with large picture windows that open. It runs four- and six-night cruises between Luxor and Aswan. It has an excellent kitchen, a gym, library and all the sophisticated touches you would expect, including a spa and treatment rooms.

M/S Sun Boat III (www.sanctuaryretreats.com) Sanctuary's most intimate cruiser, the beautiful *Sun Boat III* has 14 cabins and four suites decorated in contemporary Egyptian style, and all pretty as a picture. The seven-night itinerary includes visits to Dendara and Abydos. Dinner on board is à la carte or a set menu with two European choices and one Egyptian. There's also the option of in-room dining. The boat is impeccably run and operates a no-mobile-phone policy in public areas. Facilities include a pool and exercise machines. Sanctuary boats, formerly owned by Abercrombie & Kent, also include the larger *M/S Sun Boat IV*, which runs between Cairo and Aswan when water levels permit. All Sanctuary boats have excellent Egyptologists as guides and private mooring docks in Luxor, Aswan and Kom Ombo.

M/S Viking Ra (www.vikingrivercruises.co.uk; 12 nights from £5295) Viking stripped the *Ra* back to its shell and rebuilt it in 2017. Most of the 24 suites open onto small verandahs and the ship has all the facilities of a good hotel, including a spa. It is currently only available as part of a 12-day Egypt itinerary.

M/S Darakum (www.movenpick.com) Spacious and top-end, though not super-luxurious, the *Darakum* has 44 cabins and eight suites, plus a swimming pool. The decor is more 1970s than New Kingdom and you have to be quick to get a sunbed, but food and service is good, as you would expect from Mövenpick, who operate the boat.

Nubian woman, Aswan (p240)

Lake Nasser

Of the handful of boats currently cruising on Lake Nasser, a few stand out above the rest.

Ta Seti (☎012-2749-1892, 010-0134-2410, 097-230-9748; www.african-angler.net) Something different: Tim Baily worked in safaris south of the Sahara before setting up African Angler, the first company to run Lake Nasser safaris. He has a staff of skilled guides, expert in the flora, fauna and fish life of the lake, and owns several styles of small boat. Two-cabin houseboats have toilet and shower, the two-bunk safari boats are more basic, while the mothership carries the kitchen and supplies. Cruises can be from one to seven nights and can start from Aswan or Abu Simbel.

Nublana (p262) The *Nublana* is a small motorboat with three small cabins, a suite and a shared shower. Above is a lounge and sun deck. A speedboat can also be arranged for fishing trips or waterskiing. The same company also organises five-day boat trekking trips from Aswan to Abu Simbel.

Prince Abbas (☎010-0005-9590, 02-2690-1797; www.movenpick.com) A five-star deluxe ship operated by the Swiss chain Mövenpick, it has a library, a gym, a sun deck with a plunge pool and a jacuzzi. The spacious cabins have TV, music system, minibar, picture windows and private bathroom.

Plan Your Trip
Diving the Red Sea

The sights below Egypt's waters are just as magnificent as those above. Under the sea's surface lies a fantasia of coral mountains and shallow reefs swarming with brightly coloured fish. Submerge into this kaleidoscope world and you'll understand why the Red Sea boasts a legendary reputation among diving enthusiasts.

Best Diving Experiences

Best Diving Intro Experience
Gently submerging into Dahab's sloping Lighthouse Reef (p389), and discovering a colourful world of darting, curious fish only a few steps from the shore.

Best Famous Dive-Site Experience
Plunging into the Blue Hole (p389).

Best Wreck-Diving Experience
Exploring the underwater museum of the Thistlegorm (p383), the WWII supply ship first discovered by Jacques Cousteau.

Best Marine Life Experiences
Coming face to face with hammerheads and mantas, passing by large shoals of tuna and spotting emperor angelfish and turtles at world-renowned Elphinstone Reef (p368).

Diving with the resident pod of dolphins at Sha'ab Samadai (p369).

Best Off-the-Beaten-Track Experience
Venturing to the far south near Marsa Alam (p367), where the pristine reefs of the Fury Shoals can be accessed as day trips.

When to Dive

The Red Sea can be dived year-round, though diving conditions are at their peak during the summer months of July to September, when calm sea conditions, sea temperatures averaging 26°C, and excellent visibility make for astonishingly good diving conditions. Despite this, if you're not great at dealing with heat you should try to avoid booking a dive holiday in August, when land temperatures regularly sky-rocket to more than 40°C.

During the winter months of December and January, rough seas and strong winds can make access to some dive sites difficult and even impossible, though if you're happy to stick to shore dives you shouldn't have a problem. Visibility does take a hit during this period and sea temperatures also drop substantially. The plus side is that, unlike in summer, you'll be diving without the crowds.

If you are planning to dive in the Red Sea's southernmost sections (Marsa Alam and beyond), take into account that a plankton bloom reduces visibility for a few weeks during April and May and is best avoided.

Where to Dive

Diving tends to be concentrated at the northern end of the Egyptian Red Sea, although increasing numbers of advanced divers are pushing further south. The most popular sites are around the southern tip of the Sinai Peninsula where you'll find the jewels in the Red Sea's crown. The underwater spectacles of Ras Mohammed National Park and the Straits of Gubal led a panel of scientists and conservationists to choose the northern section of the Red Sea as one of the Seven Underwater Wonders of the World in 1989.

The thin strip of land jutting out into the sea forming Ras Mohammed National Park (p378) is home to the 'Holy Trinity' of Shark Reef, Eel Garden and the *Jolanda* wreck. Further off shore, on the western side of the Sinai Peninsula are the **Straits of Gubal**, a series of coral pinnacles just beneath the surface of the sea, famous for snagging ships trying to navigate north to the Suez Canal. This is where the majority of Egypt's shipwrecks lie, including the WWII wreck of the *Thistlegorm*, famously discovered in the 1950s by Jacques Cousteau.

Another major diving area is in the **Straits of Tiran**, which form the narrow entrance to the Gulf of Aqaba. The currents sweeping through the deep channel allow coral to grow prolifically, attracting abundant marine life.

Heading south, the best reefs are found around the many offshore islands. Although the reefs nearest to Hurghada have been damaged by tourist development, there is a plethora of pristine dive sites further south.

Where you base yourself for your Red Sea diving trip depends much on your own travelling style. Some travellers find themselves spending more time than they planned in the backpacker-friendly village

THISTLEGORM: THE RED SEA'S BEST WRECK DIVE

Built by the North East Marine Engineering Company, the 129m-long cargo ship christened the *Thistlegorm* was completed and launched in 1940 in Sunderland, England. Before setting out from Glasgow in 1941, it had previously made several successful trips to North America, the East Indies and Argentina. However, with a cargo full of vital supplies destined for North Africa, where British forces were preparing for Operation Crusader (the relief of Tobruk against the German 8th Army), the *Thistlegorm* met its end at 2am on 6 October 1941.

While the ship was waiting in the Straits of Gubal for a call sign to proceed up the Gulf of Suez, four German Heinkel He 111s that were flying out of Crete mounted an attack. The planes were returning from an armed reconnaissance mission up the Sinai coast, and targeted the ship to offload their unused bombs. One bomber scored a direct hit on the No 4 hold, which tore the ship in two and sent the two railway locomotives that the vessel was carrying hurtling through the air. Incredibly, they landed upright on the seabed, one on either side of the wreck. In less than 20 minutes, the ship sank to the ocean floor, taking with it nine sailors out of a crew of 49.

The *Thistlegorm* lay undisturbed until 1956 when legendary French diver Jacques Cousteau located the wreck, lying at a depth of 17m to 35m, to the northwest of Ras Mohammed. Cousteau found a cache of WWII cargo packed in the hold, including a full consignment of armaments and supplies, such as Bedford trucks, Morris cars, BSA 350 motorbikes and Bren gun carriers. Although Cousteau took the ship's bell, the captain's safe and a motorbike, he left the wreck as he found it and kept its location secret. However, it was rediscovered in 1993 when some divers stumbled upon its location, and it has since become one of the world's premier wreck-dive sites.

The *Thistlegorm* (p383) is best dived on an overnight trip because it takes 3½ hours each way from Sharm El Sheikh by boat; dive operators throughout Sinai can easily help you arrange this. On your first dive, you will do a perimeter sweep of the boat, which is highlighted by a swim along the soldier walkways on the side of the vessel. On your second dive, you will penetrate the ship's interior, swimming through a living museum of WWII memorabilia.

Diving the Red Sea

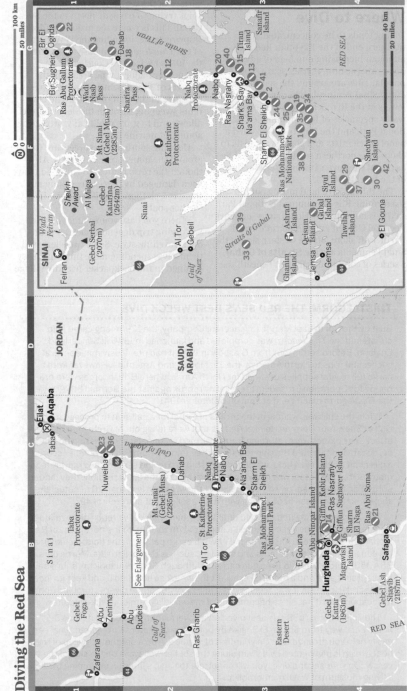

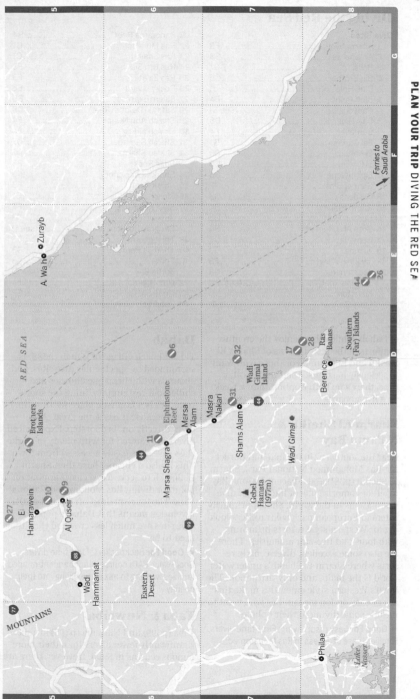

RED SEA

MOUNTAINS

Eastern Desert

Wadi Hammamat

Al Quseir

Hamarawein

Brothers Islands

Elphinstone Reef

Marsa Shagra

Mersa Alam

Masra Nakari

Shams Alam

Gebel Hamata (1977m)

Wadi Gimal Island

Wadi Gimal

Berenice

Ras Banas

Southern (Far) Islands

Philae

Lake Nasser

A Wa h o Zurayb

Ferries to Saudi Arabia

Diving the Red Sea

Dive Sites

1	Alternatives	F3
2	Amphoras	G3
3	Bells	G1
4	Big Brother	C5
	Blue Hole	(see 3)
5	Bluff Point	E4
	Canyon	(see 8)
6	Daedalus	D6
7	Dunraven	F4
8	Eel Garden	G1
9	El Kaf	C5
10	El Qadim	C5
11	Elphinstone	C6
12	Gabr el-Bint	G2
13	Gardens	G3
14	Giftun Islands	B4
15	Gordon Reef	G3
16	Gota Abu Ramada	B4
17	Hamada	D7
18	Islands	G2
19	Jackfish Alley	F3
20	Jackson Reef	G3
	Jolanda Reef	(see 35)
	Kingston	(see 33)
	Little Brother	(see 4)
21	Panorama Reef	B4
22	Ras Mumlach	G1
23	Ras Shaitan	C1
24	Ras Um Sid	F3
25	Ras Za'atir	F3
26	Rocky Island	E8
27	Salem Express	B5
28	Sataya (Dolphin Reef)	D8
29	Sha'ab Abu Nuhas	F4
30	Sha'ab al-Erg	F4
31	Sha'ab Samadai	D7
32	Sha'ab Sharm	D7
33	Shag Rock	E3
34	Shark Observatory	F3
35	Shark Reef	F3
36	Sinker	C1
37	Siyul Kebira	F4
38	Small Crack	F3
	Stingray Station	(see 1)
39	Thistlegorm	E3
40	Thomas Reef	G3
41	Tower	G3
	Turtle Bay	(see 2)
42	Umm Qamar	F4
43	Umm Sid	G2
44	Zabargad Island	E8

of Dahab, while others enjoy the creature comforts of the resort towns of Sharm El Sheikh and El Gouna. For those who want to seriously maximise their underwater time, there's no better option than a week on a live-aboard.

Sharm El Sheikh & Na'ama Bay

Near the southern tip of Sinai and bordering Ras Mohammed National Park, Sharm El Sheikh (p381) and adjacent Na'ama Bay together comprise one of the busiest dive destinations in the world. Sharm primarily caters to European package travellers looking for Western-style resorts brimming with four- and five-star amenities. There are also some excellent diver-centric resorts where Sharm El Sheikh's underwater world is the main, and only, attraction. The town's Western-style amenities make this a very easy option for families who want to include some diving in their holiday.

➡ **Good For** Easy resort living; First-time divers; Families; Ease of access to Ras Mohammed; Wreck diving

Dahab

The laid-back village of Dahab (p388) is surrounded by spectacular dive sites, and abounds with cheap guesthouses and chilled-out restaurants lining the shorefront. It's is a fantastic place for first-time divers because it has some great shore dives directly on its doorstep. Experienced divers are catered for with plenty of world-class dive sites easily accessed from town. This is also a cheaper base than Sharm El Sheikh to serve as an easy jumping-off point for diving Ras Mohammed National Park. The tourism drop-off since the 2011 revolution means that Dahab's popular dive sites are much less crowded than they used to be.

➡ **Good For** Backpackers; First-time divers; Good-value PADI courses; Independent-minded families wanting to mix some diving into their holiday

Taba & Nuweiba

Taba (p399) and Nuweiba (p395) attract significantly fewer divers than their more famous cousins in Sinai. However, there are a handful of excellent dive sites in the area (although the diving here is not as rich and as varied as other spots in Sinai and the Red Sea), and they are a suitable base for independent-minded divers looking for low-key ambience and minimal crowds. For an even more relaxed experience, some divers also base themselves at one of the beach camps on the Nuweiba–Taba coastal highway. Tourism has taken a significant hit in this area since the 2011 revolution and would-be divers should keep up-to-date with their government's travel advisories before planning a trip here.

➤ **Good For** Escaping the crowds

Hurghada & El Gouna

Egypt's original resort strip, ageing Hurghada (p357), has been plagued by over-development and poor environmental management, while glossy El Gouna (p354) just to the north is a five-star tourist enclave that seems aeons apart from the rest of Egypt. Although the reefs close to both towns have been heavily damaged by unfettered tourist development, both towns are well-placed bases for easy access to the popular dive sites of the Giftun Islands, as well as the diving in the Straits of Gubal. Because of mass tourism, dive trips (and hence dive sites) tend to be crowded. On a positive note, conservation measures are finally being implemented, spearheaded by local NGOs, and the situation has begun to improve.

➤ **Good for** Resort-style living; Cheap package deals; Combined Red Sea diving and Nile Valley holidays; Straits of Gubal wreck diving

PLAN YOUR TRIP DIVING THE RED SEA

> ### RED SEA STATS
>
> **Depth** 4m to 40m
>
> **Visibility** 15m to 40m
>
> **Water Temperature** Averages 21°C to 30°C, with January the coldest month and August the warmest.
>
> **Access** Shore, boat and live-aboard

Safaga

For the most part, Safaga (p364) defies the tourist hordes, which is a good thing as there are some pristine reefs offshore from this rather unattractive port town. Unlike nearby Hurghada and El Gouna, resorts here are extremely low-key, and cater almost exclusively to dedicated divers.

➤ **Good For** Dive-centric holidays; Technical diving training

Al Quseir

A historic trade and export hub with a history stretching back centuries, the sleepy town of Al Quseir (p365) holds a charm absent from most other Red Sea destinations. The comparative lack of tourist development means that the offshore dive sites here are generally empty, though you will have to contend with strong winds and rough seas.

➤ **Good For** Escaping the crowds

Marsa Alam

The closest base to the south-coast dive sites, Marsa Alam (p367) still manages to hold on to its remote-outpost ambience

MARE ROSTRUM

Surrounded by desert on three sides, the Red Sea was formed some 40 million years ago when the Arabian Peninsula split from Africa, allowing the waters of the Indian Ocean to rush in. Bordered at its southern end by the 25km Bab Al Mandab Strait, the Red Sea is the only tropical sea that is almost entirely closed. No river flows into it and the influx of water from the Indian Ocean is slight. These unique geographical features, combined with the arid desert climate and high temperatures, make the sea extremely salty. It is also windy – on average the sea is flat for only 50 days a year.

In regard to the etymology of its name (the Red Sea is in fact deep blue), there are two competing schools of thought. Some believe that the sea was named after the surrounding red-rock mountain ranges. Others insist it was named for the periodic algae blooms that tinge the water a reddish-brown. Whatever the spark, it inspired ancient mariners to dub these waters *Mare Rostrum* – the Red Sea.

ACCESSING THE MARINE PARK ISLANDS

For experienced divers the remote dive sites of Egypt's Marine Park Islands (**Big Brother**, **Little Brother**, **Daedalus Reef**, **Zabargad**, and **Rocky Island**) are home to some of the Red Sea's most pristine coral and abundant sealife. Accessing these dive sites is strictly regulated. Divers must have completed a minimum of 30 dives before entering; night diving or landing on the islands is prohibited; and fishing, spear fishing and the use of gloves are banned.

Because of these restrictions, permission must be given for each trip, and a park ranger will often accompany boats to ensure that the rules are being enforced. To carry divers, boats must have special safety equipment, which national park and Red Sea governorate officials inspect before each trip.

If you've been offered a trip to this area, check thoroughly that the boat is licensed. If you are caught on an unlicensed boat, you could have your own equipment or belongings confiscated and find yourself in custody.

despite the resort construction drive of recent years. It's great if you want to experience some of Egypt's most far-flung dives without the cost of a live-aboard. The reefs along this southernmost stretch of the coast lack the crowds further north, though be aware that high winds and strong currents make many of the dives more suitable for experienced divers. Veterans of these parts will tell you, once you've dived here, nothing else will compare.

➡ **Good For** Dive-centric holidays; Intermediate and advanced divers; Escaping the crowds

Live-Aboards

The vast majority of larger dive operators in Egypt organise dive safaris to sites ranging from one night to two weeks' duration. The cost of these live-aboard dive safaris (also known as marine safaris) varies according to the boat and the destination, with the more remote sites in the far south generally the most expensive. While you won't see much of terrestrial Egypt, they allow you to access a greater range of dive sites, including many more distant areas that are too far to explore as day trips.

As a general rule, you should always ask to see the boat before agreeing to sail on it. Also, if a trip is very cheap, check whether the costs of diving and food are included. Furthermore, check that your live-aboard complies with the following two rules:

➡ There should be a diver-guide ratio of one guide to every 12 divers (or every eight divers in marine park areas).

➡ Divers on live-aboards entering marine park areas must be experienced, with a minimum of 30 logged dives, as well as insurance coverage.

While it's quite possible to book yourself a basic package on a live-aboard after arriving in Egypt, there are numerous agencies that specialise in Red Sea diving holidays. Here is a small sampling:

Emperor Divers (www.emperordivers.com) Emperor Divers offer live-aboard itineraries starting from Sharm El Sheikh, Hurghada and Marsa Alam.

Blue O Two (www.blueotwo.com) This UK-based dive-holiday operator specialises in luxury live-aboards with its own fleet of ships based in Hurghada and Marsa Alam.

Crusader Travel (www.crusadertravel.com) Live-aboard diving packages in the Red Sea, including diving for people with disabilities.

Oonasdivers (www.oonasdivers.com) Well-priced live-aboard trips from this dive centre based at Na'ama Bay in Sharm El Sheikh.

What You'll See

The Red Sea is teeming with more than a thousand species of marine life, and is an amazing spectacle of colour and form. Fish, sharks, turtles, stingrays, dolphins, corals, sponges, sea cucumbers and molluscs all thrive in these waters. Around 20% of the fish species to be found in the Red Sea are endemic to the region.

Coral This is what makes a reef a reef – though thought for centuries to be some form of flowering plant, it is in fact an animal. Both hard and

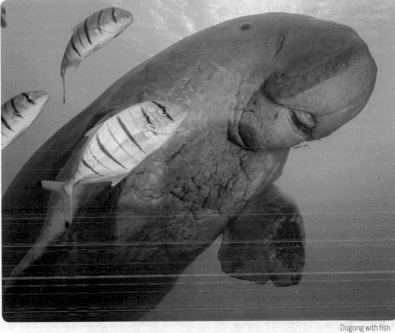

VERDE MASSIMO/SHUTTERSTOCK ©

Dugong with fish

soft corals exist, their common denominator being that they are made up of polyps, which are tiny cylinders ringed by waving tentacles that sting their prey and draw it into their stomach. During the day corals retract into their tubes, only displaying their real colours at night.

Fish Most of the bewildering variety of fish species in the Red Sea – including many that are found nowhere else – are closely associated with the coral reef, and live and breed in the reefs or nearby seagrass beds. These include such commonly sighted species as the grouper, wrasse, parrotfish and snapper. Others, such as tuna and barracuda, live in open waters and usually only venture into the reefs to feed or breed.

Manta rays Spotting the graceful, frolicking form of a manta during a Red Sea dive is a major highlight for any diver lucky enough to have this experience. Mantas are easily recognisable for their pectoral 'wings' and huge bulk. They can grow to nearly 7m and can weigh up to 1400kg. They are usually sighted near the surface, where they feed on the plankton present there.

Sharks When diving, the sharks you're most likely to encounter include white- or black-tipped reef sharks. Tiger sharks, as well as the enormous, plankton-eating whale sharks, are generally found only in deeper waters. If you're skittish about these top predators, you can take comfort in the

THE RED SEA'S DUGONG

Little is known about the distribution and numbers of these enigmatic marine mammals in the Red Sea. Weighing up to 500kg, the dugong are easily recognisable for their fusiform (spindle-like) shape and dolphin-like tail. These gentle herbivores are found in shallow coastal waters where they feed on seagrass and other plant forms. This makes them especially vulnerable to coastal degradation and pollution. Most dugong sightings in Egypt have occurred at sites along the coast south of Hurghada, with the Marsa Abu Dabab dive site (to the north of Marsa Alam) known for dugong-spotting. To help preserve the area and protect the resident dugong of the bay, zoning laws and access restrictions have now been put in place around this dive site.

RESEARCHING BEFORE YOU GO

The Chamber of Diving & Watersports (www.cdws.travel) Egyptian licensing body for dive operators. Its website provides a list of reputable dive centres in Egypt, although it is unfortunately not kept up to date.

HEPCA (www.hepca.org) The Hurghada Environmental Protection & Conservation Association is a local NGO extremely active in promoting conservation issues throughout the Red Sea region. Its website is packed full of information on the Red Sea and a great resource for travellers.

Dive Site Directory (www.divesitedirectory.co.uk) Reviews of dive sites throughout the Red Sea.

Egypt Tourism Authority (www.egypt.travel) The official website of Egypt's Tourist Board has some good basic information to get you started planning a Red Sea diving trip.

fact that shark attacks in the Red Sea are rare (though not unheard of).

Turtles The most common type of turtle found in these waters is the green turtle, although the leatherback and hawksbill are occasionally sighted. Turtles are protected in Egypt, and although they're not deliberately hunted, they are sometimes caught in nets and end up on menus in restaurants in Cairo and along the coasts.

➡ **Marine life you're better off avoiding**
As intriguing as they may seem, there are some creatures that should be given a wide berth, especially moray eels, sea urchins, fire coral, blowfish, triggerfish, feathery lionfish, turkeyfish and stonefish. To help protect yourself, it's a good idea to familiarise yourself with pictures of all these creatures before snorkelling or diving – single-page colour guides to the Red Sea's common marine hazards can be bought in hotel bookshops around diving areas.

Responsible Diving

The Red Sea's natural wonders are just as magnificent as the splendours of Egypt's Pharaonic heritage, and appear all the more stunning when contrasted with their barren desert backdrop. However, care is needed if the delicate world of coral reefs and fish is not to be permanently damaged. Almost the entire Egyptian coastline in the Gulf of Aqaba is now a protectorate, as is the Red Sea coast from Hurghada south to Sudan. Divers and snorkellers should heed the requests of instructors *not* to touch or tread on coral – if you kill the coral, you'll eventually kill or chase away the fish, too.

Overall, the paramount guideline for preserving the ecology and beauty of reefs is to take nothing with you, leave nothing behind. Other considerations:

➡ Never use anchors on the reef, and take care not to ground boats on coral.

➡ Avoid touching or standing on living marine organisms or dragging equipment across the reef. Polyps can be damaged by even the gentlest contact. If you must hold on to the reef, only touch exposed rock or dead coral.

➡ Be conscious of your fins. Even without contact, the surge from fin strokes near the reef can damage delicate organisms. Take care not to kick up clouds of sand, which can smother organisms.

➡ Practise and maintain proper buoyancy control. Major damage can be done by divers descending too fast and colliding with the reef.

➡ Take great care in underwater caves. Spend as little time within them as possible as your air bubbles may be caught within the roof and cause damage. Take turns to inspect the interior of a small cave.

➡ Resist the temptation to collect or buy corals or shells or to loot marine archaeological sites (mainly shipwrecks).

➡ Ensure that you take home all your rubbish and any litter you may find as well. Plastics in particular are a serious threat to marine life.

➡ Do not feed fish, and minimise your disturbance of marine animals.

➡ Report any violations of responsible diving practices by dive centres and diving groups to HEPCA.

Learning to Dive

Most dive clubs in Egypt offer PADI certification, though you'll occasionally find NAUI, SSI, CMAS and BSAC as well.

PADI Scuba Diver (two days) and PADI Open Water (four intensive days) dive courses are offered by most dive centres in Egypt. PADI Scuba Diver courses usually cost from €200 and PADI Open Water courses cost from €270. When comparing prices, check to see whether the certification fee and books are included.

Beginner courses are designed to drum into you things that have to become second nature when you're underwater. They usually consist of classroom work, where you learn the principles and basic knowledge needed to dive, followed by training in a confined body of water, such as a pool, before heading out to the open sea. If you want to give it a try before you commit yourself, all dive clubs offer introductory Discover Scuba dives for between €45 and €95, including equipment.

In addition to basic certification, most of the well-established clubs on the coast offer a variety of more advanced courses as well as professional-level courses or training in technical diving.

CLIMBING & DIVING: A WORD OF WARNING

Altitude can kill, particularly if your body is full of residual nitrogen. If you've been diving recently, be advised that Mt Sinai is high enough to induce decompression sickness. As a general rule, avoid climbing the mountain for 12 hours after one dive, or 18 hours if you've been on multiple dives. Although this may complicate your travel plans, trust us – you'll be delayed a lot longer if you end up confined in a hyperbaric chamber. And, of course, decompression sickness is anything but fun.

Choosing a Dive Operator

Whether you choose to plunge into the Red Sea with a small local centre, an established resort or a live-aboard, you will have no problem finding a dive operator. Almost all of the large resorts and hotels along the Red Sea have attached dive centres, and there are a vast number of smaller, independent dive centres in the main coastal towns. Some centres and live-aboards are laid-back and informal, while others are slick and structured.

READING UP

Red Sea Diver's Guide from Sharm El Sheikh to Hurghada (Shlomo and Roni Cohen) Has excellent maps and descriptions of sites around Ras Mohammed, the Straits of Gubal and Hurghada. The book is unfortunately out of print but it's quite easy to find secondhand copies.

Sinai Dive Guide (Peter Harrison) Has detailed maps and explanations of the main Red Sea sites.

Sinai Diving Guide (Alberto Siliotti) Has maps and ratings of numerous sites around Sharm El Sheikh and Ras Mohammed National Park. Although the book can be hard to source outside of Egypt, shops in Sharm El Sheikh usually have it in stock.

Red Sea Diving Guide (Andrea Ghisotti and Alessandro Carletti) Covers Egyptian sites, as well as others in Sudan, Israel and Eritrea.

The Red Sea: Underwater Paradise (Angelo Mojetta) One of the better glossy coffee-table books, with beautiful photos of the flora and fauna of Egypt's reefs.

The Official HEPCA Dive Guide Details 46 sites with artists' drawings and a small fish index. Proceeds from the sale of this guide go towards maintaining mooring buoys on the Red Sea.

Diving coral reefs

Obviously, with diving a huge cash-cow in this area, there are invariably a few fly-by-night outfits. Avoid them by doing your research first. Look for a dive operator that has a high PADI rating or equivalent, and ask other divers for recommendations. When deciding which dive centre to use, consider the operator's attention to safety and its sensitivity to environmental issues.

The Chamber of Diving & Watersports (CDWS; www.cdws.travel) is Egypt's only legal dive centre licensing agency. Since the 2011 revolution the CDWS has been in disarray but it's still worthwhile to check the validity date of your dive centre's CDWS licence before choosing to dive with them.

Because of Egypt's tourism slowdown since the revolution, it is more important than ever to make sure your dive-centre's equipment is in good condition. Because of a lack of business, some dive centres are not replacing old, worn-out equipment.

Accidents still occasionally happen and are usually the result of neglect and negligence. Before making any choices, consider the following factors:

➡ Take your time when choosing clubs and dive sites, and don't let yourself be pressured into accepting something, or someone, you're not comfortable with.

➡ Don't choose a club based solely on cost. Safety should be the paramount concern; if a dive outfit cuts corners to keep prices low, you could be in danger.

➡ If you haven't dived for more than three months, take a check-out dive. This is for your own safety and all reputable operators will make this a requirement. The cost is usually applied towards later dives.

➡ If you're taking lessons, ensure that the instructor speaks your language well. If you can't understand them, you should request another.

➡ Check that all equipment is clean and stored away from the sun, and check all hoses, mouthpieces and valves for cuts and leakage.

➡ Confirm that wetsuits are in good condition. Some divers have reported getting hypothermia because of dry, cracked suits.

➡ Check that there is oxygen on the dive boat in case of accidents.

➡ If you're in Sinai, ask if the club donates US$1 per diver each day to the hyperbaric chamber; this is often a reflection of the club's safety consciousness. If you're diving in Hurghada, El Gouna or Marsa Alam, check that the club is a HEPCA (www.hepca.org) supporter. HEPCA lists all its supporting dive centres on its website.

Plan Your Trip
Travel with Children

Visiting Egypt with children can be a delight. For them, seeing ancient monuments – or a camel for that matter – up close can be a fantasy made real. For you, the incredibly warm welcome towards young ones can smooth over many small practical hassles.

Egypt for Kids

Attitudes

What Egypt lacks in kiddie infrastructure, such as playgrounds and nappy-changing tables, it more than makes up for in its loving attitude towards little ones. In all but the finest restaurants, waiters are delighted to see kids – don't be surprised if your baby even gets passed around the place for everyone to hug and kiss, or your toddler is welcomed onto laps and fed sweets. (Yes, probably right before bedtime. Egyptians often have a different concept of 'bedtime'.)

Teenagers are less subject to this kind of attention, though their Egyptian counterparts will likely seem a bit younger and more sheltered. By adolescence, separation of the sexes is more typical, so teens should abide by grown-up etiquette when meeting Egyptians of their age.

Practicalities

Safety standards may make visitors nervous: don't expect car seats (or even seat belts, for that matter) in taxis or private cars, or child-size life preservers on boats.

Hygiene in food preparation can be inconsistent, so be prepared for diarrhoea or other stomach problems (and have a plan for when you're struck down and the kids are still raring to go). Rehydration salts, available very cheaply at all pharmacies

Best Regions for Kids

Cairo

Intensely crowded Cairo isn't obviously kid-scale, but children may delight in finding exotic trinkets in the souq. In mosques, they're welcome to roam barefoot on carpets (but not to yell). Kids love to ride horses, or a camel, around the pyramids, or enter the deep narrow corridor that leads to the heart of a pyramid.

Southern Nile Valley

All of Upper Egypt, from Luxor southwards, is straight out of picture books: temples, camels and old-time boats. Many of the family-friendly hotels have pools to recover from the sightseeing and the heat.

Western Desert

The slow pace of the oases is well suited to children. Aside from in Bawiti, there's virtually no hassle, and out in the desert, kids can roll down sand dunes, find fossils and sleep in a tent.

Red Sea Coast

Plenty of beaches here, and plenty of entertainment for kids. Teens can learn to dive, and little ones can snorkel.

(ask for Rehydran), can be a life-saver, as children can lose fluid rapidly in Egypt's hot, dry climate.

Keep kids away from stray animals, which can spread disease – street cats in particular are everywhere and liable to scratch if approached.

In resort towns formula is readily available, as are disposable nappies, but these can be hard to find in out-of-the-way places. High chairs are often available in better restaurants. Babysitting facilities are usually available in top-end hotels. Snacks such as peanuts, sesame-seed bars, dried fruit and dates are common; stock up for outings, though, as it's possible to wind up somewhere with no other services than someone selling sugary drinks and chips.

If you need more enticements during your trip, stop by the bookshop in any five-star hotel – they're usually stocked with good Egypt-themed books and toys.

For more practical advice, pick up a copy of Lonely Planet's *Travel with Children,* written by a team of parent-writers.

Children's Highlights

Desert Life

Siwa Oasis Siwa's mellow atmosphere is perfect for kids, though the bus ride is very long. Once there, they can dive-bomb into springs and graze on fresh dates. (p292)

Wadi Al Hittan How did a whale wind up in the desert? Find out in Wadi Al Hittan, where fossils are set in the sand. Trips here often include sand-boarding on nearby dunes. (p154)

Fayoum Pottery School Hands-on pottery in the Fayoum oasis. (p152)

Nobi's Arabian Horse Stables Ride a camel into the desert from the west bank in Luxor, with one of Nobi's expertly trained attendants to watch over you. (p215)

Ancient & Awesome

Great Pyramid of Khufu Older children will be astounded to enter the Great Pyramid of Khufu at Giza – though test for a tendency for claustrophobia beforehand. (p122)

Egyptian Museum Devise a virtual treasure hunt for children at the Egyptian Museum. Can they find King Tut's wig box? How many miniature oarsmen does it take to row a miniature boat? Where are the baboon mummies? (p131)

Mummification Museum Children are fascinated by mummies, so learn all about the processes in Luxor or visit the Royal Mummies Halls at the Egyptian Museum in Cairo. (p195)

Tombs of the Nobles Let them feel like Tintin uncovering the mysteries of the pharaohs at the temples in Aswan (p246) or at the Valley of the Kings. (p200)

Bibliotheca Alexandrina Bookworms can inspect antique manuscripts, while science fans can

---

PLANNING

Before You Go

If they're not already, get kids reading about ancient Egypt. As a starter, Zilpha Keatley Snyder's classic fantasy *The Egypt Game* may get tweens hooked. For budding Egyptologists, the British Museum (www.ancientegypt.co.uk) website is loaded with games and other material; www.greatscott.com introduces hieroglyphics.

For modern Egypt, look for *The Day of Ahmed's Secret,* by Florence Parry Heide and Judith Heide Gilliland, a wonderful picture book set in one of Cairo's poor neighbourhoods. Teens may like *Aunt Safiyya and the Monastery,* by Bahaa' Taher; *Life Is More Beautiful than Paradise,* by Khaled Al Berry; or *I Want to Get Married!* by Ghada Abdel Aal.

Also make sure children are up-to-date with routine vaccinations, and discuss possible travel vaccinations with your doctor well before departure.

What to Pack

Stock up your first-aid kit, pack good sun hats and don't skimp on the sunscreen or rehydration salts. For infants, you'll want a sling or back carrier – strollers will get you nowhere. Bring your own car seat if travelling by car.

KANUMAN / SHUTTERSTOCK ©

Camels, Giza Pyramids (p122)

explore the science museum. And everyone loves the planetarium. (p314)

All Aboard!

Sailing a felucca (Cairo, Luxor or Aswan) You can sail in Luxor and Aswan in the afternoon, but don't forget you can escape the traffic madness of Cairo by sailing and letting the kids play pirate. (p30)

Train to Tanta Egypt's trains are seldom crowded in 1st class, making a trip into the Delta region – perhaps to Tanta, famous for its sweets – a low-stress half-day out. (p160)

Boating to Qanater On a Friday, join Egyptian families on the boat to Qanater, the Nile Barrages just outside of Cairo. (p159)

Riding the West Bank (Luxor) Hop on a bike on Luxor's west bank – it's a great way to catch whatever breeze there is. (p195)

Tramming in Alexandria Ride the tram in Alexandria from end to end for a cheap, low-stress view of the city. (p330)

On the Water

Snorkelling (Red Sea Coast) Snorkelling in the Red Sea is a dazzling introduction to the underwater world. Seek out sites – in Sharm and Al Quseir, for instance – where kids can drift along the side of a reef, rather than directly over it. (p36)

Shipyards (Alexandria) Boats of all sizes get worked on in these shipyards. Ask aspiring captains which they'd like to helm. Round it out with a visit to the fish market, then dinner at one of many family-friendly restaurants. (p314)

Suez Canal (Port Said) For shipping on an even larger scale, stop in Port Said and watch the massive freighters go through the Suez Canal. (p342)

Regions at a Glance

Cairo

Entertainment
History
Shopping

People Watching
Cairo, the very model of a modern megalopolis, is perfect for watching the human parade at night. Hit the town to see belly dancers in a dive bar or a luxury-hotel cabaret, embark on a Downtown bar crawl or find some live music.

Beyond the Pyramids
The Egyptian Museum is so crammed with thrilling artefacts that it's a destination in itself. Fast-forward through time to visit the early churches in Coptic Cairo, or stroll through picturesque Islamic Cairo, with its awesome mosques and palaces.

Souqs & Boutiques
Heaving with commerce for more than a millennium, the souq of Khan Al Khalili is a great browse. If nothing strikes your fancy there, try the city's many boutiques for stylish souvenirs, from vintage movie posters to leather-bound books.

p54

Cairo Outskirts & the Nile Delta

Ancient History
Rural Life
Sufi Tradition

The Other Pyramids
The vast complex of Saqqara, with Zoser's experimental Step Pyramid, is a full-day outing from Cairo. Dedicated Egyptomaniacs can also visit Tanis, set between lush fields and desert.

Oases & Farms
Just an hour from Cairo is the semi-oasis of Al Fayoum, where the arts colony of Tunis harbours ceramicists and other creative types. In the fertile Nile Delta, there are few tourist sites, but the countryside is lush.

Birthday Celebrations
The birthday of 13th-century religious leader Al Sayyed Ahmed Al Badawi draws up to a million people each year to the town of Tanta.

p141

Northern Nile Valley

Ancient History
Coptic Heritage
Urban Charm

Temples & Tombs
You might think you'll see everything ancient worth seeing between Cairo, Luxor and Aswan, but the temples and tombs here – such as Beni Hasan and Tell Al Amarna – are well worth visiting and Abydos is in itself worth a journey to Egypt.

Coptic Churches
At Deir Al Muharraq, in the oldest church of the world, monks conduct Mass in the Coptic language. At the beautiful Red Monastery, near Sohag, the walls still display 4th-century frescoes.

Minya
Minya, the official gateway to Upper Egypt, is a surprisingly elegant mid-size city with faded early-20th-century architecture.

p162

Luxor

Ancient History
More History
Museums

Luxor & Karnak

Luxor has the highest concentration of ancient Egyptian monuments: the astonishing temples of Karnak, and Luxor Temple, open till late for atmospheric sightseeing. And that's just the east bank of the Nile.

Valley of the Kings

On the Nile's west bank, it just gets better: the Valley of the Kings, of King Tut fame, the Temple of Hatshepsut, cut out of the cliffs; and, oh, the 1000-tonne Colossi of Memnon just standing by.

Luxor Museum

More than a means to enjoy the airconditioning, the exemplary Luxor Museum has an excellent and beautifully displayed collection of finds from nearby temples – including two royal mummies, displayed unwrapped.

p182

Southern Nile Valley

Ancient History
Rural Landscapes
Nubian Heritage

Tremendous Temples

The Temple at Edfu is one of the best preserved in Egypt, and the quarries of Gebel Silsila are where so many monuments got their start. In the southernmost spot is the grand Ramses II temple at Abu Simbel.

Lake Nasser & Aswan

A cruise along Lake Nasser's banks reveals crocodiles and gazelles, while around Aswan the birdwatching is exceptional, especially in winter.

Nubian Heritage

Trance-like folk music, elegant mudbrick architecture and distinctive clothing are characteristics of the unique culture in this part of Egypt.

p229

Siwa Oasis & the Western Desert

Ancient History
Wilderness
Ecotourism

Graeco-Roman Traces

Ruined garrisons hint at the lively trade routes that criss-crossed the Western Desert in Roman times. Well before that, the Oracle of Amun foretold destruction in the 6th century BC.

Wild Deserts

'Desert' doesn't convey the full variety of wild land here: soak in hot springs or cold pools, and explore the White Desert gleaming like a snowfield in full moon.

Ecotourism

Few trips are lower impact than to walk out of an oasis and into the desert. Try Siwa or Dakhla, where you can round out the adventure with a stay at a lodge designed to integrate seamlessly with the desert landscape.

p266

Alexandria & the Med Coast

Nostalgia
Ancient History
Fun in the Sun

Alexandria Cafes

Traces of Alexandria's cosmopolitan glamour can still be found in scores of old cafes where writers Lawrence Durrell, Constantine Cavafy and others once mused.

Port-City History

The Bibliotheca Alexandrina only opened in 2002, but it was inspired by the ancient library that once drew scholars from all over the Mediterranean. For a portrait of the city from Graeco-Roman times on, visit the excellent Alexandria National Museum.

Coastal Leisure

Seafront pleasures here include freshfish dinners on Alexandria's corniche and beaches strung out to the west, mobbed in summer as Egyptians escape the heat.

p305

Suez Canal

Nostalgia
Ancient History
Industry

Ismailia & Port Said

Squint just right in downtown Ismailia and Port Said and you can almost see the pashas and European dandies who built the canal, strolling in front of the decaying French-colonial buildings.

Ancient Waterways

Before the British and French opened up the shipping channel between Africa and Asia, the pharaohs and the Persians dug waterways here. See the archaeological traces at the Ismailia Museum.

Cruise the Canal

Watch global commerce in action as giant container ships transit through the newly enlarged canal. In Port Said hop on a free ferry to get a glimpse of the action.

p340

Red Sea Coast

Fun in the Sun
Ancient History
Wilderness

Resorts & Beach Camps

The concrete resort town of Hurghada is offset by the sophistication of El Gouna and the simpler pleasures of beach camps around Marsa Alam, or if you're a kitesurfer, the windy coast at Safaga.

Historic Outposts

The Coptic monasteries of St Anthony and St Paul, the world's first Christian hermitages, are adorned with 13th-century wall paintings. In the photogenically crumbling port of Al Quseir, visit an Ottoman fortress.

Eastern Desert

Tourist infrastructure in the Eastern Desert is sparse but with a guide you can trek to abandoned Roman mines, spot migratory birds and even visit a remote camel market.

p350

Sinai

History
Fun in the Sun
Wilderness

Mt Sinai

God is said to have given Moses the law here at Mt Sinai, traditionally a popular hike for religious and secular travellers alike. St Katherine's Monastery, at the base of the peak, is home to early Byzantine icons.

Beach Camps & Resorts

The beach camps between Taba and Dahab are relaxed and low-key. At the other end of the scale, Sharm El Sheikh serves up a glitzy, international holiday scene.

Deserts & Reefs

The interior of the Sinai is the place for starlit treks with Bedouin guides, while Ras Mohammed National Park is a coral wonderland.

p373

On the Road

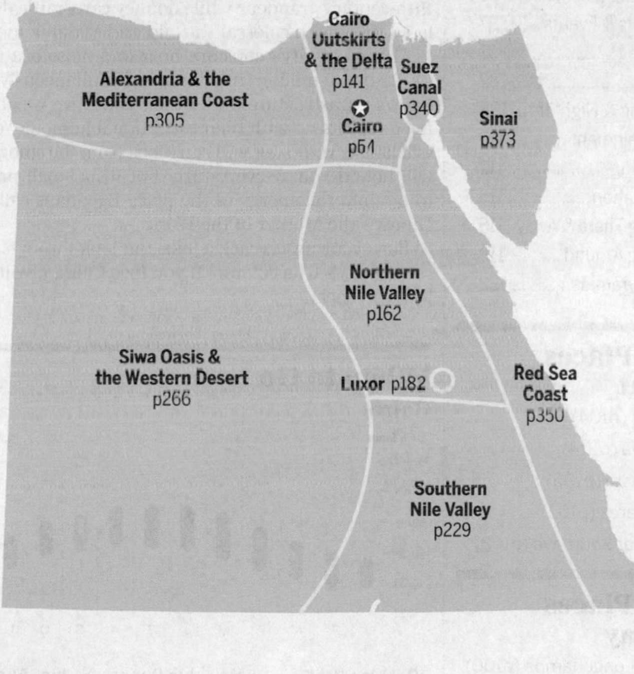

Cairo
Outskirts
& the Delta
p141

Suez
Canal
p340

Sinai
p373

Alexandria & the
Mediterranean Coast
p305

Cairo
p64

Northern
Nile Valley
p162

Siwa Oasis &
the Western Desert
p266

Luxor p182

Red Sea
Coast
p350

Southern
Nile Valley
p229

Cairo

02 / POP 22 MILLION

Best Places to Eat

➜ Zööba (p104)

➜ Sabaya (p104)

➜ O's Pasta (p105)

➜ Abu Tarek (p102)

➜ Fasahat Soumaya (p103)

Best Places to Stay

➜ Hotel Longchamps (p100)

➜ Pension Roma (p98)

➜ Golden Hotel (p99)

➜ Steigenberger Hotel El Tahrir (p100)

➜ Sofitel El Gezirah (p101)

Why Go?

Cairo is chaos at its most magnificent, infuriating and beautiful. From above, the distorted roar of the *muezzins'* call to prayer echoes out from duelling minarets. Below, car horns bellow tuneless symphonies amid avenues of faded 19th-century grandeur while donkey carts rattle down dusty lanes lined with colossal Fatimid and Mamluk monuments.

This mega-city's constant buzz and noise is a product of its 22-or-so million inhabitants simultaneously crushing Cairo's infrastructure under their collective weight and lifting its spirits up with their exceptional humour. Your nerves will jangle, your snot will run black from the smog and touts will hound you at every turn, but it's a small price to pay to tap into the energy of the place Egyptians call Umm Ad Dunya – the Mother of the World.

Blow your nose, crack a joke and look through the dirt to see the city's true colours. If you love Cairo, it will definitely love you back.

When to Go
Cairo

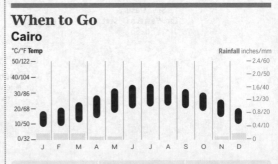

Oct–Jan Best time to visit: cooler weather means you can enjoy sightseeing without sweating.

May–Jun During Ramadan, once the sun has set, every night is street-party night in Cairo.

Jun–Aug The temperature dials up to boiling, but in good news, it's mango season.

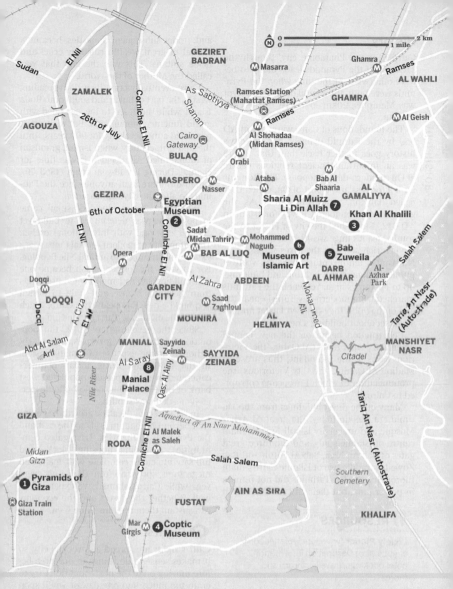

Cairo Highlights

1 **Pyramids of Giza** (p122) Experiencing one of the world's great wonders.

2 **Egyptian Museum** (p131) Taking in the awe-inspiring clutter of this legendary museum.

3 **Khan Al Khalili** (p70) Trawling alleyways for deals then recharging at an *ahwa*.

4 **Coptic Museum** (p66) Admiring a fascinating collection of Coptic Christian artistry.

5 **Bab Zuweila** (p78) Climbing the minaret's spiral staircase to see the city sprawl beneath you.

6 **Museum of Islamic Art** (p78) Examining this

museum's world-class collection.

7 **Sharia Al Muizz Li Din Allah** (p71) Reliving the splendour of Cairo's glorious past.

8 **Manial Palace** (p64) Imagining the gilded lives of royalty in ornate salons and the glittering gold throne room.

History

Cairo is not a Pharaonic city, though the presence of the Pyramids leads many to believe otherwise. At the time when the Pyramids were built, the capital of ancient Egypt was Memphis, 20km southeast of the Giza Plateau.

The foundations of Cairo were laid in AD 969 by the Fatimid dynasty, but the city's history goes further back than that. There was an important ancient religious centre at On (modern-day Heliopolis). The Romans built a fortress at the port of On, which they called Babylon, while Amr Ibn Al As, the general who conquered Egypt for Islam in AD 642, established the city of Fustat to the south. Fustat's huge wealth was drawn from Egypt's rich soil and the taxes imposed on Nile traffic. Tenth-century travellers wrote of public gardens, street lighting and buildings up to 14 storeys high. Yet when the Fatimids marched from modern-day Tunisia near the end of the 900s, they spurned Fustat and instead set about building a new city.

Construction began on the new capital when the planet Mars (Al Qahir, 'the Victorious') was in the ascendant; thus arose Al Madina Al Qahira, 'the City Victorious', the pronunciation of which Europeans corrupted to Cairo.

Many of the finest buildings from the Fatimid era remain today: the great Al Azhar Mosque and university is still Egypt's main centre of Islamic study, and the three great gates of Bab An Nasr, Bab Al Futuh and Bab Zuweila straddle two of Islamic Cairo's main thoroughfares. The Fatimids did not remain in power long, but their city survived them

and, under subsequent dynasties, became a capital of great wealth, ruled by cruel and fickle sultans. This was the city that was called the Mother of the World.

Cairo eventually burst its walls, spreading west to the port of Bulaq and south onto Roda Island, while the desert to the east filled with grand funerary monuments. But at heart it remained a medieval city for 900 years, until the mid-19th century, when Ismail, grandson of Mohammed Ali, decided it was time for change. During his 16-year reign (1863–79), Ismail did more than anyone since the Fatimids to alter the city's appearance.

When the French-educated Ismail came to power, he was determined to build yet another city, one with international cachet. The future site of modern central Cairo was a swampy plain subject to annual Nile flooding. For 10 years the former marsh became one vast building site as Ismail invited architects from Belgium, France and Italy to design and build a new European-style Cairo, which earned the nickname 'Paris on the Nile'.

Since the revolution of 1952, the population of Cairo has grown spectacularly, although at the expense of Ismail's vision. In the 1960s and 1970s, urban planners concreted over the sparsely populated west bank of the Nile so they could build desperately needed new suburbs.

In more recent decades, growth has crept well beyond Muqattam Hills to the east and the Pyramids to the west. Luxe gated communities, sprawling housing blocks and full satellite cities, complete with malls and megastores, spring up from the desert every year while Cairo's slums have expanded as well. Whether the desert and the economy can sustain them remains to be seen.

RESOURCES

Lonely Planet (www.lonelyplanet.com/egypt/cairo) Destination information, hotel bookings, traveller forum and more.

Cairo 360 (www.cairo360.com) Restaurant and nightlife reviews and what's on guide for the capital.

Cairobserver (www.cairobserver.com) Smart articles on Cairo's urban fabric.

Cairo Scene (www.cairoscene.com) Contemporary lifestyle and culture plus news, reviews and events.

Egy.com (www.egy.com) For 19th- and 20th-century Cairo history.

Sights

Cairo's sights are spread all over the city, so it makes sense to do things in one area before moving on to the next – but don't try to cram too much into one day, or you'll soon be overwhelmed. The awe-inspiring but cluttered Egyptian Museum (p131) requires at least half a day, and ideally two or three shorter visits. Khan Al Khalili and most of the medieval monuments are in Islamic Cairo, and you'll need a full day or several visits at different times of the day. Definitely allow a few hours of aimless wandering in this area (even if it comes at the expense of 'proper' sightseeing), as the back lanes give the truest sense of the city.

CAIRO IN...

Two Days

Start with the magnificent **Egyptian Museum** (p131), followed by Egyptian street food done right at **Abu Tarek** (p102). Hop on the metro to Coptic Cairo to marvel at the wonders of the **Coptic Museum** (p66) and the area's clutch of churches, and then head to **Manial Palace** (p64) for a glimpse of the long-gone lifestyle of royalty amid the ornate salons. On day two make an early start for the **Pyramids of Giza** (p122). Afterwards dive into Islamic Cairo. Head to the **Museum of Islamic Art** (p78) first, then stroll via **Bab Zuweila** (p78) along **Sharia Al Muizz Li Din Allah** (p71), lined by glorious monuments. Put your haggling hat on for **Khan Al Khalili** (p70), then rest up amid the vintage interior of **Fishawi's** (p109).

Four Days

With two more days, further explore Islamic Cairo's maze. Don't miss walking from the **Mosque-Madrassa of Sultan Hassan** (p82) to the **Mosque of Ibn Tulun** (p83), taking in the gorgeous dervish theatre of the **Museo Mevlevi** (p83) and the **Gayer Anderson Museum's** (p84) restored finery along the way. Head to the **Citadel** (p81) for city views and the domed extravagance of the **Mosque of Mohammed Ali** (p81) before leaving the old medieval city's chaos behind, heading Nileside to stroll Garden City's looping lanes or heading out on the mighty river itself for a sunset **felucca ride**.

The Pyramids of Giza can be visited in four or five hours, but with the 10km trip to the edge of the city and back, it's inevitably a full-day outing. Coptic Cairo can be toured in a morning – made especially easy by metro access – and you'll likely soak up Downtown's atmosphere just by going to and from your hotel, or by hanging out there in the evenings.

◉ Downtown

Though the Egyptian Museum is found here, the part of town between Midan Ramses and Midan Tahrir, which locals call Wust Al Balad, is better known for its practical offerings: budget hotels, plenty of restaurants, cultural venues and a dazzling stream of shop window displays. (Don't rely on that shoe store/ lingerie shop/prosthetic-limbs dealer as a landmark – there's another one just a block away.) Occasionally try to look away from the traffic and fluorescent-lit shops and up at the dust-caked but elegant Empire-style office and apartment buildings that drip faded glamour (or is that an air-conditioner leaking?). It's a wonderful part of town to explore – just be prepared for sensory overload and loads of perfume-shop touts.

Midan Tahrir   SQUARE
(Map p62) Midan Tahrir (Liberation Sq) gained world renown in early 2011, when millions of Egyptians converged here to oust then-president Hosni Mubarak. On a regular day, it's just your average giant roundabout (traffic circle), albeit one where half-a-dozen major arteries converge. The main reason you'll pass through is to visit the powder-pink puffball bulk of the Egyptian Museum (p131).

One of the most distinctive orientation aids is the Ritz-Carlton Hotel. The modernist slab, with its mod-hieroglyphic facade, was built in 1959. Due north is the Egyptian Museum. Behind it used to be the blackened shell of Mubarak's National Democratic Party (NDP) headquarters, torched during the revolution and demolished in 2015.

South of the hotel, the **Arab League Building** (Map p62; closed to the public) is the occasional gathering place of leaders from around the Middle East, and now sometimes the site of smaller demonstrations. South across Sharia Tahrir you'll see the ornate white palace of the **Ministry of Foreign Affairs**, and the adjacent **Omar Makram Mosque** (Map p62; Midan Simon Bolivar), where anybody who's anybody has their funeral. The rest of the south side is occupied by the monstrous Mogamma (p116), home to 18,000 civil servants and notorious nationwide as the epicentre of the country's infernal bureaucracy. Comedian Adel Imam lampooned the place in his classic 1992 film *Irhab Wal Kabab* (Terrorism and Kebab), in

Cairo

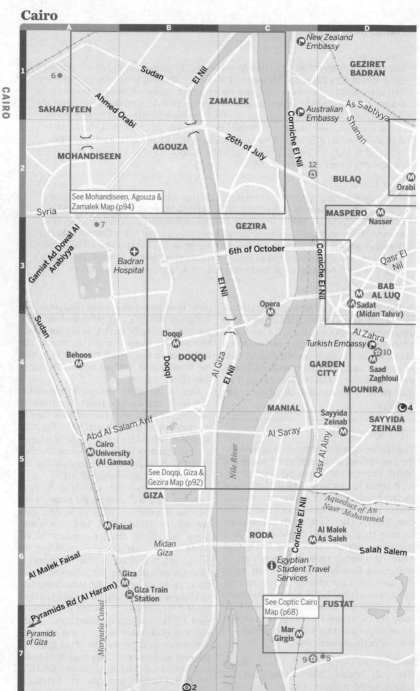

New Zealand Embassy

GEZIRET BADRAN

Sudan

El Nil

ZAMALEK

As Sabtiyya

Australian Embassy

SAHAFIYEEN

Ahmed Orabi

Corniche El Nil

Shanan

●6

MOHANDISEEN

AGOUZA

26th of July

12

BULAQ

Orabi

Syria

See Mohandiseen, Agouza & Zamalek Map (p94)

GEZIRA

MASPERO

Nasser

●7

Gamiat Ad Dowal Al Arabiyya

Badran Hospital

6th of October

El Nil

Corniche El Nil

Qasr El Nil

BAB AL LUQ

Sadat (Midan Tahrir)

Opera

Sudan

Behoos

Doqqi

Doqqi

DOQQI

El Giza

El Nil

Al Zahra

Turkish Embassy

●10

GARDEN CITY

Saad Zaghloul

MOUNIRA

Abd Al Salam Arif

Cairo University (Al Gamaa)

See Doqqi, Giza & Gezira Map (p92)

MANIAL

Al Saray

Sayyida Zeinab

Sayyida Zeinab

●4

SAYYIDA ZEINAB

Nile River

Qasr Al Ainy

GIZA

Faisal

Midan Giza

Aqueduct of An Nasr Mohammed

RODA

Corniche El Nil

Al Malek As Saleh

Salah Salem

Al Malek Faisal

Giza

Giza Train Station

Egyptian Student Travel Services

Pyramids Rd (Al Haram)

Maryutia Canal

See Coptic Cairo Map (p68)

FUSTAT

Pyramids of Giza

Mar Girgis

9 ● ●5

●2

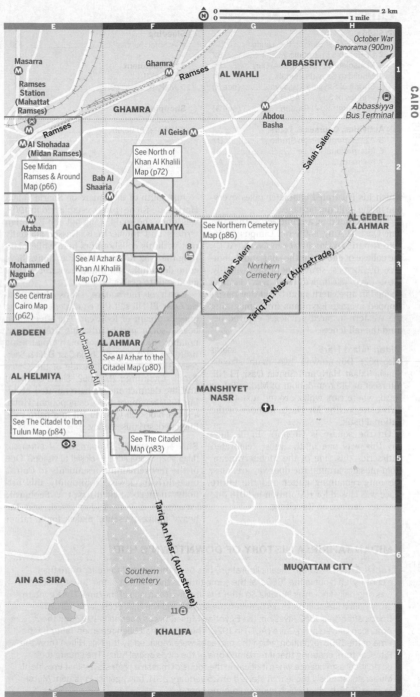

October War
Panorama (900m)

ABBASSIYYA

Masarra Ⓜ

Ghamra Ⓜ Ramses

AL WAHLI

**Ramses
Station
(Mahattat
Ramses)**

Abbassiyya
Bus Terminal

GHAMRA

Abdou
Basha Ⓜ

Ⓜ Al Shohadaa
(Midan Ramses)

Ⓜ Ramses

Al Geish Ⓜ

Salah Salem

See Midan
Ramses & Around
Map (p66)

Bab Al
Shaaria Ⓜ

See North of
Khan Al Khalili
Map (p72)

**AL GEBEL
AL AHMAR**

Ⓜ
Ataba

AL GAMALIYYA

See Northern Cemetery
Map (p86)

8

**Mohammed
Naguib** Ⓜ

See Al Azhar &
Khan Al Khalili
Map (p77)

(Salah Salem

Northern
Cemetery

Tariq An Nasr (Autostrade)

See Central
Cairo Map
(p62)

ABDEEN

**DARB
AL AHMAR**

See Al Azhar to the
Citadel Map (p80)

Mohammed Ali

AL HELMIYA

**MANSHIYET
NASR**

✞1

See The Citadel to Ibn
Tulun Map (p84)

◉3

See The Citadel
Map (p83)

Tariq An Nasr (Autostrade)

MUQATTAM CITY

AIN AS SIRA

Southern
Cemetery

11🏛

KHALIFA

Cairo

which his frustrated character takes everyone in the building hostage.

The next building around, across the four-lane Qasr Al Ainy, is the old campus of the elite American University in Cairo (AUC), the college of choice for the sons and daughters of Egypt's stratospherically wealthy. Most have decamped to a new campus opened in an eastern suburb, but that hasn't stopped average Egyptians from imagining the Western-inspired privileges enjoyed behind the tall fences.

Midan Talaat Harb   SQUARE
(Map p62) Downtown's two main streets, Sharia Talaat Harb and Sharia Qasr El Nil, intersect at the roundabout of Midan Talaat Harb, where cars whizz around a statue of tarboosh-sporting Mr Harb, founder of the national bank.

On the square is Groppi's. In its heyday this was one of the most celebrated patisseries this side of the Mediterranean. Gold mosaics around the doorway are, alas, the only remaining glitter and the entire place was closed for restoration in 2016 due to water damage on its ceiling.

Just south of the square on Sharia Talaat Harb, Café Riche (p104), established in 1908, was once the main hang-out for Egyptian writers and intellectuals. Nasser allegedly met with his collaborators here while planning the 1952 Revolution. Today things have gone downhill somewhat, though it's still a good spot to grab a beer.

North of the square, shops along Sharia Qasr El Nil sell the equivalent of a drag queen's dream of footwear. The street itself boasts some particularly fine architecture, notably the moorish Italian Insurance building (Map p62; cnr Sharia Qasr El Nil & Sherifeen), the neo classical facade of the Cairo Stock Exchange (Map p62; Sharia Sherifeen) and the defunct and being-renovated building that was once the Cosmopolitan Hotel, a short block off Qasr El Nil in a palm-tree-lined pedestrianised alley.

Shar Hashamaim Synagogue   SYNAGOGUE
(Map p62; Sharia Adly; ⊙closed to visitors) One of the few remaining testaments to Cairo's once-thriving Jewish community, this art-nouveau-meets-ancient-Egypt Sephardic synagogue is very seldom used, and the heavy police presence makes for a rather

---

MIDAN TAHRIR: A HISTORY OF DOWNTOWN'S HUB

Tahrir Square ('*tahrir*' means liberation) has been the heart of Cairo for more than a century. Laid out in the 1860s, at the same time as the building of the Suez Canal, it was originally known as Ismailia Sq after the khedive (or ruler) of the time. The Egyptian army built a sizeable barracks between the square and the Nile, occupied by British troops after their 1882 invasion; the Egyptian Museum was opened in 1902 and the American University in Cairo (AUC) in 1920. The square had been renamed Tahrir by the time of the 1952 revolution, when the barracks were replaced by the Nile Hilton (now the Ritz-Carlton), ensuring that it remained one of the city's social hubs. The square took on political significance when it became the focus of massive protests against President Mubarak, famously those that started on 25 January 2011, and against President Morsi in June 2013, both of which ended in regime change.

tense scene. When it opened in 1899, there was a large Jewish community in Cairo, but the last time the synagogue was full was in the 1960s. Casual visitors, unfortunately, haven't been able to enter for years, but you can admire the beautiful facade in full from across the road.

Abdeen Palace   MUSEUM
(Qasr Abdeen; Map p62; ☑2391 0042; Midan Al Gomhuriyya; adult/student LE100/50, camera LE10; ☺10am-2.30pm Sat-Thu; Ⓜ Mohammed Naguib) Unless you're into armaments (or over-the-top golden objects gifted to various Egyptian presidents), Abdeen Palace can easily be missed. Today the once regal salons are home to a military museum, the unintentionally funny presidential-gift rooms complete with gold palm tree and a painting of President Sisi made entirely from thumb tacks, and also a museum that holds some highly elaborate 18th- and 19th-century silverware.

Begun in 1863, the palace was a centrepiece of Khedive Ismail's plan for a modern Cairo, inspired by Paris' then-recent makeover; the khedive even called in mastermind French planner Baron Haussmann as a consultant. He wanted the palace finished for the 1869 opening of the Suez Canal, to impress visiting dignitaries, but its 500 rooms weren't completed until 1874. It was the royal residence until the monarchy was abolished in 1952.

The museum's entry is on the east side. The ticket office is in the building across the road.

Midan Ataba   SQUARE
(Map p62; off Sharia Al Gomhuriyya; Ⓟ) This traffic-clogged area of park, markets and transit hub is the transition point from European-built Cairo, particularly its theatre and entertainment district, to the medieval Cairo of Saladin (Salah Ad Din), the Mamluks and the Ottomans. You'll likely find yourself at the Midan because it's a convenient walk from here to Islamic Cairo.

On the southwest side of Midan Ataba, past the flyovers, the domed main post office has a pretty courtyard. The 'Commemorative Stamp Office' just inside the post office entrance is where you buy tickets to the neighbouring **Postal Museum** (Map p62; ☑2391 0011; 2nd fl, Central Post Office, Midan Ataba; LE2; ☺8am-3pm Sun-Fri). The quirky collection of miniature models of post offices, old postal uniforms, aerogram envelopes and stamps is worth a brief look for anyone who enjoys an eccentric museum.

RAMSES' COLOSSUS

The eponymous Ramses, a multistorey Pharaonic colossus of red granite, stood on Midan Ramses, amid the traffic, until 2006, when he was removed, with much complex machinery, road closures and some emotion. He now stands swaddled in plastic wrap on the edge of the desert north of the city, waiting to stand sentry at the yet-to-be-opened Grand Egyptian Museum, no doubt missing his old view over the action.

Just off Midan Ataba is Ezbekiyya. By night the crowded stalls of the **Ezbekiyya Book Market** (Map p62; Ezbekiyya Gardens; ☺11am-9pm) are busy with browsers. By day **Ezbekiyya Gardens** (Map p62; Sharia Al Gomhuriyya; LE2; ☺8am-10pm) are a dusty urban respite. The famous Shepheard's Hotel, the preferred accommodation of the British colonists, was once located opposite – it was destroyed by Black Saturday rioters in 1952. Next to the gardens, Midan Opera marks the site of the old opera house, which burnt down in 1971, and was rebuilt as a towering car park.

◉ Midan Ramses

The northern gateway into central Cairo, Midan Ramses is a byword for bedlam. The city's main north–south access collides with overpasses and arterial roads to swamp the square with an unchoreographed slew of vehicles. Commuters swarming from the train station add to the melee.

Ramses Train Station   NOTABLE BUILDING
(Mahattat Ramses; ☑2575 3555; Ⓜ Al Shohadaa) Cairo's main train station, built in its current style in 1892, is an attractive marriage of Islamic style and industrial-age engineering – at least on the outside. Its interior was redone with gaudy Dubai-mall aesthetics in a massive refit completed in 2014. At its eastern end is the quirky **Egyptian Railways Museum** (☑2576 3793; Ramses Station; LE50, camera LE10; ☺9am-4pm; Ⓜ Al Shohadaa), heaven for railway-geeks and model-building hobbyists, which traces the history of transportation in Egypt from the Pharaonic era to the modern age through models, replicas, documents and old photos.

Central Cairo

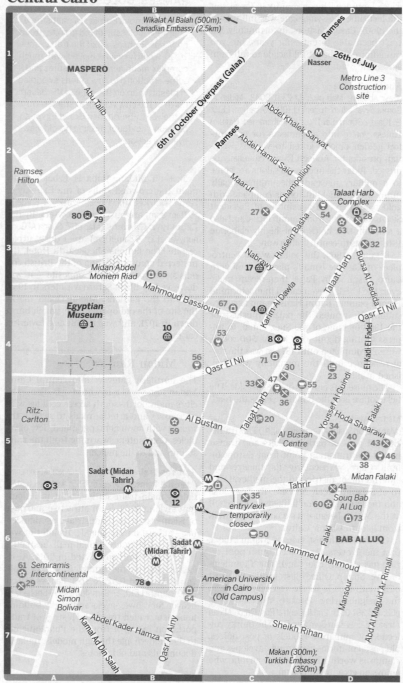

MASPERO

Wikalat Al Balah (500m);
Canadian Embassy (2.5km)

Ramses

26th of July

Nasser

Metro Line 3
Construction
site

Abul Talib

6th of October Overpass (Galaa)

Ramses

Abdel Khalek Sarwat

Ramses
Hilton

Abdel Hamid Said

Maaruf

Champollion

Talaat Harb
Complex

27

54

28

63

18

32

Hussein Bacha

Nabrawy

17

Talaat Harb

Bursa Al Gedida

Midan Abdel
Moniem Riad

65

Mahmoud Bassiouni

Egyptian
Museum
1

10

67

4

Karim Al Dawla

Qasr El Nil

8

13

El Kadi El Fadel

53

Qasr El Nil

56

71

30

23

Ritz-
Carlton

33

47

55

36

59

Al Bustan

20

Talaat Harb

34

Youssef Al Guindi

Hoda Shaarawi

Falaki

40

43

46

Al Bustan
Centre

38

Midan Falaki

Sadat (Midan
Tahrir)

72

Tahrir

41

3

12

35

entry/exit
temporarily
closed

60

Souq Bab
Al Luq

73

BAB AL LUQ

50

Mohammed Mahmoud

Falaki

Mansour

Abd Al Maguid Ar Rimali

14

Sadat
(Midan Tahrir)

61 Semiramis
Intercontinental

29

Midan
Simon
Bolivar

78

American University
in Cairo
(Old Campus)

64

Abdel Kader Hamza

Kamal Ad Din Salah

Qasr Al Ainy

Sheikh Rihan

Makan (300m);
Turkish Embassy
(350m)

80 79

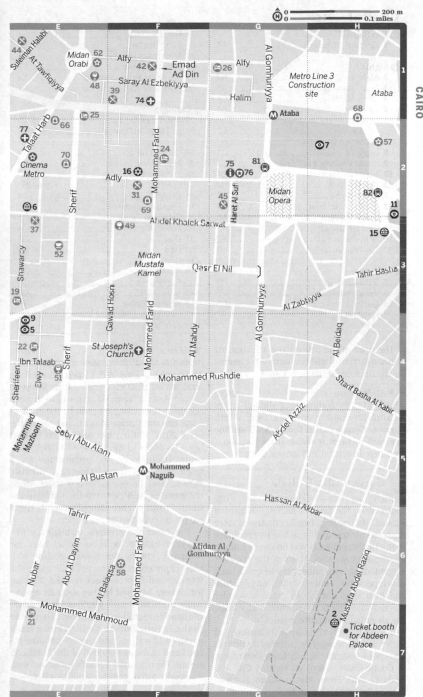

Central Cairo

The prize of the collection is the original railway carriage built for Empress Eugénie for the opening of the Suez Canal.

Al Fath Mosque   MOSQUE
(Map p66) On the south side of Midan Ramses is Cairo's pre-eminent orientation aid, Al Fath Mosque. Completed in the early 1990s, the mosque's minaret is visible from just about anywhere in central and Islamic Cairo.

◉ Garden City & Roda

Garden City was developed in the early 1900s along the lines of an English garden suburb. Its curving, tree-lined streets were designed for tranquillity, while its proximity to the British embassy was no doubt intended to convey security. Many of the enclave's elegant villas have fallen prey to quick-buck developers, but enough grand architecture and lush trees survive to make a wander through the streets worthwhile – at sunset, the air of faded romance is palpable.

The island of Roda is quiet, its banks lined with plant nurseries. If you're very dedicated, you could walk all the way from Downtown to Coptic Cairo (5 km) via Garden City and Roda (2 km). From Midan Talaat Harb to Manial Palace (2.8 km) is about 40 minutes.

★**Manial Palace**   MUSEUM
(Mathaf Al Manial, Palace-Museum of Mohammed Ali; Map p92; ☑ 2368 7495; 1 Sharia Al Saray, Roda; adult/student LE100/50; ⊗9am-4pm; Ⓜ Sayyida Zeinab) After a years'-long restoration period, this palace complex, built by the uncle of King Farouk, Prince Mohammed Ali, in the early 20th century, has once again thrown open its doors to the public as a quirky museum. Its interiors and architecture are a fascinating merging of Ottoman, Moorish, Persian and European rococo styles, while the gardens (still closed to the public at the time of research) are planted with rare tropical plants collected by the prince.

You enter the grounds through the **Reception Palace**, with its grand halls for receiving guests decorated lavishly with tiles, chandeliers and carved ceilings. In the **Residential Palace** check out the Blue Salon, where battered leather sofas sit against walls decorated with glorious blue faience tiles and Orientalist oil paintings. Then head to the **Throne Palace** for the Throne Hall's gaudy gold-styling, and the eye-popping rococo and baroque overload of the Aubusson Room. Even Manial Palace's **mosque** (with rococo-inspired ceiling) and **clock tower** (based on Moroccan Almohad-era minaret design) are a marvellous mesh of influences.

Umm Kulthum Museum & Monastirli Palace
MUSEUM

(Map p68; 📞 2363 1467; Sharia Al Malek As Salih, Roda Island; adult/student LE6/3, camera LE20; ⊙ 9am-4pm) Set in a peaceful Nileside garden, Monastirli Palace was built in 1851 for an Ottoman pasha whose family hailed from Monastir, in northern Greece. The *salamlik* (greeting area) that he built for public functions is an elegant venue for concerts, while the other part is the Umm Kulthum Museum, a shrinelike space dedicated to the most famous Arab diva.

The singer's signature rhinestone-trimmed glasses and glittery gowns are hung under spotlights, and you can listen to her music and watch a fascinating biographical film (with English subtitles), which traces her career from the beginning when she performed disguised as a Bedouin boy, to her magnetic performances that brought Cairo to a standstill. The documentary's footage of her funeral, when millions of mourners flooded Cairo's streets, is worth a visit alone.

Nilometer
HISTORIC SITE

(Map p68; Sharia Al Malek As Salih, Roda Island; LE15; ⊙ 9am-4pm; Ⓜ Mar Girgis) At the very southern tip of Roda, inside the Monastirli Palace compound, the Nilometer was constructed in AD 861. Like others built millennia before, it measured the rise and fall of the river, and predicted the fortunes of the annual harvest. The Turkish-style pencil-point dome is a Farouk-era reconstruction of an earlier one wrecked by Napoleon's troops.

If the water rose to 16 cubits (a cubit is about the length of a forearm), the harvest was likely to be good, inspiring one of the greatest celebrations of the medieval era. Any higher, though, and the flooding could be disastrous, while lower levels presaged hunger. The measuring device, a graduated column, sits below the level of the Nile at the bottom of a flight of precipitous steps, which you can descend right to the bottom. The entrance is on Sharia Al Malek As Salih. You buy your ticket there off the site guard who will then accompany you down the path to the Nilometer building as it's usually kept shut between visits.

⊙ Coptic Cairo

A maze of ancient and modern churches and monasteries, set within the walls of the fortress of Babylon founded in 6th century BC and expanded by the Roman Emperor Trajan in AD 98, Coptic Cairo is a fascinating

CAIRO SIGHTS

Midan Ramses & Around

Midan Ramses & Around

◎ Sights
1 Al Fath Mosque...................................B2

⊕ Activities, Courses & Tours
2 Studio Emad Eddin B3

⊗ Eating
3 At Tabei Ad Dumyati...........................A3

counterpoint to the rest of the city, and holds the beautiful Coptic Museum. You can visit the oldest church, the oldest mosque and the oldest synagogue in Cairo, while nearby is the newly opened (but rather bare of exhibits and still unfinished at the time of research) National Museum of Egyptian Civilisation (p69).

There are four entrances to the Coptic compound. The main gate in the centre of Sharia Mar Girgis (directly opposite the metro exit) is for the Coptic Museum. Just to the south, another doorway leads to the Hanging Church, while to the north is the entrance into the Church of St George. On the street outside, a sunken staircase gives access to a section of narrow cobbled alleyways leading to the other churches and the synagogue. At one time there were more than 20 churches clustered within less than 1 sq km.

★ **Coptic Museum** MUSEUM
(Map p68; ☎2363 9742; www.coptic-cairo.com/museum; 3 Sharia Mar Girgis; adult/student LE100/50, camera LE50; ◷8am-4pm; Ⓜ Mar Girgis) This museum, founded in 1908, houses Coptic art from the earliest days of Christianity in Egypt right through to early Islam. It is a beautiful place, as much for the elaborate woodcarving in all the galleries as for the treasures they contain. These include sculpture that shows obvious continuity from the Ptolemaic period, rich textiles and whole walls of monastery frescoes. Allow at least a couple of hours to explore the 1200 or so pieces on display.

The 2nd- to 5th-century funerary stelae from Kom Abou Billou clearly show the transition between Pharaonic and Coptic art, with the first crosses shaped like the ankh, key of life. The 4th- and 5th-century sculpture equally marks this transition, where Christian symbolism was influenced by Graeco-Roman mythology as well as older Pharaonic subjects. Rebirth through baptism of water is suggested by Aphrodite emerging from the waters on a seashell. Look out for the wonderful 7th- to 8th-century work of three mice asking a cat for peace. In Egypt the depiction of animals behaving like humans dates back to 1500 BC.

DOWNTOWN ARTS SCENE

Cairo's art scene is more active and diverse than ever, and much of the action is Downtown. In addition to these arts spaces, the city's cultural centres (p110) often mount interesting shows, and Darb 1718 (p110) is worth a trip.

Cairo Atelier (Atelier du Caire; Map p62; ☑ 2574 6730; www.facebook.com/groups/ 216621056906; 2 Sharia Karim Al Dawla; ☉10am-1pm & 5-10pm Sat-Thu) FREE Off Sharia Mahmoud Bassiouni, as much a clubhouse as an exhibition space.

Contemporary Image Collective (Map p62; ☑ 2396 4272; www.ciccairo.com; 4th fl, 22 Abdel Khalek Sarwat; ☉10am-6pm Sun-Thu) FREE Often hosts excellent temporary art and photography exhibitions documenting Egyptian life, plus film and photo workshops.

Mashrabia Gallery (Map p62; ☑ 2578 4494; www.facebook.com/mashrabiagallery; 8 Sharia Champollion; ☉11am-8pm Sat-Thu; Ⓜ Sadat) FREE A bit cramped but represents the bigger names in painting and sculpture.

Studio Emad Eddin (SEE; Map p66; ☑ 2576 3850; www.seefoundation.org; 18 Sharia Emad Ad Din) Rehearsal and workshop space for performing artists; sometimes stages events and workshops.

Townhouse Gallery (Map p62; ☑ 2576 8086; www.thetownhousegallery.com; 3 Sharia Hussein Basha; ☉noon-9pm Sat-Wed; Ⓜ Sadat) FREE Cairo's most cutting-edge space, set amid car-repair shops, has launched many Egyptian artists. There's a regular program of temporary exhibitions, along with events, seminars and performances.

Upstairs are two large rooms with exquisite 4th- to 7th-century Coptic textiles, woven and embroidered, and a room with the Nag Hammadi manuscripts, the primary source for Gnosticism, and the oldest book of psalms in the world, the Psalms of David, with two original wooden covers.

Hanging Church
CHURCH

(Al Kineesa Al Mu'allaqa; Map p68; www.coptic-cairo.com; Sharia Mar Girgis; donations welcome; ☉8am-4pm, Coptic Mass 8-11am Wed & Fri, 9-11am Sun; Ⓜ Mar Girgis) FREE Just south of the Coptic Museum on Sharia Mar Girgis (the main road parallel with the metro), a stone facade inscribed with Coptic and Arabic marks the entrance to the 9th-century (some say 7th-century) Hanging Church, so named because it is suspended over the Water Gate of Roman Babylon. With its three barrel-vaulted, wood-roofed aisles, the interior of the church feels like an upturned ark, resting on 13 elegant pillars representing Christ and his apostles.

Steep stairs lead to a 19th-century facade topped by twin bell towers. In a small inner courtyard, vendors sell taped liturgies and videos of the Coptic pope, Shenouda III. The interior feels very similar to that of a mosque. The ebony- and ivory-inlaid screens hiding the altar show the same intricate geometric designs that are distinguishable from Islamic patterns only by the tiny crosses worked on

them. One of the columns is darker than the rest; it is believed to represent Judas.

The church has 110 icons, including a series describing the life and torture of St George and the life of St John the Baptist, and a very sacred painting of Virgin Mary known as the Coptic 'Mona Lisa'. In the baptistery, off to the right, a panel has been cut out of the floor to reveal the Water Gate below. Still in use, the church is equally crowded with tourists and parishioners who come to pray over a collection of saints' relics and an icon of Mary.

Roman Towers
MONUMENT

(Map p68; Sharia Mar Girgis; Ⓜ Mar Girgis) In AD 98 the Roman emperor Trajan enlarged an existing fortress here, called Babylon, likely a corruption of Per-hapi en on (Estate of the Nile God at On), a Pharaonic name for the area. What remains are two round towers of Babylon's western gate. These were part of riverfront fortifications, and the Nile would have lapped right up against them. Emperor Trajan also reopened the canal that ran through this town connecting the Nile with the Red Sea.

Visitors can peer down around the southern tower, where excavations have revealed part of the ancient quay, several metres below street level. The Greek Orthodox Monastery and Church of St George sit on top of the northern tower.

Coptic Cairo

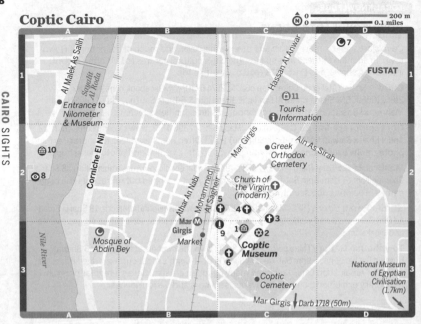

Coptic Cairo

Greek Orthodox Monastery & Church of St George
CHURCH

(Map p68; Sharia Mar Girgis; donations welcome; ⊙8am-4pm) FREE The first doorway north of the Coptic Museum gate leads to the Greek Orthodox Monastery and Church of St George. St George (Mar Girgis) is one of the region's most popular Christian saints. A Palestinian conscript in the Roman army, he was executed in AD 303 for resisting Emperor Diocletian's decree forbidding the practice of Christianity. There has been a church dedicated to him in Coptic Cairo since the 10th century; this one dates from 1909.

The neighbouring monastery is closed to visitors. The Coptic *moulid* (saints' festival) of Mar Girgis is held here on 23 April.

Church of St Sergius & Bacchus
CHURCH

(Abu Sarga; Map p68; www.coptic-cairo.com/old cairo/church/sarga/sarga.html; off Sharia Haret Al Kidees Girgis; donations welcome; ⊙8am-4pm; ⓂMar Girgis) FREE This is the oldest church inside Coptic Cairo's walls, built in the 11th century with 4th-century pillars. It honours the Roman soldiers Sergius and Bacchus, who were martyred in Syria for their Christian faith in AD 296. It is built over a cave where Joseph, Mary and the infant Jesus are said to have taken shelter after fleeing to Egypt to escape persecution from King Herod of Judea, who had embarked upon a 'massacre of the first born'.

Abu Sarga is based on a basilica structure with a nave and two side aisles. The nave is defined by 12 columns, 11 in white marble and one in red granite, with some showing traces of images of saints. The church houses some great icons representing the life of Christ, various saints and the Virgin Mary. The cave of the Holy Family, now a crypt, is reached by descending steps in a chapel to the left of the altar (usually locked). Every year, on 1 June, a special Mass is held here to commemorate the event. To get here, walk down the central lane (Haret Al Kidees Girgis), turning right at the T, then left as it turns; stairs lead down to the entrance, below street level.

Church of St Barbara
CHURCH
(Map p68; www.coptic-cairo.com/oldcairo/church/barbara/barbara.html; off Sharia Haret Al Kidees Girgis; donations welcome; ⊙8am-4pm; Ⓜ Mar Girgis) FREE At the corner past Abu Sarga, the Church of St Barbara is dedicated to a martyr who was beaten to death by her father for trying to convert him to Christianity. Her supposed relics rest in a small chapel left of the altar, along with a few other saints' remains. The church houses some rare icons of St Barbara, the Virgin Mary and Jesus Christ. Beyond the church an iron gate leads to the peaceful (if somewhat litter-strewn) Coptic cemetery

Ben Ezra Synagogue
SYNAGOGUE
(Map p68; off Sharia Haret Al Kidees Girgis; donations welcome; ⊙8am-4pm; Ⓜ Mar Girgis) FREE Just outside the walls of the Coptic enclave, the 9th-century Ben Ezra Synagogue occupies the shell of a 4th-century Christian church. Tradition marks this as the spot where the prophet Jeremiah gathered the Jews in the 6th century after Nebuchadnezzar destroyed the Jerusalem temple. The adjacent spring is supposed to mark the place where the pharaoh's daughter found Moses in the reeds, and also where Mary drew water to wash Jesus.

In the 12th century the synagogue was restored by Abraham Ben Ezra, rabbi of Jerusalem. In 1890 a cache of more than 250,000 historic papers, known as the Geniza documents, was uncovered in the synagogue. From them, researchers have been able to piece together details of the life of the North African Jewish community from the 11th to 13th centuries.

Mosque of Amr Ibn Al As
MOSQUE
(Map p68; Sharia Sidi Hassan Al Anwar; Ⓜ Mar Girgis) FREE The first mosque built in Egypt, this structure was established in AD 642 by the general who conquered Egypt for Islam. Built on the site where Ibn Al As pitched his tent, the original structure was only palm trunks thatched with leaves. It expanded to its current size in AD 827, and has been continually reworked since then – most recently, a wood roof was installed to mimic the original style more closely.

The oldest section is to the right of the sanctuary; the rest of the mosque is a forest of some 200 different columns, the majority taken from ancient sites. There's little else to see, but the vast space is a pleasant place to rest. To reach it, head north on Sharia Mar Girgis, beyond the Coptic compound and past Souq Al Fustat (p112), a covered market with quality craft shops and a cafe.

National Museum of Egyptian Civilisation
MUSEUM
(NMEC; ☑2525 5588; www.nmec.gov.eg; Sharia Al Fustat, Fustat; adult/child LE60/30, camera LE50; ⊙9am-4pm; Ⓜ Mar Girgis) This megalithic new building, sitting behind a massive white-stone plaza, is intending to walk visitors through the vast breadth of Egyptian civilisation. It was only partially open when we visited, with construction ongoing on the huge outdoor terrace area that runs down to the shore of Ayn As Sirah Lake and has views across to the Citadel. Only one gallery was open, exhibiting a small display of some beautiful textiles, ceramics and jewellery.

Do check the website to see if it's fully open when you're in town as, when finished, the planned galleries here will hopefully help throw light on the wealth of culture Egypt has amassed through the ages and its importance in world history.

ⓘ COPTIC CAIRO PRACTICALITIES

➡ Mar Girgis metro station is directly in front of the compound.

➡ Visitors must have shoulders and knees covered to enter churches or mosques.

➡ Churches celebrate Mass on Sunday, and some on Friday as well.

➡ Bring small change for church donation boxes.

➡ A few basic cafes, with toilets, are scattered among the churches. There are also toilets at the Coptic Museum and the Hanging Church.

➡ For cheap street snacks, cross the metro tracks to the west side.

➡ Check out the website of nearby art centre Darb 1718 (p110) for listings of events, and seek out **Souq Al Fustat** (p112) for contemporary local craft shopping.

Islamic Cairo

Despite the number of minarets on the skyline in this part of the city, 'Islamic' Cairo is a bit of a misnomer, as this area is not significantly more religious than other districts. But for many centuries it was one of the power centres of an Islamic empire, and its monuments are some of the most significant architecture inspired by Islam. Today it is still a more traditional part of town, the *galabeya* (men's full-length robes) still outnumber jeans; buildings and crowds press closer, and the din comes less from car traffic and more from the cries of street vendors and the clang of small workshops. Here the streets are a warren of blind alleys, and it's easy to lose not just a sense of direction but also a sense of time.

An ambitious restoration program is making over monuments as well as streets and everyday buildings, with fresh paint and turned-wood window screens. Return visitors may be shocked by the extent of change. Although many projects came to a standstill with the downfall of President Mubarak, renovations have revved up again so do expect a smattering of wooden-scaffolding-covered facades. The changes have, for the most part, greatly benefited residents. Vast Al Azhar Park, once an enormous rubbish heap, is hard to argue with as an improvement.

Midan Al Hussein & Around

Midan Al Hussein   SQUARE
(Map p77) The square between the two venerated mosques of Al Azhar and Sayyidna Al Hussein was one of the focal points of Mamluk Cairo and remains an important space at feast times, particularly on Ramadan evenings and during the *moulids* of Hussein and the Prophet Mohammed. The square is a popular meeting place, and the restaurants (mains LE30 to LE120) with outdoor seating on the western side, at the entrance to the Khan Al Khalili, are often packed with equal parts locals and tourists.

Mosque of Sayyidna Al Hussein   MOSQUE
(Map p77; Midan Al Hussein; ⊘ closed to non-Muslims) One of the most sacred Islamic sites in Egypt, this mosque is the reputed burial place of the head of Hussein, the grandson of Prophet Mohammed. Most of the building dates from about 1870, except for the beautiful 14th-century stucco panels on the minaret. The modern metal sculptures in front are elegant Teflon canopies

that expand to cover worshippers during Friday prayers. This is one of the few mosques where non-Muslims can't enter.

The death of Hussein in Karbala, Iraq, cemented the rift between the Sunni and Shiite branches of Islam. It has to be said that the Umayyad Mosque in Damascus also claims Hussein's head, a Shiite relic, even though both mosques were established by Sunnis.

★ **Khan Al Khalili**   MARKET
(Map p77; off Sharia Al Azhar & Al Gamaliyya) The skinny lanes of Khan Al Khalili are basically a medieval-style mall. This agglomeration of shops – many arranged around small courtyards – stocks everything from soap powder to semiprecious stones, not to mention tacky toy camels and alabaster pyramids. Most shops and stalls open from around 9am to well after sundown (except Friday morning and Sunday), although plenty of the souvenir vendors are open as long as there are customers, even on Sunday.

Cairenes have plied their trades here since the khan was built in the 14th century, and parts of the market, such as the gold district, are still the first choice for thousands of locals. The khan used to be divided into fairly rigid districts, but now the only distinct areas are the gold sellers, the coppersmiths and the spice dealers. Apart from the clumsy 'Hey mister, look for free' touts, the merchants of Khan Al Khalili are some of the greatest smooth-talkers you will ever meet. Almost anything can be bought here and if one merchant doesn't have what you're looking for, he'll happily find somebody who does.

Midaq Alley   STREET
(Zuqaq Al Midaq; Map p77) This tiny alley is Islamic Cairo's literary star thanks to being immortalised in Naguib Mahfouz's famous novel named after the street. Although the stepped lane may not be populated with the same colourful characters as the book, the way of life here is little changed from the author's 1940s depictions. Because of the street's fame, the street sign is kept in the coffeehouse at the foot of the steps and produced only on payment of baksheesh.

Sharia Al Gamaliyya   STREET
(Map p72) Sharia Al Gamaliyya was the heart of a trading district in medieval Cairo, and a major thoroughfare. Today it's more like a back alley with a real local residential feel. At its southern end, running off Midan Al Hussein, many facades above the shopfronts

ℹ️ VISITING ISLAMIC CAIRO

➡ Appropriate dress is not just polite but necessary if you want to enter mosques; legs and shoulders must be covered. Wear sturdy shoes that can be easily slipped off.

➡ Caretakers are usually around from 9am until early evening. Mosques are often closed to visitors during prayer times.

➡ Bring small change to tip caretakers at mosques – a bit of baksheesh for looking after shoes, pointing out details or climbing a minaret is typical. But be firm and don't pay more than you wish.

➡ With the exception of Sultan Hassan and Ar Rifai, all mosques are free to enter, but some caretakers will claim an admission fee. If you're not sure, ask if there is a ticket ('fee taz-kar-a?') and politely refuse payment if there is none.

➡ In ticketed monuments, some guards will attempt to resell a previous visitor's ticket (cadged by another guard inside, assuring the visitor it's 'normal' to hand it over). If it is not torn out of the book in front of you, it's reused.

➡ Some caretakers have even claimed guidebooks aren't permitted in mosques, to prevent you from reading these very warnings.

are obscured by webs of restorers' wooden scaffolding. Heading north, one completed project is the 1408 **Mosque of Gamal Ad Din**, cleaned up to reveal a row of shops below, the rent from which contributed to the mosque's upkeep.

Right at the northern end of the street is the **Wikala of Sultan Qaitbey** which was undergoing an extensive restoration at the time of research. Through the scaffolding though you can still admire the fine entranceway of this large Mamluk-era merchant's inn.

Khanqah & Mausoleum of Sultan Beybars Al Gashankir
MOSQUE, TOMB

(Sufi Monastery; Map p72; Sharia Al Gamaliyya; ⊙9am-5pm) FREE Built in 1310, this *khanqah* (Sufi monastery) is one of the city's first. It's distinguished by its stubby minaret, topped with a small ribbed dome. The multipart 'baffled' entrance orients the rooms away from the street. The interior is in a sorry state, in part due to the flocks of pigeons roosting here. If you're not a bird fan, it's probably best not to enter.

Mamluk sultan Beybars Al Gashankir is entombed in a room that shimmers with black-and-white marble panelling and light from stained-glass windows. His name was excised from the building facade by order of his successor.

Wikala Al Bazara
HISTORIC BUILDING

(Map p72; Sharia Al Tombakshiyya; adult/student LE40/20; ⊙8am-5pm) This is one of about 20 remaining *wikala* (merchants' inn) in the medieval city, from about 360 in the 17th century, when this one was built. All were built to the same plan: storerooms and stables surrounding a courtyard, with guestrooms for traders on the upper floors. Heavy front gates (check out the inlaid-wood door lock, and the anachronistic Lancashire fire badge) protected the merchandise at night. Climb upon the roof for the view.

⭐ Sharia Al Muizz Li Din Allah
STREET

(Map p77) Sharia Al Muizz, as it's usually called, named after the Fatimid caliph who conquered Cairo in AD 969, was Cairo's grand thoroughfare, once chock-a-block with storytellers, entertainers and food stalls. The part of Sharia Al Muizz just north of Khan Al Khalili's gold district is known as **Bein Al Qasreen** (Palace Walk; Map p72), a reminder of the great palace complexes that flanked the street during the Fatimid era. Today the great Mamluk complexes provide one of Cairo's most impressive assemblies of minarets, domes and striped-stone facades.

The Bein Al Qasreen section of the street has been redone, from new pavement to the tips of the minarets of the monuments along its length. During daytime vehicle-free hours (9am to 10pm), visitors may comfortably gawk at the sites without fear of being flattened by traffic. One stretch of the street is occupied by small places selling shishas (water pipes), braziers and pear-shaped cooking pots for *fuul*. Soon the stock expands to crescent-moon minaret tops, coffee ewers and other copper products, hence its more popular name, Sharia An Nahaseen (Street of the Coppersmiths). Stroll along and admire the medieval architecture mixed with Cairo's hustle and bustle.

Several monuments, starting from the Madrassa and Mausoleum of Qalaun, and heading north, share a combination entrance ticket.

★ Madrassa & Mausoleum of Qalaun   HISTORIC BUILDING

(Map p72; Sharia Al Muizz Li Din Allah multisite ticket adult/student LE100/50; ⊗9am-5pm) Built in just 13 months, the 1279 Madrassa and Mausoleum of Qalaun is both the earliest and the most splendid of the vast religious complexes on this street. The mausoleum, on the right, is a particularly intricate assemblage of inlaid stone and stucco, patterned with stars and floral motifs and lit by stained-glass windows. The complex also includes a *maristan* (hospital), which Qalaun ordered to be built after he visited one in Damascus, where he was cured of colic.

The Arab traveller and historian Ibn Battuta, who visited Cairo in 1325, was impressed that Qalaun's hospital contained 'an innumerable quantity of appliances and medicaments'. He also described how the mausoleum was flanked by Quran reciters day and night chanting requiems for the dead within.

Madrassa & Mausoleum of As Salih Ayyub   HISTORIC BUILDING

(Map p72; Sharia Al Muizz Li Din Allah; Sharia Al Muizz Li Din Allah multisite ticket adult/student LE100/50; ⊗9am-5pm) This complex was built between 1242 and 1244 by the last Ayyubid sultan of Egypt, Al Salih Najm Al Din Ayyub, who died defending Egypt against the Crusader attack that was led by Louis IX. His grandfather was the famous Salah Al Din Ayyub, known in the West as Saladin.

It is the first known example of a mausoleum attached to a madrassa, and it was in many ways a trendsetter for the Mamluk buildings that followed, and that can be visited further along the street. The madrassa was also the first to house all four of the Sunni legal schools. The adjoining tomb, where Sultan Ayyub resides, was built by his Turkic wife, Shagaret Al Durr (Tree of Pearls), in 1250, well after the sultan's death, which she had concealed to keep the French Crusader armies in Damietta from sensing weakness. Shagarat Al Durr managed to defeat the Crusaders, then ruled on as sultana

North of Khan Al Khalili

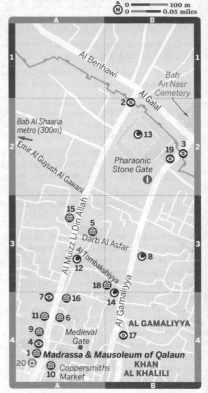

and ushered in the Mamluk era, when the Turkic janissaries took power.

Madrassa & Mausoleum of An Nasir Mohammed   HISTORIC BUILDING

(Map p72; Sharia Al Muizz Li Din Allah; Sharia Al Muizz Li Din Allah multisite ticket adult/student LE100/50; ⊗9am-5pm) Sultan An Nasir ('the Victor'), was both despotic and exceedingly accomplished. His madrassa was built in 1304 in part with a Gothic doorway An Nasir plundered from a church in Acre (now Akko, Israel) after he and his army ended Crusader domination there in 1290. Buried in the mausoleum (on the right as you enter, ask the site guardian for the key) is An Nasir's mother and favourite son; the sultan himself is next door in the mausoleum of his father, Qalaun.

North of Khan Al Khalili

Madrassa & Mausoleum of Barquq
HISTORIC BUILDING

(Map p72; Sharia Al Muizz Li Din Allah; Sharia Al Muizz Li Din Allah multi-site ticket adult/student LE100/50; ⊙9am-5pm) Sultan Barquq seized power in 1382, when Egypt was reeling from plague and famine; his Sufi school was completed four years later. Enter through the bold black-and-white marble portal into a vaulted passageway. To the right, the inner court has a lavish blue-and-gold ceiling supported by four porphyry Pharaonic columns. Barquq's daughter is buried in the splendid domed tomb chamber; the sultan himself preferred to rest in the Northern Cemetery, surrounded by Sufi sheikhs.

Egyptian Textile Museum
MUSEUM

(Map p72; Sharia Al Muizz Li Din Allah; adult/student LE20/10; ⊙9am-4.30pm) The only one of its kind in the Middle East, this interesting museum features textiles from ancient Egypt and the Roman, Coptic and Islamic eras. The collection starts at the very beginning, with Pharaonic diapers, and moves on through beautifully embroidered Coptic tunics and great embroidered *qiswat* (the panels that adorn the Kaaba in Mecca). It's a small museum, but well worth a peek for anyone with an affinity for weaving and fabric.

Hammam Inal
HAMMAM

(Map p72; Sharia Al Muizz Li Din Allah; Sharia Al Muizz Li Din Allah multisite ticket adult/student LE100/50; ⊙9am-4.30pm) One of the few well restored examples of Cairo's once vibrant hammam (bathhouse) culture, the Hammam Inal dates from 1456. The marble-clad central room is topped by a traditional domed ceiling studded with tiny coloured glass windows that allow in shafts of light.

Sabil-Kuttab of Abdel Rahman Katkhuda
HISTORIC BUILDING

(Map p72; Sharia Al Muizz Li Din Allah; Sharia Al Muizz Li Din Allah multisite ticket adult/student LE100/50; ⊙9am-4pm) The Sabil-Kuttab of Abdel Rahman Katkhuda is one of the iconic structures of Islamic Cairo, depicted in scores of paintings and lithographs. Building this fountain-school combo was an atonement for sins, as it provided two things commended by the Prophet: water for the thirsty and enlightenment for the ignorant. This one was built in 1744 by an emir notorious for his debauchery. There's nice ceramic work inside.

Qasr Beshtak
HISTORIC BUILDING

(Map p72; off Sharia Al Muizz Li Din Allah; Sharia Al Muizz Li Din Allah multisite ticket adult/student LE100/50; ⊙9am-5pm) At the Sabil-Kuttab of Kathkuda, take the little alleyway that leads to Qasr Beshtak (Palace of Amir Beshtak), a rare example of 14th-century domestic architecture originally five floors high. The main hall here (which is occasionally used as a concert venue) has been beautifully restored.

Mosque of Al Aqmar
MOSQUE

(Map p72; Sharia Al Muizz Li Din Allah) **FREE** This petite mosque, the oldest in Egypt with a stone facade, was built in 1125 by one of the last Fatimid caliphs. Several features appear here that became part of the mosque builders' essential vocabulary, including *muqarna* (decorative stalactite-type stone carvings) vaulting and the ribbing in the hooded arch.

LOCAL KNOWLEDGE

ISLAMIC CAIRO: PLANNING A WALK

The district is quite large and packed with notable buildings, so we've subdivided it into several smaller areas:

Midan Al Hussein & Around Includes Khan Al Khalili, the northern section of Sharia Al Muizz Li Din Allah (known as Bein Al Qasreen), and the northern walls and gates.

Al Azhar to the Citadel Monuments on the south side of Sharia Al Azhar, such as the Al Ghouri buildings and Bab Zuweila.

Darb Al Ahmar Between the street of the same name and Al Azhar Park.

Citadel The hillside fortress compound.

Citadel to Ibn Tulun The southern section of Islamic Cairo from the mosque of Sultan Hassan to Ibn Tulun.

Northern Cemetery East of the ring road, including the best Mamluk dome.

Each area is good for a half-day wander, and ideally you'll visit several times, perhaps once on a weekday to feel the throb of commerce and again on a Friday morning, or on Sunday when most shops are shut and it's easier to admire architectural details.

There are many more medieval buildings than we can identify here. For more detail, pick up the guide-maps published by the Society for the Preservation of the Architectural Resources of Egypt (SPARE), on sale at the AUC Bookshop (p112).

There are several good approaches. One is to come on foot from Downtown, so you can see the transition from the modern city; from Midan Ataba, bear east on the market street of Sharia Al Muski. (To bypass this and cut straight to Khan Al Khalili, hail a taxi and ask for 'Al Hussein', or hop on a microbus at Ataba.)

The Bab Al Shaaria metro stop deposits you on the northwest edge of the medieval city – walk due east on Sharia Emir Al Guyush Al Gawani, and you'll reach the northern stretch of Sharia Al Muizz Li Din Allah.

Another strategy is to start at Al Azhar Park, where you get a good view over the district, then exit through the downhill park gate and head north through Darb Al Ahmar.

If you climb to the roof, you'll have a great view along the Bein Al Qasreen section of Sharia Al Muizz Li Din Allah.

Beit El Suhaymi   HISTORIC BUILDING
(Map p72; Darb Al Asfar; adult/student LE50/25; ⊙9am-5pm) With its fully restored paving stones and elaborate *mashrabiyya* (wooden lattice screens), **Darb Al Asfar** alley conjures up the Middle Ages – if the Middle Ages were clean. The first few buildings you pass are part of Beit El Suhaymi, a family mansion and caravanserai built in the 17th and 18th centuries. After jogging through a narrow hall, you arrive at a peaceful courtyard surrounded by grand reception halls, bedrooms, storerooms and baths.

The house has been thoroughly restored, though barely furnished (the fire extinguishers, a precaution required by the extensive new woodwork, are the most prominent item on display). As a result it can feel a bit ghostly. The changes on Darb Al Asfar have been heavily debated, as they displaced at least 30 families in the name of restoration, but it has brought some peace to this crowded area for the residents who were allowed to stay.

Mosque-Sabil of Suleiman Silahdar   HISTORIC BUILDING
(Map p72; Sharia Al Muizz Li Din Allah; Sharia Al Muizz Li Din Allah multisite ticket adult/student LE100/50) This 19th-century complex, built by Mohammed Ali's chief of armoury, combines a baroque-styled *kuttab* (Quranic school) and *sabil* (public fountain) at ground level, a mosque above and a cistern below. You'll need to ask the site guardian to unlock the cistern for you (tip appreciated), so you can take the 49 steps down into the vast and soaring 15-metres-high space, which once provided water to the *sabil*.

Mosque of Al Hakim   MOSQUE
(Map p72; Sharia Al Muizz Li Din Allah; ⊙9am-5pm) **FREE** Completed in 1013, the vast and starkly plain Mosque of Al Hakim built into the northern walls, is one of Cairo's older mosques, but it was rarely used for worship. Instead it functioned as a Crusaders' prison, a stable, a warehouse, a boys' school

and, most appropriately considering its notorious founder, a madhouse. The real masterpieces are the two stone minarets, the earliest surviving in the city (thanks in part to a post-earthquake restoration in 1304 by Beybars Al Gashankir).

Sultan Al Hakim, the sixth Fatimid ruler of Egypt, took the throne at the age of 11 and his tutor nicknamed him 'Little Lizard' because of his frightening looks and behaviour. His 24-year reign was marked by violence and behaviour that went far beyond the usual court intrigues; modern historians speculate he may simply have been insane. Those nearest to him lived in constant fear for their lives. He had his nicknaming tutor killed, along with scores of others. Hakim reputedly often patrolled the streets in disguise, riding a donkey. Most notoriously, he punished dishonest merchants by having them dealt with by a well-endowed black servant. His death was as bizarre as his life. On one of his solitary nocturnal jaunts up onto the Muqattam Hills, Hakim simply disappeared; his body was never found. To one of his followers, a man called Al Darizy, this was proof of Hakim's divine nature. From this seed Al Darizy founded the sect of the Druze that continues to this day. An Ismaili Shiite group restored the mosque in the 1980s, but with its open-plan square and spare decoration, it's not nearly as interesting as the man behind it.

Bab Al Futuh   GATE
(Gate of Conquests; Map p72; Sharia Al Muizz Li Din Allah) The rounded Bab Al Futuh with its delicate carved stone arch and the square-towered **Bab An Nasr** (Gate of Victory; Map p72; Sharia Al Gamaliyya) were built in 1087 as the two main northern entrances to the walled Fatimid city of Al Qahira. Although they never repelled a military attack, until the French adapted them to their cannons, if you walk along the outside you'll see what an imposing bit of military architecture the whole thing is.

At the time of research, the gates were being extensively restored. When finished, visitors should be able to get access to the top of the walls and inside the gates themselves, and see inscriptions left by Napoleon's troops as well as carved animals and Pharaonic figures on the stones scavenged from the ruins of ancient Memphis.

Al-Azhar to the Citadel

South of Sharia Al Azhar, Sharia Al Muizz Li Din Allah continues as a market street 400m down to the twin-minareted gate of Bab Zuweila. From here, you can carry on south through Sharia Al Khayamiyya another 30 minutes to Midan Salah Ad Din and the Mosque-Madrassa of Sultan Hassan. Or turn west on Darb Al Ahmar to head directly to the Museum of Islamic Art.

★ **Al Azhar Mosque**   MOSQUE
(Gami' Al Azhar; Map p77; Sharia Al Azhar; ⊘24hr)
FREE Founded in AD 970 as the centrepiece of the newly created Fatimid city, Al Azhar is one of Cairo's earlier mosques, and its sheikh is considered the highest theological authority for Egyptian Muslims. The building is a harmonious blend of architectural styles, the result of numerous enlargements over more than 1000 years. The tomb chamber, located through a doorway on the left just inside the entrance, has a beautiful *mihrab* (a niche indicating the direction of Mecca) and should not be missed.

The central courtyard is the earliest part, while from south to north the three minarets date from the 14th, 15th and 16th centuries; the latter, with its double finial, was added by Sultan Al Ghouri, whose mosque and mausoleum stand nearby.

ℹ CAIRO TOP TIPS

➜ Early-morning, late-night and all-day-Friday arrivals/departures at Cairo Airport are preferable (to avoid traffic).

➜ Keep small coins and bills (LE20 and under) for change and tips in an easily accessible pocket.

➜ Strangers who approach you around Midan Talaat Harb, the Egyptian Museum and Khan Al Khalili almost certainly want to sell you something.

➜ Most Cairo residents drink the tap water. If your system can handle it, help yourself to cold water outside mosques to cut down on plastic-bottle use.

➜ Unless you don't mind blackened, dirty feet, avoid wearing flip-flops. There's a reason the majority of Cairenes wear closed shoes.

➜ There is no such thing as a Papyrus Museum. It's a shop.

A madrassa was established here in AD 988, growing into a university that is the world's second-oldest educational institution (after the University of Al Kairaouine in Fez, Morocco). At one time the university was one of the world's preeminent centres of learning, drawing students from Europe and all over the Islamic empire. The large modern campus (due east) is still the most prestigious place to study Sunni theology.

Although visitors could still enter, Al Azhar was undergoing restoration at the time of research – with the minarets masked in scaffolding and sections of the mosque blocked off. Work seemed to be going full steam ahead, which means hopefully it should all be finished by the time you're in town.

Beit Zeinab Al Khatoun ARCHITECTURE
(House of Zeinab Khatoun; Map p80; ☑ 2735 7001; 3 Sharia Mohammed Abduh; LE20; ⊘ 9am-5pm) Beit Zeinab Al Khatoun is a small but interesting Ottoman-era house with a rooftop affording superb views of the surrounding minaret-studded skyline. The courtyard has a traditional *ahwa*, much frequented by young Cairenes. The house is on a little piazza at the end of a narrow street behind the Al Azhar Mosque.

Across the plaza, Beit Al Harrawi is another fine 18th-century mansion, but its sparse interior isn't worth the entry fee. Both houses are often used as concert venues, and Beit Al Harrawi is home to the Arabic Oud House, a music school; at night it's often open and you can wander in for free.

Wikala of Al Ghouri ARCHITECTURE
(Map p77; ☑ 2511 0472; Sharia Mohammed Abduh; LE40; ⊘ 9am-5pm Sat-Thu) Built in AD 1504 by the Mamluk sultan Al Ghouri, this *wikala* was originally designed as an inn for traders following the caravan routes from the east and the west. The impressive stone facade has been beautifully restored. The upper rooms are artists' ateliers while the former stables were turned into craft shops. The courtyard here in the evening is the theatre for the Sufi dance performances by Al Tannoura Egyptian Heritage Dance Troupe (p110).

Mausoleum of Al Ghouri TOMB
(Map p77; Sharia Al Muizz Li Din Allah; adult/student LE30/20; ⊘ 9am-5pm) The penultimate Mamluk sultan Al Ghouri built his funerary complex in 1504, on both sides of Sharia Al Muizz. At the age of 78, Al Ghouri was beheaded in Syria, and his body was never recovered. The elegant mausoleum actually contains the body of Tumanbey, his successor, hanged by the Turks in 1517. There is a weekly musical event on Sundays at 9pm, not to be confused with the Sufi concert at the Wikala of Al Ghouri up the street.

Mosque-Madrassa of Al Ghouri MOSQUE
(Map p77; Sharia Al Muizz Li Din Allah; ⊘ 9am-5pm) **FREE** On the western side of Sharia Al Muizz, opposite the mausoleum, is the second part of Al Ghouri's funerary complex, the intimate and richly decorated mosque-madrassa. The interior reveals gilt and painted wood-panelling, panels of white and black marble, soaring ceilings and intricate geometric paving. Four *iwans* (vaulted halls) surround a small sunken courtyard. It's also possible to climb the four-storey, red-chequered minaret (for baksheesh; ignore claims of 'tickets').

Carpet & Clothes Market MARKET
(Map p77; off Sharia Al Muizz Li Din Allah; ⊘ approx 10am-sunset Mon-Thu & Sat) The street between Al Ghouri's mosque and the mausoleum, and the area around, was historically the city's silk market. While it isn't a particularly great place to buy anything, it's worth walking through the busy clothes market for its colourful atmosphere. Less than 50m south of the mosque is Cairo's last **tarboosh (fez) maker** (Map p77; Sharia Al Muizz Li Din Allah; ⊘ 10am-6pm Mon-Thu & Sat), who shapes the red felt hats on horse brass presses. Once worn by every *effendi* (gentleman), the tarboosh is now mainly bought by tourists.

Sabil of Muhammed Ali Pasha ARCHITECTURE
(Map p80; Sharia Al Muizz Li Din Allah; LE10; ⊘ 8.30am-5pm) This elegant 1820 *sabil* (public fountain) was the first in Cairo to have gilded window grilles and calligraphic panels in Ottoman Turkish. It has been meticulously restored, with interesting displays about Muhammed Ali, who had the complex built to honour his son Tusun, who died of the plague. Nifty details include access to the cistern below and desks in the *kuttab* (Quranic school) upstairs, which welcomed students until 1992.

Mosque of Al Mu'ayyad Shaykh MOSQUE
(Map p80; Sharia Al Muizz Li Din Allah; ⊘ 9am-5pm) **FREE** Built into the Fatimid walls between 1415 and 1421, the red-and-white-striped Mosque of Al Mu'ayyad Shaykh was laid out on the site of a prison where its patron Mamluk sultan had earlier languished. Its

Al Azhar & Khan Al Khalilii

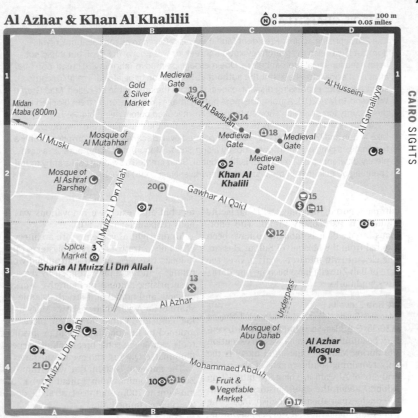

Al Azhar & Khan Al Khalilii

CAIRO'S GRAFFITI ART

The 2011 uprising against President Mubarak was referred to as the Facebook revolution, but it was also the graffiti revolution. Street art was known in Egypt, but it had not been used for social protest before. One message painted in Tahrir in 2011 read 'don't be afraid – it's only street art', but the authorities had reason to be afraid: graffiti became a key medium for expressing dissent, especially from the time of the so-called 'Mad Graffiti Weekend' in May 2011. Among the most potent images was one, on a street blocked by the security forces, which showed the street as it looked before being blocked.

Graffiti is still a popular way to express dissent, but the authorities are now quick to take action and most street art is quickly painted over. Because of the clampdown, only a few vestiges cling on Downtown, mostly along Sharia Mohammed Mahmoud. On a completely different scale, French-Tunisian artist eL Seed created a swirling calligraphy mural spanning 50 buildings in the district of Manshiyet Nasr (p88) in 2016.

entrance portal, dripping with stalactite vaulting, is particularly grand. The enormous bronze door is thought to have been pilfered from the Mosque of Sultan Hassan. The elegant twin minarets soaring over the gate of Bab Zuweila have become one of the city's landmarks.

★ Bab Zuweila   GATE
(Map p80; Sharia Al Muizz Li Din Allah; adult/student LE30/15; ☺8.30am-5pm) Built in the 11th century, beautiful Bab Zuweila was an execution site during Mamluk times, and today is the only remaining southern gate of the medieval city of Al Qahira. There are interesting exhibits about the gate's history, all with thorough explanations in English, inside the gate, while up on the roof you get panoramic vistas that stretch out to the citadel. Those with a head for heights can also wind their way up to the top of the two minarets.

The spirit of a healing saint was (and still is) said to reside behind one towering wooden door, which supplicants have studded with nails and teeth as offerings over the centuries.

★ Museum of Islamic Art   MUSEUM
(☑2390 1520; www.islamicmuseum.gov.eg/museum.html; Midan Bab Al Khalq; adult/student LE100/50, camera LE50; ☺9am-5pm Sat-Thu, 9am-noon & 2-5pm Fri) This museum, on the edge of Islamic Cairo holds one of the world's finest collections of Islamic art and is Egypt's (and one of the entire Middle East's) most beautifully curated museums. What's on display is only a sliver of the 80,000 objects the museum owns, but the selected items are stunning. The museum was heavily damaged in January 2014 in a car-bomb attack on nearby police headquar-

ters but after extensive renovations was finally reopened in early 2017.

To the right as you enter are architectural details – frescoes, carved plaster so fine it looks like lace, an intricate inlaid-wood ceiling – and ceramics grouped by dynasty. A surprising amount of figurative work is on view, and not all of it strictly Islamic – a shard of an Ayyubid bowl shows Mary holding a crucified Christ. To the left, pieces are grouped by function and medium: medical tools, astrolabes, some breathtaking carpets, illuminated Qurans, and even headstones.

The museum is 500m due west from Bab Zuweila. Coming from Midan Ataba, the museum is 700m southeast, straight down Sharia Mohammed Ali.

★ Tentmakers Market   MARKET
(Map p80; Sharia Al Khayamiyya; ☺9am-6pm Mon-Sat) The 'Street of the Tentmakers' is one of the remaining medieval speciality quarters – it takes its name from the artisans who produce the bright fabrics used for the ceremonial tents at wakes, weddings and feasts. They also hand-make intricate appliqué wall hangings, cushion covers and bedspreads, and print original patterns for tablecloths. The highest concentration of artisans along the road is directly south after Bab Zuweila, in the covered tentmakers market.

Darb Al Ahmar

In its heyday in the 14th and 15th centuries, Darb Al Ahmar ('Red Road') and neighbouring alleys and cul-de-sacs had a population of about 250,000, and the district is still nearly as dense. It is also dense with historic monuments, most from the late Mamluk era, as the city expanded outside the Fatimid gates. As part of the Al Azhar Park project, this neighbourhood has in parts been beautifully restored, along with various social programs to boost income in this long-poor area. It's a fascinating jumble and rewarding for an aimless wander. The historic street itself is now known as Ahmad Mahir Pasha on the north end and At Tabana on its southern stretch.

Mosque of Qijmas Al Ishaqi   MOSQUE
(Map p80; Sharia Ahmad Mahir Pasha; ☺9am-5pm) FREE This remarkable mosque, built in 1481 by Prince Sayf Al Din Qijmas, above a row of shops, is one of Cairo's best examples of Mamluk architecture. Its plain but wonderful facade and minaret feature on the LE50 note. The craftsmanship is exquisite. Note in particular the stunning multicoloured marble panel above the entrance, and if it's open when you pass by (it was closed when we last visited), check out the interior's beautiful stained-glass windows and stunning decorated wooden ceiling.

Mosque of Al Maridani   MOSQUE
(Map p80; Sharia At Tabana; ☺9am-5pm) FREE This 1339 building incorporates architectural elements from several different periods: eight granite columns were taken from a Pharaonic monument; the arches contain Roman, Christian and Islamic designs; and the Ottomans added a fountain and wooden housing. Trees in the courtyard, attractive *mashrabiyya* (wooden lattice screens) and a lack of visitors make this a peaceful place to stop.

Mosque-Madrassa of Umm Sultan Sha'aban   MOSQUE
(Map p80; Sharia At Tabana; ☺9am-5pm) FREE With its towering red-and-white-striped facade and entrance trimmed with a triangular arrangement of *muqarnas* vaulting, this complex is more interesting on the outside than in. But it is worth entering briefly, through a long hallway, to see the interior of the building oriented away from the street, to align with Mecca. It was built in 1369 by Khawand Baraka, the mother of the reigning Mamluk, after completing the hajj. Ask at the Blue Mosque for the keys.

Blue Mosque   MOSQUE
(Mosque of Aqsunqur; Map p80; Sharia At Tabana; ☺9am-5pm) FREE Built in 1347 and well restored in 2015, this building is highly touted by would-be guides, but it's nothing like its Istanbul namesake. It's classic Mamluk architecture throughout, except for one wall of flowery blue Ottoman tiles, looking a bit out of place, as they were installed 300 years later. The minaret affords an excellent view of

the Citadel, as well as the remains of Saladin's city walls, to the east behind the mosque.

Khayrbek Complex   MOSQUE, TOMB
(Map p80; Sharia At Tabana; ☺9am-5pm) FREE Emir Khayrbek, governor of Aleppo under Sultan Al Ghouri, defected to the Ottoman side in 1516, which effectively ended Mamluk rule. He then became the governor of Egypt under Selim I. Khayrbek's mausoleum and a mosque, built in 1521, are the anchors of this clutch of buildings, but what's interesting is how other structures – the 13th-century Alin Aq Palace, plus several later Ottoman houses – are all interconnected. The mosque's brick minaret sits on a Pharaonic stone block with hieroglyphs.

Despite official opening hours, it is often kept locked.

Mosque of Aslam Al Silahdar   MOSQUE
(Map p80; Midan Aslam, off Darb Al Ahmar; ☺9am-5pm) FREE As the closest monument to the Bab Al Mahruq entrance to Al Azhar Park, this mosque makes a good landmark for finding your way there. The 14th-century structure is distinguished by beautiful stone-inlay floors, intricate carved-stucco medallions in the walls and a beautiful tiled dome. Across the square is a gallery selling neighbourhood handicrafts. Coming from Bab Zuweila, to find the mosque (and Bab Al Mahruq) walk east behind the Mosque of Qijmas Al Ishaqi.

★ Al Azhar Park   PARK
(Map p80; ☎2510 3868; www.azharpark.com; Sharia Salah Salem; admission Mon-Wed/Thu-Sun LE7/10; ☺9am-10pm) With funds from the Aga Khan Trust for Culture, what had been a mountain of garbage, amassed over centuries, was in 2005, almost miraculously, transformed into the city's first (and only) park of significant size. Cairenes stroll

---

ⓘ PLAYING CHICKEN

It may sound silly, but the greatest challenge most travellers face in Cairo is crossing the street. Traffic seldom stops, so you have to trust the cars will avoid you. Our advice: position yourself so that one or more locals forms a buffer between you and oncoming traffic, then cross when they do – they usually don't mind being used as human shields. Never ever hesitate or turn back once you've stepped off the pavement, and cross as if you own the road. But do it fast!

Al Azhar to the Citadel

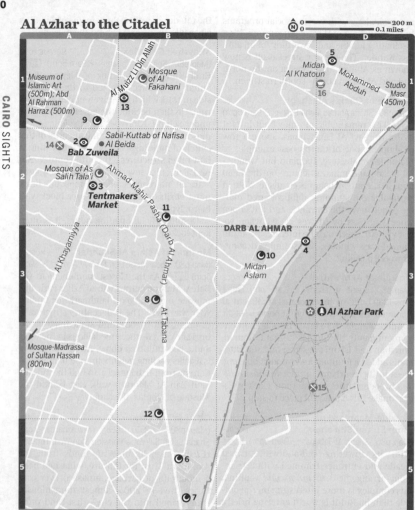

N
0 ————— 200 m
0 ————— 0.1 miles

Museum of Islamic Art (500m); Abd Al Rahman Harraz (500m)

Al Muizz Li Din Allah

Mosque of Al Fakahani

Midan Al Khatoun

5

16

Mohammed Abduh

Studio Masr (450m)

13

9

14

2
Bab Zuweila

Sabil-Kuttab of Nafisa Al Beida

Mosque of As Salih Tala'i

Ahmad Mahir Pasha

3
Tentmakers Market

11

Ahmad Mahir Pasha (Darb Al Ahmar)

DARB AL AHMAR

10
Midan Aslam

4

Al Khayamiyya

At Tabana

8

17 1
Al Azhar Park

Mosque-Madrassa of Sultan Hassan (800m)

15

12

6

7

through a profusion of gardens, emerald grass and fountains, or sit beside the lake or on the terraces of one of the restaurants, admiring the superb views over Cairo. It's most fun on weekends, when families day-trip with picnics.

Depending on your outlook, the park is a gorgeous respite or a middle-class play-ground. This was offset slightly when the **Bab Al Mahruq** entrance, through a medi-eval gate in the old Ayyubid walls, finally opened in 2009. This granted easier access for residents of the lower-income Darb Al Ahmar district. You can enter here be-

fore 6pm, but after dark you can only exit through the main park gates on Sharia Salah Salem (taxis wait but overcharge; microbus-es go to Ataba for LE2). If you enter from Darb Al Ahmar, check out the ongoing ex-cavations of the Ayyubid walls – one major achievement was the rediscovery of Bab Al Barqiya, which had long ago been lost under the trash heap.

In addition to a couple of small cafes and the open-air theatre **El Genaina** (☎ 02-2751-0771; http://mawred.org/programs-and-activities/el-genaina-theater), the restaurant **Studio Masr** (mains LE70-250; ⊙10am-1am) in the northern

Al Azhar to the Citadel

section of the park capitalises on the views across the medieval city and beyond. The **Lakeside Cafe** (☑ 02-2510-9162; mezze LE15-30, mains LE35-90), on the other side of the park, has a tranquil lake-edge setting.

The Citadel

Sprawling over a limestone spur on the city's eastern edge, the **Citadel** (Al Qala'a; Map p83; ☑ 02-2512-1735; Sharia Salah Salem; adult/student LE120/60; ⊙ 9am-5pm, mosques closed during prayers Fri), started by Saladin in 1176 as a fortification against the Crusaders, was home to Egypt's rulers for 700 years. Their legacy is a collection of three very different mosques, several palaces (housing some either underwhelming, or nearly-always closed museums) and a couple of terraces with superb Cairo views – on a clear day you'll see Giza's Pyramids poking up in the far distance.

Following their overthrow of Saladin's Ayyubid dynasty, the Mamluks enlarged the complex, adding sumptuous palaces and harems. Under the Ottomans (1517–1798) the fortress expanded westward and a new main gate, the Bab Al Azab, was added, while the Mamluk palaces deteriorated. Even so, when Napoleon's French expedition took control in 1798, the emperor's savants regarded these buildings as some of the finest Islamic monuments in Cairo. This didn't stop Mohammed Ali – who rose to power after the French – from drastically remodelling, and crowning the complex with the Ottoman-style mosque that dominates Cairo's eastern skyline. After Mohammed Ali's grandson Ismail moved his residence to the Abdeen Palace, the Citadel became a military garrison. The British army was barracked here during WWII, and Egyptian soldiers still have a small foothold, although most of the Citadel has been given over to tourists.

Mosque of Mohammed Ali   MOSQUE
(Map p83; ⊙ closed to visitors during Fri midday prayers) **FREE** Modelled on classic Ottoman lines, with domes upon domes upon domes, this alabaster-white mosque within the Citadel took 18 years to build (1830–48) and its interior is all twinkling chandeliers and luridly striped stone, the main dome a rich emerald green. Mohammed Ali lies in the tomb on the right as you enter.

The glitzy clock in the entrance courtyard was a gift from King Louis-Philippe of France in return for the obelisk that adorns the Place de la Concorde in Paris, but it arrived damaged and was never repaired.

Mosque of An Nasir Mohammed   MOSQUE
(Map p83) **FREE** Dwarfed by Mohammed Ali's mosque, this beautiful 1318 mosque is the only Mamluk work that Mohammed Ali didn't demolish – instead, he used it as a stable. Before that, Ottoman sultan Selim I stripped its interior of its marble, but the old wood ceiling and *muqarnas* show up nicely, and the twisted finials of the minarets are interesting for their covering of glazed tiles, something rarely seen in Egypt.

Police Museum   MUSEUM
(Map p83; ⊙ 9am-5pm) The quirky but fly-blown Police Museum is located within the Citadel's old prison building. Inside are displays of famous political assassinations, complete in some cases with the murder weapon. It's worth a quick peek, though the main interest here is the neighbouring grand terrace with superb views all the way to the Pyramids at Giza.

Site of the Massacre
of the Mamluks   HISTORIC SITE
(Map p83) From the terrace near the Police Museum you can look down into the narrow entrance where 470 Mamluk beys (governors) were killed by Mohammed Ali's troops in 1811, thus ending Mamluk influence in

Egypt and consolidating his rule. The Mamluks had been summoned to the citadel for a celebration but once they had entered, the gates were shut, trapping them in the defile and allowing troops loyal to Mohammed Ali to easily slaughter them.

Gawhara Palace & Museum   MUSEUM
(Map p83) South of Mohammed Ali's mosque is the Gawhara Palace & Museum, a lame attempt to evoke 19th-century court life, but it's most often closed. There are excellent views over the city from the nearby terrace.

National Military Museum   MUSEUM
(Map p83) Mohammed Ali's one-time Harem Palace is now the lavish National Military Museum. It was closed for restoration on our last visit though unlike the other neglected Citadel museums, its popularity with visiting school groups means it's likely to have reopened by the time you're here. Endless plush-carpeted halls are lined with dioramas depicting great moments in warfare, from Pharaonic times to the 20th-century conflicts with Israel – kitschy fun to start, then eventually a bit depressing. There is a cafe nearby.

The Citadel to Ibn Tulun
South of Darb Al Ahmar, the late-Ottoman-era Citadel complex watches over the city. At its base, on Midan Salah Ad Din and along Sharia Al Saliba, is another important historic quarter, with two of Cairo's largest mosques, plus several other smaller monuments (many closed) which have interesting facades to admire as you wander through. Although restoration works have started, in

contrast with historic quarters further north this area has yet to see much revitalisation.

★ Mosque-Madrassa of Sultan Hassan   MOSQUE
(Map p84; Midan Salah Ad Din; incl Mosque of Ar Rifai adult/student LE60/30; ⊘8am-4.30pm) Massive yet elegant, this grand structure is regarded as the finest piece of early Mamluk architecture in Cairo. It was built between 1356 and 1363 by Sultan Hassan, a grandson of Sultan Qalaun; he took the throne at the age of 13, was deposed and reinstated no less than three times, then assassinated shortly before the mosque was completed. Beyond the striking recessed entrance, a dark passage leads into a peaceful square courtyard surrounded by four soaring *iwans* (vaulted halls).

The *iwans* were dedicated to teaching the four main schools of Sunni Islam. At the rear of the eastern *iwan*, an especially beautiful *mihrab* is flanked by stolen Crusader columns. To the right, a bronze door leads to the sultan's mausoleum. During construction, one of the minarets collapsed and killed some 300 onlookers sparking superstitious rumours that Sultan Hassan's rule was at an end. They weren't wrong. Just over a month later, he was murdered by his army commander.

Mosque of Ar Rifai   MOSQUE
(Map p84; Midan Salah Ad Din; incl Mosque-Madrassa of Sultan Hassan adult/student LE60/30; ⊘8am-4.30pm) Opposite the grand Mosque-Madrassa of Sultan Hassan, the Mosque of Ar Rifai is constructed on a similarly imposing scale, begun in 1869 and not finished

---

ⓘ HOW TO BLEND IN
....

Even if your appearance allows it, it's next to impossible to 'pass' as a native Cairene. But you can look more like a resident foreigner, thus deflecting hustler attention onto the more obvious tourists walking behind you and leaving you free to enjoy the good things about Cairo. Here's how:

➡ Carry your stuff in a plastic shopping bag or a generic tote. Nothing screams 'tourist' like a multipocketed, zippered, heavy-duty-nylon backpack with visible water bottle.

➡ Cover your legs – this goes for men and women. Islamic rules aside, Egyptians have a high level of modesty, and it's clear you haven't been here long if you don't feel embarrassed to show your knees in public.

➡ Eating on-the-go is rarely seen. Munch on your shawarma (meat sliced off a spit and stuffed in a bread roll with chopped tomatoes and garnish) or *ta'amiyya* either at the benches of the fast food canteen or standing just outside, watching the world go by.

➡ Carry a copy of *Al Ahram Weekly* – or the Arabic *Al Ahram*, if you want to go deep undercover.

The Citadel

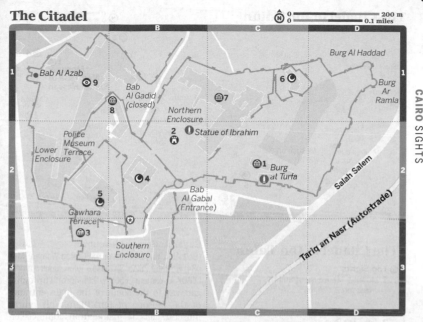

until 1912. Members of modern Egypt's royal family, including Khedive Ismail and King Farouk, are buried inside, as is the last shah of Iran. Their tombs lie to the left of the entrance.

Amir Taz Palace HISTORIC BUILDING
(Map p84; ☎2514 2581; 17 Sharia Suyufiyya; ⊗9am-4pm) FREE Walking west along busy Sharia Al Saliba eventually leads to the Mosque of Ibn Tulun. A short detour north on Sharia Suyufiyya brings you to this restored home of one of Sultan Al Nasir Muhammad's closest advisers, who later controlled the throne through Sultan Hassan. The palace is now used as a cultural centre but you're free to enter and view the salons.

Museo Mevlevi MUSEUM
(Sama'khana; Map p84; Sharia Suyufiyya; ⊗9am-2pm) FREE Just north of the Amir Taz Palace, behind a green door with an Italian Institute sign, this museum is essentially a meticulously restored Ottoman-era *sama khane* (ritual hall) where Mevlevi whirling dervishes would hold their ritual whirling dance (the *sama*). The beautiful wooden structure, with intricate painted decoration, is hidden behind stone facades; entering feels like discovering a secret little jewel box.

The Citadel

Downstairs are the remains of the 14th-century *madrassa* that forms the building's foundation, and which was discovered during restoration of the hall; the thorough notes are a rare model of thoughtful excavation.

Mosque of Ibn Tulun MOSQUE
(Map p84; Sharia Al Saliba; ⊗8am-4pm) FREE The city's oldest intact, functioning Islamic monument is easily identified by its high walls topped with neat crenulations that resemble a string of paper dolls. It was built between AD 876 and 879 by Ibn Tulun, who was sent to rule the outpost of Al Fustat in the 9th century by the Abbasid caliph of Baghdad. Its geometric simplicity is part of

The Citadel to Ibn Tulun

Ⓝ 0 ——————————— 200 m
0 ——————————— 0.1 miles

Sayyida Zeinab Ⓜ Metro Station (750m)

Ibn Tulun
Al Khalifa area (20m)

The Citadel to Ibn Tulun

its beauty and is best appreciated from the top of the minaret.

The mosque covers 2.5 hectares, large enough for the whole community of Al Fustat to assemble for Friday prayers. An outer moatlike courtyard, originally created to keep the secular city at a distance, was at one time filled with shops and stalls. Ibn Tulun drew inspiration from his homeland, particularly the ancient Mosque of Samarra (Iraq), on which the spiral minaret is modelled, as well as the use of brick. The minaret is accessed from the moat. He also added some innovations of his own: according to architectural historians, this is the first structure to use the pointed arch, a good 200 years before the European Gothic arch.

Note that sometimes one of the caretakers here can be overly forceful in asking for donations.

Gayer-Anderson Museum MUSEUM
(Beit Al Kritliyya, House of the Cretan Woman; Map p84; ☎ 2364 7822; Sharia Ibn Tulun; adult/student LE60/30, camera LE50; ⊙ 9am-4pm) Through a gateway to the south of the main entrance of the Mosque of Ibn Tulun, this quirky museum gets its name from John Gayer-Anderson, the British major and army doctor who restored the two adjoining 16th-century houses between 1935 and 1942, filling them with lovely antiquities, artworks and knick-knacks acquired on his travels in the region. The house was used as a location in the James Bond film *The Spy Who Loved Me*.

On his death in 1945, Gayer-Anderson bequeathed the lot to Egypt. The puzzle of rooms is decorated in a variety of styles: the Persian Room has exquisite tiling, the Damascus Room has lacquer and gold, and the Queen Anne Room displays ornate furniture and a silver tea set. The enchanting *mashrabiyya* gallery looks down onto a magnificent *qa'a* (reception hall), which has a marble fountain, decorated ceiling beams and carpet-covered alcoves. The rooftop terrace has been lovingly restored, with more complex *mashrabiyya*.

From here, it's rewarding to keep walking another 750m west to the popular quarter of Sayyida Zeinab, where there's a metro station.

Northern Cemetery
The Northern Cemetery is half of a vast necropolis called Al Qarafa or, more common among tourists, the City of the Dead. The titillating name conjures a vision of morbid slums, of tomb structures bursting with living families. But the area is more 'town' than

A WALK THROUGH AL KHALIFA

A short walk south from the Mosque of Ibn Tulun, the district of Al Khalifa (also known as Al Mashahed) retains an authentic if downtrodden atmosphere, packed with markets and workshops.

Over the past few years a project, funded by the US and carried out by heritage conservation initiative Athar Lina (www.atharlina.com) has restored several of the sites along the main thoroughfare of Sharia Al Khalifa. Although lacking the regal bling of Islamic Cairo's many Mamluk buildings, these modest monuments are important as surviving architectural examples of the Fatimid era.

The twin-domed **Shrines of Sayyida Atika & Mohammed Al Gaafari** (Map p58), the prophet's aunt and one of his descendants respectively, date from the mid-12th century. The fluted dome that tops Sayyida Atika's shrine is thought to be the earliest-surviving example of that style in Cairo. Just to the south is the larger **Shrine of Sayyida Ruqayya**, the prophet's granddaughter. Inside, the stucco *mihrab* has been painstakingly restored. Directly across the road is the **Mausoleum of Shagaret Al Durr**, wife of Sultan Ayyub, and, after his death, Egypt's first Islamic-era female ruler. Shagaret Al Durr's body was never interred here though, as she was murdered after only 80 days of rule – one story has it that her assassins slapped her to her death using hammam slippers – and her body thrown from the Citadel walls to be eaten by Cairo's wild dogs. The interior of the dome has rare blue-green-painted geometric decoration.

'shanty', complete with power lines, a post office and multistorey buildings. Thanks to a near-complete absence of cars, it's also a fairly peaceful part of the city, with a friendly neighbourhood feel and some flawless Mamluk monuments.

The easiest way to the Northern Cemetery is walking east from Midan Al Hussein along Sharia Al Azhar. At Sharia Salah Salem, cross via the overpass. In addition to the three main monuments, several others have been well restored, but are not reliably open.

★ **Mosque of Qaitbey**　MOSQUE
(Map p86; ⊙9am-4pm) **FREE** Sultan Qaitbey was as ruthless as any Mamluk sultan, but he was also something of an aesthete. His mosque, completed in 1474 as part of a much larger funerary complex, is widely agreed to mark the pinnacle of Islamic architecture in Cairo. The interior is one of the most pleasant places to sit and relax, but the true glory is the exterior of the dome, carved with the finest, most intricate floral designs anywhere in the Islamic world.

Qaitbey ruled for 28 years and was the last Mamluk leader with any real power in Egypt. He was a prolific builder, and with some 80 buildings in his name, he truly refined the Mamluk style. Behind the boldly striped facade, the interior has four *iwans* around a central court lit by large, lattice-screened windows. The interior is panelled in cool marble with a mesmerising decorative wood

ceiling. The adjacent tomb chamber contains the cenotaphs of Qaitbey and his two sisters. The elegant and slender stone minaret, carved with a star pattern and an intricate floral arabesque, is one of the city's most beautiful. Climb up for the best view.

Khanqah-Mausoleum of Farag Ibn Barquq　TOMB
(Map p86; ⊙9am-4pm) **FREE** Built by a son of Sultan Barquq, whose great madrassa and mausoleum stand on Bein Al Qasreen, this tomb complex was completed in 1411 because Barquq wished to be buried near some particular illustrious Sufi sheikhs. The *khanqah* (Sufi monastery) is a fortress-like building with high, sheer facades and twin minarets and domes, the largest stone domes in Cairo. Inside, the ceilings are painted in mesmerising red-and-black geometric patterns.

Complex of Sultan Ashraf Barsbey　MAUSOLEUM
(Map p86; tip the site guard for entry) Enclosed by a stone wall midway between Barquq's Mausoleum and the Mosque of Qaitbey is the funerary complex of Barsbey, who ruled from 1422 to 1438. Most of the compound is crumbling, but the dome of his mausoleum is carved with a beautiful star pattern, and there is some fine marble flooring and an ivory-inlay *minbar* (pulpit in a mosque). The guard will let you in for baksheesh.

Northern Cemetery

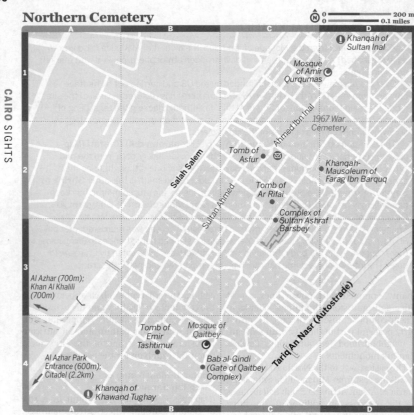

Gezira & Zamalek

Uninhabited until the mid-19th century, Gezira (Arabic for 'island') was a narrow strip of alluvial land rising up out of the Nile. After he built modern-day Downtown, Khedive Ismail dedicated his energy to a great palace on the island, with the rest of the land as a royal garden. During the development boom of the early 20th century, the palace grounds were sold off, while the palace was made into a hotel. Much of the island is occupied by sports clubs and parks, while the northern third is stylish Zamalek, a leafy neighbourhood of old embassy mansions and 1920s apartment blocks. It has few tourist sites, but it's a pleasant place to wander around and an even better place to eat, drink and shop.

★ **Cairo Tower** MONUMENT
(Burg Misr; Map p92; ☑ 2735-7187; www.cairo tower.net; Sharia Hadayek Al Zuhreya, Gezira; adult/child under 6yr LE70/free; ⊙ 8am-midnight, to 1am summer; Ⓜ Opera) This 187m-high tower is the city's most famous landmark after the Pyramids. Built in 1961, the structure, which resembles a stylised lotus plant with its latticework casing, was a thumb to the nose at the Americans, who had given Nasser the money used for its construction to buy US arms. The 360-degree views across the city from the top are clearest in the late morning, after the haze burns off, or late afternoon when you can often spy the Pyramids.

You might encounter a queue for the elevator at dusk, as the tower is extremely popular with Cairenes. The **Sky Window** cafe, one floor down from the observation deck, serves not-too-exorbitant drinks and food (beer LE47, sandwiches LE53 to LE65), and although mains are served with the saddest side salad known to man, the actual sandwiches are quite nice. The **360 Revolving Restaurant** just below that is a bit pricier (mains LE120 to LE220).

If you're walking from Downtown, turn right onto Sharia Saraya Al Geriza after walking across Qasr El Nil Bridge, and then take the second left.

Museum of Modern Egyptian Art   MUSEUM

(Map p92; ☑2736-6667; Gezira Exhibition Grounds, Gezira; ⊗10am-2pm & 5-8pm Sat-Thu; Ⓜ Opera) FREE This vast collection of 20th- and 21st-century Egyptian art is set in the green, well-groomed Gezira Exhibition Grounds, across from the Cairo Opera House. The museum's highlights are Mahmoud Mukhtar's deco-elegant bronze *Bride of the Nile*, along with Mahmoud Said's painting *Al Madina* (The City, 1937). The museum was partially open (just the ground floor gallery; hence the free entry) due to ongoing restoration at the time of research. It's well worth a peek though if you're into art.

Mahmoud Mukhtar Museum   MUSEUM

(Map p92; ☑2736-6665; Sharia Tahrir, Gezira; LE15; ⊗10am-2pm & 5-10pm Tue-Sun; Ⓜ Opera) Mukhtar (1891–1934) was the sculptor laureate of independent Egypt, responsible for Saad Zaghloul on the nearby roundabout and the *Egypt Reawakening* monument outside the Cairo Zoo. Collected in this little-visited museum, his work ranges from tiny caricatures (look for *Ibn Al Balad*, a spunky city kid) to life-size portraits. Mukhtar's tomb sits in the basement. The museum was closed for renovation when we

last visited, though we were assured that it would reopen soon.

Cairo Marriott Hotel   ARCHITECTURE

(Map p94; 16 Sharia Saray Al Gezira, Zamalek) The core of this luxury hotel (p101) is a lavish palace built by Khedive Ismail to house Empress Éugenie when she visited for the opening of the Suez Canal in 1869. A stroll inside gives a sense of its original grandeur. Head straight through and down the stairs to grand old sitting rooms, then into the garden and right to the next entrance and the fantastic former ballroom, with triple-height ceilings and an enormous staircase for making that dramatic entrance.

★ Aisha Fahmy Palace   ARTS CENTRE

(Mogamma Al Funoon; Map p94; Sharia Al Shaer Aziz Abaza, Zamalek; ⊗9am-9pm when exhibitions are on) FREE Shuttered for years, the Aisha Fahmy Palace was built in 1907 for Egyptian aristocrat Ali Fahmy, who was King Farouk's army chief. Reopened as an arts centre in mid-2017, the sublime rococo interior of silk-clad and frescoed walls, carved-wood fireplaces, painted lacquerwork and a wonderful triple-arched stained-glass window overlooking the grand staircase has all been fabulously restored to finery. The mansion's grand salons are now to be used as a gallery, with a program of temporary exhibitions.

When we were last in town the palace had only just been reopened, and there seemed to be some confusion over whether the house would be open to the public all the time or only when an art exhibition was showing. Exhibitions are advertised on the fence

---

THE CITY OF THE DEAD

Some estimates put the number of living Cairenes in the Northern and Southern Cemeteries at half a million; others, perhaps more realistic, guess only 50,000. As Max Rodenbeck notes in *Cairo: The City Victorious*, some of the tomb dwellers, especially the paid guardians and their families, have lived here for generations. Others have moved in more recently – there was a spike in 1992, following the earthquake that flattened cheaply built high-rises, and others may have opted for a more central Qarafa home over forced relocation to a bleak low-income suburb. On Fridays and public holidays, visitors flock here to picnic and pay their respects to the dead – a lively time to visit.

The cemetery first appealed to Mamluk sultans and emirs because it afforded ample building space. The vast mausoleums they built were more than just tombs; they were also meant as places for entertaining – a continuation of the Pharaonic tradition of picnicking among the graves. Even the humblest family tombs included a room for overnight visitors. The dead hoped they would be remembered; the city's homeless thanked them for free accommodation. This coexistence of the living and the dead was happening as far back as the 14th century, though these days in some tomb-houses, cenotaphs serve as tables and washing is strung between headstones.

MANSHIYET NASR: CAIRO'S 'GARBAGE CITY'

Looking around some parts of Cairo, you might think garbage is never collected – but it certainly is, by some 65,000 people of the Coptic Christian Zaraeeb community. Known (derogatorily) to most Cairenes as the *zabbalin* ('garbage people'), this community makes a living by collecting rubbish from Cairene homes, sorting and recycling the salvaged materials while feeding the organic waste to their pigs. Managing to recycle approximately 80% of the waste they collect, their recycling methods have been recognised as among most efficient in the world. Despite this, in 2004 under Mubarak, Cairo's waste collection was handed out to multinationals, seriously threatening the Zaraeeb's livelihood. In 2014, because of the failure of the official waste-collection system, the government partially reversed the policy, officially reinstating the community's role, registering around 60 Zaraeeb companies to take charge of waste disposal in part of the city.

The Zaraeeb live in the district of Manshiyet Nasr (known also as 'Garbage City') at the base of the Muqattam Hills. This densely populated area is also where the rubbish gets sorted, with apartment block roofs piled high with plastic waste in various states of sorting for recycling, and huge bags of salvaged waste being sifted through in the narrow alleys.

The area is home to two rather extraordinary sights:

Church of St Simeon the Tanner (Kineesat Samaan Al Kharraz; Map p58; ☑ 02-2512-3666; www.samaanchurch.com; Moqattam, Manshiyet Nasr) FREE Built in the 1970s into a vast cave on the ridge of the Muqattam Hills above Manshiyet Nasr, the Church of St Simeon the Tanner is thought to be the largest church in the Middle East, seating 17,000 worshippers. It's part of a complex of churches here, all built into caves on the escarpment. The church is named in honour of St Simeon, a 10th-century ascetic who prayed to make Muqattam move at the behest of Fatimid caliph Al Muizz Li Din Allah. Crowds throng here on Fridays and Sundays, when Mass is held.

Perception In 2016, French-Tunisian street artist eL Seed created one of the most astonishing pieces of street art in the Middle East here in Manshiyet Nasr. Perception covers 50 buildings in an exuberant swirl of Arabic calligraphy that quotes St Athanasius: 'Anyone who wants to see the sunlight clearly, needs to wipe his eyes first'. It is, eL Seed has said, a reminder to those who perceive the district, and people themselves, as dirty, of the vital work this community do clearing the Cairo streets of rubbish.

The mural can only be seen in full from one viewpoint (behind a block of buildings, up a staircase and an easy scramble over a wall onto a ledge), just a short walk from the Church of St Simeon the Tanner. It is, though, difficult to find by yourself. Local Manshiyet Nasr guide **Maged** (☑ 012-2464-1223) speaks excellent English and can guide you around all the churches here, as well as lead you to the viewpoint (ask for the 'graffiti').

outside. The entry gate is just off Sharia 26th of July. You'll need to leave your passport with the gate-security policeman for entry.

Museum of Islamic Ceramics MUSEUM (Map p94; ☑ 2737-3298; 1 Sharia Sheikh Al Marsafy, Zamalek; adult/student LE25/15; ⊙ 10am-1.30pm & 5.30-9pm Sat-Thu) This museum has been closed for renovation for the past few years. When it reopens, it's worth a peek for its collection of colourful plates, tiles and even 11th-century hand grenades. Give it a walk-past when you're in the neighbourhood, as equally appealing is the gorgeous 1924 villa it's housed in.

The garden and back of the building are home to the **Gezira Arts Centre** (⊙ 10am-2pm & 5-9pm Sat-Thu), with galleries hosting rotating contemporary exhibitions, but this too was closed on our last visit.

◎ Mohandiseen, Agouza & Doqqi

A map of Cairo in Baedecker's 1929 guide to Egypt shows nothing on the Nile's west bank other than a hospital and the road to the Pyramids. The hospital is still there, set back from the corniche, but it's now hemmed in on all sides by mid-rise buildings. This is the sprawl of Giza governorate – not technically part of Cairo at all – and it reaches all the way out to the foot of the Pyramids (they're not isolated in the desert, as you might have imagined). In the 1960s and 1970s, the neighbourhoods of Mohandiseen, Agouza and Doqqi, the closest areas to the

Nile, were created to house Egypt's emerging professional classes. They remain middle-class bastions, home to families who made good under Sadat's open-door policy – though some pockets of Mohandiseen are Cairo's ritziest.

Unless you happen to find concrete and traffic stimulating, the main reason to come here are some good restaurants, a few embassies and upscale shopping on Sharia Suleiman Abaza and Sharia Libnan.

What little history there is since the pharaohs floats on the river in the form of houseboats moored off Sharia El Nil, just north of Zamalek Bridge in Agouza. These floating two-storey structures once lined the Nile all the way from Giza to Imbaba. During the 1930s some boats became casinos, music halls and bordellos. Many of the surviving residences still have a bohemian air, as chronicled in Naguib Mahfouz' novel *Adrift on the Nile*.

Mr & Mrs Mahmoud Khalil Museum   MUSEUM
(Map p92; ☑ 3338-9720; 1 Sharia Kafour, Doqqi) In 2010 this museum gained global notoriety when art thieves nicked Van Gogh's *Poppy Flowers* (valued at US$50 million) right off the wall in broad daylight. The painting has yet to be recovered and the museum has been closed (ostensibly for renovations) ever since. If it has reopened by the time you're in town, the galleries of fine art here are definitely worth a visit, even if you didn't come to Egypt to see 19th- and 20th-century European and Japanese art.

⊙ Heliopolis

This pretty suburb shows a different, more relaxed side of the city and is a nice antidote to central Cairo's tourist pressure. With all its trees and outdoor cafes, it's a pleasant place for an evening's wander. Many Egyptians think so too, as Heliopolis has become 'Downtown' for people living in dull satellite cities further east.

Belgian industrialist and baron Édouard Empain laid out Heliopolis in the early 20th century as a 'garden city' for the colonial officials who ruled Egypt. Its whitewashed Moorish-style buildings with dark-wood balconies, grand arcades and terraces are the European vision of the 'Orient' set in stone. Since the 1950s, overcrowding has filled in the green spaces with apartment buildings festooned with satellite dishes, and those

ornate arcades have become rather dilapidated and grubby, but the area still has a relaxed, vaguely Mediterranean air.

Sharia Al Ahram runs through Korba, 'downtown' Heliopolis. At the south end, **Uruba Palace** (Qasr Ittihadiya; Map p94; Sharia Al Ahram; Ⓜ Al Ahram) was once the grand Heliopolis Palace hotel, opened in 1910 and graced by the likes of King Albert I of Belgium. During the world wars the British appropriated it for use as a military hospital. In the 1960s the hotel closed, and during the 1980s President Mubarak revamped this plush pad to use as the official presidential palace. Today, it continues this role under President Sisi and – alas – only visiting dignitaries get to gawk at its regal interiors.

From the palace, at the first intersection with Sharia Ibrahim Laqqany (detour left for some pretty arcades), is the open-air cafeteria **L'Amphitrion** (Map p94; ☑ 02-2258-1379; 181 Sharia Ibrahim Laqqany; ◷ noon-2am), as old as Heliopolis itself and a popular watering hole for Allied soldiers during the world wars. Towards the northern end of Sharia Al Ahram, turn right into **Sharia Ibrahim** to view the once glorious, now shabby, ornate arcades lining the street. The northern end of Sharia Al Ahram comes to a stop at the **Basilica** (Map p94); a miniature version of Istanbul's famous Aya Sofya. Baron Empain is buried here.

The easiest way to get here is using metro line 3, which runs from Attaba station. Alight

THE HELIOPOLIS COLOSSUS DISCOVERY

In early March 2017, archaeologists working on the site of ancient Heliopolis (in the working-class district of Matareya, to the north of modern Heliopolis) discovered a mammoth 8m bust and head of a statue submerged in the mud. First thought to be a statue of Ramses II, the discovery made headlines around the world. Later on, after the colossus had been excavated, archaeologists corrected their initial assumptions and thought the statue more probable to depict 26th-dynasty ruler Psammetich I (664–610 BC). If so, it will be the largest Late Period statue ever found. The colossus is currently undergoing restoration work and when finished will be exhibited at the Egyptian Museum.

CAIRO ACTIVITIES

Heliopolis

Heliopolis

at Al Ahram station (currently the end of the line, though this line will eventually run all the way to Cairo Airport), which is conveniently placed on Sharia Nazih Khalifa, two blocks down from Heliopolis Basilica.

Baron's Palace   NOTABLE BUILDING
(Qasr Al Baron; Sharia Al Uruba, Heliopolis) Baron Empain lived in a fantastical and highly eccentric Hindu temple–inspired mansion, with the facade bedecked with elephants and serpents. Unfortunately it has been closed to the public since 1997 when 'Satanists' were allegedly holding rituals here; it turned out they were a bunch of upper-class teenage metalheads. Good news, though, is on the horizon. Restoration work has began on this architectural oddity, and it's planned to become a cultural centre, with the finishing date pegged for late 2019.Until then, it's not worth a dedicated trip, but keep an eye out for it on your way to and from the airport.

The palace is due east from Heliopolis Basilica, at the end of Sharia Nazih Khalifa.

October War Panorama   MUSEUM
(📞2402-2317; Sharia Al Uruba; LE30; ⊙shows 11am, 12.20pm, 6pm & 7.30pm Wed-Mon) Built with help from North Korean artists, the October War Panorama is a memorial to the 1973 'victory' over Israel. A large 3D mural and diorama depicts the Egyptian forces' breaching of the Bar Lev Line on the Suez Canal, while a stirring commentary (in Arabic only) recounts the heroic victories. Interestingly it skips over the successful Israeli counterattacks. Both sides accepted a UN-brokered ceasefire, and Sinai was returned by negotiation six years later.

🏃 Activities

Boat Rides
One of the most pleasant things to do on a warm day is to go out on a **felucca**, Egypt's ancient broad-sail boat, with a supply of beer and a small picnic just as sunset approaches. Because it's near a wider spot in the river, the best place for hiring is the **Dok Dok landing stage** (Map p92; Corniche El Nil), and the dock just to the south, on the corniche in Garden City, across from the Four Seasons. Subject to haggling, a boat and captain should cost between LE70 and LE100 per hour; your captain will appreciate additional baksheesh.

Once night falls, light-festooned **party boats** crowd the docks near Maspero, the east bank of the Nile north of 6th of October Bridge. A 45-minute or hour-long ride usually costs LE20 or so per person, and boats go whenever they're full.

Swimming
Finding a place to cool off in the city can be difficult. Cairenes who can afford it swim in members-only clubs. Some hotels do allow day use for nonguests, but most are pricey. The best bargains are in Mohandiseen,

DIY WALKING CAIRO

Contrary to first impressions, Cairo is an excellent city for walking. The terrain is level, the scenery changes quickly, and you'll never accidentally wander into a 'bad' neighbourhood. We encourage getting a little lost in Cairo's back lanes, and, at least once, accepting a stranger's invitation to tea. These are some of the best places to stroll over the course of a day.

Islamic Cairo in the Morning

Start before 7am with tea at **Fishawi's** (p109) cafe and watch the Khan Al Khalili slowly wake up. Take a stroll down **Bein Al Qasreen** (p71) to admire the buildings without the crush of commerce, then follow **Sharia Al Muizz Li Din Allah** (p71) south and at **Bab Zuweila** (p78) take a left towards Darb Al Ahmar and **Al Azhar Park** (p79), roughly following the old walls built by Saladin. Tiny workshops here produce shoes, parquet flooring, mother-of-pearl inlay boxes and more. But it's also a residential district, where families on upper floors run baskets down to the *ba'al* (grocer) for supplies, and knife-sharpeners and junk traders (the men who shout 'Beee-kya!') roll through the lanes. Keeping your bearings with the park to your left, you can wander all the way to the **Citadel** (p81). To loop back to Sharia Al Azhar, go via Sharia Al Khayamiyya.

Garden City at Twilight

The interlocking circles that form the streets of Garden City are maddening if you want to get anywhere, but they're perfect for admiring the crumbling mansions in this colonial-era district. The best time to visit is the hour before sundown, when the dust coating the architectural curlicues turns a warm gold and the starlings shrill in the trees.

Start at the north end (get the brutalist concrete Canadian embassy behind you right away!), keeping an eye out for wrought-iron dragons on cobwebbed gates, a rare Turkish-style wood-front home and the last real garden in Garden City, behind the Four Seasons hotel. Nearby at 10 Sharia Tulumbat is **Grey Pillars**, the British residency during WWII, with a beautiful birdcage elevator inside. Stop for a coffee at the peaceful **Falak** (Map p92; 7 Sharia Gamal Ad Din Abu Al Mahasin, Garden City; ☺10am-midnight) cafe. You wind up, conveniently, near the **Dok Dok felucca landing stage** (p90) for a sailboat ride.

Downtown at Night

A jaunt Downtown is less walking than cafe-hopping. After dark the air is cool and the streets are thronged. Start at Midan Orabi where you can perch on any random planter and someone will come and sell you tea. From here Sharia Alfy and the smaller streets on either side are your playground for snacking and shisha smoking. A more contemporary cafe night scene is found at **Eish + Malh** (p103) on Sharia Adly, directly opposite the beautiful imposing facade of the **Shar Hashamaim Synagogue** (p60). No matter how late you're out, you can wind up the night at the 24-hour **Odeon Palace Hotel** (p108) bar.

---

where a minimum charge at the cafes at **Atlas Zamalek Hotel** (Map p94; ☏3346-7230; www.atlaszamalek.com; 20 Sharia Gamiat Ad Dowal Al Arabiyya; minimum LE120) and **Nabila Hotel** (Map p94; ☏3303-0302; 4 Sharia Gamiat Ad Dowal Al Arabiyya; minimum LE60; ☺10am-5pm) give you access to their small rooftop pools. Much nicer, and still very affordable, is the sculpted dip pool with a Nile view at the **Hilton Zamalek Residence** (Map p94; ☏2737-0055; 21 Sharia Mohammed Mazhar, Zamalek; day use LE200 Sun-Thu, LE250 Fri & Sat; ☺7am-6pm).

For a bigger day outing, **Mohamed Ali Club** (☏3345-0228, 012-2211-3681; Km 13, Upper Egypt Agriculture Rd; day use incl lunch LE200; ☺9am-2am) is a major social scene – a mix of foreign residents and Egyptians – with house music, good Lebanese food and beers. It's located 3km south on the Nile's west bank, about even with Ma'adi.

🎓 Courses

Arabic

International House LANGUAGE
(International Language Institute (ILI); Map p58; ☏3346-3087; www.arabicegypt.com; 4 Sharia Mahmoud Azmy, Mohandiseen; 2-week course from US$190) This is the largest school in Cairo, so it's able to offer the biggest range of levels. Two-week and four-week courses in both Egyptian-colloquial and Modern-standard

Doqqi, Giza & Gezira

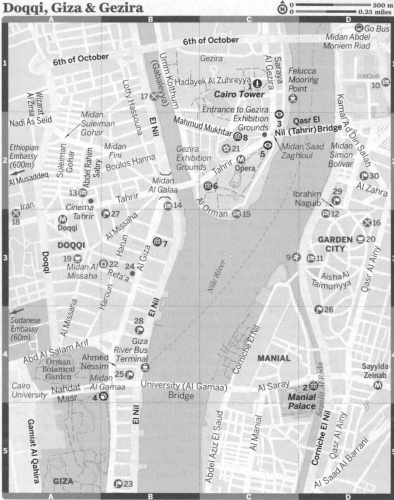

Arabic with possibility to study both concurrently. Excellent Egyptian-colloquial textbooks. Also has online courses.

Kalimat LANGUAGE
(Map p58; ☑3761-8136; www.kalimategypt.com; 22 Sharia Mohammed Mahmoud Shaaban, Mohandiseen; 4-week course from US$260) Small language school with four-week courses in both Modern-standard Arabic and Egyptian-colloquial.

Arts & Crafts

Azza Fahmy Design Studio ART
(Map p58; ☑010-9012-7641; www.facebook.com/TheDesignStudiobyAzzaFahmy; Sharia Qasr Al Shama; ⊙10am-6pm) Both long- and short-term jewellery design courses by internationally renowned jeweller Azza Fahmy (p113). Next door to Darb 1718, which also organises many arts and crafts workshops.

Art Cafe ART
(☑2380-1113; www.artcafe-egypt.com; 10b Rd 11, Ma'adi; ⊙10am-10pm Sat-Thu) Organises Arabic

Doqqi, Giza & Gezira

calligraphy classes (four classes, once per week LE580) from beginner to advanced levels, along with many other art workshops. Also hosts excellent arts and crafts sessions for children from storytelling (in English and German as well as Arabic) to pottery.

Belly Dancing

The more service-minded tourist hotels can arrange belly-dancing classes, and this is the most flexible option. Many of the big-name dancers on the Cairo scene offer one-on-one instruction with an hour's tuition usually costing between US$40 and US$100 per hour. Some of the city's gyms and health centres sometimes also offer group courses.

Raqia Hassan (☏3748-2338, 012-2329-2386; www.raqiahassan.net; 40 Sharia Messaha, Doqqi; per hr US$70-150) A respected name in the Cairo belly-dance scene, Raqia Hassan teaches one-on-one workshops at her private studio in Doqqi. She also organises the Ahlan wa Sahlan belly-dancing festival, one week of workshops, competitions and shows. Check her website for festival details.

Raqs of Course (www.raqsofcourse.com; ☉Jul) A week-long belly-dancing festival of instruction workshops, competitions and shows that hosts belly-dance instructors and dancers from across the world as well as Egypt. It's organised by Rana Kamel, one of Cairo's biggest belly-dancing names. She can also be contacted through the website for private lessons.

Yasmina of Cairo (☏012-2746-5185; www.yasminaofcairo.com) Organises belly-dance classes, workshops and tours. She runs a small studio in her Doqqi apartment, where either she or one of her protégés will give you (or a group, if you can get one together) lessons.

☞ Tours

Nearly everybody in your hotel will want to sell you a day tour in Cairo (the most popular option touted being a combo Giza Pyramids and Saqqara outing).

To hire a taxi for the day and dispense with a guide, try **Aton Amon** (☏010-0621-7674; aton_manos@yahoo.com; full day taxi transport to Saqqara, Memphis & Giza Pyramids US$50), who speaks excellent English and French; he also does airport pickups. The first female cabbie in Cairo **Nour Gaber** (☏011-4888-5561; full day taxi transport to Saqqara, Memphis & Giza Pyramids

Mohandiseen, Agouza & Zamalek

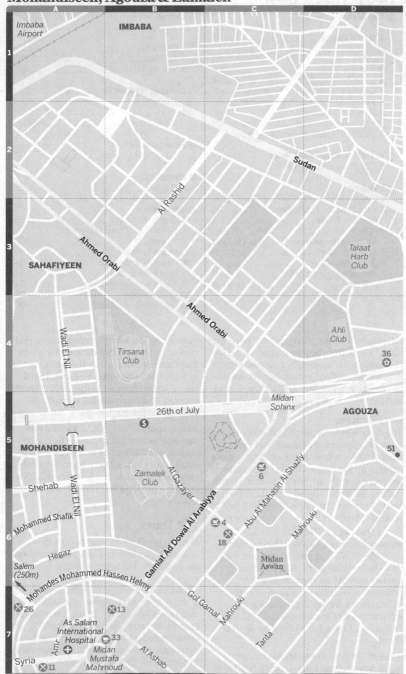

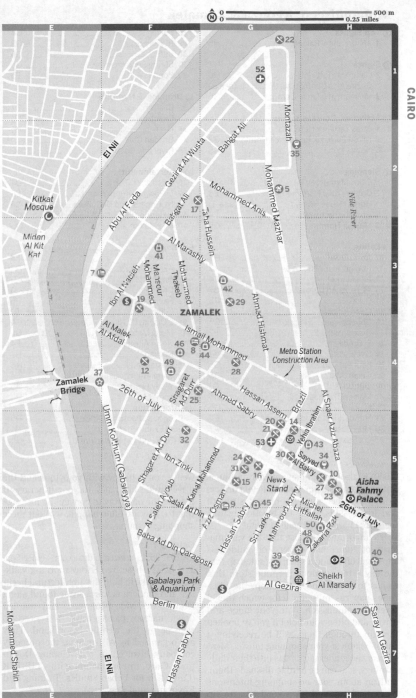

Mohandiseen, Agouza & Zamalek

LE500) is also a great day-tour driver. She is setting up an academy for female taxi drivers to improve their English, mental strength and driving skills, partly as a reaction against the sexual harassment against women.

It's important to realise that the vast majority of guides and drivers (on guide-less trips) will often add a shopping side-trip into the day – the spurious perfume store that claims to supply the Body Shop; the illustrious papyrus 'museum' – for which they'll receive a commission. Both your guide and driver, and often your hotel if you've booked the trip through them, will be receiving a cut of whatever your shopping tally is. Most drivers and guides factor this into their daily earnings, so it can be hard to dissuade them. Be firm about your no-shopping intentions when booking, and it's a good idea to tip

well if you're happy with your tour and the driver/guide has stuck to your itinerary. It may be the only way to convey the message that tourists are often happier without these shopping detours.

Cairo D-Tour   TOURS
(📞 2391-9651; www.cairo-dtour.com; ⊙ Fri Sep-Jun) **FREE** These free Friday morning walking tours take in both the architectural heritage and modern cultural scene found along Downtown's wide boulevards and snaffled down narrow passageways. You need to register on the website beforehand. They are organised by Al Ismaelia, the property company involved in redeveloping Downtown Cairo, in conjunction with CLUSTER (Cairo Lab for Urban Studies, Training and Environmental Research).

Backpacker Concierge   TOURS
(☑ 010-6350-7118;   www.backpackerconcierge.
com) This boutique travel agency dishes up
tailor-made itineraries with a cultural and
environmentally responsible focus. Its excellent guides and drivers for day tours in and
around Cairo will never take you on unscheduled shopping stops, and it can also put together custom trips with a more adventurous
twist, such as temple cycling tours in Luxor.

Real Egypt   TOURS
(☑ 011-0002-2242; www.realegypt.net) Samir
Abbass and his team get consistently recommended by travellers for their tailor-made
tours. Can arrange both Cairo day tours as
well as longer Egypt itineraries.

Cairo Urban Adventures   TOURS
(☑ 010-9799-9534; www.urbanadventures.com/
destination/Cairo-tours; Cairo guided tours US$28-
53) As well as typical Pyramid excursions and
Islamic Cairo tours, Cairo Urban Adventures
offers evening walks through Downtown,
introducing you to central Cairo's bustling
modern vibe as well as its historic 19th-
century architecture. The Home Cooked
Cairo tour offers travellers a chance to dig
a little deeper into Cairene local life, with a
dinner at a local family's home.

Manal Helmy   TOURS
(☑ 012-2313-9045; noula.helmy@gmail.com; guiding fee per day US$100) Excellent female guide
for the Pyramids and the Egyptian Museum.

Samo Tours   TOURS
(☑ 02-2187-8629, 012-2313-8446; www.samotours
egypt.com; 59 Sharia Aziz Al Masry, El Nozha;
☺ 8am-4pm Sun-Thu) Reliable tour company, with excellent English-speaking guides,
Egyptologists and drivers. Can arrange
everything from day trips to Nile cruises and
multiday Egypt tours.

⭐ Festivals & Events

Moulid of Sayyida Zeinab   RELIGIOUS
(Map p58; Midan Sayyida Zeinab, Sayyida Zeinab;
Ⓜ Sayyida Zeinab) In the last week of the Islamic month of Ragab (March to April 2018
to 2020), this veneration of the prophet's
granddaughter is a great neighbourhood
event, behind the mosque of the same name.

D-CAF   PERFORMING ARTS
(Downtown Contemporary Arts Festival; http://d-caf.
org; ☺ Mar-Apr) Going from strength to
strength, this three-week contemporary arts
festival draws the focus on Downtown Cairo

with both local and international acts staging music and dance events, as well as an
art, film and literature program in venues
across the central district. Events all have individual tickets which can be booked online
or (in some cases) bought at the door.

Citadel Festival   MUSIC
(☑ 02-2739-0188; www.cairoopera.org; ☺ Aug-
Sep) Some of the biggest names in classical
Arab music, plus more contemporary artists,
perform at this two-week festival which is
organised by the Cairo Opera House. Performances take place at both the Cairo Opera
House and within the Citadel.

Cairo Jazz Festival   MUSIC
(www.cairojazzfest.com; ☺ Sep-Oct) A three-day
celebration of jazz, bringing acclaimed local
and international musicians to Cairo. Most
performances are held at the venue halls of
the **GrEEK Campus** (Map p62; www.thegreek
campus.com; 28 Sharia Falaki, Bab Al Luq, Downtown) as well as the Cairo Jazz Club (p110).

Cairo International Film Festival   FILM
(https://ciff.org.eg; ☺ Nov) One of the longest-running cultural events in the Arab
world, this annual festival celebrates film
from across the world but with a focus on
Arab and African contributions. As well as
the festival competition, with glitzy award
ceremony, there are plenty of film screenings mostly held in the Cairo Opera House
(p110) venues.

Panorama European Film Festival   FILM
(☺ Nov) A celebration of art-house cinema,
with a program of film screenings from
Europe and across the Arab world (many
showing with English subtitles) at venues
throughout central Cairo, including **cinema
Zawya** (Map p62; ☑ 012-8320-0888; www.zawya
cinema.com; Cinema Odeon, 4 Sharia Abdel Hamid
Said, Downtown).

Moulid of Sayyidna Al Hussein   RELIGIOUS
(Map p77; Midan Al Hussein, Islamic Cairo) On the
square in front of the Mosque of Al Hussein,
this Sufi gathering celebrates the birthday
of the prophet's grandson. If the crowds get
too intense, you can watch from one of the
rooftop cafes. It's near the end of the Islamic
month of Rabei Al Tani (December to January 2018 to 2020).

🛏 Sleeping

Cairo is chock-a-block with budget crashpads, including a few really good ones, but midrange gems are rarer. At the upper end, luxury hotels line the banks of the Nile.

It pays to reserve in advance for your first night or two. Cairo is no place to haul your luggage around comparing room rates. Many budget hotels offer better rates if you book directly rather than using big online booking agencies.

Downtown

This is primarily budget territory, though there are a few noteworthy upper-end sleeps. Either way, you'll be in the thick of things and near great cheap restaurants. Most hotels are located on or around Sharia Talaat Harb in old apartment blocks. Don't be alarmed by grimy stairs and shaky elevators – they aren't necessarily a reflection of the hotels above. Many have balconies and windows overlooking noisy main streets; request a rear room if you're a light sleeper, with earplugs as backup.

★ **Pension Roma**   PENSION $

(Map p62; ☑2391-1088; www.pensionroma. eg; 4th fl, 169 Sharia Mohammed Farid; d LE250-320, tr LE325-420, with shared bathroom s LE125-180, d LE195-273, tr LE275-370; ❈🛜) Run by a French-Egyptian woman with impeccable standards, the Roma brings dignity, even elegance, to the budget-travel scene. The towering ceilings, fresh white-painted walls, antique furniture and filmy white curtains create a feeling of timeless calm while everything's kept neat as a pin. Most rooms share toilets, though many have showers. Rooms in the new extension have full bathroom and air-con.

You'll never be pressured to buy a tour here (they're not even an option), and staff are genuinely friendly and welcoming. Unsurprisingly, this place is popular with repeat guests, many of whom could afford more expensive places but prefer the old-Cairo atmosphere here.

Bella Luna Hotel   HOSTEL $

(Map p62; ☑2393-8139; www.hotelluna cairo.com; 3rd fl, 27 Sharia Talaat Harb; s/d/tr/q US$20/32/38/45; ❈🛜) Modern, backpacker-friendly Bella Luna offers great value for money with bright and large simply furnished rooms, all with bathrooms that come with piping-hot water. In the cleanliness stakes for Downtown's budget hotels, this place really stands out. Small comforts missing elsewhere (bedside lamps and bathmats) are also provided. The (signed) entry is down an alleyway between two watch shops.

For those watching their pennies, there are also cheaper, slightly aged rooms upstairs in their older **Luna Hostel** (Map p62; ☑02-2396-1020; 5th fl, 27 Sharia Talaat Harb; s/d/tr/q US$15/19/22/25, with shared bathroom US$11/15/18/21, dm US$4-6; ❈🛜).

CAIRO FOR CHILDREN

Cairo can be exhausting for kids, but there is much they will enjoy. Be aware the pavements and traffic can be a nightmare for parents with little ones, so backpack-style child carriers are a much better idea for toddlers than pushchairs. The heat can be a serious drain on kids, as well as frazzle parents, so visit in the cooler winter months if possible and time outdoor sightseeing for the morning. It's worth buying *Cairo, the Family Guide*, by Lesley Lababidi and Lisa Sabbahy (AUC Press), revised in 2010.

Children of all ages will like an excursion on a Nile **felucca** or a night-time party boat, gawking at Tut's treasures in the **Egyptian Museum** (p131), and investigating the **Pyramids of Giza** (p122) and the brilliant solar barque at the nearby **Cheops Boat Museum** (p124), as well as exploring the mazelike market of **Khan Al Khalili** (p70). For evening entertainment, most kids will be mesmerised by a rambunctious and colourful performance of the **Al Tannoura Egyptian Heritage Dance Troupe** (p110), while the **Cairo Puppet Theatre** (p110) shows should enchant younger ones.

Parents with smaller children should head to **Al Azhar Park** (p79) on a Friday or Saturday, when local families flock here for picnics. It's a great chance to mingle with local children. Although a full-tilt tourist trap, many little ones will also enjoy **Dr Ragab's Pharaonic Village** (Map p58; ☑3572 2533; www.pharaonicvillage.com; 3 Sharia Al Bahr Al Azam; family of 4 entry and tour program from LE255; ⊙9am-5pm, to 7pm Jul & Aug). A little tattered, it's good for sparking the imagination about what life in ancient Egypt was like. In Ma'adi, the **Art Cafe** (p92) runs child-friendly arts and crafts sessions, as well as storytelling events that are a good way to balance out all the history.

Museum House Hotel
HOSTEL $

(Map p92; ☑02-2574-6672, 010-9108-8968; museumhousehotel@gmail.com; 2 Sharia Champollion; s/d/tr LE350/450/550, d/tr with shared bathroom LE350/450; ❈ 🛜) With only nine rooms, this is an intimate choice in a prime position just off Midan Tahrir. There's a cheery blue-and-white theme running throughout with pot plants adding a cosy home-from-home feel. Rooms are simple but clean, with good bathrooms, and management are super helpful. They were making a dorm (LE100 per person) when we were last in town.

Berlin Hotel
HOSTEL $

(Map p62; ☑2395 7502; www.facebook.com/berlinhotelcairo; 4th fl, 2 Sharia Shawarby; s/d with aircon US$20/25, without air-con US$14/20, all with shared bathroom; ❈ 🛜) The high-ceilinged, colour-saturated rooms at this old-school hostel are exceedingly simple but brim with old-fashioned character. All share toilets but air-con rooms have shower cubicles, and some now come with satellite TV. Owner Hisham is a fount of knowledge on all things Cairo, and when arranging tours only uses drivers who don't do 'shopping' stops.

There's a teensy shared kitchen too and good long-stay rates.

Travelers House Hotel
HOSTEL $

(Map p62; ☑2396-4362; travelershousehotel@yahoo.com; 4th fl, 43 Sharia Sherif; s/d/tr LE200/280/320, s/d with shared bathroom LE170/230; 🛜) With only five rooms (three with private bathroom), this place is a cosy choice. All rooms are large, high-ceilinged, very simple and clean. There's a cute lounge to hang out in, scattered with kitsch Egyptian souvenirs, and with a dinky balcony where you can overlook the madness of Sharia 26th of July from above. Breakfast is an extra LE10.

Hotel Royal
HOTEL $

(Map p62; ☑2391-7203; www.cairohotelroyal.com; 1st fl, 10 Sharia Elwy; s US$21, d US$24-28; ❈ 🛜) The Royal's rooms take a minimalist approach to furnishings and come with mini fridges, office-style desk chairs and frosted-glass cubicles as in-room bathrooms. Unfortunately, service and cleaning are haphazard at best, which is a shame, because with a bit of polish this could be a winner.

Meramees Hostel
HOSTEL $

(Map p62; ☑2396-2318; 5th fl, 32 Sharia Sabri Abu Alam; s/d LE250/450, dm/s/d with shared bathroom LE100/200/400; ❈ 🛜) This well-positioned hostel is easy-going, and the rooms have high ceilings, wooden floorboards, large windows and balconies – though those on the 5th floor are noticeably better kept than those on the 6th. Communal bathrooms and kitchen are kept clean, and the management seems to have travellers' interests in mind.

★ Golden Hotel
HOTEL $$

(Map p62; ☑2390-3815; www.goldenhotelegypt.com; 13 Sharia Talaat Harb; s/d $30/40, new wing $40/50; ❈ 🛜) A serious step-up in room quality for Downtown, Golden's fresh, modern rooms are tiny but come with blue-tiled contemporary bathrooms and good facilities: fridge, satellite TVs, and (miracles never cease) a decent amount of powerpoints. Splash an extra US$10 to grab a recently refurbished room in the new wing for way more space and funky burnt-orange walls with stone accents.

When we stopped by last, the roof terrace was being renovated to create a cool bar area.

Windsor Hotel
HISTORIC HOTEL $$

(Map p62; ☑2591-5810; www.windsorcairo.com; 19 Sharia Alfy; s US$46-62, d US$58-74, s/d with shower & hand basin US$37/46; ❈ 🛜) Ride the hand-cranked elevator up to rooms that ooze old-timer charm, with dark furniture and scuffed-wood floors (room 25 is our favourite). The air-con is noisy, and management is prone to adding surprise extra charges, but the faded romance of the place – including the restaurant where the dinner bell chimes every evening at 7.30pm – is nostalgia-buff heaven.

City View Hotel
HOTEL $$

(Map p92; ☑2773-5980; www.cityview-hotel.com; 1 Sharia Al Bustan; s/d US$40/50; ❈ 🛜) Just a step from the madness of Midan Tahrir, City View is a well-run place with friendly, helpful management and views across to the Egyptian Museum. Rooms are cosy and come with good facilities of mini-fridge, satellite TV and balcony, though the frou-frou drapes and soft furnishings are straight out of grandma's house.

Hotel Osiris
HOTEL $$

(Map p62; ☑010-0531-1822, 2794-5728; www.hotelosiris.fr; 12th fl, 49 Sharia Nubar; s/d/tr US$40/75/90, s with shared bathroom US$25; ❈ 🛜) On the top floor of a commercial building, the Osiris enjoys great city views. In the spotless rooms, colourful appliqué bedspreads and palm-frond shelves add dashes of traditional flavour, though the single rooms are cramped for the price. Bag

CAIRO HOTEL SCAMS

In short, all scams are attempts to distract you from your lodging of choice. Hotels do not open and close with any great frequency in Cairo, and if it's a known place, it is very unlikely to have gone out of business by the time you arrive.

At the airport, you may be approached by a person with an official-looking badge, claiming to be a government tourism representative. (There are no such true reps at the airport.) They'll ask if you've booked a hotel and then offer to call to confirm that a room is waiting for you. Of course, they don't call the hotel – they call a friend, who says there is no booking and that his establishment is full. Concerned, the tout will offer to find you an alternative.

Some taxi drivers will stall by saying they don't know where your hotel is. In that case tell them to let you out at Midan Talaat Harb – from here it's a short walk to most budget hotels. Other lines include telling you the hotel you're heading for is closed/very expensive/horrible/a brothel and suggesting a 'better' place, for which they earn a commission, which will then be added to your bill.

The most elaborate scam is when a stranger (often on the airport bus) chats you up and asks your name and where you're staying. Then the person says goodbye and isn't seen again. What they next do is call a friend who goes and stands outside the hotel you've booked. When you arrive, he or she will ask 'Are you...?', using the name you volunteered back at the airport. Then you'll be told that the hotel has been closed by the police/flooded because of plumbing issues/totally booked out, and that the owners have organised a room for you elsewhere.

Finally, when checking in without a prior reservation, never pay for more than a night in advance. No decent hotel will ask for more, and this gives you recourse if the place doesn't meet your needs.

a double with balcony if you can. Breakfast involves fresh juice, crêpes and omelettes.

★ **Steigenberger Hotel El Tahrir** HOTEL $$$
(Map p92; ☑ 2575-0777; www.eltahrir.steigen berger.com; 2 Sharia Qasr El Nil; r from US$116; ❄ 🛜 ≋) This sophisticated customer has been shaking up the Downtown hotel scene since it opened in early 2017. From the vast, modern minimalist lobby with casual bar to the spacious, contemporary styled rooms, the Steigenberger is a soothing oasis right in the heart of the city. Service here is stellar, and it's also excellent value in comparison to other top-end options.

🛏 Garden City

Just south of Midan Tahrir, this area is quieter and less congested than elsewhere in Cairo, but there aren't many hotels to choose from.

Four Seasons at Nile Plaza HOTEL $$$
(Map p92; ☑ 2791-7000; www.fourseasons.com/ caironp; 1089 Corniche El Nil; r from US$300; ❄ 🛜 ≋) Of the two Four Seasons in Cairo (the other is in Giza), this one has a more modern vibe (check out the cool Omar Nagdi painting behind reception), and a handier location, 15 minutes' walk from the Egyptian Museum.

The impeccable rooms have windows that actually open (unfortunately rare in luxury hotels). Plus: three (!) swimming pools.

Kempinski Nile HOTEL $$$
(Map p92; ☑ 2798-0000; www.kempinski.com; 12 Sharia Ahmed Ragab; r from US$150; ❄ 🛜 ≋) You enter this Nileside tower through a rather cramped, bland lobby, but things definitely get better in the rooms, which are bright and modern, with nice art hung on the walls and skinny balconies. Compared to its rivals, though, service can be a little off, and the swimming pool is a bit small.

🛏 Zamalek

The relatively quiet enclave of Zamalek offers the best night's sleep in the city, though not the cheapest. Many of Cairo's best restaurants, shops, bars and coffee shops are here, but sights are a taxi ride away over traffic-jammed bridges.

★ **Hotel Longchamps** BOUTIQUE HOTEL $$
(Map p94; ☑ 2735-2311; www.hotellongchamps. com; 5th fl, 21 Sharia Ismail Mohammed; r US$84-96; ❄ 🛜) Hotel Longchamps is a favourite of returning visitors to Cairo. The comfortable, stylish rooms are spacious, well maintained and come with full mod-cons of a flat-screen

TV, a minibar, and, lo and behold, kettles (a rarity in Egypt). Bathrooms are generously sized and modern. The greenery-covered, peaceful rear balcony, where guests gather to chat at sunset, is a major bonus.

Horus House Hotel
HOTEL $$

(Map p94; ☑2735-3634; www.horushouse hotel.4t.com; 4th fl, 21 Sharia Ismail Mohammed; s/d/tr old-wing US$75/95/115, s/d new-wing US$85/105; ✻⊕) The newly renovated rooms at this homely option are a great option – all large and classically styled with kettles, brand new mattresses on the beds, and chic beige-tiled bathrooms. Older rooms are much simpler but are kept scrupulously clean. All come with mini-fridges and satellite TV. Staff here are courteous and friendly, and go out of their way to help.

Golden Tulip Flamenco Hotel
HOTEL $$

(Map p94; ☑2735-0815; www.flamencohotels. com; 2 Sharia Gezirat Al Wusta; s/d/tr from US$90/100/130; ✻⊕) This popular place is a reasonable alternative to five-star heavyweights. Rooms are comfortable and well equipped, if rather cramped. An extra US$10 for 'superior' class gives you interior space and a balcony overlooking the houseboats on the Nile.

Mayfair Hotel
HOTEL $$

(Map p94; ☑2735-7315; www.mayfaircairo.com; 2nd fl, 9 Sharia Aziz Osman; s/d/tr US$42/48/58, s/d with shared bathroom US$29/34; ✻⊕) Pleasantly old fashioned with high ceilings and a wrap-around terrace for breakfasts, the Mayfair is the cheapest sleep in the neighbourhood and on a quiet street. Single rooms are teensy, but doubles are a good size. All could do with a modern spruce up, but they're clean and come with (exceedingly old) TVs and mini-fridges.

Sofitel El Gezirah
HOTEL $$$

(Map p92; ☑2737-3737; www.sofitel.com; Sharia Al Orman, Gezira; r from US$130; ✻⊕⊠) Tired from long travels? Rest up here in a room with superb views and let the staff look after you. This hotel, on the tip of Gezira island, is delightfully quiet, but it can be hard to get a cab out. There are several good restaurants, including the hotel's new Indian restaurant Manipuri (p106).

Cairo Marriott Hotel
HOTEL $$$

(Map p94; ☑2728-3000; www.marriott.com/ caieg; 16 Sharia Saray Al Gezira; r from US$130; ⒫✻⊕⊠) Historical atmosphere is thick in the lobby and public areas, which all occupy a 19th-century palace. The rooms, though, are all in two modern towers; many have tiny bathrooms, but touches like plasma-screen TVs and extra-plush beds make up for them. It also has a popular garden cafe (p109) – a great place to people-watch – and a good pool.

Doqqi

One step removed from the all-out-bustle, Doqqi has a more residential feel. There's not huge amounts of choice in accommodation or restaurants, but the Doqqi metro station means you're only a hop from Downtown.

King Hotel
HOTEL $$

(Map p92; ☑3335-9455; www.kinghotelcairo.com; 20 Sharia Abdel Rahim Sabry; s/d US$50/65; ✻⊕) This modern mid-rise does a lot right; one of the reasons it's used by many tour groups. Staff here are charming and on the ball, and while the large rooms may be boring beige, they all come with TV, mini-fridge, powerful air-con and clean bathrooms. A major bonus is the rooftop Nomad Bar (p109) where your beer comes with a Pyramids view.

Sheraton Cairo
HOTEL $$$

(Map p92; ☑3336-9700; www.sheratoncairo.com; Midan Galaa; r from US$205; ⒫✻⊕⊠) After a very swish head to tail refurbishment, Cairo's Nileside Sheraton reopened in mid-2017 and is now home to some of the city's chicest rooms. Spacious and well designed all soothing neutral tones and elegant furnishings – they come with big, comfy beds and wide balconies; some have exceptional cityscapes. Service is as slick as you'd expect.

Islamic Cairo

The negatives: no immediate metro access, touts like locusts, nowhere to get a beer and more than the usual number of mosques with loudspeakers. But this is the place to plunge in at Cairo's deep end.

Arabian Nights
HOTEL $

(Map p58; ☑2924-0924; www.arabian nights.hostel.com; 10 Sharia Al Addad; s/d/tr US$20/25/28, with shared bathroom US$12/18/25; ✻⊕) Distinctly out of the tourist fray. Some rooms are quite dark, but standards are generally good and the place is kept shipshape and clean. The challenge is finding it: turn north on Sharia Al Mansouria (east along Sharia Al Azhar from Midan Hussein);

300m on, turn left at the ruined shell of cinema Kawakeb.

El Hussein
HOTEL $

(Map p77; 2591-8089; off Midan Al Hussein; s/d LE200/250; ❄) Off either side of an open-ended hallway where street noise reverberates, the rooms here are dreary and the service surly. But the view from the front-facing rooms with balconies affords mesmerising people-watching on Midan Al Hussein below. There's a top-floor restaurant too. Entrance is in the back alley, one block off the square.

🍴 Eating

In Cairo, you can spend LE5 or LE500 on dinner.

Many midrange and top-end restaurants double as bars.

Too tired to leave the hotel? You can get just about anything delivered, and even order online through www.otlob.com, with service from more than 120 of the city's most popular restaurants.

At the budget end of the spectrum are the street carts, *kushari* (mix of noodles, rice, black lentils, fried onions and tomato sauce) canteens, and fruit-and-veg markets where the majority of Cairenes feed themselves. One step up are the Egyptian fast-food operations – forget KFC and Pizza Hut – that serve some of the most delicious and cheapest meals you'll have. As with the hotel scene, reliable midrange options are in short supply, but the few good ones offer great value, especially for traditional food.

At the upper end, Cairo dining can be quite cosmopolitan, with the chefs usually imported straight from the relevant country, along with all the ingredients. Dinner reservations are generally recommended.

✕ Downtown

This is predominantly cheap-and-cheerful territory, plus a few nostalgic favourites. It's by far the best place to get good authentic Egyptian street food.

★ Abu Tarek
EGYPTIAN $

(Map p62; 40 Sharia Champollion; kushari LE10-25; ⊙8am-midnight; ✒) 'We have no other branches!' proclaims this temple of *kushari*. No, the place has just expanded, decade by decade, into the upper storeys of its building, and continues to hold on to Cairo's unofficial 'best *kushari*' title. Eat in, rather than takeaway, to check out the elaborate decor upstairs.

Order the 'special' for the all-important extra chickpeas and fried onions.

★ At Tabei Ad Dumyati
EGYPTIAN $

(Map p66; 2579-7533; 31 Sharia Orabi; ta'amiyya, shawarma & sandwiches LE2.50-23, dishes LE4.50-51; ⊙7am-1am; ✒) The takeaway section out front does a roaring trade in shawarma (meat sliced off a spit and stuffed in a bread roll with chopped tomatoes and garnish) and *ta'amiyya* (Egyptian variant of falafel), while out back is a sit-down canteen that bustles with families and offers some of Cairo's cheapest meals with a popular salad bar and friendly waiters.

Pick your salads, eat some *fuul* and tuck into crisp-outside, fluffy-inside *ta'amiyya*. There are branches on **Talaat Harb** (Map p62; Talaat Harb Complex, Sharia Talaat Harb; ⊙9am-midnight) and in **Mohandiseen** (Map p94; 02-3304-1124; 17 Sharia Gamiat Ad Dowal Al Arabiyya; ⊙7am-1am).

Koshary Goha
EGYPTIAN $

(Map p62; 4 Sharia Emad Ad Din; mains LE7-15; ⊙10am-midnight; ✒) Egyptian families know a good deal when they see one, and that's why Koshary Goha's outdoor tables are often packed solid in the evening. The *kushari* here is seriously good with liberal sprinklings of fried onions and a proper hot sauce on the side. But the real treat is the *makaroneh bi lahm*, a baked pasta casserole with spicy tomato sauce.

Greek Club
MEDITERRANEAN $

(Map p62; 2575-0822; 21 Sharia Mahmoud Bassiouni; minimum LE30, cover charge for non-Greek LE5, dishes LE10-70; ⊙5pm-midnight) The Greek Club is a Downtown institution and a popular hangout with liberal Egyptians, artists and foreign residents. A cold beer on the outdoor terrace is a joy during summer months. The food is nothing special but more than adequate, and the main dining room oozes vintage charm with high ceilings and tall columns.

Gad
EGYPTIAN $

(Map p62; 2576-3583; 13 Sharia 26th of July; ta'amiyya & shawarma LE2.50-24, mains LE15-46; ⊙9am-2am; ✒) Gad's lighthouse logo is fitting: it's a beacon in the night for hungry Cairenes whether they're in the mood for *fiteer* (sweet or savoury flaky pizza), shawarma, salads or European-style pizza. The ground floor is for takeaway; order and pay at the till and then take the receipts to the relevant counters. Or eat in upstairs.

The one on **Sharia Abdel Khalek Sarwat** (Map p62; 02-2396-4621; Sharia Abdel Khalek Sarwat; 9am-2am) is typically less crowded. There are also branches on **Sharia Al Azhar** (Map p80; 9am-2am) and **Midan Falaki** (Map p62; 24hr).

El Abd
BAKERY $

(Map p62; 35 Sharia Talaat Harb; pastries LE2-10; 8.30am-midnight) For Arabic-style pastries head for Cairo's most famous bakery, easily identified by the crowds of people outside tearing into their croissants, sweets and savoury pies. It's a great place to augment your ho-hum hotel breakfast. There is another **branch** (Map p62; 8.30am-midnight) on the corner of Sharia 26th of July and Sherif

Fatatri At Tahrir
EGYPTIAN $

(Map p62; 166 Sharia Tahrir; fiteer from LE35; 7am-1am) This basic canteen just off Midan Tahrir has been serving delicious, filling, though greasy *fiteer* (sweet or savoury flaky pizza) to Downtown residents and legions of backpackers for decades. There's no menu as such. The *fiteer* cook will just reel off the ingredients for you to choose from. They can make them decently spicy as well if asked.

Sudan Restaurant
AFRICAN $

(Map p62; Sharia Haret Al Sufi; dishes LE8-40; 10am-10pm) One of several Sudanese restaurants and cafes in this alley, this is the tidiest and perhaps serves the most delicious dishes. Try *salata iswid* ('black salad'), a spicy mix of eggplant and peanuts, and *qarassa*, stew served in a bread bowl, among other treats

It's in the alley connecting Sharia Adly and Sharia Abdel Khalek Sarwat, in a courtyard off the southern end. Sign is Arabic only – yellow letters on a red background

Fasahat Soumaya
EGYPTIAN $$

(Map p62; 020-9873-8637; 15 Sharia Youssef Al Guindi; mains LE35-75; 1-10.30pm;) This restaurant is squiggled down a little pedestrian alley. All the staples are here, prepared like an Egyptian mother would make: various stuffed veggies, hearty stews and extra odd bits (rice sausage, lamb shanks) on Thursdays. The sign is in Arabic only, green on a white wall, with a few steps down to the basement space.

Eish + Malh
CAFE $$

(Map p62; 010-9874-4014; 20 Sharia Adly; breakfasts LE35-65, mains LE39-89; 8am-midnight;) This high-ceilinged cafe, with its original arched windows framed by floor-to-ceiling city scenes, is a favoured hang-out for hip, young Cairenes. The menu has an Italian bent with decent pizza, plenty of pasta options and really good ice cream, while in a major bonus to caffeine-fans, it also makes the best flat white (along with other espresso-based coffees) in Downtown.

Hati Al Geish
EGYPTIAN $$

(Map p62; 23 Sharia Falaki; mains LE30-180; 11am-11pm) This temple to charcoal-grilled meat does excellent *kastileeta* (lamb chops) and tender *moza* (shanks) – good for gnawing. The *moza fatta,* with a side of rice-and-pita casserole, is also good plus there's *tagens* (stews cooked in a deep clay pot) and multiple mezze dishes and salads for hearty Egyptian family feasting.

Gomhouriya
EGYPTIAN $$

(Map p62; 42 Sharia Falaki; pigeons LE55; noon-midnight) Roast, stuffed pigeon is the star of the show here – just tell the waiter how many birds you want, and they arrive crisp and hot, along with salad and all-you-can-drink mugs of peppery, lemony broth. The small English sign says 'Shalapy'.

Felfela Restaurant
EGYPTIAN $$

(Map p62; 2392-2833; 15 Sharia Hoda Shaarawi; dishes LE12-105; 8am-midnight;) Attracting tourists, coach parties and locals since 1963, Felfela is an institution that can deliver a reliable, if not wildly delicious, meal with good service. A bizarre jungle theme rules the decor, but the food is straight-down-the-line Egyptian and consistently decent, especially the mezze and grilled chicken.

Le Bistro
FRENCH $$

(Map p62; 2392-7694; 8 Sharia Hoda Shaarawi; mains LE60-110; noon-11pm) Tucked away below street level, Le Bistro is a surprisingly fancy outpost Downtown. The food may not quite match its European ideal, but Cairenes love it, and steak frites can make a nice change from kebab. The restaurant entrance is to the right; you can also order off the food menu at the bar (enter to the left).

Estoril
EGYPTIAN $$

(Map p62; 2574-3102; off Sharia Talaat Harb; mezze LE21-52, mains LE60-120; noon-midnight;) There are clouds of cigarette smoke and tables crammed with Cairo's arts-and-letters set here, but once seated, you'll feel like one of the club, scooping up simple mezze and ordering cold beer after beer. Food is nothing special, but the atmosphere is old school.

ⓘ SELF CATERING

Sunny Supermarket (Map p94; ☑16848; 11 Sharia Aziz Osman, Zamalek; ⊙7:30am-midnight daily) This small high-end supermarket has excellent fresh produce, bakery and deli sections, and stocks plenty of international products. It also makes its own line of smoothies.

Alfa Market (Map p94; ☑02-2737-0801; 4 Sharia Al Malek Al Afdal, Zamalek; ⊙8am-10pm) A good range of local foods and imported items.

Souq At Tawfiqiyya (Sharia At Tawfiqiyya; Map p62; Downtown; ⊙7am-9pm) Blocks-long fruit-and-veg market, open late. There's a good dairy store at the corner with Talaat Harb selling fresh cheese.

Women can come for a drink alone here, and the bar in the back is a good place to perch too.

Café Riche   EGYPTIAN $$
(Map p62; ☑2392 9793; 17 Sharia Talaat Harb; mezze LE8-25, mains LE50-90; ⊙10am-midnight; ☑) This narrow restaurant, allegedly the oldest in Cairo, was the favoured drinking spot of the intelligentsia. It's gone to seed somewhat since then, though a certain old guard still sits under the ceiling fans. The mains of slightly Frenchified Egyptian dishes aren't great, so partner your cold beer with a couple of mezze instead.

🍴 Garden City

This is the place to come for a formal feast. The luxury hotels lining the banks of the Nile here have some truly excellent restaurants.

Mahrous   EGYPTIAN $
(Map p92; Sharia Al Haras, Garden City; meals LE20; ⊙4pm-4am; ☑) Perhaps Cairo's best *fuul*, and worth elevating to dinner status (note the atypical hours). With each plate of beans, you get a spread of salads and fresh potato chips. It's just a tiny stand on a residential block. Turn in to Garden City at the Co-op gas station, make the first left and then a hard left at the next intersection.

★ Sabaya   LEBANESE $$$
(Map p62; ☑2795-7171; Corniche El Nil, Semiramis InterContinental; mezze LE40-95, mains LE145-265; ⊙1pm-1am) Delicious Lebanese food in a sumptuous but relaxed atmosphere. There's plenty of grilled meat mains, but the mezze here is the real star of the show. Order old favourites hummus and *sambousek* (stuffed pastry triangles), some salads, chicken livers in pomegranate molasses, and *bel kawarma* (mashed potato doused in lamb's fat), and you've got yourself a real Levantine feast.

Everything comes with fresh-baked pillows of pita, and sharing is the name of the game; all the better for sampling more mezze dishes. To top it off, service here is head and shoulders above most other places in town.

Osmanly   TURKISH $$$
(Map p92; ☑2798-0000; Corniche El Nil, Kempinski Nile; mezze LE45-65, mains LE160-200; ⊙noon-midnight; ☑) Exceptionally good Turkish food, served with elan, starting with handwashing in jasmine-scented water and moving on to a dazzling selection of cold mezze, impeccably grilled kebab plates and the odd riff on Ottoman palace cuisine, such as chicken legs stuffed with rice and pine nuts. Save room for the *kunafa* (sweet cheese and vermicelli-like pastry) dessert.

Bird Cage   THAI $$$
(Map p62; ☑02-2795-7171; Corniche El Nil, Semiramis InterContinental; dishes LE75-190; ⊙noon-midnight) This soothing, wood-panelled space is a favourite with wealthy Cairenes. Grilled foods don't have the proper char, but other preparations, such as whole sea bass wrapped in banana leaves, are good and beautifully presented. The chef will make it truly Thai-spicy if you ask.

🍴 Zamalek

Zamalek has some of Cairo's best and most stylish restaurants. Cheap dining is not one of the island's fortes, but there are a few possibilities, such as the **Baraka shawarma stand** (Map p94; ☑02-2736-8737; 9 Sharia Brazil; shawarma & sandwiches LE18-30; ⊙9am-2am) on Sharia Brazil.

Several shops on 26th of July sell very good quality fresh produce.

★ Zööba   EGYPTIAN $
(Map p94; ☑16082; www.facebook.com/ZoobaEats; Sharia 26th of July; dishes LE3-36; ⊙8am-1am; ☑) Egyptian street food gets a modern makeover. Zööba has taken the country's classic cheap eats and given them contemporary twists. Whole-grain *kushari*, beetroot *baladi* bread, pickled lemon and spicy pepper *ta'amiyya* sandwiches, and some seriously

good salads and shawarma. Eat in at the zinc-clad table amid the most eclectic of decors, or take out – this is ideal picnic fodder.

It's not just locals who are loving Zööba's take on Egyptian fast food either. The team won first place at London's 2016 Falafel Festival with its *ta'amiyya*.

Copenhagen
CAFE $

(Map p94; ☑ 2737-4796; 118 Sharia 26th of July; pastries LE15-45, sandwiches LE30-75; ⊗ 7am-11pm; ☜ ☑) A strong latte and avocado toast for a light lunch – well, well Cairo, how times change. This teensy place, with just two high bar-tables and eight seats, is our new favourite coffee hangout in Zamalek. It does a selection of salads and sandwiches (which also make excellent day-out picnic fodder), plus has a ridiculously tempting display case of patisserie goodies.

The early opening hours, fresh croissants and good coffee make it a beacon for travellers who've lost all enthusiasm for the typical Cairo hotel bread roll/cheese triangle/hard boiled egg/fig jam breakfast combo.

Four Fat Ladies
DESSERTS $

(Map p94; ☑ 16679; 8 Sharia Brazil; LE9-30; ⊗ 8am-midnight) Not the place for maintaining your diet. This coffee and cake joint is sugar-rush heaven with brownies, always at least six different cakes – including our favourite carrot cake in town – and a good selection of muffins and biscuits.

★ O's Pasta
ITALIAN $$

(Map p94; ☑ 2739-5609; www.facebook.com/ospasta; 159 Sharia 26th of July, Zamalek; mains LE68-155; ⊗ 4pm-midnight; ☑) A few years ago, Cairo was a-tizz with new sushi joints; now all the newbie restaurants are Italian and O's Pasta is our pick of the bunch. Squeeze – and we mean squeeze, there are only five tables – into the blue-and-green room to munch on Red Sea calamari pasta doused in spinach and cream sauce, or pecan-basil-pesto chicken pasta.

The kitchen is right in front of you so you can watch the chefs at work, and service is friendly and efficient. The menu is nearly all pasta, with a few salads thrown in for good measure and with a rather delectable sweet-potato soup as a starter. There's no alcohol so sup on a tart lemon-and-mint juice instead.

It's just off Sharia 26th July, on the alleyway between Diwan bookshop and Maison Thomas; look for the blue door.

Abou El Sid
EGYPTIAN $$

(Map p94; ☑ 2735-9640; www.abouelsid.com; 157 Sharia 26th of July; mains LE19-58, mains LE56-120; ⊗ noon-1am) Cairo's first hipster Egyptian restaurant (and now a national franchise), Abou El Sid is as popular with tourists as it is with upper-class natives. You can get better *molokhiyya* (garlicky leaf soup, speciality of Egypt) elsewhere, but here you wash it down with a wine or beer and lounge on kitschy gilt 'Louis Farouk' furniture.

The entrance is just off Sharia 26th of July; take the street between Diwan bookstore and Maison Thomas, and look for the tall wooden doors. Reservations are a good idea.

Maison Thomas
PIZZA $$

(Map p94; ☑ 02-2735-7057; 157 Sharia 26th of July; pizzas LE35-114; ⊗ 24hr) A little slice of the Continent, with loads of brass and mirrors, and friendly waiters in long white aprons, Maison Thomas has been serving up Cairo's best thin-crust pizza for decades. Puritans should opt for the authentic Neapolitan, but we're rather partial to the Leonardo (with artichokes and marinated peppers) as well.

Sufi
CAFE $$

(Map p94; ☑ 2738-1643; 1st fl, 12 Sharia Sayyed Al Bakry; mains LE35-80; ⊗ 9am-1am; ☜) Young Cairenes tap on their laptops while sipping coffee or munching on pasta, pizza and filling sandwiches, amid creaky wood-floored rooms rimmed by shelves stuffed to the brim with old books. It's an arty-flavoured, quiet space and, continuing with the cultural theme, there's occasional exhibitions and film screenings.

Cairo Kitchen
EGYPTIAN $$

(Map p94; ☑ 2735-4000; 118 Sharia 26th of July; salads LE15, mains LE21-79; ⊗ 10am-midnight; ☑) Dig into contemporary versions of traditional wholesome Egyptian home cooking. Order from the counter – brown-rice *kushari*, *molokhiyya* or a typical Egyptian stew. The salad bar here provides some of the tastiest vegetarian meals in town. Grab a four-salad mix and pair it with a side of spicy potatoes.

The decor is colourful, prices are good and the place is popular with Cairenes. Despite the address, the entrance is one block down Sharia Aziz Osman.

Crave
INTERNATIONAL $$

(Map p94; 22 Sharia Taha Hussein; mains LE43-189; ⊗ 11am-midnight; ☜) Most definitely not a place for vegetarians; Crave specialises in meaty comfort dishes that the clientele of

CAIRO EATING

ZAMALEK ICE CREAM STOP

Gelato Mio (Map p94; ☎2737-1527; 6 Sharia Brazil; scoop from LE20; ⊙noon-1am) On a sweltering summer's day, we make a beeline here to cool off with a mixed scoop of watermelon and prickly pear. For chocoholics, the Twix and chilli-chocolate flavours are bliss.

Rigoletto (Map p94; ☎010-2666-3110; www.rigolettoicecream.com; Yamama Center, 3 Sharia Taha Hussein; per scoop LE15; ⊙10am-midnight) Delicious ice cream to cool you down on a hot day. For the young (and young at heart) there are fun flavours like banana milk and butterscotch, while those pining for something a tad more sophisticated can try the *mastik* (Arabic gum), salted peanut, or cardamom.

Mandarine Koueider (Map p94; ☎2735-5010; 17 Sharia Shagaret Ad Durr; per scoop LE10; ⊙9am-11pm) This ice cream parlour is a hit with local families taking the kids out for a treat. For a fruity kick, get stuck into the *zabadi bi tut* (yoghurt with blackberry).

Egyptian families and big groups of friends lap up. There are sandwiches, pizza and salads too but what people come here for are big-portioned dishes, such as pepper steak and chicken breast in lemon-dill sauce, all served with veggies and mash.

Left Bank BRASSERIE $$
(Map p94; ☎2735-0014; www.leftbankonline.com; 53 Sharia Abu Al Feda; mains LE35-195; ⊙8am-midnight; P) The Nileside terrace is a great place for breakfast with options ranging from French toast to a traditional Cairene plate with *fuul* and feta. Later in the day there is a wide selection of salads, pasta, and mains such as grilled sea bass and chicken stuffed with mushrooms and mozzarella.

Peking CHINESE $$
(Map p94; ☎2736-3894; 23B Sharia Ismail Mohammed; dishes LE18-100; ⊙noon-midnight) Sometimes you just need steamed dumplings. Luckily when that craving hits in Cairo you can head to Peking. Order the delicious chilli cabbage, and a bowl of hot and sour soup while you're at it, and you've got yourself the perfect antidote to *kushari* and shawarma overload. The bar here (beer LE43, cocktails from LE70) is rather nice too.

Five Bells EGYPTIAN $$
(Map p94; ☎2735-8980; 13 Sharia Ismail Mohammed; mezze LE29-88, mains LE77-165; ⊙12.30pm-1am) A pretty place to rest up after a long stroll through Zamalek, this garden restaurant serves traditional Egyptian mezze to a soundtrack of Edith Piaf and other wistful European tunes, along with plinky-plonky live piano in the evenings. The bar here is a relaxed spot to snack on meatballs and fresh fried potato crisps while sinking a cold beer.

Makani SUSHI $$
(Map p94; ☎2736-1486; 118 Sharia 26th of July; dishes LE39-110; ⊙10am-2am) A cafe selling sushi and pasta shouldn't work, right? But Makani does. The sushi, though, is the pick of the menu (which also includes sandwiches), with a vast selection of classic maki rolls, fusion sushi rolls and sashimi.

Manipuri INDIAN $$$
(Map p92; ☎2737-3737; www.sofitel.com; Sharia Al Orman, Gezira, Sofitel Gezirah; dishes LE50-280; ⊙7pm-1am Tue-Sun; ✍) Although we'd prefer a more liberal hand with the spicing, this is probably Cairo's best Indian restaurant. The menu mostly focuses on tandoori, but there are still plentiful vegetarian curries to choose from and some seafood specialities from Kerala. If you can, eat on the outdoor terrace with its great views of the bank of the Nile.

Mohandiseen & Doqqi

These concrete suburbs look bland and flavourless, but it's possible to find some excellent restaurants.

Abu Ammar Al Souri SYRIAN $
(Map p94; ☎3336-0887; 8 Sharia Syria, Mohandiseen; salads & mezze LE8-12, sandwiches & shawarma LE9-35, mains LE18-74; ⊙24hr) At this thronged fast-food operation, pantalooned men work the shawarma skewers, folding meat slices into huge pieces of Syrian-style *saj* flatbread. It's also good for trying out Arabic specialities more usually seen in Syria and Jordan, such as *freek* (a pilaf made from *freekah*, green wheat) and *mansaf* (Bedouin lamb dish doused in a sauce made from fermented dried yoghurt).

Yemen Restaurant
YEMENI $

(Map p92; ☑3338-8087; 10 Sharia Iran, Doqqi; dishes LE15-80; ☺noon-2am) This fluorescent-lit place has all the ambience of a car showroom, but it does have great authentic Yemeni dishes, served without cutlery, and huge rounds of flaky flatbread for scooping. Everything-in-the-pot *salta* (stew) is standard, but almost everything on the cryptic menu is richly spiced, even the 'choped meat'. Sharia Iran is one block north of Midan Doqqi, running west.

El Omda
EGYPTIAN $

(Map p94; ☑3346-2701; 6 Sharia Al Gazayer, Mohandiseen; dishes LE2.50-80; ☺24hr; ☎) A mini-empire taking up the better part of a block, El Omda offers numerous ways to put grilled meats into your system. At the takeout joint on the corner, get a *shish tawouq* (marinated chicken grilled on skewers) sandwich with spicy pickles.

Mori Sushi
JAPANESE $$

(Map p94; ☑11112; www.mori-sushi.com; 30 Sharia Mohandes Mohammed Hassen Helmy, Mohandiseen; sushi 4-8 pieces LE28-120; ☺noon-1am) Egypt's favourite sushi haunt (with several branches across the country) is always buzzing thanks to its reasonable prices and vast menu selection. From *temaki* and *gunkan* rolls to *nigiri* and simple maki rolls, it's sure to solve all your Japanese-cuisine cravings.

Sea Gull
SEAFOOD $$

(Map p92; ☑3749-4244; 106 Sharia El Nil, Agouza; meals LE120-170; ☺11am-1am; ☎) There's no menu here, just select your fish from the iced-down display, and then retire to your table to admire the view and tuck into a spread of salads while everything is grilled.

The crowd is almost entirely Egyptian families. Outside seating is great on a balmy night; there's air-con inside if you want it.

✕ Islamic Cairo

There are plenty of fast-food joints around Midan Al Hussein, but the restaurants in this part of town are limited – you really have to like grilled meat, and not be too squeamish about hygiene.

Al Halwagy
EGYPTIAN $

(Map p77; ☑2591-7055; off Sharia Gawhar Al Qaid; dishes LE6-45; ☺24hr) This good *ta'amiyya*, *fuul* and salad place has been around for nearly a century. You can eat at pavement tables or hide away upstairs.

Khan El Khalili Restaurant & Mahfouz Coffee Shop
EGYPTIAN $$

(Map p77; ☑2590-3788; 5 Sikket Al Badistan; sandwiches & mains LE40-70; ☺noon-3am; ☎☎) The tranquil Moorish-style interior of this cafe-restaurant, with its strong air-con and tarboosh-hatted waiters, is a popular haven from the khan's bustle. Although geared to capture tourist trade, the food is decent, particularly the *hawashi* (meat patty) and spiced *baladi* sausage sandwiches, and their version of Egypt's bread-based dessert, *umm ali*. The juices are also excellent.

Farahat
EGYPTIAN $$

(Map p77; 126a Sharia Al Azhar, Islamic Cairo; pigeons LE55-60; ☺noon-4am) In an alley off Sharia Al Azhar, this place is legendary for its pigeon, available stuffed or grilled. It doesn't look like much – just plastic chairs outside – but once you start nibbling the succulent, spiced birds, you'll believe the hype.

LOCAL KNOWLEDGE

FIND YOUR OWN AHWA

Cairo's *ahwas* – traditional coffeehouses – are essential places to unwind, chat and breathe deeply over a shisha. Dusty floors, rickety tables and the clatter of dominoes and *towla* (backgammon) define the traditional ones. But newer, shinier places – where women smoke as well – have expanded the concept, not to mention the array of shisha flavours, which now include everything from mango to bubblegum.

There's an *ahwa* for every possible subculture. We review a couple of the most famous ones, but half the joy of the *ahwa* is discovering 'yours'. Look in back alleys all over Downtown. Sports fans gather south of Sharia Alfy; intellectuals at Midan Falaki. There's a nice traditional joint down the lane behind Al Azhar Mosque, and a cool mixed crowd next to Townhouse Gallery. Most *ahwas* are open from 8am to 2am or so, and you can order a lot more than *shai* (tea) and coffee: try *karkadai* (hibiscus, hot or cold), *irfa* (cinnamon), *kamun* (cumin, good for colds), *yansun* (anise) and, in winter, hot *sahlab* (milky drink made from orchid tubers).

♀ Drinking & Nightlife

Cairo isn't a 'dry' city, but locals tend to run on caffeine, available at both traditional *ahwas* (coffeehouses) and European-style cafes. Drinking beer or spirits typically doesn't start till the evening hours, and then it's limited to Western-style bars and some cheaper, more locals-only dives. For the former, Zamalek is the best place to go boozing; the latter are all Downtown.

Liquor is expensive, local wine is drinkable but not great, but beer is widely available and cheap. Beers range from LE25 to LE45, while cocktails are typically only served at more upscale bars and range from LE70 to more than LE200. The fancier places can have door policies as strict as the nightclubs, so dress well and go in mixed groups. Many places also have full menus, so you can snack as you go.

♀ Downtown

Zahret Al Bustan   COFFEE
(Map p62; Sharia Talaat Harb; ⊙8am-2am) This traditional *ahwa* is a bit of an intellectuals' and artists' haunt, though also firmly on many backpackers' lists, so be alert to scam artists. It's in the lane just behind Café Riche.

Windsor Bar   BAR
(Map p62; ✆2591-5810; 19 Sharia Alfy, Windsor Hotel; ⊙6pm-1am) Alas, most of the regular clientele of the Windsor Hotel's bar has passed on, leaving a few hotel guests, a polyglot bartender and a faint soundtrack of swing jazz and Umm Kulthum. Colonial history has settled in an almost palpable film on the taxidermist's antelope heads, the barrel-half chairs and the dainty wall sconces. Solo women will feel comfortable here.

Kafein   CAFE
(Map p62; ✆010-0302-5346; 28 Sharia Sherif; ⊙7am-1.30am; 🛜) This teensy cafe-restaurant, tucked in the little alley off Sharia Sherif, does good coffee and shisha, as well as yummy fresh juices and milkshakes. Many a foreign journalist enjoys the air-con confines upstairs, the free wi-fi and the caffeine-hit here. Also good for lunch, with a menu of sandwiches and salads.

Cilantro   CAFE
(Map p62; www.cilantrocafe.net; 31 Sharia Mohammed Mahmoud; ⊙9am-2am; 🛜) Egypt's home-grown answer to Starbucks, this popular chain does all the usual hot and cold coffee drinks, teas and juices, plus packaged sandwiches and cakes. If it weren't for the gaggles of headscarf-wearing teenage girls who crowd the banquettes after school, it would be easy to forget you're in Egypt. The latte frappé is heaven on a hot day.

There are other branches scattered throughout the city: **Zamalek** (Map p94; 157 Sharia 26th of July; ⊙10am-11pm; 🛜), **Mohandiseen** (Map p94; ✆02-3303-0645; cnr Sharia Gamiliat Ad Dowal Al Arabiyya & Wadi El Nil; ⊙8am-2am) and **Doqqi** (Map p92; Midan Al Missaha; ⊙7am-1am; 🛜), to name a few. All offer free wi-fi, strong air-con, and a well-separated non-smoking area.

Odeon Palace Hotel   ROOFTOP BAR
(Map p62; ✆02-2577-6637; www.hodeon.com; 6 Sharia Abdel Hamid Said; ⊙24hr) Its fake turf singed from shisha coals, this slightly dilapidated rooftop bar is favoured by Cairo's heavy-drinking theatre and cinema clique, and is a great place to watch the sun go down (or even better, come up).

Le Grillon   BAR
(Map p62; ✆02-2574-3114; 8 Sharia Qasr El Nil; ⊙11am-2am) Nominally a restaurant, this bizarre faux patio is all about beer, shisha and gossip about politics and the arts scene. The illusion of outdoors is created with wicker furniture, fake vines and lots of ceiling fans. The entrance is in the back of a courtyard between two buildings.

Zigzag   BAR
(Map p62; ✆012-7560-2411; www.facebook.com/zigzagCairo49; 6 Sharia Qasr El Nil; ⊙10pm-6am) This bar-club, set in the old Arabesque restaurant, hosts local bands on weekday nights while Thursday and Friday nights are DJ sets with electronica, R&B, hip-hop and grime. There's a strict couples and mixed groups only entry policy. In July and August, when most of Cairo's party-set have upped sticks for the beach, it is only open for occasional events.

♀ Zamalek & Doqqi

Deals   BAR
(Map p94; ✆2736-0502; 2 Sharia Sayyed Al Bakry; ⊙4pm-2am; 🛜) This classic Zamalek hangout can get crammed, and seriously smoke-filled, late in the evening, but we still love its laid-back, casual vibe. Also check out its larger, newer sister cafe next door, No Big Deal, with a slightly old-fashioned vibe

LOCAL KNOWLEDGE

BALADI BAR CRAWL

Bar-hopping in Cairo typically takes you to Western-style lounges. But there's a parallel drinking culture in cheaper *baladi* (local) bars. These 'cafeterias', as they're often signed, have a slightly seedy, old-fashioned air. Renovations funded by beer company Stella have taken a layer of grime off a few, and there's even an (out-of-date but still fun) online guide at www.baladibar.com. Entrances are often hidden or screened off. A few Downtown classics:

Cafeteria El Horreya (Map p62; ☑ 02-2392-0397; Midan Falaki, Downtown; ⊗ 2pm-1am) A Cairo institution, and quite wholesome as it's big, brightly lit and welcoming to women. No beer served on the side with the chessboards.

Cafeteria Stella (Map p62; cnr Sharia Hoda Shaarawi & Sharia Talaat Harb; ⊗ 1pm-midnight) Ceilings are higher than the room is wide, with tables crammed with a mix of characters from afternoon on. Look for the entrance behind a kiosk. Free nibbles are served with beer.

Cap d'Or (Map p62; ☑ 02-2123-8957; Sharia Abdel Khalek Sarwat, Downtown; ⊗ 4pm-2am) Quite run-down and lit with fluorescent bulbs. The staff are used to seeing foreigners, but usually male only.

Greek Club (p102) Cool beer on a terrace, and an air-kissing crowd talking about art, revolution and politics.

Cairo (Map p62; ☑ 02-2574-1479, 3 Sharia Saray Al Ezbekiyya, Downtown; ⊗ 10am-3am) Walk through the grill restaurant to the 1st-floor bar. The sign is in Arabic only, blue letters on a red background.

Gemayka (Map p62; 16 Sharia Sherif, Downtown; ⊗ 11am-2am) That's Egyptian for 'Jamaica'. In the pedestrian area around the stock exchange.

and a menu of sandwiches and coffees; open throughout the day.

Sequoia LOUNGE
(Map p94; ☑ 2576-8086; www.sequoiaonline.net; 53 Sharia Abu Al Feda; ⊗ 1pm-1am) At the very northern tip of Zamalek, this sprawling Nileside lounge is a swank scene, with low cushions for nursing a shisha while downing a few beers or sipping a cocktail. The char-grilled mains don't tend to live up to the great setting so snack on a range of mezze instead. There's a LE200 minimum fee.

Garden Café CAFE
(Map p94; ☑ 2728-3000, 16 Sharia Saray Al Gezira, Cairo Marriot; ⊗ 6.30am-10pm) The garden terrace at the Marriott is one of the most comfortable spots in town to relax over a drink. Big cane chairs, fresh air and good-quality wine and beer make it deservedly popular. The food is pricey and not very special.

Nomad Bar ROOFTOP BAR
(Map p92; 20 Sharia Abdel Rehim Sabry, King Hotel, Doqqi; ⊗ 1pm-4am; ⊛) This bar, on the rooftop of the King Hotel, comes with the bonus of Pyramid views. It's a casual and relaxed place to hang out with a beer and shisha during the evening.

Riverside Cairo BAR
(Map p94; ☑ 012-1280-1290; www.riversidecairo.com; 16 Sharia Al Montazah; ⊗ noon-1am) Super-fashionable bar and restaurant in a top spot in Zamalek with regular live music and DJs on weekend evenings. Expect expensive cocktails and good sushi, but the thing here is to see and be seen. You'll need to dress up to fit in here. There's a minimum charge of LE200.

Islamic Cairo

★ **Fishawi's** COFFEE
(Map p77; Khan Al Khalili; ⊗ 24hr, during Ramadan 5pm-3am) Probably the oldest *ahwa* in the city, and certainly the most celebrated, Fishawi's has been a great place to watch the world go by since 1773. It's all clouded mirrors and copper tabletops that ooze old-world ambience. Although swamped by foreign tourists and equally wide-eyed out-of-town Egyptians, it is a regular *ahwa*, serving tea and shisha to stallholders and shoppers alike.

Prices tend to vary so confirm with your waiter.

Coffeeshop Al Khatoun COFFEE
(Map p80; Midan Al Khatoun, Islamic Cairo; ⊗ 3pm-1am) Tucked away in a quiet square behind

Al Azhar, this modern outdoor *ahwa* is a great place to rest up after a walk, with tea and snacks and comfortable pillow-strewn benches. In the evenings it attracts an arty crowd – students from the Arabic Oud House school on the square and others.

☆ Entertainment

Cairo has a small, but growing, live-music scene, some good cultural performance spaces and a smattering of belly-dancing. Check out www.cairo360.com for listings. Not that you need to head inside – street life can be entertainment enough. Lots of Cairenes take an evening stroll along the Nile corniche Downtown or on Qasr El Nil Bridge. Pop-up tea kiosks provide refreshments.

Live Music & Performance

Makan   TRADITIONAL MUSIC
(Map p58; ☑2792-0878; http://egyptmusic.org; 1 Sharia Saad Zaghloul, Mounira; concert tickets LE40; ⊙concerts Tue & Wed; Ⓜ Saad Zaghloul) The Egyptian Centre for Culture & Art runs this intimate space dedicated to folk music. Don't miss the traditional women's *zar,* a sort of musical trance and healing ritual on Wednesday nights (doors open at 8.30pm). Tuesday evening has various performances of folk music, often an Egyptian-Sudanese jam session (doors open at 7.30pm).

To find the space, walk north on Sharia Mansour from Saad Zaghloul metro. Advance booking is a good idea due to limited space.

El Dammah Theatre   TRADITIONAL MUSIC
(Map p62; ☑2392-6768; www.el-mastaba.org; 30a Sharia Al Balaqsa, Abdeen, Downtown; tickets LE30; ⊙doors open 8pm, concerts 9.30pm) Regular Thursday, Friday and Saturday shows by musical ensembles such as Rango, a trancey Sudanese folk group, and the El Tanboura Band, playing *simsimiyya,* a musical style from the Suez Canal region, as well as other folk bands from Egypt (check the website for listings).

Al Tannoura Egyptian Heritage Dance Troupe   DANCE
(Map p77; ☑2512 1735; Wikala of Al Ghouri, Sharia Mohammed Abduh, Islamic Cairo; show LE30; ⊙performances 7.30pm Mon, Wed & Sat) Egypt's only Sufi dance troupe – more raucous and colourful than the better-known white-clad Turkish dervishes – puts on a mesmerising performance three times weekly at the Wikala of Al Ghouri just off Sharia Al Azhar.

It's a great opportunity to see one of the medieval spaces in use; arrive about an hour ahead to secure a seat.

El Sawy Culture Wheel   LIVE MUSIC
(El Sakia; Map p94; ☑2736-8881; www.culturewheel.com; Sharia 26th of July, Zamalek; ⊙8am-midnight) Egyptian rock and jazz bands play at this lively and very active complex of a dozen performance spaces and galleries tucked under a bridge overpass. There are also regular performances by the El Sakia Puppet Theatre (great for kids) and various seminar events. The main entrance is on the south side of 26th of July; there's a nice outdoor cafe too.

Darb 1718   ARTS CENTRE
(Map p58; ☑2361 0511; www.darb1718.com; off Sharia Qasr Al Shama, Fustat; ⊙11am-10pm Sat-Wed, from 4pm Fri) This super-cool creative space aims to be a 'trampoline' for contemporary art, which gives an idea of the fun to be found here – there's a regular program of concerts by Egyptian bands and movie screenings at night as well as a schedule of creative workshops. During the day there's sometimes an art show on. For listings check out the website.

To reach Darb, walk south on Sharia Mar Girgis and follow the road as it bears left. At the end of the street, turn left on Sharia Qasr Al Shama and then turn right two streets on – Darb 1718 is at the end.

Cairo Opera House   OPERA
(Map p92; ☑2739-8144; www.cairoopera.org; Gezira Exhibition Grounds, Gezira; Ⓜ Opera) Performances by the Cairo Opera and the Cairo Symphony Orchestra are held in the 1200-seat Main Hall, where jacket and tie are required for men (travellers have been known to borrow them from staff). The Small Hall and Open Air Theatre are casual.

Cairo Jazz Club   JAZZ
(Map p94; ☑010-6880-4764; www.cairojazzclub.com; 197 Sharia 26th of July, Agouza; ⊙9pm-3am) The Cairo Jazz Club has kept up with the beat, and it has one of the city's liveliest stages, with modern Egyptian folk, electronica, fusion and more, seven nights a week, usually starting around 10pm. You must book a table ahead (online is easiest), and no one under 25 is admitted.

Cairo Puppet Theatre   PUPPET THEATRE
(Map p62; ☑2591 0954; Sharia Masrah Al Ara'is, Downtown, behind Ezbekiyya Gardens; adult/child

LE20/15; ☉ performances usually 6.30pm Thu-Fri; Ⓜ Ataba) Keeping Cairene kids entertained since 1959, this is the Arab world's biggest puppet theatre. Shows are in Arabic but are colourful and animated enough to entertain all ages. It's a bit tricky to locate; take the fenced-in footpath that runs around the south of Ezbekiyya Gardens, turn left at the mosque and duck down the first alleyway on your left.

Belly Dancing

If you see only one belly dancer in your life, it had better be in Cairo, the art form's true home. The best dancers perform at Cairo's five-star hotels, usually to an adoring crowd of wealthy Gulf Arabs. Shows typically begin around 10pm, although the star might not take to the stage until midnight or later. Admission is steep. There's either a show-plus-meal fee (with drinks extra) or a per person minimum charge. At the very top venues, prepare for the evening to cost you more than LE1000. A less-overpriced alternative is the Nile-boat evening cruise belly dancing shows. Be aware that the crooning lounge-singer-style warm up acts on these boats can be hilariously dire. Cairo's divas are often getting in tiffs with their host hotels or their managers, so their venues may change.

At the other end of the scale, you can watch a less nuanced expression of the art form at several clubs around Sharia Alfy in Downtown Cairo. They're seedy (prostitution is definitely a sideline), the mics are set on the highest reverb, and most of the dancers have the grace of amateur wrestlers. But it can be fun, especially if you can maintain enough of a buzz to join in the dancing onstage (a perk if you shower the dancer and the band with enough LE5 notes), but not so fun if you fall for the myriad overcharging tactics, including beer prices being hiked up and fees for unordered snacks and even napkins.

Bab El Nil   CABARET
(☎ 02-2461-9494; www.fairmont.com/nile-city-cairo/dining/bab-el-nil; Nile City Towers, 2005b Corniche El Nil, Fairmont Nile City Hotel; minimum per person LE1000-1200; ☉ shows 10pm-1am) The Fairmont Nile City's restaurant is one of the classier venues to take in a belly dancing show with long-time Cairo favourite Soreya regularly performing here. Unlike many other joints, there's no menu-plus-show price, and instead a minimum charge for your drinks and dinner (the more expensive minimum charge is for the seats closer to the stage).

Nile Maxim   CABARET
(Map p94; ☎ 2738-8888, 012-2241-9500; www.maximrestaurants.com; Sharia Saray Al Gezira, Zamalek; show & dinner LE480-730; ☉ sailings at 8.30pm & 10.30pm) The best of the Nile cruisers, run by the Marriott, is a relatively economical way to see a big-name belly-dancing star such as Randa or Farah, along with a choice of à la carte menu options (drinks not included). Go for the later sailing, as that show tends to have less crooning singer warm-up and more actual belly dancing. Opposite Cairo Marriott Hotel.

Shahrazad   CABARET
(Map p62; 1 Sharia Alfy, Downtown; incl 2 drinks LE150; ☉ 10pm-2am) Worth visiting for the gorgeous interior alone, this old-school hall got a makeover in recent years, and its Orientalist fantasia, complete with red-velvet drapes, feels substantially less seedy than other Downtown dives. This doesn't necessarily inspire a classier air in the patrons, however. Occasionally the venue hosts a DJ night for an artier crowd.

Haroun El Rashid Nightclub   CABARET
(Map p62; ☎ 2798-8000; www.ihg.com; Corniche El Nil, 3rd fl, Semiramis InterContinental, Garden City; show incl dinner from LE1140; ☉ 11pm-4am) This five-star club is all red curtains and white marquee lights. Top seats, at tables nearest the stage go for LE1900 (drinks not included), with the price tag getting cheaper the further back you sit. The eye-watering cost is because this is where the famous Dina undulates, but – handy hint – Dina only ever dances on Thursday nights.

Cultural Centres

Netherlands-Flemish Institute   ARTS CENTRE
(NVIC; Map p94; ☎ 2738-2520; www.nvic.leidenuniv.nl; 1 Sharia Mahmoud Azmy, Zamalek; ☉ weekly film & lecture series Sep-May) This excellent cultural centre hosts Sunday evening films (7.30pm), ranging from Dutch art-house features to the latest works by young Egyptian directors (all with English subtitles), plus weekly lectures on Thursdays (6pm), often in English, and regular exhibitions.

Istituto Italiano Di Cultura   ARTS CENTRE
(Map p94; ☎ 2735-8791; www.iiccairo.esteri.it; 3 Sharia Sheikh Al Marsafy, Zamalek; ☉ library 10am-4pm Sun, Tue & Thu) One of Cairo's most active cultural centres, the Italian institute hosts

a busy program of art house films plus lectures (sometimes in English) and art exhibitions, and has a library.

Goethe Institut ARTS CENTRE
(Map p62; ☑ 2575-9877; www.goethe.de; 5 Sharia Al Bustan, Downtown; ⊙library 1-7pm Sun-Wed) Seminars and lectures in German on Egyptology and other topics, plus visiting music groups, art exhibitions and film screenings. The library has more than 15,000 (mainly German) titles.

🛍 Shopping

Faced with the mountains of chintzy souvenirs and over-eager hustlers trying to sell them to you over endless glasses of tea, it's tempting to keep your wallet firmly shut in Cairo. But then you'd be missing out on some of Egypt's most beautiful treasures. The trick is knowing where to look.

🏠 Downtown

★**Oum El Dounia** ARTS & CRAFTS
(Map p62; ☑ 2393-8273; 1st fl, 3 Sharia Talaat Harb; ⊙10am-9pm) At a great central location, Oum El Dounia sells an exceptionally taste-

LOCAL MARKETS

Souq Al Gomaa (Friday Market; Map p58; Southern Cemetery; ⊙6am-noon Fri) South of the Citadel, this sprawling weekly market is all the craziness of a medieval bazaar in a modern setting. Under a highway flyover, expect bicycles, live donkeys and broken telephones. Savvy pickers can find some funky objects and vintage clothes. Go before 10am to avoid the crush of people. Tell the taxi driver 'Khalifa', the name of the neighbourhood.

Wikalat Al Balah (Souq Bulaq; Map p58; Sharia 26th of July, Bulaq; ⊙8am-6pm) This street market specialises in secondhand clothing, mostly well organised, clean and with marked prices (especially on Sharia Al Wabur Al Fransawi). It starts beside the Corniche, under the 26th of July overpass.

Souq Bab Al Luq (Map p62; Midan Falaki, Downtown; ⊙7am-7pm) Big indoor neighbourhood market with produce and meat; surrounding shops sell dry goods.

ful and good-value selection of locally made crafts. These include glassware, ceramics, jewellery, cotton clothes made in Akhmim, and other interesting trinkets. Illustrated postcards by cartoonist Golo make a nice change. One room is dedicated to books on Egypt in French.

★**American University in Cairo Bookshop** BOOKS
(Map p62; ☑ 2797-5929; www.aucpress.com; Sharia Sheikh Rihan; ⊙10am-6pm Sat-Thu; Ⓜ Sadat) The best English-language bookshop in Egypt, with a huge selection of material on the politics, sociology and history of Cairo, Egypt and the wider Middle East, as well as other more general non-fiction titles. There are plenty of guidebooks and maps, and a decent fiction section. This is also a great place to find titles by Arab writers in translation.

You need to show your passport (or another kind of ID) to gain entry.

Lehnert & Landrock BOOKS
(Map p62; ☑ 2392-7606; www.lehnertandlandrock.net; 44 Sharia Sherif; ⊙10am-7pm Mon-Sat) Old maps, books about Cairo and Egypt (some secondhand), great vintage postcards and reprints of wonderful old photographs.

Drinkies DRINKS
(Map p62; ☑ 19930; 41 Sharia Talaat Harb; ⊙11am-midnight) Spiffy modern booze sellers; no need to sneak behind a curtain, and even offers delivery. A small Stella is LE12, a large Sakara is LE17. There's another Downtown branch (Map p62; ⊙11am-midnight) on Sharia Mahmoud Bassouni.

🏠 Coptic Cairo

Souq Al Fustat MARKET
(Map p68; Sharia Al Anwar, Fustat; ⊙10am-7pm) It's a shame more travellers don't venture to this modern market-complex after their Coptic Cairo visit as there are some interesting boutiques here – nearly all focused on modern Egyptian handicrafts. There are funky interpretations of Bedouin embroidery at **Bidouin Handmade**, embroideries and recycled crafts at the **Association for the Protection of the Environment shop** and a branch of Abd El Zaher (p115).

🏠 Zamalek & Doqqi

Fair Trade Egypt ARTS & CRAFTS
(Map p94; ☑ 2736-5123; 1st fl, 27 Sharia Yehia Ibrahim; ⊙10am-8pm) 🌱 Crafts sold here are

LOCAL KNOWLEDGE

ANTIQUES ROADSHOW: CAIRO EDITION

Evidence of Cairo's glam years can be found in dusty warehouses and glittery shops. These are some of the best.

Ahmed El Dabba & Sons (Map p77; ☑ 02-2590-7823; 5 Sikket Al Badistan, Islamic Cairo; ☺ 10am-7pm Mon-Sat) The most respected antiques dealer in Khan Al Khalili, filled with Louis XV furniture, jewellery and snuff boxes.

Amgad Naguib (Map p62; ☑ 012-8668-0908; off Sharia Mahmoud Bassiouni, Downtown; ☺ by appointment) Make an appointment to visit Amgad's dusty treasure house Downtown. Along with vintage sunglasses, movie posters and groovy glass, you get some great stories.

Kerop (Map p62; 116 Mohammed Farid, Downtown; ☺ 9am-1pm Mon-Fri) Vintage Cairo photos, from original plates, in a time-warp office.

King Saleh Bazaar (Map p72; 80 Sharia Al Muizz Li Din Allah, Islamic Cairo; ☺ 10am-7pm Mon-Sat) Immediately south of the Madrassa & Mausoleum of Qalaun. The more you look through the dust, the more pops out.

Nostalgia (Map p94; 6 Sharia Zakaria Rizk, Zamalek; ☺ 10am-6pm) From framed Arabic ad prints to escargot forks.

L'Orientaliste (Map p62; ☑ 2575 3418; 15 Sharia Qasr El Nil, Downtown; ☺ 10am-8pm) Find rare books on Egypt and the Middle East, as well as lithographs, maps and engravings.

produced in income-generating projects throughout the country. Items for sale include Bedouin rugs, hand-woven cotton, pottery from Al Fayoum and beaded jewellery from Aswan. The cotton bedspreads and shawls are particularly lovely, and prices are very reasonable.

L'Oiseau du Nil　　　　GIFTS & SOUVENIRS
(Asfour El Nil; Map p94; ☑ 2735-1458; 23a Sharia Ismail Mohammed; ☺ 11am-10pm Sat-Thu) A little treasure trove with original gifts made in Egypt, great cotton clothing, funky bags and accessories, and wonderful Egyptian-cotton bed linen by Malaika.

Azza Fahmy　　　　JEWELLERY
(Map p94; ☑ 010-6664-2365; www.azzafahmy. com; 15c Sharia Dr Taha Hussein, cnr of Sharia Marashly; ☺ 10am-10pm) World-renowned contemporary jeweller inspired by Islamic and Pharaonic designs. Azza Fahmy also organises design workshops (p92) to make fabulous jewellery.

Nomad　　　　ARTS & CRAFTS
(Map p94; ☑ 2736-1917; www.nomadgallery.net; 1st fl, 14 Sharia Saray Al Gezira; ☺ 9am-8pm) Specialists in jewellery and traditional Bedouin crafts and costumes. Items include appliqué tablecloths and cushion covers, dresses made in the oases, woven baskets, silk slippers and chunky silver jewellery. To find it, go past the Egyptian Water Works office to the 1st floor

and ring the bell. There is a smaller branch in the Cairo Marriott (p87).

Sami Amin　　　　FASHION & ACCESSORIES
(Map p94; ☑ 2738-1837; www.sami-amin.com; 15a Sharia Mansour Mohammed; ☺ 10.30am-10pm Mon-Sat) Cool brass-and-enamel jewellery as well as various homewares including chunky metal photo and mirror frames. Just down the street, at number 13, are leather bags, belts and other accessories, many imprinted with tribal patterns, and all very well priced.

Diwan　　　　BOOKS
(Map p94; ☑ 2736-2578; www.diwanegypt.com; 159 Sharia 26th of July; ☺ 9am-11.30pm) Fabulous English, French and German titles, from novels to travel guides to coffee-table books. It also has a kids' section, plenty of non-fiction titles about Egypt and Arabic writers in translation, and a small cafe.

Nevin Altmann　　　　CLOTHING
(Map p94; ☑ 2736-5431; www.nevinaltmann.com; 3 Sharia Hassan Assem; ☺ 10am-10pm) Delightful intricately embroidered accessories, on cotton and linen, all made in different regions in Egypt. Look out for the beautiful fabric dolls, too, which make great gifts.

Al Qahira　　　　HOMEWARES
(Map p94; ☑ 011-1313-3932; www.facebook.com/Alqahiragallery; 1st fl, 6 Sharia Bahgat Ali; ☺ noon-9pm) Al Qahira sells well-made Egyptian

LOCAL KNOWLEDGE

CAIRO CRAFTS: WHERE TO SHOP

These are the best districts for certain goods.

Gold and silver Head to the gold district on the west end of Khan Al Khalili (p70).

Backgammon and shisha pipes Shops line Sharia Al Muizz Li Din Allah (p71) around Bein Al Qasreen. Another set of shisha dealers are just east and west of Bab Zuweila (p78).

Appliqué Best buys are at the Tentmakers Market (p78), south of Bab Zuweila.

Carpets The carpet bazaar south of the Mosque-Madrassa of Al Ghouri (p76) has imports; flat-weave Bedouin rugs are the only local style.

Spices Most dealers in the Khan are more trouble than they're worth. Try Abd Al Rahman Harraz or shops around Midan Falaki.

Perfume In addition to the southwest corner of Khan Al Khalili, try shops around Midan Falaki.

Inlay Artisans in Darb Al Ahmar sell from out of their workshops.

Muski glass Available everywhere, but interesting to see the glassblowing studios in the district north of Bab Al Futuh (p75).

crafts, often with a little quirky element. Brilliant jewellery by Suzanne El Masry, embroidered jewellery, fabrics printed with vintage photos of movie stars and some fun homewares.

Wady Craft Shop   ARTS & CRAFTS
(Map p94; ☑ 2735-4350; 5 Sharia Michel Lutfallah; ◷ 10am-5pm Mon, Tue & Fri, 10am-10pm Wed, Thu & Sat, 11am-10pm Sun) ✒ This charity store run by the Anglican church sells work done by refugee organisations and disadvantaged families. There are plenty of kitchen linens and wooden inlay products but the traditional wooden children's toy trains, planes, trucks and block-pyramids are the real standouts. Despite the address (the main gate to the church complex), the shop's entrance is located on Sharia Zakaria Rizk.

Mix & Match   CLOTHING
(Map p94; 11 Sharia Hassan Sabry; ◷ 10am-10pm) Well made and locally designed, these separates for women in wool, silk and cotton are reasonably priced and often feature subtle Middle Eastern details.

Nagada   CLOTHING, CERAMICS
(Map p92; ☑ 3748-6663; www.nagada.net; 13 Sharia Refa'a, Doqqi; ◷ 10am-6.30pm) High-quality handwoven, colour-saturated silks, cottons and linens are the mainstay of this delightful shop. Buy by the yard, or in boxy, drapey women's and men's apparel. There's also very pretty pottery from Al Fayoum.

Loft   HOMEWARES
(Map p94; ☑ 2736-6931; www.loftegypt.com; 1st fl, 12 Sharia Sayyed Al Bakry; ◷ 10am-10pm Mon-Sat) In a rambling apartment, this eclectic store stocks local regional curiosities from small brass candlesticks to antique divans, as well as large painted tabletop trays as seen in chic restaurants around town.

Drinkies   DRINKS
(Map p94; ☑ 19330; 157 Sharia 26th of July; ◷ 10am-midnight) Cold beer, wine and more to take away.

🕌 Islamic Cairo

Abd Al Rahman Harraz   FOOD
(☑ 2512-6349; 1 Midan Bab Al Khalq; ◷ 10am-10pm) Established in 1885, this is one of the most esteemed spice traders in Cairo, with a brisk business in medicinal herbs as well (upstairs, herbalists diagnose and prescribe). There's no English sign: look for dioramas of Egyptian village life in the corner shop windows. It's about 450m west of Bab Zuweila.

Khan Misr Touloun   ARTS & CRAFTS
(Map p84; ☑ 2365-2227; Midan Ibn Tulun; ◷ 10am-5pm Mon-Sat) This shop opposite the Mosque of Ibn Tulun is stacked with a desirable jumble of reasonably priced crafts, wooden chests, jewellery, pottery, puppets and scarves.

It closes for vacation in August and sometimes in July too, so if you're here in summer it's best to ring and check it's open before trooping out here.

Abd El Zaher STATIONERY
(Map p77; https://abdelzahers.com; 31 Sharia Mohammed Abduh, Islamic Cairo; ⊙9am-11pm) Cairo's last working bookbinder also makes beautiful leather- and oil-paper-bound blank books, photo albums and diaries. Gold monogramming is included in the prices, which are heartbreakingly low considering the work that goes into them. Getting your own books bound starts around LE100 and takes a few days.

Atlas CLOTHING, HANDICRAFTS
(Map p77; ☑2591-8833; Sikket Al Badistan, Islamic Cairo; ⊙10am-8pm Mon-Sat) In business since 1948, the Atlas family specialises in silk moiré kaftans and slippers. You can also order the fabric by the yard, or in custom-tailored clothing.

Mahmoud Abd El Ghaffar FASHION & ACCESSORIES
(Map p77; ☑2589-7443; 73 Sharia Gawhar Al Qaid, Islamic Cairo; ⊙11am-11pm Mon-Sat) One of the best dealers in belly-dancing outfits in the city. Look for the entrance at the end of a short lane just off the main street, and walk upstairs where the really good stuff is.

Out of the Centre

Citystars Centre MALL
(☑2480-0500; www.citystars-heliopolis.com.eg; Sharia Omar Ibn Khattab, Nasr City; ⊙11am-1am) Cairo's most lavish mall is the current landing spot for every new international chain, from Starbucks to Zara. There's a kids' theme park and a big cinema. It's about 12km east of Downtown. Just hop in a taxi and say, 'Citystars'.

ℹ Information

DANGERS & ANNOYANCES
Despite a rise in petty crime following the 2011 revolution, Cairo is still a pretty safe city, with crime rates likely much lower than where you're visiting from.
➡ For female visitors, sexual harassment continues to be a problem.
➡ Pickpockets and bag-snatchers are rare but do sometimes operate in crowded spots such as Khan Al Khalili, the metro and buses.
➡ Touts operate around Midan Tahrir and Midan Talaat Harb. Be wary of anyone who approaches you in these areas.
➡ If anything does get stolen, go straight to the tourist police rather than the normal police.

Bogus Tours
Cairo's worst scams are associated with tours. Rather than making arrangements in Cairo, you are almost always better off booking tours in the place you'll be taking them. Stick with reputable agencies. Even your hotel is not a good place to book anything except typical day trips from Cairo. Never book with a random office Downtown (many are fronts) or with the help of someone you meet on the street.

Street Hassle
Contrary to media reports, women are generally safe walking alone in Cairo. Although minor harassment is rampant, actual physical assault remains much rarer than in many European or 'western' countries. After about 11pm, however, solo women travellers will probably feel more comfortable buddying-up while strolling the streets, and at all times avoid the cheapest buses (notorious for frottage, to female commuters' chagrin) and endeavour to steer clear of large groups of aimless men: political demonstrations and any kind of football-related celebration tend to bring out the testosterone. Also be a bit wary of men (or boys) who want to escort you across a street – it's a prime groping opportunity. Women should always sit in the back seat in Cairo's taxis. If you'd like to book a female cabbie, call Nour Gaber (p93).

EMERGENCY
Main Tourist Police Office (Map p62; ☑126, 2395-9116; Sharia Adly, Downtown; ⊙9am-2pm) On the 1st floor of a building in the alley just left of the main tourist office in Downtown. Come here first for minor emergencies, including theft.

There are various other offices scattered around the city:
Tourist Police (Map p58; ☑126; Midan Al Hussein, Islamic Cairo; ⊙9am-5pm) Near Khan Al Khalili.
Tourist Police (Map p83; ☑126; Citadel; ⊙9am-5pm) Within the Citadel.
Tourist Police (☑126; Pyramids Rd, Giza; ⊙8am-5pm) Across from the Mena House Hotel.

Ambulance	☑123
Fire	☑180
Police	☑122

MEDICAL SERVICES
Many of Cairo's hospitals suffer from antiquated equipment and a cavalier attitude to hygiene, but there are several exceptions. Your embassy should be able to recommend doctors and hospitals.

As Salam International Hospital (☑ 2524-0250, emergency 19885; www.assih.com; Corniche El Nil, Ma'adi; ☺ 24hr)

Badran Hospital (Map p58; ☑ 3337-8823; 3 Sharia Al Ahrar, Doqqi; ☺ 24hr) Just northwest of 6th of October Bridge in Doqqi.

These pharmacies operate 24 hours, have English-speaking staff and will deliver to your hotel.

Al Ezaby Pharmacy (Map p94; ☑ 19600; 46 Sharia Bahgat Ali, Zamalek; ☺ 24hr) Other branches all over Cairo.

Delmar Pharmacy (Map p62; ☑ 2575-1052; Sharia 26th of July, Downtown; ☺ 24hr)

Misr Pharmacy (Map p62; ☑ 19110; 44 Sharia Talaat Harb, Downtown; ☺ 24hr) Modern pharmacy; other branches throughout the city. Also well-stocked with skin care products, with plenty of hard-to-find-elsewhere international brands.

New Victoria Pharmacy (Map p94; ☑ 2735-1628; 6 Sharia Brazil, Zamalek; ☺ 24hr)

MONEY

Hotel bank branches can change cash, but rates are slightly better at independent exchange bureaux, of which there are several along Sharia Adly in Downtown and on Sharia 26th of July in Zamalek. These tend to be open from 10am to 8pm Saturday to Thursday. ATMs are numerous, except in Islamic Cairo – the most convenient machine here is below El Hussein hotel in Khan Al Khalili.

TOILETS

Public toilets in Cairo are a rarity. Most large museums and monuments have passable facilities. You can stop in to fast-food places like Gad where the toilets usually have an attendant; tip LE2. In Khan Al Khalili, head for the Khan El Khalili Restaurant & Mahfouz Coffee Shop (p107).

TOURIST INFORMATION

Main Tourist Office (Ministry of Tourism; Map p62; ☑ 2391-3454; 5 Sharia Adly, Downtown; ☺ 9am-6pm)

Tourist Information Office (Ramses Train Station, Midan Ramses, Downtown; ☺ 9am-7pm) Inside the train station. The most helpful office.

Tourist Information Office (☑ 3383-8823; Pyramids Rd, Giza; ☺ 8.30am-5pm) Opposite Mena House Hotel, before the Pyramids' main entrance gate

VISA EXTENSIONS

All visa business (extensions plus multiple-entry stamps) is carried out at the **Mogamma** (Passport Office; Map p62; Mogamma Bldg, Midan Tahrir; ☺ 8am-1.30pm Sat-Wed).

For visa extensions, head to the 1st floor, and turn right. Pick up a form from the police officers at the table in the hallway, fill it in and return it to the police officers to be signed. Take the form (plus two passport photos and two copies of your passport's visa and information pages) to window 12. Then collect stamps from window 43 and file all back at window 12. Next-day pickup is at window 38.

Convert your single-entry visa into a multiple-entry visa (LE61) at the well-signed window on the opposite side the hall.

If your hotel is in Giza (this includes Doqqi), you will need to go to the **Agouza Passport Office** (Map p94; ☑ 3338-4226; El Shorta Tower, Sharia Nawal; ☺ 8am-1.30pm Sat-Wed) for your visa extension or multiple-entry stamp. Enter at the side entrance of the police station and head to window 4 on the 2nd floor.

ⓘ Getting There & Away

AIR

Cairo International Airport (p489) is 20km northeast of the city centre. There are ATMs in all terminal arrival halls.

Terminal 1 Services most international airlines. The terminal is three buildings, all within view of each other, though only arrivals halls 1 and 3 receive commercial flights.

Terminal 3 EgyptAir's hub for both international and domestic flights, and also home to all services for other Star Alliance international airlines. The terminal is 2km south of T1.

Terminal 2 Partially reopened after a long renovation and now servicing several international airlines, with more set to move there in the future.

A free shuttle (service every 30 minutes) connects the terminals.

BUS
Cairo Gateway Bus Station

The main bus station is **Cairo Gateway** (Turgoman Garage; Sharia Al Gisr, Bulaq; Ⓜ Orabi), 400m west of the Orabi metro stop – or pay LE5 or so for a taxi from Tahrir or Sharia Talaat Harb.

Tickets are sold at different windows according to company and destination.

East Delta Travel Co (☑ 2419-8533; Cairo Gateway, Sharia Al Gisr, Bulaq), for Suez and Sinai, and **Super Jet** (☑ 02-3572-5032, 2290-9017; Cairo Gateway, Sharia Al Gisr, Bulaq), for Hurghada, Luxor and Sharm El Sheikh, are to the right.

West & Mid Delta Bus Co (☑ 2432-0049; http://westmidbus-eg.com; Cairo Gateway, Sharia Al Gisr, Bulaq), for Alexandria, Marsa Matruh and Siwa, and **Upper Egypt Travel Co** (☑ 2576-0261; Cairo Gateway, Sharia Al Gisr, Bulaq), for Western Desert oases and Luxor, are to the left. (Note that the train is better for Alexandria and Luxor.)

It is advisable to book most tickets in advance, particularly for popular routes such as Sinai, Alexandria and Marsa Matruh in summer.

Student discounts are not offered on bus tickets.

There are also bus services to Israel and Jordan.

Because of security issues, foreign travellers are not allowed to take the direct road from Cairo to Taba, which cuts through the middle of the Sinai Peninsula. Instead, if they're planning to travel to Taba or Nuweiba, they must take the longer south Sinai coastal route via Al Tor to Sharm El Sheikh and Dahab where they can transfer onto the Nuweiba–Taba bus.

This means that the East Delta Travel Co was not issuing tickets along the direct Cairo–Taba route to any foreigners at the time of research. You can check for updates on the situation at its booth at Cairo Gateway.

Go Bus Station

Go Bus (Map p92; ☎ 19567; www.gobus-eg. com; Midan Abdel Moniem Riad, Downtown) runs regular services to Alexandria, Dahab, El Gouna, Hurghada, Luxor, Marsa Alam, Marsa Matruh, Qena and Sharm El Sheikh. Tickets – and even specific seats – can be booked online.

Buses come in a baffling array of service classes with the higher-priced 'Elite' buses offering bigger seats, wi-fi and a free snack. The 'Deluxe'

services are pretty much on par with Super Jet and East Delta buses, though Go Bus tend to have shorter journey times (particularly on the Sinai routes) as it gets waved through most of the security checkpoints.

Sample ticket prices:

Dahab Economic/Deluxe/Elite LE145/175/330

Hurghada Economic/Deluxe/Elite LE115/140/275

Sharm El Sheikh Economic/Deluxe/Elite LE125/140/275

Services depart/arrive from the Tahrir office on Midan Abdel Moniem Riad (behind the Egyptian Museum, opposite the Ramses Hilton).

Abbassiyya Bus Station

Buses from Taba (which foreigners can't take) and, sometimes, from St Katherine's still terminate at **Abbasslyya Bus Terminal** (Sinai Station; Map p58; Sharia Ramses, Abbassiyya; Ⓜ Abbassiyya), 4km northeast of Ramses Train Station; take the nearby metro to the centre.

Abboud Bus Station

Abboud Bus Terminal (Khazindar; Sharia Al Tir'n Al Doulaqia, Shubra, Ⓜ Mezallal) Services to the Delta and Wadi Natrun. It's 5km north of

BUSES FROM CAIRO GATEWAY

DESTINATION	COMPANY	PRICE	DURATION	TIMES
Alexandria	West & Mid Delta	LE55	3hr	hourly 5am 12.05am
Al Kharga	Upper Egypt Travel	LE150	8-10hr	9.30pm & 10.30pm
Al Quseir	Upper Egypt Travel	LE120	10hr	1.30pm, 6.30pm & 11pm
Bahariya (Bawiti)	Upper Egypt Travel	LE100	4-5hr	7.30am & 6pm
Dahab	East Delta	LE140	9hr	8am, 1.30pm, 7.30pm & 11pm
Dakhla	Upper Egypt Travel	LE120	8-10hr	7.30am & 6pm
Farafra	Upper Egypt Travel	LE120	8-10hr	7.30am & 6pm
Hurghada	Super Jet	LE120	6hr	7.30am, 12.30pm & 11pm
	Upper Egypt Travel	LE120	6-7hr	1.30pm, 6.30pm & midnight
Ismailia	East Delta	LE25	4hr	hourly 6.30am-7.30pm
Luxor	Super Jet	LE150	11hr	1.30pm, 5.30pm & 11.30pm
	Upper Egypt Travel	LE150	11hr	9pm
Marsa Matruh	West & Mid Delta	LE105	5hr	15 services 6.30am-midnight
Port Said	East Delta	LE40	4hr	hourly 6.30am–9.30pm
Sharm El Sheikh	East Delta	LE120	7hr	6.30am, 8am, 1.30pm, 4.30pm, 7.30pm, 11pm & 1am
	Super Jet	LE125	7hr	7.30am, 1.15pm, 6.15pm & 11.30pm
Siwa	West & Mid Delta	LE150	11hr	11.45pm Sat, Mon & Thu
St Katherine	East Delta	LE90	7hr	11am
Suez	East Delta	LE25	2hr	hourly 6.30am-7.30pm
Taba & Nuweiba	East Delta	LE110	8hr	9.30am & 12.45pm (tourists not allowed on this route)

Ramses Train Station – walk east from Mezallat metro, about 800m.

MICROBUS & SERVEES

You can get a seat in a microbus or servees (shared taxi) to most destinations, including **Alexandria**, destinations in the Delta, and **Suez** (Map p66), from the blocks between Ramses Station and **Midan Ulali** (Map p66).

For Al Fayoum and the western oases, head to Moneib, on Sharia El Nil in Giza, under the ring road overpass (take a taxi or walk 800m east from the Sakkiat Mekki metro stop). Midan Al Remaya in Giza, near the Pyramids, is another starting point for Al Fayoum and western Delta towns; hop on a microbus from the Giza metro station.

TRAIN

Trains to Alexandria, Upper Egypt and major towns in the Delta are the most efficient and comfortable.

Train travel to smaller towns is recommended for rail fans only, as it's often quite slow and scruffy.

Ramses Station is Cairo's main train station. It has a left luggage office, a post office, ATMs and a helpful information office (p116) with English-speakers on hand.

Secondary stations include **Giza** (Mahattat Giza; Pyramids Rd, Giza; Ⓜ Giza), where all services to Upper Egypt also stop: **Giza Suburban**, next to the metro stop of the same name, for Al Fayoum; and **Ain Shams**, in the northeast part of the city, for Suez.

For 1st- and 2nd-class air-con services, visit the Egyptian National Railways website (https://enr.gov.eg), where you can check schedules and purchase tickets for trains on the main Alexandria–Aswan line. Purchasing tickets at Ramses Station requires getting to the right set of windows for your destination and knowing the time and/or train number you want. Confirm at the **information office** (p116), where the clerk can write your preference in Arabic to show the ticket seller.

To Alexandria

There are two classes of trains. Special class makes fewer stops than the Spanish ones.

In both, a first class (ula) ticket gets you a roomier assigned seat and usually a much cleaner bathroom.

To Luxor & Aswan

Tourists used to be restricted to travelling on the privately run sleeper train to Luxor and Aswan but are now allowed to travel on any of the normal, much cheaper seater-only day and night services. If you do encounter a desk clerk who does not want to sell you a ticket, you can always purchase a ticket on board from the conductor, for a small additional fee, or in advance online.

There are two different categories of seater trains (Spanish, and the more expensive Special), which both offer 1st- and 2nd-class air-con seating. There is no difference in journey time between them, despite the jump in ticket price, so your choice mainly comes down to which departure time you prefer. The Special service is just newer rolling stock with slightly bigger

MAJOR TRAINS FROM CAIRO

Prices are for a 1st-class air-con seat, unless otherwise noted.

DESTINATION	PRICE	DURATION	TIMES
Alexandria (direct)	LE70-100	2½hr	8am, 9am, 11am, 2pm, 3pm, 6pm, 7pm & 10.30pm
Alexandria (stopping)	LE50	3-3½hr	6am, 8.10am, 10am, noon, 1pm, 2.20pm, 3.10pm, 4pm, 5.10pm, 8.15pm & 9pm
Ismailia	LE25 (2nd class)	3hr	6.15am, 1.45pm, 2.40pm, 5.45pm & 7.50pm
Luxor/Aswan (Spanish)	LE109/135	10½hr/14hr	noon, 7pm, 8pm & 10pm
Luxor/Aswan (Special)	LE200/240	10½hr/14hr	8am, 10am, 5.30pm, 9pm & 11pm
Luxor/Aswan (Watania Sleeper)	2-/1-berth cabin US$80/110	9½hr/13hr	Train 84: 8pm (Giza-only departure); Train 86: 8.15pm (Ramses) & 8.30pm (Giza)
Marsa Matruh (Watania Sleeper)	US$43	7hr	11.30pm Sat, Mon & Wed mid-Jun–mid-Sep
Port Said	LE30 (2nd class)	4hr	6.15am, 1.45pm & 7.50pm
Tanta	LE30-45	1-1½hr	6am, 8.10am, 10am, 11am, noon, 1pm, 2.20pm, 3.10pm, 4pm, 5.10pm, 6pm, 8.15pm, 9pm & 10.30pm
Zagazig	LE15 (2nd class)	1½hr	5.15am, 6.15am, 1pm, 1.45pm, 3.40pm, 7.50pm & 10pm

Ramses Station

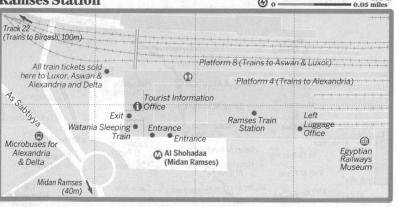

seats. It's also supposed to offer wi-fi but (in reality) doesn't. The 8am departure is the most scenic option.

Watania Sleeper Train to Luxor & Aswan

The overnight Wagon-Lits service to Luxor and Aswan is operated by a private company, Watania (p495). You can purchase tickets at its office in Ramses Station, which can take credit cards (for a surcharge), as well as cash in euros, dollars or Egyptian pounds. Tickets can also be purchased at Giza Station, in the trailer to the right of the entrance, as well as online.

Book before 6pm for the same day, but in high season (October to April) book several days in advance.

To Marsa Matruh

Watania (p495) runs a train to the Mediterranean coast three times a week during the summer season.

To Suez Canal Region

Delays on this route are common, going by bus is more efficient. If you're determined to travel by train, the best option is to Ismailia.

ℹ Getting Around

TO/FROM THE AIRPORT
Airport Pick-up Services

For a smooth arrival, arrange an airport pick-up through your hotel or book a prearranged pick-up online with **Cairo Airport Travel** (☑ 19970; www.cairoshuttlebus.com; Terminals 1 & 3, Cairo International Airport; ☺ 24hr). There are desks at Terminal 1, Arrivals 1, and Terminal 3 (though the service can pick you up from anywhere in the airport); it charges LE220 per car.

Bus

Don't believe anyone who tells you there is no bus to the city centre. **Air-con buses** (Map p62) 400 and 500 (LE2.50, plus LE2 per large luggage item, one to two hours) run at 20-minute intervals between Midan Abdel Moniem Riad (behind the Egyptian Museum) in central Cairo and the airport bus station. Bus 400 runs 24 hours, while 500 services finish at 10pm. Be aware that these buses are a crowded and not particularly-comfortable option. There was talk of introducing a modern, comfortable coach-style bus service (costing LE5) between Downtown and the airport on our last visit, though there was no confirmed starting date.

A free shuttle connects air terminals and the airport bus station. At Terminal 1, Arrivals 1, the shuttle stops in the first lane of the car park, a little to your right as you come out of the doors. In Terminal 1, Arrivals 3, bear left outside – the shuttle stops in the outer lane, under the skybridge to the Air Mall. The shuttle drops you across the road from the bus complex just after a right turn at the petrol station. In Terminal 3, bear right out the doors, to the far end of the outer lane. From here, the shuttle drives straight into the bus terminal.

Taxi

Metered taxis are rarely seen at Cairo Airport (and if you do find one, they're not going to put the meter on), so you'll need to negotiate with one of the mob of drivers clustered around the door when you exit. Most drivers charge LE120 to Downtown, though many will start out by quoting LE150. It's better to walk away a bit before starting negotiations, as it can sometimes bring the price down. Triple-check the agreed fare, as there is an irritating tendency for drivers to nod at what you say and claim a higher fare later. (Heading to the airport from the centre,

Cairo Metro

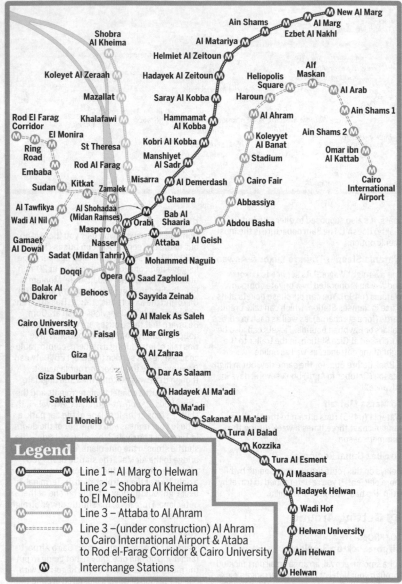

Legend

- Ⓜ────────Ⓜ Line 1 – Al Marg to Helwan
- Ⓜ────────Ⓜ Line 2 – Shobra Al Kheima to El Moneib
- Ⓜ────────Ⓜ Line 3 – Attaba to Al Ahram
- Ⓜ┅┅┅┅┅┅Ⓜ Line 3 –(under construction) Al Ahram to Cairo International Airport & Ataba to Rod el-Farag Corridor & Cairo University
- Ⓜ Interchange Stations

you can easily get a metered taxi; you'll have to pay LE5 to enter the airport grounds.)

In the arrivals halls, there are also car desks offering airport 'limo service' transfers into the central city for around LE175 to LE200.

In the traffic-free early hours of the morning, the journey to central Cairo takes 20 minutes. At busier times of the day it can take more than an hour.

BUS

Cairo is thoroughly served by a network of lumbering sardine-cans-on-wheels and smaller shuttle-size minibuses (on which, theoretically, there's no standing allowed), but visitors will find only a few uses for them: they're good for slow but cheap trips to the Pyramids or from the airport, but elsewhere you can travel more efficiently and comfortably by metro and/or taxi. Signs are in Arabic only, so you'll have to know your numerals. There is no known map of any of the city's bus routes. Just hop on and pay the conductor when he comes around selling tickets, which cost between LE1.50 and LE2.50 depending on distance and whether there's air-con (mint-green buses sometimes have it, as do the big white CTA buses). New, more comfortable air-con buses (LE5) started to ply some longer routes from the centre to the suburbs in 2017.

Major bus hubs are **Midan Abdel Moniem Riad** (Map p62), behind the Egyptian Museum, and Midan Ataba.

CAR

Driving in Cairo can't be recommended – not only is it harrowing, but you're only contributing to the hideously clogged streets. Lane markings are ignored, indicators are rarely used and traffic lights are discretionary unless enforced by a police officer. At night some drivers use their headlights exclusively for flashing oncoming vehicles.

But Cairo drivers do have road rules: they look out for each other and are tolerant of driving that elsewhere might provoke road rage. Things only go awry when an inexperienced driver – like an international visitor, perhaps – is thrown into the mix.

METRO

The metro (www.cairometro.gov.eg) is blissfully efficient, inexpensive and, outside rush hours (7am to 9am and 3pm to 6pm), not too crowded. Given the impossible car traffic in Cairo, if you can make even a portion of your journey on the metro, you'll save time and aggravation.

Metro stations have signs with a big red 'M' in a blue M star. Tickets cost LE2 to any stop; keep yours handy to feed into the turnstile (or, more likely, hand in to the turnstile attendant) on the way out. Trains run every five minutes or so from around 6am until 11.30pm.

Two carriages in the centre of each train are reserved for women. Look for the blue 'Ladies' signs on the platform marking where you should stand.

Metro Lines

Line 1 Stretches 43km along the east bank of the Nile via Downtown, Coptic Cairo and Ma'adi.
Line 2 Crosses to the west bank, passing through Downtown and across Gezira en route.

USEFUL METRO STATIONS

Ataba Convenient for Downtown.
Bab Al Shaaria Closest to Islamic Cairo, on the north side.
Opera By the Cairo Opera House, closest to Zamalek.
Giza Next to Giza train station, handy for buses to the Pyramids.
Mar Girgis In the middle of Coptic Cairo.
Mohammed Naguib Close to Abdeen Palace.
Al Shohadaa Beneath Midan Ramses and Ramses Railway Station.
Nasser Sharia 26th of July and Sharia Ramses; closest to Downtown nightlife.
Sadat Beneath Midan Tahrir, close to the Egyptian Museum.

Line 3 Long-awaited Line 3 has opened partially from Ataba in Downtown to Al Ahram station in Heliopolis, and eventually will run west to the airport and east to Imbaba via Zamalek.

MICROBUS

Cairenes use the private microbus (meekrobas) – a small van with 12 or so seats – as much as the public bus. No destinations are marked, which can make them hard to use at first. But they're quite useful for major routes: from the Giza metro to the main gate of the Pyramids and to Midan Al Remaya (for long-distance microbuses); and from Midan Ataba to **Sharia Sayyida Aisha** (Map p62) for the Citadel, and to **Midan Al Hussein** (Map p62) for Islamic Cairo.

Locals use coded hand gestures to communicate their destination to passing microbuses; if the van has a free seat, it will stop. Fares vary according to distance, from LE2 to LE5, paid after you take your seat. This often requires passing your money to passengers ahead and receiving your change the same way (which is always done scrupulously).

RIVERBUS

It's of limited utility, but it's scenic; the river bus runs from the Corniche near Downtown Cairo to **Giza** (Map p92), by the zoo and Cairo University. The Downtown terminal is located at Maspero, 250m north of the Ramses Hilton, in front of the big round TV building. Boats depart every 15 minutes. The trip takes 30 minutes and the fare is LE1.50.

TAXI

Outside the midafternoon rush, taxis are readily available and will come to a screeching halt with the slightest wave of your hand. For hailing off the street, the whole Cairo cab experience has been transformed by new white taxis with meters and even, on occasion, air-con. Older, unmetered black-and-white taxis still ply the streets, but although there's the potential for getting a cheaper fare in them, the discomfort and near-inevitable argument at the end make them not worth your while.

Meter rates start at LE2.50, plus LE1.25 per kilometre and LE0.25 waiting. A tip of 10% or so is very much appreciated, and it's good to have small change on hand, as drivers are often short of it. Some people have reported taxis with suspiciously fast-running meters, or drivers who claim the meter is broken. If you encounter either situation, simply stop the car, get out and flag down another – the vast majority are legitimate and won't give you trouble.

Occasionally, to make extra fares, taxi drivers pick up multiple passengers, although this isn't standard practice. This will usually result in a more roundabout journey. Feel free to wave on any driver who stops for you and already has passengers.

Hiring a taxi for a longer period runs from LE30 to LE40 per hour, depending on your bargaining skills; LE350 to LE400 for a full day is typical.

Female taxi driver Nour Gaber (p93) can be booked in advance, offers good rates and speaks English.

If you prefer not to hail off the street, both Uber and Middle East–based Careem (www.careem.com/cairo) operate taxi services in Cairo.

GIZA PYRAMIDS

Technically all of Cairo on the west bank of the Nile is Giza, though the name is inextricably linked with the Pyramids, 9km from the river, on the edge of the desert. Truly time-strapped sightseers could conceivably stay out here and bypass Cairo entirely, but that's missing a lot of the fun. More realistically, you'll probably come out here on a day outing. Sharia Al Haram (Pyramids Rd) leads straight to the site and the village of Nazlet As Samaan at its base and south of Pyramids Rd.

◉ Sights

The last remaining wonder of the ancient world; for nearly 4000 years, the extraordinary shape, impeccable geometry and sheer bulk of the **Giza Pyramids** (illustration p126; adult/student LE120/60; ⊘8am-4pm) have invited the obvious questions: 'How were we built, and why?'. Centuries of research have given us parts of the answers. Built as massive tombs on the orders of the pharaohs, they were constructed by teams of workers

tens-of-thousands strong. Today they stand as an awe-inspiring tribute to the might, organisation and achievements of ancient Egypt.

Ongoing excavations on the Giza Plateau, along with the discovery of a pyramid-builders' settlement, complete with areas for large-scale food production and medical facilities, have provided more evidence that the workers were not the slaves of Hollywood tradition, but an organised workforce of Egyptian farmers. During the flood season, when the Nile covered their fields, the farmers could have been redeployed by the highly structured bureaucracy to work on the pharaoh's tomb. In this way, the Pyramids can almost be seen as an ancient job-creation scheme. And the flood waters made it easier to transport building stone to the site. But, despite the evidence, some still won't accept that the ancient Egyptians were capable of such achievements. So-called pyramidologists point to the carving and placement of the stones, precise to the millimetre, and argue the numerological significance of the structures' dimensions as evidence that the Pyramids were constructed by angels or aliens. It's easy to laugh at these out-there ideas, but when you see the monuments up close, especially inside, you'll better understand why so many people believe such awesome structures must have unearthly origins. Most visitors will make a beeline straight to the four most famous sights; the **Great Pyramid of Khufu**, the **Pyramid of Khafre**, the **Pyramid of Menkaure** and the **Sphinx**. But for those who want to explore further, the desert plateau surrounding the Pyramids is littered with tombs, temple ruins and smaller satellite pyramids.

Great Pyramid of Khufu ARCHAEOLOGICAL SITE (Great Pyramid of Cheops; interior adult/student LE300/150; ⊘8am-noon & 1-4pm) The oldest pyramid in Giza and the largest in Egypt, Khufu's Great Pyramid stood 146m high when it was completed around 2570 BC. After 46 windy centuries, its height has been reduced by 9m.

There isn't much to see inside the pyramid, but the experience of climbing through the ancient structure is unforgettable – though impossible if you suffer from the tiniest degree of claustrophobia. The elderly and unfit should not attempt the climb, as it is very steep.

First you clamber up the face of the pyramid a bit, up rudimentary stairs to the left

Giza Plateau

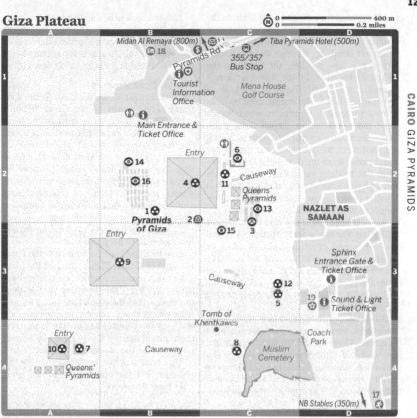

Giza Plateau

of the entrance. Leave your camera with the guard if you have one, then crouch down to enter. At a juncture in the tunnel, a passage descends to an unfinished tomb (usually closed) about 100m along and 30m deep in the bedrock. From here, another passage, 1.3m high and 1m wide, ascends for about 40m to reach the Great Gallery, an impressive narrow space 47m long and 8.5m high. At the start of the gallery, a small horizontal passage leads into the so-called Queen's Chamber.

As you climb up through the Great Gallery, notice how precisely the blocks in the ceiling fit together. In the 10m-long King's Chamber at the end, the walls are built of red granite blocks. The ceiling itself consists of nine huge slabs of granite, which weigh more than 400 tonnes. Above these slabs, four more slabs are separated by gaps, which are designed to distribute the enormous weight away from the chamber. Good airflow from the modern ventilation system (built into two tiny ancient air shafts) will help you breathe easier as you contemplate the tremendous weight suspended above you.

East of the pyramid is a ruin of a different era: **King Farouk's Rest House**, a grand neo-Pharaonic structure built in 1946 by Mustafa Fahmy. It's now an unfortunate shambles, but there's a good view of the city from the adjacent yard and in mid-2017 the government announced it had been pegged for restoration.

Along the pyramid's east face, three small structures, some 20m high, resemble piles of rubble. These are the **Queens' Pyramids**, the tombs of Khufu's wives and sisters. You can enter some of them, but they're quite steamy inside. Note also the **solar barque pits** between the pyramids, which held giant ritual boats.

Western Cemetery CEMETERY

Private cemeteries are tucked into the hill alongside the causeways, as well as arrayed in neat rows around the Pyramids in a grid pattern. Only a few of the tombs are open to the public at any given time. At the northern end of the Western Cemetery, the **Tomb of Senegemib-Inti** contains interesting inscriptions, including a rather vicious looking hippopotamus, rippling with muscle.

Eastern Cemetery CEMETERY

In this cemetery, on the eastern flank of the Queen's Pyramids, you can still see the perfectly smooth limestone facing along the bases of some structures. The 4th-dynasty **Tomb of Meresankh III** (adult/student LE50/25), after 25 years of closure, has been reopened to help boost tourism. The bas-reliefs of daily life inside – scenes depict farming and craftspeople as well as Meresankh's family – provide a colourful contrast with the stark, unadorned interiors of the Pyramids.

Just to the south, the **Tomb of Seshemnufer IV** is almost always open. Just inside the columned entrance, carved deer adorn the walls of the entrance room and there's a burial chamber you can climb down into.

Cheops Boat Museum MUSEUM

(adult/student 80/40, camera LE50; ☉9am-4pm) Immediately south of the Great Pyramid (p122) is this fascinating museum with exactly one object on display: one of Cheops' five solar barques (boats), buried near his pyramid, and unearthed in 1954. This huge, stunning ancient wood vessel, possibly the oldest boat in existence, was carefully restored from 1200 pieces of Lebanese cedar and encased in this museum to protect it from the elements. Visitors to the museum must help this process by donning protective footwear to keep sand out.

Five large pits were found near the Great Pyramid of Khufu. They contained the pharaoh's solar barques, which may have been used to convey the mummy of the dead pharaoh across the Nile to the valley temple, from where it was brought up the causeway and into the tomb chamber. The boats were then buried around the pyramid to provide transport for the pharaoh in the next world.

This boat was put back together for this museum, but the others were buried again after their discovery.

Pyramid of Khafre ARCHAEOLOGICAL SITE

(Pyramid of Chephren; adult/student LE60/30; ☉8am-4pm) Khafre, the second pyramid, seems larger than that of Khafre's father, Khufu (p122). At just 136m high, it's not, but it stands on higher ground and its peak is still capped with the original polished limestone casing. Originally all three pyramids were totally encased in this smooth white stone, which would have made them gleam in the sun. Over the centuries, this casing has been stripped for use in palaces and mosques, exposing the softer inner-core stones to the elements.

The chambers and passageways of this pyramid are less elaborate than those in the Great Pyramid, but almost as claustrophobic. The entrance descends into a passage and then across to the burial chamber, which still contains Khafre's large granite sarcophagus. At the time of research the interior of this pyramid was closed; it usually alternates opening with the Pyramid of Menkaure.

ℹ PYRAMID PRACTICALITIES

Entrance & Tickets

The main **entrance** is at the end of Pyramids Rd (Sharia Al Haram), though if you come on a tour bus, you may enter through the **gate** below the Sphinx, in the village of Nazlet As Samaan.

Additional tickets are required for the **Cheops Boat Museum**, the **Tomb of Meresankh III** and the pyramid interiors. The **Great Pyramid** (p122) is always open, along with one of the other two (they alternate every year or so). Pyramid interior and Tomb of Meresankh III tickets can only be purchased at the main entrance ticket office. Secondary-pyramid tickets are sold all day. At peak times, Great Pyramid tickets (300 per day available in summer, 500 per day in winter) are sold in two lots, first thing in the morning and at 1pm. In winter, you may need to queue, especially on Wednesday and Thursday, when tour groups come from the Red Sea. These days, though, with fewer tourists in Egypt, tickets are usually available all day, without queues. If you exit the site to purchase additional tickets, let the guards know so there's no trouble when you come back through.

Cameras are allowed all over the site, including in the museum (for a fee), but not inside pyramids and tombs. Guards will watch your camera at the pyramid entrances in exchange for LE5 or so baksheesh; some will also permit photos inside tombs for a tip.

Facilities & Food

Clean, well-maintained **toilets** are right beside the main entrance's ticket office (tip the attendant LE2 or so). On the plateau, there's one decent one in the Cheops Boat Museum and a row of less nice options in a dodgy trailer near the Great Pyramid. At the base of the Sphinx, there's a decent toilet block (LE2 fee).

The open-air **cafe** (drinks LE20, sandwiches LE25 to LE65) at the base of the Sphinx wasn't operating when we were last here. For food, it's grossly overpriced, and the waiters are easily 'confused' when making change. For the same amount, you can refresh at the nearby Pizza Hut or far lovelier **Mena House**, though this means a hike back up the hill to the main entrance gate. For **cheap eats**, from the Sphinx gate walk a bit northeast on the main road through Nazlet As Samaan, and you'll pass various snack options.

Horses & Camels

Considering the pressure, it's tempting to ignore the camel touts; however, the distance between the three pyramids is significant, so the service is a real one. 'Official' prices (LE50 per 30 minutes) exist, but, as one tourist police officer said with an apologetic shrug, 'You're still expected to bargain.' Realistically, you can't ride an animal any distance for less than LE50, and LE20 is the minimum for a short trot and photo op. Choose only healthy-looking animals, and if you're asked to pay more than agreed before you're let down, call over the nearest tourist police, or go to the **tourist police office** (p115) by Mena House and complain. For longer rides, hiring a horse from one of the village stables is a far better option than taking one from inside the Pyramids complex.

Back outside, to the east of the pyramid, are the substantial remains of Khafre's funerary temple and the flagged paving of the causeway that provided access from the Nile to the tomb.

Pyramid of Menkaure ARCHAEOLOGICAL SITE
(Pyramid of Mycerinus; adult/student LE60/30; ⊘8am-4pm) At 62m (originally 66.5m), this pyramid is the smallest of the trio, only about one-tenth the bulk of the Great Pyramid (p122). The pharaoh Menkaure died before the structure was finished – around the

bottom are several courses of granite facing that were never properly smoothed. Inside, you descend into three distinct levels – the largest surprisingly vast – and you can peer into the main tomb.

Outside the pyramid you'll see the excavated remains of **Menkaure's Funerary Temple** and, further east, the ruins of his **valley temple**. To the south is a set of **Queens' Pyramids**. If you hike this far, horse and camel touts will want to lure you out into the desert for better photo ops of all three pyramids. If you go, keep your general-

The Pyramids of Giza

TACKLING THE SITE

Constructed more than 4000 years ago, the Pyramids are the last remaining wonder of the ancient world. The giant structures – the ❶ **Great Pyramid of Khufu**, the smaller ❷ **Pyramid of Khafre** and the ❸ **Pyramid of Menkaure** – deservedly sit at the top of many travellers' to-do lists. But the site is challenging to explore, with everything, including the smaller ❹ **Queens' Pyramids** and assorted tombs such as the ❺ **Tomb of Senegemib-Inti**, spread out in the desert under the hot sun. And it all looks, at first glance, a bit smaller than you might have thought.

It helps to imagine them as they were: originally, the Pyramids gleamed in the sun, covered in a smooth white limestone casing. These enormous mausoleums, each devoted to a single pharaoh, were part of larger complexes. At the east base of each was a 'funerary temple', where the pharaoh was worshipped after his demise, with daily rounds of offerings to sustain his soul. In the ground around the pyramids, wooden boats – so-called solar barques – were buried with more supplies to transport the pharaoh's soul to the afterlife (one of these has been reconstructed and sits in the ❻ **Cheops Boat Museum**). From each funerary temple, a long stone-paved causeway extended down the hill.

At the base of the plateau, a lake covered the land where the village of Nazlet as-Samaan is now – this was fed by a canal and enlarged with flood waters each year. At the end of each causeway, a 'valley temple' stood at the water's edge to greet visitors. Next to Khafre's valley temple, the lion-bodied ❼ **Sphinx** stands guard.

So much about the Pyramids remains mysterious – including the whereabouts of the bodies of the pharaohs themselves. But there's still plenty for visitors to see. Here we show you both the big picture and the little details to look out for, starting with the ❽ **ticket booth and entrance**.

Pyramid of Khafre
Khufu's son built this pyramid, which has some surviving limestone casing at the top. Scattered around the base are enormous granite stones that once added a snappy black stripe to the lowest level of the structure.

Khafre's Valley Temple

❼

Eastern Cemetery

The Sphinx
This human-headed beast, thought to be a portrait of Khafre, guards the base of the plateau. The entrance is only through Khafre's valley temple. Come early or late in the day to avoid the long queue.

Pyramid of Menkaure (Mycerinus)

This pyramid opens alternately with the Pyramid of Khafre. The gash in the exterior is the folly of Sultan al-Aziz Uthman, who tried to dismantle the pyramid in 1196.

Cheops Boat Museum

Preserved in its own modern tomb, this 4500-year-old cedar barge was dug up from in front of the Great Pyramid and reassembled by expert craftspeople like a 1224-piece jigsaw puzzle.

③

②

Tomb of Senegemib-Inti

The Giza Plateau is dotted with small tombs like this one. Opening schedules vary each year. Duck inside to look for delicate wall carvings and enjoy a bit of shade.

Western Cemetery

Khafre's Funerary Temple

Ticket Booth & Entrance

Buy tickets, marked with a hologram sticker, here and only here. All other options are counterfeit. Clean bathrooms, the only good facilities, are in a building just to the east.

⑥

⑤

①

⑧

④

Great Pyramid of Khufu (Cheops)

Clamber inside the corridors to marvel at the precision engineering of the seamless stone blocks, each weighing 2.5 tonnes. Pause to consider the full weight of 2.3 million of them.

Queens' Pyramids

These smaller piles were built as the tombs of Khufu's sister, mother and wife. They're in bad shape, but some show the original limestone casing at the base – feel how smoothly the stones are fitted.

admission ticket handy in case police ask for it when you return.

Khafre's Valley Temple
ARCHAEOLOGICAL SITE

You approach the Sphinx through this temple that once sat at the edge of a small artificial lake, connected to the Nile by a canal – it was in this way that construction materials were brought to the area at the start, and later it was how worshippers came to visit the temple. The sturdy building is filled with beautiful pink-granite columns and alabaster floors.

Look in the corners, where the pink-granite stones fit together like pieces of a jigsaw puzzle. The temple originally held 23 statues of Khafre, which were illuminated with the ancient version of mood lighting, through slits between the top of the wall and the flat roof. Only one of these statues, all carved in the hard black stone diorite, has been found intact – it is now in the Egyptian Museum.

Sphinx
ARCHAEOLOGICAL SITE

Known in Arabic as Abu Al Hol (Father of Terror), this sculpture of a man with the haunches of a lion was dubbed the Sphinx by the ancient Greeks because it resembled their mythical winged monster who set riddles and killed anyone unable to answer them. A geological survey has shown that it was most likely carved from the bedrock at the bottom of the causeway during Khafre's reign, so it probably portrays his features.

As is clear from the accounts of early Arab travellers, the nose was hammered off sometime between the 11th and 15th centuries, although some still like to blame Napoleon for the deed. Part of the fallen beard was carted off by 19th-century adventurers and is now on display in the British Museum in London. These days the Sphinx has potentially greater problems: pollution and rising groundwater are causing internal fractures, and it is under a constant state of repair.

Legends and superstitions about the Sphinx abound, and the mystery surrounding its long-forgotten purpose is almost as intriguing as its appearance. On seeing it for the first time, many visitors agree with English playwright Alan Bennett, who noted in his diary that seeing the Sphinx is like meeting a TV personality in the flesh: he's smaller than one had imagined.

Wissa Wassef Art Centre
ARTS CENTRE

(☑ 02-3381-5746; www.wissawassef.com; Saqqara Rd, Harraniyya; ⊙10am-5pm Tue-Sun, by appointment only Mon) FREE The artisans of the Wissa Wassef Art Centre, who work in open studios, are known for their distinctive tapestries depicting rural scenes. Crude imitations are standard in souvenir shops; the ones for sale and on display in the museum here are in a completely different class, like paintings in wool. There's pottery and batik fabric, done to equally good effect. The place has the feeling of a sanctuary – quiet and refreshingly green, especially after a dusty Pyramids visit.

The centre is housed in a beautiful mud-brick complex, the work of its founder, architect Ramses Wissa Wassef. It won an Aga Khan prize for its refined traditional style.

To get here, take a Saqqara-bound microbus (LE3) or taxi from Pyramids Rd at Maryutia Canal – a giant flyover runs above it. Get off when you see the blue 'Harraniyya' sign, after about 3.5km, and about 600m after the flyover turns away. The centre is by the canal on the west side of the road.

🏃 Activities

There's only one thing to do around the Pyramids, and you'll never stop hearing about it. But a desert horse ride at sunset, with the Pyramids as a background, is unforgettable.

All of the stables are strung along the road south of the coach park by the Sphinx gate.

Expect to pay around LE150 per person per hour at a good place; a reputable operation won't ask for money till the end of the ride. Others may charge less, but often their horses are very poorly kept. Tip your guide an additional LE10 to LE15, and keep your Pyramids site ticket or you'll be charged again to enter. Moonlit rides around the Pyramids are another favourite outing but under new regulations you can't ride anywhere close to the site after 6pm.

NB Stables
HORSE RIDING

(☑ 02-3382-0435, 012-2746-2565; www.facebook. com/NasserBreeshStables; Nazlet As Samaan; rides per hr LE150) General Cairo foreign resident opinion holds that this is the best stables near the Sphinx. It's owned by Nasser Breesh, who's praised for his healthy steeds and good guides.

His place can be tricky to find: head down the street by the Sphinx poster off the main square where horses are gathered, or ask for directions to the Sphinx Club, as the stables are just behind.

FB Stables HORSE RIDING
(☑ 010-6507-0288; www.fbstablesgiza.co.uk; Sharia Gamal Abdul Nasser; rides per hr LE150; ⊙ 24hr) This stables for horse rides at the Pyramids is recommended for its healthy, well cared for horses.

🛏 Sleeping

Tiba Pyramids Hotel HOTEL $
(☑ 3358-1659; www.tibapyramidshotel.com; 33 Pyramids Rd; r from LE320; ❄ 🛜) The best deal within walking distance of the Pyramids, though not great quality. The traffic noise is intense as it's at a major intersection. Only stay here if you're on a budget and planning a surgical strike on the Pyramids.

Barceló HOTEL $$
(☑ 3582-3300; www.barcelo.com; 229 Pyramids Rd; r from €66; ❄ 🛜 🏊) Well placed for a strategic visit to the Pyramids, without totally giving up on the city. The Giza metro stop is about 3km away, and the Pyramids are 4km. It's a standard chain, but modern and well kitted-out, with good breakfast and a nice rooftop pool.

Mena House Hotel HISTORIC HOTEL $$$
(☑ 3377-3222; www.menahousehotel.com; Pyramids Rd; s/d from US$315/345; ❄ 🛜 🏊) Built in 1869 as Khedive Ismail's hunting lodge, Mena House dazzles with intricate gold decoration and air that perpetually smells of jasmine. The grandest palace-wing rooms are borderline-kitschy Arabian Nights style, but the view of the Great Pyramid filling your window is a treat. Rooms in the garden wing are more typically modern. The swimming pool is suitably capacious.

🍴 Eating

Khan Al Khalili EGYPTIAN $$
(Pyramids Rd, Mena House Hotel; mains LE73-165; ⊙ 1-3pm & 7.30-10pm) This casual restaurant at Mena House has huge windows opening on to the Pyramids – a great place to rest up for lunch after a morning of Pyramids sightseeing. The menu offers plenty of mezze

---

THE PYRAMIDS HUSTLE

Usually crammed with tour buses, gargling camels, and camel- and horse-carriage touts, the Pyramids is an intense tourist scene and many visitors find it the most gruelling part of their trip. Unfortunately, until the site is better managed and the people in the village by the Pyramids have some other income besides selling horse and camel rides, there is no way to avoid the sales pressure and scam attempts. It does help, however, to know what you're up against. These days, however, with fewer tourists around, there are fewer vendors, but among these the desperation to make some money is even greater.

The hustle can start before you even leave your hotel, where someone tries to sell you a 'sunrise tour' of the Pyramids: really just a way of delivering you early to the horse touts, as you can't enter the site before 8am. En route, someone will chat you up at the Giza metro, or a man will jump in your taxi while it's stuck in traffic on Pyramids Rd. The road ahead is closed, he warns, and the best way to proceed is on a horse. (The road *is* closed, sort of; about 1km from the site, all outbound traffic must detour north on Sharia Al Mansouria. Don't panic – you'll loop back to the Pyramids soon.) If you've been dropped at the bottom of the hill at the main entrance gate, while you're walking up to the ticket office horse touts will try to convince you the entrance has moved, only vehicles are allowed to enter this way, or point you to a secret back route. Counterfeit tickets aren't unheard of – buy yours only from the ticket-office windows.

Once through the turnstiles, police might direct you to a waiting man, or men will ask for your ticket in an official tone. Ignore them, as they're just attempting to become your guide. You need only show your additional tickets at the Great Pyramid, at whichever secondary pyramid is open, and at the Tomb of Meresankh III (and guards should take only half the ticket, not the whole thing). Guards also sometimes check your general ticket at the Sphinx. Attendants at smaller tombs will ask for a ticket, hoping you'll assume you need to buy one – flash your general ticket and you should be fine.

Even knowing all this won't stop touts from approaching you, and no matter how tersely and frequently you say no, these guys won't stop – it's the only job they've got. So it's key for your own happiness not to snap, but to smile and just keep walking. It also helps to remember that the Pyramids have been attracting tourists since day one, and a local was probably already waiting to sell a souvenir.

ℹ THE PYRAMIDS AFTER DARK

Narrated by the Sphinx, the **sound and light show** (☎02-3385-7320; www.sound andlight.com.eg; Sphinx Entrance Gate; LE150-175; ⊙shows at 7pm & 8pm Oct-Apr, 7.30pm & 8.30pm May-Sep) is a rather dated spectacular. It's not worth a special trip, but fine if you're in the area – it is neat to see the Pyramids so dramatically lit. The first show (in English; free translation headsets available) always runs; the second (in either Italian, French, German or Spanish) runs with a minimum of five spectators.

The entrance and **ticket office** is on the Sphinx side. Though there's officially no student discount, some readers report negotiating a small one.

plus traditional mains of stuffed pigeon, *molokhiyya* (garlicky leaf soup, a speciality of Egypt) and pan-fried Nile perch.

Andrea   EGYPTIAN **$$**
(☎010-0353-2000; New Giza Rd, New Giza; mains LE35-120; ⊙noon-midnight) Long a favoured post-Pyramids dining spot, Andrea has moved out to a new hilltop spot in New Giza, where you eat in the garden while overlooking the city-sprawl. It's justly famous for its spit-roasted chicken and tasty mezze dishes, though it's a bit of a hike by taxi (about 20 to 30 minutes depending on traffic) from the Pyramids now.

Moghul Room   INDIAN **$$$**
(☎3377-3222; www.menahousehotel.com; Pyramids Rd, Mena House Hotel; mains LE70-185; ⊙7.30-11pm; 🚗) Mena House's long-running Indian restaurant specialises in tandoori dishes and mild North Indian-style curries with a good range of vegetarian dishes too. Though it's a long taxi ride from Downtown, the opulent decor, good food and live sitar music make it worthwhile. Not entirely authentic but pleasant and beautiful surroundings.

ℹ Getting There & Away

The most efficient traffic-beating way to reach the Pyramids is to go via metro to Giza (LE2), then by taxi (about LE20), microbus (LE5) or bus (LE2.50).

Microbuses cluster at the bottom of the west-side stairs from the metro (drivers are yelling 'Haram'). The driver will drop you at the roundabout, right outside the main entrance gate to the Pyramids. You just need to walk up the hill to the ticket office.

Buses stop on the north side of Pyramids Rd, just west of the metro underpass. Hop on any headed for Midan Al Remaya and get off at Sharia Al Mansouria, or look out for buses **355 or 357**, which terminate in front of Mena House, about 250m from the site entrance.

Returning to Cairo, if you want to take a microbus or bus back to Giza metro, it's easiest to exit back through the main gate and flag one down at the roundabout just outside the gate. Taxis will try to convince you to go for a flat fare, rather than on the meter. Walking out further helps. You could also take a tuk-tuk from near the Sphinx gate out to Pyramids Rd for about LE3.

Egyptian Museum

One of the world's most important collections of ancient artefacts, the **Egyptian Museum** (adult/student LE120/60, after 5.30pm Sun & Thu LE180/90, Royal Mummies Room LE150/75, camera LE50; ⊙ 9am-7pm Mon-Wed, to 9pm Sun & Thu, to 4pm Fri & Sat; Ⓜ Sadat) takes pride of place in Downtown Cairo, on the north side of Midan Tahrir. Inside the vast domed powder-pink building, the glittering treasures of great pharaohs lie alongside the grave goods, mummies, jewellery, bowls and toys of Egyptians whose names are lost to history. To walk around the museum is to embark on an adventure through time.

This is in part due to the museum structure itself. There's nary an interactive touch-screen to be found; many of the smaller items are in the same vitrines in which they were first placed when the museum opened in 1902. The lighting is so poor in some halls that by late afternoon you have to squint to make out details and read the words on the cryptic typed display cards placed on a few key items.

In this way, the Egyptian Museum documents not just the time of the pharaohs, but also the history of Egyptology. Some display cards have turned obsolete as new discoveries have busted old theories. And the collection rapidly outgrew its sensible layout, as, for instance, Tutankhamun's enormous trove and the tomb contents of Tanis were both unearthed after the museum opened, and then had to be shoehorned into the space. Now more than 100,000 objects are wedged into about 15,000 sq m.

Like the country itself, the museum is in flux. Most objects are still on display, although some are being moved to the Grand Egyptian Museum. While rooms are being refurbished the objects are deposited elsewhere in the museum, usually in the room next door. This museum will remain a major sight, very much the same as it is now with many of the master pieces but less clutter. However it is not clear just how much will stay the same, and when the GEM will open.

This makes the Egyptian Museum somewhat challenging. A rewarding strategy is simply to walk around and see what catches your eye. But it's hard to shake the sense that something even more stunning is waiting in the next room. We recommend some highlights, but be sure to stop and see some of the lesser items, as they often do just as well if not better in bringing the world of the pharaohs back to life.

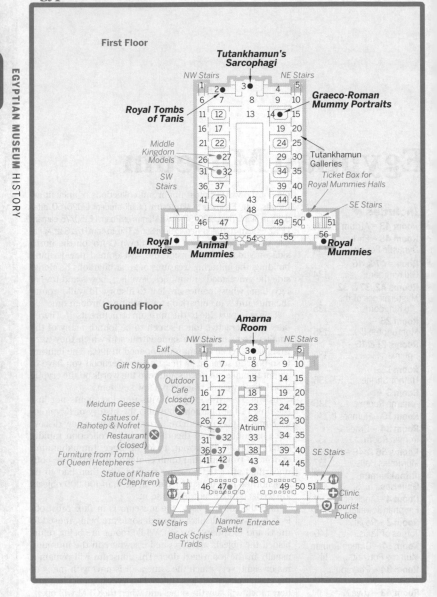

First Floor

Tutankhamun's Sarcophagi

NW Stairs — *NE Stairs*

Royal Tombs of Tanis

Graeco-Roman Mummy Portraits

Middle Kingdom Models

Tutankhamun Galleries

Ticket Box for Royal Mummies Halls

SW Stairs

SE Stairs

Royal Mummies **Animal Mummies** **Royal Mummies**

Ground Floor

Amarna Room

NW Stairs — *NE Stairs*

Exit

Gift Shop ●

Outdoor Cafe (closed)

Meidum Geese

Statues of Rahotep & Nofret

Restaurant (closed)

Atrium

Furniture from Tomb of Queen Hetepheres

Statue of Khafre (Chephren)

SE Stairs

Clinic

Tourist Police

SW Stairs

Black Schist Triads

Narmer Palette

Entrance

History

The current museum has its origins in several earlier efforts at managing Egypt's ancient heritage, beginning in 1835, when Egyptian ruler Mohammed Ali banned the export of antiquities. Not that anyone heeded this – French archaeologist Auguste Mariette was busy shipping his finds from Saqqara to the Louvre when he was empowered to create the Egyptian Antiquities Service in 1858.

Mariette's growing collection, from some 35 dig sites, bounced around various homes in Cairo until 1902, when the current building was erected in a suitably prominent position in the city. There it has stood, in its original layout, a gem of early museum design. But the lack of upkeep, and the ever-expanding field of Egyptology, has strained the place. For decades, the museum's basement store was a notorious morass, as neglected sculptures sank into the soft flooring and needed to be excavated all over again.

Until 1996, museum security involved locking the door at night. When an enterprising thief stowed away overnight and helped himself to treasures, the museum authorities installed alarms and detectors, at the same time improving the lighting on many exhibits. During the 2011 revolution, the museum was broken into and a few artefacts went missing. To prevent further looting, activists formed a human chain around the building to guard its contents. By most reports, they were successful.

GROUND FLOOR

Before entering the museum, wander through the garden. To your left lies the **tomb of Auguste Mariette** (1821–81), with a statue of the archaeologist, arms folded, shaded under a spreading tree. Mariette's tomb is overlooked by an **arc of busts** of two dozen Egyptological luminaries including Jean-François Champollion, who cracked the code of the hieroglyphs; Gaston Maspero, Mariette's successor as director of the Egyptian Antiquities Service; and Karl Lepsius, the pre-eminent 19th-century German Egyptologist.

The ground floor of the museum is laid out roughly chronologically in a clockwise fashion starting at the entrance hall.

Room 43 – Atrium

The central atrium is filled with a miscellany of large and small Egyptological finds. In the area before the steps lie some of the collection's oldest items. In the central cabinet No 8, the double-sided **Narmer Palette**, found

---

ⓘ MUSEUM PRACTICALITIES

Entrance & Tickets
Getting into the **Egyptian Museum** is an exercise in queuing: at peak times, you'll wait to have your bag X-rayed, to buy tickets, and then to pass through the turnstiles and to have your bag checked again. Last tickets are sold one hour before closing time.

Additional tickets for the **Royal Mummies Halls** are purchased upstairs near Room 56.

Photography tickets can be bought when you buy your main entry ticket. If you don't have a photography ticket you have to will check your camera in at the front gate – in the kiosk adjacent to the first X-ray machine. A small tip (LE1 or LE2) is nice when you claim your items. Return promptly at closing time, or you may find the room locked up.

Timing
Tour buses usually hit the museum between 10.30am and 2pm. It's a good idea to either go early or visit late afternoon. Friday mornings are also quieter, as are the evenings on Sunday and Thursday when the museum closes at 9pm. It can be quite dim during the evening; you may want to bring a small torch (flashlight).

Guides
Quite a few official guides troll for business in the garden area. No doubt they will approach you if you are not in a group, and will suggest to take you around for upwards of LE100 per hour. Some are better than others, but many have a fairly standard knowledge of what's on show at the museum. For those with more than a passing interest in Egyptology, wanting to go a bit deeper into the history, a visit in the company of a guide such as Manal Helmy (p97) is highly recommended.

Facilities & Food
Toilets are on the mezzanine of each southern staircase. A sign says tips are not accepted but, well, they are – LE5 is good. The plaza on the west side of the building holds a simple **cafe**, with cold drinks, ice cream and basic sandwiches, but it was shut during our last visit. Make sure to bring water with you. You can only re-enter the museum at the front, and with much sweet-talking of the guards.

HIGHLIGHTS OF THE EGYPTIAN MUSEUM

The following are our favourite must-see exhibits, for which you need at least half a day but preferably a little more.

Tutankhamun Galleries (1st fl) Top on everyone's list, King Tut's treasures occupy a large chunk of the museum's upper floor. Go first to Room 3 to see his sarcophagi while the crowds are light.

Old Kingdom Rooms (Ground fl, Rooms 42, 37 & 32) After peeking at Tutankhamun, return to the ground floor for a chronological tour. Look out for the statue of well-muscled Khafre – you may also recognise him from the Sphinx.

Amarna Room (Ground fl, Room 3) Stepping into this room feels like visiting another museum entirely – the artwork commissioned by Akhenaten for his new capital at Tell Al Amarna is dramatically different in style from his predecessors. Say hi to his wife, Nefertiti, while you're here.

Royal Tombs of Tanis (1st fl, Room 2) While everyone else is gawking at Tutankhamun's treasure down the hall, this room of gem-encrusted gold jewellery, found at the largest ruined city in the Nile Delta, is often empty.

Graeco-Roman Mummy Portraits (1st fl, Room 14) An odd interlude in mummy traditions, from very late in the ancient Egypt game, these wood-panel portraits were placed over the faces of embalmed dead, staring up in vividly realistic style.

Animal Mummies (1st fl, Rooms 53 & 54) Tucked in an odd corner of the museum, this long, dim room contains the bundled remains of the ancients' beloved pets, honoured gods and even their last meals.

Middle Kingdom Models (1st fl, Rooms 32 & 27) When you've had your fill of gold and other royal trappings, stop in these rooms to get a picture of common life in ancient Egypt, depicted in miniature dioramas made to accompany the pharaoh to the other world.

Royal Mummies Halls (1st fl, Rooms 56 & 46) Visit these around lunch or near closing time to avoid the crowds – they don't require more than half an hour, but they do put a human face on all the stunning objects you've seen.

at the Temple of Horus in Kom Al Ahmar near Edfu, is of great significance. Dating from around the 1st dynasty, it depicts Pharaoh Narmer (also known as Menes, c 3100 BC) wearing, on one side, the crown of Upper Egypt and, on the other side, the crown of Lower Egypt, suggesting the first union of Upper and Lower Egypt under one ruler. Egyptologists take this as the birth of ancient Egyptian civilisation and Narmer's reign as the first of the 1st dynasty. This, then, is the starting point of more than 3000 years of Pharaonic history in which more than 170 rulers presided over 30 dynasties and produced almost everything in this building. In this sense, the Narmer Palette is the foundation stone of the Egyptian Museum. In the sexagonal cabinet to the right is a small clay head from the 4th millennium BC, one of the earliest human representations found in Egypt. There are several other exquisite objects from the pre-Pharaonic period.

Room 48 – Early Dynastic Period

In glass cabinet No 16 is the **limestone statue of Zoser** (Djoser; 2667–2648 BC), the 3rd-dynasty pharaoh whose chief architect Imhotep designed the revolutionary Step Pyramid at Saqqara. The statue, discovered in 1924 in its *serdab* (cellar) in the northeastern corner of the pyramid, is the oldest statue of its kind in the museum. The seated, near-life-size figure has lost its original inlaid eyes but is still impressive in a tight robe and striped head cloth over a huge wig.

Rooms 47 & 46 – Old Kingdom

Look for the three exquisite **black schist triads** that depict the pharaoh Menkaure (Mycerinus; 2532–2503 BC), builder of the smallest of the three Pyramids of Giza, flanked either side by a female figure. The hardness of the stone makes the sculptor's skill all the greater and has helped ensure the triads' survival through the ages. The figure to the pharaoh's right is the goddess Hathor, while each of the figures on his left represents a nome (administrative division) of Egypt, the name of which is given by the symbol above their head. These triads (plus one other that is not held by this museum) were discovered at the pharaoh's valley temple, just east of his pyramid at Giza.

Rooms 42, 37 & 32 – Masterpieces of the Old Kingdom

In the centre of Room 42 is one of the museum's masterpieces, a smooth, black statue of Khafre (Chephren; 2558–2532 BC). The builder of the second pyramid at Giza sits on a lion throne, and is protected by the wings of the falcon god Horus. The use of the stone diorite, which is harder than marble or granite, suggests the pharaoh's power. In fact, Khafre had 23 identical pieces carved for his valley temple at the Giza Plateau, though this is the only survivor.

Slightly to the left in front of Khafre, the core of the stunning wooden statue of Ka-Aper (No 40) was carved out of a single piece of sycamore (the arms were ancient additions; the legs, modern restorations). The sycamore was sacred to the goddess Hathor, while Ka-Aper's belly suggests his prosperity. His eyes are amazingly lifelike, set in copper lids with whites of opaque quartz and corneas of rock crystal, drilled and filled with black paste to form the pupils. When this statue was excavated at Saqqara in 1870, local workmen named him Sheikh Al Balad (Headman), for his resemblance to their own local leader. Behind you, to the left of the door, sits the Seated Scribe (No 44), a wonderful painted limestone figure, hand poised as if waiting to take dictation, his inlaid eyes set in an asymmetrical face giving him a very vivid appearance.

Room 32 is dominated by the beautiful statues of Rahotep and Nofret (No 27), a noble couple in the 4th-dynasty reign of Sneferu, builder of the Bent and the Red Pyramids at Dahshur. Almost life-size with well-preserved painted surfaces, the limestone sculptures have simple lines making them seem almost contemporary, despite having been around for a staggering 4600 years.

In a cabinet off to the left, a limestone group shows Seneb, 'chief of the royal wardrobe', and his family (No 39). Seneb is notable for being a dwarf: he sits cross-legged, his two children strategically placed to cover his short legs. His full-size wife Senetites places her arms protectively and affectionately around his shoulders. Rediscovered in their tomb in Giza in 1926, the happy couple and their two kids were more recently used in Egyptian family-planning campaigns.

Also here is a panel of Meidum geese (No 138), part of an extraordinarily beautiful wall painting from a mudbrick mastaba (bench above a tomb) at Meidum, near the oasis of Al Fayoum. Though painted around 2500 BC, the pigments remain vivid and the degree of realism, even within the distinct Pharaonic style, is astonishing – ornithologists have had no trouble identifying the species.

Room 37, entered via Room 32, contains furniture from the Giza Plateau tomb of Queen Hetepheres, wife of Sneferu and mother of Khufu (Cheops), including a carrying chair, bed, bed canopy and a jewellery box. Her mummy has not been found but her shrivelled internal organs remain inside her Canopic chest. A glass cabinet holds a miniature ivory statue of her son Khufu, found at Abydos. Ironically, at under 8cm, this tiny figure is the only surviving representation of the builder of Egypt's Great Pyramid.

Room 26 – Montuhotep II

The seated statue in the corridor on your right, after leaving Room 32, represents Theban-born Montuhotep II (2055–2004 BC; No 136), first ruler of the Middle Kingdom period. He is shown with black skin (representing fertility and rebirth) and the red crown of Lower Egypt. This statue was discovered by Howard Carter under the forecourt of the pharaoh's temple at Deir Al Bahri in Thebes in 1900, when the ground gave way under his horse – a surprisingly common means of discovery in the annals of Egyptology.

Rooms 21 & 16 – Sphinxes

These grey-granite sphinxes are very different from the great enigmatic Sphinx at Giza – they look more like the Cowardly Lion from The Wizard of Oz, each with a fleshy human face surrounded by a great shaggy mane and big ears. Sculpted for Pharaoh Amenemhat III (1855–1808 BC)

THE (NOT-SO-) GRAND EGYPTIAN MUSEUM

In 2002, amidst much pomp and circumstance, then-President Hosni Mubarak laid the ceremonial foundation for the Grand Egyptian Museum (GEM; www.gem.gov.eg), the cornerstone of an ambitious project aimed at redefining the Giza Plateau. Fifteen years on, and the project looks like one of the more blatant boondoggles of the dictator's reign. Plenty of cash has been thrown at it, yet progress has been been grindingly slow and beset with financial difficulties. In 2015 Egypt's Ministry of Antiquities announced that another US$300 million would need to be found to finish it, bringing the estimated total cost of building the museum to US$1.1 billion.

Located 2km from the Great Pyramids, the GEM is meant to be a state-of-the-art showcase for the country's finest antiquities. But since the 2011 revolution, the fate of the project has been uncertain. Slowly, certain pieces are being moved from the old to the 'Grand' museum, and from various other sites, but no one knows exactly what will eventually be shown where. The latest official statements hope for the GEM to partially open in mid-2018, with a full opening in either 2020 or 2022. In the meantime, enjoy the fresh paint job here in the Egyptian Museum – that's likely the only real improvement in antiquities exhibits that tourists will see for a while.

during the 12th dynasty, they were moved to Avaris by the Hyksos and then to the Delta city of Tanis by Ramses II. Also here, in Room 16, is an extraordinary wood figure of the ka (spirit double) of the 13th-dynasty ruler Hor Auibre.

Room 12 – Hathor Shrine

The centrepiece of this room is a remarkably well-preserved, vaulted **sandstone chapel**, found near the Theban temple of Deir Al Bahri. Its walls are painted with reliefs of Tuthmosis III (1479–1425 BC), his wife Meritre and two princesses, making offerings to Hathor, who suckles the pharaoh. The life-size cow statue suckles Tuthmosis III's son and successor Amenhotep II (1427–1400 BC), who also stands beneath her chin.

Hatshepsut (1473–1458 BC), who was co-regent for part of Tuthmosis III's reign, eventually had herself crowned as pharaoh. Her life-size **pink granite statue** stands to the right of the chapel. Although she wears a pharaoh's headdress and a false beard, the statue has definite feminine characteristics. In the corridor outside this room, the large reddish-painted limestone head is also of Hatshepsut, taken from one of the huge Osiris-type statues that adorned the pillared facade of her great temple at Deir Al Bahri. Also in Room 12, on the north wall, are decorations from the same temple showing the famed expedition to Punt, which scholars posit may be current-day Somalia or perhaps the Arabian Peninsula.

Room 3 – Amarna Room

Akhenaten (1352–1336 BC), the 'heretic pharaoh', did more than build a new capital at Tell Al Amarna, close the temples of the traditional state god Amun and promote the sun god Aten in his place. He also ushered in a period of great artistic freedom, as a glance around this room will show. Compare these great torsos and their strangely bulbous bellies, hips and thighs, their elongated faces and thick lips, with the sleek, hard-edged Middle Kingdom sculptures of previous rooms.

Perhaps most striking of all is the **unfinished head of Nefertiti** (No 161, in the left alcove), wife of Akhenaten. Worked in brown quartzite, it's an incredibly delicate and sensitive portrait and shows the queen to have been extremely beautiful – unlike some of the relief figures of her elsewhere in the room, in which she appears with exactly the same strange features as her husband. The masterpiece of this period, the finished bust of Nefertiti, can be seen in the Neues Museum in Berlin.

Room 10 – Ramses II

At the foot of the northeast stairs is a fabulous large **grey-granite representation of Ramses II** (1279–1213 BC), builder of the Ramesseum and Abu Simbel. But here in this statue he is tenderly depicted as a child with his finger in his mouth nestled against the breast of a great falcon, in this case the Canaanite god Horus.

Room 34 – Graeco-Roman Room

It is best to visit these last rooms after seeing the first floor, because this is the end of the ancient Egyptian story. By the 4th century BC, Egypt had been invaded by many nations, most recently by the Macedonian Alexander the Great. Egypt's famously resistant culture had become porous, as will be obvious from the statue situated immediately to the left as you enter this room: a typically Greek face with curly beard and locks, but wearing a Pharaonic-style headdress.

Nearby on the right-hand wall, you'll see a large sandstone panel inscribed in three languages: official Egyptian hieroglyphic; the more popularly used demotic; and Greek, the language of the new rulers. This trilingual stone is similar in nature to the more famous Rosetta Stone that is housed in London's British Museum. A cast of the Rosetta Stone stands near the museum entrance (Room 48)

FIRST FLOOR

Exhibits here are grouped thematically and can be viewed in any order, but if you come up the southeast stairs, you'll enter the Tutankhamun Galleries at Room 45 and experience the pieces in roughly the same order that they were laid out in the tomb (a poster on the wall outside Room 45 illustrates the tomb and treasures as they were found). But first, directly above the stairs, are the Royal Mummies Halls.

Rooms 56 & 46 – Royal Mummies Halls

These rooms house the remains of some of Egypt's most illustrious pharaohs and queens from the 17th to the 21st dynasties, 1650 to 945 BC. They lie in individual glass showcases (kept at a constant 22°C) in two rooms at either corner of the museum. The mood is suitably sombre, and talking above a hushed whisper is forbidden (though, somewhat counterproductively, the guards are often chatting loudly on their mobile phones). Tour guides are not allowed to enter, although some do.

Displaying dead royalty has proved controversial. Late President Anwar Sadat took the royal mummies off display in 1979 for political reasons, but the subsequent reappearance of 11 of the better-looking mummies in 1994 did wonders for tourism figures, inspiring the opening of a second mummy room with second-tier but no less interesting personages. The ticket price is steep, but you certainly won't see so many mummies in any other single museum, nor get to peer at them so closely. Parents should be aware that the mummies can be a frightening sight for young children.

Room 56

Take time to study some of the first room's celebrated inmates, beginning with the brave Theban pharaoh Seqenenre Taa II who died violently, possibly during struggles to reunite the country at the end of the Second Intermediate Period, around 1560 BC. His wounds are still visible beneath his curly hair, and his twisted arms reflect his violent death. The perfectly wrapped mummies of Queen Merit Amun and Amenhotep I (1525–1504 BC) show how all royal mummies would once have looked, bedecked with garlands.

On the opposite side of the room, Tuthmosis II (1525–1504 BC) lies next to his sister-wife, Hatshepsut – the great queen and female pharaoh, rendered so grandly in stone in Room 12, is here reduced to an 'obese female with bad teeth', according to the descriptive text. Their son, Tuthmosis III (1479–1425 BC), occupies the last case, looking not too bad considering he'd been severely damaged by grave robbers centuries ago.

In the centre of the room, Ramses II is strikingly well preserved, his haughty profile revealing the family's characteristic curved nose, his grey hair tinged with henna and his fingernails long. By contrast, his 13th son and successor, Merenptah (1213–1203 BC), has a distinctly white appearance caused by the mummification process. Amenhotep II rests in the next case, finally settled after a particularly tumultuous century of being shipped up and down the Nile and stolen from his tomb in the Valley of the Kings. Tuthmosis IV (1400–1390 BC) sports beautifully styled hair; he was also the first pharaoh to have his ears pierced. With his smooth black skin and square chin, Seti I (1294–1279 BC) rivals Ramses II in flawless preservation.

Room 46

The second mummy room (same ticket) is located across the building, off Room 47. The corridor display relates some of the most famous mummy discoveries, including the 1881 Deir Al Bahri cache, and displays the body of **Queen Tiye**, with long flowing hair. Many of the mummies in this section date from the 20th and 21st dynasties, the end of the New Kingdom and the start of the Third Intermediate Period (c 1186–945 BC). You first pass **Ramses III** (1184–1153 BC) and **Ramses IV** (1153–1147 BC), and around the corner, the face of **Ramses V** (1147–1143 BC) is marked with small raised spots, likely caused by smallpox. In the centre of the room, **Nedjmet** (c 1070–946 BC) wears a lavish curly wig and has black-and-white stones for eyes. Next to her, **Queen Henettawy** (c 1025 BC), in a linen shroud painted with an image of Osiris, is a product of modern restorers, who repaired her cheeks, which had burst from overpacking by ancient embalmers. In the final section, the mummy of **Queen Nesikhonsu** still conveys the queen's vivid features, while **Queen Maatkare** lies with her pet baboon.

Tutankhamun Galleries

The treasures of the young New Kingdom pharaoh Tutankhamun, who ruled for only nine years during the 14th century BC (1336–1327 BC), are among the world's most famous antiquities. English archaeologist Howard Carter unearthed the tomb in 1922. Its well-hidden location in the Valley of the Kings, below the much grander but ransacked tomb of Ramses VI, had long prevented its discovery. Many archaeologists now believe that up to 80% of these extraordinary treasures were made for Tutankhamun's predecessors, Akhenaten and Smenkhkare – some still carry the names of the original owners. Perhaps with Tutankhamun's death everything connected with the Amarna Period was simply chucked in with him to be buried away and forgotten.

About 1700 items are spread throughout a series of rooms on the museum's 1st floor, and although the gold shines brightest, sometimes the less grand objects give more insight into the pharaoh's life. Some rooms are being refurbished.

Room 45

Flanking the doorway as you enter are two life-size **statues of Tutankhamun**, found in the tomb antechamber. The statues are made of wood coated in bitumen, their black skin suggesting an identification with Osiris and the rich, black river silt, symbolising fertility and rebirth.

Rooms 35 & 30

The **pharaoh's lion throne** (No 179) is one of the museum's highlights. Covered with sheet

KING TUT GOES TO THE LAB

Though we have much concrete evidence of the pharaoh Tutankhamun, in the form of his tomb contents, the boy king still remains elusive in some ways. How did he die? Who were his parents? Who was his wife? Advances in DNA analysis finally inspired a test of Tut and other mummies thought to be his relatives, and the results were revealed in 2010.

The DNA tests confirmed the predominant theory that Tut's grandparents were Amenhotep III and Queen Tiye. This in turn showed that Tut's father was almost certainly the 'heretic' pharaoh Akhenaten. Finally, the team was able to confirm that another unidentified mummy was Tut's mother – as well as Akhenaten's sister.

The researchers also looked for congenital disease markers. Had Tut and his forebears suffered from an ailment that caused the distorted face shape and androgynous look depicted so famously in Akhenaten's portraiture? In fact, the DNA showed no such abnormality – so Akhenaten's odd appearance may have been just a stylistic choice.

But Tutankhamun was likely affected by inbreeding all the same. Two mummified foetuses buried with him are almost certainly his unborn daughters. And a separate theory posits that his wife was Ankhesamun, his half-sister. This all suggests the foetuses were too deformed to live.

Finally, while preparing Tutankhamun's mummy for the DNA analysis, a CT scan revealed a club foot and necrosis in one toe – which accounts for the numerous canes found in his tomb, despite his death at age 19. The samples also tested positive for parasites associated with malaria, which may have killed him.

So not every mystery is yet solved – but researchers are still at work on other mummies, which may untangle more of Tutankhamun's complex family history.

gold and inlaid with lapis, cornelian and other semiprecious stones, the wooden throne is supported by lion legs. The colourful tableau on the chair back depicts Ankhesenamun applying perfume to her husband, under the rays of the sun (Aten), the worship of which was a hangover from the Amarna period. Evidence of remodelling of the figures suggests that this was actually the throne of Akhenaten, Tutankhamun's father and predecessor. The royals' robes are modelled in beaten silver, their hair of glass paste.

Opposite the throne, on the east wall, **Tutankhamun's wig box** is made of dark wood, with strips of blue and orange inlay. The mushroom-shaped wooden support inside once held the pharaoh's short curly wig.

Many **golden statues** were placed in the tomb to help the pharaoh on his journey in the afterlife, including a series of 28 gilt-wood protective deities and 413 shabti, attendants who would serve the pharaoh in the afterlife. Only a few of them are displayed here.

Room 20

This room contains exquisite **alabaster jars** and **vessels** carved into the shape of boats and animals. Some critters have lifelike pink tongues sticking out – as if the artist just wanted to show he could render such a thing in stone.

Rooms 10 & 9

The eastern end of this gallery is filled with the pharaoh's three elaborate **funerary couches**, one supported by the cow-goddess Mehetweret, one by two figures of the goddess Ammit, 'the devourer', who ate the hearts of the damned, and the third by the lioness god Mehet. The huge **bouquets** of persea and olive leaves in Room 10, near the top of the stairs, were originally propped up beside the two black-and-gold guardian statues in Room 45. A cross-section plan on the wall next to the stairs shows how all the furniture was arranged in the tomb.

At the west end of Room 9, an alabaster chest contains four **Canopic jars**, the stoppers of which are in the form of Tutankhamun's head. Inside these jars, four miniature gold coffins (now in Room 3) held the pharaoh's internal organs. The chest was placed inside the golden Canopic shrine with the four gilded goddesses: Isis, Neith, Nephthys and Selket, all portrayed with protective outstretched arms.

Most people walk right past Tutankhamun's amazing **wardrobe**, laid out along the south wall. The pharaoh was buried with a range of sumptuous tunics covered in gold discs and beading, ritual robes of 'fake fur', a large supply of neatly folded underwear and split-toe socks to be worn with the 47 pairs of flip-flop–type sandals. From these and other objects, the Tutankhamun Textile Project has worked out that the pharaoh's vital statistics were: chest 79cm (31in), waist 74cm (29in) and hips 109cm (43in).

Rooms 8 & 7

These galleries just barely accommodate four massive **gilded wooden shrines**. These fitted one inside the other, like a set of Russian dolls, encasing at their centre the sarcophagi of the boy pharaoh.

Room 3

Everybody wants to see this room as it contains the pharaoh's golden sarcophagus and jewels; at peak times, prepare to queue. Tutankhamun's astonishing **death mask** has become an Egyptian icon. Made of solid gold and weighing 11kg, it covered the head of the mummy, and lay inside a series of three sarcophagi. The mask is an idealised portrait of the young pharaoh; the eyes are fashioned from obsidian and quartz, while the outlines of the eyes and the eyebrows are delineated with lapis lazuli. The mask made international headlines in 2015 when its beard was knocked off during work on the exhibit case and was simply glued back on. Experts were eventually called in to fix the botched job and have restored it to its original finery.

No less wondrous are the two **golden sarcophagi**, the inner two of the burial. The outermost coffin, along with the pharaoh's mummy, remains in his tomb in the Valley of the Kings. The smallest coffin is, like the mask, cast in solid gold and inlaid in the same fashion. It weighs 110kg. The slightly larger coffin is made of gilded wood.

Room 4 – Ancient Egyptian Jewellery

Even after Tutankhamun's treasures, this stunning collection of **royal jewellery** takes the breath away. The collection covers the period from early dynasties to the Romans and includes belts, inlaid beadwork, necklaces, semiprecious stones and bracelets. Among the most beautiful is a piece from the Pyramid of Al Lahun: the diadem of Queen Sit-Hathor-Yunet, a golden headband with a rearing cobra inset with semiprecious stones. Also of note is Pharaoh Ahmose's gold dagger and Seti II's considerable gold earrings.

Room 2 – Royal Tombs of Tanis

This glittering collection of gold- and silver-encrusted objects came from six intact 21st- and 22nd-dynasty tombs unearthed at the Delta site of Tanis by the French in 1939. The tombs rivalled Tutankhamun's in riches, but news of the find was overshadowed by the outbreak of WWII. The gold death mask of Psusennes I (1039–991 BC), with thick black eyeliner, is shown alongside his silver inner coffin and another silver coffin with the head of a falcon belonging to the pharaoh Shoshenq II (c 890 BC).

Room 14 – Graeco-Roman Mummy Portraits

This room contains a small sample of the stunning portraits found on Graeco-Roman mummies, popularly known as the Fayoum Portraits. Painted on wooden panels, often during the subject's life, and placed over the mummies' embalmed faces, these portraits express the personalities of their subjects better than the stylised elegance of most other ancient Egyptian art, and are recognised as the link between ancient art and the Western portrait tradition.

Room 34 – Pharaonic Technology

Interesting for gadget buffs, this room contains a great number of everyday objects that helped support ancient Egypt's great leap out of prehistory. Some, such as the hand tools for farming, are still in use in parts of Egypt today, and others – needles and thread, combs, dice – look remarkably like our own. Pharaonic boomerangs were apparently used for hunting birds.

Room 43 – Yuya & Thuyu Tomb

Before Tutankhamun's tomb was uncovered, the tomb of Yuya and Thuyu (the parents of Queen Tiye, and Tutankhamun's great-grandparents) had yielded the most spectacular find in Egyptian archaeology. Found virtually intact in the Valley of the Kings in 1905, the tomb contained a vast number of treasures, including five ornate sarcophagi and the remarkably well-preserved mummies of the two commoners who became royal in-laws. Among many other items on display is the fabulous gilded and bead-trimmed death mask of Thuyu, at the front of the room.

Room 53 – Animal Mummies

Animal cults grew in strength throughout ancient Egypt, as the mummified cats, dogs, crocodiles, birds, monkeys and jackals in Room 53 suggest. Tucked in a dim, dusty wing of the museum, their rigid forms are a bit creepier than their human counterparts. Some edible beasts became 'victual mummies', preserved as food and 'browned' with resin, to offer the pharaoh an eternal picnic.

Room 37 – Model Armies

Discovered in the Asyut tomb of governor Mesheti and dating from about 2000 BC (11th dynasty), these are two sets of 40 wooden warriors marching in phalanxes. The darker soldiers (No 72) are Nubian archers from the south of the kingdom, each wearing brightly coloured kilts of varying design, while the lighter-skinned soldiers (No 73) are Egyptian pikemen.

Rooms 32 & 27 – Middle Kingdom Models

These lifelike models were mostly found in the tomb of Meketre, an 11th-dynasty chancellor in Thebes, and, like some of the best Egyptian tomb paintings, they provide a fascinating portrait of daily life almost 4000 years ago. They include finely modelled servants (especially in Room 32), fishing boats, kitchens, and carpentry and weaving workshops. In Room 27, a model of Meketre's house includes fig trees in the garden, and a 1.5m-wide scene shows Meketre sitting with his sons, four scribes and others, counting cattle.

Cairo Outskirts & the Delta

Best Places for History

→ Serapeum (p148)

→ Imhotep Museum (p144)

→ Bent Pyramid (p149)

→ Pyramid of Meidum (p155)

→ Tanis (p161)

Best Sights off the Beaten Track

→ Medinat Madi (p154)

→ Wadi Rayyan (p153)

→ Karanis (p153)

→ Birqash Camel Market (p159)

Why Go?

If you want to dig a little deeper into Egyptian culture and history, the area surrounding the capital is home to several intriguing and important sites rarely included on typical Egypt itineraries. Although few can honestly be put in the 'must-see' category – except of course for the majestic ancient site of Saqqara, which lies on the city's southern edge – those with time up their sleeve will enjoy delving into this lesser-seen region.

The Coptic monasteries of Wadi Natrun have roots 17 centuries deep, while a morning at Birqash camel market provides plenty of not-for-the-squeamish, chaotic action. Wadi Al Hittan's prehistoric whale skeletons are one of the most important evolutionary sites in the world, while you'll have the rest of this region's scattered slumping ruins and lonely fallen colossi all to yourself.

Every destination here can be visited as an easy day trip or a leisurely overnight excursion from Cairo.

When to Go
Medinat al Fayoum

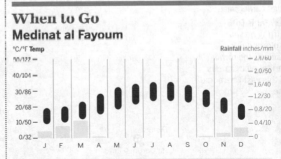

Dec–Feb Cooler weather; best time for day-tripping to this region's shadeless ancient sites.

Jun–Aug Paralysing summer heat. Take a slow pace and plenty of water if exploring here.

Oct The *moulid* (saint's festival) of Al Sayyed Badawi in Tanta draws a million Egyptians.

Cairo Outskirts & the Delta Highlights

1 Saqqara (p143) Taking a spin back in time within this ancient Old Kingdom necropolis of pyramids and intricately decorated tombs.

2 Dahshur (p149) Heading down the steep staircase, deep into the heart of the Red Pyramid.

3 Wadi Al Hittan (p154) Delving into a history far older than the pharaohs amid the whale fossils scattered across the orange-hued desert sands.

4 Deir Abu Makar (p158) Furthering your understanding of Egypt's rich monastic traditions with a monk-led tour of the churches, monk cells and fortress of this monastery.

5 Birqash Camel Market (p159) Diving into the stinky pandemonium of this huge camel sale.

6 Tanis (p161) Putting on your explorer hat to discover the tombs and toppled statues of this vast Pharaonic site.

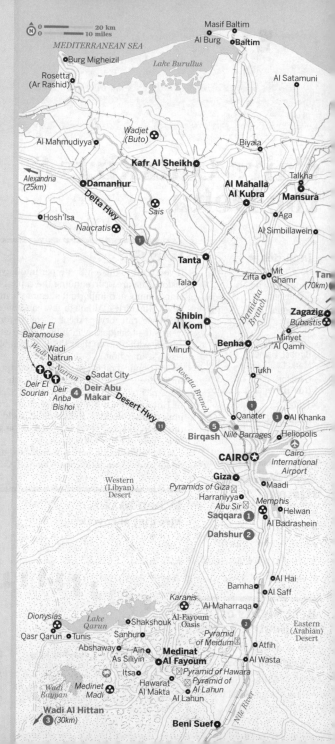

DESERT ENVIRONS

Saqqara, Memphis & Dahshur

Although most tourists associate Egypt with the Pyramids of Giza, there are known to be at least 118 ancient pyramids scattered around the country, with more being discovered every few years or so. The majority of these monuments are spread out along the desert between the Giza Plateau and the semi-oasis of Al Fayoum. They include the must-see Step Pyramid of Zoser at Saqqara, and the Red Pyramid and Bent Pyramid of Dahshur. These three pyramids represent the formative steps of architecture that reached fruition in the Great Pyramid of Khufu (Cheops).

History

The story of these pyramids begins with the ancient city of Memphis, which barely survives today. Around 3100 BC, the legendary pharaoh Narmer (Menes) unified the two lands of Upper and Lower Egypt and founded Memphis, symbolically on the spot where the Nile Delta met the valley. For most of the Pharaonic period, Memphis was the capital of Egypt, though the seat of power was later moved to Thebes (now Luxor) during the era of the New Kingdom.

Originally known as Ineb-hedj, meaning 'white walls', the contemporary name of Memphis derives from Men-nefer, meaning 'established and beautiful'. Indeed, the city was filled with palaces, gardens and temples, making it one of the greatest cities of the ancient world. In the 5th century BC, long after its period of power, Greek historian and traveller Herodotus still described Memphis as 'a prosperous city and cosmopolitan centre'. Even after Thebes became the capital during the New Kingdom, Memphis remained Egypt's second city, and prospered until it was finally abandoned during the first Arab invasions in the 7th century AD.

Although the city was once an area replete with royal pyramids, private tombs and the necropolises of sacred animals, centuries of builders quarrying for stone, annual floods of the Nile and greed-stricken antiquity hunters succeeded where even the mighty Persians failed: the city of Memphis itself has almost completely vanished.

The foundations have long since been ploughed under, and even the enormous temple of the creator god, Ptah, is little more than a few sparse ruins frequently waterlogged due to the high water table. Today, at the village of Mit Rahina, there are few clues as to Memphis' former grandeur and importance and, sadly, it's difficult to imagine that any sort of settlement once stood here. The only solid traces of Memphis remain the funerary complexes – the pyramids – that lie around the fringes.

◉ Sights

◉ Saqqara

★ Saqqara   ARCHAEOLOGICAL SITE
(adult/student LE120/60, parking LE2; ⊘8am-4pm, to 3pm during Ramadan) Covering a 7km stretch of the Western Desert, Saqqara, the huge cemetery of ancient Memphis, was an active burial ground for more than 3500 years and is Egypt's largest archaeological site. The necropolis is situated high above the Nile Valley's cultivation area, and is the final resting place for deceased pharaohs and their families, administrators, generals and sacred animals. The name Saqqara is most likely derived from Sokar, the Memphite god of the dead.

Old Kingdom pharaohs were buried within Saqqara's 11 major pyramids, while their subjects were buried in the hundreds of smaller tombs. Most of Saqqara, except for the Step Pyramid, was buried in sand until the mid-19th century, when the great French Egyptologist Auguste Mariette uncovered the Serapeum (p148). Since then, it has been a gradual process of rediscovery: the Step Pyramid's massive funerary complex was not exposed until 1924, and it is in a constant state of restoration. French architect Jean-Philippe Lauer, who began work here in 1926, was involved in the project for an incredible 75 years until his death in 2001. More recently, there has been a string of new discoveries, including a whole slew of mummies and even a new pyramid.

If you keep up a good pace, you can see the high points of Saqqara in about half a day. Start with a quick visit to the Imhotep Museum (p144), to get the lay of the land. Head for Zoser's funerary complex, entering through the hypostyle hall, and gaze on the Step Pyramid (p144), the world's oldest pyramid. Walk south towards the Causeway of Unas then drive to the Pyramid of Teti

LOCAL KNOWLEDGE

VISITING THE 'OTHER PYRAMIDS'

After the Pyramids of Giza, a trip to Saqqara and the surrounding sites is the most popular day outing from Cairo, and you should have no trouble arranging a tour through your accommodation. For more freedom, simply hire a taxi for the day.

Just getting out of the city can be half the battle, so ideally go on a Friday or Saturday, when the traffic is lighter. In any case, get a very early start. In winter, when daytime temperatures are manageable, visit Dahshur first, as it's the furthest away (about an hour in light traffic). Then you reach Saqqara at midday, when many of the tour buses have moved on. But if the day is at all hot, start with Saqqara to avoid the peak heat, and pace yourself.

Pack a picnic lunch (takeaway sandwiches, for instance), as there are no real places to eat.

(p148) to see some of the famous Pyramid Texts inside. Afterwards, pop into the nearby Tomb of Kagemni (p148) before ending with the most wonderful tomb of all, the Mastaba of Ti (p148), with its fascinating reliefs of daily life.

★ Imhotep Museum   MUSEUM

In the complex at the entrance (p151) to the Saqqara site is this beautiful collection of some of the best finds from Saqqara, and one of the finest small museums in Egypt. It is framed as a tribute to the architect Imhotep, who served Pharaoh Zoser and is credited with creating ancient Egypt's first comprehensive vision of stone architecture (he also happens to be considered the world's first physician). His solid wood coffin is on display in one room.

There's a good installation of the turquoise-green faience tiles from inside Zoser's pyramid and the striking carvings of starving people, complete with bony ribs and sagging breasts, found on the causeway of Unas. You'll also see some beautifully realistic portrait heads and statues, and a mummy (Merrenre I) with his toes and head exposed – the oldest complete royal mummy, from 2292 BC.

As an interesting counterpoint to all the ancient stuff, one room is a recreation of the library of Jean-Philippe Lauer, who spent most of his life excavating Saqqara.

Step Pyramid of Zoser   MONUMENT

In the year 2650 BC, Pharaoh Zoser (2667–2648 BC) asked his chief architect, Imhotep (later deified), to build him a Step Pyramid. This is the world's earliest stone monument, and its significance cannot be overstated. The Step Pyramid is 60m high and is surrounded by a vast funerary complex, enclosed by a 1645m-long panelled limestone wall. Part of the enclosure wall survives today, and a section near the entrance was restored to its original 10m height.

Previously, temples were made of perishable materials, while royal tombs were usually underground rooms topped with a mudbrick mastaba (a structure in the shape of a bench). However, Imhotep developed the mastaba into a pyramid and built it in hewn stone. From this flowed Egypt's later architectural achievements.

The pyramid was transformed from mastaba through six stages of construction, the builders gaining confidence in their use of the new medium and mastering techniques required to move, place and secure the huge blocks. This first pyramid rose in six steps to a height of 60m, and was encased in fine white limestone.

You enter the complex at the southeastern corner via a colonnaded corridor and a broad **hypostyle hall**. The 40 pillars in the corridor are 'bundle columns', ribbed to resemble a bundle of palm or papyrus stems. The walls have been restored, but the protective ceiling is modern concrete. After the entrance, you pass through a large, false, half-open ka (attendant spirit) door – note the stone 'hinge' near the bottom. There were 14 such doors in the complex, in previous eras made of wood but here carved for the first time from stone and painted to resemble wood. They allowed the pharaoh's ka to come and go at will.

The hypostyle hall leads into the **Great South Court**, a huge open area flanking the south side of the pyramid, with a section of wall featuring a frieze of cobras (the rest are in the Imhotep Museum). The cobra (uraeus) represented the goddess Wadjet, a fire-spitting agent of destruction and protector of the pharaoh. It was a symbol of Egyptian royalty, and a rearing cobra always appeared on the brow of a pharaoh's headdress or crown.

Near the base of the pyramid is an altar, and in the centre of the court are two stone D-shaped boundary markers, which delineated the ritual race the pharaoh had to run, a literal demonstration of his fitness to rule. The race was part of the Jubilee Festival (Heb-Sed), which usually occurred after 30 years' reign and showed the pharaoh's symbolic rejuvenation and the recognition of his supremacy by officials from all over Egypt. The construction of the Heb-Sed within Zoser's funerary complex was therefore intended to perpetuate his revitalisation for eternity.

The buildings on the eastern side of the pyramid are also connected with the royal jubilee, and include the **Heb-Sed (Jubilee) Court**. Buildings on the east side of the court represent the shrines of Lower Egypt, and those on the west represent Upper Egypt. All were designed to house the spirits of Egypt's gods when they gathered to witness the rebirth of the pharaoh during his jubilee rituals.

North of the Heb-Sed Court are the **House of the South Court** and **House of the North Court**, representing the two main shrines of Upper and Lower Egypt, and symbolising the unity of the country. The heraldic plants of the two regions were chosen to decorate the column capitals: papyrus for the north and lotus for the south.

The House of the South also features one of the earliest examples of tourist graffiti. In the 47th year of Ramses II's reign, nearly 1500 years after Zoser's death, Hadnakhte, a treasury scribe, recorded his admiration for Zoser while 'on a pleasure trip west of Memphis' in about 1232 BC. His hieratic script, written in black ink, is preserved behind perspex just inside the building's entrance.

A stone structure right in front of the pyramid, the *serdab* (a small room containing a statue of the deceased to which offerings were presented) contains a slightly tilted wooden box with two holes drilled into its north face. Look through these and you'll have the eerie experience of coming face to face with Zoser himself. Inside is a lifelike statue of the long-dead pharaoh, gazing stonily out towards the stars. However, this is only a copy – the original is in Cairo's Egyptian Museum.

The original entrance to the Step Pyramid is directly behind the *serdab*, and leads down to a maze of subterranean tunnels and chambers quarried for almost 6km through the rock. The pharaoh's burial chamber is vaulted in granite, and others are decorated with reliefs of the jubilee race and feature some exquisite blue faience tile decoration. Although the interior of the pyramid is unsafe and closed to the public, part of the

North Saqqara

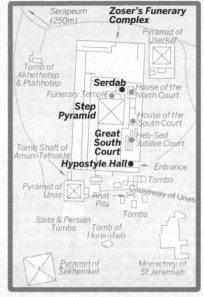

blue-tiled decoration can be seen in the Imhotep Museum at the site entrance.

Pyramid of Userkaf   MONUMENT

Northeast of the Step Pyramid is the Pyramid of Userkaf, the first pharaoh of the 5th dynasty (closed to the public for safety reasons). Although the removal of its limestone casing has left it a mound of rubble, it once rose to a height of 49m. Furthermore, its funerary temple was once decorated with the most exquisite naturalistic relief carvings, judging from one of the few remaining fragments (now in the Egyptian Museum) showing birds by the river.

Pyramid of Unas   MONUMENT

To the southwest of Zoser's funerary complex is the Pyramid of Unas, last pharaoh of the 5th dynasty (2375–2345 BC). Built only 300 years after the inspired Step Pyramid, this unassuming pile of loose blocks once stood 43m high, and its interior marked the beginning of a significant development in funerary practices. For the first time, the royal burial chamber was decorated, its ceiling adorned with stars and its white alabaster-lined walls inscribed with beautiful blue hieroglyphs.

The aforementioned hieroglyphs are some of the earliest examples of the funerary

> **ℹ SAQQARA PRACTICALITIES**
>
> ➡ The main monuments are in an area around the Step Pyramid known as North Saqqara.
>
> ➡ About 1km south of the Step Pyramid is a group of monuments known as South Saqqara, with no official entry fee or opening hours.
>
> ➡ The only toilets at the site are at the main entrance to North Saqqara.
>
> ➡ Check at the ticket office to see which monuments are open – this constantly changes.

inscriptions that are now known as the **Pyramid Texts** (later compiled into the Egyptian Book of the Dead). Covering the walls of a number of the pyramids at Saqqara, the hieroglyphs are 'spells' to protect the soul of the deceased. Of the 283 separate phrases in Unas' tomb, most are prayers and hymns and lists of items, such as food and clothing the pharaoh would require in the afterlife.

The 750m-long **causeway** running from the east side of Unas' pyramid to his valley temple (now marked by little more than a couple of stone columns at the side of the road leading up to the site) was originally roofed and decorated with a great range of painted relief scenes, including a startling image of people starving, thought to be due to a famine during Unas' reign. A portion of the relief is on display in the Imhotep Museum.

The two 45m-long **boat pits** of Unas lie immediately south of the causeway, while on either side of the causeway are numerous **tombs** – more than 200 have been excavated. Of the several better-preserved examples usually open to visitors are the tombs of one of Unas' queens, Nebet, and that of Princess Idut, who was possibly his daughter. There are also several brightly painted tombs of prominent 5th- and 6th-dynasty officials. These include the Tomb of Mehu, the royal vizier (minister), and the Tomb of Nefer, the supervisor of singers.

Several beautiful tombs have been cleared in the area east of the Pyramid of Unas. Although not quite as famous as the tombs north of the Step Pyramid, this set includes a number of interesting Pharaonic attendants. These include the joint **Tomb of Niankhkhnum and Khnumhotep**, overseers of the royal manicurists to Pharaoh Nyuserra; the **Tomb of Neferherenptah**, the overseer

of the royal hairdressers; and the **Tomb of Irukaptah**, overseer of the royal butchers.

Around the sides of the Pyramid of Unas are several **large shaft tombs** built much later, in the Saite era (664–525 BC) and the Persian period (525–404 BC). These are some of the deepest tombs in Egypt, although as with just about everywhere else in the country, precautions against grave robbers failed. However, the sheer size of the tombs and the great stone sarcophagi within, combined with their sophisticated decoration, demonstrate that the technical achievements of the later part of ancient Egyptian history were equal to those of earlier times.

Monastery of St Jeremiah RUINS
Uphill from the causeway of Unas, southeast of the boat pits, are the half-buried remains of this Coptic monastery, which dates from the 5th century AD. Unfortunately, little is left of the structure, which was ransacked by invading Arabs in 950. More recently, the wall paintings and carvings were moved to the Coptic Museum (p66) in Cairo.

Pyramid of Sekhemkhet MONUMENT
Closed to the public because of its dangerous condition, the unfinished pyramid of Zoser's successor Sekhemkhet (2648–2640 BC) is a short distance west of the ruined Monastery St Jeremiah. The project was abandoned for unknown reasons when the great limestone enclosure wall was only 3m high, despite the fact that the architects had already constructed the underground chambers in the rock beneath the pyramid as well as the deep shaft of the south tomb.

Tomb of Horemheb TOMB
Originally designated as the final resting place of General Horemheb, this tomb became irrelevant in 1323 BC when its intended occupant seized power from Pharaoh Ay. Soon afterwards, Pharaoh Horemheb (1323–1295 BC) commissioned the building of a new tomb in the Valley of the Kings (p200). The tomb at Saqqara was never put to use, but it yielded a number of exquisite reliefs that are displayed around the world.

Tomb of Akhethotep & Ptahhotep TOMB
This joint mastaba for Akhethotep and his son Ptahhotep has two burial chambers, two chapels and a pillared hall. The painted reliefs in Ptahhotep's section of the tomb are particularly beautiful, and portray a wide range of animals, from lions to hedgehogs to the domesticated cattle and fowl that were brought

The Pyramids of Abu Sir & Saqqara

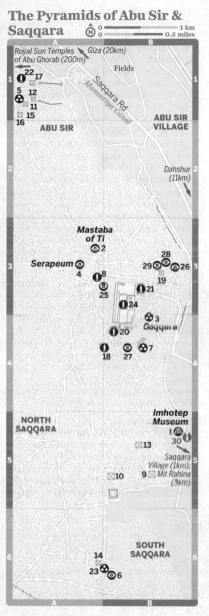

as offerings to the deceased. Ptahhotep himself is portrayed resplendent in a panther-skin robe inhaling perfume from a jar.

Akhethotep and his son Ptahhotep were senior royal officials during the reigns of Djedkare (2414–2375 BC) and Unas at the end of the 5th dynasty. Akhethotep served as vizier, judge and supervisor of pyramid cities and supervisor of priests, though his titles were eventually inherited by Ptahhotep, along with his tomb.

Philosophers' Circle   MONUMENT
This quite sad-looking group of Greek statues, the remnant of a collection of philosophers and poets set up as a wayside shrine by Ptolemy I (323–283 BC) as part of his patronage of learning, is arranged in a semi circle and sheltered by a spectacularly ugly concrete shelter. From left to right are Plato, Heraclitus, Thales, Protagoras, Homer, Hesiod, Demetrius of Phalerum and Pindar.

★ Serapeum   TOMB

The Serapeum, dedicated to the sacred Apis bull, is one of the highlights of visiting Saqqara. The first Apis burial took place in the reign of Amenhotep III (1390–1352 BC), and the practice continued until 30 BC. The enormous granite and limestone coffins weighed up to 80 tonnes each. When it died, the bull was mummified at Memphis, then carried in a stately procession to the Serapeum's subterranean galleries and placed in a huge stone sarcophagus.

The Apis, it was believed, was an incarnation of Ptah, the god of Memphis, and was the calf of a cow struck by lightning from heaven. The Apis bulls were by far the most important of the cult animals entombed at Saqqara. Once divinely impregnated, the cow could never again give birth, and her calf was kept in the Temple of Ptah at Memphis and worshipped as a god. The Apis was always portrayed as black, with a distinctive white diamond on its forehead, the image of a vulture on its back and a scarab-shaped mark on its tongue.

Until the mid-19th century, the existence of the sacred Apis tombs was known only from classical references. In 1851, Auguste Mariette, after finding a half-buried sphinx at Saqqara, and using the description given by the Greek historian Strabo in 24 BC, uncovered the avenue leading to the Serapeum. However, only one Apis sarcophagus was found intact.

★ Mastaba of Ti   TOMB

The Mastaba of Ti was discovered by Auguste Mariette in 1865. This grand and detailed private tomb is not only Old Kingdom art at its best but also one of our main sources of knowledge about life in Old Kingdom Egypt. Its owner, Ti, was overseer of the Abu Sir pyramids and sun temples (among other things) during the 5th dynasty. In fact, the superb quality of his tomb is in keeping with his nickname, Ti the Rich.

A life-size statue of the deceased stands in the tomb's offering hall (the original is in Cairo's Egyptian Museum). Ti's wife, Neferhetpes, was priestess and 'royal acquaintance'. Together with their two sons, Demedj (overseer of the duck pond) and Ti (inspector of royal manicurists), the couple appears throughout the tomb alongside detailed scenes of daily life. As men and women are seen working on the land, preparing food, fishing, building boats, dancing, trading and avoiding crocodiles, their images are accompanied by chattering hieroglyphic dialogue, all no doubt familiar to Ti during his career as a royal overseer: 'Hurry up, the herdsman's coming', 'Don't make so much noise!', 'Pay up – it's cheap!'.

Pyramid of Teti   MONUMENT

The Pyramid of Teti (2345–2323 BC), the first pharaoh of the 6th dynasty, was built in step form and cased in limestone, but today only a modest mound remains. In the interior you can see portions of the hieroglyphic spells of the Pyramid Texts up close, as well as a shower of stars. Within the intact burial chamber, Teti's basalt sarcophagus is well preserved, and represents the first example of a sarcophagus with inscriptions.

Tomb of Kagemni   TOMB

The plump-looking chief justice under Teti, Kagemni appears in his own mastaba tomb as though he enjoyed the riches of the land, if the splendid and lively friezes inside are anything to go by. Look for catfish and eels thriving in the Nile, cows being milked, men

---

STEP PYRAMID: AT RISK OF COLLAPSE

In 2006, the Step Pyramid was under threat of 'imminent' collapse as a result of a 1992 earthquake. A British team deployed giant 'air-bags' to support the ceiling of the pyramid as the government initiated plans for more permanent repairs. After the 2011 revolution and continuing economic crisis, the restoration stopped.

In 2014, the works were handed to a construction company with no experience at all in restoring archaeological sights. The first thing they did was to build a new wall around the pyramid as if it were a modern construction, completely against international standards of restoration, and added further pressure to the pyramid itself. Activists of the Non-Stop Robberies Movement have demanded the government employ an adequate construction company, to stop the further deterioration of the site. However, the government's answer was that the worries were unfounded, and nothing more than rumours spread by the deposed Muslim Brotherhood. The future for the oldest pyramid in the world is sadly very unsure.

feeding puppies, even dragonflies and other insects. Particularly vivid are the scenes of a crocodile and hippo fighting, and a row of vigorous dancers and acrobats.

Next door, the tomb of **Mereruka** (adult/student LE80/40) contains similarly precise scenes, while the tomb of **Ankhmahor** is closed because of deteriorating conditions.

◉ South Saqqara

South Saqqara   ARCHAEOLOGICAL SITE

South Saqqara is home to several Old Kingdom tombs, pyramids and mounds of rubble, interesting to the more dedicated pyramid fans.

The most remote site in South Saqqara is the unusual funerary complex called the **Mastaba of Al Faraun**, also called the Pharaoh's Bench. It belongs to the last 4th-dynasty pharaoh, the short-lived Shepseskaf (2503–2498 BC). Shepseskaf was the son of Menkaure (builder of Giza's third great pyramid), though he failed to emulate the glory of his father. Occupying an enclosure once covering 700 sq metres, Shepseskaf's rectangular tomb was built of limestone blocks, and originally covered by a further layer of fine, white limestone and a lower layer of red granite. Inside the tomb, a 21m-long corridor slopes down to storage rooms and a vaulted burial chamber.

Working your way back north, you pass the **Pyramid of Pepi II** (2278–2184 BC). The pharaoh's 94-year reign at the end of the 6th dynasty was probably the longest in Egyptian history. Despite Pepi's longevity, his 52m-high pyramid was of the same modest proportions as those of his predecessor, Pepi I. The exterior is little more than a mound of rubble, but the interior is decorated with more passages from the Pyramid Texts.

South Saqqara is also home to the pyramids of **Djedkare**, **Merenre** and **Pepi I**. Known as the 'Pyramid of the Sentinel', the 25m-high Djedkare pyramid contains the remains of the last ruler of the 5th dynasty, and can be penetrated from the north side. The pyramids of Merenre and Pepi I are little more than slowly collapsing piles of rock, though the latter is significant as 'Memphis' appears in one of its names.

◉ Dahshur

Dahshur   ARCHAEOLOGICAL SITE

(adult/student LE60/30, parking LE2; ☉8am-4pm, to 3pm during Ramadan) About 10km south of Saqqara lies this impressive 3.5km-long field of 4th- and 12th-dynasty pyramids.

Although there were originally 11 pyramids here, only the two Old Kingdom ones remain intact. Pharaoh Sneferu (2613–2589 BC), father of Khufu, built Egypt's first true pyramid here, the Red Pyramid, as well as an earlier version, the Bent Pyramid. These two striking pyramids are the same height, and together are also the third-largest pyramids in Egypt after the two largest at Giza.

The pyramids here are just as impressive as their counterparts at Giza, but the site is much more peaceful (no camel touts in sight). Before founding the necropolis at Dahshur, Sneferu also began the Pyramid of Meidum in Al Fayoum. The Red Pyramid can be entered. Tickets are purchased at a small gatehouse on the edge of the site; there are no other facilities.

★ Red Pyramid   MONUMENT

(North Pyramid) The world's oldest true pyramid, the Red Pyramid probably derives its name from the red tones of its weathered limestone, after the better-quality white limestone casing was removed. The architects had learned from their experiences building the rather deformed Bent Pyramid, so carried on where they had left off, building the Red Pyramid at the same 43-degree angle as the Bent Pyramid's more gently inclining upper section. Penetrating its somewhat dank interior is a true Indiana Jones experience.

The entrance – via 125 extremely steep stone steps up, up, up, then down again, plus a 63m-long passage – takes you down to two antechambers with stunning 12m-high corbelled ceilings and a 15m-high corbelled burial chamber in which fragmentary human remains, possibly of Sneferu himself, were found. Also look for charcoal graffiti, left by British explorers in the early 19th century. Take your ticket with you up to the entrance, along with a little baksheesh ('tip') for the bored attendant.

Bent Pyramid   MONUMENT

Trying to create a true smooth-sided pyramid, Sneferu's architects began with the same steep angle and inward-leaning courses of stone they used to create step pyramids. When this began to show signs of stress and instability around halfway up its eventual 105m height, they had to reduce the angle from 54 degrees to 43 degrees and begin to lay the stones in horizontal layers. This explains why the structure has the unusual shape that gives it its name.

READING THE PHARAONIC SCENES

When visiting temples and tombs, the endless scenes of pharaohs – standing sideways, presenting a never-ending line of gods with the same old offerings – can start to get a bit much. Look closer, however, and these scenes can reveal a few surprises.

As the little figures on the wall strike their eternal poses, a keen eye can find anything from pharaohs ploughing fields to small girls pulling at each other's hair. A whole range of activities that we consider modern can be found among the most ancient scenes, including hairdressing, perfumery, manicures and even massage – the treasury overseer Ptahhotep certainly enjoyed his comforts. There are similar scenes of pampering elsewhere at Saqqara, with a group of men in the Tomb of Ankhmahor enjoying both manicures and pedicures.

With the title 'overseer of royal hairdressers and wigmakers' commonly held by the highest officials in the land, hairdressing scenes can also be found in the most unexpected places. Not only does Ptahhotep have his wig fitted by his manservants, similar hairdressing scenes can even be found on coffins, as on the limestone sarcophagus of 11th-dynasty Queen Kawit (in Cairo's Egyptian Museum), which shows her wig being deftly styled.

Among its wealth of scenes, the Theban Tomb of Rekhmire, on Luxor's West Bank, shows a banquet at which the female harpist sings, 'Put perfume on the hair of the goddess Maat.' And nearby in the Deir Al Medina tomb of the workman Peshedu, his family tree contains relatives whose hair denotes their seniority: the eldest shown has the whitest hair.

As in many representations of ancient Egyptians, black eye make-up is worn by both male and female, adult and child. As well as its aesthetic value, it was also used as a means of reducing the glare of the sun – think ancient sunglasses. Even manual workers wore it: the Deir Al Medina Tomb of Ipy once contained a scene in which men building the royal tombs were having eye paint applied while they worked.

Most of its outer casing is still intact, and inside (closed to visitors) are two burial chambers, the highest of which retains its original ancient scaffolding of great cedar beams to counteract internal instability. There is also a small subsidiary pyramid to the south as well as the remains of a small funerary temple to the east. About halfway towards the cultivated area to the east are the ruins of Sneferu's valley temple, which yielded some interesting reliefs.

Black Pyramid   MONUMENT

You can only peer at this structure from the parking area by the Bent Pyramid. The oddly shaped, tower-like pyramid was built by Amenemhat III (1855–1808 BC), but has completely collapsed. The mudbrick remains contain a maze of corridors and rooms designed to deceive tomb robbers. Thieves did manage to penetrate the burial chambers but left behind a number of precious funerary artefacts that were discovered in 1993.

⊙ Memphis

Mit Rahina   MUSEUM

(adult/student LE60/30, parking LE5; ⊘ 8am-4pm, to 3pm during Ramadan) The only remaining evidence of Memphis is this noteworthy open-air museum, built around a magnificent fallen colossal limestone **statue of Ramses II**. Its position on its back gives a great opportunity to inspect the carving up close – even the pharaoh's nipples are precise. Its twin is the statue that stood in Midan Ramses in Cairo until 2006 when it was moved to stand guard by the Grand Egyptian Museum construction site.

Other highlights of the museum include an alabaster sphinx of the New Kingdom, two statues of Ramses II that originally adorned Nubian temples, and the huge stone beds on which the sacred Apis bulls were mummified before being placed in the Serapeum at Saqqara.

⊙ Abu Sir

Abu Sir ARCHAEOLOGICAL SITE
(off Saqqara Rd; adult/student LE80/40; ⊘8am-4pm) Surrounded by sand dunes, the pyramids of Abu Sir form the necropolis of the 5th dynasty (2494–2345 BC). Most of the remains are less impressive than those in Giza or Saqqara, but it is bliss to enjoy a moment of peace at the humble ruins, and revel in the serene desolation of the surrounding desert. Of the four pyramid complexes at Abu Sir, Sahure's is the most complete.

There is an official **entrance gatehouse** at the site but no ticket fee. In lieu of this, ad hoc guides lounge out front and will show you around for baksheesh.

Pyramid of Sahure MONUMENT

Sahure (2487–2475 BC) was the first of the 5th-dynasty pharaohs to be buried at Abu Sir. His pyramid, originally 50m high, is now badly damaged. From the entrance you can walk through a 75m-long corridor before crawling 2m on your stomach through Pharaonic dust and spiderwebs to reach the burial chamber. Sahure's funerary temple must have been an impressive temple, with black-basalt-paved floors, red-granite date-palm columns and walls decorated with 10,000 sq m of superbly detailed reliefs.

It was connected by a 235m-long causeway to the valley temple, which was built at the edge of the cultivation and bordered by water. From the pyramid, on a clear day you can see some 10 other pyramids stretching out to the horizon.

Pyramid of Nyuserra MONUMENT

The most dilapidated of the finished pyramids at Abu Sir belonged to Nyuserra (2445–2421 BC). Originally some 50m high, this pyramid has been heavily quarried over the millennia. In fact, Nyuserra reused his father Neferirkare's valley temple, and then redirected the causeway to lead not to his father's pyramid, but to his own.

Pyramid of Neferirkare MONUMENT

Neferirkare (2475–2455 BC) was the third pharaoh of the 5th dynasty and Sahure's father. His burial place originally resembled the Step Pyramid at Saqqara. However, the present-day complex is only the core as the original outer casing has been stripped away, reducing the pyramid from its original planned height of 72m to today's 45m.

In the early 20th century in Neferirkare's funerary temple, archaeologists found the so-called Abu Sir Papyri, an important archive of Old Kingdom documents written in hieratic script, a shorthand form of hieroglyphs. They relate to the cult of the pharaohs buried at the site, recording important details of ritual ceremonies, temple equipment, priests' work rotas and the temple accounts.

South of Neferirkare's pyramid lies the badly ruined **Pyramid of Queen Khentkawes II**, wife of Neferirkare and mother of both Raneferef and Nyuserra. In her nearby funerary temple, Czech archaeologists discovered another set of papyrus documents. In addition, two virtually destroyed pyramids to the south of the queen's pyramid may have belonged to the queens of Nyuserra.

Pyramid of Raneferef MONUMENT

(Pyramid of Neferefre) The Pyramid of Raneferef (2448–2445 BC), who is believed to have reigned for four years before Nyuserra, is unfinished, and was only completed as a mastaba. In the adjoining mudbrick cult building, Czech archaeologists found fragments of statuary, including a superb limestone figurine of Raneferef protected by Horus (now in Cairo's Egyptian Museum) along with papyrus fragments relating to the Abu Sir temple archives.

Royal Sun Temples of Abu Ghorab MONUMENT

Just northwest of the Abu Sir pyramids lies the site of Abu Ghorab, which is home to two temples dedicated to the worship of Ra, the sun god of Heliopolis. Built for Pharaohs Userkaf (2494–2487 BC) and Nyuserra, these temples follow the traditional plan of a valley temple, and contain a causeway and a large stone enclosure. This enclosure contains a large limestone obelisk standing some 37m tall on a 20m-high base.

☞ Tours

For experienced riders, a popular outing is a horse or camel ride from Giza to Saqqara, a trip of about three hours.

At Saqqara, it's also possible to hire a camel, horse or donkey from near the Serapeum to take you on a circuit of the sites for between LE75 and LE100. You'll need to pay more the further into the desert from North Saqqara you go.

ℹ Information

DANGERS & ANNOYANCES

Some of the site guardians in the outer pyramid sites can be overly forceful asking for tips. Abu

WORTH A TRIP

TUNIS VILLAGE

Near the southwest end of Lake Qarun, this tiny village is all about bougainvillea tumbling over high stone walls that hide curvaceous mudbrick villas built in the style of Hassan Fathy, Egypt's most influential modern architect. Tunis has been a getaway for Cairene artists and intellectuals since the 1970s, and it's also well known as a pottery centre with a handful of independent potters' studios found within its squiggle of quiet lanes. It's a peaceful and laid-back place to while away a few days, and a good base for exploring the greater Fayoum area. The village holds an annual festival in early November for pottery and crafts.

Sights

Fayoum Pottery School (☑084-682-0405; ⊙10am-6pm) Established in the 1970s by Swiss artists, Evelyne Porret and Michel Pastore, this school, which trains children and adults in the local potting traditions, is set in a beautiful mudbrick compound. Its architecture – very much in the Egyptian vernacular style – is as attractive as the students' creations from clay, which are on sale here. From the school, ask for directions to the workshop of **Ahmed Abou Zeid**, another noted local potter.

Fayoum Art Center Residency (☑012-2338-2810; www.facebook.com/fayoumartcenter) This project run by painter Mohamed Abla hosts classes and resident artists from around the world in the cooler months of January and February; email him for information on upcoming workshops. For the casual visitor, the onsite **Caricature Museum** holds an interesting collection of Egyptian political cartoons.

Sir can be a particular problem. Some readers have reported that the guides who hang out at the gatehouse sometimes charge hefty fees for tours and don't allow travellers into the precinct without first paying it.

ⓘ Getting There & Away

Because of extremely limited public transport options, this area is typically visited as part of an organised tour, or with a private taxi from Cairo hired for the day (LE350 to LE450, plus parking at each site).

Moreover, the sites of Saqqara and Dahshur are quite vast, and it's an asset to have a car to drive you around them.

For the truly determined, you can reach Saqqara and Mit Rahina by public transport, but only with a great deal of trouble; Dahshur and Abu Sir are not at all accessible this way. Take a microbus or bus down Pyramids Rd in Cairo to Maryutia Canal (under the ring-road flyover), then hop on a microbus bound for Saqqara village; ask to be let off at 'Haram Saqqara'. It's a 1.5km walk to the ticket office (p151), though you may be able to get a tuk-tuk to take you there, and even down the road to Mit Rahina.

Al Fayoum

☑ 084 / POP 3 MILLION

Less than two hours from Cairo, the vast salty Lake Qarun comes into view and the arid monotonous plains are replaced with a lush patchwork of farming plots, sunflowers swaying in the breeze, and tall date palms with water buffalo lounging in the shade beside them.

This large fertile basin, about 70km wide and 60km long, is often referred to as an oasis, though technically it's watered not by springs but by the Nile via hundreds of capillary canals, many dug in ancient times. The area harbours a number of small but important archaeological sites; slumped, stubby remains of pyramids and crumbled remnants of once vast Ptolemaic cities that were major centres of crocodile worship. Fayoum is also the base for adventures out to Wadi Rayyan's desert lakes and to Wadi Al Hittan, where prehistoric whale skeletons sit amid a sweep of rock-outcrop dotted sand.

As a visitor, you'll deal primarily with two towns in the oasis. **Medinat Al Fayoum**, a city of half a million, is built along one of the largest canals and offers the usual Egyptian urban chaos. It's the main transit hub and has all the services you might need, including hotels. The downtown area is along the Bahr Yusuf, the main canal through the oasis. The village of Tunis, an arts colony on the west edge of Al Fayoum, is the more typical place to spend the night – or on the nearby shores of Lake Qarun.

◉ Sights

Karanis
ARCHAEOLOGICAL SITE

(Kom Aushim; adult/student LE60/30; ⊘9am-4pm) The vast, slumping ruins of ancient Karanis lie 25km north of Medinat Al Fayoum, on the edge of the oasis depression, along the road to Cairo. Founded by Ptolemy II's mercenaries in the 3rd century BC, this was once a mudbrick settlement with a population in the thousands. Today, little of the ancient city remains intact aside from half-buried, crumbling walls scattered across the sand, though Karanis is home to two well-preserved **Graeco-Roman temples**.

The larger and more interesting temple was built in the 1st century BC and is dedicated to two local crocodile gods, Pnepheros and Petesouchos. In front of the east entrance is a large square container – essentially a giant swimming pool for the holy crocs. Inside, niches in the wall are where crocodile mummies would've been stowed, and a block-like structure was the 'house' for the gods. The temple is also adorned with inscriptions dating from the reigns of the Roman emperors Nero, Claudius and Vespasian.

It's a trek to the north temple, and there is far less structure here – but you can see an ancient pigeon tower, off to the east, not so different from the ones that dot Al Fayoum today. In the ruined domestic area north of the temple, you'll find a bathtub adorned with frescoes.

The **museum** on-site, next to Lord Cromer's one-time field house, holds an eclectic collection of artefacts from sites around Fayoum that cover the Pharaonic, Graeco-Roman, Coptic and Islamic eras. Just at the start of the ruins area, there's also a small open-air 'museum' of columns and stone statuary remnants rescued from Kiman Faris (ancient Crocodilopolis) which has been consumed by the modern city of Medinat Al Fayoum.

The best way to get here is by taxi as the site sign is only in Arabic and only labelled with its Arabic name 'Kom Aushim'. The driver (and anyone else you ask in Fayoum) is also more likely to know the site by this name.

Lake Qarun
LAKE

Lake Qarun is a popular weekend spot for Cairenes looking to cool down, and the lake edge is dotted with cafes and wedding pavilions. It's not a big swimming spot, but even the sight of an expansive lake on the edge of the desert is refreshing, and you can rent a rowing boat. The lake is now an important bird area where thousands of migratory birds rest during their winter migration pattern south, including large numbers of flamingos.

Before the 12th-dynasty reigns of Sesostris III and his son Amenemhat III, the area that's now known as Al Fayoum was entirely covered by Lake Qarun. In an early effort at land reclamation, both pharaohs dug a series of canals linking Qarun to the Nile, and drained much of the lake.

Over the past few centuries, the lake has regained some of its former grandeur due to the diversion of the Nile to create more agricultural land, and it now stretches for 42km. However, since it presently sits at 45m below sea level, the water has suffered from increasing salinity. Remarkably, the wildlife has adapted, and today the self-proclaimed 'world's most ancient lake' supports a unique ecosystem. Chances are that you'll spot countless varieties of birds here, particularly in autumn, including a large colony of flamingos, grey herons, spoonbills and many duck species.

Qasr Qarun
MONUMENT

(adult/student LE60/30; ⊘8am-4pm) At the western end of Lake Qarun, just east of the village of Qasr Qarun, are the ruins of ancient Dionysias, once the starting point for caravans to the Western Desert oasis of Bahariya. All that remains of the ancient settlement is a Ptolemaic temple, known as Qasr Qarun, built in 4 BC and dedicated to Sobek, the crocodile-headed god of Al Fayoum. There are excellent views from the rooftop.

Wadi Rayyan Protected Area
NATIONAL PARK

(LE40, plus LE5 per vehicle; ⊘9am-5pm) The 'waterfalls' in the Wadi Rayyan Protected Area are a major attraction for weekend picnickers from Cairo. The waterfalls, where one lake drains into another, are about 20km away from the reserve's gate, on the left side of the road. Along the lakefront is a visitors centre, toilets and some cafes. From here, big wooden rowboats take, for about LE50 to LE75, a one-hour trip out to the middle of the lake and then back up close to the falls.

The wider Wadi Rayyan area is rich in wildlife, including white gazelles, Egyptian gazelles, sand foxes and fennec foxes, as well as rare species of resident birds, migrant birds and various kinds of eagles and falcons. It's well worth exploring this fascinating area further. Five kilometres further along the road from the lake turn off is the rocky outcrop of

Medinat Al Fayoum

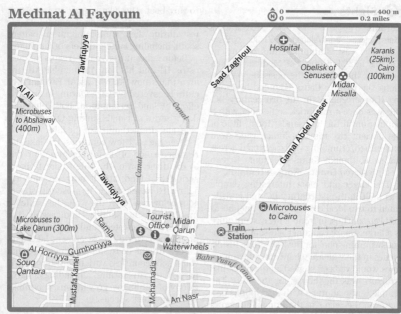

Jabal Al Modawara, fairly easy to climb and a great place to spot eagles or falcons.

In the 1960s, Egyptian authorities created three lakes in the Wadi Rayyan depression, southwest of Lake Qarun, to hold excess water from agricultural drainage. This was intended to be the first step in an ambitious land-reclamation project, though not everything went to plan when the water started to become increasingly brackish. On the bright side, these man-made lakes became particularly conducive to large colonies of birds, leading to the entire depression being administered as a national park.

Wadi Al Hittan (officially part of the Wadi Rayyan Protected Area) is reached by taking the signposted turn off just past Jabal Al Modawara. You can camp here for LE15 per night.

★ **Wadi Al Hittan**   NATIONAL PARK
(Valley of the Whales; LE40, plus LE5 per vehicle; ⊙9am-5pm) This Unesco World Heritage Site is home to the earliest prehistoric whale fossils ever discovered. The more than 400 basilosaurus and dorodontus (both rather fierce water predators) skeletons found here are around 40 million years old and show the clear evolution of land-based mammals into sea-going ones, as they have vestigial front and back legs.

The sands are also studded with the remains of manatees and big bony fish – which look very out of place in the vast desert.

From the central site complex a small network of walking tracks leads out to more than a dozen skeleton sites. Although it doesn't sound like much, the desert setting is dramatic and it's a great destination for a day or overnight outing, usually combined with Wadi Rayyan.

The site complex has toilets, a wilderness campground and the excellent **Wadi Al Hittan Fossil & Climate Change Museum** (⊙9am-2pm Sat-Thu) FREE. The circular one-room museum does a good job of explaining the geological history and nature of the area with a series of information boards and fossil displays that surround the crowning exhibit, an 18-metre long skeleton of a Basilosaurus Isis whale. There's also a short documentary on Wadi Al Hittan.

Wadi Al Hittan is reached by an unsealed corrugated desert track that runs off the main Wadi Rayyan road; a 4WD is necessary. From the turn off, it's 37 kilometres to the main site complex.

Medinat Madi   ARCHAEOLOGICAL SITE
(adult/student LE50/25) This ancient city is one of the most isolated in Al Fayoum, but this is part of its appeal, as you're often alone

out in the blowing sand that drifts over the heads of the stone sphinxes. Medinat Madi (Arabic for 'City of the Past') is noted for a well-preserved Middle Kingdom temple, few of which have survived in Egypt. It is dedicated to the crocodile god Sobek and the cobra goddess Renenutet, built by Amenemhat III and Amenemhat IV.

Italian excavations in the early 20th century uncovered an archive of Greek texts, that refer to the city as Narmouthis. They also found a separate crocodile-cult temple where the beasts appear to have been bred in captivity – a cache of eggs was found, along with bodies of the creatures in various stages of development. Often they were sacrificed when still quite young.

Visiting requires a 4WD vehicle, as there is no real track to the site.

Pyramid of Meidum ARCHAEOLOGICAL SITE
(adult/student LE40/20; 8am-4pm) About 30km northeast of Medinat Al Fayoum is the ruin of the first true pyramid attempted by the ancient Egyptians. It began as an eight-stepped structure, with the steps later filled in and an outer casing added to form the first pyramid shell. There were design flaws and, sometime after completion (possibly as late as the last few centuries BC), the pyramid's own weight caused the sides to collapse. Today, only the core stands, though it is still an impressive sight.

Pharaoh Huni (2637–2613 BC) commissioned the pyramid, although it was his son Sneferu who was responsible for the actual building, Sneferu's architects then went on to build the more successful Bent Pyramid and Red Pyramid at Dahshur.

The guard will unlock the entrance of the pyramid, from where steps lead 75m down to the empty burial chamber. Near the pyramid are the large mastaba tombs of some of Sneferu's family and officials, including his son Rahotep and wife Nofret.

The pyramid is hard to reach. The best option is to hire a taxi and visit as part of a larger tour.

Pyramid of Hawara ARCHAEOLOGICAL SITE
(adult/student LE60/30; 8am-4pm) About 8km southeast of Medinat Al Fayoum, on the north side of the canal Bahr Yusuf, the canal that connects Al Fayoum to the Nile, stands the dilapidated second pyramid of Amenemhat III, built at a gentler angle than his first one (the towerlike Black Pyramid at Dahshur). Herodotus described this temple (300m by 250m) as a 3000-room labyrinth that surpassed even the Pyramids of Giza. Strabo claimed it had as many rooms as there were provinces.

Although the Pyramid of Hawara was originally covered with white limestone casing, sadly only the mudbrick core remains today, and even the once-famous temple has been quarried. The interior of the pyramid, now closed to visitors, revealed several technical developments: corridors were blocked using a series of huge stone portcullises; the burial chamber is carved from a single piece of quartzite; and the chamber was sealed by an ingenious device using sand to lower the roof block into place.

Microbuses between Medinat Al Fayoum and Beni Suef pass through the town of Hawarat Al Makta. From here, it is just a short walk to the pyramid. Alternatively, you can visit in a taxi as part of a circuit.

THE FAYOUM PORTRAITS

Al Fayoum may not be famous for much these days, but it was here that caches of what are some of the world's earliest portraits were found. These extraordinarily lifelike representations, known as the Fayoum Portraits, were painted on wooden panels and put over the faces of mummies, or painted directly onto linen shrouds covering the corpses. This fusion of ancient Egyptian and Graeco-Roman funerary practices laid the foundation for the Western tradition of realistic portraiture.

Dating from 30 BC to AD 395, the paintings were executed in a technique involving a heated mixture of pigment and wax. Remarkable for the skill of the anonymous artists who painted them, the realistic and eerily modern-looking faces bridge the centuries. The haunting images are made all the more poignant by their youth (some are only babies) – a reflection of the high infant-mortality rates at the time.

More than a thousand of these portraits have been found, not just in Al Fayoum but throughout Egypt. They now reside in numerous museums around the world, including the Egyptian Museum (p131) in Cairo.

Pyramid of Al Lahun ARCHAEOLOGICAL SITE
(adult/student LE60/30; ⊙8am-4pm) About
10km southeast of Hawara are the ruins of
this mudbrick pyramid, built by Pharaoh Sesostris II (1880–1874 BC). It's not worth a separate trip, but if you're driving by, look out for
its strangely lumpen shape, set on an existing
rock outcropping for extra stature. Ancient
tomb robbers stripped it of all its rock and
treasures, except for the amazing solid-gold
cobra that is now displayed in the jewellery
room of the Egyptian Museum in Cairo.

Tours

Hany Zaki TOURS
(☑010-0166-6979; www.facebook.com/Rahhala
Expeditions) Hani Zaki, founder of Rahha-
la Expeditions, has over 30 years' experience in the Western Desert, and organises
bird-watching trips, desert safari and sand-
boarding on the dunes. He can provide
transport to see sights around Al Fayoum.

Etman Abood TOURS
(☑010-0133-3781) Etman Abood can organise sandboarding and trips into the desert
around Al Fayoum and Wadi Rayyan.

Sleeping & Eating

Bedding down amid the bustle of Medinat
Al Fayoum is not the most scenic option; it's
far better to head to Lake Qarun or Tunis.

There may not be much accommodation
to choose from, but what Tunis does have is
wonderfully eclectic and characterful, with
bohemian-flavoured budget guesthouses
and a couple of high-end countryside retreats. Wherever you stay bring bug spray;
the mosquitoes are ferocious.

All the lodges in Tunis and along the lake-
shore have their own restaurants.

Tunis

Zad Al Mosafer GUESTHOUSE $
(☑010-0639-5590, 084-282-0180; www.facebook.
com/zad-elmosafer-guest-house-2304123
60350291/; r without/with air-con LE180/350, s with
shared bathroom LE80; ✳✖) The quintessential
groovy hang-out in Tunis. Zad Al Mosafer's
basic mudbrick-and-stone bungalows are
bedecked with Bedouin rag-rugs and palm-
frond furnishings. In the grounds there are
oodles of cushion-strewn areas to crash out
with a beer. What it lacks in amenities it
makes up for in character, plus the menu of
traditional Egyptian meals (LE20 to LE50)
and the company are excellent.

Sobek Lodge GUESTHOUSE $
(☑010-6888-5423; www.facebook.com/Sobek-
lodge; s/d/tr LE250/450/500; ✖) The few basic but clean rooms here are part of a larger
potters' compound, in a nice green spot with
plenty of space to lounge around and a small
pool. Even if you're not staying, it's worthwhile booking a meal (LE50 to LE120) here
while you're in Fayoum as the home cooking
(particularly the local duck dishes) is highly
recommended.

Kom el Dikka Agri Lodge VILLA $$
(☑012-2244-0012; www.facebook.com/komel
dikkaagrilodge; ste US$80, 3-6 person villas from
US$250; ⊙Oct-Jun; ✳✖) This 45-acre or-
ganic olive farm overlooking Lake Qarun
offers self-catering accommodation in suite-
style rooms and two villas, all designed in
a minimalist-modern mudbrick style with
curvy walls, domed roofs and modern kitch-
ens (the suites have kitchenettes) and bath-
rooms. A great getaway for families, with
plenty of activities specifically targeted at
kids.

The lodge provides organic produce from
its gardens and guests can get involved with
planting and crop harvesting if they like.

Lazib Inn RESORT $$$
(☑084-682-0000; www.lazibinn.com; ste from
US$200; ✳✖✖) The earth-toned walls here
hide a pampering hideaway of spacious
suites, all elegantly attired with local crafts
and the odd antique adding artistic accents.
Wake up to Lake Qarun vistas from your
terrace and relax in your jacuzzi after Fayoum explorations, though with a spa and
two infinity pools onsite you may find it
hard to leave.

Lake Qarun

Helnan Auberge Fayoum HOTEL $$
(☑084-698-1200; www.helnan.com; near Shak-
shouk, Lake Qarun; r from US$50; ✳✖✖) Built
in 1937 as King Farouk's private hunting
lodge, this hotel was where world leaders
met after WWII to decide the borders of the
Middle East. There are still wisps of coloni-
al glamour clinging on in the regally long
corridors and high-ceilinged rooms, but the
service leaves a lot to be desired.

❶ Information

DANGERS & ANNOYANCES
Al Fayoum was long notorious for its
heavy-handed security for independent travel-
lers. In recent years, however, this seems to have

lifted, and few travellers have reported issues. Police at checkpoints seldom inspect passports (though you should carry yours just in case), and often if you're a lone tourist in a microbus full of Egyptians, you're waved on through without question. Occasionally individual travellers may be appointed a police escort, but this rarely happens these days. The only sign of police escorts we saw on our last visit was on the Wadi Al Hittan access road; and that only seemed to be the case for large tour groups.

If you avoid Medinat Al Fayoum and head for the sights elsewhere in the area, you may not be troubled by anything at all.

TOURIST INFORMATION

The **Fayoum Tourism Authority** (☎ 084-634-2313; www.fayoumegypt.com; Midan Qarun, Sharia Tawfiqiyya) has an office next to the waterwheels in Al Fayoum's main town, but it's not always staffed; the same goes for a kiosk by the Helnan Auberge Fayoum on Lake Qarun.

ⓘ Getting There & Away

Microbuses (LE10 to LE15, 1½ to two hours) are the quickest way to travel from Cairo to Al Fayoum. Catch them at Midan Al Remaya in Giza, from Ulali near Ramses Station or from the ring-road underpass in Moneib. In Medinat Al Fayoum, ask to be dropped at Bahr Yusuf. If you're heading for Lake Qarun or Tunis, take a microbus direct from Midan Al Remaya in Giza to Abshaway, just south of the lake; from there you can hire a microbus driver, a tuk-tuk or a taxi to take you onward.

Returning microbuses leave Medinat Al Fayoum from north of the train station and head to various main stations in Cairo; the fare depends on the destination.

ⓘ Getting Around

To visit the lake and various archaeological sites, you can hire a taxi for between LE300 and LE400 for the day, in which time you could feasibly visit Karanis, Lake Qarun, the pyramids and Wadi Rayyan.

If you want to spend more time in the desert or visit Wadi Al Hittan and Medinat Madi, you'll need a 4WD. All of the lodges in Tunis and lakeside can help organise trips.

Microbuses connect most of the smaller villages with Medinat Al Fayoum – you can get to **Shakshouk**, the closest settlement to the hotels on Lake Qarun, for LE2. To reach Qasr Qarun or Tunis, head to **Abshaway** (LE2) where you can hire a microbus (as a private fare), taxi or tuk-tuk driver to take you further on.

Wadi Natrun

Wadi Natrun is known for its Coptic monasteries where thousands of Christians escaped from Roman persecution in the 4th century. Of the 60 or so original compounds in the valley, only four remain. These monastery buildings are impressive, as they were fortified after Arab raids in 817, although unlike at the Monastery of St Anthony in the Eastern Desert, only scraps of fresco art remain.

Your experience here largely depends on when you visit – most days are quiet, but visitors mob the churches on Christian and public holidays, yielding a glimpse into contemporary Coptic traditions. The monastic tradition is thriving, and the Coptic pope is still chosen from the Wadi Natrun monks.

The area was also important to the ancient Egyptians because the valley's salt lakes dry up in the summer and leave natron, a substance crucial to the mummification process.

⊙ Sights

Deir Anba Bishoi MONASTERY
(☎ Cairo head office 02 2591-4448; donation appreciated; ⊙ 9am-6pm, to 7pm summer) **FREE** St Bishoi came to the desert in AD 340 and founded two monasteries in Wadi Natrun: this one and neighbouring Deir El Sourian. The fortified keep is entered via a drawbridge. Just past the entry is a small reception office. The friendly monk here will organise a tour for you taking in the refectory, the fortress (where monks used to shelter from attack) and the church where St Bishoi's body is kept; it is said to be perfectly preserved in its tube-like container.

Each year on 15 July, the tube is carried in procession around the church. According to the monks, the bearers clearly feel the weight of a whole body. On our last visit, the monks were busy making repairs to the older mudbrick structures because of damage caused by recent rains. The damage had also revealed fragments of frescoes, long buried under layers of plaster, in the chapel. It's hoped that restoration works will reveal the extent of these long-forgotten frescoes. From the roof of the fortress (usually kept locked but your monk guide will unlock it for you) you can get excellent views over the monastery compound with its internal palm shaded gardens.

Adjacent to the complex is an enormous new cathedral. Outside the keep in a separate building is a shop selling monastery products: olive oil, honey, candles and, oddly, cleaning supplies.

Deir El Sourian   MONASTERY

(☑ Cairo head office 02-2590-5161; www.st-mary-alsourian.com; donation appreciated; ☺ 9am-6pm, to 7pm summer) FREE About 500m northwest of Deir Anba Bishoi, Deir El Sourian is the most picturesquely situated of the monasteries. It is named after wandering Syrian monks who bought the monastery from the Copts in the 8th century, though the Copts took it back in the 16th century. Its Church of the Virgin contains 11th-century wall paintings and older icons with the eyes scratched out, including one saint in a distinctly Pharaonic-looking robe.

The church was built around the 4th-century cave where St Bishoi resided and tied his hair to the ceiling to keep himself awake during prayers. Elsewhere in the compound is a second ancient church, the tamarind tree of St Ephraim, allegedly sprung from the Syrian holy man's cane, and some slightly unfortunate mannequins of monks illustrating daily life at the monastery.

Deir Abu Makar   MONASTERY

(St Macarius Monastery; ☑ Cairo head office 02-2577-0614; www.stmacariusmonastery.org; donation appreciated; ☺ 9am-6pm, closed during fasting periods) FREE Deir Abu Makar was founded around the cell where St Macarius spent his last 20 or so years. Although structurally it suffered more than other monasteries at the hands of raiding Bedouin, it has been carefully restored and the monks here give excellent tours of the complex for visitors. Deir Abu Makar is famous as most of the Coptic popes have been selected from among its monks, and most are buried here.

Inside the main Church of St Macarius, an intricately carved 10th-century sycamore door leads into the apse (kept locked but your guide will usually open it up for you), which you can peek into to see the domed roof and a surviving 7th-century cherub fresco in one corner. In the nave, a trapdoor reveals the crypt, discovered during restoration works, where the monks found relics claimed to be of St John the Baptist. The tiny and stark original monk cells are also possible to visit, along with a small square-domed chapel, the refectory and the impressively restored fortress.

Deir Al Baramouse   MONASTERY

(☑ Cairo head office 02-592-2775; donation appreciated; ☺ 9am-6pm Fri-Sun, closed during fasting periods) FREE Once quite isolated because of a bad road, Deir Al Baramouse now has more than 100 monks in residence, plus six modern churches in addition to its restored medieval fortress (not open to the public). The gardens and entire complex here are beautiful and well-maintained, with a serene ambience. There's a wonderfully restored millstone in an alcove and, nearby, in it's oldest chapel, the Church of the Virgin Mary, there are remnants of 13th-century wall frescoes.

🛏 Sleeping & Eating

Men are welcome to spend the night at any of the monasteries but must have written consent from the Cairo offices. Even if you're not devout, it is good manners to attend religious services and to leave a generous donation with the monks on departure.

There are simple cafes selling tea, cold drinks and snacks outside each of the monastery complexes. As well as this, Deir Anba Bishoi runs a free restaurant inside the monastery grounds where everyone is welcome to sit down for a basic meal of bread and *fuul*.

ℹ Information

Some of the monasteries close during the three major fasting periods: Lent (40 days before Easter Week), Advent (40 days before Christmas) and the Dormition (two weeks in August).

ℹ Getting There & Away

Wadi Natrun lies on the desert side of the Cairo–Alexandria Desert Hwy, which roughly separates the green fields of the Delta and the harsh sands of the Western Desert, though the area is now dotted with farms and new satellite towns.

Alexandria-bound West & Mid Delta Co buses from Cairo Gateway can drop you on the Desert Hwy close to Wadi Natrun (tell the driver you want to get off at Master Mall and Rest), but charge the full price to Alex (LE55). Cheaper are microbuses (LE15, one hour) from Midan Al Remaya near the Pyramids of Giza; the buses go into the less-than-lovely town of Wadi Natrun. Tuk-tuks and taxis wait at the highway and the bus depot. A tuk-tuk to Deir Anba Bishoi and Deir El Sourian (you can walk between the two), with pickup a couple of hours later, will cost around LE50. To visit all four monasteries, you'll need a taxi; expect to pay around LE50 per hour.

A full-day taxi trip from Cairo should cost between LE500 and LE600, including driving around to all the monasteries.

THE NILE DELTA

North of Cairo, the Nile River divides into two branches that enter the Mediterranean at the old ports of Damietta and Rosetta, forming one of the most fertile and most cultivated regions in the world. Laced with countless waterways, the lush Delta region is a relaxing counterpoint to Cairo's grit and the desert's austerity. Very few tourists make it here, and there is little infrastructure in the way of hotels; police may even be a bit suspicious of your motives. But just a day visit can be rewarding for travellers who prefer aimless exploration to actual sightseeing.

Birqash Camel Market

Egypt's largest camel market is held at **Birqash** (pronounced Bir'ash; (Souq Al Gimaal; Birqash; LE25, camera LE20; ⊗6am-noon Fri & Sun)), a small village 35km northwest of Cairo, just on the edge of the Delta's cultivated land. The camel market is not for the faint of heart – these beasts are not treated like beloved pets. But it can make an unforgettable day trip, especially if you're a keen photographer. Hundreds of camels are sold here every market day, with the liveliest action between 7am and 10am.

Most of the animals are brought up the Forty Days Rd from western Sudan to just north of Abu Simbel by camel herders, and from there to the market in Daraw in Upper Egypt. Unsold camels are then hobbled and crammed into trucks for the 24-hour drive to Birqash. By the time they arrive, many are emaciated, fit only for the knacker's yard, and some expire at the market itself. Traders stand no nonsense, and camels that get out of line are beaten relentlessly.

In addition to those from Sudan, there are camels from various parts of Egypt (including Sinai, the west and the south) and sometimes from as far away as Somalia. They are traded for cash or other livestock, such as goats, sheep and horses, and sold for farm work or slaughter. Smaller camels go for as little as LE750, but bigger beasts can sell for LE6000 and up.

While at the market, watch out for pickpockets. Women should dress conservatively – the market is very much a man's scene, with the only female presence being the local tea-lady. But traders here are accustomed to tourists and are generally happy to answer questions and have their photos taken if you

ask nicely. Always be alert to bolting camels – even hobbled, they can move pretty fast.

Microbuses and trucks (LE2) run from the site of the old camel market at Imbaba. To get to Imbaba, take a microbus from Midan Abdel Moniem Riad in Downtown Cairo, then ask around for a connecting service to the old market – Imbaba airport (matar Imbaba) is the nearest landmark. Or you could take a taxi to the old market site. Returning to Cairo, microbuses for Imbaba leave when full.

The easiest option to get here is to simply hire a taxi from Cairo, with waiting time – one hour in the market is usually enough for most people. The full trip will cost around LE200. You could also combine this with a trip to the Nile Barrages and have the taxi drop you there, then return on the river bus.

Qanater (Nile Barrages)
📞 02 / POP 66,350

Half the appeal of Qanater ('Barrages'), is the two-hour trip on a ramshackle river bus, best done on Fridays or public holidays. Large groups of young people and smaller family parties pack the boats to picnic in the scraggly public gardens at Qanater, a 1km patch of land between the two branches of the Nile where the 19th-century barrages are handsome pieces of engineering. On the boats, Arabic pop blares and the younger passengers sing along, clap, dance and decorously flirt.

It's an enjoyable, sociable jaunt, though prepare yourself for attention. Tourists are a rare and intriguing sight, and Qanater is a popular destination for young males who relish cruising the promenade between the two barrages on their motor scooters. Solo females would be better off buddying up before making the trip here.

The barrages themselves are a series of basins and locks built to guarantee a year-round flow of water into the Delta region, thus leading to a great increase in cotton production. The barrage on the Damietta branch consists of 71 sluices stretching 521m across the river; the Rosetta Barrage is 438m long with 61 sluices.

ℹ Getting There & Away

River buses (p121) (LE12) go from the dock in front of the TV building (Maspero), just north of the Ramses Hilton in central Cairo. They depart when full, from 7am to about 10am. You can return by microbus (LE20) if the boat departures aren't convenient, or if you need a little quiet.

Qanater is very close to Birqash, so you could hire a taxi to drive you to the camel market and then leave you at Qanater so you can take the boat back; pay about LE200.

Tanta

📞 040 / POP 429,000

The largest city in the Delta, Tanta doesn't have much to actually see but is an easy place to sample provincial town life, as it's accessible by good trains. It's a major centre for Sufism, and home to a large mosque dedicated to Al Sayyed Ahmed Al Badawi, a Moroccan Sufi who fought the Crusaders in the 13th century. The *moulid* held in his honour follows the cotton harvest, usually held the last week in October. It is one of the biggest in Egypt, drawing crowds of more than a million people for the eight days of chanting, rituals and the sweets for which Tanta is best known.

If visiting during the *moulid,* prepare yourself for mayhem (women should not go alone as sexual harassment is rife) and book accommodation well in advance.

History

This area of the western Delta was once home to the ancient cities of Sais, Naucratis and Wadjet. Although these cities have been wiped off the map, anyone with a historical interest in the Delta region might be intrigued as to where they once stood.

Northwest of Tanta, on the east bank of the Rosetta branch of the Nile, once stood the legendary city of Sais (Sa Al Hagar), Egypt's 26th-dynasty capital. Sacred to Neith, goddess of war and hunting, and protector of embalmed bodies, Sais dates back to the start of Egyptian history and was replete with palaces, temples and royal tombs. However, the city was destroyed in 525 BC by the Persian emperor Cambyses, who reportedly exhumed the mummies of previous rulers from the ground and had them publicly whipped and burned.

West of Tanta, more than halfway along the road to Damanhur, is where the city of Naucratis once stood. The city was given to the Greeks to settle during the 7th century BC.

Northeast of Damanhur and northwest of Tanta was the Egyptian cult centre of Wadjet (known as Buto to the Greeks), which honoured the cobra goddess of Lower Egypt. Cobras were once worshipped here by devout followers.

◉ Sights

The road that leads to the mosque is lined with sweets-sellers; the local speciality is a type of nougat studded with nuts or dried chickpeas. Behind the mosque is Tanta's **old market district**, good for an aimless stroll.

**Mosque of Al Sayyed
Ahmed Al Badawi** MOSQUE

(⊘24hr) FREE Al Badawi, born in Morocco, came to Tanta in 1234, and founded one of Egypt's largest Sufi orders, the Badawiya. Once you're inside the mosque, to the left is Al Badawi's shrine lit with green fluorescent lights and circled by pilgrims snapping photos on their mobile phones. The mosque is 300m from the train station – bear right across the parking area in front of the station and then you'll see it at the end of the first major street.

🛏 Sleeping

New Arafa Hotel HOTEL $

(📞040-340-5040; Midan Al Mahatta; s/d from LE350/500; ❋ 🛜) The not-so-new New Arafa Hotel is your best bet in Tanta. Get your no-expectations hat on and this place is fine for a night. The rooms are nothing special, but staff are nice and there is a decent bar and restaurant on the premises. It's the tall pink building across the road, and to the right, from the train station.

ℹ Getting There & Away

Tanta is on the Cairo–Alexandria line so is well served by train. Comfortable air-con trains (LE30 to LE45, one to 1½ hours) head to Tanta from Ramses Station in Cairo 14 times daily between 6am and 10.30pm. Coming back to Cairo there are 13 services with the last at 10.55pm. The trains are far preferable to a microbus (which leave from outside Tanta Station), as they're not subject to traffic whims.

Zagazig & Bubastis

📞 055 / POP 319,700

On the outskirts of the delightfully named city of Zagazig (Egyptians say 'za'-a-*zi'*) are the ruins of Bubastis, one of the country's most ancient cities. Its temple, now reduced to piles of scattered stone blocks, was dedicated to the resident deity, the elegant cat goddess Bastet. For serious Egyptology buffs, an outing from Cairo taking in both Bubastis and Tanis (70km further northeast) is an interesting day trip to two of Egypt's rarely visited sites.

⊙ Sights

Temple of Bubastis   ARCHAEOLOGICAL SITE
(Tell Basta; Sharia Al Shohaada; adult/student LE60/30; ⊙8am-4pm) Festivals held at the Temple of Bubastis once attracted more than 700,000 revellers who sang, danced, feasted, consumed great quantities of wine and offered sacrifices to the goddess Bastet. Khufu and Khafre started building the temple during the 4th dynasty, but additions were made over about 17 centuries. Many fine stelae and pieces of statuary found here have been re-erected in a sculpture garden, while the temple itself (to the right) is now just a pile of rubble.

To the left of the sculpture garden are the slumping mudbrick remains of a palace and the cemetery with five tombs (kept locked) where many bronze statues of cats were found.

The site is roughly 2.5km south of the train station. Ask taxi and tuk-tuk drivers for 'Tell Basta'. If you're coming from Cairo by taxi, the site is on the southern edge of town, head along the main entry road until you get to the mammoth overpass and turn right.

① Getting There & Away

The cheapest and fastest way to go to Zagazig is by bus or microbus. There are frequent departures in both directions between Zagazig's train station and Cairo's Abboud terminal (LE10 to LE15, 1½ to two hours).

By train, from Cairo's Ramses Station, trains leave at 6am, 7am, 9am, 2.30pm, 5.30pm and 7.30pm (LE20, two to three hours). These are 3rd-class trains, and delays are common.

A day trip from Cairo to Bubastis and Tanis by taxi should cost around LE450 to LE500. Tourist police at Bubastis sometimes do not allow travellers of American and most western Europe nationalities to continue on by car to Tanis from Zagazig without a police escort. This (and the waiting around it entails) can be avoided by heading to Tanis first.

Tanis

Just outside the village of San Al Hagar, 70km northeast of Zagazig, are the partly excavated ruins of Tanis (San Al Hagar; adult/student LE25/15; ⊙8am-5pm), a city known as Djanet to the ancient Egyptians and Zoan to the Hebrews. Some call it the Saqqara of the Delta because of its impressive scale. Although it is not so well preserved as that ruin and only shattered remnants of its temples remain, the statuary, obelisks and stelae

scattered across the vast sands here are incredibly atmospheric.

For several centuries Tanis was one of the largest cities in the Delta, and became a site of great importance after the end of the New Kingdom, especially during the Late Period (747–332 BC).

The earliest buildings at Tanis are from the reign of Psusennes I (1039–991 BC), who surrounded the **Temple of Amun** with a great enclosure wall. His royal tomb and five others from the 21st dynasty were unearthed by the French in 1939, and the treasures are some of the most spectacular ever found in Egypt. The trove, which includes gorgeous jewellery, is on view in the Egyptian Museum. Psusennes I and later kings reused blocks and statues from earlier eras – so much of the stone actually dates from the Old and Middle Kingdoms. His successors added a temple to Mut, Khons and the Asiatic goddess Astarte, together with a sacred lake, and temple building continued until Ptolemaic times.

With Egypt's glut of Pharaonic sites, Tanis rightly falls low on the priority list for Egyptology fans, but for those with plenty of time on their hands, a visit here is rewarding. Cinema buffs are also quick to point out that Tanis is where Indiana Jones discovered the 'Lost Ark'.

Local site guide, Ezzat, is usually found at the ticket office and is well worth touring the site with (tip appreciated). You won't get an in-depth rundown on Tanis' history, but he's very knowledgeable about the hieroglyphs on display and can point out many of the details you would otherwise miss if you were rambling the site by yourself. Some readers have run into aggressive wild dogs here; this is another good reason to accept Ezzat's services rather than go it alone in this huge site.

You can reach Tanis by taking a microbus or East Delta bus from Ulali or Abboud in Cairo (LE15, two hours) to the town of Faqus, which is about 35km south of Tanis. From Faqus, take a service taxi or bus (LE5 to LE7) to the village of San Al Hagar, or hire a taxi (LE35) to take you to the site.

Alternatively, and much more slowly, the train takes about 3½ hours to get to Abu Kabir (LE20), the nearest station to Faqus. These old, non-air-con trains leave from the far east end of Cairo's Ramses Station (ask for 'Sharq' or 'Limun') approximately every two hours. If you're coming from Zagazig, the train is slightly more appealing. It takes just 45 minutes to Abu Kabir, and there are more options, with service every hour or so.

Northern Nile Valley

Includes →

Best Places to Eat

→ Bondookah Restaurant (p167)

→ Al Watania Palace Hotel (p174)

→ El Khalil Grill (p167)

Best Places to Stay

→ New Hermopolis (p170)

→ Horus Resort (p166)

→ House of Life (p179)

→ Al Watania Palace Hotel (p174)

→ Al Safa Hotel (p176)

Why Go?

If you're in a hurry to reach the treasures and pleasures of the south, it is easy to dismiss the places between Cairo and Luxor. But these less touristed parts of the country almost always repay what can be the considerable effort of a visit.

Some of this region remains less developed – you will see farmers still working by hand – but everyone here also has to grapple with modernity and its problems, with water and electricity shortages and, since the downfall of the Muslim Brotherhood, tension and security issues.

However much a backwater today, this region played a key role in Egypt's destiny and there are archaeological sites to prove it – from the lavishly painted tombs at Beni Hasan and the remains of the doomed city of Akhetaten, where Tutankhamun was brought up, to the Pharaonic-inspired monasteries of the early Christian period.

When to Go
Asyut

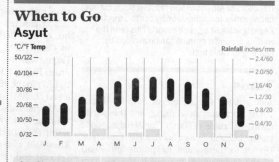

Apr Sham El Nessim, the spring festival, is celebrated in style in the region.

Aug Millions of people arrive to celebrate the Feast of the Virgin outside Minya.

Oct–Nov The ideal touring time, when the light is particularly beautiful.

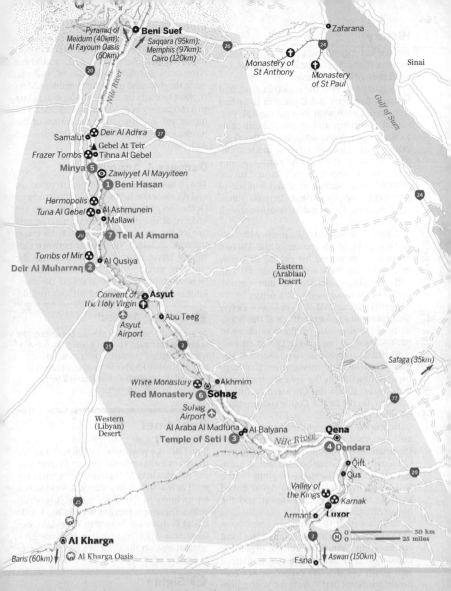

Northern Nile Valley Highlights

1 **Beni Hasan** (p167) Admiring lithe dancers, hunters and even wrestlers in these finely painted tombs.

2 **Deir Al Muharraq** (p173) Visiting the Coptic monastery to see why Copts claim to be heirs to the ancient Egyptians.

3 **Temple of Seti I** (p177) Gazing upon some of ancient Egypt's finest temple reliefs in Abydos.

4 **Dendara** (p180) Marvelling at the Temple of Hathor, one of Egypt's best-preserved temple complexes.

5 **Minya** (p165) Hanging out in the colonial-era centre.

6 **Red Monastery** (p175) Seeing the frescoes at one of the finest buildings from late antiquity.

7 **Tell Al Amarna** (p170) Wandering through the lush countryside around the doomed city of the heretic king Akhenaten.

History

For ancient Egyptians, Upper Egypt began south of the ancient capital of Memphis, beyond present-day Saqqara.

Egyptians divided the area that stretched between Beni Suef and Qena into 15 nomes (provinces), each with its own capital. Provincial governors and notables built their tombs on the desert edge, above the flood plain. Abydos, located close to modern Sohag, was once the predominant religious centre in the region as well as one of the country's most sacred sites and a place of pilgrimage: Egypt's earliest dynastic rulers were interred there and it flourished well into the Christian era.

When New Kingdom Pharaoh Akhenaten tried to break the power of the Theban priesthood, he moved his capital to a new city, Akhetaten (near modern Mallawi), one of the few places along the Nile that was not, at that point, associated with a deity.

Christianity arrived early in Upper Egypt. Sectarian splits in Alexandria and the popularity of the monastic tradition established by St Anthony in the Eastern Desert encouraged priests to settle in the provinces. The many churches and monasteries that continue to function in the area are testament to the strength of the Christian tradition: this area has the largest Coptic communities outside Cairo.

Dependent on agriculture, much of the area remained a backwater throughout the Christian and Islamic periods, although Qena and Asyut flourished as trading hubs: Qena was also the jumping-off point for the Red Sea port of Safaga, while Asyut linked the Nile with the Western Desert and the Sudan caravan route.

Today much of the region remains poor. Agriculture is still the mainstay of the local economy but cannot sustain the exploding population. The lack of any real industrial base south of Cairo has caused severe economic hardship, particularly for young people who drift in increasing numbers into towns and cities in search of work. Resentment at their lack of hope was compounded by the loss of remittances from Iraq: many people from this region who had found work abroad in the 1980s lost it with the outbreak of the first Gulf War. Religious militants exploited the violent insurrection that exploded in the 1990s, directing it towards the government in a bid to create an Islamic state. The insurrection was violently crushed. The Muslim Brotherhood found much support here after 2011, and there have been regular outbreaks of violence since the downfall of former president Morsi, most recently an attack on Copts heading to a monastery near Minya in May 2017. The unrest will continue until the causes of the unrest – poverty and thwarted hopes – are addressed.

Dangers & Annoyances

Travel restrictions have been in place on and off since the 1990s Islamic insurrection. Outbreaks of violence mean restrictions are in force at the time of writing, making this one of the most difficult regions to travel through, although Nile cruises between Cairo and Luxor have resumed. Although the situation remains fluid, some areas, particularly south of Sohag (Abydos and Dendara, for instance), can be visited without trouble.

ℹ Getting Around

Trains are the best way of moving between cities in this part of Egypt. Foreign visitors are currently not permitted to travel by microbus, so the only alternative for shorter journeys is private taxi, and you might then find yourself being escorted by armed police.

Beni Suef

♪ 082 / POP 272,850

Beni Suef is a provincial capital and a major transport hub between Cairo and Luxor, and the Red Sea and Al Fayoum. From antiquity until at least the 16th century, it was famous for its linen. In the 19th century, it was still sufficiently important (at least in the textile trade) to have an American consulate, but there is now little to capture the traveller's interest beyond the sight of a provincial city at work.

◉ Sights

Beni Suef Museum   MUSEUM
(adult/student LE20/10; ⏱ 8am-4pm) Next to the governorate building and behind the zoo, this museum is Beni Suef's main attraction. There is a small but worthwhile collection of objects from the Old Kingdom to the Mohammed Ali period with good Ptolemaic carvings, Coptic weavings and 19th-century table-settings.

🛌 Sleeping

City Center Hotel HOTEL $
(☑ 011-1007-2326; www.cityhotel.net; Midan Al Mahatta; s/d LE265/295; ❋ 🛜) Around the corner from the forlorn Semiramis Hotel and across the square from the train station, this three-star 45-room hotel is popular with managers and white-collar workers posted to Beni Suef. Rooms are basic but have aircon, fridges and TVs. The 6th-floor restaurant serves a mixed menu including pizzas, chicken and pigeon for lunch and dinner, although you might need to order in advance.

Tolip Inn HOTEL $$
(☑ 088-236-6993; www.tolipinnbns.com; Sharia Ahmed Orabi; s/d US$60/80; P ❋ 🛜 ≋) The newest and smartest address in Beni Suef, with spacious rooms, all with large flat-screen TVs, mini-bar, good internet and tea and coffee facilities. The restaurant serves a dull but reliable menu of local and European dishes, and there's a large pool.

❶ Getting There & Away

The bus station is along the main road, Sharia Bur Said, south of the town centre. Buses run to Cairo, Minya, Al Fayoum and Zafarana. Microbuses also run the same routes. Depending on the security situation, you may be obliged to take a train or hire a private taxi.

There are frequent train connections north to Cairo and Giza (1st/2nd class LE39/23, 90 minutes to two hours), and south to Minya (LE39/23, 1½ hours).

Gebel At Teir & Frazer Tombs

Deir Al Adhra MONASTERY
(☼ 8am-dusk) The clifflike Gebel At Teir (Bird Mountain) rises east of the Nile, some 93km south of Beni Suef and 20km north of Minya. The mountain takes its name from a legend that all Egyptian birds paused here on the monastery's annual feast day. Deir Al Adhra (Monastery of the Virgin) is perched 130m above the river and was formerly known as the Convent of the Pulley, a reminder of the time when rope was the only way of reaching the cliff top.

Coptic tradition claims that the Holy Family rested here for three days on their journey through Egypt. A cave-chapel built on the site in the 4th century AD is ascribed to Helena, mother of Byzantine Emperor Constantine. A 19th-century building encloses the cave, whose icon of the Virgin is said to have miraculous powers. The monastery, unvisited for most of the year, is mobbed by many thousands of pilgrims during the week-long Feast of the Assumption, culminating on 22 August.

You can get to the monastery by public transport (servees or microbus from Minya to Samalut and a boat across the river), but a private taxi from Minya shouldn't cost more than LE100 to LE150 for the return trip.

Frazer Tombs TOMB
(adult/student LE30/15; ☼ 8am-4pm) Five kilometres south of Tihna Al Gebel, the Frazer Tombs date back to the 5th and 6th dynasties. These Old Kingdom tombs are cut into the east bank cliffs and overlook the valley. Only two tombs are open and both are very simple, with eroded images and hieroglyphs but no colourful scenes. They are likely to appeal only if you have a passion for rarely visited sites.

Minya

☑ 086 / POP 283,000
Minya, the 'Bride of Upper Egypt' (Arousa As Sa'id), sits on the boundary between Upper and Lower Egypt. A provincial capital, its broad tree-lined streets, wide corniche and some great, if shabby, early-20th-century buildings make this one of the most pleasant town centres in Upper Egypt.

Once the hub of the Upper Egyptian cotton trade, its factories now process sugar, soap and perfume. The downturn in the local economy helped fuel an Islamist insurgency in the 1990s, which the government sent tanks and armoured personnel carriers to suppress. They did this again in 2013 to quell pro-Muslim Brotherhood protests. More recently, security was tightened in May 2017 following an attack on Coptic visitors to a monastery outside Minya in which 28 people died. In spite of the tension, Minya remains a good place to visit and its city centre retains the air of a more graceful era.

◉ Sights

Beyond the pleasure of strolling around the town centre and along the Nile corniche, against the background of the Eastern Hills, Minya doesn't have many sights. That will change when the new Akhenaten Museum eventually opens. There is a **souq** (market) at the southern end of the town centre and

Minya

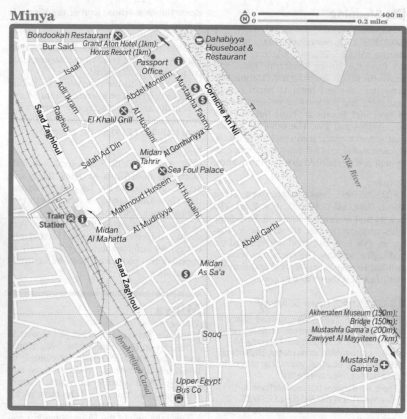

Bondookah Restaurant
Bur Said
Grand Aton Hotel (1km);
Horus Resort (1km)
Isaaf
Passport Office
Dahabiyya Houseboat & Restaurant
Adli Ikram
Abdel Moneim
Mustapha Fahmy
Corniche An Nil
Ragheb
Saad Zaghloul
El Khalil Grill
Al Hussaini
Salah Ad Din
Midan Al Gomhuriyya
Midan Tahrir
Sea Foul Palace
Mahmoud Hussein
Al Hussaini
Al Mudiriyya
Train Station
Midan Al Mahatta
Saad Zaghloul
Abdel Garhi
Midan As Sa'a
Souq
Akhenaten Museum (150m); Bridge (150m); Mustashfa Gama'a (200m); Zawiyyet Al Mayyiteen (7km)
Mustashfa Gama'a
Ibrahimiyya Canal
Upper Egypt Bus Co
Nile River

the streets that run from it to Midan Tahrir are among the liveliest.

Hantours (horse-drawn carriages; per hour LE30 to LE40) can be rented for a leisurely ride around the town centre or along the corniche. **Feluccas** (Egyptian sailing boats; per hour LE50) can be rented at the landing opposite the tourist office for trips along the river.

Zawiyyet Al Mayyiteen CEMETERY
On the east bank about 7km southeast of town, this large Muslim and Christian cemetery, called Zawiyyet Al Mayyiteen (Place of the Dead), consists of several hundred mudbrick mausoleums, many with beehive roofs. Stretching for 4km from the road to the hills and said to be one of the largest cemeteries in the world, it is an interesting sight.

Akhenaten Museum MUSEUM
The new Akhenaten Museum on the east bank is now complete, but no date has been

set for its opening. If the Egyptian authorities can swing it, it will be home, for some months at least, to the iconic bust of Queen Nefertiti (now in Berlin) as well as treasures from the nearby Tell Al Amarna excavations.

🛏 Sleeping

⭐ **Horus Resort** HOTEL $$
(☎ 086-231-6660; www.horusresortminia.com; Corniche An Nil; s/d US$40/60; ❄️🛜🏊) On the Nile about 1km from the centre, this remains our top-pick hotel although that is mostly because of the lack of competition. Staff are friendly and views of the Nile are good, but cleanliness and food standards have dropped since our last visit. The large riverside swimming pool and the playground make it popular with kids.

The popular riverside terrace serves cold beers, fresh juices and shisha; the restaurant serves a dire breakfast but some standard

Egyptian as well as Italian dishes in the evening.

Grand Aton Hotel HOTEL $$$
(📞 086-234-2993, 086-234-2994; Corniche An Nil; s/d US$100/120; 🅿🛜❄) Still referred to locally as the Etap (its former incarnation), the Grand Aton has emerged from a major renovation with the best rooms in town but the atmosphere of a mall more than a hotel. On the west bank of the Nile, many of the well-equipped bungalow rooms have great river views. Restaurants, a cafe/bar and pool.

✖ Eating & Drinking

★ Bondookah Restaurant EGYPTIAN $
(Sharia Masaken El Gamaa; mains from I F45; ⊘ noon-11pm) The best grilled meat in Minya in an unfussy 2nd-floor restaurant. Grilled chicken, lamb chops, *tagen* (a stew cooked in a deep clay pot) and, best of all, kofta. There are salads, rice and bread, soft drinks and a good view through the large windows onto the busy street. Not somewhere to spend the evening, but good to refuel. The menu is in Arabic.

Sea Foul Palace EGYPTIAN $
(Midan Tahrir; mains from LE20) Some of the best *fuul* and *ta'amiyya* in town from this takeaway beside the old Palace Hotel. Grab a bag-full and sit in the square, or up the road on the corniche, and watch the world go by.

El Khalil Grill EGYPTIAN $$
(📞 086-233-4433; Sharia Abdel Moneim; mains around LE65; ⊘ 11am-2am) A popular, no-nonsense, reliable kebab and grill restaurant for when you need a meat fix, El Khalil is something of a legend in Minya. Kebabs (LE250 a kilo) are the main item. No alcohol, but there's a really good juice bar next door.

Dahabiyya Houseboat & Restaurant CAFE
(📞 086-236-5596; Corniche An Nil; ⊘ noon-11pm) This old Nile sailing boat has been moored along the corniche near the tourist office for many years and is one of Minya's most unusual addresses. The bedrooms downstairs are no longer for hire, but the top-deck cafe-restaurant remains popular with locals, especially for a coffee or cool drink on a warm evening.

ℹ Information

The **tourist office** (Map p166; 📞 086-236-0150; Corniche An Nil; ⊘ 9am-3.30pm Sat-Thu) in the centre of town and facing the Nile might look derelict, but the willing staff should be able to help with basic information regarding hotels, excursions and onward travel. There's also a **branch** (Map p166; 📞 086-234-2044) at the train station, although it is often closed.

ℹ Getting There & Away

BUS & MICROBUS

The **Upper Egypt Bus Co** (Map p166; 📞 086-236-3721; Sharia Saad Zaghloul) has hourly services to Cairo (LE30, four hours) from 6am. Buses leave for Hurghada at 10.30am and 10.30pm (LE80, six hours).

A seat in a microbus or servees, if you are allowed to take one, will cost LE20 to Cairo and LE15 to Asyut.

TRAIN

Trains to Cairo (1st/2nd class LE62/36, three to four hours) leave at least every 1½ hours starting at 4.25am. Trains heading south also leave fairly frequently, with the fastest trains departing from Minya between 11pm and 1am: Luxor (LE86/47, six to eight hours) and Aswan (LE109/59, eight to 11 hours), stopping at Asyut (LE39/26, two hours), Sohag (LE55/34, three to four hours) and Qena (LE78/44, five to seven hours).

Beni Hasan

The necropolis of **Beni Hasan** (adult/student LE60/40; ⊘ 8am-4pm) occupies a range of east-bank limestone cliffs some 20km south of Minya. It is a superb and important location and has the added attraction of a rest house, although these days it is only occasionally open for drinks; you should bring your own water and food. Most tombs date from the 11th and 12th dynasties (2125–1795 BC), the 39 upper tombs belonging to nomarchs (local governors). Many remain unfinished and only four are currently open to visitors, but they are well worth the trouble of visiting for the fascinating glimpse they provide of the daily life and political tensions of the period.

A guard will accompany you from the ticket office, so baksheesh is expected (at least LE20). Try to see the tombs chronologically.

◉ Sights

Tomb of Baqet (No 15) TOMB
(adult /student LE60/40 incl all Beni Hasan tombs; ⊘ 8am-4pm) Baqet was an 11th-dynasty governor of the Oryx nome (district). His rectangular tomb chapel has seven tomb shafts

and some well-preserved wall paintings. They include Baqet and his wife on the left wall watching weavers and acrobats – mostly women in diaphanous dresses in flexible poses. Further along, animals, presumably possessions of Baqet, are being counted. A hunting scene in the desert shows mythical creatures among the gazelles.

The back wall shows a sequence of wrestling moves that are still used today. The right (south) wall is decorated with scenes from the nomarch's daily life, with potters, metalworkers and a flax harvest, among others.

Tomb of Kheti (No 17)   TOMB
Kheti, Baqet's son, inherited the governorship of the Oryx nome from his father. His tomb chapel, with two of its original six papyrus columns intact, has many vivid painted scenes that show hunting, linen production, board games, metalwork, wrestling, acrobatics and dancing, most of them watched over by the nomarch. Notice the yogalike positions on the right-hand wall, between images of winemaking and herding. On the west-facing wall are images of 10 different trees.

★Tomb of Amenemhat (No 2)   TOMB
Amenemhat was a 12th-dynasty governor of Oryx. His tomb is the largest and possibly the best at Beni Hasan and, like that of Khnumhotep, its impressive facade and interior decoration mark a clear departure from the more modest earlier ones. Entered through a columned doorway, and with its six columns intact, it contains beautifully executed scenes of farming, hunting, manufacturing and offerings to the deceased, who can also be seen with his dogs.

As well as the fine paintings, the tomb has a long, faded text in which Amenemhat addresses the visitors to his chapel: 'You who love life and hate death, say: Thousands of bread and beer, thousands of cattle and wild fowl for the ka of the hereditary prince...the Great Chief of the Oryx Nome...'

Tomb of Khnumhotep (No 3)   TOMB
Khnumhotep was governor during the early 12th dynasty, and his detailed 'autobiography' is inscribed on the base of walls that contain the most detailed painted scenes. The tomb is famous for its rich, finely rendered scenes of plant, animal and bird life. On the left wall farmers are shown tending their crops while a scribe is shown recording the harvest. Also on the left wall is a representation of a delegation bringing offerings from Asia – their clothes, faces and beards are all distinct.

Speos Artemidos   MONUMENT
(Grotto of Artemis; ⊘ 8am-4pm) If the guardian allows, you can follow a cliffside track that leads southeast for about 2.5km and then some 500m into a wadi to the rock-cut temple called the Speos Artemidos, and referred to locally as Istabl Antar (Stable of Antar, an Arab warrior-poet and folk hero), but actually dedicated to the ancient Egyptian lion-goddess Pasht.

Dating back to the 18th dynasty, the small temple was started by Hatshepsut (1473–1458 BC) and completed by Tuthmosis III (1479–1425 BC). There is a small hall with roughly hewn Hathor-headed columns and an unfinished sanctuary. On the walls are scenes of Hatshepsut making offerings and, on its upper facade, an inscription describing

---

PLUNDERING THE PAST

Antiquity theft is nothing new in Egypt – people have been robbing tombs and other sites for millennia. But in the security void that followed Mubarak's 2011 downfall, many sites were plundered across the country. With continuing economic hardship, more people have a motive to go digging, and looting continues to be widespread throughout Egypt. Famous sites, including the Egyptian Museum in Cairo, have suffered losses, but many more lesser-known places, including El Hibeh and Mallawi's museum, have been plundered too. Although the unit of the Egyptian government charged with recovering antiquities has struggled to cope with the challenge, some major pieces have been recovered from salesrooms abroad. One of the loudest activists has been Dr Monica Hanna, an Egyptologist who happened to be inside the Mallawi Museum in 2013 when most of its 1000-plus antiquities were looted (the majority have since been recovered). Dr Hanna created Egypt's Heritage Taskforce, one of several organisations helping to protect antiquities, but the threat remains.

how she restored order after the rule of the Hyksos, even though she reigned long after.

Expect to be accompanied by a police escort and a guard (who will want baksheesh).

ℹ Getting There & Away

It may be possible to take a microbus from Minya to the east bank and then another heading south to Beni Hasan, but as elsewhere, this will take time and is often forbidden. A taxi from Minya will cost anything from LE200 to LE400, depending on your bargaining skills and how long you stay at the site.

Beni Hasan to Tell Al Amarna

Hermopolis

Hermopolis is the site of the ancient city of Khemenu. Capital of the 15th Upper Egyptian nome, its original Egyptian name, which translates as Eight Town, refers to four pairs of snake and frog gods that, according to one Egyptian creation myth, existed here before the first earth appeared out of the waters of chaos. This was also an important cult centre of Thoth, god of wisdom and writing, whom the Greeks identified with their god Hermes, hence the city's Greek name, 'Hermopolis'.

Although little remains of the wealthy ancient city, there are some wonderful things to see in and around its nearby cemetery, Tuna Al Gebel, although the seventeen mummies discovered in May 2017 will not be shown for some time.

◉ Sights

★ **Tuna Al Gebel** MONUMENT
(Map p171; adult/student LE60/30; ☺8am-4pm) Tuna Al Gebel was the necropolis of Hermopolis; about 5km past the village of Tuna Al Gebel you'll find the catacombs and tombs of the residents and sacred animals. The dark catacomb galleries once held many thousands of mummified ibis and baboons, both seen as the 'living image of Thoth'. This wonderfully atmospheric subterranean cemetery is on two levels and extends for at least 3km, perhaps even all the way to Hermopolis.

There is an impressive shrine to the baboon god and a single human burial on the lowest level. You need a torch to get the most out of the galleries.

At one time Tuna Al Gebel belonged to Akhetaten, the short-lived capital of Pharaoh Akhenaten, and along the road you pass one of 14 stelae marking the boundary of the royal city. The large stone stele carries Akhenaten's vow never to expand his city beyond this western limit of its farmlands and associated villages, nor to be buried anywhere else, although it seems he was eventually buried in the Valley of the Kings at Luxor. To the left, two damaged statues of the pharaoh and his wife Nefertiti hold offering tables; the sides are inscribed with figures of three of their daughters.

The most striking ruins at Hermopolis itself are two colossal 14th-century-BC quartzite statues of Thoth as a baboon. These supported part of Thoth's temple, which was rebuilt throughout antiquity. A Middle Kingdom temple gateway and a pylon of Ramses II, using stone plundered from nearby Tell Al Amarna, also survive. There is also the remains of a Coptic basilica, which reused columns and even the baboon statues, though first removing their giant phalluses.

The site is several kilometres south of Hermopolis and then 5km along a road into the desert.

Tomb of Petosiris TOMB
(☺8am-4pm) The Tomb of Petosiris, a high priest of Thoth from the late period (between the Persian and Greek conquests), is unusual because it copies the form of what has come to be labelled as a Ptolemaic temple. Like his elaborate sarcophagus in the Egyptian Museum in Cairo, Petosiris's tomb is a fascinating mix. Although built in the reign of Nectanebo II, it shows both Persian and Greek influence. There are wonderful coloured reliefs of farming and of the deceased being given offerings, as well as others of daily life. The rectangular inner chamber is supported by four pillars. The burial chamber is beneath the centre of this space.

Tomb of Isadora TOMB
Isadora was a wealthy woman who drowned in the Nile during the rule of Antoninus Pius (AD 138–161). Her tomb has few decorations but it does contain the unfortunate woman's mummy, with her teeth, hair and fingernails clearly visible.

SUSTAINABLE TOURISM

A rarity in Egypt, **New Hermopolis** (www.newhermopolis.org; half board per person UK£60-90 depending on group size; ☉ Oct-May; P ☎) is a sustainable farm and lodge run as a not-for-profit to provide educational opportunities for the local community. Accommodation is in bee-hive-domed rooms, water is drawn from the farm's well, and power is mostly from solar panels. The centre has meeting rooms and currently only accepts groups of 12 to 24 people. It has some senior foreign Egyptologists as its patrons.

❶ Getting There & Away

The slow village train service from Minya stops at Mallawi. From there, a network of microbuses runs around the villages. But unless you have time to burn, the only way to get around these sites is by taxi from Minya, perhaps continuing on to Asyut. Expect to pay up to LE1000, depending on the time you want to spend, the distance you want to travel and your bargaining skills.

Tell Al Amarna

In the fifth year of his reign, Pharaoh Akhenaten (1352–1336 BC) and his queen Nefertiti abandoned the gods and priests of Karnak and established a new religion based on the worship of a single deity, Aten, god of the sun disc.

They also built a new capital, Akhetaten (Horizon of the Aten), now known as Tell Al Amarna. This beautiful crescent-shaped plain, about 10km from north to south, sits between the river and a bay of high cliffs. After Akhenaten's death, his successor changed his name from Tutankhaten to Tutankhamun (1336–1327 BC), re-established the cult of Amun and moved the capital back to Thebes. Akhetaten, capital of Egypt for some 30 years, fell into ruin.

Akhenaten's doomed project is a complex site and the ruins, scattered across the desert plain, are hard to understand. Pre-trip planning helps: more detailed information is available on the excavation site www.amarnaproject.com.

◉ Sights

Two groups of cliff tombs, about 8km apart, make up the **Tell Al Amarna necropolis**

(adult/student LE60/30; ☉ 8am-4pm Oct-May, to 5pm Jun-Sep), which features colourful, albeit defaced, wall paintings of life during the Aten revolution. Remains of temples and private or administrative buildings are scattered across a wide area: this was, after all, an imperial city. Buy tickets at the ticket office.

◉ Central Ruins

Central City   TEMPLE
The centre of Akhetaten contained the temple complex, the Great Palace and the King's House. The temple complex contained two main buildings, a sanctuary and the Long Temple, 190m in length and divided into six courts. Along the south wall of the Long Table, archaeologists found the remains of 920 offering tables. This was separated from the King's House by storerooms. The palace was built of stone and decorated with great care, with faience mouldings and tiles, and alabaster balustrades.

Archaeologists value the site because, unlike most places in Egypt, it was occupied for just one reign. Also, it has proved to be one of the most useful sites for understanding how people lived in this early period.

◉ Northern Tombs

Tomb of Huya (No 1)   TOMB
Huya was the steward of Akhenaten's mother, Queen Tiye, and relief scenes to the right and left of the entrance to his tomb show Tiye dining with her son and his family. On the right wall of this columned outer chamber, Akhenaten is shown taking his mother to a small temple he has built for her and, on the left wall, sitting in a carrying chair with Nefertiti.

Tomb of Meryre II (No 2)   TOMB
Meryre II was scribe, steward and 'Overseer of the Royal Harem of Nefertiti'. To the left of the entrance, you will find a scene that shows Nefertiti pouring wine for Akhenaten.

Tomb of Ahmose (No 3)   TOMB
Ahmose, whose title was 'True Scribe of the King, Fan-Bearer on the King's Right Hand', was buried in the northern cemetery. Much of his tomb decoration was unfinished: the left-hand wall of the long corridor leading to the burial chamber shows the artists' different stages. The upper register shows the royal couple on their way to the Great Temple of Aten, followed by armed guards.

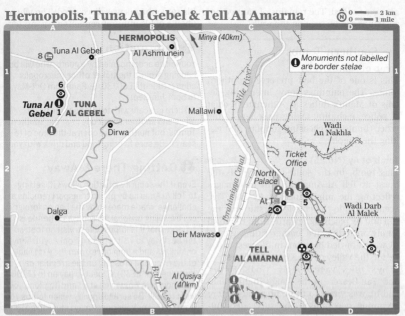

The lower register shows them seated in the palace listening to an orchestra.

Tomb of Meryre I (No 4)   TOMB
High priest of the Aten, Meryre is shown, on the left wall of the columned chamber, being carried by his friends to receive rewards from the royal couple. On the right-hand wall, the royal couple are shown making offerings to the Aten disc; note here the rare depiction of a rainbow.

Tomb of Penthu (No 5)   TOMB
Penthu, the royal physician and 'First under the King', was buried in a simple tomb. The left-hand wall of the corridor is decorated with images of the royal family at the Great Temple of Aten and of Pentu being appointed their physician.

Tomb of Panehsy (No 6)   TOMB
The tomb of Panehsy, chief servant of the Aten in Akhetaten, retains the decorated facade most others have lost. Inside, scenes of the royal family, including Nefertiti driving her chariot and, on the right wall of the entrance passage, Nefertiti's sister Mutnodjmet, later married to Pharaoh Horemheb (1323–1295 BC), with dwarf servants. Panehsy appears as a fat old man on the left

wall of the passage between the two main chambers.

With the end of the ancient rites, Copts created a Christian community around these tombs and Panehsy's tomb was converted to a church. Two of the first chamber's four columns were removed by the Copts and an apse was added. The remains of painted angel wings can be seen on the walls.

Southern Tombs

Tomb of Mahu (No 9)   TOMB

This is one of the best preserved southern tombs. The paintings show interesting details of Mahu's duties as Akhenaten's chief of police, including taking prisoners to the vizier (minister), checking supplies and visiting the temple.

Tomb of Ay (No 25)   TOMB

This tomb, in the southern group, is the finest at Tell Al Amarna, with the images reflecting the importance of Ay and Tiyi. Scenes include the couple worshipping the sun and Ay receiving rewards from the royal family, including red-leather riding gloves. Ay wasn't buried here, but in the west valley beside the Valley of the Kings at Thebes.

Ay's titles were simply 'God's Father' and 'Fan-Bearer on the King's Right Hand', and he was vizier to three pharaohs before becoming one himself (he succeeded Tutankhamun and reigned from 1327 to 1323 BC). His wife Tiyi was Nefertiti's wet nurse.

Royal Tomb of Akhenaten

Royal Tomb of Akhenaten   TOMB

(additional ticket adult/student LE40/20) Akhenaten's tomb (No 26) is in a ravine about 12km up the Royal Valley (Wadi Darb Al Malek), which divides the north and south sections of the cliffs and where the sun was seen to rise each dawn. It is similar in design and proportions to the royal tombs in the Valley of the Kings but with several burial chambers. The tomb decoration was painted on plaster, most of which has fallen, so very little remains.

The right-hand chamber has damaged reliefs of Akhenaten and his family worshipping Aten. A raised rectangular outline in the burial chamber once held the sarcophagus, which is now in the Egyptian Museum in Cairo (after being returned from Germany).

A well-laid road leads up the bleak valley. The guard will need to start up the tomb's generator before allowing you inside. Akhenaten himself was probably not buried here, although members of his family certainly were. Some believe he was buried in KV 55 in Luxor's Valley of the Kings, where

his sarcophagus was discovered. The whereabouts of his mummy remains are a mystery.

ℹ Information

You will be accompanied by a guard, who will be hanging around the **ticket office** (necropolis adult/student LE60/30; ☉ 8am-4pm Oct-May, to 5pm Jun-Sep).

There is a cafe with toilets near the ticket office and another newer one near the Southern Tombs, but neither were open at the time of research. Be sure to bring food and drink with you.

ℹ Getting There & Away

Even if the security situation allows it, getting to Tell Al Amarna by public transport remains a challenge; made more so by the ban on foreigners travelling on local microbuses. The site is so large that it is impossible to visit on foot, so the best way to visit is by taxi from Asyut, Minya or Mallawi and a long drive down the east bank of the river, or a crossing on the irregular car ferry (per car LE30). Expect to pay up to LE1000 depending on where you start and how long you want to stay. Be sure to specify which tombs you want to visit or your driver may refuse to go to far-flung sites.

Tombs of Mir

The necropolis of the governors of Cusae, the **Tombs of Mir** (adult/student LE40/20; ☉ 9am-4pm Sat-Wed) as they are commonly known (sometimes also Meir), were cut into the barren escarpment during the Old and Middle Kingdoms. Nine tombs are decorated and open to the public; six others were unfinished and remain unexcavated.

Tomb No 1 and the adjoining tomb No 2 are inscribed with 720 Pharaonic deities, but as the tombs were used as cells by early Coptic hermits, many faces and names of the gods were destroyed. In tomb No 4, you can still see the original grid drawn on the wall to assist the artist in designing the layout of the wall decorations. Tomb No 3 features a cow giving birth.

The tombs are about 50 minutes' drive from Asyut towards Minya. The bus will drop you at Al Qusiya. Few vehicles from Al Qusiya go out to the Tombs of Mir, so you'll have to hire a taxi to take you there. Expect to pay at least LE70, depending on how long you spend at the site. A taxi from Asyut to Mir will cost LE20 to LE300. Ideally, you could combine this with a visit to Deir Al Muharraq.

Deir Al Muharraq

Deir Al Muharraq MONASTERY
(Burnt Monastery; ☉ 6am-dusk) Deir Al Muharraq, an hour's drive northwest of Asyut, is a place of pilgrimage, refuge and vows, where the strength of Coptic traditions can be experienced. Resident monks believe that Mary and Jesus inhabited a cave on this site for six months and 10 days after fleeing from Herod, their longest stay anywhere they are said to have rested in Egypt. Tradition states that the Church of Al Azraq (the Anointed) sits over the cave and is the world's oldest Christian church, consecrated around AD 60.

There has been monastic life here since the 4th century, although the current building dates from the 12th to 13th centuries. Unusually, the church contains two iconostases; the one to the left of the altar came from an Ethiopian Church of Sts Peter and Paul, which used to sit on the roof. Other objects from the Ethiopians are displayed in the hall outside the church.

The keep beside the church is an independent 7th-century tower, rebuilt in the 12th and 20th centuries. Reached by drawbridge, its four floors can serve as a mini-monastery, complete with its own small Church of St Michael, a refectory, accommodation and even burial space behind the altar.

Monks believe the monastery's religious significance is given in the Book of Isaiah (19:19–21). The monastery has done much to preserve Coptic tradition: monks here spoke the Coptic language until the 19th century (at that time there were 190 of them) and, while other monasteries celebrate some of the Coptic liturgy in Arabic (for their Arabic-speaking congregation), here they stick to Coptic.

Also in the compound, the Church of St George (Mar Girgis) was built in 1880 with permission from the Ottoman sultan, who was still the official sovereign of Egypt. It is decorated with paintings of the 12 apostles and other religious scenes, its iconostasis is made from marble and many of the icons are in Byzantine style. Tradition has it that the icon showing the Virgin and Child was painted by St Luke.

Remember to remove shoes before entering either church and respect the silence and sanctity of the place. For a week every year (usually 21 to 28 June), thousands of pilgrims attend the monastery's annual feast, a time when non-pilgrim visitors may not be admitted.

You will usually be escorted around the monastery and, while there is no fee, donations are appreciated. Visits sometimes finish with a brief visit to the new church built in 1940 or the nearby gift shop or, sometimes, with a cool drink in the monastery's reception room.

The monastery is about 50 minutes' drive from Asyut towards Minya. The bus will drop you at Al Qusiya, but currently you are not allowed to take a microbus, so you would have to walk. A taxi is the obvious alternative.

Asyut

🔗 088 / POP 429,538
Asyut offers a very different view of Egypt than one might gain from Cairo or Luxor: it belongs to the provinces, a capital not of the country but of the area's farming communities. Settled during Pharaonic times on a fertile plain west of the Nile, it has preserved an echo of antiquity in its name: as Swaty it was the ancient capital of the 13th nome of Upper Egypt. Sitting at the end of one of the great caravan routes from south of the Sahara via Sudan and then Al Kharga Oasis, it has always been important commercially, if not politically. For centuries, slaves were one of the main commodities traded here and caravans stopped to quarantine them before they were traded, a period in which slavers used to prepare some of their male slaves for the harem.

◎ Sights

For a city of such history, Asyut has surprisingly little to show for itself. In part, this is because much of what survives of ancient Asyut is either unexcavated or survives in the hills on the edge of the irrigation, which is currently off-limits to foreigners. Spiritual tourists did flock to Asyut in 2000 after the Virgin Mary was seen by both Copts and Muslims floating above the Church of St Mark. The apparitions continued for some months.

Asyut Barrage LANDMARK
Until the Nile-side Alexan Palace, one of the city's finest 19th-century buildings, has been renovated and reopened, the Asyut Barrage serves as the most accessible introduction to Asyut's period of wealth. Built over the Nile

Asyut

between 1898 and 1902 to regulate the flow of water into the Ibrahimiyya Canal and assure irrigation of the valley as far north as Beni Suef, it also serves as a bridge across the Nile.

As the barrage still has strategic importance, photography is forbidden, so you should keep your camera out of sight.

Banana Island   ISLAND
(Gezirat Al Moz) Banana Island, to the north of town, is a shady, pleasant place to picnic. You'll have to bargain with a felucca captain for the ride: expect to pay at least LE40 an hour.

Convent of the Holy Virgin   CONVENT
(☺6am-6pm) At Dirunka, some 11km southwest of Asyut, this convent was built near a cave where the Holy Family are said to have taken refuge during their flight into Egypt.

Some 50 nuns and monks live at the convent, built into a cliff situated about 120m above the valley. One of the monks will be happy to show you around. You will need to go by taxi (LE60 to LE80).

During the Moulid of the Virgin (a festival held in the second half of August), many thousands of pilgrims come to pray, carrying portraits of Mary and Jesus.

🛏 Sleeping

As a large provincial centre, Asyut has a selection of hotels, but many are overpriced and noisy. While prices have risen in the past few years, standards have not.

YMCA   HOSTEL $
(☎088-230-3018; Sharia Salah Ad Din Al Ayyubi; dm LE30; ❄) This hostel with a large garden offers basic rooms with fridges. A popular stop for Egyptian youth groups, make sure to book ahead.

Al Watania Palace Hotel   HOTEL $$
(☎088-228-7981; Sharia Al Gomhuriyya; s/d US$60/80; ❄🐾🛜) The newest, smartest and largest hotel in Asyut is already looking a little worn. Part of a property development by a Gulf-backed consortium, it has an impressive lobby, spacious rooms, various function rooms and more stars than anywhere else in town. What you lose in location and atmosphere is made up for with comfort and service.

Assiutel Hotel   HOTEL $$
(☎088-231-2121; 146 Corniche An Nil (Thawra); s/d LE620/840; ❄@) Overlooking the Nile and the noisy corniche, this was once the best place in town, but it now looks drab. There are two levels of rooms, but neither are particularly welcoming and the cheaper ones are worn. All have satellite TV, fridge and private bathroom. There is a dull restaurant and one of Asyut's only bars.

🍴 Eating

The mid-priced rooftop restaurant at Al Watania Palace Hotel is among the more reliable places for a sit-down meal. There are several good fast food places along nearby Sharia Al Gomhuriyya. There are the usual *fuul* and *ta'amiyya* stands around the train station, and some more upmarket options along the Nile, where there is also a very friendly cafe.

★ **Koshari Alaa Eldin**   EGYPTIAN $
(Sharia Al Gomhuriyya; mains LE6-10; ⊘10am-11pm) Excellent *kushari* from this friendly, simple place on one of the main streets in town.

La Poire   PASTRIES $$
(Sharia Al Gomhurriya; ⊘10am-9pm Sat-Thu) Excellent Egyptian and international pastries and ice cream in an offshoot of an upmarket Cairo patisserie. The *kunafa* (vermicelli-like pastry over a vanilla base soaked in syrup) with dates and almonds (LE110 a kilo) is particularly good.

ⓘ Information

There are ATMs at Midan Talaat Harb and along Sharia Port Said.

The very welcoming staff at the **tourist office** (⌨088-231-0010; Governorate Bldg, Corniche An Nil (Thawra), which can look derelict when the doors are shut, can provide maps of the city and help arrange onward travel.

ⓘ Getting There & Away

Asyut is a major hub for all forms of transport, although if you want to go by road to Luxor and the south you will have to change at Sohag.

BUS

The Upper Egypt **bus station** (⌨088-233-0460) near the train station has services to Cairo (LE80, five to six hours), Hurghada (LE80, 5½ hours), Sharm El Sheikh (LE130, 10 hours) and Alexandria (LE110, eight hours).

MICROBUS & TAXI

There are no microbuses to Luxor. You might be able to take one to **Mallawi**, but this is sometimes forbidden. A private taxi to Luxor will cost up to LE1000.

TRAIN

There are several daytime trains to Cairo (1st/2nd class LE79/44, four to five hours) and Minya (LE39/26, one hour), and about 10 daily south to Luxor (LE70/40, five to six hours) and Aswan (LE95/52, eight to nine hours). All stop in Sohag (LE33/21, one to two hours) and Qena (LE59/35, three to four hours).

Sohag

⌨093 / POP 211,181
Sohag is one of the major Coptic Christian areas of Upper Egypt. Although there are few sights in the city, the nearby White and Red Monasteries are well worth a visit, and

the town of Akhmim, across the river, is of interest.

⊙ Sights

To get to the monasteries, you'll have to take a taxi (about LE100 per hour).

★ **Red Monastery**   MONASTERY
(Deir Al Ahmar; LE20; ⊘7am-dusk) The Red Monastery, 4km southeast of the White Monastery and hidden at the rear of a village, is one of the most remarkable Christian buildings in Egypt. It was founded by Besa, a disciple of Shenouda who, according to legend, was a thief who converted to Christianity; he dedicated it to St Bishoi. Opening hours might be affected by services and Coptic holidays.

The older of the monastery's two chapels, the Chapel of St Bishoi and St Bigol, dates from the 4th century AD and some 80% of its surfaces are still covered with painted plaster and frescoes, giving a good idea of how all late antique religious buildings might have looked. An extensive restoration by the American Research Center in Egypt and United States Agency for International Development (USAID) has revealed them in full glory. The quality and extent of the surviving work has led this chapel to be likened to the Aya Sofya in Istanbul and the church of Ravenna as one of the great surviving monuments of late antiquity. The chapel of the Virgin, across the open court, is a more modern and less interesting structure, but the services held here, with much incense, can be atmospheric.

White Monastery   MONASTERY
(Deir Al Abyad; LE20; ⊘7am-dusk) On rocky ground above the old Nile flood level, 6km northwest of Sohag, the White Monastery was founded by St Shenouda around AD 400 and dedicated to his mentor, St Bigol. White limestone from Pharaonic temples was reused, and ancient gods and hieroglyphs still look out from some of the blocks. The design of the outer walls echoes ancient temples.

The monastery once supported a huge community of monks and boasted the largest library in Egypt. Research is finally underway on the manuscripts, while the monastery is currently home to 23 monks. The fortress walls still stand though they failed to protect the interior, most of which is in ruins. Nevertheless, it is easy to make out the plan of the church inside the enclosure

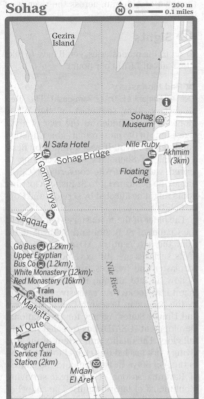

Sohag

- Gezira Island
- Sohag Museum
- Al Safa Hotel
- Nile Ruby
- Akhmim (3km)
- Sohag Bridge
- Floating Cafe
- Al Gomhuriyya
- Saqqafa
- Go Bus (1.2km); Upper Egyptian Bus Co (1.2km); White Monastery (12km); Red Monastery (16km)
- Train Station
- Al Mahatta
- Al Qute
- Moghaf Qena Service Taxi Station (2km)
- Midan El Aref
- Nile River

0 — 200 m
0 — 0.1 miles

walls. Made of brick and measuring 75m by 35m, it follows a basilica plan, with a nave, two side aisles and a triple apse. The nave and apses are intact, the domes decorated with the Dormition of the Virgin and Christ Pantocrator. Nineteen columns, taken from an earlier structure, separate the side chapels from the nave. Visitors wanting to assist in services may arrive from 4am.

Akhmim

RUINS

(Meret Amun; adult/child LE40/20) The satellite town of Akhmim, on Sohag's east bank, covers the ruins of the ancient Egyptian town of Ipu, itself built over an older predynastic settlement. It was dedicated to Min, a fertility god often represented by a giant phallus, equated with Pan by the Greeks (who later called the town Panopolis). A taxi to Akhmim should cost around LE50 per hour. The microbus, if you are allowed to take it, costs LE6 and takes 15 minutes.

The current name echoes that of the god Min, but more definite links to antiquity were uncovered in 1982 when excavations beside the Mosque of Sheikh Naqshadi revealed an 11m-high statue of **Meret Amun**. This is the tallest statue of an ancient queen to have been discovered in Egypt. Meret Amun (Beloved of the Amun) was the daughter of Ramses II, wife of Amenhotep and priestess of the Temple of Min. She is shown here with flail in her left hand, wearing a ceremonial headdress and large earrings. Nearby, the remains of a seated statue of her father still retain some original colour.

Little is left of the temple itself, and the statue of Meret Amun now stands in a small archaeological park, among the remains of a Roman settlement and houses of the modern town. Another excavation pit has been dug across the road and a more extensive excavation is underway nearby.

Akhmim was famed in antiquity for its textiles – one of its current weavers calls it 'Manchester before history'. The tradition continues today and opposite the statue of Meret Amun, across from the post office, a green door leads to a small weaving factory (knock if it is shut). Here you can see weavers at work and buy hand-woven silk and cotton textiles straight from the bolt (silk LE200 per metre, cotton LE90 to LE125) or packets of ready-made tablecloths and serviettes.

Sohag Museum

MUSEUM

(adult/child LE60/30) At the time of writing, the new Sohag Museum had not yet opened, but it will eventually display local antiquities, including those from ongoing excavations of the temple of Ramses II in Akhmim.

🛏 Sleeping

Al Safa Hotel

HOTEL $

(☎ 093-230-7701, 093-230-7702; Sharia Al Gomhuriyya, west bank; s/d LE300/400; ❋🐾) This well-placed west-bank spot across the river from the new museum is the best hotel in town (which isn't saying much). Rooms are comfortable and the riverside terrace is very popular in the evening for snacks, soft drinks and water pipes. Prices vary according to demand.

Nile Ruby

HOUSEBOAT $$

(☎ 012-2223-5440) The downturn in Nile cruising has seen a number of boats converted to hotels, the latest being the Nile Ruby, moored near the bridge in Sohag. The boat was being cleaned up at the time of our last

THE KING LIST

Ancient Egyptians constructed their history around their pharaohs. Instead of using a continuous year-by-year sequence, events were recorded as happening in a specific year of a specific ruler: at each pharaoh's accession they started at year one, continuing until the pharaoh died, and then began again with year one of the next pharaoh.

The sequence of pharaohs was recorded on so-called king lists. These can be seen in the Egyptian Museum in Cairo, the Louvre in Paris and the British Museum in London. But the only one remaining in its original location can be found in Seti I's Temple at Abydos. With an emphasis on the royal ancestors, Seti names 75 of his predecessors beginning with the semi-mythical Menes (usually regarded as Narmer). But the list is incomplete: Seti rewrites history by excluding pharaohs considered 'unsuitable', omitting the foreign Hyksos rulers of the Second Intermediate Period, the female pharaoh Hatshepsut and the Amarna pharaohs. So Amenhotep III is immediately followed by Horemheb, and in the process Akhenaten, Smenkhkare, Tutankhamun and Ay are simply erased from the record.

visit, and prices for the 70 cabins had not yet been fixed.

✗ Eating & Drinking

The best food options are in the two main hotels. Budget *kushari, fuul* and *ta'amiyya* places line the roads near the train station. For something more romantic, there is a cafe on Gezira Island, reached by boat from the north side of the Hotel Al Nil.

Floating Cafe   CAFE
(☉noon-midnight) Moored on the west bank of the Nile, close to the bridge, this Nileboat-turned-cafe looks tired, but still attracts crowds on a warm evening. There is a basic menu and sometimes a buffet, but avoid eating and stick to the nonalcoholic drinks. It can be a fun place to people-watch.

ℹ Information

There are banks along Sharia Al Gomhuriyya.

The helpful **tourist office** (☎093-460-4913; Governorate Bldg; ☉8.30am-3pm Sun-Thu), in the building beside the museum on the east bank, can help arrange visits to the monasteries.

ℹ Getting There & Away

Go Bus has a twice daily service to Cairo (LE135). The **Upper Egyptian Bus Co** has regular departures to Cairo between 7.30am and 9.30pm (LE85 to LE120).

There is a frequent train service north and south along the Cairo-Luxor main line, with a dozen daily trains to Asyut (1st/2nd class LE34/21, one to two hours) and Luxor (LE94/63, three to four hours). The service to Al Balyana (3rd class only, one to two hours) is very slow.

Abydos

There were shrines to Osiris, god of the dead, throughout Egypt, each one the supposed resting place of another part of his body, but the main cult centre of Osiris was Abydos (adult/student LE80/40; ☉8am-4pm). This was where his head was believed to rest and it became somewhere Egyptians tried to visit on pilgrimage during their lives and also the place to be buried: it was used as a necropolis for more than 4500 years from predynastic to Christian times (c 4000 BC–AD 600). Most tombs remain unexcavated, a fact reflected in the Arabic name for the place, Arabah El Madfunah ('the buried Arabah'). The area behind the Temple of Seti I, known as Umm Al Qa'ab (Mother of Pots), contains the tombs of many early pharaohs including Djer (c 3000 BC) of the 1st dynasty. With excavations ongoing, this area is closed to the public.

◉ Sights

★**Temple of Seti I**   MONUMENT
(Cenotaph; Map p179; adult/student LE80/40; ☉8am-4pm) The first structure you'll see at Abydos is the Great Temple of Seti I, which, after a certain amount of restoration work, is one of the most complete, unique and beautiful temples in Egypt. With exquisite decoration and plenty of atmosphere, it is the main attraction here, although the nearby Osireion is also wrapped in mystery and the desert views are spectacular.

This great limestone structure, unusually L-shaped rather than rectangular, had seven great doorways and was dedicated to the six

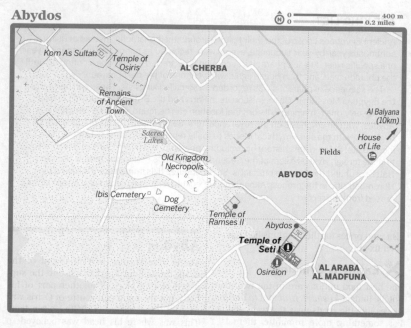

major gods – Osiris, Isis, Horus, Amun-Ra, Ra-Horakhty and Ptah – and also to Seti I (1294–1279 BC) himself. Less than 50 years after the end of the Amarna 'heresy' – when Pharaoh Akhenaten broke with tradition by creating a new religion, capital and artistic style – this is a clear attempt to revive the old ways. As you roam through Seti's dark halls and sanctuaries, an air of mystery surrounds you.

The temple is entered through a largely destroyed pylon and two open courtyards, built by Seti I's son Ramses II, who is depicted on the portico killing Asiatics and worshipping Osiris. Beyond, originally with seven doorways but now only entered through the central one, is the first hypostyle hall, also completed by Ramses II. Reliefs depict the pharaoh making offerings to the gods and preparing the temple building.

The second hypostyle hall, with 24 sandstone papyrus columns, was the last part of the temple to have been decorated by Seti, who died before the work was completed. The reliefs here are of the highest quality and hark back to the finest Old Kingdom work. Particularly outstanding is a scene on the rear right-hand wall showing Seti standing in front of a shrine to Osiris, upon which sits the god himself. Standing in front of him are the goddesses Maat, Renpet, Isis, Nephthys and Amentet. Below is a frieze of Hapi, the Nile god.

At the rear of this second hypostyle hall are sanctuaries for each of the seven gods (right to left: Horus, Isis, Osiris, Amun-Ra, Ra-Horakhty, Ptah and the deified Seti), which once held their cult statues. The Osiris sanctuary, third from the right, leads to a series of inner chambers dedicated to the god, his wife and child, Isis and Horus, and the ever-present Seti. More interesting are the chambers off to the left of the seven sanctuaries: here, in a group of chambers dedicated to the mysteries of Osiris, the god is shown mummified with the goddess Isis hovering above him as a bird, a graphic scene which records the conception of their son Horus.

Immediately to the left of this is the corridor known as Gallery of the Kings, carved with the figures of Seti I, his eldest son the future Ramses II, and a long list of the pharaohs who preceded them. The stairway leads out to the Osireion and the desert beyond.

One of the temple's most recent residents was Dorothy Eady. An Englishwoman better known as 'Omm Sety', Eady believed she was a reincarnated temple priestess and lover of Seti I. For 35 years she lived at Abydos and provided archaeologists with information about the workings of the temple, in which she was given permission to perform the ancient rites. She died in 1981 and is buried in the desert.

Osireion
MONUMENT

Directly behind the Temple of Seti I, the Osireion is a weird and wonderful structure, unique in Egypt and still baffling for Egyptologists. The entire structure is closed to visitors, making inspection of the funerary and ritual texts carved on its walls impossible, but you can look down on it from the rear of Seti's temple, from where there is a good overview of the cenotaph and its surrounding waters.

Originally thought to be an Old Kingdom construction, on account of the great blocks of granite, it has now been dated to Seti's reign and is usually interpreted as a cenotaph to Osiris, or more specifically to Seti as Osiris. Its design is believed to be based on the rock-cut tombs in the Valley of the Kings. Reached by a 120 ft subterranean passage, the centre of its 10-columned 'burial chamber', which lies at a lower level than Seti's temple, is a dummy sarcophagus. This chamber is surrounded by water channels to simulate an island.

Temple of Ramses II
TEMPLE

Northwest of Seti I's temple, this smaller, less well-preserved, roofless structure was built by his son Ramses II (1279–1213 BC). Following the rectangular plan of a traditional temple, it has sanctuaries for each god Ramses considered important, including Osiris, Amun-Ra, Thoth, Min, the deified Seti I and Ramses himself. The reliefs still retain a significant amount of colour, clearly seen on figures of priests, offering bearers and the pharaoh anointing the gods' statues. The site is occasionally placed off limits.

🛏 Sleeping

House of Life
HOTEL $$

(☑ 010-1000-8912, 093-494-4044; www.houseoflife.info; s/d €55/70; ❄@🛜🏊) This large Dutch-Egyptian-run complex with a mock-Pharaonic facade is on the road leading to the Temple of Seti I. Spacious, quiet and well-equipped rooms have walk-in showers. Most look onto the swimming pool or surrounding countryside (no temple views). There is a healing centre using ancient remedies and an outdoor cafe serving soft drinks and water pipes.

Temple of Seti I

Seven Sanctuaries
1 Chapel of Horus
2 Chapel of Isis
3 Chapel of Osiris
4 Chapel of Amen-Ra
5 Chapel of Ra-Harakhty
6 Chapel of Ptah
7 Chapel of the deified Seti

Entrance
First Courtyard
Terrace
Second Courtyard
Portico
First Hypostyle Hall
Second Hypostyle Hall
Seven Sanctuaries
7 6 5 4 3 2 1
Gallery of the Kings
Corridor of the Bulls
Osireion

ℹ Getting There & Away

Al Araba Al Madfuna is 10km from the nearest train station, at Al Balyana. Most people arrive from Luxor, where many companies offer day-long coach tours. A private taxi from Luxor will cost from LE900 return, depending on bargaining skills and how long you want at the temple. A train leaves Luxor at 8.25am (1st/2nd class LE52/42, three hours). A private taxi from Al Balyana to the temple will cost about LE60 depending on the wait time. A microbus from Al Balyana costs LE3.

Qena

☑ 096 / POP 257,939

Qena sits on a huge bend of the river, and at the intersection of one of the main Nile roads and the road running across the desert to the Red Sea port of Port Safaga and resort town of Hurghada. A market town and provincial capital, it is a useful junction for a visit to the nearby spectacular temple complex at Dendara. It's also the place to be on the 14th of the Islamic month of Sha'ban, when the city's 12th-century patron saint, Abdel Rehim Al Qenawi, is celebrated.

◉ Sights

★ **Dendara**   TEMPLE

(adult/student LE80/40; ☉7am-6pm) Dendara was an important administrative and religious centre as early as the 6th dynasty (c 2320 BC). Although built at the very end of the Pharaonic period, the Temple of Hathor is one of the iconic Egyptian buildings, mostly because it remains largely intact, with a great stone roof and columns, dark chambers, underground crypts and twisting stairways, all carved with hieroglyphs.

All visitors must pass through the **visitors centre** with its ticket office and bazaar. While it is still mostly unoccupied, before long this may involve running the gauntlet of hassling traders to get to the temple. One advantage is a clean, working toilet. At the time of our visit, it was not possible to buy food or drinks at the site.

Beyond the towering gateway and mud walls, the temple was built on a slight rise. The entrance leads into the **outer hypostyle hall**, built by Roman emperor Tiberius, the first six of its 24 great stone columns adorned on all four sides with Hathor's head, defaced by Christians but still an impressive sight. The walls are carved with scenes of Tiberius and his Roman successors presenting offerings to the Egyptian gods: the message here, as throughout the temple, is the continuity of tradition, even under foreign rulers. The ceiling at the far left and right side of the hall is decorated with zodiacs. One section has now been cleaned and the colours are very bright.

The inner temple was built by the Ptolemies. The smaller **inner hypostyle hall** again has Hathor columns and walls carved with scenes of royal ceremonials, including the founding of the temple. But notice the 'blank' cartouches that reveal much about the political instability of late Ptolemaic times – with such a rapid turnover of pharaohs, the stonemasons seem to have been reluctant to carve the names of those who might not be in the job for long. Things reached an all-time low in 80 BC when Ptolemy XI murdered his more popular wife and stepmother Berenice III after only 19 days of co-rule. The outraged citizens of Alexandria dragged the pharaoh from his palace and killed him in revenge.

Beyond the second hypostyle hall, you will find the **Hall of Offerings** leads to the **sanctuary**, the most holy part of the temple, home to the goddess' statue. A further Hathor statue was stored in the crypt beneath her temple, and brought out each year for the New Year Festival, which in ancient times fell in July and coincided with the rising of the Nile. It was carried into the Hall of Offerings, where it rested with statues of other gods before being taken to the roof. The **western staircase** is decorated with scenes from this procession. In the open-air kiosk on the southwestern corner of the roof, the gods awaited the first reviving rays of the sun-god Ra on New Year's Day. The statues were later taken down the **eastern staircase**, which is also decorated with this scene.

The theme of revival continues in two suites of rooms on the roof, decorated with scenes of the revival of Osiris by his sister-wife, Isis. In the centre of the ceiling of the **northeastern suite** is a plaster cast of the famous 'Dendara Zodiac', the original now in the Louvre in Paris. Views of the surrounding countryside from the roof are magnificent.

The exterior walls feature lion-headed gargoyles to cope with the very occasional rainfall and are decorated with scenes of pharaohs paying homage to the gods. The most famous of these is on the rear (south) wall, where Cleopatra stands with Caesarion, her son by Julius Caesar.

Facing this back wall is a small **temple of Isis** built by Cleopatra's great rival Octavian (the Emperor Augustus). Walking back towards the front of the Hathor temple on the west side, the palm-filled **Sacred Lake** supplied the temple's water. Beyond this, to the north, lie the mudbrick foundations of the **sanatorium**, where the ill came to seek a cure from the goddess.

Finally there are two *mammisi* (birth houses): the first was built by the 30th-dynasty Egyptian pharaoh, Nectanebo I (380–362 BC), and decorated by the Ptolemies; the other was built by the Romans and decorated by Emperor Trajan (AD 98–117). Such buildings celebrated divine birth, both of the young gods and the pharaoh himself as the son of the gods. Between the *mammisi* lie the remains of a 5th-century-AD **Coptic basilica**.

Dendara

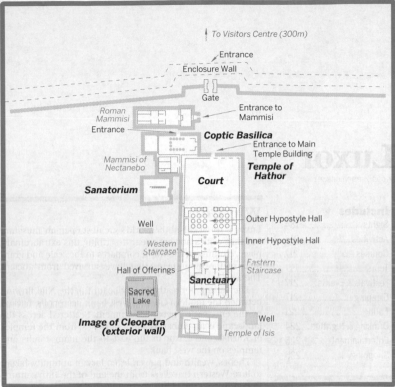

To Visitors Centre (300m)

Entrance

Enclosure Wall

Gate

Roman Mammisi

Entrance to Mammisi

Entrance

Coptic Basilica

Entrance to Main Temple Building

Mammisi of Nectanebo

Temple of Hathor

Court

Sanatorium

Well

Outer Hypostyle Hall

Western Staircase

Inner Hypostyle Hall

Hall of Offerings

Eastern Staircase

Sacred Lake

Sanctuary

Image of Cleopatra (exterior wall)

Well

Temple of Isis

Dendara is 4km southwest of Qena on the west side of the Nile. Most visitors arrive from Luxor. A return taxi from Luxor will cost you about LE200. There is also a day cruise to Dendara from Luxor. If you arrive in Qena by train, you will need to take a taxi to the temple (LE40 to the temple and back with some waiting time).

ⓘ Getting There & Away

BUS

The **Upper Egypt Bus Co** (Midan Al Mahatta), at the bus station opposite the train station, runs regular services to Cairo via the Red Sea, Hurghada and Suez.

MICROBUS

At the time of writing, foreigners were not allowed to use microbus services. When this changes, from the station, 1km inland from the bridge, you will be able to get south to Luxor and Aswan, east to Hurghada, Marsa Alam and Suez, and north to Nag Hamadi, Sohag and Asyut.

TRAIN

All main north–south trains stop at Qena. There are 1st-/2nd-class air-con trains to Luxor (from LE27/19, 40 minutes) and trains to Al Balyana (2nd/3rd class LE18/12, two hours).

Luxor

📞 095 / POP 1,088,911

Best Places to Eat

➡ Sofra Restaurant & Café (p222)

➡ Al Moudira (p224)

➡ Nile Valley Hotel (p223)

➡ As Sahaby Lane (p222)

➡ Koshari Alzaeem (p222)

Best Places to Stay

➡ Al Moudira (p221)

➡ Hilton Luxor Resort & Spa (p219)

➡ Nefertiti Hotel (p218)

➡ Beit Sabée (p220)

➡ Bob Marley Peace Hotel (p217)

➡ Winter Palace Hotel (p219)

Why Go?

Luxor is often called the world's greatest open-air museum, but that comes nowhere near describing this extraordinary place. Nothing in the world compares to the scale and grandeur of the monuments that have survived from ancient Thebes.

The setting is breathtakingly beautiful, the Nile flowing between the modern city and west-bank necropolis, backed by the enigmatic Theban escarpment. Scattered across the landscape is an embarrassment of riches, from the temples of Karnak and Luxor in the east to the many tombs and temples on the west bank.

Thebes' wealth and power, legendary in antiquity, began to lure Western travellers from the end of the 18th century. Depending on the political situation, today's traveller might be alone at the sights, or be surrounded by coachloads of tourists from around the world. Whichever it is, a little planning will help you get the most from the magic of Thebes.

When to Go
Luxor

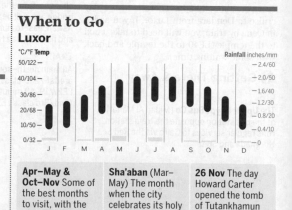

Apr–May & Oct–Nov Some of the best months to visit, with the richest light.

Sha'aban (Mar–May) The month when the city celebrates its holy man, Youssef Abu Al Haggag.

26 Nov The day Howard Carter opened the tomb of Tutankhamun in 1922.

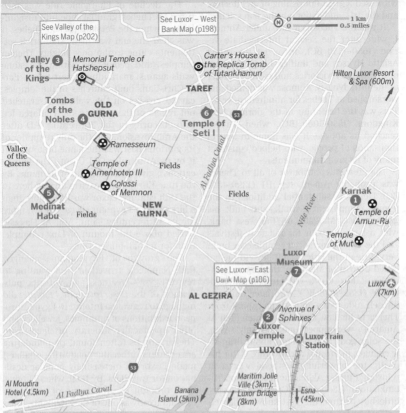

Luxor Highlights

1 Karnak (p185)
Wandering around the exotic stone thickets of gigantic papyrus-shaped columns in the great hypostyle hall.

2 Luxor Temple (p192)
Marvelling at the stunning architecture and returning later at night to see the beautifully lit carvings on the walls.

3 Valley of the Kings (p200) Being led by the gods into the afterworld, like the pharaoh.

4 Tombs of the Nobles (p214) Glimpsing the good life of an ancient Egyptian aristocrat on the tomb walls.

5 Medinat Habu (p210) Wandering through the best-preserved Theban temple in the soft late-afternoon light.

6 Temple of Seti I (p214) Sensing the spirituality of this rarely visited temple.

7 Luxor Museum (p193) Seeing the treasures in this beautiful museum.

History

Thebes (ancient Waset) became important in the Middle Kingdom period (2055–1650 BC). The 11th-dynasty Theban prince Montuhotep II (2055–2004 BC) reunited Upper and Lower Egypt, made Thebes his capital and increased Karnak's importance as a cult centre to the local god Amun with a temple dedicated to him. The 12th-dynasty pharaohs (1985–1795 BC) moved their capital back north, but much of their immense wealth from expanded foreign trade and agriculture, and tribute from military expeditions made into Nubia and Asia, went to Thebes, which remained the religious capital. This 200-year period was one of the richest times throughout Egyptian history, which witnessed a great flourishing of architecture and the arts, and major advances in science.

It was the Thebans again, under Ahmose I, who, after the Second Intermediate Period (1650–1550 BC), drove out the ruling Asiatic Hyksos and unified Egypt. Because of his military victories and as the founder of the 18th dynasty, Ahmose was deified and worshipped at Thebes for hundreds of years. This was the beginning of the glorious New Kingdom (1550–1069 BC), when Thebes reached its apogee. It was home to tens of thousands of people, who helped construct many of its great monuments.

The greatest contributor of all to Thebes was probably Amenhotep III (1390–1352 BC). He made substantial additions to the temple complex at Karnak, and built his great palace, Malqata, on the west bank, with a large harbour for religious festivals and the largest memorial temple ever built. Very little of the latter is left beyond the so-called Colossi of Memnon, the largest monolithic statue ever carved. His son Amenhotep IV (1352–1336 BC), who later renamed himself Akhenaten, moved the capital from Thebes to his new city of Akhetaten (Tell Al Amarna), worshipped one god only (Aten, the solar god), and brought about dramatic changes in art and architecture. After his death, the powerful priesthood was soon reinstated under Akhenaten's successor, Tutankhamun (1336–1327 BC), who built very little but became the best-known pharaoh ever when his tomb was discovered full of treasure in 1922. Ramses II (1279–1213 BC) may have exaggerated his military victories, but he too was a great builder and added the magnificent hypostyle hall to Karnak, other halls to Luxor Temple, and built the Ramesseum and two magnificent tombs in the Valley of the Kings for himself and his many sons.

ℹ️ RESOURCES

Luxor Travel Guide (http://luxor-news. blogspot.co.uk) Information on Luxor.

Theban Mapping Project (www.theban mappingproject.com) History, images and news from the Valley of the Kings.

Flat Rental (www.flatsinluxor.co.uk) Accommodation, guide and tour bookings.

Luxor Times (http://luxortimesmag azine.blogspot.co.uk) The local English-language paper.

The decline of Pharaonic rule was mirrored by Thebes' gradual slide into insignificance: when the Persians sacked Thebes, it was clear the end was nigh. Mud-brick settlements clung to the once mighty Theban temples, and people hid within the stone walls against marauding desert tribes. Early Christians built churches in the temples, carved crosses on the walls and scratched out reliefs of the pagan gods. The area fell into obscurity in the 7th century AD after the Arab invasion, and the only reminder of its glorious past was the name bestowed on it by its Arab rulers: Al Uqsur (The Fortifications), giving modern Luxor its name. By the time European travellers arrived here in the 18th century, Luxor was little more than a large Upper Egyptian village, known more for its 12th-century saint, Abu Al Haggag, buried above the mound of Luxor Temple, than for its half-buried ruins.

The growth of Egyptomania changed that. Napoleon arrived in 1798 wanting to revive Egypt's greatness and, with the publication of the *Description de l'Egypte*, did manage to reawaken interest in Egypt. European exhibitions of mummies, jewellery and other spectacular funerary artefacts from Theban tombs (often found by plundering adventurers rather than enquiring scholars) made Luxor an increasingly popular destination for travellers. By 1869, when Thomas Cook brought his first group of tourists to Egypt, Luxor was one of the highlights. Mass tourism had arrived and Luxor regained its place on the world map.

The 1960s saw the start of modern mass tourism on the Nile with Luxor as its epicentre, and more hotels and sights than anywhere else in southern Egypt. The town has since grown into a city of several hundred thousand people, almost all of them dependant on tourism. In the past couple of decades, there have been booms and crashes, the latest crash brought on by the riots that ended the presidencies of Hosni Mubarak and Mohammed Morsi. Tourist numbers have been down since then, and people in Luxor and elsewhere in the south have suffered.

◉ Sights

Luxor sights are spread on the east and west banks of the Nile. Start on the east bank, where visitors will find most of the hotels, the modern city of Luxor and the temple complexes of Luxor and Karnak. The west bank, traditionally the 'side of the dead', is

LUXOR IN...

Two Days

If you've only got two days in Luxor, your schedule will be full on. Start the first day on the east bank with an early morning visit to the **Temples of Karnak** (p185). After Karnak stroll along the corniche to the **Luxor Museum** (p193). After a late lunch at **Sofra** (p222), visit **Luxor Temple** (p192) in the golden glow of the afternoon. Return after dinner to see the temple floodlit. The next day take a taxi for a day to the west bank, starting early again to avoid the crowds at the **Valley of the Kings** (p200). On the way back visit **Howard Carter's House** (p214), with its brilliant replica of Tutankhamun's burial chamber, and the **Memorial Temple of Hatshepsut** (p211). After lunch visit the **Tombs of the Nobles** (p213), or the wonderful temple of Ramses III at **Medinat Habu** (p210).

Four Days

Four days allows for a more leisurely schedule. On the west bank, you could visit the **Tombs of the Nobles** (p214), the **Ramesseum** (p211) and the **Temple of Seti I** (p214), and on the last day revisit Karnak in the morning and cross the river to see the ancient workers' village and tombs at **Deir Al Medina** (p209). Alternatively you could make a day-trip to the amazing temples of **Dendara** (p180) and **Abydos** (p177).

where the mortuary temples and necropolis are located.

◉ East Bank

Karnak

Karnak (☑095-238-0270; Sharia Maabad Al Karnak; adult/student LE120/60, incl open-air museum LE150/75; ⊙6am-6pm; 🅿) is an extraordinary complex of sanctuaries, kiosks, pylons and obelisks dedicated to the Theban triad but also to the greater glory of the pharaohs. The site covers over 2 sq km; it's large enough to contain about 10 cathedrals. At its heart is the Temple of Amun, the earthly 'home' of the local god. Built, added to, dismantled, restored, enlarged and decorated over nearly 1500 years, Karnak was the most important place of worship in Egypt during the New Kingdom.

The complex is dominated by the great **Temple of Amun-Ra** – one of the world's largest religious complexes – with its famous **hypostyle hall**, a spectacular forest of giant papyrus-shaped columns. This main structure is surrounded by the houses of Amun's wife Mut and their son Khonsu, two other huge temple complexes on this site. On its southern side, the **Mut Temple Enclosure** was once linked to the main temple by an avenue of ram-headed sphinxes. To the north is the **Montu Temple Enclosure**, which honoured the local Theban war god. The 3km paved avenue of human-headed sphinxes that once linked the great Temple of Amun at Karnak with Luxor Temple is now again being cleared. Most of what you can see was built by the powerful pharaohs of the 18th

to 20th dynasties (1570–1090 BC), who spent fortunes on making their mark in this most sacred of places, which was then called Ipet-Sut, meaning 'The Most Esteemed of Places'. Later pharaohs extended and rebuilt the complex, as did the Ptolemies and early Christians. The further into the complex you venture, the older the structures. The light is most beautiful in the early morning or later afternoon, and the temple is quieter then, as later in the morning tour buses bring day trippers from Hurghada. It pays to visit more than once, to make sense of the overwhelming jumble of ancient remains.

★**Amun Temple Enclosure**   TEMPLE
Amun-Ra was the local god of Karnak (Luxor) and during the New Kingdom, when the princes of Thebes ruled Egypt, he became the preeminent state god, with a temple that reflected his status. At the height of its power, the temple owned 421,000 head of cattle, 65 cities, 83 ships and 276,400 hectares of agricultural land and had 81,000 people working for it. The shell that remains, sacked by Assyrians and Persians, is still one of the world's great archaeological sites, grand, beautiful and inspiring.

The **Quay of Amun** was the dock where the large boats carrying the statues of the gods moored during festivals. From paintings in the tomb of Nakht and elsewhere we know that there were palaces to the north of the quay and that these were surrounded by lush gardens. On the east side, a ramp slopes down to the processional **avenue of**

LUXOR

Luxor – East Bank

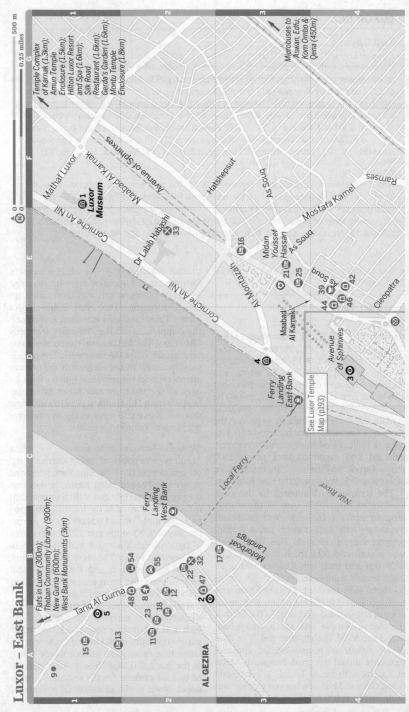

500 m
0.25 miles

Temple Complex of Karnak (1.3km);
Amun Temple Enclosure (1.5km);
Hilton Luxor Resort and Spa (1.6km);
Silk Road Restaurant (1.6km);
Gerda's Garden (1.6km);
Montu Temple Enclosure (1.8km)

Microbuses to Aswan, Edfu, Kom Ombo & Qena (450m)

Mathaf Luxor

Maabad Al Karnak

Avenue of Sphinxes

Hatshepsut

As Souq

Mostafa Kamel

Ramses

Cleopatra

Corniche An Nil

Dr Labib Habashi

33

Luxor Museum **1**

Al-Montazah

Midan Youssef Hassan

16

21 **25**

As Souq

39

44 **46** **42**

Maabad Al Karnak

Avenue of Sphinxes

3

Corniche An Nil

4

Ferry Landing East Bank

See Luxor Temple Map (p193)

Local Ferry

Nile River

Ferry Landing West Bank

Motorboat Landings

Flats in Luxor (300m);
Theban Community Library (900m);
New Gurna (600m);
West Bank Monuments (3km)

Tariq Al Gurna

5

15

13

48 **8** **18**

23 **12**

11

54

55

22 **47**

32

17

2

AL GEZIRA

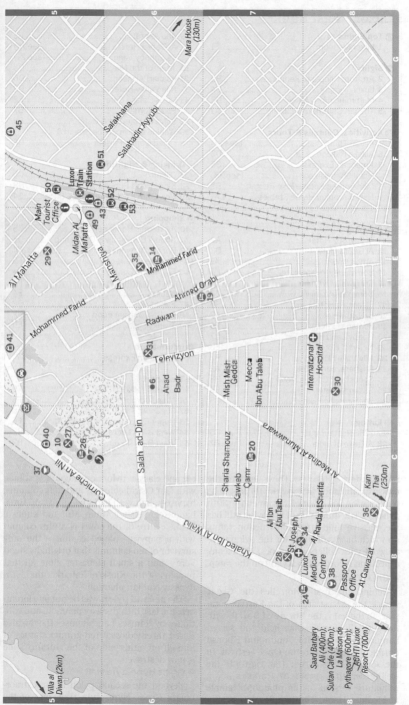

LUXOR

Mara House (130m)

Salakhana

Salahadin Ayyubi

45

51

Luxor Train Station

50

Main Tourist Office

52

Midan Al Mahatta

49   43   53

Al Mahatta

29

35   14

Mohammed Farid

Mohammed Farid

Ahmad Orabi   19

Radwan

41

31

Televizyon

International Hospital

6   Anad   Badr

30

Mish Mish Gedca

Mecca

Ibn Abu Taleb

Salah ad-Din

40   27

10   26

7

Al Medina Al Munawwara

Corniche An Nil

37

Sharia Shamouz

Kawkeb

Qamr   20

Khaled ibn Al Walid

Ali Ibn Abu Taleb

Kam Thai (250m)

36

St Joseph

28   34

Al Rawda Al Sharifa

Luxor Medical Centre

Passport Office

Al Gawazat

38

24

Saad Barbary Ali (400m); Sultan Cafe (400m); La Maison de Pythagore (600m); ACHTI Luxor Resort (700m)

Villa al Diwan (2km)

Luxor - East Bank

⊚ Top Sights
1 Luxor Museum F1

⊚ Sights
2 Art from People to People B2
3 Luxor Temple D4
4 Mummification Museum D3
5 Theban Community Library A1

⊕ Activities, Courses & Tours
Aladin Tours .... (see 21)
6 Alaska Balloon D6
7 American Express C5
Hotel Sheherazade .... (see 23)
8 Mohammed Setohe Bike Rental B2
9 Nobi's Arabian Horse Stables A1
10 Travel Choice Egypt C5

⊜ Sleeping
11 Al Fayrouz Hotel A2
12 Al Gezira Hotel B2
13 Amon Hotel A1
14 Bob Marley Peace Hotel E6
15 Cleopatra Hotel A1
16 Domina Inn Emilio E3
17 El Mesala Hotel B3
18 El Nakhil Hotel A2
19 Fontana Hotel E6
20 Happy Land Hotel C7
21 Nefertiti Hotel E3
22 Nile Valley Hotel B2
23 Sheherazade Hotel A2
24 Sonesta St George Hotel B8
25 Susanna Hotel E3
26 Winter Palace Hotel C5

⊗ Eating
27 1886 Restaurant C5
28 A Taste of India B7
29 Abu Ashraf E5
Al Gezira Hotel .... (see 12)
As Sahaby Lane .... (see 21)
30 Jewel of the Nile D8
31 Koshari Alzaeem D6
32 Nile Valley Hotel B2
33 Oasis Palace Cafe E2
34 Pizza Roma.It B7
35 Sofra Restaurant & Café E6
36 Wenkie's German Ice Cream &
Iced Coffee Parlour B8

⊜ Drinking & Nightlife
37 Cilantro C5
38 Kings Head Pub B8
39 New Oum Koulsoum Coffee Shop E4

⊜ Shopping
40 AA Gaddis Bookshop C5
41 Aboudi Bookshop & Coffeshop D5
42 Bazaar Al Ayam E4
43 Drinkies F5
44 Fair Trade Centre E4
45 Fruit & Vegetable Souq F5
46 Habiba E4
47 Sandouk B2
48 Sa-Re Gourmet Food B2
49 Twinky E5

⊙ Information
American Express .... (see 7)

⊙ Transport
50 Go Bus Ticket Office F5
51 Main Microbus Station F5
52 Super Jet Ticket Office F6
53 Upper Egypt Bus Co Ticket Office F6
54 West Bank Microbus Parking Lot B2
55 West Bank Taxis B2

ram-headed sphinxes. These lead to the massive unfinished **first pylon**, the last to be built, during the reign of Nectanebo I (30th dynasty). The inner side of the pylon still has the massive mud-brick construction ramp, up which blocks of stone for the pylon were dragged with rollers and ropes. Napoleon's expedition recorded blocks still on the ramp.

➡ **Great Court**

Behind the first pylon lies the **Great Court**, the largest area of the Karnak complex. To the left is the **Shrine of Seti II**, with three small chapels that held the sacred barques (boats) of Mut, Amun and Khonsu during the lead-up to the Opet Festival. In the southeastern corner (far right) is the well-preserved **Temple of Ramses III**, a miniature version of the pharaoh's temple at Medinat Habu. The temple plan is sim-

ple and classic: pylon, open court, vestibule with four Osirid columns and four columns, hypostyle hall with eight columns and three barque chapels for Amun, Mut and Khonsu. At the centre of the court is a 21m column with a papyrus-shaped capital – the only survivor of ten columns that originally stood here – and a small alabaster altar, all that remains of the Kiosk of Taharka, the 25th-dynasty Nubian pharaoh.

The **second pylon** was begun by Horemheb, the last 18th-dynasty pharaoh, and continued by Ramses I and Ramses II, who also raised three colossal red-granite statues of himself on either side of the entrance; one is now destroyed.

➡ **Great Hypostyle Hall**

Beyond the second pylon is the extraordinary **Great Hypostyle Hall**, one of the greatest religious monuments ever built. Covering 5500 sq m – enough space to contain both Rome's St Peter's Basilica and London's St Paul's Cathedral – the hall is an unforgettable forest of 134 towering stone pillars. Their papyrus shape symbolise a swamp, of which there were so many along the Nile. Ancient Egyptians believed that these plants surrounded the primeval mound on which life was first created. Each summer when the Nile began to flood, this hall and its columns would fill with several feet of water. Originally, the columns would have been brightly painted – some colour remains – and roofed, making it pretty dark away from the lit main axis. The size and grandeur of the pillars and the endless decorations can be overwhelming, so take your time, sit for a while and stare at the dizzying spectacle.

The hall was planned by Ramses I and built by Seti I and Ramses II. Note the difference in quality between the delicate raised relief in the northern part, by Seti I, and the much cruder sunken relief work, added by Ramses II in the southern part of the hall. The cryptic scenes on the inner walls were intended for the priesthood and the royalty who understood the religious context, but the outer walls are easier to comprehend, showing the pharaoh's military prowess and strength, and his ability to bring order to chaos.

On the back of the **third pylon**, built by Amenhotep III, to the right the pharaoh is shown sailing the sacred barque during the Opet Festival. Tuthmosis I (1504–1492 BC) created a narrow court between the **third** and **fourth pylons**, where four obelisks stood, two each for Tuthmosis I and Tuthmosis III (1479–1425 BC). Only the bases remain except for one, 22m high, raised for Tuthmosis I.

➡ Inner Temple

Beyond the fourth pylon is the **Hypostyle Hall of Tuthmosis III** built by Tuthmosis I in precious wood, and altered by Tuthmosis III with 14 columns and a stone roof. In this court stands one of the two magnificent 30m-high obelisks erected by Queen Hatshepsut (1473–1458 BC) to the glory of her 'father' Amun. The other is broken, but the upper shaft lies near the sacred lake. The **Obelisk of Hatshepsut** is the tallest in Egypt, its tip originally covered in electrum (a commonly used alloy of gold and silver). After Hatshepsut's death, her stepson Tuthmosis III eradicated all signs of her reign and had them walled into a sandstone structure.

The ruined **fifth pylon**, constructed by Tuthmosis I, leads to another colonnade now badly ruined, followed by the small **sixth pylon**, raised by Tuthmosis III, who also built the pair of red-granite columns in the vestibule beyond, carved with the lotus and the papyrus, the symbols of Upper and Lower Egypt. Nearby, on the left, are two huge statues of Amun and the goddess Amunet, carved in the reign of Tutankhamun.

The original **Sanctuary of Amun**, the very core of the temple and the place of darkness where the god resided, was built by Tuthmosis III. Destroyed when the temple was sacked by the Persians, it was rebuilt in granite by Alexander the Great's successor and half-brother, the fragile, dim-witted Philip Arrhidaeus (323–317 BC).

East of the shrine of Philip Arrhidaeus is the oldest-known part of the temple, the **Middle Kingdom Court**, where Sesostris I built a shrine, of which the foundation walls have been found. On the northern wall of the court is the **Wall of Records**, a running tally of the organised tribute the pharaoh exacted in honour of Amun from his subjugated lands.

➡ Great Festival Hall of Tuthmosis III

At the back of the Middle Kingdom Court is the **Great Festival Hall of Tuthmosis III**. It is an unusual structure with carved stone columns imitating tent poles, perhaps a reference to the pharaoh's life under canvas on his frequent military expeditions abroad. The columned vestibule that lies beyond, generally referred to as the Botanical Gardens, has wonderful, detailed relief scenes of the flora and fauna that the pharaoh had encountered during his campaigns in Syria and Palestine, and had brought back to Egypt.

➡ Secondary Axis of the Amun Temple Enclosure

The courtyard between the Hypostyle Hall and the **seventh pylon**, built by Tuthmosis III, is known as the **cachette court**, as thousands of stone and bronze statues were discovered here in 1903. The priests had the old statues and temple furniture they no longer needed buried around 300 BC. Most statues were sent to the Egyptian Museum in Cairo, but some remain, standing in front of the seventh pylon, including four of Tuthmosis III on the left.

The well-preserved **eighth pylon**, built by Queen Hatshepsut, is the oldest part of the north–south axis of the temple, and one of the earliest pylons in Karnak. Carved on it

Amun Temple Enclosure

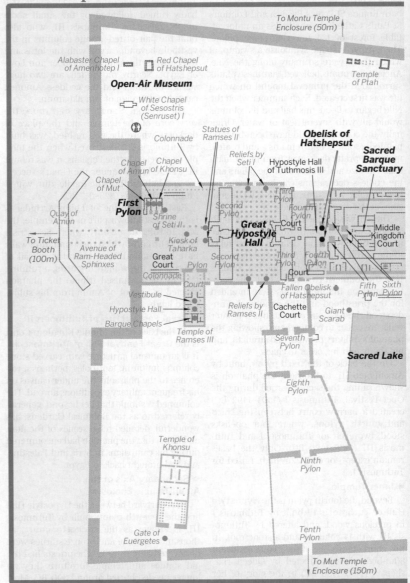

is a text she falsely attributed to Tuthmosis I, justifying her taking the throne of Egypt.

East of the seventh and eighth pylons is the sacred lake, where, according to Herodotus, the priests of Amun bathed twice daily and nightly for ritual purity. On the northwestern side of the lake is part of the Fallen Obelisk of Hatshepsut showing her coronation, and a giant scarab in stone dedicated by Amenhotep III to Khepri, a form of the sun god.

The temple, mostly the work of Ramses III and enlarged by later Ramesside rulers, lies north of **Euergetes' Gate** and the avenue of sphinxes leading to Luxor Temple. The temple pylon leads via a peristyle court to a hypostyle hall with eight columns carved with figures of Ramses XI and the High Priest Herihor, who effectively ruled Upper Egypt at the time. The next chamber housed the sacred barque of Khonsu.

Mut Temple Enclosure   TEMPLE

(adult/student LE40/20) From the 10th pylon, an avenue of sphinxes leads to the partly excavated southern enclosure – the Precinct of Mut, consort of Amun. The Temple of Mut was built by Amenhotep III and consists of a sanctuary, a hypostyle hall and two courts. It has been restored and officially opened to the public.

Amenhotep also set up more than 700 black granite statues of the lioness goddess Sekhmet, Mut's northern counterpart, which are believed to form a calendar, with two statues for every day of the year, receiving offerings each morning and evening. The main avenue of sphinxes from Luxor Temple enters the Karnak complex at the front of the Mut Temple.

Montu Temple Enclosure   TEMPLE

Inside the Amun Temple Enclosure there is a gate in the northern wall (on your left as you enter) near the Temple of Ptah. The gate, which is usually locked, leads to the Montu Temple Enclosure. Montu, the falcon-headed warrior god, was one of the original deities of Thebes and this temple was one of the original Middle Kingdom structures at Karnak. The ruins that survive were rebuilt by Amenhotep III and modified by others. The complex is very dilapidated.

Open-Air Museum   MUSEUM

(adult/student LE60/30, incl Amun Temple Enclosure LE150/70; ☻ 6am-5.30pm summer, to 4.30pm winter) Off to the left (north) of the first court of the Amun Temple Enclosure (p185) is Karnak's open-air museum. The word 'museum' and the fact that there is so much else to see in Karnak means that most visitors skip this collection of stones, statues and shrines, but it is definitely worth a look.

The well-preserved chapels include the **White Chapel of Sesostris I**, one of the oldest and most beautiful monuments in Karnak, which has wonderful Middle Kingdom reliefs; the **Red Chapel of Hatshepsut**, its red quartzite blocks reassembled

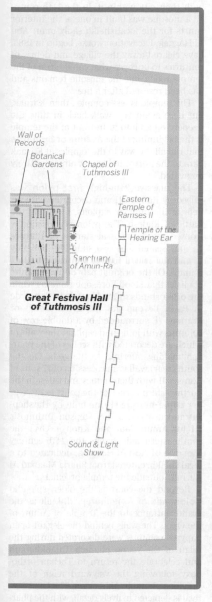

Wall of Records

Botanical Gardens

Chapel of Tuthmosis III

Eastern Temple of Ramses II

Temple of the Hearing Ear

Sanctuary of Amun-Ra

Great Festival Hall of Tuthmosis III

Sound & Light Show

In the southwestern corner of the enclosure is the **Temple of Khonsu**, god of the moon, and son of Amun and Mut. It can be reached from a door in the southern wall of the Hypostyle Hall of the Temple of Amun, via a path through various blocks of stone.

LUXOR SIGHTS

AVENUE OF SPHINXES

A 3km-long alley of sphinxes connecting Luxor and Karnak is being excavated. Most of the buildings covering the sphinxes have been demolished, including some that were important to the development of 19th- and early-20th-century Luxor. The avenue will eventually be completely revealed, although it remains to be seen how many people will want to walk from Luxor to Karnak temples.

in 2000; and the **Alabaster Chapel of Amenhotep I**. The museum also contains a collection of statuary found throughout the temple complex. Buy the combo ticket at the main ticket office.

Luxor Temple & Museums

Luxor Temple   TEMPLE
(☑ 095-237-2408; Corniche An Nil; adult/student LE100/50; ☺ 6am-9pm) Largely built by the New Kingdom pharaohs Amenhotep III (1390–1352 BC) and Ramses II (1279–1213 BC), this temple is a strikingly graceful monument in the heart of the modern town. Also known as the Southern Sanctuary, its main function was during the annual Opet celebrations, when the statues of Amun, Mut and Khonsu were brought from Karnak, along the Avenue of Sphinxes, and reunited here during the inundation.

Visit early when the temple opens, before the crowds arrive, or later at sunset when the stones glow. Whenever you go, be sure to return at night when the temple is lit up, creating an eerie spectacle as shadow and light play off the reliefs and colonnades.

Amenhotep III greatly enlarged an older shrine built by Hatshepsut, and rededicated the massive temple as Amun's southern *ipet* (harem), the private quarters of the god. The structure was further added to by Tutankhamun, Ramses II, Alexander the Great and various Romans. The Romans constructed a military fort around the temple that the Arabs later called Al Uqsur (The Fortifications), which was later corrupted to give modern Luxor its name.

In ancient times the temple would have been surrounded by a warren of mud-brick houses, shops and workshops, which now lie under the modern town, but after the decline of the city people moved into the – by

then – partly covered temple complex and built their city within it. In the 14th century, a mosque was built in one of the interior courts for the local sheikh (holy man) Abu Al Haggag. Excavation works, begun in 1885, have cleared away the village and debris of centuries to uncover what can be seen of the temple today, but the mosque remains and has been restored after a fire.

The temple is less complex than Karnak, but here again you walk back in time the deeper you go into it. In front of the temple is the beginning of the **Avenue of Sphinxes** that ran all the way to the temples at Karnak 3km to the north, and is now almost entirely excavated.

The massive 24m-high **first pylon** was raised by Ramses II and decorated with reliefs of his military exploits, including the Battle of Kadesh. The pylon was originally fronted by six colossal statues of Ramses II, four seated and two standing, but only two of the seated figures and one standing remain. Of the original pair of pink-granite obelisks that stood here, one remains while the other stands in the Place de la Concorde in Paris. Beyond lies the **Great Court of Ramses II**, surrounded by a double row of columns with lotus-bud capitals, the walls of which are decorated with scenes of the pharaoh making offerings to the gods. On the south (rear) wall is a procession of 17 sons of Ramses II with their names and titles. In the northwestern corner of the court is the earlier **triple-barque shrine** built by Hatshepsut and usurped by her stepson Tuthmosis III for Amun, Mut and Khonsu. Over the southeastern side hangs the 14th-century **Mosque of Abu Al Haggag**, dedicated to a local sheikh, entered from Sharia Maabad Al Karnak, outside the temple precinct.

Beyond the court is the older, splendid **Colonnade of Amenhotep III**, built as the grand entrance to the Temple of Amun of the Opet. The walls behind the elegant open papyrus columns were decorated during the reign of the young pharaoh Tutankhamun and celebrate the return to Theban orthodoxy following the wayward reign of the previous pharaoh, Akhenaten. The Opet Festival is depicted in lively detail, with the pharaoh, nobility and common people joining the triumphal procession. Look out for the drummers and acrobats doing backbends.

South of the Colonnade is the **Sun Court of Amenhotep III**, once enclosed on three sides by double rows of towering papyrus-

Luxor Temple

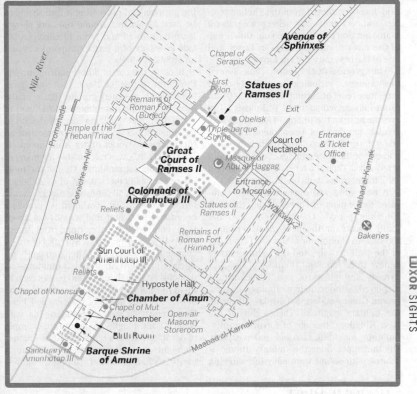

bundle columns, the best preserved of which, with their architraves extant, are those on the eastern and western sides. In 1989 workmen found a cache of 26 statues here, buried by priests in Roman times, now displayed in the Luxor Museum.

Beyond lies the **Hypostyle Hall**, the first room of the original Opet temple, with four rows of eight columns each, leading to the temple's main rooms. The central chamber on the axis south of the Hypostyle Hall was the **cult sanctuary of Amun**, stuccoed over by the Romans in the 3rd century AD and painted with scenes of Roman officials: some of this is still intact and vivid. Through this chamber, either side of which are chapels dedicated to Mut and Khonsu, is the four-columned antechamber where offerings were made to Amun. Immediately behind the chamber is the **Barque Shrine of Amun**, rebuilt by Alexander the Great,

with reliefs portraying him as an Egyptian pharaoh.

To the east a doorway leads into two rooms. The first is Amenhotep III's '**birth room**' with scenes of his symbolic divine birth. You can see the moment of his conception, when the fingers of the god touch those of the queen and 'his dew filled her body', according to the accompanying hieroglyphic caption. The **Sanctuary of Amenhotep III** is the last chamber; it still has the remains of the stone base on which Amun's statue stood, and although it was once the most sacred part of the temple, the busy street that now runs directly behind it makes it less atmospheric.

★**Luxor Museum**   MUSEUM
(Map p186; Corniche An Nil; adult/student LE120/60; ◷9am-2pm & 5-9pm) This wonderful museum has a well-chosen and brilliantly displayed and explained collection of

antiquities dating from the end of the Old Kingdom right through to the Mamluk period, mostly gathered from the Theban temples and necropolis. The ticket price puts off many, but don't let that stop you: this is one of the most rewarding sights in Luxor and one of the best museums in Egypt.

The **ground-floor gallery** has several masterpieces, including a well-preserved limestone relief of Tuthmosis III (No 140), an exquisitely carved statue of Tuthmosis III in greywacke from the Temple of Karnak (No 2), an alabaster figure of Amenhotep III protected by the great crocodile god Sobek (No 155), and one of the few examples of Old Kingdom art found at Thebes, a relief of Unas-ankh (No 183), found in his tomb on the west bank.

A **new wing** was opened in 2004, dedicated to the glory of Thebes during the New Kingdom period. The highlight, and the main reason for the new construction, is the two royal mummies, Ahmose I (founder of the 18th dynasty) and the mummy some believe to be Ramses I (founder of the 19th dynasty and father of Seti I), beautifully displayed without their wrappings in dark rooms. Other well-labelled displays illustrate the military might of Thebes during the New Kingdom, the age of Egypt's empire-building, including chariots and weapons. On the upper floor the military theme is diluted with scenes from daily life showing the technology used in the New Kingdom. Multimedia displays show workers harvesting papyrus and processing it into sheets to be used for writing. Young boys are shown learning to read and write hieroglyphs beside a display of a scribe's implements and an architect's tools.

Back in the old building, moving up via the ramp to the **1st floor**, you come face-to-face with a seated granite figure of the legendary scribe Amenhotep (No 4), son of Hapu, the great official eventually deified in Ptolemaic times and who, as overseer of all the pharaoh's works under Amenhotep III (1390–1352 BC), was responsible for many of Thebes' greatest buildings. One of the most interesting exhibits is the Wall of Akhenaten, a series of small sandstone blocks named *talatat* (threes) by workmen – probably because their height and length was about three hand lengths – that came from Amenhotep IV's contribution at Karnak before he changed his name to Akhenaten and left Thebes for Tell Al Amarna. His building was demolished and about 40,000 blocks used to fill in Karnak's ninth pylon were found in the late 1960s and partially reassembled here. The scenes showing Akhenaten, his wife Nefertiti and temple life are a rare example of decoration from a temple of Aten. Further highlights are treasures from Tutankhamun's tomb, including shabti (servant) figures,

MAKING MUMMIES

Although the practice of preserving dead bodies can be found in cultures across the world, the Egyptians were the ultimate practitioners of this highly complex procedure that they refined over a period of almost 4000 years. Their preservation of the dead can be traced back to the very earliest times, when bodies were simply buried in the desert away from the limited areas of cultivation. In direct contact with the sand that covered them, the hot, dry conditions allowed the body fluids to drain away while preserving the skin, hair and nails intact. Accidentally uncovering such bodies must have had a profound effect upon those who were able to recognise people who had died years earlier.

So began a long process of experimentation to preserve the bodies without burying them in the sand. It wasn't until around 2600 BC that internal organs, which is where putrefaction actually begins, began to be removed. As the process became increasingly elaborate, all the organs were removed except the kidneys, which were hard to reach, and the heart. The latter, which was considered the source of intelligence rather than the brain, was left in place, often with a heart amulet inscribed with an invocation from the Book of the Dead. The brain was removed by inserting a metal probe up the nose and whisking to reduce the organ to a liquid that could be easily drained away. All the rest – lungs, liver, stomach, intestines – were removed through an opening cut in the left flank. Then the body and its separate organs were covered with piles of natron salt and left to dry out for 40 days, after which they were washed, purified and anointed with a range of oils, spices and resins. All were then wrapped in layers of linen, with the appropriate amulets set in place over the various parts of the body as priests recited the incantations needed to activate the protective functions of the amulets.

model boats, sandals, arrows and a series of gilded bronze rosettes from his funeral pall.

A ramp back down to the **ground floor** leaves you close to the exit and beside a black-and-gold wooden head of the cow deity Mehit-Weret, an aspect of the goddess Hathor, which was also found in Tutankhamun's tomb.

On the left just before the exit is a **small hall** containing 16 of 22 statues that were uncovered in Luxor Temple in 1989. All are magnificent examples of ancient Egyptian sculpture, but pride of place at the end of the hall is given to an almost pristine 2.45m-tall quartzite statue of a muscular Amenhotep III, wearing a pleated kilt.

Mummification Museum MUSEUM
(Map p186; Corniche An Nil; adult/student LE80/40; ⊙ 9am-?pm) Housed in the former visitors centre on Luxor's corniche, the Mummification Museum has well-presented exhibits explaining the art of mummification. The museum is small and some may find the entrance fee overpriced. Also, although it should be open throughout the day, a lack of visitors means that it sometimes closes for several hours after midday.

On display are the well-preserved mummy of a 21st-dynasty high priest of Amun, Maserharti, and a host of mummified animals. Vitrines show the tools and materials used in the mummification process – check out the small spoon and metal spatula used for scraping the brain out of the skull. Several artefacts that were crucial to the mummy's journey to the afterlife have also been included, as well as some picturesque painted coffins. Presiding over the entrance is a beautiful little statue of the jackal god, Anubis, the god of embalming who helped Isis turn her brother-husband Osiris into the first mummy.

◉ West Bank

The **West Bank** (illustration p196) is a world away from the noise and bustle of Luxor town on the east bank. Taking a taxi across the bridge, 6km south of the centre, or crossing on the old ferry, you are immediately in lush countryside, with bright-green sugarcane fields along irrigation canals and clusters of colourful houses, all against the background of the desert and the Theban hills. Coming towards the end of the cultivated land, you start to notice huge sandstone blocks lying in the middle of fields, gaping black holes in the rocks and giant sandstone forms on the edge of the cultivation below. Magnificent memorial temples were built on the flood plains here, where the pharaoh's cult could be perpetuated by the devotions of his priests and subjects, while his body and worldly wealth, and the bodies of his wives and children, were laid in splendidly decorated tombs hidden in the hills.

From the New Kingdom onwards, the necropolis also supported a large living population of artisans, labourers, temple priests and guards, who devoted their lives to the construction and maintenance of this city of the dead, and who protected the tombs full of treasure from eager robbers. The artisans perfected the techniques of tomb building, decoration and concealment, and passed the secrets down through their families. They all built their own tombs here.

Until a generation ago, villagers used tombs to shelter from the extremes of the desert climate and, until recently, many lived in houses built over the Tombs of the Nobles. These beautifully painted houses were a picturesque sight to anyone visiting the west bank. However, over the past 100 years or so the Supreme Council of Antiquities has been trying to relocate the inhabitants of Al Gurna. In 2007, their houses were demolished, and the families were moved to a huge new village of small breeze-block houses 8km north of the Valley of the Kings. A few houses have been left standing, although it has not been decided what use they should be put to.

Tickets

The **Antiquities Inspectorate ticket office** (Map p198; main road, 3km inland from ferry landing; ⊙ 6am-5pm), beyond the Colossi of Memnon (p198), sells tickets to most sites except for the Temple at Deir Al Bahri, the Assasif Tombs (available at Deir Al Bahri ticket office), the Valley of the Kings and the Valley of the Queens. Check here first to see which tickets are available, and which tombs are open. All sites are officially open from 6am to 5pm.

Photography is not permitted in any tombs, and guards may confiscate film or memory cards. Alternatively, they might see you using a camera or phone as an opportunity to extract some extra cash. Tickets are valid only for the day of purchase, and no refunds are given.

Luxor's West Bank

Sometimes there is no way around the crowds of visitors and hawkers in the Valley of the Kings, but try to go early, before it gets hot. Stop off at the ❶ **Colossi of Memnon** as you pass them, taking a look at the ongoing excavation of the ruins of the Temple of Amenhotep III, whose entrance they once flanked. From the royal tombs, drive around the hillside to visit the massive terraced ❷ **Temple of Hatshepsut**, almost entirely reconstructed but still good to see as it is the best surviving example of classical-style Egyptian architecture in Luxor.

The Theban hillside further to the south is pitted with thousands of tomb openings. The Tombs of the Nobles in what was ❸ **Gurna Village** and the nearby ❹ **Workers' Tombs** at Deir al-Medina are very different in style and construction from the royal burials. In some ways, their views of everyday life are more impressive than the more orthodox scenes on the walls of the royal tombs.

In the afternoon, drop down towards the line between desert and agriculture to see two royal temples. The Ramesseum is dedicated to the memory of Ramses II and contains the upper half of a massive statue of the pharaoh. In midafternoon, when the light starts to soften, head over to ❺ **Medinat Habu**, the temple of Ramses III. The last of the great imperial temples built during the New Kingdom, the temple has retained much of its grandeur, as well as extensive (and often exaggerated) records of the king's reign.

TOP TIPS

➜ Allow at least one day.

➜ Tickets for everything except the Valley of the Kings must be bought at the ticket office.

➜ Bring a hat, sunscreen and plenty of water.

➜ Photography is not allowed inside the tombs, but there is plenty to see – and photograph – outside.

Medinat Habu
Original paintwork, applied more than 3000 years ago, can still be seen on lintels and inner columns. Some of this was preserved by the mudbrick houses and chapels of early Christians (since destroyed).

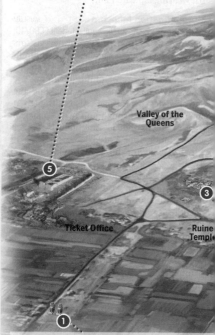

Valley of the Queens

Ticket Office

Ruine Temple

Colossi of Memnon
Although the Greeks called him Memnon, the colossi were built for Pharaoh Amenhotep III, who built the largest of all funerary temples here on the west bank (its ruins are only now being excavated).

BLACKMAC / SHUTTERSTOCK ©

DMITRY PETRENKO / SHUTTERSTOCK ©

'orkers' Tombs (Deir al-Medina)

'hat to do with your spare time if you were an :cient Egyptian tomb worker? Cut a tomb and ·corate it with things you didn't have in this life, :cluding ceilings decorated with rug patterns.

Temple of Hatshepsut

Hatshepsut's funerary temple is unlike any other in Luxor. Built on three terraces with its back to the hill that contains the Valley of the Kings, it was once as grand as the pharaoh-queen.

Valley of the Kings

②

Tombs of the Nobles (all this hillside)

Ramesseum (Temple of Ramses II)

Gurna Village

Rumours of treasure beneath houses in Gurna led the government to move the villagers and demolish their houses in the early 2000s. Some Gurna houses dated back to at least the beginning of the 19th century.

Luxor – West Bank

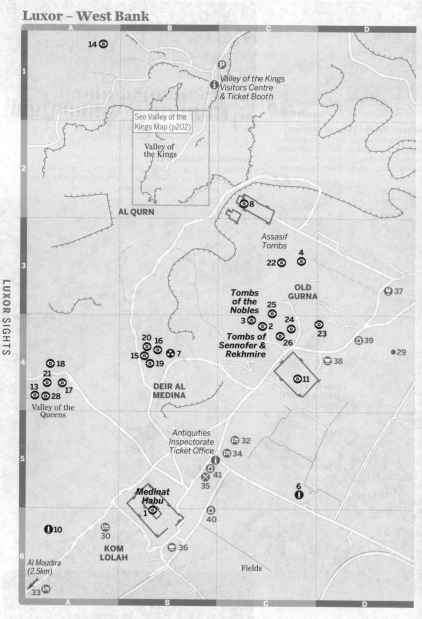

Valley of the Kings Visitors Centre & Ticket Booth

See Valley of the Kings Map (p202)

Valley of the Kings

AL QURN

Assasif Tombs

OLD GURNA

Tombs of the Nobles

Tombs of Sennofer & Rekhmire

DEIR AL MEDINA

Valley of the Queens

Antiquities Inspectorate Ticket Office

Medinat Habu

KOM LOLAH

Al Moudira (2.5km)

Fields

LUXOR SIGHTS

Gezira Village to Ticket Office

Art from People to People   ARTS CENTRE
(Map p186; ☎ 095-231-5529, 012-2079-7310; https://art-frompeople.com; Gezira; ⊙ 4-8pm Sat, Mon & Thu) A new venture in Luxor, this art gallery and centre is located in a small place behind the Nile Valley Hotel (p220). Run by Eiad Oraby, it showcases local artists as well as holding art classes and events for kids, providing a much-needed creative hub.

general books in Arabic and English, and a good collection on archaeology and issues related to conservation. There are regular evening lectures. More information is available from the librarian, Ahmed Hassan, or via their website or Facebook page.

Open to all, the library is used by local archaeologists and guides, school children (there is no other library that serves them) and people from the villages. The latest additions include books on diet and pre-natal care for local mothers. The library is self-funding and welcomes donations.

New Gurna   VILLAGE

(Map p198) Hassan Fathy's mud-brick village lies just past the railway track on the road from the ferry to the Antiquities Inspectorate ticket office. Although built between 1946 and 1952 to rehouse the inhabitants of Old Gurna, who lived above and around the Tombs of the Nobles, the village became a showcase of utilitarian mud-brick design. The stunning buildings had Hassan Fathy's signature domes and vaults, thick mud-brick walls and natural ventilation.

The project failed in its original intention because most inhabitants of Old Gurna refused to move into the new houses, unhappy at the idea of being moved from their old homes and their livelihoods, which some claim was selling trinkets to tourists and others claim was digging up treasures from the ancient burials beneath the houses. Today much of Fathy's work is in tatters, the original houses increasingly replaced with breeze block, although the beautiful mud-brick mosque and theatre survive. Unesco has recognised the need to safeguard the village, but its plans have stalled. A short film about the village is available at https://vimeo.com/15514401.

Colossi of Memnon   MONUMENT

(Map p198) **FREE** The two faceless Colossi of Memnon, originally representing Pharaoh Amenhotep III, rising majestically about 18m from the plain, are the first monuments tourists see when they visit the west bank. These magnificent colossi, each cut from a single block of stone and weighing 1000 tonnes, sat at the eastern entrance to the funerary temple of Amenophis III, the largest on the west bank. Egyptologists are currently excavating the temple and their discoveries can be seen behind the colossi.

The colossi were already a great tourist attraction during Graeco-Roman times, when

Theban Community Library   LIBRARY

(Map p186; ☎ 010-0523-8113; www.tmp-library.org; near New Gourna; ☉ 3.30-8.30pm; ♠) **FREE** The latest project from Professor Kent Weeks and the Theban Mapping Project is the first open library in Luxor, a free service with

Luxor – West Bank

the statues were attributed to Memnon, the legendary African king who was slain by Achilles during the Trojan War. The Greeks and Romans considered it good luck to hear the whistling sound emitted by the northern statue at sunrise, which they believed to be the cry of Memnon greeting his mother Eos, the goddess of dawn. She in turn would weep tears of dew for his untimely death. All this was probably due to a crack in the colossus' upper body, which appeared after the 27 BC earthquake. As the heat of the morning sun baked the dew-soaked stone, sand particles would break off and resonate inside the cracks in the structure. After Septimus Severus (193–211 AD) repaired the statue in the 3rd century AD, Memnon's plaintive greeting was heard no more.

The colossi are just off the road, before you reach the Antiquities Inspectorate ticket office, and are usually being snapped and filmed by an army of tourists. Yet few visitors have any idea that these giant enthroned figures are set in front of the main entrance to an equally impressive funerary temple, the largest in Egypt, the remains of which are slowly being brought to light.

Some tiny parts of the temple that stood behind the colossi remain and more is being uncovered now that the excavation is underway. Many statues, among them the huge dyad of Amenhotep III and his wife Tiye that now dominates the central court of the Egyptian Museum in Cairo, were later dragged off by other pharaohs, but much still remains beneath the silt. A stele, also now in the Egyptian Museum, describes the temple as being built from 'white sandstone, with gold throughout, a floor covered with silver, and doors covered with electrum'. No gold or silver has yet been found, but if you wander behind the colossi, you can see the huge area littered with statues and masonry that had long lain under the ground.

Valley of the Kings

The west bank of Luxor had been the site of royal burials since around 2100 BC, but it was the pharaohs of the New Kingdom period (1550–1069 BC) who chose this isolated valley dominated by the pyramid-shaped mountain peak of Al Qurn (The Horn). Once called the Great Necropolis of Millions of Years of Pharaoh, or the Place of Truth, the **Valley of the Kings** (Wadi Biban Al Muluk; Map p202; www.thebanmappingproject.com; adult/student for 3 tombs LE160/80; ⊘ 6am-5pm, last ticket sold at 4pm) has 63 magnificent royal tombs.

The tombs have suffered greatly from treasure hunters, floods and, in recent years, mass tourism: carbon dioxide, friction and the humidity produced by the average 2.8g of sweat left by each visitor have affected the reliefs and the stability of paintings that were made on plaster laid over limestone. The Department of Antiquities has installed dehumidifiers and glass screens in the worst-affected tombs. They have also introduced a rotation system: a limited number of tombs are open to the public at any one time. The entry ticket gains access to three tombs, with extra tickets to see the tombs of Ay, Tutankhamun, Seti I and Ramses VI.

The road into the Valley of the Kings is a gradual, dry, hot climb, so be prepared, especially if you are riding a bicycle. Also be ready to run the gauntlet of the tourist bazaar, which sells soft drinks, ice creams and snacks alongside the tat. The air-conditioned **Valley of the Kings Visitors Centre & Ticket Booth** (Map p198) has a good model of the valley, a movie about Carter's discovery of the tomb of Tutankhamun and toilets (there are Portakabins higher up, but this is the one to use). A tuf-tuf (a little electrical train) ferries visitors between the visitors centre and the tombs (it can be hot during summer). The ride costs LE4. It's worth having a torch to illuminate badly lit areas but you cannot take a camera – photography is forbidden in all tombs.

The best source of information about the tombs, including detailed descriptions of their decoration and history, can be found on the Theban Mapping Project website. Some tombs have additional entry fees and tickets.

Highlights include the Tomb of Ay, Tomb of Horemheb (KV 57), Tomb of Ramses III (KV 11), Tomb of Ramses VI (KV 9) and Tomb of Seti I (KV 17).

Tomb of Ramses VII (KV 1)   TOMB

Near the main entrance is the small, unfinished tomb of Ramses VII (1136–1129 BC). Only 44m long – short for a royal tomb because of Ramses' sudden death – it consists of a corridor, a burial chamber and an unfinished third chamber. His architects hastily widened what was to have been the tomb's second corridor, making it a burial chamber, and the pharaoh was laid to rest in a pit covered with a sarcophagus lid.

Niches for Canopic jars are carved into the pit's sides, a feature unique to this tomb. Walls on the corridor leading to the chamber are decorated with fairly well preserved excerpts from the Book of Caverns and the Opening of the Mouth ritual, while the burial chamber is decorated with passages from the Book of the Earth. It was later used by Coptic hermits, as their graffiti suggests.

Tomb of Ramses IV (KV 2)   TOMB

Originally intended to be much larger, KV 2 was cut short at 89m on the early death of the pharaoh (1147 BC) and a pillared hall was converted to be the burial chamber. The sarcophagus is in place with a magnificent goddess Nut filling the ceiling above it. Close to the entrance of the valley, this tomb was opened in antiquity and inhabited (there is Greek, Roman and Coptic graffiti), and used as a hotel by many 18th and 19th century visitors.

The paintings in the burial chamber have deteriorated, but there is a wonderful image of the goddess Nut, stretched across the blue ceiling, and it is the only tomb to contain the text of the Book of Nut, with a description of the path taken by the sun every day. The red-granite sarcophagus, though empty, is one of the largest in the valley. The discovery of an ancient plan of the tomb on papyrus (now in the Turin Museum) shows the sarcophagus was originally enclosed by four large shrines similar to those in Tutankhamun's tomb. The mummy of Ramses IV was later reburied in the tomb of Amenhotep II

LUXOR SIGHTS

> ### ℹ TACKLING THE WEST BANK
>
> Take more than a day to visit the west bank, if you can. Plan your day in advance as tickets for most sights must be bought from the central ticket office, and are only valid for that day. Early morning visits are ideal, but that is unfortunately when most tour groups visit the **Memorial Temple of Hatshepsut** or the **Valley of the Kings**. So try to leave these two to the afternoon to avoid the crowds and visit other sights such as the **Tombs of the Nobles** or the **Ramesseum** in the morning.

Valley of the Kings

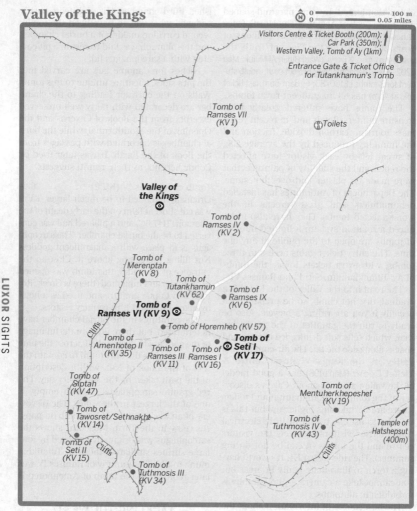

(KV 35), and is now in the Egyptian Museum in Cairo.

Tomb of Ramses IX (KV 6) TOMB

Only half decorated at the time of the king's death and open since antiquity, this is not the most interesting tomb in the valley, but it is one the most popular because it has a very gently shelving shaft and is near the entrance to the valley. Its large antechamber is decorated with animals, serpents and demons from the Book of the Dead. There is also a pillared hall and short hallway before the burial chamber.

On either side of the gate on the rear wall are two figures of priests, both dressed in panther-skin robes and sporting a ceremonial sidelock. The walls of the burial chamber feature the Book of Amduat, the Book of Caverns and the Book of the Earth; the Book of the Heavens is represented on the ceiling. Although it is unfinished, it was the last tomb in the valley to have so much of its decoration completed, and the paintings are relatively well preserved.

Tomb of Merenptah (KV 8)   TOMB

The second-largest tomb in the valley, Merenptah's tomb has been open since antiquity and has its share of Greek and Coptic graffiti. Floods have damaged the lower part of the walls of the long tunnel-like tomb, but the upper parts have well-preserved reliefs. The corridors are decorated with the Book of the Dead, the Book of Gates and the Book of Amduat. Beyond a shaft is a false burial chamber with two pillars decorated with the Book of Gates.

Ramses II lived for so long that 12 of his sons died before he did, so it was finally his 13th son, Merenptah (1213–1203 BC), who succeeded him in his 60s. The pharaoh was originally buried inside four stone sarcophagi: three of granite (the lid of the second is still in situ, with an effigy of Merenptah on top), and the fourth and innermost of alabaster. In a rare mistake by ancient Egyptian engineers, the outer sarcophagus did not fit through the tomb entrance and its gates had to be hacked away. Much of the decoration in the burial chamber has faded, but it remains an impressive room, with a sunken floor and brick niches on the front and rear walls.

Tomb of Tutankhamun (KV 62)   TOMB

(Map p202; Valley of the Kings; adult/student LE200/100, plus Valley of the Kings ticket; ☺6am 5pm) The story of the celebrated discovery of the famous tomb and all the fabulous treasures it contained far outshines the reality of the small tomb of a short-lived pharaoh. Tutankhamun's tomb is one of the least impressive in the valley and bears all the signs of a rather hasty completion and inglorious burial, as well as significant damage to the decorations. In spite of this and of the existence of a more instructive replica, many people choose to visit.

The Egyptologist Howard Carter slaved away for six seasons in the valley and in the end was rewarded with the discovery of the resting place of Tutankhamun, with all its treasures, the most impressive haul ever made in Egypt. The first step was found on 4 November 1922, and on 5 November the rest of the steps and a sealed doorway came to light. Carter wired Lord Carnarvon to join him in Egypt immediately for the opening of what he hoped was the completely intact tomb of Tutankhamun. When he looked inside, he saw what he famously described as 'wonderful things'.

The son of Akhenaten and one of Akhenaten's sisters, Tutankhamun ruled briefly

DON'T MISS

THE BEST TOMBS

With so many tombs to choose from, these are the highlights of the Theban necropolis:

Valley of the Kings
➡ Tuthmosis III (p205)
➡ Amenhotep II (p205)
➡ Horemheb (p205)
➡ Seti I (KV 17) (p206)

Valley of the Queens
➡ Amunherkhepshef (p209)
➡ Nefertari (p208)

Tombs of the Nobles
➡ Nakht (p215)
➡ Sennofer (p215)
➡ Ramose (p215)

Deir Al Medina
➡ Sennedjem (p209)

(1336–1327 BC) and died young, with no great battles or buildings to his credit, so there was little time to build a tomb. The tomb had been partially robbed twice in antiquity, but its priceless cache of treasures vindicated Carter's dream beyond even his wildest imaginings. Four chambers were crammed with jewellery, furniture, statues, chariots, musical instruments, weapons, boxes, jars and food. Even the later discovery that many had been stuffed haphazardly into the wrong boxes by necropolis officials 'tidying up' after the ancient robberies does not detract from their dazzling wealth. Some archaeologists believe that Tutankhamun was perhaps buried with all the regalia of the unpopular Amarna royal line, as some of it is inscribed with the names of his father Akhenaten and the mysterious Smenkhkare (1388–1336 BC), who some Egyptologists believe was Nefertiti ruling as pharaoh.

Most of the treasure is in the Cairo Museum, with a few pieces in Luxor Museum: only Tutankhamun's mummy in its gilded wooden coffin and his sarcophagus are in situ. The burial chamber walls are decorated by chubby figures of the pharaoh before the gods, painted against a yellow-gold background. The wall at the foot end of the sarcophagus shows scenes of the pharaoh's funeral; the 12 squatting apes from the Book

❶ WHAT TO BRING

When visiting the west bank sights, bring plenty of water (it is available at some sights, but you should overestimate the amount you will need). A sun hat, sunglasses and sun protector are also essential. Small change for baksheesh is much needed, as guardians rely on tips to augment their pathetic salaries; LE10 or LE20 for each should be enough for them to either leave you in peace, or to open a door or reflect light on a particularly beautiful painting. A torch (flashlight) can come in handy.

of Amduat, representing the 12 hours of the night, are featured on the opposite wall.

The extra ticket needed to enter the tomb can be bought at the **Entrance Gate & Ticket Office for Tutankhamun's Tomb** (Map p202).

An exact replica of the tomb and sacrophagus, as well as a full explanation of the rediscovery of the tomb, has been installed in the grounds of Howard Carter's house (p214).

Work was underway at the time of writing to determine whether there is another chamber beyond the back wall of the burial chamber: Egyptologist Nicholas Reeves has suggested that the tomb might originally have been used to bury Nefertiti, whose remains – and perhaps her treasure – might lie beyond the wall.

★ **Tomb of Ramses VI (KV 9)** TOMB
(Map p202; Valley of the Kings; adult/student LE80/40, plus Valley of the Kings ticket; ⊙6am-5pm) With some of the broadest corridors, longest shafts (117m) and greatest variety of decoration, KV 9 is one of the most spectacular tombs in the valley. Started by Ramses V and finished by Ramses VI, it is a feast for the eyes, much of its surface covered with intact hieroglyphs and paintings. The burial chamber has an unfinished pit in the floor and a magnificent figure of Nut and scenes from the Book of the Day and Book of the Night.

Tutankhamun's tomb remained intact until 1922 largely thanks to the existence of the neighbouring tomb of Ramses VI, which acted as an unwitting cloak for the older tomb's entrance. KV 9 was begun for the ephemeral Ramses V (1147–1143 BC) and continued by Ramses VI (1143–1136 BC), with both pharaohs apparently buried here; the names and titles of Ramses V still appear in the first half of the tomb. Following the tomb's

ransacking a mere 20 years after burial, the mummies of both Ramses V and Ramses VI were moved to Amenhotep II's tomb where they were found in 1898 and taken to Cairo.

Although the tomb's plastering was not finished, its fine decoration is well preserved, with an emphasis on astronomical scenes and texts. Extracts from the Book of Gates and the Book of Caverns cover the entrance corridor. These continue into the midsection of the tomb and well room, with the addition of the Book of the Heavens. Nearer the burial chamber the walls are adorned with extracts from the Book of Amduat. The burial chamber itself is beautifully decorated, with a superb double image of Nut framing the Book of the Day and Book of the Night on the ceiling. This nocturnal landscape in black and gold shows the sky goddess swallowing the sun each evening to give birth to it each morning in an endless cycle of new life designed to revive the souls of the dead pharaohs. The walls of the chamber are filled with fine images of Ramses VI with various deities, as well as scenes from the Book of the Earth, showing the sun god's progress through the night, the gods who help him and the forces of darkness trying to stop him reaching the dawn. Look out for the decapitated kneeling figures of the sun god's enemies around the base of the chamber walls and the black-coloured executioners who turn the decapitated bodies upside down to render them as helpless as possible.

Tomb of Ramses III (KV 11) TOMB
One of the most popular tombs in the valley, KV 11 is also one of the most interesting and best preserved. Originally started by Sethnakht (1186–1184 BC), the project was abandoned when workers hit the shaft of another tomb (KV10). Work resumed under Ramses III (1184–1153 BC), the last of Egypt's warrior pharaohs, with the corridor turning to the right, then left. It continues deep (125m overall) into the mountain and opens into a magnificent eight-pillared burial chamber.

The wonderful decorations include colourful painted sunken reliefs featuring the traditional ritual texts (Litany of Ra, Book of Gates etc) and Ramses before the gods. Unusual here are the secular scenes, in the small side rooms of the entrance corridor, showing foreign tributes, such as highly detailed pottery imported from the Aegean, the royal armoury, boats and, in the last of these side chambers, the blind harpists that gave the tomb one of its alternative names: 'Tomb of the Harpers'. When the Scottish traveller James Bruce included a copy of this image in his *Travels to Discover the Source of the Nile,* he was laughed out of London after its publication in 1790.

In the chamber beyond is an aborted tunnel where ancient builders ran into the neighbouring tomb. They shifted the axis of the tomb to the west and built a corridor leading to a pillared hall, with walls decorated with scenes from the Book of Gates. There is also ancient graffiti on the rear right pillar describing the reburial of the pharaoh during the 21st dynasty (1069–945 BC). The remainder of the tomb is only partially excavated and structurally weak.

Ramses III's sarcophagus is in the Louvre in Paris, its detailed lid is in the Fitzwilliam Museum in Cambridge and his mummy – found in the Deir Al Bahri cache – is now in Cairo's Egyptian Museum. It was the model for Boris Karloff's character in the 1930s film *The Mummy.*

Tomb of Horemheb (KV 57)   TOMB

Horemheb was Tutankhamun's general, who succeeded Ay, Tutankhamun's briefly reigning tutor. His tomb has beautiful decoration that shows the first use of bas-relief in the valley. This was also the first time the Book of Gates was used to decorate a tomb in the burial chamber. Some 128m long and very steep, this was also the first tomb to run straight and not have a right-angle bend. Horemheb, who was not of royal birth, ruled for 28 years and restored the cult of Amun.

This tomb was discovered filled with ransacked pieces of the royal funerary equipment, including a number of wooden figurines that were taken to the Egyptian Museum in Cairo. Horemheb (1323–1295 BC) brought stability after the turmoil of Akhenaten's reign. He had already built a lavish tomb in Saqqara, but abandoned it for this tomb. The various stages of decoration in the burial chamber give a fascinating glimpse into the process of tomb decoration.

From the entrance, a steep flight of steps and an equally steep passage lead to a well shaft decorated with superb figures of Horemheb before the gods. Notice Hathor's blue-and-black striped wig and the lotus crown of the young god Nefertum, all executed against a grey-blue background. The six-pillared burial chamber, decorated with part of the Book of Gates, remains partially unfinished, showing how the decoration

was applied by following a grid system in red ink over which the figures were drawn in black prior to their carving and painting. The pharaoh's empty red-granite sarcophagus carved with protective figures of goddesses with outstretched wings remains in the tomb; his mummy is missing.

Tomb of Amenhotep II (KV 35)   TOMB

This 91m-long tomb was built for Amenhotep II (sometimes also called Amenophis II), who succeeded his father, the great king Tuthmosis III. Amenophis died around 1400 BC after a 26-year reign, long enough to excavate this large and complicated tomb with its six-pillared inner hall leading to the burial chamber. The pharaoh's remains were found here along with many other royal mummies when the tomb was opened by French archaeologist Victor Loret in 1898.

One of the deepest structures in the valley, this tomb has more than 90 steps down to a modern gangway, built over a deep pit designed to protect the inner, lower chambers from both thieves (which it failed to do) and from flash floods.

Stars cover the entire ceiling in the huge burial chamber and the walls feature, as if on a giant painted scroll, text from the Book of Amduat. While most figures are of the same stick-like proportions as in the tomb of Tuthmosis III, this is the first royal tomb in the valley to present figures with more rounded proportions, as on the pillars in the burial chamber showing the pharaoh before Osiris, Hathor and Anubis. The burial chamber is also unique for its double level; the top level was filled with pillars, the bottom contained the sarcophagus.

Although thieves breached the tomb in antiquity, Amenhotep's mummy was restored by the priests, put back in his sarcophagus with a garland of flowers around his neck, and buried in the two side rooms with 13 other royal mummies, including Tuthmosis IV (1400–1390 BC), Amenhotep III, Merenptah, Ramses IV, V and VI, and Seti II (1200–1194 BC), most of which are now at the Egyptian Museum.

Tomb of Tuthmosis III (KV 34)   TOMB

Hidden in the hills between high limestone cliffs, and reached only via a steep staircase that crosses an even steeper ravine, this tomb demonstrates the lengths to which the ancient pharaohs went to thwart the cunning of the ancient thieves. Tuthmosis III (1479–1425 BC), an innovator in many fields, and whose military exploits and stature earned him the description 'the Napoleon of ancient Egypt', was one of the first to build his tomb in the Valley of the Kings.

It is a steep climb up and down, but secrecy was the pharaoh's utmost concern: he chose the most inaccessible spot and designed his burial place with a series of passages at haphazard angles and fake doors to mislead or catch potential robbers. The shaft, now traversed by a narrow gangway, leads to an antechamber supported by two pillars, the walls of which are adorned with a list of more than 700 gods and demigods. As the earliest tomb in the valley to be painted, the walls appear to be simply giant versions of funerary papyri, with scenes populated by stick men. The burial chamber has curved walls and is oval in shape; it contains the pharaoh's quartzite sarcophagus, which is carved in the shape of a cartouche.

Tomb of Siptah (KV 47) TOMB

Discovered in 1905, the tomb of Siptah (1194–1188 BC) was never completed, but the upper corridors are nonetheless covered in fine paintings. The tomb's entrance is decorated with the sun disc, and figures of Maat, the goddess of truth, kneel on each side of the doorway. There are further scenes from the Book of Amduat, and figures of Anubis, after which the tomb remains undecorated.

Tomb of Tawosret/ Sethnakht (KV 14) TOMB

Tawosret was the wife of Seti II and after his successor Siptah died, she took power herself (1188–1186 BC). Egyptologists think she began the tomb for herself and Seti II, but their burials were removed by her successor, the equally short-lived Sethnakht (1186–1184 BC), who added a second burial chamber for himself. The tomb has been open since antiquity and some decoration has deteriorated.

The change of ownership can be seen in the tomb's decoration; the upper corridors show the queen, accompanied by her stepson Siptah, in the presence of the gods. Siptah's cartouche was later replaced by Seti II's. But in the lower corridors and burial chambers, images of Tawosret have been plastered over by images or cartouches of Sethnakht. The colour and state of the burial chambers remains good, with astronomical ceiling decorations and images of Tawosret and Sethnakht with the gods. The final scene from the Book of Caverns adorning Tawosret's burial chamber is par-

ticularly impressive, showing the sun god as a ram-headed figure stretching out his wings to emerge from the darkness of the underworld.

Tomb of Seti II (KV 15) TOMB

Adjacent to the tomb of Tawosret/Sethnakht is a smaller tomb where it seems Sethnakht buried Seti II (1200–1194 BC) after turfing him out of KV 14. Open since ancient times, judging by the many examples of classical graffiti, the tomb's entrance area has some finely carved relief scenes, although the rest was quickly finished off in paint alone. The walls have extracts from the Litany of Ra, the Book of Gates and the Book of Amduat.

One unusual feature of the decoration here can be found on the walls of the well room: images of the type of funerary objects used in pharaohs' tombs, such as golden statuettes of the pharaoh within a shrine.

Tomb of Ramses I (KV 16) TOMB

Unfinished at the time of his death in 1294 BC after a two-year reign, Ramses I's simple tomb has the shortest entrance corridor; it leads to a single, almost square, burial chamber, containing the pharaoh's open pink-granite sarcophagus. Discovered and excavated (like many others) in 1817 by the Italian adventurer Giovanni Belzoni, the quartzite sarcophagus is in place and some of the wall paintings are still fresh.

Only the chamber is superbly decorated, very similar to Horemheb's tomb (KV 57), with extracts from the Book of Gates, as well as scenes of the pharaoh in the presence of the gods, eg the pharaoh kneeling between the jackal-headed 'Soul of Nekhen' and the falcon-headed 'Soul of Pe', symbolising Upper and Lower Egypt.

★Tomb of Seti I (KV 17) TOMB

(Map p202; Valley of the Kings; LE1000, plus Valley of the Kings ticket; ⏱ 6am-5pm) One of the great achievements of Egyptian art, this cathedral-like tomb is the finest in the Valley of the Kings. Long closed to visitors, it is now re-opened and if you can afford the ticket, it is money well spent. The 137m-long tomb was completely decorated and beautifully preserved when Giovanni Belzoni opened it in 1817, and although it has suffered since, it still offers an eye-popping experience – art from Seti's reign is among the finest in Egypt.

Seti I, who succeeded Ramses I and was father of Ramses II, ruled some 70 years

KV 5: THE GREATEST FIND SINCE TUTANKHAMUN

In 1995 American archaeologist Dr Kent Weeks discovered the largest tomb in Egypt, believed to be the burial place of the many sons of Ramses II. It was immediately hailed as the greatest find since that of Tutankhamun, or as one London newspaper put it: 'The Mummy of all Tombs'.

In 1987 Weeks had located the entrance to tomb KV 5, which James Burton Carter had uncovered in the 1820s but had thought was a small tomb as it was filled with silt and sand. The entrance to the tomb was then lost beneath debris from other excavations. When Weeks and his team cleared the entrance chambers, they found pottery, fragments of sarcophagi and wall decorations, which led the professor to believe it was the tomb of the Sons of Ramses II.

Then, in 1995, Weeks unearthed a doorway leading to an incredible 121 chambers and corridors, making the tomb many times larger and more complex than any other found in Egypt. One chamber has 16 pillars, more than any other in the Valley of the Kings. Clearing the debris from this unique and enormous tomb has been a painstaking and dangerous task. Not only does every bucketful have to be sifted for fragments of pottery, bone and reliefs, but major engineering work had to be done to shore up the structure of the 440m-long tomb. Progress is slow, but Weeks speculates that it has as many as 150 chambers. The excavation can be followed on the excellent website www.thebanmappingproject.com.

after the death of Tutankhamun. After the chaos of the Akhenaten years at Tell Al Amarna, Seti I's reign was a golden age that saw a revival of Old Kingdom-style art, best seen at his temple in Abydos and here in his tomb. The tomb suffered after Belzoni made copies of the decoration by laying wet papers over the raised reliefs and lifting off some of the colour. Subsequent visitors did more damage, with Champollion, the man who deciphered hieroglyphs, even cutting out some of the wall decoration. The tomb was reopened in 2016 and its walls are filled with fabulous images from many ancient texts, including the Litany of Ra, Book of the Dead, Book of Gates, Book of the Heavenly Cow and many others. The sarcophagus, one of the finest carved in Egypt and taken by Belzoni, now sits in the Sir John Soane's Museum, London, while two of its painted reliefs showing Seti with Hathor are now in the Louvre in Paris and Florence's Archaeological Museum.

Tomb of Mentuherkhepeshef (KV 19)   TOMB

The only tomb of a prince that you can visit in the Valley of the Kings (others are closed), this was decorated for Prince Rameses Mentuherkhepeshef (c 1000 BC), a son of Rameses IX. When Giovanni Belzoni discovered it in 1817, he found a number of later mummies buried here. Mentuherkhepeshef's remains have not been found. There are good wall paintings, although they are now behind glass since a 1994 flood damaged the lower parts of the walls.

Mentuherkhepeshef's name translates as 'The Arm of Mentu is Strong'. The entrance corridor to his tomb is adorned with life-size reliefs of various gods, including Osiris, Ptah, Thoth and Khonsu, receiving offerings from the young prince, who is shown in all his finery, wearing exquisitely pleated fine linen robes and a blue-and-gold 'sidelock of youth' attached to his black wig – not to mention his gorgeous make-up (as worn by both men and women in ancient Egypt).

Tomb of Tuthmosis IV (KV 43)   TOMB

The tomb of Tuthmosis IV (1400-1390 BC) is one of the largest and deepest tombs constructed during the 18th dynasty. It is also the first in which paint was applied over a yellow background, beginning a tradition that was continued in many tombs. It was discovered in 1903 by Howard Carter, 20 years earlier than the tomb of Tuthmosis IV's great-grandson, Tutankhamun.

It is accessed by two long flights of steps leading down and around to the burial chamber where there's an enormous sarcophagus covered in hieroglyphs. The walls of the well shaft and antechamber are decorated with painted scenes of Tuthmosis before the gods, and the figures of the goddess Hathor are particularly fetching in a range of beautiful dresses decorated with beaded designs.

On the left (south) wall of the antechamber there is a patch of ancient Egyptian graffiti dating back to 1315 BC. It was written by government official Maya and his assistant Djehutymose, and refers to their inspection and restoration of Tuthmosis IV's burial on the orders of Horemheb, following the first wave of robbery in the eighth year of Horemheb's reign, some 67 years after Tuthmosis IV died.

Tomb of Ay
TOMB

(Map p198; adult/student LE40/20, plus Valley of the Kings ticket; ☺6am-5pm) Although only the burial chamber is decorated, this tomb, tucked away in the West Valley, is noted for its scenes of Ay hunting hippopotamus and fishing in the marshes (scenes usually found in the tombs of nobles not royalty), and for a wall featuring 12 baboons, representing the 12 hours of the night, after which the West Valley or Wadi Al Gurud (Valley of the Monkeys) is named.

Although he succeeded Tutankhamun, Ay's brief reign from 1327 to 1323 BC tends to be associated with the earlier Amarna period and Akhenaten (some Egyptologists have suggested he could have been the father of Akhenaten's wife Nefertiti). Ay abandoned a grandiose tomb in Amarna and took over another here in the West Valley. The valley played an important part in the Amarna story, as it was chosen as a new burial ground by Amenhotep III for his own enormous tomb (KV 22, part way up the valley), and his son and successor Akhenaten also began a tomb here, before he relocated the capital at Amarna, where he was eventually buried.

It seems Tutankhamun also planned to be buried in the West Valley, until his early death saw his successor Ay 'switch' tombs. Tutankhamun was buried in a tomb (KV 62) in the traditional section of the Valley of the Kings, while Ay himself took over the tomb Tutankhamun had begun at the head of the

West Valley. The tomb is accessed by a dirt road that leads off from the car park at the Valley of the Kings and winds for almost 2km up a desolate valley past sheer rock cliffs. Recapturing the atmosphere (and silence) once found in the neighbouring Valley of the Kings makes it worth the visit.

Valley of the Queens
At the southern end of the Theban hillside, the **Valley of the Queens** (Biban Al Harim; Map p198; adult/student LE80/40; ☺6am-5pm) contains at least 75 tombs that belonged to queens of the 19th and 20th dynasties as well as to other members of the royal families, including princesses and the Ramesside princes. Four of the tombs are open for viewing. The most famous of these, the tomb of Nefertari, was only reopened to the public in late 2016. The other tombs are those of Titi, Khaemwaset and Amunherkhepshef.

An additional ticket is required for Tomb of Nefertari.

Tomb of Nefertari
TOMB

(Map p198; LE1000, plus Valley of the Queens ticket; ☺6am-5pm) Nefertari's tomb is hailed as one of the finest in the Theban necropolis – and all of Egypt for that matter. Nefertari was one of five wives of Ramses II, the New Kingdom pharaoh known for his colossal monuments, but the tomb he built for his favourite queen is a shrine to her beauty and, without doubt, an exquisite labour of love. Every centimetre of the walls in the tomb's three chambers and connecting corridors is adorned with colourful scenes.

Nefertari, known as the 'Most Beautiful of Them', is depicted wearing a divinely transparent white gown and a golden headdress featuring two long feathers extending from the back of a vulture. The ceiling of the tomb is festooned with golden stars. In many places the queen is shown in the company of the gods and with associated text from the Book of the Dead.

Like most of the tombs in the Valley of the Kings, this one had been plundered by the time it was discovered by archaeologists. Only a few fragments of the queen's pink-granite sarcophagus remained, and of her mummified body, only traces of her knees were left.

A replica of the tomb is planned to be installed, alongside the replica of Tutankhamun's burial chamber, near Howard Carter's house.

LUXOR SIGHTS

ℹ TIMING YOUR VISIT

At busy periods, coaches bringing daytrippers from the Red Sea arrive in Luxor around 10am. They head directly to either the Valley of the Kings or the Temple of Karnak, so avoid those sights late morning if you don't like being overrun.

Tomb of Amunherkhepshef   TOMB

If you can't afford entry to the Tomb of Nefertari, the valley's showpiece is the tomb of Amunherkhepshef, with beautiful, well-preserved reliefs. Amunherkhepshef, a son of Ramses III, was in his teens when he died. On the walls of the tomb's vestibule, Ramses holds his son's hand to introduce him to the gods who will help him on his journey to the afterlife. Amunherkhepshef wears a kilt and sandals, with the sidelock of hair typical of young boys.

The mummified five-month-old foetus on display in the tomb is the subject of many an inventive story, among them the suggestion that the foetus was aborted by Amunherkhepshef's mother when she heard of his death. It was actually found by Italian excavators in a valley to the south of the Valley of the Queens.

Tomb of Khaemwaset   TOMB

Like his neighbour Amunherkhepshef, Khaemwaset was a son of Ramses III who died young; there is little information about his age or cause of death. His tomb follows a linear plan and is decorated with well-preserved, brightly coloured scenes of Ramses introducing his son to the gods, and scenes from the Book of the Dead. The vestibule has an astronomical ceiling, showing Ramses III in full ceremonial dress; Khaemwaset wears a tunic, the sidelock of hair signifying his youth.

Tomb of Titi   TOMB

(Map p198; Valley of the Queens; adult/student LE50/25; ⊙6am-5pm) The tomb of Queen Titi has a corridor leading to a square chapel, off which is the burial chamber and two smaller rooms. The paintings are faded, but you can still make out a winged Maat kneeling on the left-hand side of the corridor, and the queen before Thoth, Ptah and the four sons of Horus opposite. Inside the burial chamber are a series of animal guardians: a jackal and lion, two monkeys, and a monkey with a bow.

Egyptologists are not sure which Ramesside pharaoh Titi was married to; in her tomb she is referred to as the royal wife, royal mother and royal daughter. Some archaeologists believe she was the wife of Ramses III, and her tomb is in many ways similar to those of Khaemwaset and Amunherkhepshef, perhaps her sons.

Deir Al Medina

Deir Al Medina (Monastery of the Town or Workmen's Village; Map p198; adult/student LE80/40; ⊙6am-5pm) takes its name from a Ptolemaic temple, later converted to a Coptic monastery – the Monastery of the Town – but the real attraction here is the unique **Workmen's Village**. Many of the skilled workers and artists who created tombs in the Valley of the Kings and Valley of the Queens lived and were buried here. Archaeologists have uncovered more than 70 houses in this village and many tombs; the most beautiful of these are now open to the public.

About 1km off the road to the Valley of the Queens and up a short, steep paved road, the small Ptolemaic-era temple, measuring only 10m by 15m, was built between 221 and 116 BC. It was dedicated to Hathor, the goddess of pleasure and love, and to Maat, the goddess of truth and personification of cosmic order. In front of the temple are the remains of the workmens' village, mostly low walls although there are also remains of ancient irrigation pipes. More impressive, however, are the nearby tombs of Sennedjem, Peshedu, Inherka and Ipuy. Originally these were all topped by small mud-brick pyramids, one of which has been rebuilt.

➡ Tomb of Sennedjem

The tomb of Sennedjem is stunningly decorated and contains two small chambers with some exquisite paintings. Sennedjem was a 19th-dynasty artist who lived during the reigns of Seti I and Ramses II, and it seems he ensured his own tomb was as finely decorated as those of his masters. Images include Sennedjem farming with his wife, his mummification and a particularly beautiful image of Osiris with crook and flail.

➡ Tomb of Inherka

Inherka was a 19th-dynasty servant who worked in the Place of Truth in the Valley of the Kings. His beautifully adorned one-room tomb has magnificent wall paintings, including a famous scene of a cat (representing the sun god Ra) killing a snake (representing the evil serpent Apophis) under a sacred tree, on the left wall. There are also beautiful domestic scenes of Inherka with his wife and children.

➡ Tomb of Ipuy

Ipuy was a sculptor during the reign of Ramses II. Here the artist dispenses with the usual scenes of religious ritual and instead is shown farming and hunting. There is also a depiction of Ipuy's house and its flower- and fruit-filled garden.

LUXOR SIGHTS

➡ Tomb of Peshedu

Peshedu was another 19th-dynasty servant in the Place of Truth and had himself portrayed praying under a palm tree beside a lake, an image that has become iconic.

West Bank Temples & Monuments

★ Medinat Habu   TEMPLE
(Adult/student LE40/20; ⊘6am-5pm) Ramses III's magnificent memorial temple of Medinat Habu, fronted by sleepy Kom Lolah village and backed by the Theban mountains, is one of the west bank's most underrated sites. This was one of the first places in Thebes closely associated with the local god Amun. At its height, Medinat Habu contained temples, storage rooms, workshops, administrative buildings, a royal palace and accommodation for priests and officials. It was the centre of the economic life of Thebes for centuries.

Although the complex is most famous for the funerary temple built by Ramses III, Hatshepsut and Tuthmosis III also constructed buildings here. They were later added to and altered by a succession of rulers through to the Ptolemies. When the pagan cults were banned, it became an important Christian centre, and was still inhabited as late as the 9th century AD, when a plague was thought to have decimated the town. You can still see the mud-brick remains of the medieval town

that gave the site its name (medina means 'town' or 'city') on top of the enclosure walls.

The original Temple of Amun, built by Hatshepsut and Tuthmosis III, was later completely overshadowed by the enormous Funerary Temple of Ramses III, the dominant feature of Medinat Habu. But a chapel from the Hatshepsut period still stands on the right after you have passed the outer gates.

Ramses III was inspired in the construction of his shrine by the Ramesseum of his illustrious forebear, Ramses II. His own temple and the smaller one dedicated to Amun are both enclosed within the massive outer walls of the complex.

Also just inside, to the left of the gate, are the Tomb Chapels of the Divine Adorers, which were built for the principal priestesses of Amun. Outside the eastern gate, one of only two entrances, was a landing quay for a canal that once connected Medinat Habu with the Nile.

You enter the site through the unique Syrian Gate, a large two-storey building modelled after a Syrian fortress: as with the images of the pharaoh smiting his enemies, this harks back to the famous battles between Egyptians and Hittites, particularly at the time of Ramses II. If you follow the wall to the left, you will find a staircase leading to the upper floors. There is not much to see

Medinat Habu

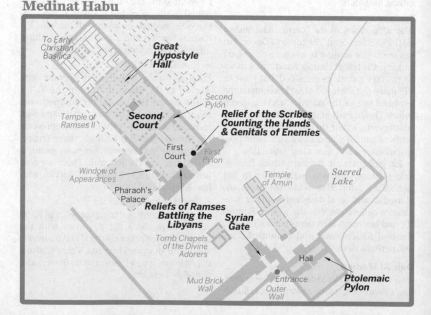

- To Early Christian Basilica
- Great Hypostyle Hall
- Temple of Ramses II
- Second Court
- Second Pylon
- Relief of the Scribes Counting the Hands & Genitals of Enemies
- First Court
- First Pylon
- Window of Appearances
- Temple of Amun
- Sacred Lake
- Pharaoh's Palace
- Reliefs of Ramses Battling the Libyans
- Syrian Gate
- Tomb Chapels of the Divine Adorers
- Hall
- Mud Brick Wall
- Entrance Outer Wall
- Ptolemaic Pylon

LUXOR SIGHTS

in the rooms but you'll get some great views out across the village in front of the temple and over the fields to the south.

The well-preserved **first pylon** marks the front of the temple proper. Ramses III is portrayed in its reliefs as the victor in several wars. Most famous are the fine reliefs of his victory over the Libyans (whom you can recognise by their long robes, sidelocks and beards). There is also a gruesome scene of scribes tallying the number of enemies killed by counting severed hands and genitals.

To the left of the **first court** are the remains of the **Pharaoh's Palace**; the three rooms at the rear were for the royal harem. There is a window between the first court and the Pharaoh's Palace known as the **Window of Appearances**, which allowed the pharaoh to show himself to his subjects.

The reliefs of the **second pylon** feature Ramses III presenting prisoners of war to Amun and his vulture-goddess wife, Mut. Colonnades and reliefs surround the **second court**, depicting various religious ceremonies.

If you have time to wander about the extensive ruins around the funerary temple, you will see the remains of an **early Christian basilica** as well as a small **sacred lake** and, on the south side of the temple, the outline of the palace and the window, looking into the temple courtyard, where Ramses would appear.

Ramesseum TEMPLE
(Map p198; adult/student LE60/30; ☉ 6am-5pm)
Ramses II called his massive memorial 'the Temple of Millions of Years of User-Maat-Ra'; classical visitors called it the tomb of Ozymandias; and Jean-François Champollion, who deciphered hieroglyphics, called it the Ramesseum. Like other memorial temples it was part of Ramses II's funerary complex. His tomb was built deep in the hills, but his memorial temple was on the edge of the cultivated area on a canal that connected with the Nile and with other memorial temples.

Unlike the well-preserved structures that Ramses II built at Karnak and Abu Simbel, his memorial temple has not survived the times very well. It has been extensively restored, but is most famous for the scattered remains of fallen statues that inspired the poem 'Ozymandias', by English poet Shelley, using the undeniable fact of Ramses' mortality to ridicule his aspirations to immortality.

Although more elaborate than many other temples, the layout of the Ramesseum is fairly orthodox, consisting of two courts, hypostyle halls, a sanctuary, accompanying chambers and storerooms. What is unusual is that the rectangular floor plan was altered to incorporate an older, smaller temple – that of Ramses II's mother, Tuya – off to one side.

The entrance is through a doorway in the northeast corner of the enclosure wall, which leads into the **second court**, where one should turn left to the first pylon. The **first and second pylons** measure more than 60m across and feature reliefs of Ramses' military exploits, particularly his battles against the Hittites. Through the first pylon are the ruins of the huge **first court**, including the double colonnade that fronted the royal palace.

Near the western stairs is part of the **Colossus of Ramses II**, the Ozymandias of Shelley's poem, lying somewhat forlornly on the ground, where it once stood 17.5m tall. The head of another granite **statue of Ramses II**, one of a pair, lies in the **second court**. Twenty-nine of the original 48 columns of the **great hypostyle hall** are still standing. In the **smaller hall** behind it, the roof, which features astronomical hieroglyphs, is still in place. Some of the wall carvings, including one showing the pharaoh's name being inscribed on a leaf, are finely done.

Memorial Temple of Hatshepsut TEMPLE
(Deir Al Bahri; Map p198; adult/student LE80/40; ☉ 6am-5pm) At Deir Al Bahri, the eyes first focus on the dramatic rugged limestone cliffs that rise nearly 300m above the desert plain, only to realise that at the foot of all this immense beauty lies a monument even more extraordinary, the dazzling Temple of Hatshepsut. The almost-modern-looking temple blends in beautifully with the cliffs from which it is partly cut – a marriage made in heaven. Most of what you see has been painstakingly reconstructed.

Continuous excavation and restoration since 1891 have revealed one of ancient Egypt's finest monuments. It must have been even more stunning in the days of Hatshepsut (1473–1458 BC), when it was approached by a grand sphinx-lined causeway instead of today's noisy tourist bazaar, when the court was a garden planted with exotic trees and perfumed plants, and when it was linked due east across the Nile to the Temple of Karnak. Called Djeser-djeseru (Most Holy of Holies), it was designed by Senenmut, a courtier at Hatshepsut's court and perhaps

Ramesseum

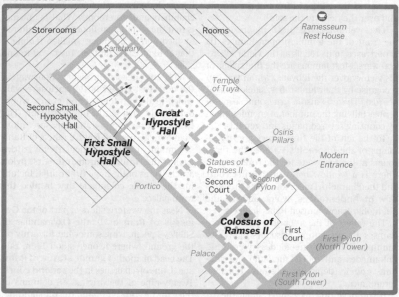

Storerooms

Sanctuary

Rooms

Ramesseum
Rest House

Temple
of Tuya

Second Small
Hypostyle
Hall

**Great
Hypostyle
Hall**

Osiris
Pillars

**First Small
Hypostyle
Hall**

Statues of
Ramses II

Modern
Entrance

Portico

Second
Court

Second
Pylon

**Colossus of
Ramses II**

First
Court

First Pylon
(North Tower)

Palace

First Pylon
(South Tower)

also her lover. If the design seems unusual, note that it did in fact feature all the things a memorial temple usually had, including the rising central axis and a three-part plan, but it had to be adapted to the chosen site: almost exactly on the same line as the Temple of Amun at Karnak, and near an older shrine to the goddess Hathor.

The temple was vandalised over the centuries: Tuthmosis III removed his stepmother's name whenever he could; Akhenaten removed all references to Amun; and the early Christians turned it into a monastery, Deir Al Bahri (Monastery of the North), and defaced the pagan reliefs.

Deir Al Bahri has been designated as one of the hottest places on earth, so an early morning visit is advisable, also because the reliefs are best seen in the low sunlight. The complex is entered via the **great court**, where original ancient tree roots are still visible. The colonnades on the lower terrace were closed for restoration at the time of writing. The delicate relief work on the **south colonnade**, left of the ramp, has reliefs of the transportation of a pair of obelisks commissioned by Hatshepsut from the Aswan quarries to Thebes, and the **north** one features scenes of birds being caught.

A large ramp leads to the two upper terraces. The best-preserved reliefs are on the **middle terrace**. The reliefs on the **north colonnade** record Hatshepsut's divine birth and at the end of it is the Chapel of Anubis, with well-preserved colourful reliefs of a disfigured Hatshepsut and Tuthmosis III in the presence of Anubis, Ra-Horakhty and Hathor. The wonderfully detailed reliefs in the **Punt Colonnade** to the left of the entrance tell the story of the expedition to the Land of Punt to collect myrrh trees needed for the incense used in temple ceremonies. There are depictions of the strange animals and exotic plants seen there, the foreign architecture and landscapes as well as the different-looking people. At the end of this colonnade is the **Hathor Chapel**, with two chambers both with Hathor-headed columns. Reliefs on the west wall show, if you have a torch, Hathor as a cow licking Hatshepsut's hand, and the queen drinking from Hathor's udder. On the north wall is a faded relief of Hatshepsut's soldiers in naval dress in the goddess' honour. Beyond the pillared halls is a three-roomed chapel cut into the rock, now closed to the public, with reliefs of the queen in front of the deities and, behind the door, a small figure of

Senenmut, the temple's architect and, some believe, Hatshepsut's lover.

The **upper terrace**, restored by a Polish-Egyptian team over the last 25 years, had 24 colossal Osiris statues, some of which are left. The central pink-granite doorway leads into the **Sanctuary of Amun**, which is hewn out of the cliff.

On the south side of Hatshepsut's temple lie the remains of the **Temple of Montuhotep**, built for the founder of the 11th dynasty and one of the oldest temples thus far discovered in Thebes, and the **Temple of Tuthmosis III**, Hatshepsut's successor. Both are in ruins.

Assasif Tombs   TOMB
(Tombs of Kheruef, Ankhor and Pabasa; Map p198; adult/student Kheruef & Ankhor LE60/30, Pabasa LE30/15; ☺6am-5pm) This group of tombs, near the Temple of Hatshepsut (p211), belongs to 18th-dynasty nobles, and 25th- and 26th-dynasty nobles under the Nubian pharaohs The area is under excavation by archaeologists, who found a new tomb as recently as 2015, so of the many tombs here only a few are open to the public. These include the **Tombs of Kheruef and Ankhhor**. The nearby tomb of Pabasa, a 26th-dynasty priest, has wonderful scenes of agriculture, including beekeeping, hunting and fishing.

Tickets are available at the ticket office of the Temple of Hatshepsut (Deir Al Bahri). Because these tombs are less visited, you may need to look for the guardian in order to have the gates opened.

Tombs of Roy & Shuroy   TOMB
(Dra Abu'l Naga; Map p198; adult/student LE40/20; ☺6am-5pm) Hidden in the desert cliffs north of Deir Al Bahri lies yet another necropolis, Dra Abu'l Naga, with more than 100 tombs of rulers and officials. Most of these date from the 17th dynasty to the late period (c 1550–500 BC), although in the summer of 2014 a royal tomb from the 11th dynasty was found (c 2081–1938 BC). The area has been extensively plundered, but two tombs, those of Roy and Shuroy, escaped with their paintings mostly intact.

The **tomb of Roy**, a royal scribe and steward of Horemheb, last pharaoh of the 18th dynasty, is small with scenes of funerary offerings and agriculture, and a beautifully painted ceiling. A few metres away, the T-shaped **tomb of Shuroy** (No 13) contains some finely executed, but in places heavily damaged, paintings of Shuroy and his wife making offerings to the gods, and a funeral procession led by a child mourner.

LUXOR SIGHTS

Memorial Temple of Hatshepsut

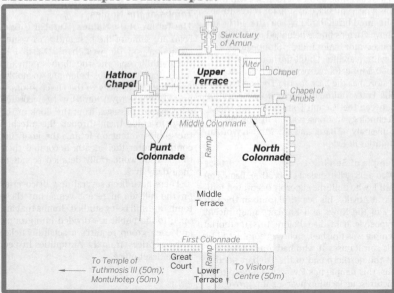

Carter's House & the Replica Tomb of Tutankhamun
MUSEUM

(Map p198; adult/student LE50/25; ⊘9am-5pm; Ⓟ) The domed mud-brick house where Howard Carter lived during his search for Tutankhamun's tomb is surrounded by a garden on what is otherwise a barren slope above the road from Deir Al Bahri to the Valley of the Kings. The house has been restored and decorated with pictures and tools of the excavation. An exact replica of Tutankhamun's burial chamber has been constructed on the edge of the garden along with an exhibition relating to the discovery of the tomb.

The replica has faithfully copied the shape of the original tomb, but only the burial chamber (right-hand side) has been reproduced here. The work is intended to challenge assumptions about our desire to see original objects and also to take some of the pressure off the original tomb. Although the young pharaoh's mummy has not been included, every detail of the burial chamber has been exactly reproduced, including dust and pitting on the walls, the wooden railing, and cracks in the sarcophagus.The left-hand storeroom (not open in the original tomb) has been used to mount displays explaining how the tomb was discovered and reproduced.

There is a cafe space on the side of Carter's House which, when it reopens, will make this a peaceful place to stop for refreshment. The mud-brick building on the little hill above Carter's house belonged to the French conservator Alexandre Stoppelaëre. An Egyptian architect built the house for him in 1950. Empty for many years, it has now been restored as the base for the Theban Necropolis Preservation Initiative, a collaboration between the Factum Foundation for Digital Technology in Conservation in Madrid, the University of Basel and the Ministry of Antiquities in Egypt.

Temple of Seti I
TEMPLE

(Map p198; adult/student LE60/30; ⊘6am-5pm) Seti I, who built the superbly decorated temple at Abydos, his beautiful tomb in the Valley of the Kings and Karnak's magnificent hypostyle hall, died before this memorial temple was finished, so it was completed by his son Ramses II who had a heavier hand. At the northern end of the Theban necropolis, this temple has few visitors, despite its picturesque location near a palm grove.

The temple was severely damaged by floods in 1994 and has been extensively restored. The entrance is through a small door in the northeast corner of the reconstructed fortress-like enclosure wall. The first and second pylons and the court are in ruins. The pharaoh's palace has also gone, but recent excavations have revealed its foundations, just south of the court, and it is therefore the earliest-surviving example of a palace within a memorial temple; its plan is similar to the better-preserved palace at the memorial temple of Ramses III at Medinat Habu.

The walls of the columned portico at the west facade of the temple, and those of the hypostyle court beyond it, contain some superbly executed reliefs. Off the hypostyle are six shrines and to the south is a small chapel dedicated to Seti's father, Ramses I, who died before he could build his own mortuary temple.

Palace of Amenhotep III
MONUMENT

(Malkata; Map p198) This open site in the desert south of Medinat Habu (p210) contains the ruins of a royal palace complex started in the 18th dynasty (14th century BC) by Amenhotep III. The palace, known in antiquity as the Palace of Joy, contained residences, a temple to Amenhotep's wife and Egypt's first glass factory. The palace was used into Byzantine times.

Tombs of the Nobles

The Tombs of the Nobles (Map p198; ⊘6am-5pm) are some of the best and least-visited attractions on the west bank. Nestled in the foothills opposite the Ramesseum are more than 400 tombs belonging to nobles from the 6th dynasty to the Graeco-Roman period. Where royal tombs were decorated with cryptic passages from the Book of the Dead to guide them through the afterlife, the nobles, intent on letting the good life continue after their death, decorated their tombs with wonderfully detailed scenes of their daily lives.

There have been several new discoveries on the hillside in recent years, but these tombs are still being studied. Tombs that are open to the public are divided into groups, and each group requires a separate ticket (various prices) from the Antiquities Inspectorate ticket office.

Tombs of Khonsu, Userhet & Benia (Nos 31, 51 & 343)   TOMB

(Map p198; adult/student LE20/10; ⊙6am-5pm) The tomb of Benia is the most colourful of this trio. Benia was a boarder in the Royal Nursery and chief treasurer during the reign of Tuthmosis III. There are many scenes of offering tables piled high with food and drinks overlooked by Benia, and sometimes by his parents. In a niche at the end of the tomb, a statue of Benia is flanked by his parents, all three with destroyed faces.

Khonsu was First Prophet in the now-vanished memorial temple of Tuthmosis III (1479-1425 BC). Inside the first chamber of Khonsu's tomb are scenes of the Montu festival at Armant, about 20km south of Luxor; this was the festival of the god of war over which Khonsu presided. The sacred barque with the shrine of Montu is towed by two smaller boats. The gods Osiris and Anubis are also honoured, and in many scenes Khonsu is seen making offerings to them. The ceiling is adorned with images of ducks flying around and nests with eggs. Next door is the less-well-preserved tomb of Userhet, a priest during the time of Seti I (1294-1279 BC).

Tombs of Menna, Nakht & Amenemope   TOMB

(Map p198; adult/student LE60/30; ⊙6am-5pm) The beautiful and highly colourful wall paintings in the tomb of Menna and the tomb of Nakht emphasise rural life in 18th-dynasty Egypt. Menna was an estate inspector and Nakht was an astronomer of Amun. Their finely detailed tombs show scenes of farming, hunting, fishing and feasting. Although this tomb is so small that only a handful of visitors are able to squeeze in at a time, the walls have some of the best-known examples of Egyptian tomb paintings.

The tomb of Amenemope is one of the most recent to be opened for visitors. The large funerary complex has previously been open since antiquity and has lost most of its decoration. Among the more recent materials found when archaeologists arrived were early Coptic manuscripts and Howard Carter's copy of the *Spectator* from 1912. Amenemope (c 1186-1069 BC) lived in the reigns of Ramses III, IV and V. His titles included Third Prophet of Amon and Greatest of the Seers of Re in Thebes. The sarcophagus in the upper corridor was dragged from the lower burial chamber.

The tomb of Nakht has a small museum area in its first chamber.

Tombs of Ramose, Userhet & Khaemhet   TOMB

(Map p198; adult/student LE40/20; ⊙6am-5pm) The tomb of Ramose, a governor of Thebes under Amenhotep III and Akhenaten, is fascinating because it is one of the few monuments dating from a period of transition between two different forms of religious worship. The exquisite paintings and low reliefs show scenes in two different styles from the reigns of both pharaohs, depicting Ramose's funeral and his relationship with Akhenaten. The tomb was never actually finished, perhaps because Ramose died prematurely.

Next door is the tomb of Userhet, one of Amenhotep II's royal scribes, with fine wall paintings depicting daily life. Userhet is shown presenting gifts to Amenhotep II; there's a barber cutting hair on another wall; other scenes include men making wine and people hunting gazelles from a chariot.

The tomb of Khaemhet, Amenhotep III's royal inspector of the granaries and court scribe, has scenes on the walls showing the deceased making offerings, the pharaoh depicted as a sphinx, the funeral ritual of Osiris and images of daily country life as well as official business.

★ Tombs of Sennofer & Rekhmire   TOMB

(Map p198; adult/student LE30/15; ⊙6am-5pm) The most interesting parts of the tomb of Sennofer, overseer of the Garden of Amun under Amenhotep II, are to be found deep underground, in the main chamber. The ceiling there is covered with clear paintings of grapes and vines, while most of the vivid scenes on the surrounding walls and columns depict Sennofer and all the different women in his life, including his wife, daughters and wet nurse. It is a short but steep climb down into the tomb.

The tomb of Rekhmire, vizier under Tuthmosis III and Amenhotep II, is one of the best preserved in the area. The long, narrow central chamber is unusual in that it slopes upwards towards a false door. The west wall shows Rekhmire inspecting the production of metals, bricks, jewellery, leather, furniture and statuary, including workers on scaffolding. The east wall shows banquet scenes, complete with lyrics; the female harpist sings: 'Put perfume on the hair of the goddess Maat'.

Tombs of Neferronpet, Dhutmosi & Nefersekheru TOMB
(Map p198; adult/student LE30/15) Discovered in 1915, the highlight of the brightly painted tomb of Neferronpet (also known as Kenro), the scribe of the treasury under Ramses II, is the scene showing him overseeing the weighing of gold at the treasury. Next door, the tomb of Nefersekheru, an officer of the treasury during the same period, is similar in style and content to its neighbours. The ceiling is decorated with a huge variety of elaborate geometric patterns.

From this long tomb, a small passage leads into the tomb of Dhutmosi, which is in poor condition.

Activities

Hot-Air Ballooning
Hot-air ballooning to see the sun rise over the ancient monuments on the west bank and Theban mountains is a great way to start the day. Flights usually last an hour and the trajectory obviously depends on the wind, so there is no guarantee you will fly over the Valley of the Kings, as some outfits suggest. Expect to pay about €100 per person in high season.

Balloon operators in Luxor have come under increased scrutiny after a number of accidents that have occurred in the last decade, the latest in January 2018 when strong winds are said to have blown a balloon off course. It then crash-landed, killing one tourist.

Alaska Balloon BALLOONING
(Map p186; 095-227-6651, 010-0568-8439; www.alaskaballoon.com; Sharia Ahad, off Sharia Televizyon; from US$50 per person) Luxor's balloon operators all offer the same sort of service, but Alaska (the local nickname for Luxor) has a good reputation.

Magic Horizon BALLOONING
(010-0568-8439, 095-227-4060; www.visitluxor inhotairballoon.com; Sharia Khaled Ibn Al Walid; from US$50 per person) A well-reputed operator of hot-air-balloon flights over the ancient monuments on the west bank and Theban mountains.

Donkey, Horse & Camel Rides
Riding a horse, a donkey or a camel through the fields and seeing the sunset behind the Theban hills is wonderful. Boys at the local ferry dock on the west bank offer donkey and camel rides for about LE40 to LE50 for an hour. There have been reports of women getting hassled and of overcharging at the end. Some west bank hotels also offer camel trips, which include visits to nearby villages for a cup of tea, and donkey treks around the west bank. These trips, which start at around 7am (sometimes 5am) and finish near lunchtime, cost about LE100 per person.

Nobi's Arabian Horse Stables HORSE RIDING
(Map p186; 095-231-0024, 010-0504-8558; www.luxorstables.com; camel or horse with helmet per hour approx LE50, donkey LE40; 7am-sunset) Excellent horses can be found at Nobi's Arabian Horse Stables, which also provides riding hats, English saddles and insurance. Nobi also has 25 camels and as many donkeys, and organises longer horse-riding and camping trips into the desert, or a week from Luxor to Kom Ombo along the west bank. Call ahead and they will collect you from your hotel.

Call ahead to book, and Nobi can arrange a hassle-free transfer to make sure you arrive at the right place, as taxi drivers often will try and take you to a friend's stable instead.

Felucca Rides
As elsewhere in Egypt, the nicest place to be late afternoon is on the Nile. Take a felucca from either bank and sail for a few hours, catching the soft afternoon light and the sunset, cooling in the afternoon breeze and relaxing after sightseeing. Felucca prices depend on your bargaining skills, but expect to pay LE50 to LE100 per boat per hour.

A popular felucca trip is upriver to Banana Island, a tiny isle dotted with palms about 5km from Luxor. The trip takes two to three hours. Plan it in such a way that you're on your way back in time to watch a brilliant Nile sunset from the boat. Be sure to agree in advance exactly what is included. Beware that some captains have been charging a fictitious 'entry fee' to the island (it's free).

Swimming
After a hot morning of tombs and temples, a dip in a pool can be heavenly. Most bigger hotels and some budget places have swimming pools. The Hilton (p219) will usually allow you to swim if you are staying for lunch (check beforehand). Domina Inn Emilio has a small rooftop pool that you can use for LE20. In the current downturn, most

other east bank hotels will also allow access for a fee. On the west bank Al Moudira (p221) has a wonderful pool set in a peaceful garden on the edge of the desert; non-guests can use it for LE100.

Volunteering

Those distressed by the state of the horses in Luxor streets may like to visit ACE (Animal Care in Egypt; ☑ 095-928-0727; www.ace-egypt. org.uk; start of Sharia Al Habil, near traffic police; by donation; ⊘ 8am-noon & 1-5pm). It's a veterinary hospital and animal welfare centre seeing up to 200 animals a day. Treatment for the working animals of Egyptians, particularly donkeys and horses, is free. Volunteers are welcome.

≋ Courses

Hotel Sheherazade   LANGUAGE
(Map   p186;   ☑ 010-0611-5939;   www.hotel sheherazade.com; Gezira Al Bayrat; €285) Bespoke Arabic courses for beginner and basic levels, run by teachers trained by and using course books from DEAC (Department for Teaching Contemporary Arabic, Institut Français). The price includes accommodation at Hotel Sheherazade, 40 hours of tuition, airport transfers and three sightseeing tours around Luxor.

⌖ Tours

Because of the bargaining and hassle involved, some people may find independent travel challenging at times, and a day tour in an air-conditioned tour bus, taking in the main sights, might be just the thing.

Most small budget hotels aggressively promote their own tours. Some are better than others and there have been complaints from a number of travellers that they ended up seeing little more than papyrus shops and alabaster factories from a sweaty car with no air-con. If you do decide to take one of these tours, expect to pay from US$30 per person.

Several of the more reliable travel agents are clustered around the Winter Palace Hotel (p219). All offer the same kind of tours, so you can easily compare the prices.

Aladin Tours   CULTURAL
(Map p186; ☑ 010-0601-6132, 095-237-2386; www. nefertitihotel.com/tours; Nefertiti Hotel, Sharia As Sahaby; ⊘ 10am-6pm) This very helpful travel agency, run by the young, energetic Aladin, organises sightseeing tours in Luxor and

around as well as in the Western Desert, plus boat trips and ferry tickets to Sinai.

American Express   CULTURAL
(Map p186; ☑ 095-237-2862; Corniche An Nil, next to Winter Palace Hotel; ⊘ 8am-8pm) Offers a large menu of tours in and around Luxor. Prices range from LE250 to LE400 per person for a half day.

Travel Choice Egypt   CULTURAL
(Map p186; ☑ 095-237-2402; www.travelchoice egypt.com; Corniche An Nil; ⊘ 9am-8pm) The former Thomas Cook office, next to the Winter Palace Hotel, still offers currency services and an array of private and group tours.

⚑ Festivals & Events

Moulid of Abu Al Haggag   CULTURAL
The town's biggest traditional festival is the Moulid of Abu Al Haggag, a raucous five-day carnival in honour of the nearest thing Luxor has to a patron saint, a 13th-century Sufi leader, Yusuf Abu Al Haggag. It takes place around Luxor Temple in the middle of Sha'aban, the month before Ramadan.

⌂ Sleeping

Luxor has a wide range of hotels for all budgets, although since the 2011 revolution and following tourism slump, visitor numbers have dropped dramatically and several places have closed their doors.

Budget hotels on the west bank are particularly good value, quieter than their east bank counterparts and offering a more authentic encounter with locals. The east bank has plenty of modern midrange hotels, with good facilities and attractive rates.

At all costs avoid hotel touts, who may pounce on you as you get off the train or bus; they will get a 25% to 40% commission for bringing you to a hotel, but that will be added to your bill. Many budget and mid range hotels offer free or cheap transfers from the airport or train station, so to avoid touts and bargaining with taxi drivers, call ahead and arrange to be picked up.

⌂ East Bank

★**Bob Marley Peace Hotel**   HOSTEL $
(Boomerang; Map p186; ☑ 095-228-0981; www. peacehotelluxor.com; Sharia Mohammed Farid; dm from LE50, s/d with shared bathroom LE140/250; ❄ ☏) The east bank's best-run budget digs, the Bob Marley Peace Hotel (also known as the Boomerang) offers great facilities on a

backpacker budget. Rooms and dorm are squeaky clean (private rooms with en suite are surprisingly spacious), breakfast is big and there's a cushion-scattered roof terrace, tour booking, free wi-fi and an easy walk with a pack from Luxor Train Station.

Happy Land Hotel
HOSTEL $

(Map p186; ☎010-0186-4922; www.facebook.com/msht12345; Sharia Qamr; s/d LE85/90, with shared bathroom LE75/80; ❊ @ ☎) The Happy Land, a backpackers' favourite, offers clean rooms and bathrooms, plus friendly service, a copious breakfast with fruit and cornflakes, and a rooftop terrace. Competition among Luxor's budget hotels is fierce, and the Happy Land does OK.

Fontana Hotel
HOSTEL $

(Map p186; ☎010-0959-8123; www.facebook.com/Fontana-Hotel; Sharia Radwan, off Sharia Televizyon; s/d/tr LE40/60/75, with shared bathroom LE30/50/65; ❊ ☎) An old stalwart of the budget-hotel scene, this 25-room hotel has clean rooms, a washing machine for guest use, a luggage storage room, a rooftop terrace and a kitchen. Bathrooms are large and clean, and toilet paper and towels are provided. The owner, Magdi Soliman, is helpful. Beware extra breakfast charges. Wi-fi in reception only.

★ Nefertiti Hotel
HOTEL $$

(Map p186; ☎095-237-2386; www.nefertitihotel.com; Sharia As Sahabi, btwn Sharia Maabad Al Karnak & Sharia As Souq; s/d/tr/f US$22/30/36/40; ❊ ☎) Aladin As Sahabi runs his family's hotel with care and passion. No wonder this hotel is popular with our readers: simple but scrupulously clean rooms come with crisp white duvets on the beds, kettles with complimentary tea and coffee, and small but spotless bathrooms. An excellent breakfast is served on the roof terrace. One of the best midrange options.

Larger new rooms on the top floors are decorated in local style. The rooftop is great for a drink or a bite, with great views of the west bank, Luxor Temple and the Avenue of Sphinxes, all lit up at night. The Aladin Tours travel agency (p217) is also in the building.

La Maison de Pythagore
GUESTHOUSE $$

(☎010-0535-0532; www.louxor-egypte.com; Al Awamiya; s/d/tr €35/50/60; ❊ ☎) This intimate guesthouse in a traditional Egyptian house is tucked away in the village behind the ACHTI Hotel, close to the Nile, but a world away from Luxor's hustle. The traditional architecture encloses simple, cosy rooms, stylishly painted in blue tones, while the garden is a small oasis planted with date palms, flowers, fruit trees and a fall of bougainvillea.

Some rooms have air-con, others fans, but all have large bathrooms. Breakfast is served on the large roof terrace. Lunch and dinner, made with local seasonal produce, are available to order and can be taken in the garden or on the roof. Run by the Belgian Anne and her son Thomas, it's a great place to stay for a few days. Mother and son are both passionate about Egypt, and run their own tailor-made half-day to one-week tours and adventures for their guests and others.

Domina Inn Emilio
HOTEL $$

(Map p186; ☎095-237-6666, 095-237-3570; www.emiliotravel.com; Sharia Yousef Hassan; s/d US$50/60; ❊ @ ☎ ❊) A good midrange hotel, the Emilio has 101 spacious rooms, all fully equipped with mini fridges, satellite TV, private bathroom, air-con and 24-hour room service. Other extras include an Astro-turfed roof terrace with plenty of shade and a large pool, a sauna and a business centre.

Susanna Hotel
HOTEL $$

(Map p186; ☎095-236-9915; 52 Sharia Maabad Al Karnak; s/d/tr from US$25/30/40; ❊ ❊ ☎) Set between the Luxor Temple and the souq, this 45-room hotel has friendly staff and worn rooms with great views. The rooftop has views over Luxor Temple and the Nile, perfect for a sunset drink as alcohol is available.

Sonesta St George Hotel
HOTEL $$

(Map p186; ☎095-238-2575; www.sonesta.com/luxor; Sharia Khaled Ibn Al Walid; s & d with city view from US$48, Nile view from US$77; ❊ @ ☎ ❊) This 322-room marble-clad hotel, with faux Pharaonic columns and a flame-like fence around the roof, has a kitsch value that should not be overlooked. It is a good, lively place to stay. The hotel is well managed, has friendly staff, comfortable rooms – some with great views – a heated swimming pool, a business centre and a good selection of restaurants.

Mara House
GUESTHOUSE $$

(☎010-2224-3661; www.marahouseluxor.com; Sharia Salahadin Ayyubi, off Sharia Salakhana; €430 per person for 3-night package; ❊ ☎) Irish Mara has built a house with spacious suites, each decorated in local style and including a sitting area and a clean bathroom. The house is open for guests taking the three-night package, which includes east and west bank tours, a day trip to Abydos and Dendara, and feasts at the house. Full details are on the website.

The modern house, in an un-touristy neighbourhood right behind the train station, can be hard to find – call for instructions or a free transfer. Mara's Salahadeen Restaurant, in the same building, was closed at the time of writing, but when it reopens it will be serving Egyptian home-style feasts for around LE225 per person.

★ Hilton Luxor Resort & Spa HOTEL $$$
(☎010-0600-1270; www.hiltonluxor.com; New Karnak; r from US$150; P ✳ 🛜 🏊) The Luxor Hilton is the slickest, most luxurious resort in Luxor. Located 2km north of Luxor centre, past the Karnak temples, the large Nileside rooms are elegant and tastefully decorated in a warm Asian-inspired style with lots of neutral colours and wood. Communal areas exude calm and tranquillity and the spa is impressive, more Thailand than Egypt.

The large grounds include two Nile-view infinity swimming pools with submerged sun loungers, a Technogym, and several top-class restaurants, including the Mediterranean Olives and a chic Asian bistro, Silk Road. The staff and management are young and very hands-on. This hotel is almost a destination in itself, albeit not very family oriented.

Winter Palace Hotel HISTORIC HOTEL $$$
(Map p188, ☎095-238-0425; www.sofitel. com; Corniche An Nil; pavillon/main wing r from US$80/136; ✳ @ 🛜 🏊) The Winter Palace was built to attract Europe's aristocracy and is one of Egypt's most famous historic hotels. A wonderfully atmospheric Victorian pile, it has a grand lobby, high ceilings and fabulous views across the Nile. The enormous garden with exotic trees and a huge swimming pool is a great place to laze at the end of a sightseeing day.

Rooms vary in size and decor, but all are very comfortable, although the building is now in need of an update. Service is generally excellent, but food can be variable, with afternoon tea a disappointment. Grand dining is still a pleasure. The newer Pavillon Wing in the garden has more functional rooms but use of the same public areas, and you can often get excellent discounts on the rooms when booking online. The pool, with its large shallow area, is particularly good for kids.

ACHTI Luxor Resort RESORT $$$
(☎095-227-4544; www.achtiresort.com; Sharia Khaled Ibn Al Walid; r from US$100; P ✳ @ 🛜 🏊) The former Sheraton Luxor is a secluded three-storey building set amid lush gardens at the southern end of Sharia Khaled Ibn Al Walid – close to some restaurants but away from street noise. Rooms are well appointed and those overlooking the Nile have great views, as does the riverside pool. A popular hotel with friendly staff and a high repeat rate.

The Italian restaurant, La Mama, remains popular. The hotel is still called the Sheraton by taxi drivers and others in Luxor.

🛏 West Bank

Nour El Gourna GUESTHOUSE $
(Map p198; ☎010-0129-5812, 095-231-1430; Old Gurna; s/d/tr €18/25/30; ✳) Set in a palm grove, easy strolling distance to Medinat Habu and the Ramesseum, Nour Al Gurna has seven large mud-brick rooms, with fans (some with air-con), mosquito nets, small stereos, locally made furniture, tiled bathrooms and traditional palm-thatch ceilings. Romantic and original, with friendly management, this is a tranquil and intimate guesthouse, conveniently located for visiting the west bank's monuments.

Even if you're not staying, stop in at their restaurant during or after your west bank exploration for one of their hearty, good-value set-menu meals (LE80; vegetarian LE50).

Marsam Hotel HISTORIC HOTEL $
(Map p198; ☎095-237-2403, 095-231-1603; www. marsamluxor.com; Old Gurna; s/d €25/35, with shared bathroom €20/25; P ✳ 🛜) The oldest hotel on the west bank, the Marsam was originally built in the 1920s as a house for archaeologists from the University of Chicago, but was later turned into a hotel by Sheikh Ali of the local Abd El Rasoul family. The family have run it ever since. Work in 2013 left the hotel looking its best.

Twenty of the 36 rooms have en-suite bathrooms and air-con, while the others have fans, but all retain the simple mud-brick design and bare furnishings. The courtyard, open to fields and the excavations of the Temple of Amenhotep III, is a lovely, shaded place to sit – a delicious breakfast with home-baked bread is served here. Atmospheric and quiet, and close to almost all the west bank sights, it remains popular with archaeologists, so you need to book ahead, particularly during the dig season (roughly from October to March). If you can't get a room, stop by for lunch or a cold beer at the end of a hot day seeing the tombs.

Al Gezira Hotel
HOTEL $

(Map p186; ✉ 095-231-0034; www.el-gezira.com; Gezira Al Bayrat; s/d/tr €15/20/25, half board extra €6 per person; ❉ ⌂) This hotel, in a modern building, is very much a home away from home – literally so for quite a few archaeologists during the winter season. The charming owners make everyone feel welcome and the 11 homey rooms, overlooking the lake or a dried-up branch of the Nile, are well maintained and pristinely clean.

Desert Paradise Lodge
LODGE $

(✉ 010-2872-1991, 095-231-3036; www.desertparadiselodge.com; Qabawi; s/d LE250/300; ❉ @ ⌂) Far from the crowds, off the road to the Valley of the Kings and on the edge of the desert, this is a place for anyone wanting to do the west bank slowly, calmly and cheaply. A beautiful small lodge built in the traditional style, it has spacious domed rooms, lots of communal space, a garden and terraces overlooking the Theban hills.

It's 1.5km from the crossroads to Valley of Kings, on the first left after Howard Carter's House.

Al Fayrouz Hotel
HOTEL $

(Map p186; ✉ 012-2277-0565, 095-231-2709; www.elfayrouz.com; Al Gezira; s/d/tr/q €10/16/19/23; ❉ ⌂) This tranquil hotel with 22 brightly painted rooms is a good base for exploring the monuments of the west bank. Under Egyptian-German management, the simple, tastefully decorated rooms are spotless and have private bathrooms; most also have balconies.

The more expensive rooms (count on around €3 more) are larger, have a sitting area and more character. Meals are served on the comfortable roof terrace or in the popular garden restaurant.

Nour El Balad
GUESTHOUSE $

(Map p198; ✉ 095-206-0111; http://nour-el-balad.luxor-hotels-eg.com; Ezbet Bisily; s/d/tr US$18/25/30; ❉) The sister hotel to Nour El Gourna (p219) is particularly quiet and has 14 spacious rooms. To get here, follow the track behind Medinat Habu for 500m.

Cleopatra Hotel
HOTEL $

(Map p186; ✉ 095-231-4545, 010-0386-8345; http://facebook.com/cleopatrahoteluxorl; Al Gezira;

s/d/tr/q LE200/250/350/400; ❉ ⌂) A newer hotel on a quieter Gezira street, all of the very clean rooms are simple but painted in bright colours, with ensuite facilities and balconies. There's a great roof terrace with views over fields.

★ Beit Sabée
BOUTIQUE HOTEL $$

(Map p198; ✉ 011-1837-5604; www.nourelnil.com/guesthouse; Bairat; d €40-100; ❉ ⌂) This is a great reinvention of a traditional-style, two-storey mud-brick house: Beit Sabée has appeared in design magazines for its cool use of local colours and furnishings with a twist. Near the farms behind Medinat Habu, it offers effortlessly chic rooms, a closer contact with rural Egypt and fabulous views of the desert and Medinat Habu from the rooftop.

Some rooms are larger and brighter than others. The bigger ones could easily take a third person (extra €10 per night). Breakfast is served in the courtyard or on the roof, and lunch and dinner are also available (LE80 for a meal with meat, LE50 for vegetarian). This is a good place to spend a calm few days.

Nile Valley Hotel
HOTEL $$

(Map p186; ✉ 095-231-1477, 012-2796-4473; www.nilevalley.nl; Al Gezira; s €22-30, d €27-35, f €35-50; ❉ ⌂ ⌂) A delightful Dutch-Egyptian hotel in a modern block near the ferry landing. Rooms in both the cheaper old wing and the new wing are filled with light and come with good facilities (air-con, satellite TV, fridge). The rooftop bar-restaurant (p223) has fantastic views over the Nile to Luxor Temple, while the garden has a pool (and children's pool) for after-temple cooling off.

Sheherazade Hotel
HOTEL $$

(Map p186; ✉ 010-0611-5939; www.hotelsheherazade.com; Al Gezira; s/d/tr US$30/35/40; ❉ ⌂ ⌂) Mohamed El Sanosy's dream of building a hotel has culminated in one of the most welcoming places to stay on the west bank and somewhere he takes great pride in. The comfortable and spacious rooms are decorated with local colour and furnishings, and all have en-suite bathrooms with water heated by solar panels. The Moorish-style building is surrounded by a garden.

Amon Hotel
GUESTHOUSE $$

(Map p186; ✉ 010-0639-4585, 095-231-0912; www.amonhotel.com; Al Gezira; from €20 per person; ❉ ⌂) Charming family-run hotel in a modern building with spotless rooms, free wi-fi, a wonderful, lush exotic garden (perfect for breakfast, lunch or a drink), extremely helpful staff and delicious home-cooked meals. This hotel is popular with archaeologists in winter, so book ahead.

In the new wing, the rooms are large with private bathrooms, ceiling fans, air-con and balconies overlooking the courtyard. In the old wing, some of the small rooms have private bathrooms, and all have air-con. On the top floor are three triple rooms with an adjoining terrace and stunning views over the Theban Hills and the east bank. There are some single and doubles with shared bathroom at €5 less.

House of Scorpion GUESTHOUSE **$$**
(Map p198; ☎010-0512-8732; www.facebook.com/Scorpion.House.Luxor; Al Taref; s/d US$22/30; ❄🛜) Charming little guesthouse in a mud-brick house with seven different themed rooms, all large with tiled bathrooms and small salons in Arab style. Tayeb, who runs the place, is very helpful and friendly. It's away from the crowds and mainly works by word of mouth. It is essential to call or book ahead for both food (lunch/dinner LE50/100) and accommodation.

El Nakhil Hotel HOTEL **$$**
(Map p186; ☎012-2382-1007, 095-231-3922; www.elnakhil.com; Al Gezira; s/d/tr €25/35/45; ❄🛜) Nestled in a palm grove, the Nakhil or 'Palm Tree' is on the edge of Al Gezira. This resort-style hotel has 17 spotless, well-finished domed rooms, all with private bathrooms and air-con. It also has family rooms, baby cots and three rooms that can cater for disabled guests. The large rooftop restaurant has great views over the Nile.

El Mesala Hotel GUESTHOUSE **$$**
(Map p186; ☎095-231-5105, 010-6253-2186; www.hotelelmesala.com; Al Gezira, near ferry landing; s/d/tr/flat €25/35/47/55, ❄🖥🛜) One of the better family-oriented hotels in Al Gezira on the west bank. The hotel is on the Nile, a stone's throw from the ferry landing, and therefore perfectly located for visits on both banks. It has 17 immaculate rooms with comfortable beds, and with balconies looking at Luxor Temple and the Nile.

The staff and the manager Mr Ahmed are all extremely welcoming, and everything is absolutely spotless. The restaurant is in the front garden, and there's a great rooftop terrace for sunbathing.

SELF-CATERING RENTAL

Families or those planning a prolonged stay in Luxor might consider a self-catering option. Flat rental is mushrooming in Luxor, on both banks; it is cheap, and many foreigners are getting involved in the business. The downside of self-catering is sex tourism, as there is very little control as to whom people can bring in, whereas in hotels foreigners are not allowed to take guests back to their room.

Several companies can arrange flat rentals, including **Flats in Luxor** (☎010-0356 4540; www.flatsinluxor.co.uk; per night from US$50; ❄@🛜), run by a British-Egyptian couple who started renting out their own flats but now also manage others. The websites www.luxor-westbank.com and www.luxor4flats.com also have a wide selection.

★ **Al Moudira** HOTEL **$$$**
(☎095-255-1440, 012-2392 8332; www.moudira.com; Daba'iyya; s/d from €150/180; ❄@🛜🖥) Al Moudira is a luxury hotel of a stylish individuality. A fantasy of pointed arches and soaring domes set amid lush gardens and birdsong, the hotel is charming and peaceful. The huge rooms are grouped around a series of verdant courtyards. There is a tranquil restaurant and vibrant bar, a large pool and hammam (bathhouse), all run by friendly staff.

Each room is different in shape, size (all are very large) and decoration, with their own hand-painted trompe l'oeil theme and with Egyptian antiques. Cushioned benches and comfortable antique chairs invite pasha-like lounging and the enormous vaulted bathrooms feel like private hammams. Public spaces are even more spectacular with traditional *mashrabiyya* (wooden latticework) combined with work by contemporary 'orientalist' artists. The staff are very helpful. Set on the edge of the cultivated land and the desert, this hotel is spectacular and unique. Don't let its isolation put you off: transport is quick and easy.

🍴 Eating

Most people come to Luxor for monuments as opposed to cuisine – a good thing as most restaurants, particularly in the hotels, have long been mediocre. But the food is improving, particularly where restaurants serve traditional Egyptian food. Outside of hotels, few places serve alcohol or accept credit cards.

Luxor has a number of good bakeries. Try the ones on Sharia Ahmed Orabi, at the beginning of Sharia Maabad Al Karnak and on Sharia Gedda. The best pastries come from **Twinky** (Map p186; Sharia Al Manshiya) near the railway station. There is also now a **Drinkies** (Map p186; www.drinkies.net; next to railway station), selling Egyptian beer and wine. On the west bank, try the food and fruit shops on the main street in Al Gezira, or head for the wonderful weekly market Souq At Talaat, in Taref opposite the Temple of Seti I. Also on the west bank is **Sa-Re Gourmet Food** (Map p186; ☑010-9750-7767; www.sa-re.net; Al Gezira; ⊙9.30am-1pm & 5pm-8.30pm Sat-Thu), a small shop near the ferry selling fresh soup, duck à l'orange and other treats.

✖ East Bank

★ **Wenkie's German Ice Cream & Iced Coffee Parlour** ICE CREAM $
(Map p186; ☑012-8894-7380; www.facebook.com/wenkies; Sharia Al Gawazat, opposite the Nile Palace; small/large scoop LE3/5; ⊙2-8pm Sat-Thu) For people who only opened up shop in 2014, Ernst and Babette Wenk have quickly become legends, serving the finest, most delicious ice cream in Luxor. Using organic buffalo milk and fresh fruit, they make and sell ices and sorbets with distinctly local flavours (think hibiscus, mango and doum palm).

The secret to their success is the quality of the product and the price. Wenkie's also serves iced coffee, milkshakes and waffles. It tends to close on holidays and for a couple of months in the summer. Their ices are also available at the Crepe Cafe near Luxor Station.

★ **Koshari Alzaeem** EGYPTIAN $
(Map p186; Sharia Al Masaken Al Shaabeya; dishes LE5-15; ⊙24hr) Probably the best *kushari* (mix of noodles, rice, black lentils, fried onions and tomato sauce) in town. The few tables tend to fill up fast. There is a second branch near Midan Youssef Hassan.

Kam Thai THAI $
(☑012-7728-2490; www.kam-thai-takeaway.jimdo.com; mains LE40-60; ⊙1-9pm; ✔) An excellent addition to the east bank dining scene is this authentic Thai. It's a tiny place tucked

away east of Sharia Khalid Ibn Al Walid, but worth finding if you hanker after hot spicy soup, stir-fried prawns or solid pad thai noodles. They also do takeaway.

Abu Ashraf EGYPTIAN $
(Map p186; ☑095-237-5936; Sharia Al Mahatta; dishes LE15-30; ⊙8am-11pm) This large, popular restaurant and takeaway is just down from the train station. It serves roast chicken, pizzas, kebabs and good *kushari*.

★ **Sofra Restaurant & Café** EGYPTIAN $$
(Map p186; ☑095-235-9752; www.sofra.com.eg; 90 Sharia Mohammed Farid; mezze LE16-25, mains LE45-85; ⊙11am-midnight) Sofra remains our favourite restaurant in downtown Luxor. Both the intimate salons and the spacious rooftop terrace are stylishly decorated, sprinkled with antique furniture, chandeliers and original tilework. The menu features excellent mezze and well-executed traditional Egyptian classics such as stuffed pigeon and excellent duck. With friendly staff and shisha to finish, the place is a treat.

The rooftop terrace is also a cafe, where you can come just for a fresh juice or coffee (alcohol is not available) and shisha.

As Sahaby Lane EGYPTIAN $$
(Map p186; ☑095-236-5509; www.nefertitihotel.com/sahabi.htm; Sharia As Sahaby, off Sharia As Souq; dishes LE13-150; ⊙9am-11.30pm) This easy-going restaurant takes over the alley way running between the souq and the street to the Karnak temples, and adjoins the Nefertiti Hotel. Fresh, well-prepared Egyptian standards like *fiteer* (sweet or savoury flaky pizza) and *tagen* (stew cooked in a deep clay pot) are served alongside good pizzas and salads, as well as more adventurous dishes such as camel with couscous.

The young staff are both friendly and efficient, and the terrace is a great place to watch the world go by, or relax after shopping in the souq.

Pizza Roma.It ITALIAN $$
(Map p186; ☑011-1879-9559; Sharia St Joseph; pizzas around LE50, meat dishes up to LE150; ⊙noon-midnight) The most popular Italian restaurant in Luxor. Run by an Italian woman and her Egyptian partner, this small ochre-painted restaurant serves a long list of pastas, pizzas, some classic Italian meat dishes and a good rocket salad. No alcohol served, but you can bring your own.

Gerda's Garden
EGYPTIAN, EUROPEAN $$
(☑012-2534-8326, 095-235-8688; opp Hilton Luxor, New Karnak; dishes LE15-45; ◷6.30-11pm) Gerda is one half of a German-Egyptian couple whose restaurant has built a strong following with European residents and regular visitors to Luxor. The decor is homely, provincial European bistro, but the menu features both Egyptian specials (kebab and delicious grilled pigeon) and very European comfort food for those slightly homesick, such as goulash and potato salad.

Oasis Palace Cafe
CAFE $$
(Map p186; Sharia Dr Labib Habashi; mains LE30-110; ◷10am-midnight; 🛜🖋) A rather charming and intimate cafe-restaurant set in a building dating back to the early 20th century, with high-ceilinged salons that still cling on to some of their original plaster lintel details. The menu is an all-round pleaser with shawarma plates, grilled meat and fish dishes, omelettes and even jacket potatoes. Service is attentive and friendly.

Jewel of the Nile
BRITISH, EGYPTIAN $$
(Map p186; ☑010-6252-2394; www.jewelofthenilerestaurant.com; Sharia Al Rawda Al Sherifa, 300m off Sharia Khaled Ibn Al Walid; mains LE45-85, set menu LE75-85; ◷noon-midnight; 🛜🖋) Laura and Mahmud have survived the tourist downturn by offering traditional Egyptian food using organic vegetables from their farm, as well as British food for homesick Brits: steaks, cottage pie and apple crumble. The menu features a good selection of vegetarian dishes. The dining room is air-conditioned, and there is a small space outside. Alcohol available.

A Taste of India
INDIAN $$
(Map p186; ☑010-9373-2727; www.facebook.com/tasteindialuxor; Sharia St Joseph, off Sharia Khaled Ibn Al Walid; dishes LE35-80; ◷noon-11pm) A small British-run Indian restaurant in neutral colours with plain wooden tables and chairs. On the menu are European versions of Indian dishes such as korma, spinach masala and *jalfrezi* (marinated meat curry with tomato, pepper and onion), as well as original Indian specials such as madras and vindaloo curries.

Silk Road
ASIAN $$$
(☑095-237-4933; www.hiltonluxor.com; New Karnak; mains LE150-250; ◷6.30-11pm; 🛜🖋) Silk Road is one of the most sophisticated dining experiences in Luxor, offering an exotic cuisine, rich in spices, sourced from India, Thailand, China and elsewhere in Asia, and prepared by the wonderful Indian chef. The setting is Asian minimal chic. If the comprehensive menu leaves you at a loss, ask for a degustation of several dishes.

1886 Restaurant
MEDITERRANEAN $$$
(Map p186; ☑095-238-0425; www.sofitel.com; Winter Palace Hotel, Corniche An Nil; mains LE160-310; ◷7-11pm) The 1886 is the fanciest restaurant in the town centre, serving inventive Mediterranean-French food and a few Egyptian dishes with a twist, all in a grand old-style dining room. The waiters are in formal attire and guests are expected to dress for the occasion – men wear a tie and/or jacket (some are available for borrowing). A grand evening out!

✖ West Bank

Marsam Restaurant
EGYPTIAN $
(Sheikh Ali's; Map p198; www.marsamluxor.com; West Bank, near the Ramesseum; mains LE50-100) A lovely place to stop for for dinner on a warm evening or for lunch while seeing the west bank sights – you can sit in the courtyard under the huge trees and look out at the backs of the Colossi of Memnon. Either way food is simple, mostly Egyptian and very good. Service is friendly and can be slow. Alcohol served.

Nile Valley Hotel
INTERNATIONAL $$
(Map p186; ☑095-231-1477; www.facebook.com/pg/Nilevalleyhotel; Al Gezira; meals LE40-80; ◷8am-11pm) A popular rooftop restaurant with a bird's-eye view of the west bank's waterfront, the river and Luxor Temple, the Nile Valley has a wide-ranging menu of Egyptian and international specialities. The falafel, moussaka and pigeon are particularly good. Come at lunch to escape the sun or after sundown for a beer with a view. They have events some evenings.

Restaurant Mohammed
EGYPTIAN $$
(Map p198; ☑012-0325-1307, 095-231-1014; Kom Lolah; mains LE40-80; ◷approx 10am-late) Mohammed's is an old-time Luxor throwback, a simple, family-run restaurant attached to the owner's mud-brick house, where charming Mohammed Abdel Lahi serves with his son Azab, while his wife cooks. The small menu includes meat grills, delicious chicken and duck as well as stuffed pigeon, a local speciality. Stella beer and Egyptian wine are usually available.

With an outdoor terrace and laid-back atmosphere, it's a great place to recharge batteries in the middle of a day exploring temples and tombs, or to linger in the evening. Call ahead to make sure it is open. They can also organise a picnic in the desert or on a felucca.

Al Gezira Hotel EGYPTIAN $$
(Map p186; ☑ 095-231-0034; Al Gezira; set menu LE35) This comfortable rooftop restaurant serves a set menu with Egyptian specialities, such as *molokhiyya* (stewed leaf soup) and *mahshi kurumb* (stuffed cabbage leaves cooked with dill and spices) that must be ordered in advance. There are great views over the Nile and the bright lights of Luxor beyond. Cool beers and Egyptian wine are on offer.

Al Moudira MEDITERRANEAN $$
(☑ 012-0325-1307; Daba'iyya; mains LE75-110; ☑ 8am-midnight) Al Moudira has the most flamboyant decor and most sophisticated (and expensive) food on the west bank. Come at lunch for great salads and grills, or at night for a more elaborate menu, which changes daily, of delicious Mediterranean-Lebanese cuisine. This is a great place for a romantic dinner in the courtyard, or by the fire in the winter. Reserve ahead.

Drinking & Nightlife

East Bank

Even without booming tourism, Luxor can be busy at night. Luxor Temple is open until 10pm and worth seeing at night; the souq is open late as well and more lively at night than during the day. In summer lots of locals stroll along the corniche. At sundown, settle onto an east bank riverside cafe or the terrace of the Winter Palace Hotel (p219) for a sundowner.

Kings Head Pub PUB
(Map p186; ☑ 010-6510-2133; www.facebook.com/ KingsHeadPubAndRestaurant; Sharia Khaled Ibn Al Walid; ☑ noon-late) A relaxed and perennially popular place to have a beer, shoot pool and watch sports on a big screen, the Kings Head tries to capture the atmosphere of an English pub without being twee. The laid-back atmosphere also means that women can come here without being harassed. At the time of writing, it had been up for sale for a long time.

Cilantro CAFE
(Map p186; lower level, Corniche An Nil; ☑ 10am-8pm) A pleasant, popular outdoor cafe, right on the Nile, in front of the Winter Palace Hotel. The former Metropolitan is now part of the Egyptian coffee chain Cilantro, serving dull though usually reliable snacks and good coffee. Away from the hassle of the corniche, right by the waterline, it's a good place to while away a moment.

New Oum Koulsoum Coffee Shop COFFEE
(Map p186; ☑ 0128 909 9909; Sharia As Souq; ☑ 10am-late) Pleasant *ahwa* (coffeehouse) right in the heart of the souq, on a large terrace with welcoming mist machines, where you can recover from shopping and haggling, and watch the crowds without any hassle. On the menu are fresh juices, hot and cold drinks and a good shisha, as well as 'professional Nespresso' coffee.

Sultan Cafe CAFE
(Sharia Khalid Ibn Al Walid; ☑ 10am-midnight) If you want an evening with the people of Luxor city, you could head for the new Sultan Cafe. From the owner of neighbouring Maxime Restaurant, this huge place has a garden with the biggest TV screen in town, indoor air-con rooms, a range of fresh juices, milkshakes, hot drinks and shisha. Egyptian women come here too.

West Bank

There are no real bars on the west bank; drinking is mostly done at restaurants or not at all.

After visiting the Tombs of the Nobles or the Ramesseum, take a break in the tree-shaded courtyard of the oldest mudbrick hotel in Luxor, the Marsam Hotel (p220). They have fresh juices and cold beers to revive the spirits.

Cafe & Restaurant Maratonga CAFE
(Map p198; ☑ 095-231-0233; Kom Lolah; ☑ 5am-11pm) This friendly outdoor cafe-restaurant, in front of Medinat Habu, is the best place to stop after wandering through Ramses III's magnificent temple. Sip a cold drink under a big tree or have a delicious *tagen* (a stew cooked in a deep clay pot) or salad for lunch. The view is superlative, the atmosphere is relaxing and the staff super friendly.

Ramesseum Rest House CAFE
(Map p198; ☑ 010-0945-0789; beside the Ramesseum, Gurna; ☑ 7am-1am) One of the oldest cafe-

restaurants on the west bank, come to this friendly, laid-back place to relax after temple viewings. In addition to the usual mineral water and soft drinks, beer and sometimes wine are available. They also serve simple food – grilled chicken, omelettes and salads.

Hatshepsut Restaurant ROOFTOP BAR
(No Galag; Map p198; ☑ 095-231-0469, 010-6975-6053; Gurna, near Temple of Hatshepsut; ⊙ noon-11pm) Facing the Theban hillside and with a sign that says 'NO GALAG' (no problem or pressure), this is the place to come sip a cold beer while watching belly dancing on the west bank – Sundays and some Thursday evenings, after 10pm. Call before you visit to be sure it is happening.

☆ Entertainment

Karnak Sound & Light Show SHOW
(☑ 02-3385-7320; www.soundandlight.com.eg; LE100, video camera LE35; ⊙ shows at 7pm, 8pm & 9pm in winter, at 8pm, 9pm & 10pm in summer) This highly kitsch sound and light show is a 1½-hour Hollywood-style extravaganza that recounts the history of Thebes and the lives of the many pharaohs who built here in honour of Amun, but it is worth a visit particularly for a chance to walk through the beautifully lit temple at night. Shows are cancelled if less than seven people arrive.

The 1st show is always in English, except for Wednesdays and Sundays, when it is the 2nd.

🔒 Shopping

For alabaster, head for the west bank. The stone is mined about 80km northwest of the Valley of the Kings, and although the alabaster factories near the Ramesseum and Deir Al Bahri sell cheap handmade cups, vases and lights in the shape of Nefertiti's head, it is possible to find higher-quality bowls and vases, often unpolished, which are great buys. Take care when buying, as sometimes what passes for stone is actually wax with stone chips. Avoid going with a tour guide as his commission will invariably be added to your bill.

The *tagen* (clay pots) that are used in local cooking make a more unusual buy. Very practical, they can be used to cook on top of the stove or in the oven, and they look good on the table too. Prices start at LE30 for a very small pot and go up to about LE80. They're on sale on the street just beside the police station in Luxor's east bank.

★ **Caravanserai** ARTS & CRAFTS
(Map p198; ☑ 012-2327-8771; www.caravanserai luxor.com; Kom Lolah; ⊙ 8am-10pm) This delightful treasure trove of Egyptian crafts, near Medinat Habu on the west bank, is run by friendly Khairy and his family. Inside you'll find beautiful pottery from the Western Oases, Siwan embroideries, a colourful selection of handwoven scarves, amazing appliqué bags and many other crafts that can be found almost nowhere else in Egypt. All at highly reasonable prices.

Recognising that making crafts was one of the few things poor Egyptian women could do to earn money, Khairy set up the shop to encourage and help them. He buys almost everything people make, telling them what sells well and suggesting ways of improving their designs. Above all, he loves people's creativity.

Habiba ARTS & CRAFTS
(Map p186; ☑ 010-0124-2026; www.habibagallery. com; Sharia Andrawes Pasha, off Sharia Al Souq, ⊙ 10am-10pm) Run by an Australian woman who promotes the best of Egyptian crafts, Habiba sells an ever-expanding selection of top quality Bedouin embroidery, jewellery, leatherwork, wonderful Siwan scarves, cotton embroidered scarves from Sohag, the best Egyptian cotton towels (usually only for export), mirrors, Aswan baskets and much more – all at fixed prices. New lines include locally made shea-butter products.

Aboudi Bookshop & Coffeshop BOOKS
(Map p186; ☑ 095-237-2390, 010-1098-7293; www. aboudi-bookstore.com; Sharia Maabad Al Karnak, behind Luxor Temple; ⊙ 9.30am-10pm) For more than a century, Aboudi has been offering an excellent selection of guidebooks, English-language books on Egypt and the Middle East, maps, postcards and fiction. If you need a read, this is the place to come. Upstairs is a coffeeshop with a great view over Luxor Temple.

Sandouk ARTS & CRAFTS
(Map p186; ☑ 010-0093-4980; Al Gezira) A new shop a short walk from the west bank ferry landing selling a selection of original and beautifully designed objects, from pottery, wood and alabaster to fashion.

Fair Trade Centre ARTS & CRAFTS
(Map p186; ☑ 095-236-0870, 010-0034-7900; Sharia Maabad Al Karnak; ⊙ 9am-10.30pm) This shop markets handicrafts from NGO projects throughout Egypt. It has well-priced

hand-carved wood and pottery from the nearby villages of Hejaza and Garagos, aromatic oils from Quz, beadwork from Sinai, hand-blown glass, Akhmim table linen, beading from the west bank in Luxor, and recycled glass and paper from Cairo.

AA Gaddis Bookshop SOUVENIRS, BOOKS
(Map p186; ☑ 095 238 7042; Corniche An Nil; ☺ 10am-9pm Mon-Sat, from 10.30am Sun, closed Jun & Jul) Next door to the Winter Palace Hotel, as it has been for generations, Gaddis has an extensive selection of books on Egypt, postcards and souvenirs.

**Abo El Hassan
Alabaster Factory** ARTS & CRAFTS
(Map p198; ☑ 010-6733-3081; west bank, opposite Tombs of the Nobles; ☺ 8am-4pm) Mohamed Yousef's shop has a wide range of alabaster and other carved stone on sale. Unlike many other alabaster shops, he will admit that the stone doesn't come from the Theban hills, but from Asyut and Minya. There is a display of stone-working techniques, no hard sell and the shop is air-conditioned. Prices range from LE100 to thousands.

Saad Barbary Ali ARTS & CRAFTS
(Sharia Khaled Ibn Al Walid) If you hanker after an old-style souvenir shop packed with dusty shelves of copper, alabaster and other Egyptian crafts, head to Saad's emporium near the ACHTI Luxor Resort (p219) turnoff. You're certain to find something to take home.

Farouk Gallery ANTIQUES
(Map p198; ☑ 010-6802-9151; www.facebook.com/ Farouk-Gallery-Luxor-932610310141883) The only real antiques shop in Luxor, recently set up on the west bank not far from the Antiquities Inspectorate ticket office. They sell a selection of objects from Luxor and the area, some early 20th century, some newer. Call ahead to make sure they are open.

Bazaar Al Ayam CLOTHING
(Map p186; Tourist Bazaar) Good place for embroidered shawls and white *galabeyas* (men's robes). This is where Egyptians come to shop.

❶ Information

DANGERS & ANNOYANCES
➡ Business has been so slow recently that Luxor's once notorious hasslers seem to have lost heart, though you will still be offered feluccas and motorboats on the corniche and a range of tat as you walk through the souq and the entrance to the Valley of the Kings.

➡ Some *calèche* (horse-drawn carriage) drivers can be persistent, pushed by the need to feed their horses, many quite malnourished.

➡ You may also be propositioned or offered sex – offers you should ignore. All this hassle is a sign of the desperate financial situation that Egypt, and particularly Luxor, is in.

EMERGENCY

Ambulance	☑ 123
Police	☑ 122
Tourist Police	☑ 095-237-6820

MEDICAL SERVICES
Dr Ihab Rizk (☑ 095-238-2525, 012-2216-0846) English-speaking cardiologist, who will come to your hotel; on the east bank.

Luxor Medical Cent (Map p186; ☑ 095-228-4092, 010-2004-7091; www.luxormedicalcenter.com; Villa Kamal, Sharia St Joseph; ☺ 24hr)re

International Hospital (Map p186; ☑ 095-228-0192, 095-227-7914; Sharia Televizyon; ☺ 24hr)

MONEY
Most major Egyptian banks have branches in Luxor, and there is no shortage of ATMs on the east bank. There are now a couple of ATMs on the west bank, but it is best not to count on them working.

American Express (Map p186; ☑ 095-237-8333; Corniche An Nil; ☺ 9am-4.30pm) Currency exchange beside the entrance to the Winter Palace Hotel.

Travel Choice Egypt (p216) Currency exchange below the entrance to the Winter Palace Hotel.

TOURIST INFORMATION
Main Tourist Office (Map p186; ☑ 095-237-3294, 095-237-2215; Midan Al Mahatta; ☺ 9am-8pm) Very helpful and well-informed tourist information opposite the train station. The office can also book hotels and tours, and sell tickets for the sound and light show in Karnak. There are branches of the tourist office in the **train station** (Map p186; ☑ 095-237-0259; Train Station; ☺ 8am-8pm) and the **airport** (☑ 095-237-2306; Luxor Airport; ☺ 8am-8pm) too, although with the lack of visitors they may not be functioning.

VISA EXTENSIONS
If you need to extend your visa, the **Passport Office** (Map p186; ☑ 095-238-0885; Sharia Khaled Ibn Al Walid; ☺ 8am-2pm Sat-Thu) is on the east bank, opposite the Sonesta St George Hotel. You will need two passport photos and two photocopies of the photo page and visa page from your passport. It is best to go first thing in

the morning and be prepared to wait, although they sometimes turn things around quickly.

❶ Getting There & Away

AIR

Luxor Airport (☎ 095-232-4455) is 7km east of central Luxor. EgyptAir (www.egyptair.com) operates regular flights to Cairo from LE730.

BUS

The **Upper Egypt Bus Co** (Map p186; ☎ 095-232-3218, 095-237-2118; Midan Al Mahatta; ⊗7am-10pm) and **Super Jet** (Map p186; ☎ 095-236-7732; Midan Al Mahatta; ⊗ 8am-10pm) have ticket offices just south of the train station. The **Go Bus office** (Map p186; ☎ 010-0779-1286; www.gobus-eg.com; Sharia Ramses) is just to the north. Most bus services leave from outside of the respective ticket office; check when booking. A taxi from downtown Luxor to the bus offices costs between LE25 and LE35.

To go to the Western Desert oases, take a train to Asyut, from where there are several buses a day to Kharga and Dakhla.

FELUCCA

You can't take a felucca from Luxor to Aswan; most feluccas leave from Esna because of the Esna Lock. Unless you have a strong wind, it can take days to go more than a few kilometres upriver and, for this reason, we recommend taking a felucca downstream from Aswan.

MICROBUS & SERVEES

The parking lot for microbuses and servees heading to towns outside of Luxor is behind, and about 1km north of, the train station. From here regular microbuses and a few servees head south to Esna (LE8), Edfu (LE12), Kom Ombo (LE20) and Aswan (LE35); and north to Qena (LE7).

Officially, foreigners are not currently allowed to use this transport, although some drivers might take you given the right financial inducement. Be aware, though, that if you're unlucky and get stopped at a checkpoint along the route, the police may ask for a bribe to allow you to carry on, make the entire microbus turn around and head back to Luxor, or, at the worst, confiscate the driver's licence.

TRAIN

The train is a comfortable and easy way to travel south to Aswan and north to Cairo. Special services have newer rolling stock and slightly bigger seats than Spanish services.

Luxor Station (☎ 095-237-2018; Midan Al Mahatta) has a tourist office, plenty of card phones and a post office. All train tickets are best bought in advance; if you buy your ticket on the train there is a surcharge of LE6.

The **Watania Sleeping Train** (www.watania sleepingtrains.com) has a ticket booking office inside the station.

❶ Getting Around

TO/FROM THE AIRPORT

There is no bus between the airport and the town, and no official price for taxis from Luxor airport into town, so the drivers set their prices, often at about LE100 or more. Quite often there is not enough work for all the drivers, so when you try to take a taxi, an argument between drivers may erupt. In short, it is a major hassle. If you want peace of mind, ask your accommodation to arrange your transfer.

BICYCLE

The compact town lends itself to cycling, and distances on the generally flat west bank are just far enough to provide some exercise but not to be exhausting (except when the weather is too hot). Cycling at night is not recommended given the local habit of driving without headlights.

Many hotels rent out bikes. Prices vary, as does the quality of bikes. You might find one for LE25 a day, or LE10 an hour. Be sure to check

BUS SERVICES FROM LUXOR

DESTINATION	PRICE	DURATION	TIME/COMPANY
Cairo	LE150-275	10-12hr	10pm (Upper Egypt); 9am, 1pm & 10.15pm (Super Jet); 1pm, 9.30pm, 11.45pm & 12.30am (Go Bus)
Dahab	LE210	18hr	5pm (Upper Egypt)
Hurghada	LE50-90	4-5hr	7am & 8.30pm (Upper Egypt); 8.30am & 7pm (Super Jet); 8am & 3.30pm (Go Bus)
Port Said	LE115	12hr	8pm (Upper Egypt)
Sharm El Sheikh	LE175	14hr	5pm (Upper Egypt)
Suez	LE90-100	9-10hr	7am & 8.30pm (Upper Egypt)

All Upper Egypt Bus Co. services heading north can drop you in Qena (LE5). Buses travelling to Hurghada can drop you in Safaga (LE50), where you can change for Al Quseir and Marsa Alam.

TRAINS FROM LUXOR

Prices are for a 1st-class air-con seat.

DESTINATION	PRICE	DURATION	TIME
Aswan	Spanish/Special LE53/94	3hr	4.30am, 7.35am, 9.45am & 10.35pm (Spanish); 2.50am, 6.20am, 6.45am, 8.15am, 6.25pm & 7.40pm (Special)
Cairo	Spanish/Special LE114/203	10hr	1.15am, 10.55am, 8pm & 11.35pm (Spanish); 9.10am, 12.30pm, 2pm, 6.20pm, 7.10pm, 9.10pm & 11.59pm (Special)
Cairo (Watania Sleeping Train)	1-/2-bed berth US$120/100	9hr	8.10pm

All trains south to Aswan stop at Esna, Edfu and Kom Ombo. All trains north to Cairo stop at Qena (for Dendara), Balyana (for Abydos) and Asyut (for the Western Desert).

roadworthiness – there's nothing worse than getting stuck with a broken chain halfway to the Valley of the Kings.

You can take bikes across to the west bank on the *baladi* (local) ferry, or pick one up for LE25 a day from the excellent **Mohamed Setouhy** (Gezira Bike Rental; Map p186; ☎ 010-0223-9710; LE25 per day; ⏰7am-7pm) on the west bank.

DONKEYS & CAMELS

Donkeys and camels with guides can sometimes be rented at the ferry landing, but it's safer to rent them from a recognised stable such as Nobi's Arabian Horse Stables (p215).

FELUCCA

There is a fleet of feluccas to take you on short trips around Luxor, leaving from various points all along the river. How much you pay depends on your bargaining skills, but expect about LE50 to LE80 for an hour of sailing.

FERRY

Most tourists on organised tours cross to the west bank by bus or taxi via the bridge, about 8km south of town. But the river remains the quickest way to go. The *baladi* ferry costs LE2 for foreigners and runs between the **dock** (Map p186) in front of Luxor Temple and the dock fronting Gezira village on the west bank. Small motor launches (locally called 'lunches') also leave from wherever they can find customers and will take you across for LE20.

HORSE-DRAWN CARRIAGES

Known as *calèche* or *hantour*, horse-drawn carriages cost from LE20 to LE100 per hour depending on your haggling skills and the desperation of the driver. Expect to pay about LE30 to get to Karnak from downtown.

MICROBUS

Microbuses are often the quickest and easiest way to get about in Luxor. They ply fixed routes and will stop whenever flagged down. Just shout your destination to the driver and if he's going that way he'll stop and pick you up. To get to the Karnak temples, take a microbus from the **main microbus station** (Map p186) directly behind Luxor Train Station, or from behind Luxor Temple, for LE1. Other routes run inside the town.

The west bank's *kabouts* (pickup trucks) have nearly all now been replaced with microbuses, which operate until around 10pm (LE1 per ride). They run back and forth between the villages so you can always flag one down on your way to one of the sites, although you will have to walk from the main road to the entrance which, in the case of the Valleys of the Kings or Queens, is quite far. The **microbus lot** (Map p186) is close to the ferry landing. All microbuses heading to Gurna can drop you at the main ticket office. Most drivers are also more than happy for you to hire the entire vehicle – private hire costs LE20 to LE30 between the ferry terminal in Gizera and the ticket office.

TAXI

There are plenty of taxis in Luxor, but passengers still have to bargain hard for trips. A short trip around town is likely to cost at least LE20. Taxis can also be hired for day trips around the west bank; expect to pay LE200 to LE300, depending on the length of the excursion and your bargaining skills. The **West Bank Taxis** (Map p186) stand is just inland from the public ferry landing.

Southern Nile Valley

Best Places to Eat

➡ Kebabgy (p250)

➡ Al Makka (p251)

➡ 1902 Restaurant (p251)

➡ Eskaleh (p265)

➡ Koshary As Safwa (p250)

Best Places to Stay

➡ Sofitel Old Cataract Hotel & Spa (p250)

➡ Eskaleh (p265)

➡ Philae Hotel (p249)

➡ Bet El Kerem (p249)

➡ Mövenpick Resort Aswan (p250)

Why Go?

The Nile south of Luxor is increasingly hemmed in by the Eastern Desert, its banks lined with grand, well-preserved Graeco-Roman temples at Esna, Edfu and Kom Ombo, and its lush fields punctuated by palm-backed villages – it's the ideal place to sail through on a Nile boat. The once-great city of Al Kab provides the perfect contrast to the grandeur of the temples, while at Gebel Silsila the river passes through a gorge sacred to the ancients, who used stone from the quarry to built the temples in Luxor. Aswan, the ancient ivory-trading post, has a laid-back atmosphere and plenty of things to see.

South of Aswan, the land is dominated by Lake Nasser, one of the world's largest artificial lakes. On its shores is one of ancient Egypt's most awesome structures: the Great Temple of Ramses II at Abu Simbel.

When to Go
Aswan

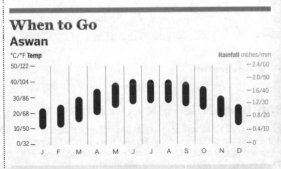

May–mid-Oct The long summers are unbearably hot in Aswan – temperatures soar well above 45°C.

Oct–Nov & Mar–Apr The best months to visit, with warm days and cooler nights.

Dec–Feb Days can occasionally be grey, and it can be too cold at night to make the most of a cruise.

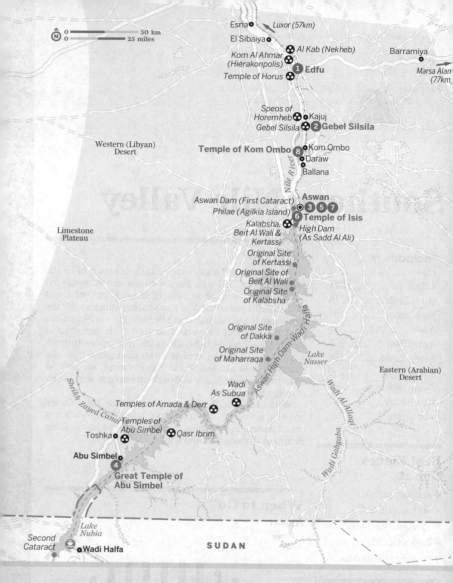

Southern Nile Valley Highlights

1 **Edfu** (p234) Marvelling at the most completely preserved temple in Egypt.

2 **Gebel Silsila** (p236) Discovering quarries where the pharaohs found stone to build ancient Thebes.

3 **Old Cataract Hotel** (p250) Sitting on the terrace and watching feluccas sail by.

4 **Great Temple** (p263) Sensing the vanity of Ramses II in the awe-inspiring temple of Abu Simbel.

5 **Ruins of Abu** (p243) Wandering around these little-visited ruins on Elephantine Island.

6 **Temple of Isis** (p257) Taking a boat out to this marvellous temple at Philae.

7 **Aswan Botanical Gardens** (p244) Strolling through Kitchener's Island in the afternoon sun.

8 **Temple of Kom Ombo** (p238) Seeing the double temple in the morning light.

History

The Nile Valley between Luxor and Aswan was the domain of the vulture and crocodile gods, a place of harsh nature and grand landscapes. Its cult places – centres such as Al Kab and Kom Al Ahmar – date back to the earliest periods of Egyptian history. The Narmer Palette, the object around which the origins of the 1st dynasty have been constructed, was found here, as was one of the earliest-known Egyptian temples, made of wood not stone. The area's Lascaux-type rock carvings and human remains have opened a window onto Egypt's remotest, pre-dynastic past.

Yet most of what one can see between Luxor and Aswan dates from the last period of ancient Egyptian history, when the country was ruled by the descendants of Alexander the Great's Macedonian general, Ptolemy I (323–283 BC). They ruled for some 300 years. Although they were based in Alexandria and looked out to the Mediterranean, the Ptolemies respected the country's ancient traditions and religion, setting an example to the Romans who succeeded them. They ensured peaceful rule in Upper Egypt by erecting temples in honour of the local gods, building in grand Pharaonic style to appease the priesthood and earn the trust of the people. The riverside temples at Esna, Edfu, Kom Ombo and Philae are as notable for their strategic locations, on ancient trade routes or at key commercial centres, as for their artistic or architectural merit.

Aswan's history was always going to be different. However much Theban, Macedonian or Roman rulers in the north may have wanted to ignore the south, they dared not neglect their southern border. Settlement on Elephantine Island, located in the middle of the Nile at Aswan, dates back to at least 3000 BC. Named Abu (Ivory) after the trade that flourished here, it was a natural fortress positioned just below the First Nile Cataract, one of six sets of rapids that blocked the river between Aswan and Khartoum. At the beginning of Egypt's dynastic history, in the Old Kingdom (2686–2125 BC), Abu became capital of the first Upper Egyptian nome (province) and developed into a thriving economic and religious centre, its strategic importance underlined by the title accorded to its rulers, Keepers of the Gate of the South. By the end of ancient history, with Egypt part of a larger Roman Empire, the southern frontier town was seen as a place of exile for anyone from the north who stepped out of line.

Climate

Heading south from Luxor, the fertile, green Nile Valley narrows considerably and becomes more and more enclosed by the desert. The climate also changes and becomes increasingly desert-like, with mostly warm, dry days in winter (December to February) – with an average temperature of about 26°C during the day – but often surprisingly cold nights. Summer (June to August) days are dry but often very hot, with temperatures hovering between 38°C and 45°C, making it difficult to visit sights outdoors. At the height of summer, temperatures hardly seem to drop during the night.

SOUTHERN UPPER EGYPT

Esna

☑ 095 / POP 82,790

Most visitors come to Esna, 64km south of Luxor on the west bank of the Nile, for the Temple of Khnum, but the busy little farming town has its own charms. Along the waterfront near the temple are several examples of 19th-century houses with elaborate *mashrabiyya* (wooden lattice screens). Immediately north of the temple is a beautiful but run-down **Ottoman caravanserai** (Wikalat Al Gedawi; next to the Temple of Khnum), the Wikalat Al Gedawi, once the commercial centre of Esna.

Esna was previously an important stop on the camel-caravan route between Sudan and Cairo, and between the oases and the Nile Valley, and the merchants stayed here. Opposite the temple is the Fatimid-era **Emari minaret** (opposite Temple of Khnum), one of the oldest in Egypt. An old oil mill, in the covered souq south of the temple, presses lettuce-seed into oil, considered an aphrodisiac since ancient times. The town makes for a pleasant morning excursion from Luxor, or a stop between Luxor and Aswan.

◉ Sights

Temple of Khnum   TEMPLE
(Map p232; adult/student LE50/25; ⊗ 8am-4.30pm) Construction of the Temple of Khnum, the ram-headed creator god who fashioned humankind on his potter's wheel,

Esna

0 — 200 m
0 — 0.1 miles

Bridge (500m)

Microbus Station
Hantours

Kabouts

Al Bahr

Nile River

Temple Ticket Office

Tourist Souq

Caravanserai

Temple of Khnum

Emari Minaret

was begun by Ptolemy VI Philometor (180–45 BC). The Romans added the hypostyle hall, the only part of the temple that is excavated and can be visited today, with well-preserved carvings from as late as the 3rd century AD.

The Temple of Khnum today sits in a 9m-deep pit, which represents 15 centuries of desert sand and debris, accumulated since it was abandoned during the Roman period. Most of the temple, similar in size to the temples of Edfu and Dendara, is still covered by the old town of Esna. A quay connecting the

temple to the Nile was built by Roman emperor Marcus Aurelius (AD 161–180).

The central doorway leads into the dark, atmospheric vestibule, where the roof is supported by 18 columns with wonderfully varied floral capitals in the form of palm leaves, lotus buds and papyrus fans; some also have bunches of grapes, a distinctive Roman touch. The roof is decorated with astronomical scenes, while the pillars are covered with hieroglyphic accounts of temple rituals. Inside the front corners, beside the smaller doorways, are two hymns to Khnum. The first is a morning hymn to awaken Khnum in his shrine; the second is a wonderful 'hymn of creation' that acknowledges him as creator of all, even foreigners: 'All are formed on his potter's wheel, their speech different in every region but the lord of the wheel is their father too.'

On the walls, Roman emperors dressed as pharaohs make offerings to the local gods of Esna. The northern wall has scenes of Emperor Commodus catching fish in a papyrus thicket with the god Khnum and, next to this, presenting the temple to the god.

The back wall, to the northeast, constructed during the Ptolemaic period, features reliefs of two Ptolemaic pharaohs, Ptolemy VI Philometor and Ptolemy VIII Euergetes (170–116 BC). A number of Roman emperors, including Septimus Severus, Caracalla and Geta, added their names near the hall's rear gateway. Outside, an underground pump struggles to move groundwater away from the structure.

The Temple of Khnum is situated about 200m from the boat landing, at the end of the tourist souq. Buy tickets at the **Temple Ticket Office**.

🛏 Sleeping & Eating

Few people linger in Esna; for most it's a stop on the road between Luxor and Aswan. There is nowhere to stay.

There are a few *ahwas* (coffeehouses) with terraces, where drinks and some basic food are served, opposite the temple.

ⓘ Getting There & Away

Trains are a pain because the train station is on the opposite (east) bank of the Nile, away from the town centre, but **kabouts** (pick-up trucks) shuttle between the two. The busy *kabout* station is beside the canal, and a block further north is the **microbus station**. A seat in a microbus to Luxor costs LE8, to Edfu LE8 and to

Aswan LE19 although foreign travellers weren't officially allowed to use microbuses in this region at the time of research. Arrivals are generally dropped off on the main thoroughfare into town, along which **hantour** (horse-drawn carriage) drivers congregate in the hope of picking up a fare. They ask LE40 for the five- to 10-minute ride to the temple and return. The best thing is to take in Esna on a day trip from Luxor to Aswan, stopping at the temples on the way.

Al Kab & Kom al Ahmar

Between Esna and Edfu are the ruins of two settlements, both dating back more than 3000 years, with traces of even earlier habitation.

Originally known as Nekheb, **Al Kab**, 26km south of Esna, was one of the most important and oldest cities of ancient Egypt, dedicated to the vulture goddess Nekhbet. The site is still being excavated and so is off limits. But the most impressive remains above ground are the mud-brick city walls, which form a square that you can walk around from the outside.

Note how the walls – 11m high, 12m thick and 550m long each side – were built in sections: if the Nile flood was particularly high, there was a chance the walls might fall. Building this way meant that sections could be repaired without rebuilding the entire wall. The oldest of the sandstone temples within the walls, dedicated to the god Thoth, was built by Ramses II (1279–1213 BC) and the adjoining Temple of Nekhbet was built during the Late Period. Both reused blocks from much earlier temples from the Early Dynastic Period (from c 3100 BC) and the Middle Kingdom (2055–1650 BC).

Nekhbet, the vulture goddess of Upper Egypt, was one of two deities who protected the pharaoh right back to the Old Kingdom.

Nearby on the waterfront is the picturesque village of Al Kab with old mud-brick houses. Across the river lies **Kom Al Ahmar** (closed to the public), ancient Nekhen or Hierakonpolis, home of the falcon god Nekheny, an early form of Horus. Although little remains of this important city, recent excavations have revealed a large settlement (with Egypt's earliest brewery!), a predynastic cemetery dating from around 3400 BC with elephant and cattle burials, together with the site of Egypt's earliest-known temple, a large timber-framed structure fronted by 12m-high imported wood pillars. A century ago, within this sacred enclosure, archaeologists discovered a range of ritual

UNCOVERING ANCIENT PAINTINGS

Most Egyptian temples were once as colourful as the tombs in Luxor, their walls, pillars and ceilings completely painted. It was long believed that the colours had been lost to time and the abrasive winds. But work inside the hypostyle hall at the **Temple of Khnum** shows that the colours are still there.

Using chemicals, archaeologists have delicately removed millennia of dust and dirt to confirm that all figures were completely painted and all backgrounds were white. There is now a debate among Egyptologists as to whether the entire temple – and other temples – should be restored, or whether the majority should be left covered, and therefore protected, for future generations.

artefacts, among them two items of huge historical significance: the Narmer Palette and a superb gold falcon head of the god Horus, both now among the highlights of Cairo's Egyptian Museum.

Cut into the ridge across the road from the village of Al Kab is a row of **tombs** (adult/student LE60/30; 8am-4pm). The most interesting is No 2, from the New Kingdom (1550–1069 BC), which belonged to Ahmose, 'Captain-General of Sailors' under Pharaoh Ahmose I (1550–1525 BC). Another Ahmose, son of Ebana, left a detailed account of his bravery in the battle against the Hyksos. All have well-preserved images.

To the north of these New Kingdom tombs, but not open to visitors, are a series of tombs from the Old Kingdom. The oldest, including one on the top of the ridge, date to around 2700 BC.

Further east into the desert from Al Kab, if you have transport, you'll see several temples dedicated to Nubian gods. You'll find a Ptolemaic temple with a staircase leading up to two columned vestibules before a chapel carved into the rock. Further south is a small chapel, locally known as Al Hammam (The Bathhouse), built by Setau, Viceroy of Nubia under Ramses II. At the centre of the wadi is a large vulture-shaped crag covered in inscriptions from predynastic times to the Old Kingdom. Some 3.5km further east into the desert is the small chapel of Nekhbet, built by Amenhotep III (1390–1352 BC) as a way station for the

STAYING AT KOM AL AHMAR

The delightful ecolodge/guesthouse **Funduk Al Shams** (010-6182-6314; www.egypt-for-you.com; Saida Bahari Al Qibli, near Kom Al Ahmar; s/d €37/80; P @ ⊙) is run by an Austrian-Egyptian team. It's constructed from mud-brick and decorated in the local style, with blue-painted rooms set around a shady garden planted with fruit trees. In the winter it is often taken by archaeologists working at Kom Al Ahmar, but this is a tranquil place to spend a few days in the Egyptian countryside.

vulture goddess's cult statue when she passed through 'The Valley'. Her protective influence was no doubt appreciated, as this was one of the supply routes to the goldmines that gave Egypt much of its wealth.

ⓘ Getting There & Away

The best way of seeing Al Kab is to take a private taxi from Esna or Edfu, or to stop on the way between Luxor and Aswan. Dahabiyyas (house boats) and some feluccas (sailing boats) travelling from Aswan to Esna stop here too, but bigger cruise boats are not able to dock.

Edfu

📋 097 / POP 133,772

Built on a rise above the broad river valley, the Temple of Horus at Edfu, having escaped destruction from Nile floods, is the most completely preserved Egyptian temple. One of the last ancient attempts at building on a grand scale, the temple dominates this west-bank town, 53km south of Esna. Its well-preserved reliefs have provided archaeologists with much valuable information about temple rituals and the power of the priesthood. Walking through the large, gloomy chambers, visitors are sometimes overwhelmed by a sense of awe at the mysteries of ancient Egypt.

Modern Edfu, a centre for sugar and pottery, is a friendly, buzzing provincial centre. Although it is an agricultural town, many people seem to live off tourism. *Hantour* drivers can be a bit of a hassle, and visitors must brave the persistent salesmen to reach the temple.

◎ Sights

★ **Temple of Horus**   TEMPLE
(adult/student LE100/50; ⊙ 8am-5pm) This Ptolemaic temple, built between 237 and 57 BC, is one of the best-preserved ancient monuments in Egypt. Preserved by desert sand, which filled the place after the pagan cult was banned, the temple is dedicated to Horus, the avenging son of Isis and Osiris. With its roof intact, it is also one of the most atmospheric of ancient buildings.

Edfu was a settlement and cemetery site from around 3000 BC onward. It was the 'home' and cult centre of the falcon god Horus of Behdet (the ancient name for Edfu), although the Temple of Horus as it exists today is Ptolemaic. Started by Ptolemy III (246–221 BC) on 23 August 237 BC, on the site of an earlier and smaller New Kingdom structure, the sandstone temple was completed some 180 years later by Ptolemy XII Neos Dionysos, Cleopatra VII's father. In conception and design it follows the general plan, scale, ornamentation and traditions of Pharaonic architecture, right down to the Egyptian attire worn by Greek pharaohs depicted in the temple's reliefs. Although it is much newer than cult temples at Luxor or Abydos, its excellent state of preservation helps to fill in many historical gaps; it is, in effect, a 2000-year-old example of an architectural style that was already archaic during Ptolemaic times.

Two hundred years ago the temple was buried by sand, rubble and part of the village of Edfu, which had spread over the roof. Excavation was begun by Auguste Mariette in the mid-19th century. Today the temple is entered via a long row of shops selling tourist tat, and a new visitors centre that houses the ticket office, clean toilets, a cafeteria and a room for showing a 15-minute film on the history of the temple in English.

➡ Touring the Temple

Beyond the Roman *mammisi* (birth house), with some colourful carvings, the massive 36m-high **pylon** (gateway) is guarded by two huge but splendid granite statues of Horus as a falcon. The walls are decorated with colossal reliefs of Ptolemy XII Neos Dionysos, who is holding his enemies by their hair before Horus and is about to smash their skulls; this is the classic propaganda pose of the almighty pharaoh.

Beyond this pylon, the **court of offerings** is surrounded on three sides by 32 columns, each with different floral capitals.

Temple of Horus

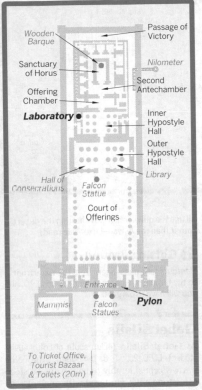

Wooden Barque

Sanctuary of Horus

Offering Chamber

Laboratory •

Passage of Victory

Nilometer

Second Antechamber

Inner Hypostyle Hall

Outer Hypostyle Hall

Library

Hall of Consecrations

Falcon Statue

Court of Offerings

Entrance

Mammisi

Falcon Statues

Pylon

To Ticket Office, Tourist Bazaar & Toilets (20m) ▼

The walls are decorated with reliefs, including the 'Feast of the Beautiful Meeting' just inside the entrance, the meeting being that of Horus of Edfu and Hathor of Dendara, who visited each other's temples each year and, after two weeks of great fertility celebrations, were magically united.

A second set of Horus falcon statues in black granite once flanked the entrance to the temple's first or **outer hypostyle hall**, but today only one remains. Inside the entrance of the outer hypostyle hall, to the left and right, are two small chambers: the one on the right was the temple library where the ritual texts were stored; the chamber on the left was the hall of consecrations, a vestry where freshly laundered robes and ritual vases were kept. The hall itself has 12 columns, and the walls are decorated with reliefs of the temple's founding.

The **inner hypostyle hall** also has 12 columns, and in the top left part of the hall

is perhaps this temple's most interesting room: the temple laboratory. Here, all the necessary perfumes and incense recipes were carefully brewed and stored, their ingredients listed on the walls.

Exit the inner hypostyle hall through the large central doorway to enter the **offering chamber**, or first antechamber, which has an altar where daily offerings of fruit, flowers, wine, milk and other foods were left. On the west side, 242 steps lead up to the rooftop and its fantastic view of the Nile and the surrounding fields. (The roof is closed to visitors.)

The **second antechamber** gives access to the sanctuary of Horus, which contains the polished-granite shrine that once housed the gold cult statue of Horus. Created during the reign of Nectanebo II (360–343 BC), this shrine, or house of the god, was reused by the Ptolemies in their newer temple. In front of it stands a replica of the wooden *barque* (boat) in which Horus' statue would be taken out of the temple in procession during festive occasions: the original is now in the Louvre, Paris.

On the eastern enclosure wall, look for the remains of the Nilometer, which measured the level of the river and helped predict the coming harvest.

🛏 Sleeping & Eating

There is a kebab joint and other simple food places on the main square, Al Midan, and several cafeterias on the waterfront, Sharia An Nil. El Massa Hotel has the best restaurant in town.

★ **El Massa Hotel** HOTEL $
(Diamond Hotel; ☎011 1136 0230, 097-471-9686; Souq Edfu; s/d/tr LE200/300/400; 🅿🛜) This

---

DON'T MISS

VICTORY PARADE IN THE TEMPLE OF HORUS

Exit the hypostyle hall to the east of the sanctuary and you come to a narrow passage between the temple and its outer enclosure wall. This ambulatory, the passage of victory, contains scenes of the dramatic battle between Horus and Seth at the annual Festival of Victory. Throughout the conflict, Seth is shown in the form of a hippopotamus, his tiny size rendering him less threatening.

Edfu

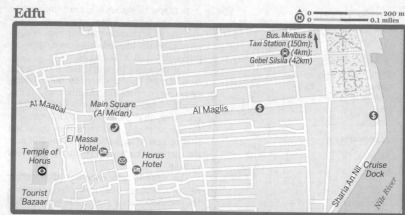

relatively new hotel has very comfortable rooms with fridge and TV, and a pleasant coffee shop that serves snacks and fresh juices. From the rooftop are excellent views over the temple and the market.

Horus Hotel HOTEL $
(☑097-471-5286, 097-471-5284; Sharia Al Gumhuriya; s/d/tr LE200/300/400; ❄🏠) On the upper floors of a building above the Baby Home clothes store and opposite the Omar Effendi department store, this hotel is basic but has OK rooms with air-con, clean bathrooms and old TVs. Try El Massa Hotel first.

ℹ Information

Bank Al Ahli Al Masri (Sharia An Nil) Has an ATM.

Banque du Caire (Sharia Al Maglis; ⊙8.30am-2pm Sun-Thu) Has an ATM.

ℹ Getting There & Away

Hiring a driver for a half-day trip to Edfu from Luxor costs around LE500.

Edfu train station is on the east bank of the Nile, about 4km from town. There are several trains heading to Luxor and Aswan throughout the day. To get to the town, you must first take a *kabout* from the train station to the bridge, then another into town. Each costs 50pt.

The microbus station is at the entrance to town, next to the bridge over the Nile. From here services depart to Luxor (LE15, two hours); Kom Ombo (LE10, 45 minutes); Aswan (LE15, 1½ hours); and Marsa Alam on the Red Sea (LE45, four to five hours). At the time of writing, foreign travellers were not officially allowed to use microbuses between Luxor and Aswan (which all use the quicker highway through the desert rather than the Aswan–Luxor Nile road).

ℹ Getting Around

Hantours take passengers from the waterfront to the temple or vice versa for LE30 to LE40, but you will have to bargain.

Gebel Silsila

At **Gebel Silsila** (42km south of Edfu; adult/student LE50/25; ⊙8am-4.30pm), the Nile narrows considerably to pass between steep sandstone cliffs, cluttered with ancient rock stelae and graffiti. The good-quality sandstone quarries here were systematically worked during the New Kingdom, when huge teams hacked out blocks that were floated down the Nile to Luxor to be used in buildings such as the temple complex of Karnak and the Ramesseum.

Known in Pharaonic times as Khenu (Place of Rowing), Gebel Silsilla was an important centre for the cult of the Nile: every year at the beginning of the inundation season, sacrifices were made here to ensure the fertility of the land. The Nile at its height flowing through the narrow gorge must have been a particularly impressive sight, and noisy, which no doubt explains why the location was chosen as a cult centre. The gorge also marks the change in the bedrock of Egypt, from limestone to sandstone. The **sandstone quarries** here were worked by thousands of men and from the 18th dynasty or earlier through to the Roman period. The quarries were for centuries the main source in Egypt of material for temple building.

The most attractive monuments are on the west bank, where the rocks are carved with inscriptions and tiny shrines from all periods, as well as adorned with larger chapels. The southern side of the site is marked by a massive pillar of rock, known as the 'Capstan', so called because locals believe there was once a chain – *silsila* in Arabic, from which the place takes its name – that ran from the east to the west bank. Nearby are the three shrines built by Merenptah, Ramses II and Seti I during the New Kingdom. Further north, the main quarry has clear masons' marks and a group of elaborate private memorial chapels. Several stelae, including a large Stelae of Shoshenq I, mark the northern limit of the quarry. Near the entry to the site is the Speos of Horemheb.

The east bank is out of bounds, but looking across from the west bank one gets a real sense of the grandeur and scale of what the pharaohs undertook, especially the huge passageway cut into the hillside.

○ Sights

Speos of Horemheb   MONUMENT
(adult/student LE50/25, incl in Gebel Silsila ticket; ⊘ 8am-4.30pm) The Speos of Horemheb was started by the New Kingdom pharaoh Horemheb (1323–1295 BC) and finished by the officials of the later Ramesside kings. The small royal shrine hewn from the sandstone is dedicated to Horemheb and a range of Egyptian deities. Their cult images are seated in a niche in the rear wall: Amun, Mut, Khonsu, Sobek, Taweret, Thoth and Horemheb.

🛈 Getting There & Away

The best way to get to Gebel Silsila is by felucca or dahabiyya between Aswan and Esna. Alternatively, hire a private taxi at Edfu and take the west-bank valley road to Silsila.

Kom Ombo

📌 097 / POP 335,642
The fertile, irrigated sugar-cane fields around Kom Ombo support not only the original community of *fellaheen* (peasant farmers), but also a large population of Nubians displaced from their own lands by the creation of Lake Nasser. It's a pleasant little place, easily accessible en route between Aswan and Luxor. A huge cattle market is held on the outskirts of town, near the railway line, on Thursdays. The main attraction these days, however, is the unique riverside temple to Horus the Elder (Haroeris) and Sobek and its attached Crocodile Museum, about 4km from the town's centre.

In ancient times Kom Ombo was known as Pa-Sebek (Land of Sobek), after the crocodile god of the region. It became important during the Ptolemaic period, when its name was changed to Ombos and it became the capital of the first Upper Egyptian nome during the reign of Ptolemy VI Philometor. Kom Ombo was an important military base

---

LASCAUX ON THE NILE

Canadian archaeologists working in the 1960s in the area of Qurta, some 15km north of Kom Ombo, discovered what they thought to be extremely old petroglyphs. Paleolithic, they thought. Ridiculous, said the experts. The matter was dropped, the site forgotten. But the images were rediscovered in 2005 by a team of archaeologists led by Dr Dirk Huyge of the Royal Museum of Art and History, Brussels (Belgium). This time the archaeologists discovered other petroglyphs that were partly covered by sediment and other deposits. These were recently dated in Belgium to the Pleistocene period of rock art, making them at least 15,000 years old, and therefore both chronologically and stylistically from the same period as the images in Lascaux, France.

The images are carved into the side of huge Nubian sandstone rocks. Most of these fine carvings are of wild horned cows in different positions, although there are also gazelles, birds, hippos and fish in a naturalistic style, and a few stylised human figures with pronounced buttocks but no other particular features. These discoveries do not just represent some of the largest and finest examples of rock art ever found in Egypt. They also pose a challenging question. How can there be such similarities between images found in Egypt and France? Was there some sort of cultural exchange between the people of Lascaux and Qurta?

Work is continuing at Qurta and no doubt more discoveries will be found. The guarded site is not currently open to the public.

and a trading centre between Egypt and Nubia. Gold was traded here, but more importantly it was a market for African elephants brought from Ethiopia, which the Ptolemies needed to fight the Indian elephants of their long-term rivals the Seleucids, who ruled Alexander's former empire to the east of Egypt.

◉ Sights

Temple of Kom Ombo & Crocodile Museum

TEMPLE

(adult/student LE80/40; ⊙ 8am-5pm) Standing on a promontory at a bend in the Nile, where in ancient times sacred crocodiles basked in the sun on the riverbank, is the Temple of Kom Ombo, one of the Nile Valley's most beautifully sited temples. Unique in Egypt, it is dedicated to two gods; the local crocodile god Sobek, and Haroeris (from *har-wer*), meaning Horus the Elder.

The temple's twin dedication is reflected in its plan: perfectly symmetrical along the main axis of the temple, there are twin entrances, two linked hypostyle halls with carvings of the two gods on either side, and twin sanctuaries. It is assumed that there were also two priesthoods. The left (western) side of the temple was dedicated to the god Haroeris, and the right (eastern) half to Sobek.

Reused blocks suggest an earlier temple from the Middle Kingdom period, but the main temple was built by Ptolemy VI Philometor, and most of its decoration was completed by Cleopatra VII's father, Ptolemy XII Neos Dionysos. The temple's spectacular riverside setting has resulted in the erosion of some of its partly Roman forecourt and outer sections, but much of the complex has survived and is very similar in layout to the Ptolemaic temples of Edfu and Dendara, albeit smaller.

➡ Touring the Temple

Passing into the temple's forecourt, where reliefs are divided between the two gods, there is a **double altar** in the centre of the court for both gods. Beyond are the shared **inner and outer hypostyle halls**, each with 10 columns. Inside the outer hypostyle hall, to the left is a finely executed relief showing Ptolemy XII Neos Dionysos being presented to Haroeris by Isis and the lion-headed goddess Raettawy, with Thoth looking on. The walls to the right show the crowning of Ptolemy XII by Nekhbet (the vulture-goddess worshipped at the Upper Egyptian town of Al Kab) and Wadjet (the snake-goddess based at Buto in Lower Egypt) with the dual crown of Upper and Lower Egypt, symbolising the unification of Egypt.

Reliefs in the **inner hypostyle** hall show Haroeris presenting Ptolemy VIII Euergetes with a curved weapon, representing the

Temple of Kom Ombo

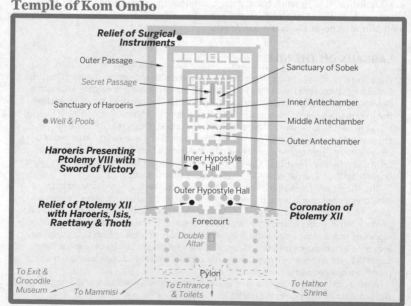

- Relief of Surgical Instruments
- Outer Passage
- Secret Passage
- Sanctuary of Haroeris
- Well & Pools
- Sanctuary of Sobek
- Inner Antechamber
- Middle Antechamber
- Outer Antechamber
- Haroeris Presenting Ptolemy VIII with Sword of Victory
- Inner Hypostyle Hall
- Outer Hypostyle Hall
- Relief of Ptolemy XII with Haroeris, Isis, Raettawy & Thoth
- Coronation of Ptolemy XII
- Forecourt
- Double Altar
- Pylon
- To Exit & Crocodile Museum
- To Mammisi
- To Entrance & Toilets
- To Hathor Shrine

DARAW

Just south of Kom Ombo is the village of Daraw, home to a remarkable camel market and local Nubian museum.

Daraw Camel Market (Souq Al Gimaal; ⊙ mornings Tue, Sat & Sun) Daraw has one of the largest camel markets in Egypt. Most of the camels come in caravans from Sudan's Darfur and Kordofan along the Darb Al Arba'een (Forty Days Rd) to just north of Abu Simbel before being trucked to Daraw. It is a picturesque sight and fascinating to see the trading; sometimes there are as many as 2000 camels.

Camels are sold here every day of the week, but the main days are Tuesday, Saturday and Sunday. Here they spend two days in quarantine before being sold by their Sudanese owners. Most go on to the camel market in Birqash, about 35km northwest of Cairo, where they are either sold to Egyptian farmers, exported to neighbouring countries or slaughtered for meat. This is no place for the squeamish.

Hosh Al Kenzi (Kenzian House; ☎ 012-8395-4911; Sharia Al Kunuz, Daraw; donations welcome; ⊙ 8am–noon) The small Nubian museum Hosh Al Kenzi, located opposite Dar Rasoul Mosque, was built in 1912 by the grandfather of the current resident, Haj Mohammed Eid Mohammed Hassanein. The house is worth seeing for its construction in traditional Nubian style, and for its decoration with objects mostly made from palm trees.

Next door is a workshop where the beaded curtains made from date pips, pieces of palm frond or various seeds are still produced for Nubian houses.

---

sword of victory. Behind Ptolemy is his sister-wife and coruler Cleopatra II.

From here, three **antechambers**, each with double entrances, lead to the sanctuaries of Sobek and Haroeris. The now-ruined chambers on either side would have been used to store priests' vestments and liturgical papyri. The walls of the sanctuaries are now one or two courses high, allowing you to see the secret passage that enabled the priests to give the gods a 'voice' to answer the petitions of pilgrims.

The **outer passage**, which runs around the temple walls, is unusual. Here, on the left-hand (northern) corner of the temple's back wall, is a puzzling scene, which is often described as a collection of 'surgical instruments'. It seems more probable that these were some of the accoutrements used during the temple's daily rituals, although the temple was certainly a place of healing, the nearest thing to an ancient hospital.

Near the Ptolemaic gateway on the southeast corner of the complex is a small shrine to Hathor, while a small **mammisi** (birth house) stands in the southwest corner. Beyond this to the north you will find the deep well that supplied the temple with water, and close by is a small pool in which crocodiles, Sobek's sacred animal, were raised.

The path out of the complex leads to the new **Crocodile Museum**. It's well worth a visit for its beautiful collection of mummi-fied crocodiles and ancient carvings, which is well lit and well explained. The museum is also dark and air-conditioned, which can be a blessing on a hot day.

🛏 Sleeping & Eating

There isn't anywhere worth staying in Kom Ombo: it is too close to Aswan for anyone to open a tourist hotel.

Cafeteria Kom Ombo   CAFETERIA $
(⊙ 8am–4pm) Between the temple and the Nile is a large garden with a cafeteria, serving cold drinks and some snacks. A pleasant place to recover from the temple visit.

ℹ Getting There & Away

The easiest way to visit the Temple of Kom Ombo is to come on a tour or by private taxi. Hiring a driver from Luxor for a day trip taking in both Edfu and Kom Ombo will cost LE900 to LE1200; moving on to Aswan instead of returning to Luxor will cost between LE900 and LE1200. A private taxi from Aswan will cost LE400 to LE500.

Trains are an option, but the station is 3.5km from the temple (take a taxi).

At the time of writing, foreigners were not allowed to travel by microbus to Aswan (LE25).

ℹ Getting Around

To get to the temple from the town centre, take a *kabout* (pickup truck) to the boat landing on the Nile about 800m north of the temple (LE1) and

HENNA TATTOOS

Henna is the natural dye derived from the leaves of the *Lawsonia inermis* shrub, grown in southern Egypt and Nubia for millennia – traces of it have even been found on the nails of mummified pharaohs.

Like their ancestors, Nubian women use henna powder for their hair and also to decorate hands and feet prior to getting married. The intricate red-brown designs adorn the skin for a fortnight or so before fading away.

Women visitors will be offered henna 'tattoos' on their hands (or feet or stomachs, from LE50 per tattoo) at some of the Nubian villages on Elephantine Island, on the west bank of Aswan or in the souq. It looks great and you get to spend time with Nubian women. Always check who will apply the tattoos; this is women's work, but would-be Lotharios see this as a great opportunity to get close to a bit of foreign flesh.

Foreigners tend to prefer black to the traditional red henna tattoos, but beware: this is in fact natural henna darkened with the very toxic hair dye PPD, which is banned in Europe. Avoid black henna completely, and visit www.hennapage.com to see the damage the dye can cause, from a light allergic reaction to chemical burns and sometimes even death.

then walk the remainder of the way. *Kabouts* to the boat landing leave from the microbus station. A private taxi between the town and temple should cost about LE35 to LE40 return.

ASWAN

📋 097 / POP 312.000

On the northern end of the First Cataract, marking ancient Egypt's southern frontier, Aswan has always been of great strategic importance. In ancient times it was a garrison town for the military campaigns against Nubia; its quarries provided the granite used for so many sculptures and obelisks.

There are plenty of things to see, but it is not a place to hurry. The river is wide, languorous and beautiful here, flowing gently down from Lake Nasser around dramatic black-granite boulders and palm-studded islands. Colourful Nubian villages run down to the water and stand out against the backdrop of the west bank's desert escarpment.

The large island of Seheyl and the village of Gharb Seheyl, situated just north of the old Aswan Dam, have various laid-back guesthouses and offer an opportunity to swim in the river. These are perfect places to linger for a few days and recover from the rigours of travelling and temple-viewing.

The best time to visit Aswan is in winter, when the days are warm and dry. In summer the temperature hovers between 38°C and 45°C; it's too hot by day to do anything but sit by a fan and swat flies, or flop into a swimming pool.

◉ Sights

With such a long history, there is plenty to see in Aswan, but somehow the sightseeing seems less urgent and certainly less overwhelming than elsewhere in Egypt, allowing more time to take in the magic of the Nile at sunset, to stroll in the exotic souq (one of the best outside Cairo) or to appreciate the gentleness of the Nubians. Most tour groups head straight for the Temple of Isis at Philae, taking in the Unfinished Obelisk and the dams on the way, but the rarely visited ruins of ancient Abu on Elephantine Island are fascinating, as are the exquisite botanical gardens and the Nubia Museum.

Aswan's sights are spread out, mostly to the south and west of the town. The souq cuts right through the centre of town, parallel to the Nile. The Nubia Museum is within walking distance, just, but all other sights require transport. The sites on the islands and on the west bank involve a short boat trip.

◉ Town & East Bank

Corniche   WATERFRONT

(Map p241) Walking along the Corniche and watching the sunset over the islands and desert across the Nile is a favourite pastime in Aswan. The view from riverside cafe terraces may be blocked by cruise boats, but plans are under way to relocate them to a dock that is being constructed at the northern end of town; for now, the best place to watch the sunset is from the Old Cataract Hotel (p250) terrace or the Sunset restaurant (p251).

Central Aswan

Central Aswan

Sharia As Souq MARKET

(Map p241) Starting from the southern end, Sharia As Souq appears very much like the tourist bazaars all over Egypt, with slightly less persistent traders than elsewhere in the country trying to lure passers-by into their shops to buy scarves, perfume, spice and roughly carved copies of Pharaonic statues. But a closer look reveals more exotic elements. Traders sell Nubian talismans for good luck, colourful Nubian baskets and skullcaps, Sudanese swords, African masks, and enormous stuffed crocodiles and desert creatures.

Aswan is also famous for the quality of its *fuul sudani* (peanuts), henna powder (sold in different qualities) and dried hibiscus flowers (used to make the much-loved local drink *karkadai*).

The pace is slow, particularly in the late afternoon; the air has a slight whiff of sandalwood; and, as in ancient times, you may feel that Aswan is the gateway to Africa.

★ **Nubia Museum** MUSEUM

(Map p244; Sharia Al Fanadeq; adult/student LE100/50; ⊙9am-1pm & 4-9pm winter, 6-10pm summer) The little-visited Nubia Museum, opposite Basma Hotel, is a treat, a showcase of the history, art and culture of Nubia. Established in 1997 in cooperation with Unesco, the museum is a reminder of what was lost beneath Lake Nasser. Exhibits are beautifully displayed in huge halls, where clearly written explanations take you from 4500 BC through to the present day.

The exhibits start with prehistoric artefacts and objects from the Kingdom of Kush and Meroe. Coptic and Islamic art displays lead to a description of the massive Unesco project to move Nubia's most important historic monuments away from the rising waters of Lake Nasser, following the building of the Aswan High Dam.

Among the museum highlights are 6000-year-old painted pottery bowls and an impressive quartzite statue of a 25th-dynasty priest of Amun in Thebes with distinct Kushite (Upper Nubian) features. The stunning horse armour found in tombs from the Ballana period (5th to 7th centuries BC) shows the sophistication of artisanship during this brief ascendancy. A fascinating display traces the development of irrigation along the Nile, from the earliest attempts to control the flow of the river, right up to the building of the old Aswan Dam. A model of a Nubian house, complete with old furniture and mannequins wearing traditional silver jewellery, attempts to portray the folk culture of modern Nubia.

★**Unfinished Obelisk** ARCHAEOLOGICAL SITE
(Map p244; Sharia Al Haddadeen; adult/student LE60/30; ☉8am-5pm) Aswan was the source of ancient Egypt's finest granite, used to make statues and embellish temples, pyramids and obelisks. The large unfinished obelisk in the Northern Quarries has provided valuable insight into how these monuments were created, although the full construction process is still not entirely clear. Three sides of the shaft, nearly 42m long, were completed except for the inscriptions. At 1168 tonnes, the completed obelisk would have been the single heaviest piece of stone the Egyptians ever fashioned.

At a late stage in the process, however, a flaw appeared, so it lies where the disappointed stonemasons abandoned it, still partly attached to the parent rock.

Upon entering the quarry, steps lead down into the pit of the obelisk, where there are ancient pictographs of dolphins and ostriches or flamingos, thought to have been painted by workers at the quarry. The Northern Quarries are about 1.5km from town, opposite the Fatimid Cemetery. Microbuses will drop you within a few minutes' walk. Private taxis will charge about LE20 to LE25.

Fatimid Cemetery CEMETERY
Among the modern graves are some ruined mud-brick domed tombs, some of which go back to the Fatimid period (9th century). The domes are built on a drum with corners sticking out like horns, a feature unique to southern Egypt. Tombs decorated with flags belong to local saints; you may see Aswanis circumambulating a tomb, praying for the saint's intercession.

The municipality of Aswan has fenced off the Fatimid Cemetery. Enter from the main gate, a 10-minute walk from the Corniche along the road to the airport, and walk right through the cemetery to join the road to the Unfinished Obelisk; just aim for the four-storey building facing the back of the cemetery. The site's caretaker will often accompany you and show you the best-preserved tombs, for which he should be given a baksheesh (tip) of a few pounds.

CROCODILES IN THE NILE?

The Nile was once synonymous with crocodiles, particularly the large ones that carry the river's name. The Nile crocodile (*Crocodylus niloticus*) is the world's second-largest reptile: an adult grows to between 4m and 4.5m, and some get as large as 6m. It's commonly held that there are none north of the Aswan Dam. Is this true? Not according to the Egyptian Environmental Affairs Agency's Crocodile Management Unit.

There is a well-known adult crocodile living around the river at Aswan. Others have been released from restaurants and houses in Aswan, where they were kept as pets while they were little – though even a small one can take off your finger. Plus there may be as many as 20,000 of them in Lake Nasser. Just when you thought it was safe to go back in the water...

The River

Elephantine Island   ISLAND
Elephantine Island's southern end comprises the site of ancient Abu. Its name meant both 'elephant' and 'ivory' in ancient Egyptian, a reminder of the important role the island once played in the ivory trade. The island's Nubian villages of **Siou** and **Koti** make a surprising counterpoint to the bustle of the city across the water.

The island lies opposite central Aswan, just north of the First Cataract. A recent building boom has changed its nature, but it remains calm and essentially rural.

At the beginning of the 1st dynasty (about 3000 BC) a fortress was built on the island to establish Egypt's southern frontier. Abu soon became an important customs point and trading centre. It remained strategically significant throughout the Pharaonic period as a departure point for the military and commercial expeditions into Nubia and the south. During the 6th dynasty (2345–2181 BC) Abu gained its strength as a political and economic centre and, despite occasional ups and downs, the island retained its importance until the Graeco-Roman period.

As well as being a thriving settlement, Elephantine Island was the main cult centre of the ram-headed god Khnum (at first the god of the inundation, and from the 18th dynasty worshipped as the creator of humankind on his potter's wheel), Satet (Khnum's wife, and guardian of the southern frontier) and their daughter Anket. Each year the rushing of the waters of the flood were first heard here on Elephantine Island. Over time religious complexes took over more and more of the island, so residential areas moved either further north on the island or to the east bank. The temple town of Abu received its coup de grâce in the 4th century AD, when Christianity was established as the imperial Roman religion. From then on, worship of the ancient gods was gradually abandoned and defensive fortifications were moved to the east bank, today's city of Aswan.

Siou and Koti villages lie between the ruins in the south and the Mövenpick Resort, which fills the northern end of the island. A north–south path crosses the middle of the island and links the two villages. Close to the wall separating the Mövenpick Resort from Siou village, facing Kitchener's Island, is Baaba Dool (p248), a gorgeous painted Nubian house, where the owner Mustapha

THE UNOFFICIAL NUBIAN MUSEUM

The small but charming museum **Animalia** (☑097-231-4152, 010-0300-5672; Main St, Siou, Elephantine Island; LE20, incl guided tour; ⊗8am-7pm) is run by Mohamed Sobhi, a Nubian guide, and his family, who have dedicated part of their large house to the traditions, flora, fauna and history of Nubia. It has a collection of stuffed animals endemic to Nubia, samples of sedimentary rocks and great pictures of Nubia before it was flooded by Lake Nasser.

There is a small shop selling Nubian crafts at fixed prices, and a lovely roof terrace where drinks and lunch are served overlooking the gardens. Mohamed Sobhi is passionate and knowledgeable about Nubian culture and the natural world. He also takes people around Elephantine Island, and on early morning **bird-watching** (p247) trips. His daughter Fatma is also an excellent English-speaking guide.

serves tea, sells Nubian handicrafts and can arrange live music and dancing performed by local women. The roof terrace is the perfect place to watch the sunset on the west bank, with a multitude of birds flying around the island opposite. Also in the villages is Animalia (p244), a charming Nubian museum.

Western women should be respectful of local tradition and wear modest clothes. More and more visitors prefer to enjoy the traditional set-up of the villages, and rent flats or houses here for a few days.

★ **Ruins of Abu**   ARCHAEOLOGICAL SITE
(Map p244; Elephantine Island; adult/student LE35/15; ⊗8am-5pm) The evocative ruins of ancient Abu and the Aswan Museum (partially closed for renovation) lie at Elephantine Island's southern tip. Numbered plaques and reconstructed buildings mark the island's long history from around 3000 BC to the 14th century AD. The largest structure on-site is the partially reconstructed Temple of Khnum (plaque numbers 6, 12 and 13). Built in honour of the god of inundation during the Old Kingdom, it was used for more than 1500 years before being extensively rebuilt in Ptolemaic times.

Aswan

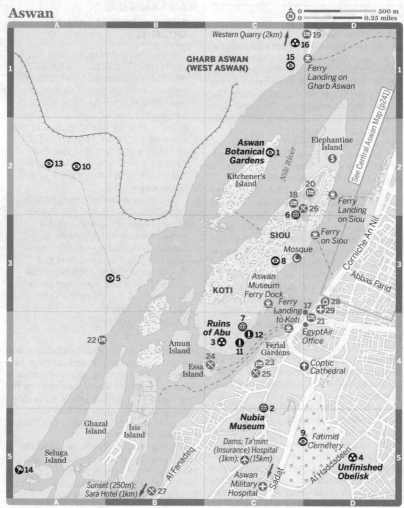

Other highlights include a small 4th-dynasty step pyramid, thought to have been built by Sneferu (2613–2589 BC; father of Khufu of Great Pyramid fame); a tiny Ptolemaic chapel (number 15), reconstructed from the Temple of Kalabsha (which is now just south of the High Dam); a reconstructed 18th-dynasty temple (number 2), built by Hatshepsut (1473–1458 BC) and dedicated to the goddess Satet; a cemetery for sacred rams (number 11), thought to have been the living embodiment of the god Khnum; and the ruins of an Aramaic Jewish colony dating from the 5th century BC.

The **Nilometer of the Temple of Khnum**, number 7, is below the southern balustrade of the Khnum temple. Heavenly portents and priestly prophecies aside, in ancient times only a Nilometer could give a real indication of the likelihood of a bountiful harvest. Built in the 26th dynasty, the Nilometer of Khnum has stone stairs leading down to a small basin for measuring the Nile's maximum level. When the nilometer here in the southern frontier town recorded a high water level of the river, it meant a good harvest, which in turn meant more taxes. Another stairway,

Aswan

with a scale etched into its wall, leads to the water from the basin's northern end.

Descending to the river's edge from beneath a sycamore tree near the Aswan Museum is the **Nilometer of the Satet Temple** (Ruins of Abu, Elephantine Island), number 10. Built in late Ptolemaic or early Roman times and restored in the 19th century, its staircase is roofed over, and niches in the walls would have had oil lamps to provide light. If you look hard as you descend to the river, you can see the names of Roman prefects carved into the left hand wall.

Aswan Museum   MUSEUM
(Map p2444; Elephantine Island, adult/student LE70/35; ⊙ 8am-5pm) The modern annexe of the museum has reopened with a delightful collection of objects, from weapons, pottery and utensils to statues, encased mummies and sarcophagi from predynastic to late Roman times. Artefacts are organised in separate glass cases, each explaining a particular facet of life on the island in ancient times.

The main part of the Aswan Museum, housed in the villa of Sir William Willcocks (architect of the old Aswan Dam), was closed for restoration at the time of writing. Built in 1898, the villa became a museum in 1912 and houses antiquities discovered in Aswan and Nubia. Although most of the Nubian artefacts rescued from the temples flooded by Lake Nasser were moved to the Nubia Museum (p241), there are some well-displayed objects here, with excellent labels in English and Arabic. At the right of the main entrance, in a room by itself, lies the sarcophagus and mummy of a sacred ram, the animal associated with Khnum.

★**Aswan Botanical Gardens**   GARDENS
(Map p244; Kitchener's Island; LE30; ⊙ 8am-6pm) Kitchener's Island, to the west of Elephantine Island, was given to Lord Horatio Kitchener in the 1890s when he was commander of the Egyptian army. Indulging his passion for beautiful palms and plants, Kitchener turned the entire island into the stunning Aswan Botanical Gardens, importing plants from the Far East, India and parts of Africa.

Covering 6.8 hectares, the gardens are filled with birds as well as hundreds of species of flora. While it may have lost some of its former glory, its majestic trees are still a stunning sight, particularly just before sunset when the light is softer and the scent of sandalwood floats on the breeze. Avoid Fridays, when the place is invaded by picnicking extended families with stereos. Instead, come late afternoon when there is hardly anyone.

The island is most easily seen as part of a felucca tour. Alternatively, take the northernmost ferry to Elephantine Island and walk through the village to the other side of the island, where a few little feluccas wait on the western edge to take visitors across to the gardens. Expect to pay at least LE50 to LE60 for a round trip.

◉ West Bank

It is easiest to visit the west bank as part of a felucca tour. The longer way is to take a ferry from Elephantine Island across to the landing for the Monastery of St Simeon.

Gharb Aswan is no longer a sleepy village, as Aswan expands ever quicker, but the Nubian settlement just north of the Tombs of the Nobles remains a tranquil place. It is particularly pleasant at night, after the souqs near the ferry landing have closed. To get to the Tombs of the Nobles, or Garb Aswan Nubian village, take the public ferry that leaves from a landing opposite the train station, on the east bank. The long way around is to take the desert road to Gharb Aswan from the bridge north of Aswan.

Aga Khan Mausoleum TOMB

(☺ closed to the public) The elegant Tomb of Mohammed Shah Aga Khan belongs to the 48th imam (leader) of the Ismaili sect. In his illustrious life he was hugely influential in the partition of India and the creation of Pakistan, and was father-in-law to Rita Hayworth. The Aga Khan liked to winter in Aswan for his health and was buried here after his death in 1957.

His fourth wife, Frenchwoman Yvonne Labrousse, known as Begum Om Habibeh, died in 2000 and is also buried here. The family's white villa is in the garden beneath the tomb. The begum was known for her charitable work: the Om Habibeh Foundation continues to work to improve healthcare in Aswan.

Monastery of St Simeon MONASTERY

(Map p244; Deir Amba Samaan; West Bank; adult/student LE40/20; ☺ 8am-4pm) The fortress-like 7th-century Monastery of St Simeon was first dedicated to the local saint Anba Hedra, who renounced the world on his wedding day. It was rebuilt in the 10th century and dedicated to St Simeon. From here the monks travelled into Nubia, in the hope of converting the Nubians to Christianity. To get there, take a private boat across the Nile then walk up the (mostly paved) desert track, or hire a camel to take you up.

Surrounded by desert sands, the monastery was built on two levels – the lower level of stone and the upper level of mud brick –

surrounded by 10m-high walls. At its height, the monastery may have housed as many as 1000 monks, but it was partially destroyed by the troops of Saladin (Salah Ad Din) in 1173. The basilica has traces of frescoes. The cells still have their *mastaba* (bench) beds. The last room on the right includes graffiti from Muslim pilgrims who stayed here en route to Mecca.

An alternative way to get here is to take the ferry to the Tombs of the Nobles and ride a camel or donkey from there. Remember to bring water.

Tombs of the Nobles TOMB

(Map p244; West Bank; adult/student LE60/30; ☺ 8am-4pm) The high cliffs opposite Aswan, just north of Kitchener's Island, are honeycombed with the tombs of the governors, the Keepers of the Gate of the South, and other dignitaries of ancient Elephantine Island. The tombs, known as the Tombs of the Nobles, are still being excavated: significant finds were made in 2014 and 2017. Six decorated tombs are currently open to the public.

The tombs date from the Old and Middle Kingdoms and most follow a simple plan, with an entrance hall, a pillared room and a corridor leading to the burial chamber. A set of stairs cutting diagonally across the hill takes you up to the tombs from the ferry landing.

The adjoining tombs of father and son **Mekhu and Sabni** (tomb numbers 25 and 26), both governors, date from the long reign of 6th-dynasty Pharaoh Pepi II (2278–2184 BC). The reliefs in Sabni's tomb record how he led his army into Nubia to punish the tribe responsible for killing his father during a previous military campaign, and to recover his father's body. Upon his return, Pepi II sent him his own royal embalmers and professional mourners, to show the importance accorded to the keepers of the southern frontier. Several reliefs in Sabni's tomb retain their original colours, and there are some lovely hunting and fishing scenes depicting him with his daughters in the pillared hall.

Sarenput was the local governor and overseer of the priesthood of Satet and Khnum under 12th-dynasty Pharaoh Amenemhat II (1922–1878 BC). The **tomb of Sarenput II** (number 31) is one of the most beautiful and best-preserved tombs, its colours still vivid. A six-pillared entrance chamber leads into a corridor with six niches holding statues of Sarenput. The burial chamber has four col-

BIRD WATCHING IN ASWAN

Bird watchers have long come to Aswan to watch the migrating flocks. But being on the Nile very early in the morning, gliding along the edge of the islands, watching birds and hearing how they fit into ancient Egyptian history or into Nubian traditions, will appeal to a much wider audience than just specialists.

Mohamed Arabi (☑012-2324-0132; www.touregypt.net/featurestories/aswanbirding.htm; per person from US$75) is known as the 'Birdman of Aswan' and no bird escapes his eye. He has been taking twitchers and documentary-makers on the Nile for many years, but is also happy to take amateurs. Call him direct. His small speedboat glides into the channels between the islands while he points out the vegetation; sunbirds; hoopoes; purple, squacco, striated and night herons; pied kingfishers; little and cattle egrets; redshanks; and many other birds.

Mohamed Sobhi (☑097-231-4152, 010-0545-6420; per person US$30, min 2 people), the owner of Nubian museum **Animalia** (p244), takes twitchers and others on nature tours along the Nile using a motor boat. He knows his birds and their significance in ancient Egypt.

---

umns and a niche with wall paintings showing Sarenput with his wife (on the right) and his mother (on the left), as well as hunting and fishing scenes.

The **tomb of Harkhuf** (number 34), governor of the south during the reign of Pepi II, is hardly decorated, except for remarkable hieroglyphic texts about his three trading expeditions into central Africa, right of the entrance. Included here is Pepi II, then only a boy of eight, advising Harkhuf to take extra care of the 'dancing pygmy' he had obtained on his travels, as the pharaoh was very keen to see him in Memphis. 'My majesty desires to see this pygmy more than the gifts of Sinai or of Punt,' Harkhuf writes. Look carefully to see the tiny hieroglyph figure of the pygmy several times in the text.

Hekaib, also known as Pepinakht, was overseer of foreign soldiers during the reign of Pepi II. He was sent to quell rebellions in both Nubia and Palestine, and was even deified after his death, as is revealed by the small shrine of Hekaib built on Elephantine Island during the Middle Kingdom (c 1900 BC). Inside the **tomb of Hekaib** (number 35), fine reliefs show fighting bulls and hunting scenes.

The court of the **tomb of Sarenput I** (number 36), grandfather of Sarenput II and governor during the 12th-dynasty reign of Sesostris I (1965–1920 BC), has the remains of six pillars, decorated with reliefs. On each side of the entrance Sarenput is shown being followed by his dogs and sandal-bearer, his flower-bearing harem, his wife and his three sons.

Qubbet Al Hawa TOMB
(Map p244; ☺8am-5pm) On the hilltop above the Tombs of the Nobles lies this small domed tomb, constructed for a local sheikh or holy man. The steep climb up is rewarded with stunning views of the Nile and the surrounding area.

Western Quarry ARCHAEOLOGICAL SITE
(Map p244) Isolated in the desert to the west of the Tombs of the Nobles is the ancient Western Quarry, where stone for many ancient monuments – possibly including the Colossi of Memnon – was quarried. A large **unfinished obelisk**, made for Seti I (1294–1279 BC), was decorated on three sides of its apex before it was abandoned.

Near the obelisk, the ancient quarry face and marks are clearly visible, along with tracks on which the huge blocks were dragged down to the Nile.

Expect to pay at least LE150, after bargaining, for the camel ride from the boat landing, 30 minutes each way. Take plenty of water, and watch out for snakes.

🏃 Activities

Feluccas

The Nile looks fabulous and magical at Aswan, and few things are more relaxing than hiring a felucca before sunset and sailing between the islands, the desert and the huge black boulders, listening to the flapping of a sail and to Nubian boys singing from tiny dugouts. On days when cruise boats dock together in town, hundreds of feluccas circle the islands, so it's a good time to take a felucca a bit further out towards Seheyl Island.

Galal
BOATING

(☎ 012-2415-4902) The trustworthy Galal, who hangs out near the ferry landing opposite the EgyptAir office, offers hassle-free tours on his family's feluccas at a fixed price (LE65 per boat for an hour, LE125 for a motor boat). Galal is from Seheyl Island and can also arrange a visit to the island and lunch (LE75) on the boat, as well as a swim on a safe beach. He has some lovely rooms for rent in his guesthouse.

Lake Nasser Day Trips

Lake Nasser is usually glimpsed from the top of the Aswan dam or seen over several days from a cruise boat, but there is nothing to stop you going out for a rewarding day trip. African Angler (p262) has small boats and offers day-fishing for perch with a fishing guide, or a mini ecosafari looking at wildlife on or along the shores of the lake. Everything is arranged for the day, including transfers to and from your hotel. Prices include rods and lunch, and get cheaper the bigger the group.

Swimming

Aswan is a hot place, and often the only way to cool down, apart from hiding in your air-conditioned room, is to swim. Joining the local kids splashing about in the Nile is not a good idea. Bilharzia or schistosomiasis (an infection of the bowel and bladder caused by a freshwater fluke) can be caught in stagnant water; boatmen know where the current is strong enough (but not too strong) for it to be safe for swimming, among them a beach on the west bank opposite Seluga Island, for which you will need to rent a motor boat.

Some hotels open their swimming pools to the public, generally from 9am to sunset and particularly if occupancy rates are low. The Mövenpick Resort Aswan (p250) on Elephantine Island charges non-guests LE180 to use its pools.

☞ Tours

Small hotels and travel agencies arrange day tours of the area's major sights. Half-day guided tours usually include the Temple of Isis at Philae, the Unfinished Obelisk and the High Dam, and start at LE400 (per person with three to five people), including admission to all sites. Some budget hotels offer cheaper tours but are not licensed to guide groups. Travel agencies will also arrange felucca trips to Elephantine and Kitchener's Islands, but it is cheaper to deal directly with the boatmen.

All travel agencies and most hotels in Aswan offer trips to Abu Simbel, but watch out for huge price differences, and check that the bus is comfortable and has air-con. Thomas Cook charges about LE1000 per person, including a seat in an air-con microbus, admission fees and guide, and LE1400 by air, including transfers, fees and guide. By contrast, budget hotels offer tours for about LE500 to LE600 in a smaller bus, though often not including the entrance fee or guide.

🛏 Sleeping

Most visitors to Aswan stay on their cruise boats, so there has been little investment in hotels, but things are slowly changing.

Hotel touts at the train station try to convince tired travellers that the hotel they have booked is now closed, so that they can take them to another hotel and collect a commission. Ignore them, as their commission will be added to your bill.

Prices vary greatly depending on the season; high-season rates run from October through to April, and peak in December and January.

Baaba Dool
GUESTHOUSE $

(Map p244; ☎ 010-0497-2608; Siou, Elephantine Island; r with shared bathroom per person €14) A great place to unwind for a few days. The rooms in this beautiful mud-brick house are painted in Nubian style, decorated with colourful carpets and local crafts, and have superb views over the Nile and the botanical gardens. It's very basic, but it's clean and there are shared hot showers. Mustapha can arrange meals. Book ahead.

Nuba Nile Hotel
HOTEL $

(Map p241; ☎ 011-4291-2224, 010-0242-2864; www.nubanilehotel.com; Sharia Abtal At Tahrir; s/d/tr/q LE200/230/280/310; ❄@🛜🖥) Although its three-star claim is amusing, to say the least, this friendly, family-run hotel, always bustling with Egyptian holidaymakers, is one of the more reliable of Aswan's budget hotels, conveniently located just north of the train station. The lobby is quite dark, but the rooms are bright and clean. Check the room before you agree, as they vary considerably.

Hathor Hotel
HOTEL **$**

(Map p241; ☎097-244-6180; Corniche An Nil; s/d LE125/200; ✳️🛜🏊) The good-sized rooms at the Hathor are no-frills and are showing some wear and tear, but they're all clean enough and come with air-con, making this a solid choice if you're watching your pennies. The rooftop terrace has a small swimming pool and spectacular Nile views.

⭐Philae Hotel
HOTEL **$$**

(Map p241; ☎011-1901-1995, 097-246-5090; philaehotel@gmail.com; Corniche An Nil; s/d/tr/ste Nile view US$70/80/105/120, s/d/tr city view US$60/70/90; ✳️🛜) By far the best midrange hotel in town. The Philae's modern, minimalist-style rooms are decorated in fabrics with Arabic calligraphy and elegant local furnishings. The hotel restaurant serves mainly vegetarian organic food from its own gardens, and at very reasonable prices for the quality (mains LE75 to LE90). It's no longer a secret, so book ahead.

⭐Happi Hotel
HOTEL **$$**

(Map p241; ☎010-0003-6522, 097-245-5032; ali.taher.rizk@gmail.com; 10 Sharia Abtal At Tahrir; s/d/tr US$30/45/55, s/d with Nile view US$40/60; ✳️@🛜) A much needed arrival on the Aswan hotel scene, the Happi hotel is well run, clean, comfortable and well located, if lacking character. All 65 rooms have TVs, air-con, a mini bar and wi-fi, and there is a 24-hour cafeteria. The superior rooms are much classier. Friendly management.

Bet El Kerem
GUESTHOUSE **$$**

(Map p244; ☎012-391-1052, 012-384-2218; www.betelkerem.com; Gharb Aswan, West Bank; s/d/f €35/45/50, s/d with shared bathroom €30/40; 🅿️✳️🛜) This modern hotel on the west side of the Nile overlooking the desert and the Tomb of the Nobles is a great find, offering quiet, clean and comfortable rooms. The hotel boasts a wonderful rooftop terrace overlooking the Nile and Nubian village, and the staff is both friendly and proud to be Nubian.

Call ahead and Shaaban will come to fetch you or give you directions. The restaurant serves delicious meals (breakfast €5, lunch €7 and dinner €10).

Marhaba Palace Hotel
HOTEL **$$**

(Map p241; ☎097-233-0102; www.marhabapalacehotel.omyhotels.club; Corniche An Nil; s/d city view US$35/60, s/d/tr Nile view US$50/70/100; ✳️🛜🏊) The homely Marhaba has sparkling clean, cosy rooms with comfortable beds,

---

ASWAN HOUSE RENTALS

A number of flats are for rent on the west bank of Aswan and on Elephantine Island, offering a good-value option for a longer stay, or even just for a night. Simply walk around on Elephantine Island and you will be offered houses for rent.

If you want to book ahead, check **Bet El Kerem** for Nubian houses, or ask Mohamed Sobhi at **Animalia** (p244). **Mohamed Arabi** (p247) has four amazing houses for rent in his 4-acre garden and orchard on the west bank, all tastefully decorated in Nubian style, with cool marble floors, clean bathrooms and a sitting room. These houses are very peaceful, and at night dinner with garden produce is served on a terrace on the Nile.

---

sumptuous bathrooms (for this price range) and satellite TV. Bright, welcoming and well run, it overlooks a park on the Corniche and has two restaurants, friendly staff and a roof terrace with excellent Nile views. Grab a room with a balcony if you can. There is a small swimming pool on the 1st floor.

Nile Hotel
HOTEL **$$**

(Map p244; ☎097-245-0222; www.nilehotel-aswan.net; Corniche An Nil; s/d/tr US$35/45/56; ✳️@🛜) Large, well-kept rooms with lots of light and very clean bathrooms. The rooms at the front, with great views over the Nile, are the ones you want.

Nubian Beach Hotel
GUESTHOUSE **$$**

(Map p244; ☎012-2169-9145; www.facebook.com/pg/Nubian-Beach-hotel-204996879841937; r US$40; ✳️🛜) Very laid-back Nubian guesthouse with simple but colourful rooms, good food at the Nubian House Restaurant (p250), and swimming in the Nile nearby, as well as sand boarding down the desert dunes.

Keylany Hotel
HOTEL **$$**

(Map p241; ☎097-231-4074; 25 Sharia Keylany; s/d/tr US$23/34/45; ✳️🛜🏊) This great little hotel used to come at budget prices, but costs have gone up and some find it expensive for what is on offer. Plus points are friendly, helpful staff and a feast of a breakfast, but the small rooms (with some en suites suitable only for the pretzel-sized) could do with a spot of maintenance for these rates.

The roof terrace doesn't have Nile views, but there is a burlap sunshade and furniture made from palm fronds, and it is a great place to hang out.

★ Sofitel Old Cataract
Hotel & Spa HISTORIC HOTEL **$$$**
(Map p244; ☑ 097-231-6000; www.sofitel.com; Sharia Abtal At Tahrir; r from US$225; ❋ 🕸 🖨 🖩) The grande dame of Aswan hotels, the Old Cataract is a destination in itself and brings you back to the days of Agatha Christie, who is said to have written part of her novel *Death on the Nile* here (the hotel certainly featured in the movie). The splendid buildings and well-tended gardens command fantastic views of the Nile and the desert.

The original building of the Old Cataract hotel, now known as the Palace Wing, has 76 rooms, of which more than half are suites. But the biggest change has been brought to the 1960s annexe, the Garden Wing, where all rooms have stunning Nile views. The 1902 Restaurant serves some of the fanciest food on the Nile, while **Kebabgy** (☺7pm-midnight) and Saraya serve simpler food in a more relaxed atmosphere. The large pool looks on to the river and the ruins of Elephantine Island, and the two-floor spa has a fitness centre, a hammam, a sauna and Thai therapists.

Mövenpick Resort Aswan RESORT **$$$**
(Map p244; ☑097-245-4455; www.movenpick. com; Elephantine Island; s/d from US$120/195; ❋ @ 🕸 🖩) Hidden in a large, lush garden but dominated by an eyesore tower, the Mövenpick sits on the northern end of Elephantine Island. The hotel has very comfortable rooms, featuring Nubian styles and colours. The swimming pool is great, as is the tower-top restaurant and bar. This is a great place for families to stay.

Guests are transported to and from the town centre by a free ferry. Book online for the best rates.

✕ Eating

Aswan is a sleepy place and most tourists eat on board the cruise boats, but there are a few laid-back restaurants. Outside the hotels, few serve alcohol and few accept credit cards.

Nubian House Restaurant EGYPTIAN **$**
(☑097-221-0125; Sharia Al Fanadek, south of the Nubian Museum; mains LE30-75; ☺8am-midnight) The Nubian House was renovated during the spring 2017, and is now more colourful than ever. The Nubian dishes served here are good, but best of all is the view at sunset looking over the First Cataract, and the peace and quiet of the place. Henna painting is on offer, and sometimes Nubian music.

Rumour has it, however, that a new high-rise next door might block the view of the Nile.

Ad Dukka EGYPTIAN **$$**
(Map p244; ☑012-2216-2379, 097-231-8293; Essa Island; mains LE45-110; ☺6.30-10pm) This Nubian restaurant, set on an island just beyond Elephantine Island, burnt down and was rebuilt in early 2017. It continues to serve excellent Nubian food in large and lavishly decorated portions. It can be a wonderfully atmospheric place to spend an evening as the setting, opposite the Old Cataract Hotel and the ruins of Abu, is spectacular.

To get here, there's a free ferry from the dock opposite the EgyptAir office (p253).

Salah Ad Din INTERNATIONAL **$$**
(Map p241; ☑097-231-0361; Corniche An Nil; mains LE35-90; ☺noon-late) One of the best of the Nileside restaurants, with several terraces and a freezing air-con dining room. The menu has Egyptian, Nubian and international dishes, a notch better than most restaurants in Aswan. The service is efficient and the beers are cold. There is also a terrace on which to smoke a shisha.

Al Makka EGYPTIAN **$$**
(Map p241; ☑097-244-0232; Sharia Abtal At Tahrir; dishes LE85-120; ☺noon-2am) Popular with meat-eating local families, this place is famous for its excellent fresh kebabs and kofta, as well as stuffed pigeon. Mains come loaded with bread, salad, tahini, rice and vegetable stew, making it a real feast. Bring your appetite.

Its sister-restaurant **Al Madina** (Map p241; ☑097-230-5696; Sharia As Souq; mains LE48-165; ☺noon-midnight) serves a similar menu.

Nubian Beach EGYPTIAN **$$**
(Map p244; ☑012-2169-9145; West Bank; set menu per person LE85; ☺noon-midnight) Nubian cafe-restaurant set in a quiet garden on the west bank of the Nile, against the backdrop of a towering sand dune and near a popular swimming spot. When it's too hot or on colder evenings, you can also chill out in its beautifully painted indoor room. The food is simple but good, and beer is sometimes served.

LOCAL EATS

Along Sharia As Souq and Sharia Abtal At Tahrir there are plenty of small restaurants and cafes, where you can take in the lively atmosphere of the souq and sample local flavours.

Marwan (Map p241; Sharia Abtal At Tahrir; LE2-5; ⊙24hr) A tiny takeaway place hidden among the low-rise apartment blocks, just off the square with the train station. This is where Aswanis go when they want good *fuul* (fava bean paste) and *ta'amiyya* (falafel).

Koshary As Safwa (Map p241; Sharia Saad Zaghloul; kushari LE8-16; ⊙10am-midnight) A good *kushari* place (a mix of noodles, rice, black lentils, fried onions and tomato sauce) that also sells takeaway shawarma and kofta (mincemeat and spices grilled on a skewer).

El Tahrer Pizza (Map p241; Midan Al Mahatta; dishes LE35-85; ⊙10am-midnight) Just off the souq in front of the train station, El Tahrer Pizza is a popular cafe serving pizza and *fiteer* (sweet or savoury flaky pizza) at rock-bottom prices. Tea and shisha are also served.

The restaurant is now part of the Nubian Beach Hotel. You can swim from the nearby beach, or go sand boarding on desert dunes.

Abeer
EGYPTIAN $$

(Map p241; ☑011 0086-4739; Sharia Abtal At Tahrir; mains LE40-76; ⊙noon-midnight) Popular Egyptian restaurant serving all the classics, including delicious stuffed pigeon, spread over various restaurant rooms in a side alley.

Sunset
PIZZA $$

(Map p244; ☑097-232-8220; Sharia Abtal At Tahrir, Nasr City; dishes LE40-90; ⊙9am-3am) A cafe terrace and restaurant to head to at sunset (if you can't get to the Cataract Hotel) for its views over the First Cataract. Sit on the huge shady terrace in a garden for a mint tea, or enjoy the small selection of grills or pizzas. Take a taxi here after dark.

Chef Khalil
EGYPTIAN $$

(Map p241; ☑097-231-0142; Sharia As Souq; meals LE90-180; ⊙noon-1am) Small but popular fish restaurant, a short walk from the train station into the souq. It serves fish from Lake Nasser and the Red Sea, chosen from a chilled display, charged by weight, and grilled, baked or fried to your choice and served with salad and rice or French fries. Sometimes it also serves lobster (LE190).

★Panorama Restaurant & Bar
INTERNATIONAL $$$

(Map p244; ☑097-230-3455; www.movenpick. com; Mövenpick Resort Aswan, Elephantine Island; mains LE140-290; ⊙noon-11pm) The Panorama is one of the best restaurants in Aswan, even though it is in the Mövenpick's eyesore tower. The food is good, the room elegant and the service friendly and efficient. The real draw, however, is the 360-degree view of Aswan, the river and the desert – spectacular at sunset, glittering at night.

The menu is mostly North African – mezze, tagines, kebabs, Red Sea fish – but also includes curries and some Italian dishes. The three-course set menu costs LE350. There's a long cocktail menu and a full wine list, too.

1902 Restaurant
FRENCH $$$

(Map p244; ☑097-231-6000; www.sofitel.com; Sharia Abtal At Tahrir; mains LE200-410; ⊙7-11pm) The revamped Old Cataract Hotel has several top-end outlets, none grander than the 1902. Under its Moorish-inspired dome, the chefs – trained here and in France – serve sophisticated, expensive and mostly nouvelle cuisine. There is usually duck and cheese from France, fish from the Red Sea and a serious wine list from around the world, with bottles costing up to $1000.

Service is as attentive as the room is grand, and guests are invited to play their part by dressing for the occasion. As a dining experience, there is simply nothing else like this south of Cairo.

🍷 Drinking & Nightlife

Strolling along the Corniche, watching the moon rise as you sit at a rooftop terrace, or having a cool drink at one of the Nileside restaurants is about all that most travellers get up to in Aswan at night. A sunset cocktail on the Old Cataract Hotel (p250) terrace is another treat.

Espresso Cafe
CAFE

(Map p241; Sharia Abtal At Tahrir; ⊙7am-midnight) Popular traditional cafe (despite the name) on a quiet backstreet behind the Banque du Caire. A good place to while away time over a shisha and tea. The Nubian owner Nouri is friendly and helpful.

☆ Entertainment

Nubian shows are sometimes performed at the Mövenpick Resort Aswan (p250) and smaller hotels such as Bet El Kerem (p249). If you're lucky, you may be invited to a Nubian wedding on a weekend night. Foreign guests are deemed auspicious additions to the ceremony, but don't be surprised if you're asked to help defray the huge costs of the band and the food.

Palace of Culture   CONCERT VENUE
(Map p241; ☑ 097-231-3390; Corniche An Nil) Between October and February/March, Aswan's folkloric dance troupe sporadically performs Nubian *tahtib* (dance performed with wooden staves) and songs depicting village life at the Palace of Culture. Call ahead to check about performances.

🛍 Shopping

Aswan's famous souq (p240) was always a good place to pick up souvenirs and crafts, but at the time of writing tourism was down and many shops were closed, while others were just selling cheap tat.

Nubia Tourist Book Centre   BOOKS
(Map p241; Sharia As Souq; ⊗9am-10pm) Good, air-conditioned bookshop near the train station with loads of books on Aswan and Egypt in English. There is another well-stocked branch in the tourist bazaar at the Unfinished Obelisk (p242).

Hanafi Bazaar   ARTS & CRAFTS
(Map p244; ☑097-231-4083; Corniche An Nil; ⊗9am-8pm) With its mock Pharaonic facade, this is the oldest, dustiest and best bazaar in town, with genuine Nubian swords, baskets, amulets, silk kaftans and beads from all over Africa, run by the totally laid-back Hanafi brothers.

ℹ Information

DANGERS & ANNOYANCES

The number of tourists is down in Aswan as elsewhere in Egypt, so several hotels and shops in the souq have closed. Aswan seems to have been relatively quiet in the last few years, however. There is no more convoy from Aswan to Abu Simbel, but foreigners should travel between 5am and 5pm; the transport company has to apply for a permission one day before.

EMERGENCY

Tourist Police (Map p241; ☑097-244-0442, 126; Corniche An Nil) Contact the tourist office (p252) first to help with translation.

MEDICAL SERVICES

Aswan Military Hospital (Map p244; ☑097-231-7985, 097-231-4739; Sharia Sadat; ⊗24hr) The top hospital in town.

Evangelical Mission Hospital (EMH; Map p244; ☑097-245-0166; Corniche An Nil) This hospital is more than a hundred years old, but it has had a revamp with the help of the Reformed Church of America. It is now considered one of the top hospitals in town.

MONEY

There are ATMs and exchange booths along the Corniche and around Sharia As Souq, as well as at the train station.

Amex Franchise (Map p244; ☑097-230-3455, 012-2223-5094; www.amexfranchise.com; Movenpick Hotel, Elephantine Island; ⊗9am-5pm)

Banque Misr (Map p241; Corniche An Nil; ⊗8am-3pm & 5-8pm) ATM and foreign-exchange booth next to main building.

Travel Choice (Map p241; ☑097-230-4011; Corniche An Nil; ⊗9am-8pm)

TOURIST INFORMATION

Main Tourist Office (Map p241; ☑097-231-2811; Midan Al Mahatta; ⊗8am-3pm Sat-Thu) This tourist office has little material, but staff can advise on timetables and give an idea of prices for taxis and feluccas.

VISA EXTENSIONS

Visa extensions are issued by the **Passport Office** (Map p244; ☑097-231-2238; 1st fl, Police Bldg, Corniche An Nil; ⊗8am-2pm & 6-8pm Sun-Thu). Use the side entrance to the north. You will need to take two passport photos and two photocopies of the photo page and visa page from your passport. It is a good idea to go first thing in the morning and be prepared to wait, although they sometimes turn things around quickly.

ℹ Getting There & Away

Travelling from Aswan did not require police convoys at the time of writing. However, foreigners are advised to travel on the sleeper trains between Aswan and Luxor and Cairo, and tickets should be booked ahead. Officially it is not allowed to travel on slow local trains, but in reality foreigners can board those trains and buy a ticket on the train.

AIR

Aswan Airport (☑097-348-2440) is located 16km southwest of town. **EgyptAir** (Map p244;

097-245-0001; Corniche An Nil; ⊘ 8am-9pm) has several flights daily to Cairo and three flights per day to Abu Simbel, Sunday to Thursday.

BOAT

Aswan is the most popular starting point for Nile cruises. It's also the best place to arrange an overnight or multiday felucca trip.

BUS

The **bus station** is 3.5km north of the train station. Services are run by Upper Egypt Bus Co. A taxi there will cost LE60, or it's LE2 in a microbus from downtown.

MICROBUS

Microbuses leave from the bus station, 3.5km north of the train station, but tourists are not allowed to use microbuses between cities. They will be stopped and returned at the checkpoints.

TRAIN

There are 10 trains daily from **Aswan Train Station** (☏ 097 231-4754; https://enr.gov.eg; Midan Al Mahatta) to Luxor and onward to Cairo. Check trains schedules beforehand at Aswan's helpful tourist office (p252) as service order does change.

The 5am, 10am, 3pm, 4.35pm, 6pm and 9pm departures use the newer rolling stock VIP 1st class to Luxor (1st/2nd class LE100/70) and Cairo (LE235/135).

The 7am, 4.15pm, 7.45pm, 8pm and 10pm are the normal Spanish service to Luxor (1st/2nd class LE51/30) and Cairo (LE135/70).

All trains stop at Daraw, Kom Ombo, Edfu and Esna. Student discounts are available on all. Tickets should be bought in advance but can be purchased on the train for an additional fee.

The **Watania Sleeping Train** (www.watania sleepingtrains.com) departs from Aswan at 7pm daily.

TO/FROM SUDAN

The Qustul land border and the Argeen land border between Egypt and Sudan reopened in 2014. There are now several Sudanese bus companies with offices at Aswan bus station offering services to Khartoum (around LE420) via Wadi Halfa (around LE280). Buses leave early in the morning between 4am and 6am (Saturday to Thursday). Which border they use to cross seems to be entirely at the driver's discretion, but the Qustul border seems to be the more popular option.

The ferry to Wadi Halfa in Sudan (1st/2nd class LE520/380) leaves every Sunday and Wednesday. Purchase tickets in advance from the **Nile River Valley Transport Corporation** (Map p241; ☏ 097-578-9256, 011-2709-2709, 097-244-0384; ⊘ 8am-2pm Sat-Thu), in the shopping arcade behind the tourist police office. The journey is supposed to take 18 hours.

With buses now running to Wadi Halfa, many travellers prefer to take the land route.

Although the ferry generally doesn't leave until 3pm, you should be at the port by 10am.

You can get to the port by taxi.

❶ Getting Around

TO/FROM THE AIRPORT

A taxi to/from the airport costs between LE100 and LE150 depending on your bargaining skills.

BICYCLE

Aswan is not a great town for cycling. However, there are a few places in the train station end of Sharia As Souq where you can hire bicycles for about LE20 a day. **Bet El Kerem** (p249) rents bikes for LE100 per day and also runs cycling trips (LE100 to LE200 per person) in the countryside and to Luxor (€595 per person for eight days).

FERRY

Two public ferries (LE1) run to Elephantine Island: the **ferry** (Map p244) departing across from EgyptAir goes to the **Aswan Museum** (Map p244), while the **ferry** (Map p241) across from the Travel Choice office (formerly Thomas Cook) goes to **Siou** (Map p244). A third public **ferry** (Map p241) goes from the ferry landing across from the train station to **West Aswan** (Map p244) and the Tombs of the Nobles for LE1. Foreigners might be expected to pay more than the local ferry fare. **Shuttleboats** (Map p241) go to and from **Mövenpick Resort Aswan** (Map p244).

SOUTHERN NILE VALLEY ASWAN

BUSES FROM ASWAN

DESTINATION	PRICE	DURATION	TIME
Abu Simbel	LE50	4hr	8am
Cairo	LE130	14hr	4pm
Hurghada	LE85	7hr	6am, 3pm & 5pm
Marsa Alam	LE50	3hr	5am

MICROBUS

Microbuses (LE1 to LE2) run along the major roads in Aswan.

TAXI

An all-day taxi tour of some of the sights near Aswan should cost between LE300 and LE400 (excluding entry tickets), depending on distances and number of sights covered.

A taxi anywhere within the town costs LE10 to LE20.

AROUND ASWAN

Aswan Dam

Completed in 1902, the **Aswan Dam** (Old Dam) was a feat of engineering for its time and the largest dam in the world, measuring 2441m across, 50m high and 30m wide. Although not an attraction in itself, the road that runs across the top of the dam (which you'll take if heading to the airport or Abu Simbel) has excellent Nile views.

Plans for the Aswan Dam began at the end of the 19th century, when Egypt's fast-growing population made it imperative to cultivate more agricultural land. This would only be possible by regulating the flow of the Nile, which would also ensure the river did not burst its banks during the flood. British engineer Sir William Willcocks started construction in 1898 above the First Cataract, with the dam structure made almost entirely of Aswan granite. It was raised twice to meet demand, not only to increase the area of cultivable land but also to provide hydroelectric power. Today the old dam generates hydroelectricity only for a nearby factory producing fertilisers. With the opening of the High Dam 6km upstream in the 1960s, though, the original dam's use was usurped.

◎ Sights

Nile Museum   MUSEUM
(next to the old Dam, Aswan–Abu Simbel Rd; adult/student LE60/30; ⊗8.30am-5pm) A three-storey building on 146,000 sq metres of land, the Nile Museum exhibits antique items that tell of the waterway's history and photos that illustrate river projects and the development of irrigation techniques since Ottoman rule. Sections are allocated within the museum for the 11 Nile Basin countries to exhibit their historical, Nile-related items.

It also includes a conference hall and a library.

Seheyl Island

Situated just north of the old Aswan Dam, the island of **Seheyl** (adult/child LE40/20; ⊗7am-4pm Oct-Apr, to 5pm May-Sep) was sacred to the goddess Anukis. Before the dam's construction, the Nile would rush noisily through the granite boulders that emerged from the riverbed just south of here, forming the First Cataract. On the island's southern tip is a cliff with more than 200 inscriptions, most dating to the 18th and 19th dynasties, of princes, generals and other officials who passed by on their journey to Nubia.

The most famous of these inscriptions is the so-called famine stele from the 3rd dynasty that recounts a terrible seven-year famine during the reign of Zoser (2667–2648 BC), which the pharaoh tried to end by making offerings to the Temple of Khnum on Elephantine Island.

Next to the inscriptions is a friendly Nubian village with brightly coloured houses. Several houses now welcome visitors, selling tea and good Nubian lunches as well as local crafts. It's a pleasant place to stroll around. Herodotus reported that an Egyptian official had told him that the First Cataract was the source of the Nile, which flowed north and south from there. Now the waters flow slowly and Seheyl makes an ideal destination for a slightly longer felucca trip.

Gharb Seheyl, the village opposite Seheyl island, has become a popular tourist attraction of late, both with excursions from Aswan and for those looking for a quieter pace of life. The colourful Nubian houses are a treat, there is a nearby beach for safe swimming, **camel rides** and a small Nubian crafts souq. A selection of laid-back guesthouses make it a popular stop to hang out for a few relaxing days.

🛏 Sleeping & Eating

★ Anakato   GUESTHOUSE $$
(☏010-1763-1212, 010-0081-8833, 097-345-1745; www.anakato.com; Gharb Seheyl; s/d LE300/550; ❄@) Anakato is Nubian for 'my house'. This small guesthouse has 12 bedrooms in the wildly coloured Nubian style, with domed roofs. It's a lovely place to hang out for a while. Meals are available, and the village of Gharb Seheyl is just there. Very pleasant terrace on the Nile.

Around Aswan

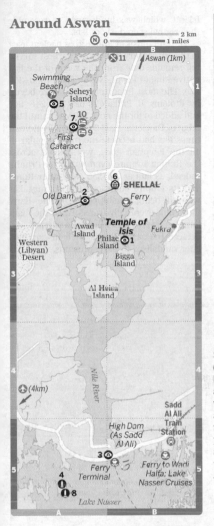

Nubian Cataract Hotel
HOTEL **$$**

(☏ 012-2272-3267; www.facebook.com/nubian-cataract; Nubian village Nag Al Makhati, opposite Seheyl Island; s/d LE550/600; ❄🛜) This new Nubian-style hotel features very comfortable rooms with great views over the Nile and Seheyl Island. The hotel has a spectacular terrace with fabulous sunset views, and a good Nubian-Egyptian restaurant (mains LE90 to LE150).

A swimming pool was being built at the time of writing.

Suheyl House
GUESTHOUSE **$**

(☏ 011-1626-2253; Seheyl Island; s/d/tr LE200/300/400; ❄🛜) Simple but very pleasant guesthouse with eight rooms equipped with aircon, mosquito net and fridge, set around a delightful terrace on the Nile, in the shade of mango trees. This is a great place to spend a few quiet days. Meals are available (LE60). There are three turtles in the garden with fruit trees; one is reputedly 360 years old.

This guesthouse is right next to the antiquities site on Seheyl.

Qaryat Gharb Seheyl
EGYPTIAN **$**

(☏ 012-2272-3126, Gharb Seheyl; mains from LE25; ⊙6am-8pm) Nasr Ad Din Abduh Es Sitar runs this beautifully restored Nubian house as a cafe-restaurant and Nubian crafts centre. Henna tattoos are also available.

❶ Getting There & Away

The best way to get here is by motor boat or felucca from the Corniche in Aswan (LE80 to LE100), or by road from the Aswan Dam.

Philae

Perched on the island of Philae (fee-*leh*), the Temple of Isis attracted pilgrims for thousands of years and was one of the last pagan temples to operate after the arrival of Christianity.

After 1902 and the building of the old Aswan Dam, the temple was flooded for six months each year, allowing travellers to row boats among the partially submerged columns to peer down through the translucent green at the wondrous sanctuaries of the mighty gods below.

After the completion of the High Dam, the temple would have entirely disappeared had Unesco not intervened. Between 1972 and 1980, the massive temple complex was disassembled stone by stone. It was then reconstructed 20m higher on nearby Agilika

Island, which was landscaped to resemble the original sacred isle of Isis.

The cult of Isis at Philae goes back at least to the 7th century BC, but the earliest surviving remains date from the reign of the last native king of Egypt, Nectanebo I (380–362 BC). The most important ruins were begun by Ptolemy II Philadelphus (285–246 BC) and added to for the next 500 years until the reign of Diocletian (AD 284–305). By Roman times Isis had become the most popular of all the Egyptian gods, worshipped across the Roman Empire even as far as Britain. Indeed, as late as AD 550, well after Rome and its empire embraced Christianity, Isis was still being worshipped at Philae. Early Christians eventually transformed the main temple's hypostyle hall into a chapel and defaced the pagan reliefs, their inscriptions later vandalised by early Muslims.

Philae (Agilika Island)

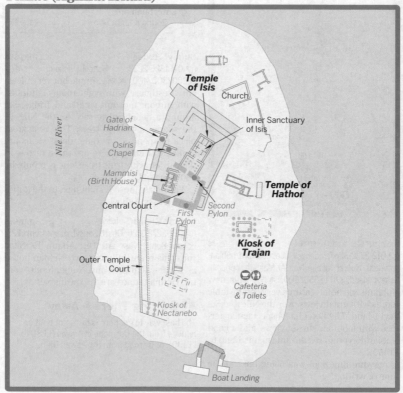

⊙ Sights

★ **Temple of Isis** TEMPLE
(adult/child LE100/50; ⊙7am-4pm Oct-May, to 5pm Jun-Sep) Built to honour the goddess Isis, this was the last temple built in the classical Egyptian style. Construction began around 690 BC, and it was one of the last outposts where the goddess was worshipped. The cult of Isis continued here until at least AD 550. The boat leaves you near the Kiosk of Nectanebo, the oldest part, and the entrance to the temple is marked by the 18m-high first pylon with reliefs of Ptolemy XII Neos Dionysos smiting enemies.

In the central court of the Temple of Isis, the *mammisi* (birth house) is dedicated to Horus, son of Isis and Osiris. Successive pharaohs reinstated their legitimacy as the mortal descendants of Horus by taking part in rituals celebrating the Isis legend and the birth of her son Horus in the marshes. The second pylon leads to a hypostyle hall, with superb column capitals. Note also the reuse of the temple as a Christian church, with crosses carved into the older hieroglyph reliefs, and images of the Egyptian gods carefully defaced. Beyond lie three vestibules, leading into the **Inner Sanctuary of Isis.** Two granite shrines stood here, one containing a gold statue of Isis and another containing the *barque* in which the statue travelled, but these were long ago moved to Florence and Paris, and only the stone pedestal for the *barque* remains, inscribed with the names of Ptolemy III and his wife, Berenice. Take a side door west out of the hypostyle hall to the **Gate of Hadrian** where there is an image of the god Hapi, sitting in a cave at the First Cataract, representing the source of the river Nile.

East of the second pylon is the delightful **Temple of Hathor**, decorated with reliefs of musicians (including an ape playing the lute) and Bes, the god of childbirth. South of this is the elegant, unfinished pavilion by the water's edge, known as the **Kiosk of Trajan** ('Pharaoh's Bed'), perhaps the most famous of Philae's monuments and one that was frequently painted by Victorian artists, whose boats were moored beneath it.

The whole complex was moved from its original location on Philae Island, to its new location on Agilkia Island, after the flooding of Lake Nasser. A major multinational Unesco team relocated Philae, and a number of other temples that now dot the shores of Lake Nasser. You can see the submerged original island a short distance away, punctuated by the steel columns used in the moving process.

Don't miss the sound and light show at night, the least cheesy of the sound and light 'extravaganzas'. On your feet, look out for the extremely creative guards who will do all in their power to get in your photos, or to point out the hieroglyphs that you can quite clearly see yourself, all for some baksheesh (tip)!

✗ Eating

There is a very pleasant waterside cafe serving overpriced drinks and snacks beneath the big tree, near the Kiosk of Trajan. Location, location!

☆ Entertainment

Sound & Light Show SHOW
(www.soundandlight.com.eg; LE125; ⊙shows 6.30pm, 7.45pm & 8.45pm Oct-Apr, 7pm, 8.15pm & 9.30pm May-Sep) Although the commentary is predictably cheesy, you really can't beat strolling through Philae's temple at night. Show times, with commentary in alternate languages, have a habit of changing, so it's best to double-check the timetable with the Aswan tourist office (p252).

(p252)

OFF THE BEATEN TRACK

FEKRA CULTURAL CENTRE

Fekra (www.fekraculture.com; Gebal Shisha, Shellal) is a farm located on 40,000 sq metres of land on the lake between the old dam and the High Dam, and overlooks Philae Island. The Fekra Cultural Centre – *fekra* means thought or idea in Arabic – is a fascinating project of artists from around the world, aiming to support Nubian and Upper Egyptian artists, and to promote an international cultural exchange through organising artistic events and workshops. It's a magical place for its energy and wonderful location.

A Nubian-style mud-brick house right on the lake, it's perfectly peaceful and a great place for swimming. It has midrange accommodation for 12 people and a few extra Bedouin tents, with shared bathrooms, but they were not welcoming guests at the time of writing.

SOUTHERN NILE VALLEY PHILAE

Shows operate with a minimum of seven spectators; at least one per day will be in English when running.

ℹ Getting There & Away

The boat landing for the Philae complex is at Shellal, south of the old Aswan Dam. The only easy way to get there is by taxi or organised trip. Combo-tours of Philae and the Aswan High Dam, including guide, can be arranged by most hotels and travel agencies in Aswan, for around LE250 per person. The return taxi fare is about LE120 to LE150.

The return boat trip should not cost more than LE20 per person, plus baksheesh for the boatman, but often costs significantly more. Organised tours usually include the boat fare, sparing you the hassle of haggling.

Aswan High Dam

Egypt's modern example of construction on a monumental scale, the controversial **Aswan High Dam** (As Sadd Al Ali; adult/child LE30/15; ⊙24hr), 13km south of Aswan, contains 18 times the material used in the Great Pyramid of Khufu and created Lake Nasser, one of the world's largest artificial lakes.

Most people visit the High Dam as part of an organised trip to sights south of Aswan. A visit here is often included with Philae's Temple of Isis (p257), but can also be combined with a trip to the Kalabsha Temple (p260).

At the dam site is a small pavilion with displays detailing the dimensions and the construction of the dam; on the western side is a monument honouring Soviet-Egyptian friendship and cooperation.

Note that video cameras and zoom lenses are not allowed onsite, although nobody seems to monitor this.

LOWER NUBIA & LAKE NASSER

For thousands of years, the First Cataract marked the border between Egypt and Nubia, the land that stretched from Aswan to Khartoum. The Nile Valley on the Egyptian side was fertile and continuously cultivated, while the banks further south in Nubia were more rugged, with rocky desert cliffs and sand separating small pockets of agricultural land.

The building of the Aswan and High Dams irrevocably changed all that, and much of Nubia disappeared under the wa-

ters of Lake Nasser. The landscape now is dominated by the contrast of smooth desert and the calm green-brown water of the lake. Apart from the beauty and the peace of the lake itself, the main attraction of this region is the temples that were so painstakingly moved above the flood waters in the 1960s.

The area between the First and the Second Cataract is generally known as Lower Nubia (ancient Egyptian Wawat), and further south between the Second and Sixth Cataracts is Upper Nubia (Kush).

To the ancient Egyptians, Nubia was Ta-Sety, the Land of Bowmen, after the weapon for which the Nubians were famous. It was a crucial route for the trade with sub-Saharan Africa, and it was the source of much-needed raw materials, such as copper, ivory, ebony and gold. The modern name is thought to come from the ancient Egyptian word *nbw*, meaning 'gold'.

Egypt was always interested in Nubia and its riches, and the two peoples' histories were always connected: when Egypt was strong it dominated Nubia and aggressively exploited its natural resources; when Egypt was weak, the Nubians enjoyed periods of growth and development.

Evidence of 10,000-year-old settlements has been found in northern Nubia. At Nabta Playa, located some 100km west of Abu Simbel, archaeologists have recently discovered the remains of houses, sculpted monoliths and the world's oldest calendar, made of small standing stones, dating from around 6000 BC.

Until 3500 BC Nubia and Egypt both developed in roughly the same way, domesticating animals, growing crops and gradually adopting permanent settlements. Both people were ethnically linked, but the darker-skinned Nubians had more African features and spoke a Nilo-Saharan language, while the ancient Egyptian language is Afro-Asiatic.

With the unification of the land north of Aswan around 3100 BC, Egypt started to impose its authority on Nubia. From the beginning of the Old Kingdom, for nearly 5000 years, expeditions were sent to extract the region's considerable mineral wealth. During the First Intermediate Period (2160–2025 BC), central authority in Egypt collapsed, while Nubia became stronger, and Nubian soldiers played an important role in Egypt's civil war.

The reunification of Egypt, at the start of the Middle Kingdom, saw Lower Nubia

NUBIAN CULTURE

The Nubians have paid the highest price for Egypt's greater good. They have lost their homes and their homeland, and with a new generation growing up far from the homeland, as Egyptians, or even Europeans, or Americans, they are now also gradually losing their distinctive identity and traditions.

What is left of Nubian culture then seems all the more vibrant. Nubian music, famous for its unique sound, was popularised in the West by musicians such as Hamza Ad Din, whose oud (lute) melodies are ethereally beautiful. In addition to the oud, two basic instruments give the music its distinctive rhythm and harmony: the *douff*, a wide, shallow drum or *tabla* that musicians hold in their hands; and the *kisir*, a type of stringed instrument.

The Nubians in Southern Egypt speak their own language, known as Nobiin, as well as Egyptian Arabic. The language seems to come from Old Nubian, and it is spoken by over 600,000 Nubians in Egypt and northern Sudan. There is no standardised orthography, so the language is written in both Latin and Arabic scripts. Part of reclaiming the Nubian identity is the plan to to revive the old Nubian alphabet.

Less known abroad is Nubia's distinctive architecture, which was the main influence on Egyptian mud-brick architect Hassan Fathy. Traditional Lower Nubian houses are made with mudbricks; unlike the Upper Egyptian houses, they often have domed or vaulted ceilings, and further south the houses usually have a flat split-palm roof. They are plastered or whitewashed and covered with decorations, including ceramic plates. The basic forms of these houses can be seen in the Nubian villages around Aswan and in Ballana, near Kom Ombo. They are often painted in plenty of colours with geometrical decorations.

Nubians also have their own marriage customs. Traditionally, wedding festivities lasted for up to 15 days, although nowadays they are a three-day affair. On the first night of the festivities, the bride and groom celebrate separately with their respective friends and families. On the second night, the bride takes her party to the groom's home and both groups dance to traditional music until the wee hours. Then the bride returns home and her hands and feet are painted with beautiful designs in henna. The groom will also have his hands and feet covered in henna but without any design. On the third day, the groom and his party walk slowly to the bride's house in a *zaffer* (procession), singing and dancing the whole way. Traditionally, the groom will stay at the bride's house for three days before seeing his family. The couple then set up home.

again annexed and a chain of fortresses built at strategic points along the Nile to safeguard trade.

During the New Kingdom, instead of fortresses, the Egyptians built temples in Nubia, dividing the whole of the region into five nomes, ruled on the pharaoh's behalf by his viceroy, who took the title King's Son of Kush. Taking advantage of Egypt's political disunity during the Third Intermediate Period (1069–945 BC), the tables were turned and Nubians extended their authority far to the north, ruling Egypt for a century as the 25th Kushite dynasty (747–656 BC). The 25th dynasty ended with the Assyrian invasion of Egypt, after which Nubian action was guided by its own best interests, sometimes siding with foreign invaders, sometimes with its Egyptian neighbours.

Christianity gradually spread to Nubia after the 5th century AD and lasted long after Islam had spread along the Egyptian Nile. In AD 652 Egypt's new Muslim authorities made a peace treaty with the Christian king of Nubia. That treaty lasted more or less until the 13th century, when Egyptians moved south again: the last Christian king of Nubia was deposed in 1305 and most of the population converted to Islam. In the 19th century Nubia was again important to Egyptian ambitions as the route for its supply of slaves. The rise of the Mahdist state in Sudan at the end of the 19th century led to Nubia being divided for the last time: with the defeat of the Mahdi and his successor, and the establishment of the Anglo-Egyptian government in Sudan in 1899, a border between Egypt and Sudan was established 40km north of Wadi Halfa.

Modern Nubia

Following the completion of the old Aswan Dam in 1902, and again after its height was raised in 1912 and 1934, the high-water level of the Nile in Lower Nubia gradually rose from 87m to 121m, partially submerging many of the monuments in the area and, by the 1930s, totally flooding a large number of Nubian villages. With their homes flooded, some Nubians moved north where, with government help, they bought land and built villages based on their traditional architecture. Most of the Nubian villages close to Aswan, such as Elephantine, Gharb Aswan (West Aswan) and Seheyl, are made up of people who moved at this time. Those who decided to stay in their homeland built houses on higher land, assuming they would be safe, but they saw their date plantations, central to their economy, destroyed. This meant that many Nubian men were forced to search for work further north, leaving the women behind to run the communities.

Less than 30 years later, the building of the High Dam forced those who had stayed to move. In the 1960s, 50,000 Egyptian Nubians were relocated to government-built villages around Kom Ombo, 50km north of Aswan. There has been a huge diaspora of Nubians, and Nubians today are doing all they can to keep their traditions and culture intact, and reclaim their Nubian identity.

Lake Nasser

Lake Nasser, one of the world's largest artificial lakes, covers an area of 5250 sq km, and is 510km long and between 5km and 35km wide. The lake was created as a result of the construction of the High Dam across the Nile between 1958 and 1970. The contrast between this enormous body of water and the remote desert stretching away on all sides makes Lake Nasser a place of austere beauty, a vast space of total tranquillity and silence. Cruise boats take several peaceful days to go from Aswan to Abu Simbel, visiting the Great Temple of Ramses II (p263) and the other temples that were moved to higher ground.

Wildlife is in abundance: keep an eye out for migratory birds, gazelles, foxes and several types of snake (including the deadly horned viper) on shore, and enormous Nile perch, crocodiles and monitor lizards in the shallows.

On average the lake contains some 135 billion cu metres of water, of which an estimated six billion are lost each year to evaporation. Its maximum capacity is 157 billion cu metres of water, which was reached in 1996 after heavy rains in Ethiopia, forcing the opening of a special spillway at Toshka, about 30km north of Abu Simbel, the first time it had been opened since the dam was built. The Egyptian government has since embarked on a controversial project to build a new canal and irrigate thousands of hectares in what is now the Nubian Desert between Toshka and the New Valley, a project ex-president Mubarak has likened to the Suez Canal and Aswan High Dam in its scale, but this has now all but failed.

Because the level of the lake fluctuates it has been difficult to build settlements around its edges. The main human presence here, apart from the fast-growing population of Abu Simbel town and the few tourists who visit, is limited to the 5000 or so fishers who spend up to six months at a time in small rowing boats, together catching about 50,000 tonnes of small fish each year.

Egyptians are very worried about the effect the Grand Ethiopian Renaissance Dam, currently under construction in Ethiopia, will have on the water flowing into Lake Nasser. The new dam will no doubt benefit Sudan and Ethiopia, but Egypt claims that it will stop the Nile River from properly filling the lake, and the diminished flow will affect the electricity generation essential for Egypt.

◉ Sights

◎ Kalabsha, Beit al Wali & Kertassi

Kalabsha Temple MONUMENT
(adult/concession LE60/30, incl Beit Al Wali & Temple of Kertassi; ☉8am-5pm) Kalabsha Temple is an impressive Ptolemaic and Roman structure, not unlike nearby Philae in its layout. The early 19th-century Swiss traveller Burckhardt (who rediscovered Abu Simbel) thought it was 'amongst the most precious remains of Egyptian antiquity'. The temple, started in the late Ptolemaic period and completed during the reign of Emperor Augustus (30 BC–AD 14), was dedicated to the Nubian solar god Merwel, known to the Greeks as Mandulis. Later it was used as a church.

An impressive stone causeway leads from the lake to the first pylon of the temple, beyond which are the colonnaded court and the eight-columned hypostyle hall. Inscriptions on the walls show various emperors or pharaohs in the presence of gods and goddesses. Just beyond the hall is the sanctuary, consisting of three chambers. Stairs from one chamber lead up to the roof, from where there are superb views of Lake Nasser and the High Dam, across the capitals of the hall and court. An inner passage, between the temple and the encircling wall, leads to a well-preserved Nilometer. The temple's original outer stone gateway was given by the Egyptian government to Germany in 1977, in thanks for helping to move this building. It is now in the Egyptian Museum, Berlin.

As a result of a massive Unesco effort, the temples here were transplanted from a now-submerged site about 50km south of Aswan. The new site is on the west bank of Lake Nasser just south of the High Dam.

When the water level is low you can sometimes walk across to the site; otherwise, you can find a motor boat on the western side of the High Dam (around LE60 for the return trip and an hour to visit).

Beit Al Wali   MONUMENT
(adult/concession LE60/30, incl Temples of Kalabsha & Kertassi; ⊙ 8am-5pm) Close to the Kalabsha Temple, the Temple of Beit Al Wali, mostly built by Ramses II, is cut into the rock and fronted by a brick pylon. On the walls of the forecourt, several fine reliefs detail the pharaoh's victory over the Nubians (on the south wall) and wars against the Libyans and Syrians (on the north wall).

Ramses is gripping the hair of his enemies before smashing their brains while women plead for mercy. The finest scenes are those of Ramses on his throne, receiving the tribute paid by the defeated Nubians, including leopard skins, gold rings, elephant tusks, feathers and exotic animals.

Temple of Kertassi   MONUMENT
(adult/concession LE60/30, incl Temple of Kalabsha & Beit Al Wali; ⊙ 8am-5pm) Just north of the Kalabsha Temple (p260) are the scant but picturesque remains of the Temple of Kertassi, with two Hathor columns, a massive architrave and four fine papyrus columns.

◉ Wadi As Subua

The temples of Wadi As Subua were moved to this site, about 4km west of the original and now-submerged location, between 1961 and 1965.

Wadi As Subua means 'Valley of Lions' in Arabic and refers to the avenue of sphinxes that leads to the Temple of Ramses II. There are two interesting New Kingdom Egyptian temples here, including a rock temple built by Ramses II.

Temple of Ramses II   MONUMENT
(adult/student LE50/25, incl Temple of Dakka & Temple of Maharraqa) Built during the reign of the energetic pharaoh, the interior of the Temple of Ramses II was hewn from the rock and fronted by a stone pylon and colossal statues. Behind the pylon is a court featuring 10 more statues of the pharaoh, beyond which lie a 12-pillared hall and the sanctuary. The central niche was once carved with relief scenes of Ramses making offerings to Amun-Ra and Ra-Horakhty.

In Christian times this part was converted into a church, the pagan reliefs plastered over and painted with saints, so that now, with part of the plaster fallen away, Ramses II appears to be adoring St Peter!

Temple of Dakka   MONUMENT
(adult/student LE50/25, incl Temple of Ramses II & Temple of Maharraqa) About 1km to the north of the Temple of Ramses II (p261) are the remains of the Temple of Dakka, begun by the Nubian pharaoh Arkamani (218–200 BC) using materials from much earlier structures and adapted by the Ptolemies and the Roman emperor Augustus. Originally situated 50km north of here, it is dedicated to the god of wisdom, Thoth, and is notable for its 12m-high pylon, which you can climb for great views of the lake and the surrounding temples.

Temple of Maharraqa   MONUMENT
(⊙ adult/student LE50/25, incl Temple of Ramses II & Temple of Dakka) The Temple of Maharraqa, the smallest of the three at Wadi As Subua, originally stood 40km north at the ancient site of Ofendina. Dedicated to Isis and Serapis, the Alexandrian god, its decorations were never finished and all that remains is a small hypostyle hall, where in the northeast corner a spiral staircase of masonry leads up to the roof.

◉ Amada

Temple of Amada   MONUMENT
(adult/student LE70/35, incl Tomb of Pennut & Temple of Derr) The Temple of Amada, moved

about 2.6km from its original location, is the oldest surviving monument on Lake Nasser. It was built jointly by 18th-dynasty pharaohs Tuthmosis III (1479–1425 BC) and his son Amenhotep II, with a hypostyle hall added by his successor, Tuthmosis IV (1400–1390 BC). Dedicated, like many temples in Nubia, to the gods Amun-Ra and Ra-Horakhty, it has some of the finest and best-preserved reliefs of any Nubian monument and contains two important historical inscriptions.

The first of these, on a stele at the left (north) side of the entrance, describes the unsuccessful Libyan invasion of Egypt (1209 BC) during Pharaoh Merenptah's reign. A second stele on the back wall of the sanctuary describes Amenhotep II's military campaign (1424 BC) in Palestine. Both were no doubt designed to impress upon the Nubians that political opposition to the powerful Egyptians was useless.

Tomb of Pennut   TOMB

(adult/student LE50/25, incl Temple of Amada & Temple of Derr) The small rock-cut Tomb of Pennut, viceroy of Nubia under Ramses VI (1143–1136 BC), was originally situated at Aniba, 40km southwest of Amada. This well-preserved Nubian tomb consists of a small offering chapel and a niche at the rear, with reliefs depicting events and personalities from Pennut's life, including him being presented with a gift by Ramses VI. It's a five-minute walk from the Temple of Derr.

Temple of Derr   MONUMENT

(adult/student LE50/25, incl Temple of Amada & Tomb of Pennut) The rock-cut Temple of Derr, built by Ramses II, stood on a curve of the Nile. The pylon and court have disappeared, but there are some well-preserved reliefs in the ruined pillared hall, illustrating the Nubian campaign of Ramses II, with the usual killing of his enemies, accompanied by his famous pet lion. Following cleaning, many of the scenes are once again brightly coloured.

◉ Qasr Ibrim

Qasr Ibrim   RUINS

The only Nubian monument visible on its original site, Qasr Ibrim once sat on top of a 70m-high cliff, about 60km north of Abu Simbel, but now has water lapping at its edges.

There is evidence that Ibrim was a garrison town from 1000 BC onward, and that around 680 BC the 25th-dynasty Pharaoh

Taharka (690–664 BC), a Nubian by birth, built a mud-brick temple dedicated to Isis.

During Roman times the town was one of the last bastions of paganism, its six temples converting to Christianity two centuries later than the rest of Egypt. It then became one of the main Christian centres in Lower Nubia and held out against Islam until the 16th century, when a group of Bosnian mercenaries, part of the Ottoman army, occupied the site. The mercenaries stayed on and eventually married into the local Nubian community, using part of the cathedral as a mosque. Among the structural remains, the most impressive is an 8th-century sandstone cathedral built over Taharka's temple. The site is closed to visitors because of ongoing archaeological work.

🏃 Activities

★ African Angler   FISHING

(☑ 010-0134-2410, 012-2749-1892; www.african-angler.net; from per person US$200, incl rods & lunch) Operates boats on Lake Nasser, running great fishing trips and safaris around the shore of the lake.

Kasr Ibrim   CRUISE

(☑ 02-2516-9656, 02-2516-9654, 02-2516-9653; www.nilecruising.com/lake-nasser-cruises.htm; from €693) The *Kasr Ibrim* and its twin the *Eugénie* were the brainchild of Mustafa Al Guindi, a Cairene of Nubian origin who is almost single-handedly responsible for getting Lake Nasser opened to tourists. The boats are stunningly designed and each has a pool, a hammam and French cuisine. Recommended.

Nubiana   CRUISE

(☑ 012-2104-0255, 012-2350-3825; www.lakenasseradventure.com) The *Nubiana* is a small motor boat with three small cabins, a suite and a shared shower. Above is a lounge and sun deck. A speedboat can also be arranged for fishing trips or waterskiing. The same company also organises five-day boat trekking trips from Aswan to Abu Simbel.

ℹ Getting There & Away

Although all the sights except Qasr Ibrim have roads leading to them, the only ones foreigners are currently allowed to drive to are Kalabsha, Beit Al Wali and Kertassi.

For the moment, the rest of the sights can only be reached by boat, which is in any case the best way to see Lake Nasser's dramatic monuments.

SAVING NUBIA'S MONUMENTS

When plans were finalised for the creation of the Aswan High Dam, worldwide attention focused on the many valuable and irreplaceable ancient monuments doomed by the waters of Lake Nasser. Between 1960 and 1980 the Unesco-sponsored Nubian Rescue Campaign gathered expertise and financing from more than 50 countries, and sent Egyptian and foreign archaeological teams to Nubia. Necropolises were excavated, many portable artefacts and relics were removed to museums and, while some temples disappeared beneath the lake, 14 were salvaged.

Ten of the temples, including the complexes of Philae (p257), Kalabsha (p260) and Abu Simbel, were dismantled stone by stone and painstakingly rebuilt on higher ground. Four others were donated to the countries that contributed to the rescue effort, including the splendid Temple of Dendur, now reconstructed in the Metropolitan Museum of Art in New York.

Perhaps the greatest achievement of all was the preservation of the temples at Abu Simbel. Ancient magnificence and skill met with equally impressive modern technology as, at a cost of about US$40 million, Egyptian, Italian, Swedish, German and French archaeological teams cut the temples up into more than 2000 huge blocks, weighing from 10 to 40 tonnes each, and reconstructed them inside an artificially built mountain, 210m away from the water and 65m above the original site. The temples were carefully oriented to face the original direction, and the landscape of their original environment was recreated on and around the dome-shaped concrete mountain.

The project took more than four years. The temples of Abu Simbel were officially reopened in 1968, while the sacred site they had occupied for more than 3000 years disappeared beneath Lake Nasser. A plaque to the right of the temple entrance eloquently describes this achievement: 'Through this restoration of the past, we have indeed helped to build the future of mankind.'

Abu Simbel

📋 097 / POP 2900

Few tourists linger in the laid-back, quiet town of Abu Simbel, staying no more than the few hours needed to visit the colossal temples for which it is famous. But anyone interested in Lake Nasser, in seeing the temples without the crowds, in wandering around a small nontouristy Nubian town, or in listening to Nubian music might choose to hang around for a day or two.

⊙ Sights

★ **Temples of Abu Simbel** TEMPLE
(adult/student incl guide LE160/80; ⊗6am-5pm Oct-Apr, to 6pm May-Sep) Overlooking Lake Nasser, the Great Temple of Ramses II (p263) and the Temple of Hathor (p264), which together make up the Temples of Abu Simbel, are among the most famous and spectacular monuments in Egypt. In a modern marvel of engineering, which matches Ramses II's original construction for sheer audacity, the temple complex was saved from being swallowed by rising waters and lost forever after the building of the High Dam (p258),

by being moved lock, stock and barrel to the position it sits upon today.

A higher price (LE240/120) is charged on 22 February and 22 October.

➡ ★ **Great Temple of Ramses II**
Carved out of the mountain on the west bank of the Nile between 1274 and 1244 BC, this imposing main temple of the Abu Simbel complex was as much dedicated to the deified Ramses II himself as to Ra-Horakhty, Amun and Ptah. The four colossal statues of the pharaoh, which front the temple, are like gigantic sentinels watching over the incoming traffic from the south, undoubtedly designed as a warning of the strength of the pharaoh.

Over the centuries both the Nile and the desert sands shifted, and this temple was lost to the world until 1813, when it was rediscovered by chance by the Swiss explorer Jean-Louis Burckhardt. Only one of the heads was completely showing above the sand, the next head was broken off and, of the remaining two, only the crowns could be seen. Enough sand was cleared away in 1817 by Giovanni Belzoni for the temple to be entered.

Great Temple of Ramses II

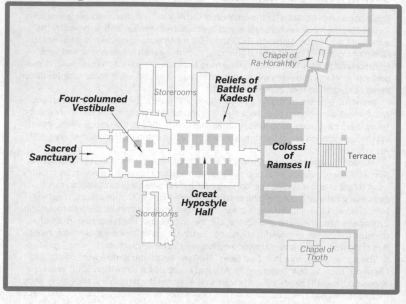

- Chapel of Ra-Horakhty
- **Reliefs of Battle of Kadesh**
- Storerooms
- **Four-columned Vestibule**
- **Sacred Sanctuary**
- **Colossi of Ramses II**
- Terrace
- **Great Hypostyle Hall**
- Storerooms
- Chapel of Thoth

From the temple's forecourt, a short flight of steps leads up to the terrace in front of the massive rock-cut facade, which is about 30m high and 35m wide. Guarding the entrance, three of the four famous **colossal statues** stare out across the water into eternity – the inner left statue collapsed in antiquity and its upper body still lies on the ground. The statues, more than 20m high, are accompanied by smaller statues of the pharaoh's mother, Queen Tuya, his wife Nefertari and some of his favourite children. Above the entrance, between the central throned colossi, is the figure of the falcon-headed sun god Ra-Horakhty.

The roof of the **large hall** is decorated with vultures, symbolising the protective goddess Nekhbet, and is supported by eight columns, each fronted by an Osiride statue of Ramses II. Reliefs on the walls depict the pharaoh's prowess in battle, trampling over his enemies and slaughtering them in front of the gods. On the north wall is a depiction of the famous Battle of Kadesh (c 1274 BC), in what is now Syria, where Ramses inspired his demoralised army so that they won the battle against the Hittites. The scene is dominated by a famous relief of Ramses in his chariot, shooting arrows at his fleeing enemies. Also visible is the Egyptian camp,

walled off by its soldiers' round-topped shields, and the fortified Hittite town, surrounded by the Orontes River.

The next hall, the **four-columned vestibule** where Ramses and Nefertari are shown in front of the gods and the solar *barques*, leads to the sacred sanctuary, where Ramses and the triad of gods of the Great Temple sit on their thrones.

The original temple was aligned in such a way that each 21 February and 21 October, Ramses' birthday and coronation day, the first rays of the rising sun moved across the hypostyle hall, through the vestibule and into the sanctuary, where they illuminate the figures of Ra-Horakhty, Ramses II and Amun. Ptah, to the left, was never supposed to be illuminated. Since the temples were moved, this phenomenon happens one day later.

➡ Temple of Hathor

Next to the Great Temple of Ramses II sits the smaller of Abu Simbel's temples. The Temple of Hathor has a rock-cut facade fronted by six 10m-high standing statues of Ramses and Nefertari, with some of their many children by their side. Nefertari here wears the costume of the goddess Hathor, and is, unusually, portrayed as the same height as her husband (instead of knee-height, as most consorts were depicted).

Inside, the six pillars of the hypostyle hall are crowned with capitals in the bovine shape of Hathor. On the walls the queen appears in front of the gods very much equal to Ramses II, and she is seen honouring her husband. The vestibule and adjoining chambers, which have colourful scenes of the goddess and her sacred *barque*, lead to the sanctuary, which has a weathered statue of Hathor as a cow emerging from the rock. The art here is softer and more graceful than in the Great Temple.

🛏 Sleeping & Eating

Few people stay the night in Abu Simbel, but there are a couple of places dedicated to package tours and a couple of others for those looking for ultimate peace and quiet.

Along Abu Simbel's main road is a line-up of cheap cafes, with the Nubian Oasis and Wadi El Nil among the most popular.

★ **Eskaleh**   GUESTHOUSE **$$**
(Beit An Nubi; ☎012-2368-0521, 097-340-1288; www.facebook.com/pg/Eskaleh; Sharia Saad Ibn Abu Wakas; d €65; ❄◉☎) Part Nubian cultural centre with a library dedicated to Nubian history, part wonderful ecolodge in a traditional mud-brick house, Eskaleh is by far the most interesting place to stay or eat in Abu Simbel. It's also a destination in its own right and a perfect base for a visit to the temples.

The friendly owner, Fikry El Kashef, a Nubian musician, was educated in Switzerland but returned to his homeland after the Abu Simbel temples were moved. In 2005, having worked for years as a guide, Fikry created this wonderful enclave beside the lake with the idea of sharing the Nubian experience with interested foreigners. Simple but comfortable rooms have local furniture, fans, aircon and good private bathrooms. Some also have a private terrace.

Nubian kitchen staff prepare delicious home-cooked meals (three-course lunch or dinner from €10 to €18) with organic produce from Fikry's garden and fish from the lake (and beer is sometimes available). These take time – be prepared to wait. At night the quiet is absolute (apart from the dogs), a rare thing on the tourist trail along the Nile. Sometimes Fikry plays music with his friends, or hosts performances of Nubian music and dance. A boat is available (approximately €50 depending on the length of time) to take you out on the lake or to the temples.

Tuya Hotel   GUESTHOUSE **$$**
(☎097-340-0002, 012-3577-7539; www.facebook.com/Tuya-Hotel-177306666061500; Sharia Ramsis, Tariq Al Maabad; s/d €35/52; ▣❄☎) Overlooking Lake Nasser, Tuya Hotel is situated 1km from Temple of Abu Simbel. The comfortable rooms are painted in strong Nubian colours, and all are equipped with clean bathrooms. There is free shuttle service to the temple.

Tuya Cafe   CAFE **$**
(☎012-357-7539; Tariq Al Maabad; breakfast LE20, mains from LE23; ⊙early-late) A simple but reliable place serving breakfast for early arrivals, and simple, local cuisine in a lovely garden or boldly painted rooms inside. It's a good place to stop for a drink or to smoke a shisha. Now part of the Tuya Hotel.

☆ Entertainment

Sound & Light Show   SHOW
(www.soundandlight.com.eg; adult/child LE150/75; ⊙shows 6.30pm & 7.30pm Oct-Apr, 7.30pm May-Sep) A sound-and-light show is performed nightly at Abu Simbel. Headphones are provided, allowing visitors to listen to the commentary in various languages. While the text is flowery and forgettable, the laser show projected on to the temples is stunning and well worth the detour.

Shows are only held with a minimum of 10 spectators; check with the tourist office.

ⓘ Getting There & Away

The vast majority of visitors to Abu Simbel come here on an organised tour from Aswan. All the hotels, cruise ships and travel agencies in Aswan can arrange tours. Budget trips – which basically just include return transport with two hours at the site – start from about LE400. There is no longer a convoy from Aswan to Abu Simbel, but foreigners should travel between 5am and 5pm, and the transport company should apply for a permission one day before.

AIR

EgyptAir has three flights to Aswan from Abu Simbel Airport per day from Sunday to Friday. All easily connect with Aswan–Cairo flights.

BUS

Buses from Abu Simbel to Aswan (LE60, four hours) leave at 6am and 1pm from Wadi El Nil restaurant on the main road. There's no advance booking – tickets are purchased on board.

Siwa Oasis & the Western Desert

Why Go?

Older than the Pyramids, as sublime as any temple, Egypt's Western Desert is a vast sweep of elemental beauty. The White Desert's shimmering vista of surreal rock formations and the ripple and swell of the Great Sand Sea's mammoth dunes are simply bewitching.

Within this intense landscape five oases, shaded by palm plantations and blessed by a plethora of natural hot and cold springs, provide a glimpse of rural Egyptian life. Get lost exploring Al Qasr's squiggling narrow lanes in Dakhla. Watch sunset sear across the countryside atop Gebel Al Ingleez in Baharia. Take a stroll amid Siwa's sprawling date palms. Once you've finished adventuring, kick back and just enjoy the laid-back pace of oasis life.

Best Natural Spring Soaks

➜ Cleopatra's Spring (p296)

➜ Bir Wahed (p296)

➜ Ain Gomma (p285)

➜ Bir Al Gebal (p281)

Best Places to Stay

➜ Adrère Amellal (p300)

➜ Al Babinshal (p299)

➜ Siwa Relax Retreat (p300)

➜ Eden Garden Camp (p292)

➜ International Hot Spring Hotel (p292)

➜ Al Tarfa Desert Sanctuary (p281)

When to Go
Siwa

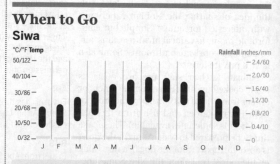

Apr–May After winter, travellers thin out and the oases prepare for the summer heat.

Sep–Oct Wander the oases' palm groves as the date harvest commences.

Nov–Mar The coolest time to be in the oases, when the hot springs are a delight.

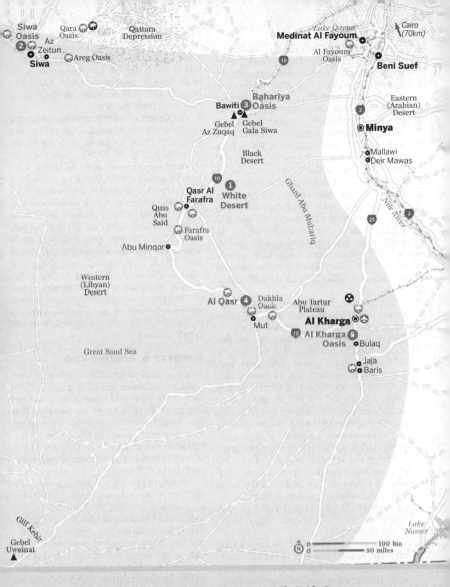

Siwa Oasis & the Western Desert Highlights

1 White Desert (p286)
Gaping in awe at this geologic wonderland.

2 Siwa Oasis (p292) Hitting the end of the road to revel in the far-from-anywhere vibe and delve into the unique Siwan culture.

3 Bahariya Oasis (p286)
Soaking off the dust in palm-shaded natural springs and pools.

4 Al Qasr (p279) Wandering through this lost-in-time, labyrinthine mud-brick town.

5 Al Kharga Oasis (p269)
Exploring the fascinating, rarely visited early Christian ruins.

History

The name Western Desert was given by the British to their share of the Libyan Desert. It doesn't really exist as a separate desert. As with the Sahara and other deserts that stretch across northern Africa, the Western Desert was once covered by the Sea of Tethys and later became a savannah that supported all manner of wildlife. Giraffes, lions and elephants roamed here in Palaeolithic times, when the landscape is thought to have looked much like the African Sahel. All that you see in the desert – the huge tracts of sand, the vast gravel plains, the fossil beds and limestone rocks – were once the happy hunting grounds that supported nomadic tribes. Gradual climate change led to desertification and turned this vast area into the arid expanse seen today. Only depressions in the desert floor have enough water to support wildlife, agriculture and human settlement.

The ancient Egyptians understood the nature of the desert, which they saw as being synonymous with death and exile. Seth, the god of chaos who killed his brother Osiris, was said to rule here. It is believed the ancient Egyptians maintained links with the oases throughout the Pharaonic era, and with the accession of a Libyan dynasty (22nd dynasty, 945–715 BC), focus increased on the oases and the caravan routes linking the Nile Valley with lands to the west.

The oases enjoyed a period of great prosperity during Roman times, when new wells and improved irrigation led to the production of wheat and grapes for export to Rome. Garrisoned fortresses that protected the oases and trade routes can still be seen in the desert around Al Kharga and Bahariya, and Roman-era temples and tombs lie scattered across all the oases.

When the Romans withdrew from Egypt, the trade routes became a target for attacking nomadic tribes. Trade suffered, the oases went into gradual decline, and the population of settlements shrank. By medieval times, raids by nomads were severe enough to bring Mamluk garrisons to the oases. The fortified villages built to defend the population can still be seen in Dakhla (Al Qasr, Balat) and Siwa (Shali).

The biggest change to the oases after the departure of the Romans occurred in 1958, when President Nasser created the so-called New Valley to relieve population pressure along the Nile. Roads were laid between the previously isolated oases, irrigation systems were modernised and an administration was established. The New Valley Governorate is the largest in Egypt and one of the least densely populated: there has never been enough work to draw significant numbers away from the Nile.

The Western Desert region has remained mostly unscathed throughout Egypt's recent years of political upheaval. Even during the 2011 revolution, Al Kharga was the only Western Desert oasis town to throw itself into the anti-Mubarak fray; after police fired into a crowd of protesters, the protesters set fire to the police station, a courthouse and other buildings. Three demonstrators were reported killed, with about 100 injured. More recently though there have been problems with smugglers crossing the desert from Libya, bringing weapons, drugs and other goods to the Nile Valley. As long as the security situation in Libya remains unstable, the travel warning from many foreign governments will remain: avoid travelling to the oases unless you have to, and no desert safaris allowed.

Dangers & Annoyances

At the time of writing the situation of travelling to the oases was fairly confused, not least in the variety of travel advisories from foreign governments. We recommend that you read the advice of your government before deciding to travel in this region. If you still want to travel, certain areas should still be avoided, including all deep desert areas, such as the Gilf Kebir.

Because of instability in neighbouring Libya, there is said to be a considerable number of smugglers crossing the desert to the Nile Valley with weapons, drugs and other goods. The Egyptian army has neither the means nor the ability to control movement in the vast desert area, something that became clear in 2015 when the army killed 12 people, mostly Mexican tourists, who had driven off the road for a rest stop. Some near-desert areas are also off limits: the tourist police currently do not allow travel agencies to use the Cairo–Bahariya desert road. This leaves the arc from Luxor to Cairo through the oases. At the time of our research, there was no problem using this route, although individuals tend to be stopped at all checkpoints and may have to travel between the oases with a police escort. Some travel agencies in Bahariya and Siwa will arrange tours into the nearby desert without problems, including overnights in the White Desert. If you are booking through an agency, make sure it has permission in advance from the authorities and that all passengers' details have been logged.

As long as the security situation in Libya remains unstable, it is unlikely there will be changes to the state of affairs in the oasis. You travel here at your own risk and are advised, before travelling, to check the latest situation with a reputable, specialist agency.

Long-Range Desert Safaris

Going on safari in the Western Desert was always one of the more rewarding experiences Egypt had to offer. However, at the time of writing, foreigners were allowed to go to the oases, but not to camp out in the desert or undertake long-range safaris. Desperate for work, some guides still offer short-range safaris into the desert, especially the White Desert, but it pays to be careful.

The Western Desert's more challenging routes such as the Great Sand Sea (p304), the remote Gilf Kebir (p304; in Egypt's southwest corner) – where you'll find the Cave of the Swimmers, made famous by *The English Patient* – and **Gebel Uweinat**, a 2000m-high peak trisected by the Egyptian, Libyan and Sudanese borders, are definitely out of reach currently. When desert travel is allowed again, remember that these adventures require extensive organisation, quality equipment and plenty of experience to properly execute; the consequences of mishaps are severe, sometimes fatal. Military permits, which are available locally for short desert treks, must be procured in Cairo for longer trips. Choose one of the operators that have a solid international reputation, are among the more reliable in Egypt, and will treat the desert with the respect it deserves.

Hisham Nessim   OUTDOORS
(☑ 010-0667-8099) Rally driver Hisham Nessim has been driving in the desert for many years. With satellite phones, GPS and six 4WDs specially rigged for long-range desert travel, he is prepared to go to all corners of Egypt. He offers 12 programs of two to 20 days, or will tailor-make tours when these are allowed again.

Dabuka Expeditions   OUTDOORS
(Map p278; ☑ 010-0355-9729; www.dabuka.de; 1 Sharia As Sawra Al Khadra) This German-based company previously arranged multiday safaris into the Great Sand Sea, Gebel Uweinat and Gilf Kebir, as well as specialised tours led by scientists and archaeologists. It also organised 4WD rental and logistics for desert do-it-yourselfers. It was only running local desert travel at the time of writing.

Al Badawiya   OUTDOORS
(Map p284; ☑ 092-751-0060, Cairo 02-2390-6429; www.badawiya.com) The three Ali brothers are Bedouin from Farafra, who have built up a significant business operating out of their Farafra-based hotel and an office in downtown Cairo (21 Sharia Youssef El Gendy). For now, they arrange trips around the oases and into the White Desert.

With considerable experience in the Western Desert, they can mount tailored camel or jeep safaris from three to 28 days in length, once these are allowed again. They have tents, cooking equipment and bedding.

Khalifa Expedition   TOURS
(☑ 012 2321 5445; www.khalifaexpedition.com) Khaled and Rose-Maria Khalifa have been running camel and jeep tours throughout the Western Desert from their base in Bahariya Oasis for more than 15 years. Rose-Maria is a qualified speech therapist and foot masseuse, which perhaps explains why they also offer meditation-retreat desert tours for people more interested in communing with nature than looking at antiquities.

AL KHARGA OASIS

As the capital of the New Valley Governorate and the closest of the oases to the Nile Valley, Al Kharga is also the most modern and therefore the least exotic. Lying in a 220km-long and 40km-wide depression, Al Kharga has long stood at the crossroads of vital desert trade routes, including the famous Darb Al Arba'een. This influential location brought it great prosperity, and with the arrival of the Romans, wells were dug, crops cultivated and fortresses built to protect caravan routes. Even as late as the 1890s, British forces were using lookout towers here to safeguard the 'back door' into Egypt.

The new road to Luxor and the airport with flights to Cairo makes it a convenient gateway to the oases, and a smattering of ancient sites here means it's a decent stopover in its own right.

Al Kharga

📞 092 / POP 80,000

The bustling city of Al Kharga is the largest town in the Western Desert and also the poster-child of the government's efforts to modernise the oases. The town's wide, bare boulevards rimmed by drab concrete housing blocks are definitely not what most travellers conjure up when they picture an oasis idyll. Despite the less than picturesque surroundings, the town is a good base for exploring a handful of unique, gently crumbling sights found around this oasis valley floor.

◎ Sights

The most popular monuments near Al Kharga lie along the good asphalt road that stretches south to Baris, but there are a few intriguing, harder-to-reach destinations north of town. Though less visited, they are hands-down the best day trips you can make around the oasis. There is an inclusive ticket for all the monuments in Kharga (adult/student LE120/60).

★ **Necropolis of Al Bagawat**   ARCHAEOLOGICAL SITE

(Map p271; adult/student LE50/25 incl Monastery of Al Kashef; ⊘8.30am-4pm) It may not look like much from afar, but this necropolis is one of the earliest surviving and best-preserved Christian cemeteries in the world. About 1km north of the Temple of Hibis, it's built on the site of an earlier Egyptian necropolis, with most of the 263 mud-brick chapel-tombs appearing to date from the 4th to the 6th centuries AD.

Some have interiors decorated with vivid murals of biblical scenes and boast ornate facades. The **Chapel of Peace** has figures of the Apostles on the squinches of the domes, just visible through Greek graffiti. The **Chapel of the Exodus**, one of the oldest tombs, has the best-preserved paintings, including the Old Testament story of Moses leading the children of Israel out of Egypt, which is visible through some 9th-century graffiti. Another large **family tomb** (No 25) has a mural of Abraham sacrificing Isaac, and the smaller **Chapel of the Grapes** (Anaeed Al Ainab) is named after the images of grapevines that cover the walls.

The site guardian will guide you around the site and unlock the doors to the decorated tombs; he'll expect a tip of about LE5.

Monastery of Al Kashef   RUINS

(Deir Al Kashef; adult/student LE50/25 incl Necropolis of Al Bagawat; ⊘8.30am-4pm) Dominating the cliffs 2km to the north of the Necropolis of Al Bagawat (p270), the ruined Monastery of Al Kashef is strategically placed to overlook what was one of the most important crossroads of the Western Desert – the point where the Darb Al Ghabari from Dakhla crossed the Darb Al Arba'een (Forty Days Rd). The magnificent mud-brick remains date back to the early Christian era. Once five storeys high, much of it has collapsed, but you can see the tops of the arched corridors that criss-crossed the building.

To get here, walk or drive on the left-hand track from the Necropolis of Al Bagawat for about 2km.

Temple of Hibis   TEMPLE

(Map p271; adult/student LE80/40; ⊘8.30am-4pm) The town of Hebet ('the Plough', now corrupted into Hibis) was the capital of the oasis in antiquity, but all that remains today is the well-preserved limestone Temple of Hibis. Once sitting on the edge of a sacred lake, the temple was dedicated to Amun of Hibis (the local version of the god, who was sometimes given solar powers, becoming Amun-Ra).

Amun-Hibis appears here with his usual companions Mut and Khons. Look for reliefs in the **hypostyle hall** showing the god Seth battling with the evil serpent Apophis. There's also an avenue of sphinxes, a court and an inner sanctuary. Construction of the temple began during the 25th dynasty, though the decorations and a colonnade were added over the following 300 years. It's 2km north of town, just to the left of the main road; pick-ups (LE1) heading to Al Munira pass this way.

Temple of An Nadura   RUINS

(Map p271) Located on a hill to the right of the main road when heading north from Al Kharga town, the Temple of An Nadura has strategic views of the area and once doubled as a fortified lookout. It was built during the reign of Roman emperor Antoninus Pius (AD 138–61) to protect the oasis. Now badly ruined, the superb vistas here are ideal for sunset adulation.

Al Kharga Museum of Antiquities   MUSEUM

(Map p272; Sharia Gamal Abdel Nasser; adult/student LE25/15; ⊘8.30am-2pm) Designed to resemble the architecture of the nearby Necropolis of Al Bagawat, this two-storey museum is an old-school dusty trove of archaeological finds from around Al Kharga and Dakhla oases. The collection is small but fairly interesting and includes artefacts from prehistoric times through the Ottoman Era, featuring tools, jewellery, textiles and other objects that sketch out the cultural history of the region.

Tours

Mohsen Abd Al Moneem TOURS
(☑010-0180-6127) Mohsen Abd Al Moneem, from Al Kharga's tourist office (p273), is an experienced tour guide highly recommended by travellers and is a mine of information on the oasis. He can arrange private transport to sights and also to Luxor or Cairo.

Sameh Abdel Rihem TOURS
(☑010-0296-2192) If you really dig archaeology, Sameh Abdel Rihem is an expert on Kharga's antiquities and has a palpable love for surrounding sights both popular and esoteric.

Sleeping

Al Kharga's accommodation scene is slim pickings. Whichever hotel you choose, you'd better recalibrate your hotel expectations – maintenance and cleanliness don't seem to be top priority for any hotel owner here.

Kharga Oasis Hotel HOTEL $
(Map p272; ☑092-2792-1206, 012-6866-6299; Midan Nasser; r LE150, bungalow LE350) This homage to the 1960s' love of concrete blocks is your best bet for bedding down for the night in Al Kharga. The main building sports large rooms with decent beds and bathrooms, but opt for one of the traditionally styled domed bungalows out back, set around a tranquil and lush palm-filled garden (beware the mosquitoes) for a bit more style.

The hotel is government-run, so service and maintenance is haphazard at best. If you can't get through to the hotel on either of the contact numbers when booking, ring Mohsen Abd Al Moneam of the Al Kharga tourist office to book on your behalf. Breakfast is not included.

El Radwan Hotel HOTEL $
(Map p272; ☑092-2792-1716; off Sharia Gamal Abdel Nasser; s/d LE110/200) One of the only decent (and we use that word loosely) budget hotels in Al Kharga. The air-con mostly works, the water runs and the rooms pass muster if you need a cheap sleep. The fa-

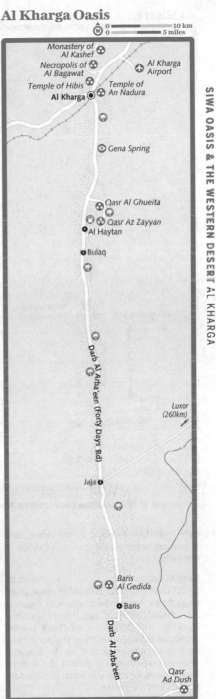

Al Kharga Oasis

0 — 10 km
0 — 5 miles

Monastery of Al Kashef
Necropolis of Al Bagawat
Al Kharga Airport
Temple of Hibis
Temple of An Nadura
Al Kharga

Gena Spring

Qasr Al Ghueita
Qasr Az Zayyan
Al Haytan

Bulaq

Darb Al Arba'een (Forty Days Rd)

Luxor (260km)

Jaja

Baris Al Gedida
Baris

Darb Al Arba'een

Qasr Ad Dush

Al Kharga

N
0   500 m
0   0.25 miles

Sol Y Mar Pioneers Hotel (400m);
Temple of Hibis (1km);
Temple of An Nadura (2km);
Necropolis of Al Bagawat (3km);
(5km);
Labakha (40km)

Aref
Midan Nasser
New Valley Tourist Office
Al Keneesa
Gamal Abdel Nasser
Al Gomhuriyya
Mosque
Port Said
Abdel Moniem Riad
Midan Abdel Moniem Riad
Abdel Moniem Riad
Gamal Abdel Nasser
Al Adel
Midan As Saha
Midan Basateen
Basateen
General Hospital
Port Said
Midan Mudares
Bus Station
Mohammed Farid
Qasr Al Ghueita (18km);
Qasr Az Zayyan (25km)
Mosque
OLD TOWN
Midan Sho'ala

cade looks like it's about to fall down, but it does get better on the inside. Breakfast is not included.

Qasr Al Bagawat
GUESTHOUSE **$$**
(☎012-0001-2669, 012-2695-5819; www.qasrelbagawat.com; opposite Necropolis of Al Bagawat; s/d half board €57/66; P) Small and charming eco-lodge with 22 domed mudbrick rooms decorated in local style. There is a hot spring for bathing, a lovely garden for shade and a Bedouin restaurant. The aim of the owners is to let guests completely relax, so no internet or TV in the rooms.

Sol Y Mar Pioneers Hotel
HOTEL **$$**
(☎092-2792-9751; Sharia Gamal Abdel Nasser; s/d/ste with half board US$60/80/100; @ 🛜 ⊠) This vast salmon-pink resort still offers the most comfortable and only properly clean rooms in Al Kharga. The staff is wonderfully friendly, the swimming pool is a godsend on a hot day, and the vast, lush gardens are a heavenly escape. Obvious wear and tear to the spacious rooms, however, makes it ridiculously overpriced.

The restaurant is the only place in town where you can count on getting alcohol.

Al Kharga

✖ Eating

There's a smattering of basic hole-in-the-wall restaurants around Midan Sho'ala, Sharia Al Adel and near Midan Basateen. Most are open for lunch and dinner. For breakfast, hit a falafel stand or a bakery.

Crepiano Cafe CRÊPES $
(Map p272; Midan Basateen; mains LE10-21; ⊘4pm-late; 🚗) Yep. It's a crêperie in Al Kharga. And the crêpes are rather good too. Choose from a plethora of ingredients (from chocolate to sausage and everything in between), seat yourself at a rickety table outside and survey the chaotic downtown Al Kharga action.

Al Ahram EGYPTIAN $
(Map p272; Sharia Basateen; mains LE15-40) This small, friendly place is a carnivore's favourite. It serves roast chicken and kofta (mincemeat and spices grilled on a skewer) accompanied by modest salads and vegetable dishes. The smell of grilled meat will lure you in. Look for the sign above with pictures of the pyramids (al ahram) to find it.

Pizza Ibn Al Balad PIZZA $
(Map p272; Midan Sho'ala; pizzas LE20-45; ⊘5pm-late; 🚗) If you're pining for a change from grilled meat and salad, make a beeline for this little place that rustles up some of the best *fiteer* (Egyptian flaky pizza) in the oases. Choose from cheese, vegetarian, tuna or beef toppings.

Wimpy EGYPTIAN $$
(Wembe; Map p272; Midan Basateen; meals LE20-35) This busy joint gets the thumbs up from Al Kharga locals for serving simple but tasty Egyptian feasts of grilled meats, salads, rice

and vegetable dishes. It's one of the town's most solid choices for a decent meal.

Estekoza EGYPTIAN $$
(Map p272; 🚗010-0091-7670; Sur As Saha Ash Shaabiya; mains LE20-45; ⊘noon-midnight) Popular restaurant selling excellent fresh fish – unlikely in the middle of the desert, but true.

🔒 Shopping

Midan Sho'ala Market MARKET
(Map p272; Midan Sho'ala) Stock up on all your fresh produce at this truly local market that runs through the alleyways off Midan Sho'ala. You'll find everything here from plastic-fantastic houseware to clucking chickens piled high in boxes. Traditional cobblers and metalworkers, and local dates by the barrelful, sit between stalls selling bawdy, cheap clothing and chintzy-tat.

It's brilliant and there's not a singing toy camel or pyramid snow-globe in sight. Come in the evening when half of Al Kharga seems to be here shopping.

ℹ Information

Banque du Caire (Map p272; off Sharia Gamal Abdel Nasser) Has an ATM.

National Bank of Egypt (Map p272; Sharia Gamal Abdel Nasser) Across from the museum; has an ATM.

New Valley Tourist Office (Map p272; 🚗010-0180-6127, 092-2792-1206; Midan Nasser; ⊘9am-2pm Sat-Thu)

Tourist Police (Map p272; 🚗092-2792-1367; Sharia Gamal Abdel Nasser) Next door to New Valley Tourist Office.

ℹ Getting There & Away

AIR
The airport is 5km north of town. The Petroleum Service Company usually has Monday and Thursday flights on a 15-seat plane, leaving Cairo at 8am and returning from Al Kharga at 3pm (LE600 one way, 1½ hours).

BUS
From the **bus station** (Map p272; 🚗092-2792-4587; Sharia Mohammed Farid), Upper Egypt Bus Co operates buses to Cairo (LE120, eight to 10 hours) daily at 9pm and 10pm. There are three services to Asyut (LE30, three to four hours) at 6am, 7am and 9am. The bus heading north to Dakhla Oasis (LE25, three hours) leaves at 2pm.

There's no direct bus service to Luxor. You can either catch a bus to Asyut and change there, or hire a private taxi.

THE WAY OF DUSTY DEATH ON THE DARB AL ARBA'EEN

Al Kharga Oasis sits atop what was once the only major African north–south trade route through Egypt's Western Desert: the notorious Darb Al Arba'een, or Forty Days Road. A 1721km track linking Fasher in Sudan's Darfur province with Asyut in the Nile Valley, this was one of Africa's great caravan trails, bringing the riches of Sudan – gold, ivory, skins, ostrich feathers and especially slaves – north to the Nile Valley and beyond to the Mediterranean.

The road is thought to date back to the Old Kingdom. The richness of the merchandise transported along this bleak track was such that protecting it was a priority. The Romans invested heavily here, building a series of fortresses – such as Qasr Ad Dush, the Monastery of Al Kashef and Qasr Al Ghueita – to tax the caravans and try to foil the frequent raids by desert tribespeople.

Despite the dangers, Darb Al Arba'een flourished until well into the Islamic era, by which time it was Egypt's main source of slaves. Untold numbers of human cargo died of starvation and thirst on the journey north. According to 19th-century European travellers, slavers travelled in the intense summer heat, preferring to expose their merchandise to dehydration on what British geographer GW Murray (author of the 1967 *Dare Me to the Desert*) called 'the way of dusty death', rather than risk the possibility of bronchitis and pneumonia from the cold desert winter.

Despite repeated attempts by the British to suppress the trade, slaves were brought north until Darfur became part of Sudan at the beginning of the 20th century. The Darb Al Arba'een withered, and today its route has been all but lost.

TAXI

Private taxis can get you to/from Luxor in about 3½ hours, using the new highway. This will set you back about LE800, but if you can get a few people to share costs it's an excellent alternative to the bus if you want to combine a trip to the Western Desert with the Nile Valley. If you want private transport to Cairo, a taxi will cost LE1350. Contact Mohsen Abd Al Moneem (p271) at the New Valley Tourist Office to arrange a car for you.

❶ Getting Around

Al Kharga oasis is fairly spread out, with the bus station in the south-central part of town, the minibus stand in the southeast near the souq, and most hotels a fair hike away from both. Microbuses (LE1) run along the main streets of Al Kharga, especially Sharia Gamal Abdel Nasser. Taxis for trips in town cost between LE5 and LE10.

Around Al Kharga

The most popular monuments near Al Kharga lie along the good asphalt road that stretches south to Baris, but there are a few intriguing, harder-to-reach destinations north of town. Though less visited, they are hands-down the best day trips you can make around the oasis.

All the ticketed monuments in this area are covered by the Kharga inclusive ticket (adult/student LE120/60).

◉ Sights

Qasr Al Ghueita FORT
(adult/student LE40/20; ⊘8am-4pm) The garrison's massive outer walls enclose a 25th-dynasty sandstone temple, dedicated to the Theban triad Amun, Mut and Khons. In later centuries, the fortress served as the perimeter for a village, with some houses surviving along the outer wall. Within the hypostyle hall a series of reliefs show Hapy, the pot-bellied Nile god, holding symbols of the nomes (provinces) of Upper Egypt.

Although you wouldn't guess it from the arid dusty landscape, during antiquity this area, some 18km south of Al Kharga, was the centre of a fertile agricultural community renowned for its grapes and winemaking – the name means 'Fortress of the Small Garden'. Settlement here has been dated back to the Middle Kingdom period when it was known as Perousekh. Today two sturdy forts from its later Roman period survive here, lording-it-up over the plains, probably utilised as garrison buildings for troops.

From the main road to Baris, an asphalted track leads 2km to this imposing mud-brick fortress. If you don't have your own vehicle, you can get to the fort from Al Kharga by taking a microbus heading for Baris (LE8) or a covered pick-up going to Bulaq (LE2.50). From the highway an asphalt road links the forts, running up the desert incline for 3km to Qasr Al Ghueita. It's an extremely long, hot hike if you're on foot – be sure to take plenty of water.

Qasr Al Zayyan   FORT
(adult/student LE40/20) One of the major monuments of the Kharga Oasis is the Grae-co-Roman temple of Qasr Al Zayyan, in the ancient village of Takhoneourit. The town, mostly unexcavated, was an important stop on the desert route to Esna. The small sand-stone temple, part of a fortress, was dedicat-ed to Amon-Hibis, and consists of a court leading to the sanctuary with a beautiful cult niche, and a chamber with a staircase to the roof.

Baris Al Gedida   ARCHITECTURE
The mud-brick houses of Baris Al Gedida lie about 2km north of the original town. Has-san Fathy, Egypt's most influential modern architect, designed the houses using tradi-tional methods and materials, intending Baris Al Gedida to be a model for other new settlements. Work stopped at the outbreak of the Six Day War of 1967, and only two houses and some public spaces have ever been completed.

The site was abandoned and never lived in.

Qasr Ad Dush   FORT
(adult/student LE40/20; ⊙8am-5pm) About 13km to the southeast of Baris, Qasr Ad Dush is an imposing Roman temple-fortress completed around AD 177 on the site of the ancient town of Kysis. A 1st-century sand-stone temple abutting the fortress was ded-icated to Isis and Serapis. The gold decora-tions that once covered parts of the temple and earned it renown have long gone, but there is still some decoration on the inner stone walls.

Dush was a border town strategically placed at the intersection of five desert tracks and was one of the southern gate-ways to Egypt. It may also have been used to guard the Darb Al Dush, an east–west track to the Esna and Edfu temples in the Nile Val-ley. As a result it was solidly built and heavi-ly garrisoned, with four or five more storeys lying underground.

★ Qasr Al Labakha   HISTORIC SITE
Set amid a desertscape of duney desola-tion, Qasr Al Labakha is a micro-oasis some 40km north of Al Kharga. Scattered among sandy swells and rocky shelves are the re-mains of a towering four-storey **Roman for-tress**, two **temples** and a vast **necropolis** where more than 500 mummies have been unearthed (you can still see human remains in the tombs). Day trips to Labakha can be arranged by Al Kharga's tourist office (p273), with prices starting at around US$150 per vehicle.

Ain Umm Al Dabadib   FORT
FREE This impressive fort sits on a ridge rising grandly out of the desert plains about 20km west of Qasr Al Labakha. It has one of the most complex underground aque-duct systems built in this area by the Ro-mans. Trips here qualify as serious desert excursions and you'll require a 4WD with experienced drivers, who can be contacted through the Al Kharga tourist office. You are only allowed to be here until sunset.

DAKHLA OASIS
📞092 / POP 90,000
With more than a dozen fertile hamlets sprinkled along the Western Desert circuit road, Dakhla lives up to most visitors' ro-mantic expectations of oasis life.

In Neolithic times, Dakhla was the site of a vast lake, and rock paintings show that el-ephants, zebras and ostriches wandered its shores. In Pharaonic times, Dakhla retained several settlements and was a fertile land producing wine, fruit and grains. The Ro-mans, and later Christians, left their mark by building over older settlements, and dur-ing medieval times the towns were fortified to protect them from Bedouin and Arab raids. Al Qasr is the best preserved of these towns – and among the most enchanting places – anywhere in the Western Desert.

The slumping mud-brick villages and palmaries, speckled with hot springs, that surround Mut capture the essence of slow-paced oasis life and are some of the Western Desert's most evocative sights.

Mut
At the centre of the oasis lies the town of Mut, named after the god Amun's consort, settled since Pharaonic times. Now a mod-ern Egyptian town of squat block concrete buildings, it has decent facilities and makes the most convenient base for travellers.

Dakhla Oasis

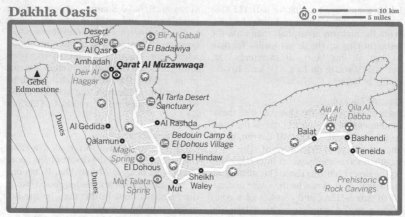

You will, however, have a richer experience of Dakhla by staying in or around Al Qasr. Mut's slumping old town remnants and the proximity of the palm groves help to give it a touch of charm – though only a touch.

◉ Sights

The labyrinth of mud-brick houses and lanes that winds up the slopes of the hill is definitely worth exploring, even if you may sometimes stumble into a trash heap.

Old Town of Mut   RUINS
(Map p278) Old Mut's visitors lived in fear of raiding Bedouin, so very few houses have outside windows, to protect against intruders and heat and dust. The labyrinthine streets had a similar purpose. On the top is Mut's old citadel (the original town centre), with great views of the new town and the oasis, and the desert beyond.

Ethnographic Museum   MUSEUM
(Map p278; ☑ 010-1484-4100, 012-2491-6379; Sharia As Salam; LE10; ⊙ on request) These days Dakhla's wonderful museum is only opened on request: ask at the tourist office (or call) and Omar Ahmad will arrange a time for your visit with the museum's manager, Ibrahim Kamel. The museum is laid out as a traditional home, with different areas for men, women and visitors. Displays of clothing, baskets, jewellery and other domestic items give an insight into oasis life.

☞ Tours

Most hotels can organise a tour of the oasis. A typical day trip includes a drive through the nearby dunes, a visit to a spring and a tour of **Al Qasr** with visits to **Al Gedida** and **Qalamun**, villages with Ottoman and modern houses, along the way. Prices start at around LE500 per car. Alternatively, Mut's taxi drivers can drive you to outlying sights for around LE400 for a full day or LE200 for a half day. If you want to go further afield, check with the tourist office to confirm whether the person taking you has the necessary permits – Dakhla is one of the closest oases to Gilf Kebir, but permits to go there are no longer issued.

Bedouin Camp &
El Dohous Village   OUTDOORS
(☑ 092-2785-0480, 010-622-1359; www.dakhla bedouins.com; Mut to Al Qasr Hwy, El Dohous; 2hr LE200, full day & overnight from LE1200) The owners of this camp are Bedouin brothers and camel experts. They can arrange short camel trips into the desert around Dakhla, but the longer trips are no longer allowed.

🛏 Sleeping

El Forsan Hotel   HOTEL $
(☑ 092-2782-1343; Sharia Al Wadi; s/d LE180/250, bungalow without air-con LE120/175; ❄ 🛜) Ignore the creepy horror-movie corridor as you enter – El Forsan is the best budget deal in town. The place is well kept and even has duvets in the air-con rooms, while out back in the garden are domed, mud-brick (rather worn) bungalows. Friendly manager Zaqaria whips up great breakfasts.

Anwar Hotel   HOTEL $
(☑ 092-2782-0070; Sharia Basateen; s/d/tr from LE100/150/220; 🛜) Friendly Mr Anwar runs this family establishment with gusto and

offers flexibly priced, relatively clean rooms with shared or private bathroom options. Noise from the nearby mosque can be an issue, and the younger Anwars are a bit over-eager to sell their tours.

El Negoom Hotel
HOTEL $

(☑ 092-2782-0014; s/d LE100/190; ☎) On a quiet street behind the tourist office, north of Sharia As Sawra Al Khadra, this friendly hotel has a homey lobby and a span of sparsely furnished and rather old-fashioned but tidy little abodes with bathrooms – some even have TV.

Bedouin Camp & El Dohous Village
HOTEL $$

(☑ 092-2785-0480, 010-0622-1359; www.dakhla bedouins.com; El Dohous; s/d half board LE250/400; P ☎ ☀) El Dohous Village, 3km from Mut centre, has a huge variety of domed and curvy rooms that give off good vibes, all decorated with local crafts. The hilltop restaurant has outstanding views, there are plenty of cushioned chill-out areas strewn about the place and there's a hot spring on-site. The friendliness of the staff is just one more reason to stay.

X Eating

There is no fancy dining in Mut, but there is some decent, fresh food (mostly of the chicken/kebab/rice variety). Most falafel takeaways close by noon.

El Forsan Cafe
EGYPTIAN $

(☑ 092-282-1343, El Forsan Hotel, Sharia Al Wadi, meals LE40-60; ☑) Behind El Forsan Hotel (you can walk through the hotel to enter), this surprisingly lush patch of grass is home to a garden cafe that serves up mammoth feasts of simple but fresh Egyptian flavours, including all manner of *mahshi* (stuffed vegetables) and the usual grilled meat. Locals hang out drinking tea here until the wee hours of the morning.

Ahmed Hamdy's Restaurant
EGYPTIAN $

(☑ 092-2782-0767; Sharia As Sawra Al Khadra; meals LE30-50) On the main road into town is Ahmed Hamdy's popular place serving delicious chicken, kebabs, vegetables and a few other small dishes inside or on the terrace. The freshly squeezed lime juice is excellent, as is the shisha.

Said Shihad
EGYPTIAN $

(Sharia As Sawra Al Khadra; meals LE30-55) Owner Said is on to a good thing here: grilling up a nightly meat-centric feast to a dedicated following of hungry locals. The shish kebab is the thing to go for – perfectly succulent and served with potatoes in a tomato sauce, rice and beans.

Fateer Al Wadi
EGYPTIAN $$

(Sharia As Sawra Al Khadra; mains LE40-70; ⊙ 6am-10pm) Fresh-from-the-oven sweet or savoury *fiteer* (flaky pizza), made to order by a friendly crew.

ℹ Information

Bank Misr (Sharia Al Wadi; ⊙ 8.30am-2pm Sun-Thu) Has an ATM, exchanges cash and makes cash advances on Visa and MasterCard.

Tourist Office (☑ 092-2782-1685, mobile 010-0180-6127; Sharia As Sawra Al Khadra; ⊙ 8am-3pm) Friendly tourist office director Omar Ahmad can help with all your oasis queries.

Tourist Police (☑ 092-2782-1687; Sharia 10th of Ramadan)

ℹ Getting There & Away

BUS

From Mut's **bus station** (☑ 092-2782-4366; Sharia Al Wadi), Upper Egypt Bus Co runs buses to Cairo (LE115, 10 hours) via Al Kharga Oasis (LE25, two to three hours) and Asyut (LE70, five hours) at 7pm and 7.30pm.

You can also travel to Cairo via Farafra Oasis (LE35, four hours) and Bahariya Oasis (LE60, seven hours) at 8pm.

All buses pick up passengers from the bus station first and then at Midan Al Tahrir, across the roundabout from the bus **booking office** kiosk.

MICROBUS

At the time of writing foreign travellers were not allowed to take microbuses between the oases.

ℹ Getting Around

Most places in Dakhla are linked by crowded pick-ups or microbuses, but working out where they all go requires a degree in astrophysics. Those heading to **Al Qasr** (LE2.50) depart from Sharia As Sawra Al Khadra. You can take pick-ups to **Balat and Bashendi** from in front of the hospital for LE2.50. Most others depart from the servees station on Sharia Tamir.

It may prove easier on occasion to bargain for a 'special' pick-up. A taxi to Al Qasr should cost LE100 with waiting time.

Mut

SIWA OASIS & THE WESTERN DESERT AROUND MUT

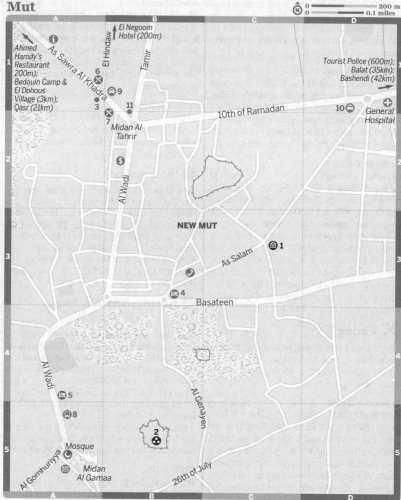

El Negoom Hotel (200m)

Ahmed Hamdy's Restaurant 200m); Bedouin Camp & El Dohous Village (3km); Qasr (21km)

As Sawra Al Khadra
El Hindaw
Tamir

Tourist Police (600m); Balat (35km); Bashendi (42km)

10th of Ramadan

General Hospital

Midan Al Tahrir

Al Wadi

NEW MUT

As Salam

Basateen

Al Wadi

Al Genayen

26th of July

Mosque
Midan Al Gamaa

Al Gomhuriyya

Around Mut

A few kilometres past the southern or western end of Mut you can have a roll around in sand dunes, which, while not the most spectacular in the desert, are easy to reach for people without their own transport (if on foot, count on at least an hour's walk each way). Almost every hotel and restaurant in Mut offers day trips that include a sand-dune stop. Sunset camel rides out to the dunes can also be arranged. There is an inclusive ticket available for the sights in Al Dakhla (adult/student LE120/60).

Balat

For a captivating glimpse into life during medieval times, pay a visit to the Islamic village of Balat, 35km east of Mut. Built during the era of the Mamluks and Turks on a site that dates back to the Old Kingdom,

Mut

Sights

1 Ethnographic Museum C3
2 Old Town of Mut B5

Activities, Courses & Tours

3 Dabuka Expeditions A1

Sleeping

4 Anwar Hotel B3
5 El Forsan Hotel A4

Eating

El Forsan Cafe .... (see 5)
6 Fateer Al Wadi A1
7 Said Shihad B2

Transport

8 Bus Station A5
9 Pick-Ups to Al Qasr B1
10 Pick-Ups to Balat & Bashendi D1
11 Upper Egypt Bus Co Booking Office B2

charismatic winding lanes weave through low-slung corridors past Gaudí-like moulded benches. Palm fronds are still used for shelter as smoothly rounded walls ease into each other. The tiny doors here were designed to keep houses cool and confuse potential invaders. A guide will happily take you onto the roof of one of the three-storey mudbrick houses for commanding views (a small tip is expected).

Sights

Qila Al Dabba RUINS

(adult/student LE40/20; 8.30am-4pm) Qila Al Dabba is Balat's ancient necropolis. The five *mastabas* (mud-brick structures above tombs that were the basis for later pyramids), the largest of which stands more than 10m high, date back to the 6th dynasty. Four are ruined, but one has been restored and is open to the public. To get here, take the dirt track that meets the main road 200m east of Balat and head north. The necropolis is 3.5km along the road, past Ain Al Asil.

Originally all five *mastabas* would have been clad in fine limestone, with three thought to have belonged to important Old Kingdom governors of the oasis. If the *mastaba* is locked, the site guardian can usually be found in the nearby buildings.

Getting There & Away

To get to Balat, take a pick-up from near the general hospital in Mut (LE2).

Bashendi

This small village of picturesque mud-brick houses to the north of the main Dakhla–Al Kharga road takes its name from Pasha Hindi, the medieval sheikh buried nearby. Five Graeco-Roman tombs were discovered here in 1947, which put the village on the map.

Sights

Tomb of Pasha Hindi SHRINE

(adult/student incl Tomb of Kitines LE30/20; 8.30am-4pm) The Tomb of Pasha Hindi is covered by an Islamic-era dome, which sits over a Roman structure, clearly visible from inside the building. Locals make pilgrimages to pray for the saint's intercession.

Tomb of Kitines TOMB

(adult/student incl Tomb of Pasha Hindi LE30/20; 8.30am-4pm) This sandstone tomb was occupied by Senussi soldiers during WWI and by a village family after that. Nevertheless, some funerary reliefs have survived and show the 2nd-century AD notable meeting the gods Min, Seth and Shu.

Carpet-Making Cooperative CULTURAL CENTRE

(LE3; 9am-1pm Sun-Thu) In Bashendi's carpet-making cooperative you can see rugs being woven and browse through the showroom.

Rock Carvings HISTORIC SITE

Carved into the weird rock formations 45km towards Al Kharga, where two important caravan routes once met, are prehistoric petroglyphs of camels, giraffes and tribal symbols. The site has recently suffered from the attentions of less-scrupulous travellers who have all but ruined most of these curious images with their own graffiti. 4WD and a good driver are necessary to get here.

Getting There & Away

It is easiest to take a taxi from Mut, or try the occasional minibus going in Bashendi's direction.

Al Qasr

One of the must-see sights in the western oases is the extraordinary medieval/Ottoman town of Al Qasr, which lies on the edge of

LOCAL KNOWLEDGE

KNOW YOUR DUNES

Classification of sand dune shapes was made in the 1970s, when scientists examined photographs of dune fields taken from space. Of the five typical shapes, four are found in Egypt.

Seif

Named for the Arabic word for sword, these long dunes form parallel to the prevailing wind. They are primarily found in the Great Sand Sea and the northern Western Desert. Usually on the move, they will even fall down an escarpment, reforming at its base.

Barchan

These are crescent-shaped dunes, with a slip face on one side. They are as wide as they are long and are usually found in straight lines with flat corridors between them. They can travel as far as 19m in one year. They are predominant in Al Kharga and Dakhla Oases and in the Great Sand Sea.

Star

Created by wind blowing in different directions, these dunes are usually found alone. Instead of moving, they tend to build up within a circle. They are rare in Egypt.

Crescent

These hill-like dunes, also called whale-back dunes, form when smaller dunes collide and piggyback on one another. With their sides pointing in different directions, these distinctive shapes can be seen between Al Kharga and Dakhla Oases.

lush vegetation at the foot of pink limestone cliffs marking the northern edge of the oasis. Portions of the old village have been thoughtfully restored to provide a glimpse of how other oasis towns looked before the New Valley development projects had their way with them; the effect is pure magic. Several hundred people still live in the town that not so long ago was home to several thousand.

Al Qasr is also a prime spot to romp around in the desert without a guide. Just north of town the plateau is textured with shallow, sandy wadis (valleys or dry riverbeds) that weave around rocky benches and weirdly hewn hills. The ground is littered with fossils, including sharks' teeth.

◉ Sights

Al Qasr's mud-brick maze of an old town is built on the ancient foundations of a Roman city and is thought to be one of the oldest inhabited areas of the oases. Most of what you can see today dates to the Ottoman period (1516–1798), although the creaky, picturesque labyrinth of narrow, covered streets harks back to its ancient origins. During its heyday, this was probably the capital of the Dakhla Oasis, easily protected by barring the fort's quartered streets.

The winding lanes manage to remain cool in the scalding summer and also serve to protect their inhabitants from desert sandstorms. Entrances to old houses can be clearly seen and some are marked by beautiful lintels – acacia beams situated above the door. Carved with the names of the carpenter and the owner of the house, the date and a verse from the Quran, these decorative touches are wonderfully preserved. The size of the houses here and the surviving fragments of decoration suggest a puzzling level of wealth and importance given to this town by the Ottomans.

There are 37 lintels in the village, the earliest of which dates to the early 16th century. One of the finest is above the Tomb of Sheikh Nasr Ad Din inside the old mosque, which is marked by a restored 12th-century mud-brick minaret. Adjoining it is Nasr Ad Din Mosque, with a 21m-high minaret. Several buildings have been renovated, including the old madrassa, a school where Islamic law was taught and which doubled as a town hall and courthouse: prisoners were tied to a stake near the entrance.

Also of interest is the restored House of Abu Nafir. A dramatic pointed arch at the entrance frames a huge studded wooden door. Built of mud brick, and on a grander scale than the surrounding houses, it incorporates massive blocks from an earlier structure, possibly a Ptolemaic temple, decorated with hieroglyphic reliefs.

Other features of the town include the **pottery factory**, a **blacksmith's forge**, a **waterwheel**, an **olive press** and a huge **old corn mill** that has been fully restored to function with Flintstone-like efficiency when its shaft is rotated. Near the entrance is the **Ethnographic Museum** (LE20; ⊙ 9am-sunset). Occupying Sherif Ahmed's house, which itself dates back to 1785, the museum's everyday objects try to give life to the empty buildings around them.

The Supreme Council for Antiquities has taken responsibility for the town, but doesn't charge an entrance fee. It's helpful to hook up with one of the Antiquities guards (if they're about) for a tour; they will expect a 'donation' of LE10. There are signposts scattered around the alleys but some of the highlights are tricky to find. A note to photographers: midday is actually a good time to take pictures here, since that's when the most light penetrates the canyon-like corridors.

For what may be the most sweeping vistas in any of the oases, hike to the top of the high bluffs that rise from the plateau – just choose the massive ramp of sand that looks most promising and trek on up! Running back down hundreds of feet of sand is an instant regression to childhood glee. From Al Qasr, it takes about two hours to reach the top, and longer if you dawdle, so bring enough water and snacks for the round trip. If the moon is full, set out before sunset and return by moonlight.

If you have your own vehicle, or driver, there are a handful of sights on the secondary road between Al Qasr and Mut that are worthy of a visit. The ruined village of **Amhadah** has several tombs nearby dating from the 2nd century. Further along towards Mut, the road passes through the sleepy villages of **Al Gedida** and **Qalamun**, both of which are home to plenty of traditional mud-brick architecture.

Bir Al Gabal   SPRING
(LE30) Set among breathtaking desert scenery, Bir Al Gabal is a gorgeous place for a soak. During the day in winter and spring any ambience here is overwhelmed by day-tripping school groups and blaring music. Come in the evening when most people have left and the stars blaze across the sky.

A sign marks the turn-off 20km north of Mut, from where it's about another 5km to the springs. It is now part of the Camp Bir Al Gabal.

If you do arrive during a busy period, there's a more serene natural spring about 500m before Bir Al Gabal on the right, concealed behind a brick pump house.

🛏 Sleeping

Al Qasr Hotel   HOSTEL $
(☎ 092-2787-6013; Main Hwy; r with shared bathroom LE90) This old backpacker favourite sits above a cafe-restaurant on the main highway through Al Qasr. Rooms are as basic as they get, but there's a breezy upstairs communal sitting area where you can play games or relax, and for LE15 you can sleep on a mattress on the roof. Owner Mohamed has a long history of fine hospitality.

Camp Bir Al Gabal   GUESTHOUSE $
(☎ 012-1043 3045; s/d LE160/200; 🅿 🛜 ♨) This guesthouse has 12 simple domed rooms with clean bathrooms in mud-brick chalets. The chalets are set in a delightful garden on the edge of the desert, but the real attraction is the hot spring Bir Al Gabal. Mud treatments are available on request. Spectacular surroundings.

★ Sosal Center for
Ethnic Arts and Crafts   GUESTHOUSE $$
(☎ 012-2323-2247; www.mervetazmi.com; r per person LE250; 🅿 🛜) This lovely villa with five bedrooms is a delightful place to stay for a few days. The house has a kitchen, comfortable living room with a fireplace, and a garden for common use. Next door is a basketry-weaving workshop. The place is self-catering, but breakfast (LE25), lunch (LE85) and dinner (LE95) can be arranged by women from the village nearby.

This is a great place to go for walks in the village, the countryside and the nearby sand dunes. It's next door to the Al Tarfa Desert Sanctuary (p282). The owner Mervat likes guests to spend an hour a day interacting with the villagers by drawing, playing football, chatting and other similar activities.

★ Al Tarfa Desert
Sanctuary   BOUTIQUE HOTEL $$$
(☎ 092-2785-1492, 010-0100-1109; www.altarfa. net; Al Qasr; s/d full board €360/440; 🅿 🛜 ♨) Taking the high end to unheard-of heights in Dakhla, Al Tarfa is flat-out desert-fabulous.

LOCAL KNOWLEDGE

ETIQUETTE FOR A SPRING SOAK

There's nothing better after a day's rambling along the dusty tracks of the oases or through the hot desert sands than a soak in one of the many natural springs.

If you're planning to bathe in the public waterholes that speckle the oases, it's important to be mindful of generally accepted spring etiquette:

➡ If local men are bathing, women should wait until they finish before entering the water.

➡ At springs within towns, women should wear a baggy T-shirt and shorts or, preferably, pants over their bathing suit. Use your best (conservative) judgment, and don't swim if the vibe is leery.

➡ Men should leave the Speedos at home.

The traditionally inspired decor is superbly tasteful and impeccably rendered, down to the smallest detail – from the embroidered bedspreads that look like museum-quality pieces to the mud-plastered walls that don't show a single crack. Private transfers to the hotel's isolated site, north of Al Qasr, can be arranged.

Even the golden dunes that flow behind the resort seem like they've been landscaped to undulating perfection. Each suite is unique, the pool is like a liquid sapphire and the spa features massage therapists brought in from Thailand.

Desert Lodge BOUTIQUE HOTEL **$$$**
(☑ 092-2772-7061, 02-2690-5240; www.desert-lodge.net; s/d/tr half board US$90/150/210; @ ⊛) This thoughtfully designed, ecofriendly mud-brick fortress of a lodge crowns the hilltop at the eastern edge of Al Qasr, overlooking the old town. Rooms are decorated in minimalist desert style incorporating tranquil pastel blues, pinks and greens. The restaurant is adequate, and there is also a bar, a private hot spring and a painting studio on the desert's edge.

🛈 Getting There & Away

Pick-ups to Al Qasr leave from opposite Said Shihad restaurant in Mut and cost LE2. Alternatively, take a microbus from Mut's microbus stand (LE2).

Deir Al Haggar & Around

Deir Al Haggar TEMPLE
(adult/student LE40/20; ☺ 8.30am-5pm) This restored sandstone temple is one of the most complete Roman monuments in Dakhla. Dedicated to the Theban triad of Amun, Mut and Khons, as well as Horus (who can be seen with a falcon's head), it was built between the reigns of Nero (AD 54–68) and Domitian (AD 81–96). Some relief panels are quite well preserved, though most are covered in bird poop.

If you look carefully in the adjacent Porch of Titus you can see the names of the entire team of Gerhard Rohlfs, the 19th-century desert explorer, carved into the wall. Also visible are the names of famous desert travellers Edmonstone, Drovetti and Houghton.

The temple is signposted 7km west of Al Qasr; from the turn-off it's a further 5km.

★ **Qarat Al Muzawwaqa** TOMB
(2km before Deir Al Haggar; adult/student LE40/20; ☺ 8am-5pm) These tombs were rediscovered by the Egyptian archaeologist Ahmed Fakri in 1971 and some have since been restored, including the tomb of **Oziri (Petosiris)** and **Badi Baset (Petubastis)**, the only ones open to the public. Featuring spectacular colours and zodiac ceilings, they are particularly interesting for their crossover between Graeco-Roman and Pharaonic styles.

More than 200 mummies were found here, but it seems the 19th-century travellers were quite happy to take them away as souvenirs.

FARAFRA OASIS

📞 092 / POP 21,930

Blink and you might just miss dusty Farafra, the smallest of the Western Desert's oases. Its exposed location made it prone to frequent attacks by Libyans and Bedouin tribes, many of whom eventually settled in the oasis and now make up much of the population. In recent years, the government has been increasing its efforts to revitalise this region, and the production of olives, dates, apricots, guavas, figs, oranges, apples and sunflowers is slowly growing. The original population of Farfarunis, about 9000, has more than doubled with an influx of Egyptians from the Nile Valley to work in agriculture.

Since the 2011 revolution, few tourists make it to Farafra, preferring to arrange the White Desert trip in Baharia, making Farafra a very sleepy place indeed.

Qasr Al Farafra

The only real town in Farafra Oasis, Qasr Al Farafra remains a barely developed speck on the Western Desert circuit. The town's tumbledown Roman fortress was originally built to guard this part of the desert caravan route, though these days all it has to show for it is a mound of rubble. Some small mudbrick houses still stand in the back alleys, their doorways secured with medieval peg locks and their walls painted with verses of the Quran.

The main reason for a stopover here is a trip to the White Desert (Sahra Al Beida), but independent travellers will find tours much easier to organise from Bahariya Oasis.

◎ Sights

Take a stroll through the palm gardens just west of 'downtown'. They're truly lovely, and full of activity during the date harvest (September/October).

★ Badr's Museum   MUSEUM
(Map p284; ☑ 092 751-0091; off Sharia Al Mardasa; donation LE20; ⊙ 8.30am-sunset) Badr Abdel Moghny is a passionate self-taught artist whose gift to his town has become its only real sight. Badr's Museum showcases his work, much of which records traditional oasis life but in the most inventive way. Badr, who seems unstoppable, continues to experiment, adding a sculpture garden on his roof and working with pigments found in his surroundings.

His distinctive style of painting and sculpture in mud, stone and sand has won him foreign admirers; he exhibited successfully in Europe in the early 1990s and later in Cairo.

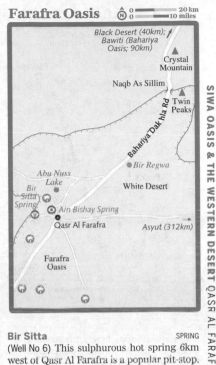

Farafra Oasis

Bir Sitta   SPRING
(Well No 6) This sulphurous hot spring 6km west of Qasr Al Farafra is a popular pit-stop. Water gushes into a jacuzzi-sized concrete pool and then spills out into a larger tank. This is a good place for a night-time soak under the stars.

Ain Bishay   SPRING
The Roman spring of Ain Bishay bubbles forth in the desert 10km southwest of Qasr Al Farafra. It has been developed into an irrigated grove of date palms together with citrus, olive, apricot and carob trees, and is a cool haven.

Abu Nuss Lake   LAKE
During the stifling heat of summer, a plunge in Abu Nuss Lake offers instant relief from hot and sweaty afternoons. There's some interesting bird life here, too. The turn-off for the lake is approximately 11km north of Qasr Al Farafra along the main road to Dakhla.

⟲ Tours

Farafra is nearer than Bahariya to the White Desert, but there is a very limited choice of desert outfits. A dearth of tourists since the 2011 revolution also means that it's not likely independent travellers will find others to hook up with for a tour. The Al Badawiya

Qasr Al Farafra

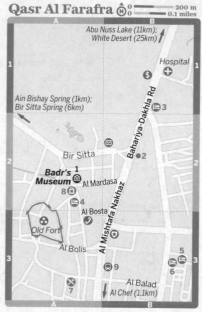

0 | 200 m
0 | 0.1 miles

Abu Nuss Lake (11km);
White Desert (25km)

Hospital

Ain Bishay Spring (1km);
Bir Sitta Spring (6km)

Bahariya-Dakhla Rd

Bir Sitta

Badr's
Museum 1
Al Mardasa

Al Bosta

Al Mishtara Nakhaz

Old Fort

Al Bolis

Al Balad
Al Chef (1.1km)

and Rahala Safari hotels can usually organise excursions around Farafra and the White Desert, with prices starting at around LE1000 per vehicle; however, with the tourism slow-down it would be prudent to contact them before your arrival to check prices and tour possibilities.

🛏 Sleeping

★ Rahala Safari Hotel
HOTEL $
(☎ 092-251-0440, 010-0306-4733; www.rahala-safari.com; s/d LE200/250; P✿🛜) This small, delightful hotel was built by the Farafaruni brothers, with domed rooms all equipped with TV, air-con, wi-fi and bathrooms. The rooms are set around a courtyard and the restaurant is Arab style, serving home-cooked food. The extremely helpful hosts also organise expert trips in the desert around the White and Black Deserts. Very warm welcome.

Beit Ad Diyafa Al Asdiqa
GUESTHOUSE $
(Badr's Guesthouse; Map p284; ☎01-2170-4710, 092-751-0091; Goshna; per person incl food & desert safari LE500; P🛜) Badr Abdel Moghny, the man who created Badr's Museum (p283), had another dream: to make a small guesthouse where creative people can find

a peaceful home away from home. This mud-brick house has six cosy rooms set in a delightful garden with local fruit trees and cacti. There's also a large room with space to create.

Al Waha Hotel
HOTEL $
(☎ 012-2720-0387; off Sharia Al Mardasa; r LE75, with shared bathroom LE60) This small, spartan hotel has acceptably clean, well-worn rooms with faux-oriental rugs. In summer the cement walls throb with heat. Newer, more comfortable rooms with kitchens and bathrooms are being prepared for when the tourists return.

Al Badawiya Safari & Hotel
HOTEL $$
(☎ 092-751-0060; www.badawiya.com; Bahariya-Dakhla Rd; s/d/tr €30/40/50, ste €40-75; P🛜🏊) The brothers who run Al Badawiya dominate Farafra tourism with their hotel and safari outfit. Comfortable domed rooms have plenty of traditional Bedouin style, though they could do with a lick of maintenance. There's a refreshing (albeit small) pool and a restaurant. The White and Western Desert tours are thoroughly professional.

🍴 Eating

Eating choices are limited in Farafra. Anyone looking for a change from the chicken/grilled meat combo is pretty much out of luck. Al Badawiya Safari & Hotel (p284) also has a restaurant.

Samir Restaurant
EGYPTIAN $

(Sharia Al Balad; meals LE30-50; ⊙10am-11pm) Samir's is the most atmospheric choice of Farafra's admittedly few dining options. Set meals of grilled meat and chicken are the same as the other restaurants in town, but your table comes complete with the fine-dining flourish of a tablecloth.

Al Chef
EGYPTIAN $

(☑010-2725-84374; Ad Da'ira Al Gadid; dishes LE20-45; ⊙noon-midnight) Road-stop restaurant on the way to Dakhla serving good basics like chicken, kofta, stews and vegetables. Very lurid decor.

🛍 Shopping

Farafra Bazaar
ARTS & CRAFTS

(☑012-8615-2165, 010-2514-5062; opposite Badr's Museum) Hany has just about the only crafts shop left in these oases. He sells goat-wool, hand-knitted sweaters and socks, rag rugs, pottery and jewellery, all handmade.

ℹ Information

For tourist information, contact Mohsen Abdel Monem at the tourist office (p277) in Mut (Dakhla).

Bank Misr (Bahariya–Dakhla Rd, ⊙9am-2pm Sun-Thu) Has an ATM, though best not to depend on it.

Tourist Police (Sharia Al Mishtafa Nakhaz) No telephone.

DANGERS & ANNOYANCES

The tourist police are strict in Farafra and check everybody coming in and out of the oasis. The official line is that foreigners should only stay in Al Badawiya Safari & Hotel, but in reality you can stay wherever you like.

ℹ Getting There & Away

There are Upper Egypt Bus Co buses from Farafra to Cairo (LE105, eight to 10 hours) via Bahariya (LE30, three hours) at 10am and 10pm. Buses from Farafra to Dakhla (LE30, four hours) originate in Cairo and leave around 2pm or 3pm and around 2am. Tickets are bought from the conductor.

Foreigners are not allowed to travel between oases on microbuses. You must take a bus or taxi.

FARAFRA OASIS TO BAHARIYA OASIS

Al Hayz

With a natural spring to cool off in and an interesting local museum where tours are given in Arabic and English, the small oasis of Al Hayz, 45km south of Bawiti, is a welcome break on the road between Farafra and Bahariya.

★ Ain Gomma
SPRING

Ain Gomma is one of the most magnificent springs around. Cool, crystal-clear water gushes into this small pool surrounded by the vast desert expanse, and the funkiest cafe in all of the oases sits beside it. Situated near the town of Al Hayz, you can take a Dakhla-bound bus here, but it's difficult to get back without your own transport. Many safari trips to the White Desert will stop here en route.

★ Al Hayz Water Education Center
MUSEUM

(www.facebook.com/El-Heiz-Water-Education-Center-726503367516623; Al Hayz Oasis; adult/student LE15/10; ⊙10am-4pm) This water museum is a real treat, with an informative introduction to Egypt's water resources and problems, the geology of the Western Desert, traditional agriculture and architecture in the oases, and what needs to be done to deal with water shortage. The museum is housed in a wonderful example of sustainable architecture, in basalt and rammed earth.

Black Desert

The change in the desert floor from beige to black, 50km south of Bawiti, signals the beginning of the Black Desert (Şahra Suda). Formed by the erosion of the mountains, which have spread a layer of black powder and stones over the peaks and plateaus, it looks like a landscape straight out of Hades. The Black Desert is a popular stop-off for tours running out of Bahariya Oasis and is usually combined with a White Desert tour.

Other sights in the region include Gebel Gala Siwa, a pyramid-shaped mountain that was formerly a lookout post for

DON'T MISS

EGYPT'S MIND-BENDING WHITE DESERT

Upon first glimpse of the 300-sq-km **White Desert National Park** (Sahra Al Beida; US$5), you'll feel like Alice through the looking-glass. About 20km northeast of Farafra, on the east side of the road, blinding-white chalk rock spires sprout almost supernaturally from the ground, each frost-coloured lollipop licked into a surreal landscape of familiar and unfamiliar shapes by the dry desert winds.

These sculptural formations are best viewed at sunrise or sunset, when the sun lights them with orangey-pink hues, or under a full moon, which gives the landscape a ghostly Arctic appearance. The sand around the outcroppings is littered with quartz and different varieties of deep-black iron pyrites, as well as small fossils. On the west side of the Farafra–Bahariya highway, away from the wind-hewn sculptures, chalk towers called inselbergs burst from the desert floor into a spectacular white canyon. Between them run grand boulevards of sand, like geologic Champs-Élysées. No less beautiful than the east side of the road, the shade and privacy here makes it a great area to camp.

About 50km north are two flat-topped mountains known as the **Twin Peaks**, a key navigation point for travellers. A favourite destination of local tour operators, the view from the top of the surrounding symmetrical hills, all shaped like giant ant-hills, is spectacular. Just beyond here, the road climbs a steep escarpment known as **Naqb As Sillim** (Pass of the Stairs); this is the main pass that leads into and out of the Farafra depression and marks the end of the White Desert.

A few kilometres further along, the desert floor changes again and becomes littered with quartz crystals. If you look at the rock formations in this area you'll see that they are also largely made of crystal. The most famous of the formations is the **Crystal Mountain**, actually a large rock made entirely of quartz. It sits right beside the main road some 24km north of Naqb As Sillim, and is easily recognisable by the large hole through its middle.

At the time of writing, foreigners were officially no longer allowed to camp overnight in the desert, but in reality many people do. The tourist police turn a blind eye, but it pays to do the trip with an experienced safari outfit. As well as the national park entry fee, you pay a LE20 fee for each night you sleep here. If you come as part of a group, the fees are included in your tour. You can usually buy tickets at the entrance to the park, but don't worry about going in without one; you can just pay the rangers when they find you. Sleeping anywhere in the park, surrounded by the white formations and visited by friendly fennecs, is an unforgettable experience.

caravans coming from Siwa, and **Gebel Az Zuqaq**, a mountain known for the red, yellow and orange streaks in its limestone base. There is an easily climbed path leading to the mountain's peak.

ℹ Getting There & Away

Ordinary vehicles are able to drive the first kilometre or so off the Bahariya–Dakhla road into the White or Black Deserts, but only 4WD vehicles can advance deeper into either area. Some travellers simply get off the bus and take themselves into the White Desert – but be sure you have adequate supplies, and remember that traffic between the neighbouring oases is rarely heavy. The megaliths west of the highway are easy to access by foot, as are the so-called mushrooms to the east; the weirdest wonderland of white hoodoos is quite far to the east, and walking there would be a real haul. Bir Regwa, a small spring situated along the highway at one of the park entrances, usually has water; it's good to know where it is (just in case), though best not to rely on it.

Even though it is not allowed to camp or go into the desert, the tourist police turns a blind eye to safari outfits in Bahariya organising short trips to the Black and White Deserts.

BAHARIYA OASIS

Bahariya is one of the more fetching of the desert circuit oases, and at just 365km from Cairo it's also the most accessible. Much of the oasis floor here is covered by sprawling shady date palms and speckled with dozens of natural springs, which beg to be plunged into. The surrounding landscape of rocky, sandy mesas is a grand introduction to the Western Desert's barren beauty.

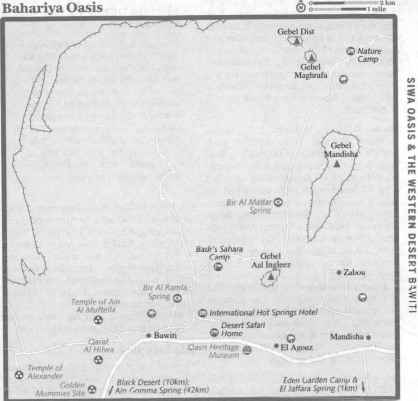

During the Middle Kingdom and especially during Roman times, the oasis was a centre of agriculture, producing wine sold in the Nile Valley and as far away as Rome. Its strategic location on the Libya–Nile Valley caravan routes ensured it prospered also throughout later ages. In recent years, stunning archaeological finds, such as that of the Golden Mummies, and easy access to the White and Black Deserts have earned Bahariya a firm spot on the tourist map.

Bawiti

📞 02 / POP 35,860

Take one look at Bawiti's dusty, unappealing main road, and you'll wonder why you came. But scratch beneath the surface and you will find a town of great charm. Stroll through its fertile palm groves, soak in one of the many hot springs or explore its quiet backstreets, where you'll meet truly hospitable people.

For many years, Bawiti was a quiet town dependent on agriculture. More recently, it became a tourist hub for trips to the White and Black Deserts, with the Golden Mummies an added draw. At the time of writing, however, it was quiet again, with many hotels closed and few travel agents operating. Everyone is waiting for tourism to the desert to return.

⊙ Sights

Qarat Qasr Salim ARCHAEOLOGICAL SITE
(Map p289; Sharia Yusef Salim; Bawiti joint site ticket adult/student LE100/50; ⊙ 8.30am-4pm) This small mound amid the houses of Bawiti is likely built upon centuries of debris. There are two well-preserved 26th-dynasty tombs here, which were robbed in antiquity and reused as collective burial sites in Roman times. Both are home to some excellently preserved and colourful wall paintings.

The rock-cut **Tomb of Zed Amun Ef Ankh** gives a glimpse of Bahariya in its heyday, the vibrant tomb paintings hinting at the wealth of its former occupant. Next to it lies the **Tomb of Bannentiu**, Zed Amun Ef Ankh's son. Consisting of a four-columned burial chamber with an inner sanctuary, it is covered in fine reliefs depicting Bannentiu with the god Khons and goddesses Isis and Nephthys.

Golden Mummies Museum   MUSEUM
(Al Mathaf; Map p289; Sharia Al Mathaf; Bawiti joint site ticket adult/student LE100/50; ⊗8am-4pm) Only 10 of Bahariya's richly decorated cache of 10,000 mummies are exhibited here. While the motifs are formulaic and the work is second-rate, the painted faces show a move away from stylised Pharaonic mummy decoration towards Fayoum portraiture. Underneath the wrappings, the embalmers' work appears to have been sloppy, so these mummies mark the beginning of the end of mummification.

The exhibit embodies that spirit and is entirely underwhelming. The museum doesn't have a sign. Look for the building resembling a wartime bunker behind a low cream-coloured wall topped with guard turrets. The ticket office (for all of Bawiti's sites) is just inside the entrance gate.

Oasis Heritage Museum   MUSEUM
(☎012-0225-0595, 02-3847-3666; Bahariya-Cairo Rd; LE15; ⊗hours vary, call ahead) The giant sandcastle-looking-thing, 3km east of town on the road to Cairo, is Mahmoud Eed's Oasis Heritage Museum. Inspired by Badr's Museum in Farafra, its creator captures, in clay, scenes from traditional village life, among them men hunting, women weaving and a painful-looking barber/doctor encounter. There's also a display of old oasis dresses and jewellery.

Sadly, Mahmoud Eed has died, leaving the exhibit very dusty and a bit in disarray.

🛏 Sleeping

There is a decent selection of budget and mid-priced hotels in Bawiti, although quite a few are now closed for lack of business.

> ### ℹ YOUR TICKET TO ANTIQUITIES
>
> Bahariya's authorities issue a one-day ticket that gives entry to five of the Bahariya Oasis' ancient sites: the **Golden Mummies Museum**, the **Tomb of Zed Amun Ef Ankh**, the **Tomb of Bannentiu**, the **Temple of Ain Al Muftella** (p291) and the **Temple of Alexander** (p291). Tickets are available at the museum's **ticket office** (Map p289; Sharia Al Mathaf; ⊗8am-4pm), so stop there first. Yup, you gotta pay for 'em all, even if you only visit one.

BAHARIYA'S GOLDEN MUMMY CACHE

Put it down to the donkey: until 1996, no one had any idea of the extent of Bahariya's archaeological treasure trove. Then a donkey stumbled on a hole near the temple of Alexander the Great, and its rider saw the face of a golden mummy peering out through the sand. Or so the story goes. (Some locals wink knowingly at what they assert is a much popularised myth.) Nevertheless, since then archaeologists have done extensive research in a cemetery that stretches over 3 sq km. Radar has revealed more than 10,000 mummies, and excavation has unearthed more than 250 of them in what has come to be called the Valley of the Golden Mummies.

These silent witnesses of a bygone age could shed new light on life in this part of Egypt during the Graeco-Roman period, a 600-year interlude marking the transition between the Pharaonic and Christian eras. Bahariya was then a thriving oasis and, with its rich, fertile land watered by natural springs, was a famous producer of wheat and wine. Greek and, later, Roman families set up home here and became a kind of expatriate elite.

Research has shown that after a brief decline when Ptolemies and Romans fought for control of the oasis, Roman administrators embarked on a major public works program, expanding irrigation systems, digging wells, restoring aqueducts and building roads. Thousands of mud-brick buildings sprang up throughout the oasis. Bahariya became a major source of grain for the empire and was home to a large garrison of troops; its wealth grew proportionately. Researchers are hoping that continued excavation of the necropolis will provide more answers about the region's early history and its inhabitants.

Bawiti

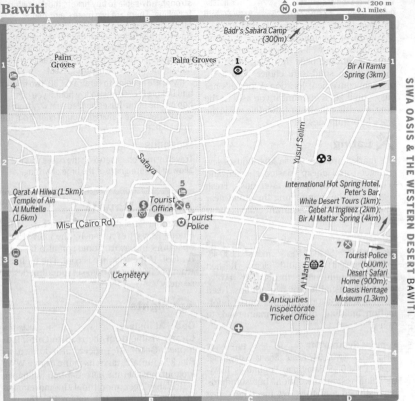

Bawiti

◉ Sights
1 Bir Al Ramla	C1
2 Golden Mummies Museum	D3
3 Qarat Qasr Salim	D2
Tomb of Bannentiu	(see 3)
Tomb of Zod Amun Ef Ankh	(see 3)

⌂ Sleeping
4 New Oasis Hotel	A1
5 Western Desert Hotel	B2

⊗ Eating
6 Popular Restaurant	B2
7 Rashed	D3

ⓘ Transport
8 Hilal Coffeehouse & Bus Stop	A3
9 Upper Egypt Bus Co Ticket Kiosk	B3

If you want to catch the mellow oasis vibe, head for one of the camps outside of town.

New Oasis Hotel HOTEL $

(Map p289, 📞 012-2847 4171; s/d LE150/240, without air-con LE140/180, ⊞ ☎) A study in curvaceous construction, this small, homey hotel has several teardrop-shaped rooms, some with balconies overlooking the expansive palm groves nearby. Inside, the rooms are in good shape, though someone seems to have been a little overzealous with the powder-blue paint. It's one of the nicer budget options in town, located next to El Beshmo spring.

Desert Safari Home HOTEL $

(Map p287; 📞 012-2731-3908; www.desertsafarihome.com; s/d LE100/150; @) This decent budget option is inconveniently located 2km from the centre of town but has good rooms. Owner Badry Khozam willingly picks up guests from the bus station.

Western Desert Hotel
HOTEL $

(Map p289; ☏ 012-2301-2155; www.western deserthotel.com; Sharia Safaya; s/d LE205/320; ☏) Right in the middle of town, this concrete block has well-kept rooms with powerful air-con and beds that even boast two sheets. It's a solid, safe choice with a supremely convenient location. When it's not busy, you'll get a discount if you ask. At the time of writing the lack of clientele made the place look quite desolate.

✖ Eating

The market area on Sharia Misr houses several good and cheap roasted chicken and kebab joints that fire up after dusk. Fresh veggies can be found along the street near Sharia Misr. As for restaurants, the scene is feeble.

Rashed
EGYPTIAN $

(Map p289; Sharia Misr; meals LE30-45; ⊗ noon-midnight) Big and clean, Rashed serves set multicourse meals that revolve around the usual meaty grill options. Head east for about 400m from the tourist information building, along the main road, to find it.

Popular Restaurant
EGYPTIAN $$

(Map p289; ☏ 02-847-2239; Sharia Safaya; set meals LE50-60; ⊗ 8am-11pm) Popular is Bawiti's main restaurant option, but standards have slipped and their set meals are now hugely overpriced. On a good note, the service is superfriendly and there's ice cold beer.

ⓘ Information

Hospital (Map p289; ☏ 02-3847-0647) Only for emergencies, otherwise head to Cairo.

National Bank of Development (Map p289; off Sharia Misr; ⊗ 9am-2pm Sun-Thu) Has an ATM and changes cash.

Tourist Office (Map p289; ☏ 02-3847-3035, 02-3847-2167; Sharia Misr; ⊗ 8.30am-2pm Sat-Thu) Run by the friendly Yehia Kandeel, who can also be contacted on 012-2321-6790.

Tourist Police (Map p289; ☏ 02-3847-6167; Sharia Misr)

ⓘ Getting There & Away

BUS

From the **bus ticket kiosk** (Map p289; ☏ 02-3847-3610; Sharia Misr; ⊗ 9am-1pm & 7-11pm) near the post office, Upper Egypt Bus Co has services to Cairo (LE85, five hours) at 6am, 8am, 10am and 3pm. They are often full, so it's strongly advisable to buy tickets the day before travelling. There are two more Cairo-bound buses that originate in Dakhla and pass through Bawiti around noon and midnight, stopping at the **Hilal Coffeehouse** (Map p289; Sharia Misr) at the western end of town. Tickets can only be bought on the bus, so hope for a seat.

If you are heading to Farafra (LE30, two hours) and Dakhla (LE50, four to five hours) you can hop on one of the buses headed that way from Cairo. They leave Bahariya around noon from the ticket office.

MICROBUS

Travel by microbus between the oases was not allowed for foreigners at the time of writing.

Around Bawiti

A number of sights in Bahariya can be included as part of a tour by the many safari operators in Bawiti. Some can also be done on foot, if the weather is cool. The main attraction, however, is the surrounding desert scenery.

◉ Sights

Gebel Al Ingleez
MOUNTAIN

Clearly visible from the road to Cairo, flat-topped Gebel Al Ingleez, also known as Black Mountain, takes its name from a WWI lookout post. From here Captain Williams, a British officer, monitored the movements of Libyan Senussi tribesmen. But the real reason to come up here is for the fantastic panoramic views, which roll out across the oasis and to the desert beyond.

At the top are the modest remains of Captain William's lookout post. Head here to watch sunset for the most atmospheric experience. A dirt track winds up to a plateau near the top, from where a footpath leads across the ridge to the summit (about a five-minute walk).

Gebel Dist
MOUNTAIN

Gebel Dist is an impressive pyramid-shaped mountain visible from most of the oasis. A local landmark, it is famous for its fossils; dinosaur bones were found here in the early 20th century, disproving the previously held theory that dinosaurs only lived in North America. In 2001 researchers from the University of Pennsylvania found the remains of a giant specimen, *Paralititan stromeri*.

The discovery of this huge herbivore, which the team deduced was standing on the edge of a tidal channel when it died 94

LOCAL KNOWLEDGE

BAHARIYA WHITE & BLACK DESERT TOURS

Business is slow in the Egyptian oases these days and many tour operators have gone out of business, or left the oasis. The hotels that are still open offer tours, as do some travel agents in Cairo.

A typical itinerary will take you to the sights in and around Bahariya – Temple of Alexander (p291), Temple of Ain Al Muftella (p291), Gebel Dist (p290) and Gebel Al Ingleez (p290) – then out through the Black Desert (p285), with a stop at the Crystal Mountain and then into the White Desert (p286).

A full day exploring the local sights of Bahariya is about LE1000; a half-day Black Desert trip costs LE500; a one-night camping trip into the White Desert will cost about LE1600. Remember, cheaper isn't always better. A reliable car and driver are well worth a few extra pounds. Before signing up, check vehicles to make sure they're roadworthy; confirm how much food and drink is supplied (and what this will be).

Many cheap Cairo hotels and hostels push their White Desert tours, but it's a much better idea to arrange things in Bawiti, where you can meet the people who will be responsible for your experience before forking over any cash. There are some well-established local safari outfits.

White Desert Tours (☎012-2321-2179; www.whitedeserttours.com; International Hot Spring Hotel) Operating since 1995, this German-owned tour company specialises in the White Desert and the area around Bahariya Oasis, but can also tailor-make multiday safaris when they are allowed again.

Eden Garden Tours (☎010-0071-0707; www.edengardentours.com; Eden Garden Camp; US$50-60 per person per day) This local tour operator's White Desert tours have been highly recommended by travellers.

---

million years ago, makes it likely that Bahariya was once a swamp similar to the Florida Everglades in the US.

About 100m away is **Gebel Maghrafa** (Mountain of the Ladle).

Temple of Ain Al Muftella   TEMPLE
(Bawiti joint site ticket adult/student LE100/50; ⊙8am-4pm) Four 26th-dynasty chapels, approximately 2km northwest of Bawiti, together form the Temple of Ain Al Muftella. The bulk of the building was ordered by 26th-dynasty high priest Zed Khonsu-ef-ankh, whose tomb (closed to the public) has been discovered under houses in Bawiti. Archaeologists suspect that the chapels could have been built during the New Kingdom, significantly expanded during the Late Period, and added to during Greek and Roman times.

All have been restored and given wooden roofs to protect them from the elements.

Qarat Al Hilwa   RUINS
(Bawiti joint site ticket adult/student LE100/50; ⊙8am-4pm) This ancient necropolis includes the 18th-dynasty Tomb of Amenhotep Huy. Overall it's a rather uninspiring site that will only interest the most avid of archaeology fans.

Temple of Alexander   TEMPLE
(Bawiti joint site ticket adult/student LE100/50; ⊙8am-4pm) The Temple of Alexander, southwest of Bawiti, is one of the few places in Egypt where Alexander the Great's cartouche has been found. Despite this fame, the site itself is small and unimpressive.

Natural Springs
El Jaffara   SPRING
A few kilometres south of the Bahariya–Cairo road, about 7km from Bawiti, lies the mini oasis of El Jaffara, where two springs – one hot, one cold – make this a prime spot in winter or summer. It's near Eden Garden Camp.

Bir Al Mattar   SPRING
At Bir Al Mattar, 7km northeast of Bawiti, cold springs pour into a viaduct and then down into a concrete pool, which you can splash in during the hot summer months. As with all Bawiti's springs, the mineral content is high, and the water can stain clothing.

Bir Al Ramla   SPRING
(Map p289) The sulphurous spring of Bir Al Ramla, 3km north of town, is very hot (45°C) and suitable for a soak, though you may feel a bit exposed to the donkey traffic passing to and fro. Women should stay well covered.

🛏 Sleeping

Badr's Sahara Camp   HUT $
(☎ 012-2792-2728; www.badrysaharacamp.com; dm/s/d/tr US$8/12/15/27; 🅿) A couple of kilometres from Bawiti, Badr's Sahara Camp has a handful of bucolic, African-influenced huts, each with two beds and small patios out front, some with air-con or fans. Hot water and electricity can't always be counted on, but cool desert breezes and knockout views of the oasis valley can. Pick-ups are available.

The atmosphere is helpful and relaxed, and there are great views from the terrace over the oasis' palm groves. Perfect to watch the sunset.

★ Eden Garden Camp   HUT $$
(☎ 010-0071-0707; www.edengardentours.com; hut per person with half board LE220, bungalow per person full board US$35) Located 7km east of Bawiti, in the small, serene oasis of El Jaffara, Eden Garden is a superfriendly place with African-style huts, a shaded lounge areas, fresh food and, best of all, two springs just outside its gates: one hot and one cold. Talaat, the owner who conceived the whole place, is a character.

This camp, with the garden and the springs, is a perfect place to wind down. Its desert safaris (p291) have a good reputation and pick-ups from Bawiti are free. You can come and hang out here for a swim, a meal (LE50 to LE150), tea and shisha or a beer.

International Hot Spring Hotel   HOTEL $$
(☎ 012-2321-2179, 02-3847-3014; www.whitedesert tours.com; s/d with half board US$50/80; 🅿🛜❄) About 3km outside Bawiti on the road to Cairo, this spa resort has 36 very comfortable rooms and eight chalets, built around a hot spring and set in a delightful pool. There's also a rooftop lounge and a good restaurant, as well as Peter's Bar. The owner Peter Wirth is an old Western Desert hand and organises recommended trips in the area.

Nature Camp   BUNGALOW $$
(☎ 012-2165-3037; naturecamps@hotmail.com; Bir Al Ghaba; r half board per person US$25; 🅿🛜❄) At the foot of Gebel Dist, 17km north of Bawiti, Nature Camp sets new standards for environmentally focused budget accommodation. The peaceful cluster of candlelit and intricately designed thatch huts looks out onto the expansive desert beside its own cold spring. The food is very good (meals LE50) and the owner, Ashraf Lotfe, is a

skilled desert hand. The perfect place away from it all.

Transport to and from Bawiti can be arranged.

🍷 Drinking & Nightlife

Peter's Bar   BAR
(☎ 012-2321-2179; International Hot Spring Hotel) This bar is as much a surprise as the hotel's own hot spring. Cold, cold beers!

SIWA OASIS
📷 046 / POP 23,000

Siwa is the stuff of desert daydreams. Just 50km from the Libyan border this fertile basin, sitting about 25m below sea level and brimming with olive trees and palms, epitomises slow-paced oasis life. Set between shady groves, squat, slouching mud-brick hamlets are connected by winding dirt lanes where trundling donkey carts are still as much a part of the street action as puttering motorbikes and 4WDs. Scattered throughout the oasis are crystal-clear springs, which are a heavenly respite from the harsh heat. At the edge of the oasis, the swells of the Great Sand Sea roll to the horizon, providing irresistible fodder for desert exploration.

Siwa's geographic isolation helped protect a unique society that stands distinctly apart from mainstream Egyptian culture. Today, local traditions and Siwi, the local Berber language, still dominate.

Well worth the long haul to get out here, Siwa casts a spell that's hard to resist.

History

Siwa has a long and ancient past: in late 2007, a human footprint was found that is thought to date back three million years, making it one of the oldest known human prints in the world. Flints discovered in the oasis show that it was inhabited in Palaeolithic and Neolithic times, but beyond that Siwa's early history remains a mystery.

The oldest monuments in the oasis, including the Temple of the Oracle, date from the 26th dynasty, when Egypt was invaded by the Assyrians. Siwa's Oracle of Amun was already famous then, and Egyptologists suspect it dates back to the earlier 21st dynasty, when the Amun priesthood became prominent throughout Egypt.

Such was the fame of Siwa's oracle that its prophecies threatened the Persians, who

Siwa Oasis

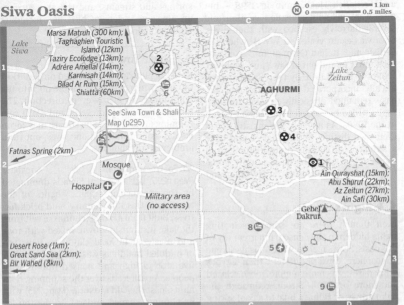

See Siwa Town & Shali Map (p295)

Siwa Oasis

◎ Sights
1 Cleopatra's Spring	D2
2 Gebel Al Mawta	B1
3 Temple of the Oracle	C1
4 Temple of Umm Ubayd	C2
Tomb of Mesu-Isis	(see 2)
Tomb of Niperpathot	(see 2)
Tomb of Si Amun	(see 2)
Tomb of the Crocodile	(see 2)

⊕ Activities, Courses & Tours
5 Sherif Sand Bath	C3

🛏 Sleeping
6 Dream Lodge Hotel	B1
7 Nanshaal	B2
8 Qasr Alzaytuna	C3
9 Siwa Shali Resort	D3

✖ Eating
Tanta Waa	(see 1)

invaded Egypt in 525 BC and ended the 26th dynasty. One of the Western Desert's most persistent legends is of the lost army of Persian king Cambyses, which was sent to destroy the oracle but disappeared completely in the desert. This only helped increase the oracle's prestige, reinforcing the political power of the Amun priesthood.

The oracle's power – and with it, Siwa's fame – grew throughout the ancient world. The young conqueror Alexander the Great led a small party on a perilous eight-day journey across the desert in 331 BC. It is believed that the priests of Amun, who was the supreme god of the Egyptian pantheon and later associated with the Greek god Zeus, declared him to be a son of the god.

The end of Roman rule, the collapse of the trade route and the gradual decline in the influence of oracles in general all contributed to Siwa's gentle slide into obscurity. While Christianity spread through most of Egypt, there is no evidence that it ever reached Siwa, and priests continued to worship Amun here until the 6th century AD. The Muslim conquerors, who crossed the desert in AD 708, were defeated several times by the fierce Siwans. However, there was a cost to this isolation: it is said that by 1203 the population had declined to just 40 men, who moved from Aghurmi to found the new fortress-town of Shali. The oasis finally converted to Islam around the 12th century, and gradually built up wealth trading date and olive crops along the Nile Valley, and also with Libyan Fezzan and the Bedouins.

European travellers arrived at the end of the 18th century – WG Browne in 1792 and Frederick Hornemann in 1798 – but most were met with a hostile reception, and several narrowly escaped with their lives. Siwa was again visited in WWII, when the British and Italian/German forces chased each other in and out of Siwa and Jaghbub, 120km west in Libya. By then Siwa was politically incorporated into Egypt, but the oasis remained physically isolated until an asphalt road connected it to Marsa Matruh in the 1980s. As a result, Siwans still speak their own distinct Berber dialect and have a strong local culture, quite distinct from the rest of Egypt. The oasis is now home to some 21,000 Siwans and a few thousand Egyptians.

⊙ Sights

Even though there are some fascinating sights hidden in the dense palm greenery of this oasis, Siwa's main attraction is its serene atmosphere. Siwa is different than Egypt's other oases; it is more remote, more relaxed and more beautiful. Strolling through the palm groves or riding a bike to a cool spring for a swim is all part of this oasis's slow, soothing, far-from-anywhere charm. Hang out with Siwans and other travellers, have a picnic, ride a donkey cart, explore the dunes by 4WD and soak it all in.

One of Siwa's most impressive sights is the oasis itself, which boasts more than 300,000 palm trees, 70,000 olive trees and a great many fruit orchards. The vegetation is sustained by more than 300 freshwater springs and streams, and the area attracts an amazing variety of bird life, including quail and falcons.

⊙ Siwa Town

Siwa is a pleasant town centred on a **market square**, where roads skedaddle off into the palm groves in nearly every direction. The proliferation of motorcycles and 4WD cars zooming around the main square may mean it's not as peaceful as it once was, but rural ambience still abounds.

★ Fortress of Shali
FORTRESS

(Map p295) FREE Central Siwa is dominated by the spectacular organic shapes of the remains of this 13th-century mud-brick fortress. Built from *kershef* (chunks of salt from the lake just outside town, mixed with rock and plastered in local clay), the labyrinth of huddled buildings was originally four or five storeys high and housed hundreds of people. A path leads over the slumping remnants, past the **Old Mosque** (Map p295) with its chimney-shaped minaret, to the top for panoramic views.

For centuries, few outsiders were admitted inside the fortress – and even fewer came back out to tell the tale. But three days of rain in 1926 caused more damage than any invader had managed and, over the last decades, inhabitants moved to newer and more comfortable houses with running water and electricity. Now only a few buildings

---

THE LOST ARMY OF CAMBYSES

Persian king Cambyses invaded Egypt in 525 BC, overthrowing Egyptian pharaoh Psamtek III and signalling the beginning of Persian rule for the next 193 years. This success, however, did not continue. In the years immediately following his conquest of Egypt, Cambyses mounted several disastrous offensives. In one, he sent a mercenary army down the Nile into Kush (now Sudan) that was so undersupplied it had to turn to cannibalism to survive, and the soldiers returned in disgrace without even encountering the enemy.

Cambyses' most famous failure remains his attempt to capture the Oracle of Amun in Siwa. Herodotus recounts how the oracle predicted a tragic end for Cambyses, and so the ruler dispatched an army of 50,000 men from Thebes, supported by a vast train of pack animals carrying supplies and weapons. The army is purported to have reached Farafra before turning west to cover the 325km of open desert to Siwa – a 30-day march without any shade or sources of water. Legend has it that after struggling through the Great Sand Sea, the men were engulfed by a fierce sandstorm, which buried the entire army.

Over the centuries, dozens of expeditions have searched in vain for a trace of Cambyses' soldiers and, especially, the treasure they reputedly carried with them. Perhaps one day the shifting sands will reveal the remnants of this ancient army.

Siwa Town & Shali

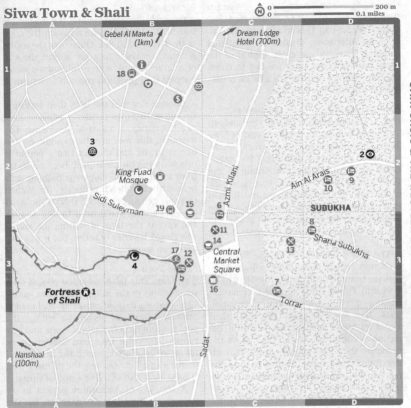

Siwa Town & Shali

⊚ Top Sights
1 Fortress of Shali A3

⊚ Sights
2 Ain Al Arais D2
3 House of Siwa Museum A2
4 Old Mosque B3

🛏 Sleeping
5 Al Babinshal Heritage Hotel B3
6 Kelany Hotel C3
7 Palm Trees Hotel C3
8 Shali Lodge D3
9 Siwa Safari Gardens Hotel D2
10 Siwa Safari Paradise D2

⊗ Eating
11 Abdu's Restaurant C3
12 Abu Ayman Restaurant B3
 Al Babinshal Restaurant .... (see 5)
 Kenooz Siwa .... (see 8)
13 Nour Al Waha C3

⊝ Drinking & Nightlife
14 Abdu Coffeeshop C3
15 Shaqraza B2
16 Zeytouna C3

⊙ Transport
17 Bicycle Hire B3
18 Bus Stop & West & Middle Delta
 Bus Co Ticket Office B1
19 Microbuses to Marsa Matruh B2

around the edges are occupied or used for storage. A pathway from the central square leads to the top for great views over the oasis. Several foreigners and Egyptians are doing up houses in the old town; some are available for overnight stays.

House of Siwa Museum
MUSEUM

(Map p295; ☑010-6513-9839; adult/student LE10; ⊙9am-2pm Sat-Thu) This small museum contains an interesting display of traditional clothing, jewellery and crafts typical of the oasis. It's worth the entry fee just to check out the wedding dresses. It's a block northwest of the King Fuad Mosque.

Gebel Al Mawta
ARCHAEOLOGICAL SITE

(Map p293; adult/student LE40/20; ⊙9am-5pm) This small hill, at the northern end of Siwa Town, is honeycombed with rock tombs peppered with wall paintings. Its name, Gebel Al Mawta, means 'Mountain of the Dead' and most of the tombs here date back to the 26th dynasty, Ptolemaic and Roman times. Only 1km from the centre of town, the tombs were used by the Siwans as shelters when the Italians bombed the oasis during WWII.

The best paintings are in the Tomb of Si Amun, where beautifully coloured reliefs portray the dead man – thought to be a wealthy Greek landowner or merchant – making offerings and praying to Egyptian gods. Also interesting are the unfinished Tomb of Mesu-Isis, with a beautiful depiction of cobras in red and blue above the entrance; the Tomb of Niperpathot, with inscriptions and crude drawings in the same reddish ink you can see on modern Siwan pottery; and finally the Tomb of the Crocodile, whose badly deteriorating wall paintings include a yellow crocodile representing the god Sobek.

⊙ Natural Springs

Siwa has no shortage of active, bubbling springs hidden among its palm groves. At all of the springs in town, women should swim in pants and a shirt and use general good judgment concerning modesty.

Cleopatra's Spring
SPRING

(Spring of the Sun; Map p293) Following the track that leads to the Temple of the Oracle and continuing past the Temple of Umm Ubayd will lead you to Siwa's most famous spring. The crystal-clear water gurgles up into a large stone pool, which is a popular bathing spot for locals and tourists alike. A couple of lovely cafes have comfortable shaded lounging areas and serve soft drinks and delicious snacks; bring your own picnic if you want to hang out for a while.

Bir Wahed
SPRING

A favourite Siwa excursion is the freshwater lake at Bir Wahed, 15km away on the edge of the Great Sand Sea. Once over the top of a dune, you come to a hot spring, the size of a large jacuzzi, where sulphurous water bubbles in a pool and runs off to irrigate a garden.

Cooling down in the lake, then watching the sun setting over the dunes while soaking in a hot spring, is a surreal experience. The thorns in this rose are the mosquitoes that bite at sunset and the fact that a permit is necessary to visit Bir Wahed. Because it's far from town, women can wear bathing suits here without offending locals. Bir Wahed can only be reached by 4WD, so if you don't have your own, you'll need to hire a guide and car. At the time of writing the spring was closed because of a fire, but it was due to reopen soon.

Fatnas Spring
SPRING

(Lake Siwa) This fairly secluded pool is on a small island in the salty Birket Siwa, accessible across a narrow causeway. Nicknamed 'Fantasy Island' for its idyllic setting, the pool is about 6km from Siwa Town, and surrounded by palm trees and lush greenery. It's an idyllic place to watch the sunset, and there's a small cafe among the palms, which is good for a spot of tea or a puff of shisha.

A Ministry of Agriculture project to try to improve the lake's drainage has left the 'island' high and dry, so sometimes the cafe may look out over salty mudflats rather than water. A tuk-tuk round trip from town will cost about LE50, with time to swim and hang out. Beware of mosquitoes at sunset.

Ain Al Arais
SPRING

(Map p295) The closest spring to central Siwa is Ain Al Arais, a cool, inviting waterhole with a grotto-like bottom, just five minutes' walk from the main market square. A casual cafe-restaurant is right beside the spring.

⊙ Aghurmi

Before Shali was founded in the 13th century, Siwa's main settlement was at Aghurmi, 4km east of the present town of Siwa. It was here that in 331 BC Alexander the Great consulted the famed oracle.

Temple of the Oracle
RUINS

(Map p293; adult/student LE30/15; ⊙9am-5pm) The 26th-dynasty Temple of the Oracle sits in the northwest corner of the ruins of

Aghurmi village. Built in the 6th century BC, probably on top of an earlier temple, it was dedicated to Amun (occasionally referred to as Zeus or Jupiter Ammon) and was a powerful symbol of the town's wealth. It is believed Alexander the Great was declared son of Amun in this temple.

There are many stories about the foundation of the temple. One tells of two priestesses who were banished from Thebes to the desert. One founded the Temple of Dodona in Greece, the other the Temple of the Oracle here in Aghurmi. One of the most revered oracles in the ancient Mediterranean, its power was such that some rulers sought its advice while others sent armies to destroy it. Although treasure hunters have been at work here and the buttressed temple was poorly restored in the 1970s, it remains an evocative site, steeped in history. Surrounded by the ruins of Aghurmi, it has awesome views over the Siwan oasis palm-tops.

Temple of Umm Ubayd RUINS
(Map p293) This almost totally ruined temple was dedicated to Amun. It was originally connected to the Temple of the Oracle by a causeway and was used during oracle rituals. Nineteenth-century travellers got to see more of it than we can; a Siwan governor blew up the temple in 1896 in order to construct the town's modern mosque and police building.

Only part of a wall covered with inscriptions survives. It's located about 200m along the track from the Temple of the Oracle.

Around Siwa

There are a few villages, ruins and springs around Siwa that are worth a trip if you've got the time. To visit these sights you'll need your own vehicle. Mahdi Hweiti at the Siwa tourist office organises trips, as does almost every restaurant and hotel in town. None of the sights, with the exception of Shiatta, require permits. Check with the tourist office (p303) before setting out.

Shiatta LAKE
Sixty kilometres west of Siwa Town, this stunning salt lake on the edge of the Great Sand Sea is ringed by palm trees. It's a popular stopover for migratory birds – including flamingos – and gazelles may be seen here too. The lake once reached all the way to Siwa Town, and an ancient boat lies somewhere 7m below the surface.

LOCAL KNOWLEDGE
RESPECTING LOCAL CUSTOMS
Take a look around, and when you see Siwan women, you probably won't glimpse more than a pair of eyes peeking out from behind a shawl. Modesty is serious business here. If a Western woman wears shorts and tank tops, it's about the same as walking naked through a stranger's home – in other words, you probably wouldn't do it. Perhaps even more than elsewhere in Egypt, travellers should dress conscientiously in Siwa. Women should cover legs, upper arms and cleavage, and men should stick to long pants rather than shorts. Displays of affection between couples should be saved for the hotel room. As with anywhere in the country, showing respect earns respect.

At the time of writing the lake was off limits for foreign visitors.

Ain Qurayshat SPRING
Ain Qurayshat, about 20km east from Siwa Town, has the largest free-flowing spring in the oasis. The best way to reach the spring is via the causeway across salty Lake Zeitun, which has striking views.

Abu Shuruf SPRING
Abu Shuruf, a clean spring said by locals to have healing properties, is 27km east of Siwa Town and 7km east of Ain Qurayshat spring in the next palm thicket. The clear water here is deliciously cold, but the ambience is somewhat spoilt by the sight and noise of the nearby Hayat water-bottling plant.

Az Zeitun RUINS
Roughly 30km east of Siwa Town, this abandoned mud-brick village, beaten by the sand and wind, sits alone on the sandy plain. Hundreds of Roman-era tombs have been discovered about 2km beyond Az Zeitun and are currently under excavation, although little of interest has been found yet.

Bilad Ar Rum RUINS
Just north of Kharmisah, around 17km northwest of Siwa Town, the City of the Romans has about 100 tombs cut into the rock of the nearby hills and the ruins of a stone temple, among the spots rumoured to be the final resting place of Alexander the

SAND BATHING AT GEBEL DAKRUR

If you thought a soak in a hot spring was invigorating, wait until you try a dip in one of the scalding-hot sand baths of **Gebel Dakrur**, several kilometres southeast of Siwa Town. From July to September, people flock here from all over the world to take turns at being immersed up to their necks in a bath of very hot sand for up to 20 minutes at a time.

Local doctors claim that a treatment regime of three to five days can cure rheumatism and arthritis – and judging by the number of repeat customers they get they might just be on to something. There are several places around the western slope of the mountain where you can get therapeutically sand-dunked. The best known is **Sherif Sand Bath** (Map p293; ☑010-0366-1905; sand bath LE100-150, with food & overnight lodging LE300-400; ☉ Jun-Sep).

The mountain also supplies the oasis with the reddish-brown pigment used to decorate Siwan pottery. Siwans believe that the mountain is haunted and claim that *afrit* (spirits) can be heard singing in the gardens at night.

Great. Nearby is **Maraqi**, once a poor village and now home to chic villas belonging to wealthy foreigners and Egyptians.

Maraqi is also where Liana Souvaltzi, a Greek archaeologist, claimed in 1995 to have found Alexander's tomb. Her findings proved controversial and the Egyptian authorities revoked her permit and closed the site.

Ain Safi   VILLAGE
Three kilometres east of the abandoned village of Az Zeitun, this is the last human vestige before the overwhelming wall of desert dunes that stretches for hundreds of kilometres, all the way south to Al Kharga Oasis. Some 30 Bedouin remain here.

Kharmisah   VILLAGE
About 15km northwest of Siwa Town, this village has five natural springs and is renowned for the quality of its olive groves.

🏃 Activities

Salt Mining Pools   SWIMMING
(Abu Shorouf) FREE Siwans always knew about the salt in their lakes, but a recent large-scale salt-mining project has created several salt water pools which are wonderful to swim in. The pools are obviously very salty, but the turquoise-blue water against the white crystals is beautiful. Several hotels offer a half-day excursion.

Taziry Stables   HORSE RIDING
(☑010-1633-3200; www.facebook.com/tazirysiwa; Taziry Ecolodge; LE300 for two hours) The Moroccan owner here is very proud of his horses. Book ahead.

👉 Tours

Almost all restaurants and hotels in Siwa offer tours in the desert around Siwa Town. Abdu's Restaurant (p301) and the Palm Trees Hotel have established a good reputation for their trips. The tourist office (p303) is also an excellent place to get help with organising tours.

All desert trips require permits, which cost LE140 per person per day and are usually obtained by your guide from the tourist office. Trip prices vary according to itineraries but the average cost of a car and driver for a full day to visit the sights around Siwa is LE200 to LE300. One of the most popular half-day trips takes you to the cold lake and hot springs at Bir Wahed (p296), on the edge of the Great Sand Sea. Palm Trees offers this with an overnight option, but you'll sleep in a camp on the edge of town, not in the dunes.

Other popular half-day itineraries include a tour of the springs Ain Qurayshat, Abu Shuruf, Az Zeitun and Ain Safi (LE200 for two people, LE300 for a bigger group); and a tour of Siwa Town and its environs (Temple of the Oracle, Gebel Al Mawta, Cleopatra's Bath, Fortress of Shali and Fatnas). Overnight trips vary in length according to destination. Most trips are done by 4WD, so ensure that the vehicle is roadworthy before you set out and that you have enough water.

Amr Baghi Tours   OUTDOORS
(☑010-0192-0465; amrshali55@yahoo.com) Amr Baghi trained as an archaeologist and organises tours in the oasis and around.

Ghazal Safari OUTDOORS
(☑010-0277-1234) If you're looking to explore the area of the Great Sand Sea surrounding Siwa, we highly recommend Ghazal Safari. Driver/guide Abd El Rahman Azmy has a kick-ass vehicle and a love for Siwa that's contagious.

⚜ Festivals & Events

Moulid At Tagmigra RELIGIOUS
(⊘Aug) Once a year, just after the corn harvest in late summer, Siwa Town's small tomb shrine of Sidi Suleiman is the scene of a *moulid* (saints' festival), known in Siwi as the Moulid At Tagmigra. Banners announce the *moulid*, and *zikrs* are performed outside the tomb.

Siyaha Festival CULTURAL
(⊘Oct) For three days around October's full moon, Gebel Dakrur is the scene of the Siyaha festival. Thousands of Siwans gather to celebrate the date harvest, renewing friendships and settling any quarrels that broke out over the previous year. Check with the tourist office to find out if it's taking place.

During the festival all Siwans, no matter what their financial or social standing, eat together at a huge feast after the noon prayer each day. The festival is intertwined with Sufism, and each evening, hundreds of men form a circle and join together in a *zikr*. Siwan women do not attend the festivities, although girls up to about the age of 12 are present until sunset.

🛏 Sleeping

Siwa Town has a great collection of places to sleep, with everything from competitively priced budget pads to dazzling top-end options. Many midrange and top-end sleeping options can also be found further afield around Gebel Dakrur and Sidi Jaafar.

The police here are very jittery about people camping close to town. If you want to sleep in the desert, it's best to organise a tour with a local guide.

▭ Siwa Town & Around

★ **Al Babinshal Heritage Hotel** BOUTIQUE HOTEL $
(Map p295; ☑010-0361-4140; www.facebook.com/Albabinshal-Heritage-Hotel-1242284019179174; Shali; s/d/tr LE285/365/475; 🛜) This gorgeous, curvy mud-brick hotel is seamlessly grafted onto, and part of, the Shali fortress with its labyrinthine architecture all built from *kershef* bricks. A maze of tunnels and stairways connects the spacious and cool rooms. Decor is distinctly desert style with date-palm furniture, local textiles and traditional wooden-shuttered windows used in abundance to add to the local vibe.

Salama keeps the place immaculate, is extremely helpful and a wise font of local knowledge. The rooftop is a great place to be at sunset, or come and have dinner under the stars.

Siwa Safari Gardens Hotel HOTEL $
(Map p295; ☑046-460-2801; www.siwagardens.com; Sharia Ain Al Arais; s/d/tr half board LE270/370/470; 🛜❄) This simple but supremely tidy hotel gets all the little things right: clean, bright rooms and a serene palm-shaded courtyard with a gleaming spring-fed pool. Ground-floor rooms are surprisingly plain, so bag a dome-ceilinged 2nd-floor room for more character. The staff here goes out of the way to help.

Dream Lodge Hotel HOTEL $
(Map p293; ☑010-0099-9255; http://siwadreamlodgehotel.net; near Gebel Al Mawta; s/d/tr/ste LE180/280/380/440; P🛜❄) Delightful small hotel with 22 rooms built in local style around a swimming pool. It's all surrounded by a shady garden, where an Egyptian breakfast is served in the morning and a fire is lit on winter nights. Very tranquil.

Palm Trees Hotel HOTEL $
(Map p295; ☑046-460-1703, 012-2104-6652; www.facebook.com/PALM-TREES-816079035146405; Sharia Torrar; s/d LE80/95, with shared bathroom LE50/60, bungalow s/d LE80/120, r with air-con LE120; 🛜) If you can handle the mosquitoes (seriously, bring bug spray), then this popular budget hotel is a lovely place to stay. It has sufficiently tidy rooms boasting screened windows, fans and balconies. The shady garden with date-palm furniture is delightful and the few ground-level bungalows have porches spilling onto the greenery.

Kelany Hotel HOTEL $
(Map p295; ☑010-2336-9627; Sharia Azmi Kilani; s/d/tr LE100/150/200; ❄🛜) Kelany's small rooms may be showing their age, but they're still a step above other budget places in Siwa; if you're looking for a cheap sleep with air-con and working wi-fi, this is your best bet. The rooftop restaurant (meals LE35) features views of the Fortress of Shali, Gebel Dakrur and everything in between. Breakfast is not included.

★ **Shali Lodge**   HOTEL $$
(Map p295; ☏010-1118-5820, 046-460-2399;
Sharia Subukha; s/d/tr/ste LE385/475/575/650;
⊙Sep-Jun; ☏) This tiny, beautiful hotel,
owned by environmentalist Mounir Neama-
tallah, is nestled in a lush palm grove about
100m from Siwa's main square. The large
comfortable rooms have lots of curvaceous
mud-brick goodness, exposed palm beams,
rock-walled bathrooms and cushioned sit-
ting nooks. Tasteful and quiet, this is how
small hotels should be.

Nanshaal   HOTEL $$
(Map p293; ☏010-6661-9586; www.facebook.com/
nanshal.siwa; Shali; r from $40; ☏) At the edge
of Shali, Nanshaal is a tranquil haven, with
a few rooms in a restored mud-brick house.
Run by the laid-back Faris Hassanein, the
rooms here are simple but authentically Siwan, using mostly natural materials. There
is a great roof terrace where you can watch
time pass.

Faris knows everyone and is very helpful
in suggesting all the delights that the oases
and surrounding desert have on offer.

Siwa Safari Paradise   HOTEL $$
(Map p295; ☏046-460-1290; www.siwaparadise.
com; Sharia Ain Al Arais; s/d LE420/550, bungalow
LE280/380, with air-con LE300/400; ☏⛱) Laid
out along a maze of garden paths, this re-
sort-style hotel mainly attracts northern Eu-
ropeans looking to sunbake by the natural
spring pool. The spacious air-con bungalows
are the pick of the bunch here with dome
ceilings and little lounge areas. The rooms
in the main building are rather bland and
formulaic.

🛏 Sidi Jaafar & Around Siwa Lake

Maraki Camp   BOUTIQUE HOTEL $
(☏012-2490-7806; www.siwawi.com; Maraqi; d
LE250; ☏) The perfect place to relax for a
few days, this small, simple and beautiful-
ly designed camp has 12 mud-brick rooms
on the lake with bathrooms, mosquito net
and solar-powered lights. The terrace is a
dream, overlooking the lake where you can
go swimming.

Next door is a beautiful villa for rent with
two bedrooms and hot water, accommodat-
ing four people (LE500 per night).

Siwa Astro Camp   TENTED CAMP $
(☏012-2410-6044; www.facebook.com/siwaastro
camp; s/d half board LE180/250) One of the few

places you can stay out in the desert is at
Astro camp, 9km from town, between two
mountains. The accommodation is in clean
tents, with a shared kitchen and bathroom,
and a large Bedouin tent for the evening.
This is a peaceful place, also perfect for yoga
and meditation. Fathi is a great host. Rec-
ommended.

★ **Siwa Relax Retreat**   HOTEL $$
(☏012-8000-0274; www.facebook.com/SiwaRelax
Retreat; s/d US$65/75, r with shared bathroom
US$30; P☏⛱) Far away from it all, this
place is a dream in which to totally relax for
a few days. Built on the edge of the lake, the
simple but comfortable rooms are covered
in bougainvillea and have floors made of
salt crystals. Some have shared bathrooms,
others are en suite. There is no electricity,
just candles.

Sun loungers surround the pool, which
is part of the lake. Ashraf is a relaxed host,
and gives excellent and expert oil and salt
massages and mudwraps on the lake shore.
You can book for a romantic dinner by the
lake (US$15).

Talist   HOTEL $$
(☏010-0114-1508, 010-0644-5881; www.talistsiwa.
com; Al Maraqi Rd; r from US$35; P☏⛱) Talist,
meaning 'lake' in the Amazig language, is a
place to get away from it all. On offer in this
family-owned ecolodge are simple but com-
fortable rooms, beauty and tranquillity. Nat-
ural materials like stone, cotton and *kershef,*
a mixture of salt and rock, are used, and
there is a great pool overlooking the lake.

A lovely candlelit dinner can be ordered
in advance (LE150). Electricity is only availa-
ble to charge devices.

★ **Adrère Amellal**   HOTEL $$$
(☏02-2736-7879; www.adrereamellal.net; Sidi
Jaafar, White Mountain; s/d/tr full board incl excursions & all drinks from US$460/605/900, ste from
US$1420; P☏⛱) Backed by the dramatic
White Mountain (called Adrère Amellal in
Siwan language), this impeccable retreat
lies in its own oasis, 13km from Siwa Town,
with stunning views over Birket Siwa salt
lake and the Great Sand Sea's dunes. It offers
the ultimate in spartan-chic. Elegantly simple suites showcase traditional architecture
techniques using *kershef.*

There is no electricity; the rooms are lit by
candles and the garden by hurricane lamps
and the moon and the stars. When sandy
adventures are done for the day, guests loll

by the natural-spring swimming pool until it's time for a gourmet dinner, mostly from their own oasis's garden, eaten under the stars. This truly magnificent – and highly romantic – hideaway is one of Egypt's most special and innovative places to stay.

Taziry Ecolodge BOUTIQUE HOTEL **$$$**
(☑ 010-1633-3200; www.facebook.com/tazirysiwa; Al Gaary; s/d/tr half board LE1200/1600/2200, chalet half board LE2200-3000; ☲) This peaceful hotel 12km west of Siwa Town was designed and built by an artist and an engineer from Alexandria. Large natural-material rooms are decorated with local crafts and Bedouin rugs. Tranquil and laid-back, with no electricity and a natural-spring pool overlooking the lake, it is a great place to unwind and experience Siwa's magic. Families can choose their own adobe chalet.

The Taziry has a relaxed lounge vibe, and is a good place to come and hang out for the day, with day use of the wonderful pool and a delicious Moroccan lunch (LE250). It organises safaris, and has stables for horse riding (p298).

Gebel Dakrur

Qasr Alzaytuna HOTEL **$**
(Map p293; ☑ 012-2222-4209, 046-460-2909; www.facebook.com/Qasr-Alzaytuna-388249304624984; s/d/tr LE150/200/240; ☲) Perfect for those who want a restful getaway, Qasr Alzaytuna has neat-as-a-pin rooms (some with dinky balconies) and a tranquil date-palm garden complete with spring-fed swimming pool. The important things are done right, like nice mattresses and modern bathrooms, and your host, Sammia, is as welcoming as could be. A great choice for families, it lies 2km southeast of town.

Siwa Shali Resort RESORT **$$**
(Map p293; ☑ 02-3974-1806, 010-0630-1017; www.siwashaliresort.com; s/d/ste half board €26/52/70; ☲) This self-contained village of traditionally styled bungalows snakes its way along a 500m spring-fed pool. While the rooms are nothing special, suites have sitting rooms with two mattresses, perfect for young kids. It's popular with European tour groups on all-inclusive packages, as it's 4km from town.

✗ Eating

Most of the restaurants and cafes in Siwa cater to tourists and are open from about 8am until late. There are a couple of falafel and *fuul* (fava bean paste) joints plus an *a'aish* (flatbread) bakery about 50m off the main square past the Kelany Hotel. For travellers looking for oasis ambience, there are several cosy palm-garden restaurants around Siwa serving the usual combination of Egyptian and Western fare.

★ Abdu's Restaurant INTERNATIONAL **$**
(Map p295; ☑ 046-460-1243; Central Market Sq; dishes LE18-50; ☺ 8.30am-midnight) Before wi-fi and smartphones, there were places like this – a village hub where people gathered nightly to catch up and swap stories. The longest-running restaurant in town remains the best eating option thanks to its friendly on-the-ball staff and a huge menu of breakfast, pasta, traditional dishes, vegetable stews, couscous, roasted chickens and pizza.

Abdu's is also prime territory for organising safaris and day trips with staff happy to dish out advice and information on all things 'Siwa'.

Al Babinshal Restaurant EGYPTIAN **$**
(Map p295; ☑ 010-0361-4140; Fortress of Shali; mains LE20-65; ☺ 8am-late) On the roof of the hotel of the same name, this might just be the most romantic dining spot in the oases. Moodily lit in the evenings, it's practically attached to the fortress of Shali and has sweeping views over all of Siwa. This is the place in town to try camel-meat stew.

Tanta Waa EGYPTIAN **$**
(Map p293; ☑ 010-1290-1337; www.facebook.com/Tanta-Waa-172058239563868; Cleopatra's Spring; mains LE30, 3-course dinner LE150-200; ☺ 10am-midnight) Tanta Waa is a great place to hang out after swimming in Cleopatra's Spring (p296). It serves delicious smoothies and fresh juices, pancakes and good paninis. The wonderful slow-cooked dinner by candlelight, features anything from leg of lamb to duck with orange or chicken baked in the sand.

Book ahead in the morning or, preferably, the night before.

Abo Ayman Restaurant GRILL **$**
(Map p295; off Sharia Sadat; meals LE18-40; ☺ 11am-midnight) Roasted on a hand-turned spit over coals in an old oil drum, the chickens at Abo Ayman are the juiciest in Siwa. They're well seasoned, and served with salad, tahini and bread. You can sit inside at low tables, but we like the tables outside with street views.

Nour Al Waha
INTERNATIONAL $

(Map p295; ☑046-460-0293; Sharia Subukha; mains LE10-30; ☺noon-midnight) This popular hang-out, in a palm grove opposite Shali Lodge, has shady tables and plenty of tea and games on hand for those who just want to while away the day in the shade. The food is a mixture of Egyptian and Western, and is generally fresh and good.

Kenooz Siwa
EGYPTIAN $

(Map p295; ☑046-460-1299; Sharia Subukha; mains LE20-45; ☺8am-midnight Sep-Jun) On the roof terrace of Shali Lodge, this cafe-restaurant is a great place to hang out while enjoying a mint tea or a cold drink. Mains include some unique Siwan specialities, such as baked lentils and eggplant with pomegranate sauce.

🍷 Drinking & Nightlife

Many of the cafes around town are no-name places where Siwan men gather to watch TV and chat, but no alcohol is served. A couple of the most enjoyable cafes are found next to Cleopatra's Bath.

Shaqraza
CAFE

(Map p295; Sharia Sidi Suleyman; ☺9am-1am; 🛜) The hippest cafe-restaurant in Siwa sits on a shaded rooftop overlooking the central square. Lounge on cushions or choose a regular table with chairs. Browse an extensive list of coffees, teas and juices, plus a full food menu. Throw in the wi-fi and this place is a sure hit.

Abdu Coffeeshop
COFFEE

(Map p295; Central Market Sq; ☺7am-midnight) Abdu's packs out nightly with local men smoking shisha, downing tea and slapping backgammon pieces with triumphant vigour.

Taghaghien Touristic Island
BAR

(☑012-8999-1991; www.facebook.com/taghaghien.island; entry incl a drink LE50; ☺10am-10pm) Desperate for a beer? This small island 12km northwest of Siwa Town and connected by a causeway is one of the few places selling the amber nectar (for a whopping LE40 a bottle). Shaded tables, paddleboat rentals and sweet sunset vistas make it great for a day trip or picnic. You'll need your own transport to get here.

Zeytouna
COFFEE

(Map p295; Central Market Sq; ☺8am-midnight) Right in town, Zeytouna is a favourite evening haunt for local men drinking tea and coffee. Its tables often spill out onto the town square.

🛍 Shopping

Siwa's rich culture is well represented by the abundance of traditional crafts that are still made for local use as well as for tourists. There are lots of shops around Siwa Town selling very similar items, so browse around a bit before you buy.

Siwan women love to adorn themselves with heavy silver jewellery and you should be able to find some interesting pieces around town. Local wedding dresses are famous for their red, orange, green and black embroidery, often embellished with shells and beads. Look for black silk *asherah nazitaf* and white cotton *asherah namilal* dresses.

GAY SIWA?

Much attention has been paid to Siwa's unique history of intimate male relations. Back when Siwa's citizens still lived in the Fortress of Shali, young men between the ages of 20 and 40 were expected to spend their nights outside the fortress to tend to the fields and protect the town from attack. These men of Siwa had a notorious reputation, not only for their bravery (they were known as *zaggalah*, or 'club bearers'), but for their love of palm wine, music and openly gay relations. Single-sex marriages were apparently still practised in Siwa right up until WWII, although they had been outlawed in Egypt decades earlier.

Even though Siwa has been listed as a place to visit in several gay travel directories, the situation today is quite different. Residents of Siwa vehemently deny that there is a local gay sex scene, and travellers coming to Siwa in hope of 'hooking up' have been faced with increasingly homophobic sentiments. Siwan men are not amused at being propositioned by passing strangers – they are much more likely than foreigners to bear the brunt of anti-gay attitudes. Violent attacks on local men accused of homosexuality are not unheard of.

A variety of baskets are woven from date-palm fronds. You can spot old baskets by their finer artisanship and the use of silk or leather instead of vinyl and polyester. The *tarkamt*, a woven plate that features a red leather centre, is traditionally used for serving sweets, the larger *tghara* is used for storing bread. Smaller baskets include the *aqarush* and the red-and-green silk-tasselled *nedibash*. You'll also find pottery coloured with pigment from Gebel Dakrur, used locally as water jugs, drinking cups and incense burners.

Siwa is also known for its dates and olives, found in every other shop around the main square. Ask to taste a few different varieties; you really can't go wrong.

❶ Information

DANGERS & ANNOYANCES
At the time of writing, it was fine to travel to the oasis of Siwa via the Marsa Matruh road, but not via the desert road from Bahariya. The oasis is calm and relaxed, but because of Libyan smugglers crossing the desert borders, it is forbidden to travel much further than Bir Wahed into the desert. Check with the tourist office for the current situation.

EMERGENCY
Tourist Police (Map p295; ☑ 046-460-2047; Siwa Town) Across the road from the tourist office.

MONEY
Banque du Caire (Map p295; Siwa Town; ⏱ 8.30am-2pm & 5-8pm) About 200m north from the King Fuad Mosque, this bank is purported to be the only all-mud-brick bank in the world. The ATM usually works but – just in case – you're better off bringing enough money to Siwa with you. It's a long way to the next bank.

PERMITS
At the time of writing, desert travel away from the oases was not permitted and the road from Siwa to Bahariya was closed. A permit is needed to venture off the beaten track from Siwa, but this is easily arranged by local guides. Mahdi Hweiti at the tourist office can also help arrange permits quickly (but not on Fridays). Permits cost LE140 per person, per day. You'll need copies of your passport.

TOURIST INFORMATION
Tourist Office (Map p295; ☑ 010-0546-1992, 046-460-1338; mahdi_hweiti@yahoo.com; Siwa Town; ⏱ 9am-2pm Sat-Thu, plus 5-8pm Oct-Apr) Siwa's tourist officer, Mahdi Hweiti, is extremely knowledgeable about the oasis

and can help arrange desert safaris or trips to surrounding villages. The office is opposite the bus station.

❶ Getting There & Away

BUS
Siwa's bus stop (Map p295) and ticket office is opposite the tourist police station; when you arrive in town, however, you'll be let off near the central market square. It's sensible to buy your ticket ahead of time as buses are often full.

From the bus stop, West & Middle Delta Bus Co buses depart for Alexandria (LE75, eight hours), via Marsa Matruh (LE40, four hours) at 7am, 10am and 10pm. The 10pm service costs LE10 more. It's direct Siwa–Cairo bus service (LE150, 11 hours) runs on Tuesday, Friday and Sunday at 8pm. Otherwise, get a bus to Alexandria and change there.

MICROBUS
Microbuses going to **Marsa Matruh** (Map p295) (LE40) leave from the main square near the King Fuad Mosque. They are more frequent and way more comfortable than the West & Mid Delta bus, and the same price.

4WD
Construction of the Siwa–Bahariya road began in 2005 and, after many delays, is now finished. However, it was closed to foreigners at the time of writing.

TO/FROM LIBYA
Though Siwa is only about 50km from the Libya, it's currently illegal to cross the border in either direction, either along this stretch of border, or via the official border crossing in Sallum.

❶ Getting Around

BICYCLE & MOTORCYCLE
Bicycles are one of the best ways to get around and can be rented from several sources, including most hotels and a number of shops dotted around the town centre. Getting a bike from one of the bicycle rentals near the Central Market Square (Map p295) gives you a better chance of finding a bike in good condition. The going rate is LE20 to LE25 per day.

Though not as enjoyable or tranquil as bicycles, motorbikes can also be rented. You can pick one up from the bike shop next to Al Babinshal Hotel, or at Palm Trees Hotel. Expect to pay between LE150 and LE200 per day.

DONKEY CART & TUK-TUK
Caretas (donkey carts) were a much-used mode of transport for Siwans, but there are not that many around anymore. Some of the boys who drive the carts speak English and can be fierce

hagglers. Expect to pay about LE40 for two to three hours, or LE20 for a short trip.

Noisy tuk-tuks have replaced the old-fashioned donkey carts. Expect to pay about LE50 for two to three hours, or LE20 for a short trip.

SERVEES

Microbuses serve as communal taxis linking Siwa Town with surrounding villages. To get to Bilad Ar Rum costs LE1 to LE2 each way. If you want to hire your own to get to more remote sites, Mahdi Hweiti at the tourist office will be able to help, or head for the petrol station and talk directly to drivers. One reliable English-speaking driver with a good-quality vehicle is Anwar Mohammed (☎ 012-2687-3261). Prices are per truck, not per passenger, and depend on the duration of the trip, the distance to be covered and, of course, your haggling skills.

BEYOND SIWA

Great Sand Sea & Gilf Kebir

Great Sand Sea   DESERT

One of the world's largest dune fields, the Great Sand Sea straddles Egypt and Libya, stretching more than 800km from its northern edge near the Mediterranean coast south to Gilf Kebir (p304). Covering a colossal 72,000 sq km, it contains some of the largest recorded dunes in the world, including one that is 140km long. It was off limits to foreigners at the time of writing.

Crescent, *seif* (sword) and *barchan* dunes are found here in abundance, and have challenged desert travellers and explorers for hundreds of years. The Persian king Cambyses is thought to have lost an army here, while the WWII British Long Range Desert Group spent months trying to find a way through the impenetrable sands to launch surprise attacks on the German army. Aerial surveys and expeditions have helped the charting of this vast expanse, but it remains one of the least-explored areas on the planet.

Gilf Kebir   DESERT

The Gilf Kebir is a spectacular sandstone plateau 150km north of Gebel Uweinat (p269), rising 300m above the desert floor. The setting feels as remote as a place can be, with a rugged beauty that used to attract the most ardent desert lovers; on the northern side, the plateau disappears into the sands of the Great Sand Sea. It is famous as a setting for Michael Ondaatje's *The English Patient*. It was off limits to foreigners at the time of writing.

In 1933, some dramatic rock carvings and paintings were discovered by the Hungarian explorer László Almásy. The stunning depictions of people who look like they are swimming – known as the Cave of Swimmers – and of abundant wildlife, including giraffes and hippopotamuses, are probably around 10,000 years old. Almásy suggested that the swimming scenes were a real depiction of their surroundings before the climate changed.

Alexandria & the Mediterranean Coast

Best Places to Eat

➡ Zephyrion (p331)
➡ Kadoura (p324)
➡ Mohammed Ahmed (p323)
➡ Greek Club (p324)

Best Places to Stay

➡ Steigenberger Cecil Hotel (p322)
➡ El Alamein Hotel (p336)
➡ Windsor Palace Hotel (p321)

Why Go?

Egypt's northern coastline runs for 500km along Mediterranean shores. Its sandy beaches and turquoise-hued sea lure floods of Egyptians here during summer and, in recent years, a number of sprawling resorts have been built facing these crystal waters. Most travellers, however, make a beeline straight to the once-great port city of Alexandria. Eulogised through the centuries, this faded old dame of a metropolis is still by far Egypt's most atmospheric city. Alexandria's fresh sea air, fantastic seafood, ancient history and crumbling gems of belle époque buildings give it a spirit distinctly different from that of Cairo.

Outside the old stomping grounds of Alexander the Great and Queen Cleopatra, foreign visitors are rarely spotted. To delve deeper into this region, take a pilgrimage to the sobering, beautifully kept WWII war memorials of El Alamein. Or amble the souq streets of Rosetta, edged by Ottoman-era architecture and brimming with time-stood-still ambience.

When to Go
Alexandria

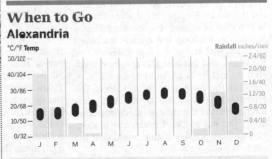

Apr–May Warm spring weather, perfect for strolling near-deserted Mediterranean shores.

Jun–mid-Sep Carnival atmosphere along sardine-packed sand as Egypt's holiday season begins.

Nov This month's film festival is the main event on Alexandria's cultural calendar.

ALEXANDRIA & THE MEDITERRANEAN COAST ALEXANDRIA

Alexandria & the Mediterranean Coast Highlights

1 Bibliotheca Alexandrina (p314) Touring the modern incarnation of an ancient wonder, where it's not just the library itself on offer but also several museums of antiquities, manuscripts and art.

2 Alexandria (p306) Tasting the last drops of 19th-century grandeur at a

period cafe and strolling the streets and souqs of soulful Anfushi at night.

3 Aboukir (p331) Eating your fill of simply grilled fresh seafood along the shore.

4 Rosetta (p331) Ambling through dusty, donkey-filled streets, where narrow lanes are rimmed by restored

Ottoman-era merchant houses and mosques.

5 El Alamein (p333) Remembering the desert battles of WWII's North Africa campaign at poignant war memorials.

6 Marsa Matruh (p336) Splashing about in stunning aqua waters at the beach.

ALEXANDRIA

03 / POP 4.4 MILLION

Founded in 331 BC by 25-year-old Alexander the Great, Alexandria (Al Iskendariyya) is the stuff of legend. Its towering Pharos lighthouse, marking the ancient harbour's entrance, was one of the Seven Wonders of the World, and its Great Library was considered the archive of ancient knowledge. Alas, fate dealt the city a spate of cruel blows. The Pharos collapsed and the Great Library was torched. Part of the ancient city disappeared under the sea and part under the modern city, so there are few visible remains of the glorious past.

The 19th century kick-started a cosmopolitan makeover and renaissance when Alexandria became one of the Mediterranean's key commercial hubs. This revival was cut short in the 1950s by President Nasser's nationalism. Today the imposing modern

library of Alexandria sits amid faded remnants of the once-grand seafront Corniche, as a symbol of the city's latest incarnation as Egypt's cultural capital.

History

Alexandria's history bridges the time between the pharaohs and the coming of Islam. The city gave rise to the last great Pharaonic dynasty (the Ptolemies), provided the entry into Egypt for the Romans, nurtured early Christianity and then rapidly faded into near-obscurity when Islam's invading armies passed it by to set up camp on a site along the Nile that later became Cairo.

The city was conceived by Alexander the Great, who arrived from Sinai having had his right to rule Egypt confirmed by the priests of Memphis. Here, on the shores of his familiar sea, he chose a fishing village as the site for a new city that he hoped would link the old Pharaonic world and the new world of the Greeks. Foundations were laid in 331 BC, and almost immediately Alexander departed for Siwa to consult the famous oracle there, before then marching for Persia. His conquering army went as far as India, and after his death at Babylon in 323 BC the rule of Egypt fell to the Macedonian general Ptolemy. Ptolemy won a struggle over Alexander's remains and buried them somewhere around Alexandria.

Ptolemy masterminded the development of the new city, filling it with architecture to rival Rome or Athens and establishing it as the cultural and political centre of his empire. To create a sense of continuity between his rule and that of the Pharaonic dynasties, Ptolemy made Alexandria look at least superficially Egyptian by adorning it with sphinxes, obelisks and statues scavenged from the old sites of Memphis and Heliopolis. The city developed into a major port and became an important stop on the trade routes between Europe and Asia Its economic wealth was equally matched by its intellectual standing. Its famed library stimulated some of the great advances of the age: this was where Herophilus discovered that the head, not the heart, is the seat of thought; Euclid developed geometry; Aristarchus discovered that the earth revolves around the sun; and Eratosthenes calculated the earth's circumference. A grand tower, the Pharos, one of the Seven Wonders of the Ancient World, was built on an island just offshore and served as both a beacon to guide ships entering the booming harbour and an ostentatious symbol of the city's greatness.

During the reign of its most famous regent, Cleopatra (51–30 BC), Alexandria rivalled Rome in everything but military power – a situation that Rome found intolerable and was eventually forced to act upon. Under Roman control, Alexandria remained the capital of Egypt, but during the 4th century AD, civil war, famine and disease ravaged the city's populace and it never regained its former glory. Alexandria's fall was sealed when the conquering Muslim armies swept into Egypt in the 7th century and bypassed Alexandria in favour of a new capital on the Nile.

Alexandria remained in decline through the Middle Ages and was even superseded in importance as a seaport by the nearby town of Rosetta (Ar Rashid). Over the centuries, its monuments were destroyed by earthquakes and their ruins quarried for building materials, so much so that one of the greatest cities of the classical world was reduced to little more than a fishing village (now Anfushi), with a population of fewer than 10,000.

The turning point in Alexandria's fortunes came with Napoleon's invasion of 1798; recognising the city's strategic importance, he initiated its revival. During the subsequent

ALEXANDRIA IN...

Two Days

Start day one at one of the city's **period cafes** and then get a taste of the past at the excellent **Alexandria National Museum** (p310). Next, stop for lunch at the bustling **Mohammed Ahmed** (p323), the king of *fuul* and falafel. Having gained a sense of the city's history, explore its future at the iconic **Bibliotheca Alexandrina** (p314). When you're done, head across the street to **Selsela Cafe** (p327) for some tea as the waves of the bay roll in alongside. Hop onto a microbus along the Corniche all the way down to **Fort Qaitbey** (p313), a scenic spot for sunset. Have a drink and dinner at the **Greek Club,** (p324) which offers fish and panoramic views over the bay.

On day two stop off for breakfast at **Delices** (p325), then head to **Kom Al Dikka** (p311) and the **Catacombs of Kom Ash Shuqqafa** (p317). Have lunch at one of the trendy restaurants at **L Passage** (p324). After lunch take the tram to the delightful **Mahmoud Said Museum** (p316), followed by the little-visited **Museum of Modern Art** (p311) in Muharram Bey. Alternatively, head for a beach along the shore to the east. For dinner try the atmospheric **Teatro Eskandariya** (p323), and finish with a beer at the old-style bar **Cap d'Or** (p326).

Four Days

On the third day add a day trip to **Rosetta** and the mouth of the Nile. The day after, head to **El Alamein** and spend the afternoon on the beach in **Sidi Abdel Rahman**.

Alexandria

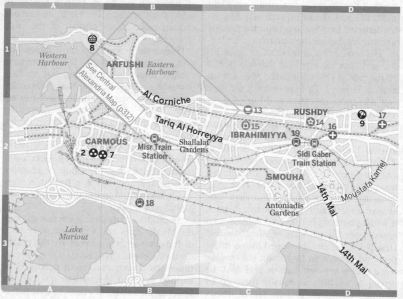

Alexandria

reign of the Egyptian reformist Mohammed Ali, a new town was built on top of the old one. Alexandria once more became one of the Mediterranean's busiest ports and attracted a cosmopolitan mix of people, among them wealthy Turkish-Egyptian traders, Jews, Greeks, Italians and many others from around the Mediterranean. Multicultural, sitting on the foundations of antiquity, perfectly placed on the overland route between

Europe and the East, and growing wealthy from trade, Alexandria took on an almost mythical quality and served as the muse for a new string of poets, writers and intellectuals. But the wave of anti-colonial, pro-Arab sentiment that swept Colonel Gamal Abdel Nasser to power in 1952 also spelt the end for Alexandria's cosmopolitan communities. Those foreigners who didn't stream out of the country in the wake of King Farouk's yacht

0
0
5 km
2.5 miles

MEDITERRANEAN SEA

1

3

SAN STEFANO
Al Corniche (Al Geish)
7 5
10 MANDARA
11
LORAN
Gamal An Nasser
GLYMM
Mahmoud Said Museum
VICTORIA
1
Sidi Bishr Train Station
Gabriel Train Station
12
6
4
Montazah Train Station
MONTAZAH
Aboukir (4km)
Malak Hefny
Rosetta (42km)

Mahmoudiyya Canal

found themselves forced out a few years later following the Suez Crisis, when Nasser confiscated foreign properties and nationalised many foreign-owned businesses.

Since that time the character of the city has changed completely. In the 1940s some 40% of the city's population was made up of foreigners, while now most of its residents are native Egyptians. Where there were 300,000 residents in the 1940s, Alexandria is now home to more than four million. In recent years more than 50,000 Syrian refugees have settled in the city, and their numbers keep rising.

Many people credit events that happened here with lighting the fuse that exploded into the 2011 revolution. In June 2010 a 28-year-old man named Khaled Said was beaten to death by police in Alexandria, apparently after he posted videos on the internet showing police pocketing drugs confiscated in a bust. Soon after the murder, a Facebook page called 'We are all Khaled Said' was created, showing photos of the young man's horribly smashed face and publicly exposing police accounts of his death as blatant fabrications. Outraged, tens of thousands of Egyptians 'friended' the page. A series of protests demanding justice were held in Alexandria. Khaled Said's killing, and the subsequent cover-up, became a symbol of everything believed to be wrong with the regime under President Mubarak. By January 2011 nearly 380,000 people had joined the Facebook page, and its moderator, Google executive Wael Ghonim, used it as a virtual megaphone to call for the demonstrations in Cairo's Tahrir Square that ultimately ousted Mubarak. Alexandria itself saw some of the largest and most intense protests in the entire country during the 2011 revolution, forcing a complete police retreat from the city's streets.

Sights

Modern Alexandria lies along a curving shoreline, stretching for 20km and rarely extending more than 3km inland. The centre of the city arcs around the Eastern Harbour, almost enclosed by two spindly promontories. The city's main tram station at Midan Ramla, where most lines terminate, is considered the epicentre of the city. Two of the city centre's main shopping streets, Sharia Saad Zaghloul and Sharia Safiyya Zaghloul, run off this square. Just west of the tram station is the larger and more formal square Midan Saad Zaghloul, with a popular garden facing the seafront. Around these two squares are the central shopping areas, the tourist office, restaurants and the majority of the cheaper hotels.

Northwest of this central area is the older, atmospheric neighbourhood of Anfushi; south-west is Carmous, which has some notable Roman ruins. Heading east, a succession of newer districts stretches along the coast to the upmarket residential area of Rushdy and the trendy suburbs of San Stefano, and further on to Montazah, with its palace and gardens (p316), which marks the eastern limits of the city. The Corniche is the long and wide coastal road that connects nearly all parts of the city, though crossing it involves playing chicken with swarms of hurtling buses and taxis.

If you're spending significant time in the city, the street map produced by **Mohandes Mostafa El Fadaly** (Map p318; 2nd fl, 49 Sharia Safiyya Zaghloul; ☺9am-4pm Sat-Thu) is very useful.

◉ Central Alexandria

As the city is sandwiched between Lake Mariout and the sea, there is relatively little space for expansion. Since the 2011 revolution a lot of old buildings are being destroyed to make way for huge new developments, and the skyline of the old Corniche has doubled in height. Right in the middle of the broad Corniche is the legendary Cecil Hotel (p322) overlooking Midan Saad Zaghloul. Built in 1930, it's an Alexandrian institution and a memorial to the city's raffish heyday, when guests included the likes of playwrights Somerset Maugham and Noël Coward and former British Prime Minister Winston Churchill. The British Secret Service operated out of a suite on the 1st floor. The hotel was immortalised in British writer Lawrence Durrell's four-novel series *Alexandria Quartet*.

★**Alexandria National Museum** MUSEUM
(Map p312; ☑03-483-5519; 110 Sharia Tariq Al Horreyya; adult/student LE80/40; ☺9am-4.30pm)
This excellent museum sets a high benchmark with its summary of Alexandria's past. Housed in a beautifully restored Italianate villa, the small but thoughtfully selected and well-labelled collection does a sterling job of relating the city's history from antiquity until the modern period. Look out especially for the beautiful *tanagra* – terracotta statues of Greek women – and the discoveries found underwater in the Mediterranean.

The museum's **ground floor** is dedicated to Graeco-Roman times, and highlights include a sphinx and other sculptures found during underwater excavations at Aboukir. Look for the small statue of the Greek god Harpocrates with a finger to his lips (representing silence); he was morphed from the original Egyptian god Horus and is also connected to Eros. Also check out the beautiful statue of a Ptolemaic queen, with Egyptian looks and a Hellenistic body.

The **basement** covers the Pharaonic period with finds from all over Egypt. Note the false doors, which were the link between the living and the dead, and the reserve heads

THE PHAROS

The Egyptian coast was a nightmare for ancient sailors, the flat featureless shoreline making it hard to steer away from hidden rocks and sandbanks. To encourage trade, Ptolemy I (323–283 BC) ordered a great tower to be built, one that could be seen by sailors long before they reached the coast. After 12 years of construction, the Pharos was inaugurated in 283 BC. The structure was added to until it acquired such massive and unique proportions that ancient scholars regarded it as one of the Seven Wonders of the Ancient World.

In its original form, the Pharos was a simple marker, probably topped with a statue, as was common at the time. The tower became a lighthouse, so historians believe, in the 1st century AD, when the Romans added a beacon, probably an oil-fed flame reflected by sheets of polished bronze. According to descriptions from as late as the 12th century, the Pharos had a square base, an octagonal central section and a round top. Contemporary images of the Pharos still exist, most notably in a mosaic in St Mark's Basilica in Venice and another in a church in eastern Libya.

In all, the Pharos withstood winds, floods and the odd tidal wave for 17 centuries; however, in 1303 a violent earthquake rattled the entire eastern Mediterranean, and the Pharos was finally toppled. More than a century later, the Mamluk sultan Qaitbey quarried the ruins for the fortress that still stands on the site.

that were placed near the corpse as a substitute for the head in the afterlife.

The **top floor** displays artefacts from the Byzantine, Islamic and modern periods, including coins, Ottoman weapons and jewels. Don't miss the exquisite silver shield. Early coexistence of Alexandria's major religions is represented by a carved wooden cross encircled by a crescent.

Kom Al Dikka
ARCHAEOLOGICAL SITE

(Map p312; Sharia Ismail Mahana; adult/student LE80/40; ⊙9am-4.30pm) Kom Al Dikka was a well-off residential area in Graeco-Roman times, with lovely villas, bathhouses and a theatre. The area was known at the time as the Park of Pan, a pleasure garden where citizens of Alexandria could indulge in various lazy pursuits. Although the ruins aren't terribly impressive in scale, they remain a superbly preserved ode to the days of the centurion and include the 13 white-marble terraces of the only Roman amphitheatre found in Egypt.

This site was discovered in 1967 when foundations were being laid for an apartment building on a site known unceremoniously as Kom Al Dikka – 'Mound of Rubble'.

In the same complex is the Villa of the Birds, a wealthy urban dwelling dating to the time of Hadrian (AD 117–138). Despite being redecorated at least four times in antiquity before being destroyed by fire in the 3rd century AD, its floor mosaic of pigeons, peacocks, quails, parrots and water hens remains astonishingly well preserved. Additional mosaics feature a panther and a stylised flower design known as a rosette.

Excavations continue to uncover more in the area. In early 2010 the ruins of a Ptolemaic-era temple were uncovered along with statues of gods and goddesses, including a number of the cat goddess Bastet.

Eliyahu Hanavi Synagogue
SYNAGOGUE

(Map p318; ☑to arrange visits 012-2703-1031; Sharia Al Nabi Daniel) Among the largest synagogues in the Middle East, this magnificent Italian-built structure served Alexandria's once-thriving and cosmopolitan Jewish community. The interior features immense marble columns and space for more than 700 people, with brass name plates still affixed to the regular seats of male worshippers. Since the wars with Israel and the 1956 Suez Crisis, the community has dwindled and rarely musters the 10 men necessary to

FINDING ALEXANDRIA'S ANCIENT CORE

Interestingly, modern Alexandria is built directly on top of the ancient city and often follows the ancient street pattern. The street now known as Sharia Tariq Al Horreyya was the ancient Canopic Way, extending from the city's Gate of the Sun in the east to the Gate of the Moon in the west. The centre of town was where it crossed the Street of the Soma (now Sharia Al Nabi Daniel).

hold a service. At the time of research, the building was awaiting renovation.

The synagogue was closed in 2012 because of security reasons. Visits to this moving reminder of the city's multicultural past must be arranged through Ben Youssef Gaon, president of the local Jewish community and, aged in his late 50s, among its youngest current members. Call Ben Youssef's mobile; if you can't make contact this way, try asking at the front gate. A donation of LE20 to LE30 is appreciated but not required.

Museum of Modern Art
MUSEUM

(Musée des Beaux Arts; Map p312; ☑010-0407-4182; 6 Sharia Manasha, Muharram Bey; 10am-6pm Tue-Thu & Sat-Sun) This wonderful and little visited collection of 16th- to 20th-century paintings reflecting the city's cosmopolitan flair is housed in an old villa. Some delightful treasures by Margot Veillon, Theodore Frère and Gerome, and well-installed sculptures by Egyptian artist Mahmoud Mokhtar, are found among more ordinary works, but the place is definitely worth visiting. Next door is a small **Calligraphy Museum**. Bring your passport to enter.

Cavafy Museum
MUSEUM

(Map p318; ☑03-486-1598; 4 Sharia Sharm El Sheikh; adult/child LE25/free; ⊙10am-5pm Tue-Sun) The Alexandrian-Greek poet Constantine Cavafy spent his last 25 years in an apartment above a brothel on the former Rue Lepsius, a flat now preserved as the Cavafy Museum, with two of the six rooms arranged as Cavafy kept them. Editions of the poet's publications and photocopies of his manuscripts, notebooks and correspondence lie spread out on tables throughout the other rooms. A collection of portraits and paintings of the poet adorns the walls of the last room.

Central Alexandria

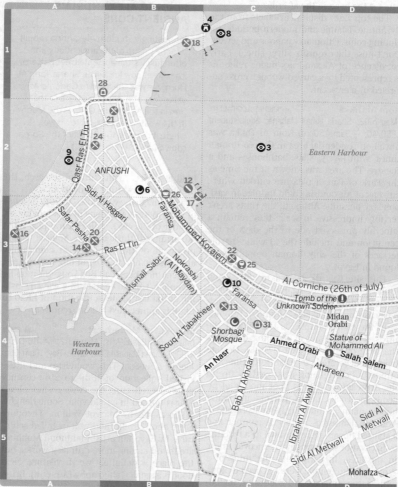

ALEXANDRIA & THE MEDITERRANEAN COAST ALEXANDRIA

With a Greek church (St Saba) around the corner and a hospital opposite, Cavafy thought this was the ideal place to live; somewhere to cater for the flesh, somewhere to provide forgiveness for sins, and a place in which to die. For those who love Cavafy's poetry this is almost a place of pilgrimage.

Anfushi & Fort Qaitbey

Charismatic Anfushi, the old Turkish part of town, was once where stuffy Alexandria came to let down its hair. While Midan Ramla and the Midan Tahrir area were developed along the lines of a European model in the 19th century, Anfushi remained untouched, an indigenous quarter standing in counterpoint to the new cosmopolitan city. This is where writer Lawrence Durrell's characters came in search of prostitutes and a bit of rough trade. Today it remains one of the poorer parts of the city, where a huge number of people live squeezed into old and decaying buildings, many of which seem to be teetering on the verge of collapse.

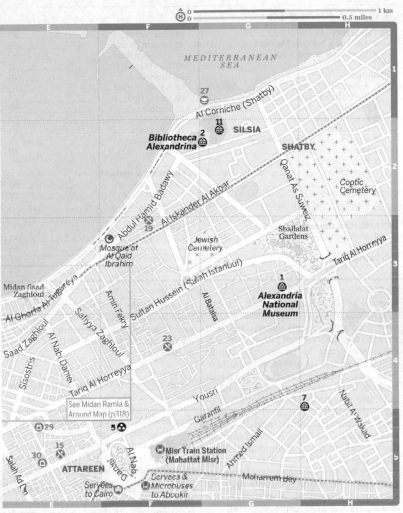

Fort Qaitbey   FORT

(Map p312; Eastern Harbour; adult/student LE40/20; ⊙9am-4pm) The Eastern Harbour is dominated by the bulky walls of Fort Qaitbey, built on a narrow peninsula over the remains of the legendary Pharos lighthouse by the Mamluk sultan Qaitbey in 1480. Finely restored, it has a warren of rooms to explore, and the walk here is just as rewarding. From Midan Ramla it's a 30- to 45-minute stroll along the Corniche with spectacular harbour views along the way.

The Pharos lighthouse, which had been in use for some 17 centuries, was destroyed by an earthquake in 1303 and lay in ruins for more than 100 years before Qaitbey ordered the fortification of the city's harbour. Material from the fallen Pharos was reused, and if you get close to the outer walls, you can pick out some great pillars of red granite, which in all likelihood came from the ancient lighthouse. Other parts of the ancient building are scattered around the nearby seabed.

If you don't feel like a seaside walk, take yellow tram 15 from Midan Ramla to get here or flag down a microbus along the Corniche. A taxi should cost LE10 to LE15.

Central Alexandria

Mosque of Abu Abbas Al Mursi MOSQUE
(Map p312; ☎ 03-480-1251; Sharia Mohammed Koraiem, Anfushi) This stately mosque was built over the tomb of a revered 13th-century Sufi saint, Abu Abbas Al Mursi, from Murcia in Spain. Several successive mosques have been built and rebuilt on the site. Though the current structure is modern, it's still an attractive octagonal building, with a soaring central tower and an interior decorated with eye-catching Islamic mosaics, tiling and woodwork. Al Mursi is one of the four master saints in Egypt, so his tomb here is a pilgrimage place.

Today, the mosque dominates a large midan, easily visible and accessible from the Corniche. Leave your shoes at the entrance and slip the attendant a little baksheesh (tip) when you collect them. Visitors can join the devotees who still flock to **Al Mursi's shrine** under the main floor. On summer nights a carnival-like atmosphere surrounds the mosque, with everything from pony rides to bumper cars to merry-go-rounds.

Terbana Mosque MOSQUE
(Map p312; Sharia Faransa, Anfushi) The beautiful little Terbana Mosque stands at the junction of Sharia Faransa and Wekalet Al Limon. This entire quarter, known as Gumruk, is located on land that was underwater during the Middle Ages. Late-17th-century builders managed to incorporate bits of ancient Al-

exandria in the mosque's structure, reusing two classical columns to support the minaret. The red-and-black-painted brickwork on the facade is typical of the Delta-style architecture.

Shipyards WATERFRONT
(Map p312; Ras El Tin) Where northern Anfushi hits the sea, you can wander among huge wooden vessels in various states of construction. In small workshops, craftspeople make accessories for the boats, such as intricately carved helms (steering wheels) and cabinets. It is off the beaten track and not recommended for women travellers on their own.

Ras El Tin Palace HISTORIC BUILDING
(Map p308; Ras El Tin) Along Alexandria's western shore, past the shipyards, you'll spot Ras El Tin Palace. It is most spectacular seen from the Mediterranean Sea. Originally built in the 1830s for Egyptian ruler Mohammed Ali, it's now part of a naval base and was an official presidential residence. It was here that King Farouk signed his abdication papers in 1952. Unfortunately it's not open to visitors.

◎ Eastern Suburbs

★ Bibliotheca Alexandrina MUSEUM
(Map p312; ☎ 03-483-9999; www.bibalex.org; Al Corniche, Shatby; adult/student LE70/35; ◎ 11am-7pm Sun-Thu, noon-4pm Sat) Alexandria's ancient

ALEXANDRIA'S UNDERWATER SIGHTS

Alexandria has sunk between 6m and 8m since antiquity, so most of what remains of the ancient city lies hidden beneath the modern city or the waters of the Mediterranean. On land, much has been destroyed as the city has grown. But underwater the story is different, and each year reveals more finds from the Ptolemaic period.

So far, exploration has been concentrated around the fortress of Qaitbey (p313), where the Pharos is believed to have stood; the south-eastern part of the Eastern Harbour, where parts of the submerged Ptolemaic royal quarter were found; and Aboukir, where remains of the two sunken cities of Herakleion-Thonis and Menouthis were found. Some of the recovered treasures can be seen in the Bibliotheca Alexandrina's Antiquities Museum (p316) and in the Alexandria National Museum (p310), but divers can also explore the submerged harbour sites with local company Alexandra Dive (p320).

If you feel like a bit of Indiana-Jones-under-the-sea action, these are Alexandria's top dive sites:

Cleopatra's Palace (Map p312) This royal-quarter area in the Eastern Harbour has yielded some of Alexandria's most interesting underwater antiquities. Today divers can see a couple of large, enigmatic sphinxes as well as red-granite columns, platforms and pavements that archaeologists speculate formed part of a former palace. There's also a remarkably complete shipwreck here that has been carbon dated to between 90 BC and AD 130. Depth: 5m. Rating: novice.

Pharos Island (Map p312) This site, just offshore from Fort Qaitbey, contains sphinxes, columns, capitals and statues dating from the Pharaonic, Greek and Roman eras as well as giant granite blocks believed to be remnants of the Pharos lighthouse, broken as if by a fall from a great height. Depth: 8m to 15m. Rating: novice.

Herakleion-Thonis (Map p308) For archaeologists the discovery of the port of Herakleion-Thonis in Aboukir has been a triumph. Excavations have revealed a huge amount of treasures, including giant 5m-high statues (raised from the site), remnants of temple buildings, and gold coins and jewellery. For the non-archaeologist diver though, the major sight in this area is the L'Orient wreck (Napoleon's flagship that sank in 1798). Depth: 14m. Rating: intermediate.

library was one of the greatest of all classical institutions, and while replacing it might seem a Herculean task, the new Bibliotheca Alexandrina manages this with aplomb. Opened in 2002, this impressive piece of modern architecture is a deliberate attempt to rekindle the brilliance of the original centre of learning and culture. The complex has become one of Egypt's major cultural venues and a stage for numerous international performers, and is home to a collection of brilliant museums.

The building takes the form of a gigantic angled discus embedded in the ground, evoking a second sun rising out of the Mediterranean. The granite exterior walls are carved with letters, pictograms, hieroglyphs and symbols from more than 120 different human scripts. Inside, the jaw-dropping main reading room can accommodate eight million books and 2500 readers under its sloping roof, with windows specially designed to let sunlight flood in but keep out rays that might harm the collection.

In addition to the very impressive main reading room, there are four specialised libraries (a children's library for ages six to 11; a youth library for ages 11 to 17; a multimedia library; a library for the blind) and a huge array of other diversions. There are four permanent museums, a planetarium, a conference centre, a range of temporary and permanent exhibitions, and a full schedule of events. To fully explore this very worthy attraction, you should allot half a day; to just gape at the astounding main reading room and do a tour, you'll need an hour or so.

The library is right on the seafront, but the main entrance and ticket office are at the back of the complex. All bags must be checked here, though you can bring your camera and wallet inside. Two of the museums inside have individual entrance tickets; these are bought within the building, next to the museums themselves.

ALEXANDRIA & THE MEDITERRANEAN COAST ALEXANDRIA

➡ The Museums

The **Antiquities Museum** (✆ 03-483-9999; http://antiquities.bibalex.org; adult/student LE50/25; ☺ 9am-6.30pm Sun-Thu, noon-3.45pm Sat) has a well-curated exhibition of artefacts cherry-picked from sites across Egypt that romp from the Pharaonic through to the Greek and Roman periods, and into the Byzantine and Islamic eras. There's a fine collection of 2nd-century coloured funerary masks, intricately decorated mummy cases and faience blue shabti (funerary statues), and some gorgeous Greek-era statuary.

Afterwards, head to the **Manuscript Museum** (adult/student LE30/15; ☺ 11am-7pm Sun-Thu, noon-4pm Sat), which holds a small but beautifully displayed collection of ancient texts and antiquarian books, including a copy of the only surviving scroll from Alexandria's ancient library. Next door is the wonderful **Impressions of Alexandria Exhibition**, which does a sterling job of documenting the city's long history through drawings, maps and early photographs.

From here, explore the Bibliotheca's exhibition halls which showcase the work of contemporary Arabic artists and are also home to a fascinating heritage collection with gorgeously displayed textiles, folk art and Arabic science equipment from the medieval period. **The World of Shadi Abdel Salam** (a cult film director, script writer and set designer born in Alexandria) shows a display of his wonderful drawings of film sets. His most famous film, *The Night of Counting the Years* (*Al Momia* in Arabic), and other films are shown regularly in the afternoon. There's also a video program on Egyptian history called the **Culturama**, displayed on nine screens.

The **Planetarium** (✆ 03-483-9999; per film adult/student LE50/10; ☺ 10am-4pm Sun-Thu) is a futuristic neon-lit sphere, looming on the plaza in front of the library like a mini Death Star from *Star Wars*. It shows 3D films focused on space exploration, the natural world and Egyptian history, all aimed at educating children, on a rotating schedule (see website). It also has an **Exploratorium**, as well as the **History of Science Museum** underneath, also targeted at groups of Egyptian school children. The museum covers the contribution to science of three key historic eras – Pharaonic Egypt, Hellenistic Alexandria and the Islamic era.

Tours of the Bibliotheca Alexandrina run every 45 minutes in English between 11.45am and 4.30pm Sunday to Thursday and on Saturdays from 12.10 to 3pm.

Note that while the library has a wide range of kid-friendly activities and diversions, little ones under the age of six are not admitted to the library room. Helpfully, day care is available during opening hours.

★**Mahmoud Said Museum**   MUSEUM
(Map p308; ✆ 03-582-1688; 6 Sharia Mohammed Pasha Said, Gianaclis; ☺ 10am-6pm Tue-Thu & Sat-Sun) **FREE** Mahmoud Said (1897–1964) was one of Egypt's finest 20th-century artists, even though he is little known outside his country. A judge by profession, he moonlighted as a painter and became a key member of a group of sophisticates devoted to forging an Egyptian artistic identity in the 1920s and '30s. This museum presents about 40 of his works in the beautiful Italianate villa in which he once lived. You will need to show a passport to get in.

One of the rooms in the museum is dedicated to female nudes, quite surprising considering the more conservative mood that Alexandria is in today. Said loved to portray various women and their sensuous bodies, adding simple accessories such as headscarves, jewellery or bracelets to celebrate their 'plebeian' Egyptian beauty. Some of his works have recently sold for millions of dollars in European auction houses.

From the San Stefano tram stop (line 2), cross the tracks and go up the steps to the raised road (opposite the huge mall). Go right and Sharia Mohammed Pasha Said is a short distance away on the left.

Montazah Palace Gardens   GARDENS
(Map p308; Montazah; gardens/beach LE15/25; ☺ 8am-midnight) The 19th-century Montazah palace is off-limits, but the surrounding lush gardens are prime strolling territory. There's an attractive sandy cove here with a semi-private beach well suited for kids (although it's not particularly clean), and an eccentric Victorian-style bridge running out to a small island of pylons. In all, it's a pleasant escape from the city centre. There are several restaurants and picnic places, and a second royal residence, the Salamlek, has been converted into a luxury hotel.

Khedive Abbas Hilmy (1892–1914) built Montazah as his summer palace, a refuge for when Cairo became too hot. It's designed in a pseudo-Moorish style, which has been given a Florentine twist with the addition of

THE GREAT LIBRARY OF ALEXANDRIA

The original Library of Alexandria was the greatest repository of books and documents in all of antiquity. Ptolemy I (323–283 BC) established the library in 283 BC as part of a larger research complex known as the Mouseion (Shrine of the Muses; the source of today's word 'museum'). This dedicated centre of learning housed more than 100 full-time scholars and, in addition to the library, boasted lecture areas, gardens, a zoo and shrines. Uniquely, this was one of the first major 'public' libraries and was open to all people with proper scholarly qualifications.

Demetrius Phalereus, a disciple of Aristotle, was charged with governing the library, and together with Ptolemy I and his successors he established the lofty goal of collecting copies of all the books in the world. Manuscripts found on ships arriving at Alexandria's busy port were confiscated by law and copied, and merchants were sent to scour the markets of other Mediterranean cities looking for tomes of all descriptions. Most books back then consisted of papyrus scrolls, often translated into Greek and rolled and stored in the library's many labelled pigeon-holes. At its height, the library was said to contain more than 700,000 works, which indicated some duplication, as this was believed to be more than the number of published works in existence. The library soon exceeded its capacity and a 'daughter library' was established in the Temple of Serapeum (p319) to stock the overflow. The vast collection established Alexandria's position as the pre-eminent centre of culture and civilization in the world.

It is uncertain exactly who was responsible for the destruction of the ancient world's greatest archives of knowledge, though there are several suspects. Julius Caesar is the first. In his scrap with Pompey in 48 BC, Caesar set fire to Alexandria's harbour, which also engulfed the part of the city in which the library stood. In AD 270, Zenobia, Queen of Palmyra (now Syria), captured Egypt and clashed with Roman emperor Aurelian here, the resulting siege destroying more of the library. At this time, Alexandria's main centre of learning moved to the daughter library in the Serapeum. Early Christians are next in line for the blame: the daughter library was finally destroyed as part of an anti-pagan purge led by Christian Roman emperor Theodosius in AD 391.

a tower modelled on one at Florence's Palazzo Vecchio.

The simplest way to get here is to stand on the Corniche or on Sharia Tariq Al Horreyya and flag down a microbus. When it slows, shout 'Montazah'; if it's going that way (most of them are), it'll stop and you can jump on. A taxi will set you back about LE40.

⊙ Carmous

Catacombs of Kom Ash Shuqqafa ARCHAEOLOGICAL SITE
(Map p308; adult/student LE60/30; ⊙9am-4.30pm) Discovered accidentally in 1900 when a donkey disappeared through the ground, these catacombs make up the largest-known Roman burial site in Egypt and one of the last major works of construction dedicated to the religion of ancient Egypt. Demonstrating Alexandria's hallmark fusion of Pharaonic and Greek styles, the architects used a Graeco-Roman approach. The catacombs consist of three tiers of tombs and chambers cut into bedrock to a depth of 35m (the bottom level is flooded and inaccessible).

Entry is through a spiral staircase; the bodies of the dead would have been lowered on ropes down the centre of this circular shaft. The staircase leads off to a **rotunda** with a central well piercing down into the gloom of the flooded lower level. When the catacombs were originally constructed in the 2nd century AD, probably as a family crypt, the rotunda would have led only to the **triclinium** (to your left) and **principal tomb chamber** (straight ahead). But over the 300 years that the tomb was in use, more chambers were hacked out until it had developed into a hive that could accommodate more than 300 corpses.

The triclinium was a banqueting hall where grieving relatives paid their last respects with a funeral feast. Mourners, who returned to feast after 40 days and again on each anniversary, reclined on the raised benches at the centre of the room around a low table.

Back in the rotunda, head down the stairs to the principal tomb, the centrepiece of the

Midan Ramla & Around

catacombs. Here, an antechamber with columns and pediment leads through to an inner sanctum. The typical Alexandrian-style decoration shows an odd synthesis of ancient Egyptian, Greek and Roman funerary iconography. The doorway to the inner chamber is flanked by figures representing Anubis, the Egyptian god of the dead, but he is dressed as a Roman legionary and sports a serpent's tail representative of Agathos Daimon, a Greek divinity.

From the antechamber a couple of short passages lead to a large U-shaped chamber lined with loculi – the holes in which the bodies were placed. After the body (or bodies, as many of the loculi held more than one) had been placed inside, the small chamber was sealed with a plaster slab.

Back up in the rotunda, four other passageways lead off to small clusters of tombs. One of these gives access to an entirely different complex, known as the **Hall of Ca-**

racalla. This had its own staircase access (long-since caved in) and has been joined to Kom Ash Shuqqafa, which it pre-dates, by industrious tomb robbers who hacked a new passageway. Beside the hole in the wall, a painting shows the mummification of Osiris and the kidnapping of Persephone by Hades, illustrating ancient Egyptian and Greek funerary myths.

As impressive as all this sounds, if you've been to the tombs on Luxor's west bank, Kom Ash Shuqqafa will surely leave you underwhelmed: most of the walls are unadorned, nearly all the paintings having faded to invisibility.

You can easily walk to the catacombs from Pompey's Pillar, which is also located in Carmous. If walking from the pillar, start from in front of the ticket office. With your back to the entrance, take the small street to the right, slightly uphill and away from the tram tracks. Follow this street for sev-

Midan Ramla & Around

eral hundred metres past a small mosque on the left; the entrance to the catacombs is in the next block on your left. A taxi from Midan Saad Zaghloul to the catacombs costs around LE35.

Pompey's Pillar & the Temple of Serapeum ARCHAEOLOGICAL SITE
(Rhakotis; Map p308; adult/student LE60/30; ⊗9am-4.30pm) A massive 30m column looms over the debris of the glorious ancient settlement of Rhakotis, the original township from which Alexandria grew. Known as Pompey's Pillar, for centuries the column, hewn from red Aswan granite, has been one of the city's prime sights: a single, tapered shaft, 2.7m at its base and capped by a fine Corinthian capital. The column rises out of the sparse ruins of the Temple of Serapeum, a magnificent structure that stood here in ancient times.

The column was named by travellers who remembered the murder of the Roman general Pompey by Cleopatra's brother, but an inscription on the base (presumably once covered with rubble) announces that it was erected in AD 291 to support a statue of the emperor Diocletian.

Underneath the column, steps lead downward to the ruins of the great temple of Serapis, the hybrid Greek and Egyptian god of Alexandria. Also here was the 'daughter library' of the Great Library of Alexandria, which was said to have contained copies and overflow of texts. These scrolls could be consulted by anyone using the temple, making it one of the most important intellectual and religious centres in the Mediterranean.

The temple was attacked during the Jewish Revolt in AD 115–117, but it was the Christians who launched a final assault on pagan intellectuals in AD 391 and destroyed the Serapeum and its library, leaving just the lonely pillar standing. The site is now very forlorn, little more than rubble pocked by trenches and holes, with a couple of narrow shafts from the Serapeum to explore below, a few sphinxes (originally from Heliopolis) and a surviving Nilometer (a structure used to measure and record the level of the Nile in ancient times). The pillar on top is the only ancient monument remaining whole and standing in Alexandria today. The guards can be slightly pushy here.

When taking a taxi here, ask for it by the Arabic name, Amoud Al Sawari. The fare should be LE30 to LE35 from Midan Saad Zaghloul.

LOCAL KNOWLEDGE

HITTING THE BEACH IN ALEXANDRIA

If you want to get in the water, there are plenty of public and private beaches along Alexandria's waterfront. But the shoreline between the Eastern Harbour and Montazah can be grubby and packed to the rafters in summer, and most locals head for beaches on the North Coast for the high season.

Women should note that at all the beaches except those owned by Western hotels, modesty prevails and covering up when swimming is strongly recommended – wear a baggy T-shirt and shorts over your swimsuit. At these and any city beaches, expect to pay an entrance fee and more for umbrellas and chairs, if desired.

Mamoura Beach (Map p308; beach/area entry LE10/5) About 1km east of Montazah, Mamoura is the 'beachiest' of Alexandria's beaches. There's a cobblestone boardwalk with a few ice-cream shops and food stalls, but what really makes this feel different from other beaches is the separation between it and the main road, meaning there's no noisy speedway behind you. To get here, flag down an Aboukir-bound microbus along the Corniche and let the driver know you want Mamoura. Local authorities are trying to keep this suburb exclusive by charging everyone who enters the area, though you might not have to pay if you walk in. A much less-crowded private beach is next to the main beach, with nice frond-type umbrellas and a LE50 per person entry fee.

Miami Beach (Map p308) Miami Beach (pronounced me-ami) has a sheltered cove with a water slide and jungle gym set up in the sea for kids to frolic on, but note that these get almost comically crowded during peak season. It's 12.5km east of Midan Saad Zaghloul along the Corniche.

Stanley Beach (Map p308; Sidi Gaber) This spectacular beach, on a tiny bay with the old Stanley Bridge soaring above it, has a modest patch of sand for bathing backed by three levels of beach cabins. The sight of the sea crashing against the bridge's concrete supports is dramatic, but this beach is not very suitable for kids because of the waves.

🏃 Activities

Alexandra Dive DIVING
(Map p312; ☎03-483-2045, mobile 012-2906-5477; www.alex-dive.com; Al Corniche, Anfushi; 2-dive package €80, with own equipment €60) Alexandria's diving experts are headed up by Dr Ashraf Sabry, who has been exploring the coastline here for decades. The company offers dive packages to the underwater archaeological sites in and around Alexandria, as well as to the WWI and WWII wreck dives offshore.

Several divers have reported that poor visibility in the bay (as little as 1m depending on the time of year) affected their enjoyment of the harbour dives. In summer, there is a lovely relaxed seafront bar in the compound.

📖 Courses

Qortoba Institute for Arabic Studies LANGUAGE
(Map p308; ☎010-0209-3065, 03-556-2959; www.qortoba.net; cnr Muhammad Nabeel Hamdy & Khalid Bin Waleed, Miami; ⊙7am-11pm) Offers modern standard and colloquial Arabic courses, private tuition and online courses for everyone from absolute beginners to experienced speakers. The institute can also arrange accommodation nearby in good-value student apartments.

👉 Tours

Michael Mitchell WALKING
(☎012-2085-2916; egyptianmitch@gmail.com; US$30-50) Michael Mitchell organises personal guided walking tours highlighting the city's rich architecture, history and culture, particularly of the Egyptian belle époque era. Call him to see what's on, or he can offer you a customised walk.

Tamer Zakaria TOURS
(☎012-2370-8210; tamerzakaria@yahoo.com) A highly recommended English-speaking guide and Egyptologist, friendly and knowledgeable, available for day guiding. He can also organise trips and tours along the coast or elsewhere in Egypt.

✨ Festivals & Events

Alexandria International
Film Festival
FILM

(🕙Nov) The Alexandria International Film Festival takes place every November and is a key event in Egypt's cinematic calendar. Independent filmmakers from across the world showcase their work here. The main venue is the Bibliotheca Alexandrina (p314), but screenings and Q&As with directors also take place at several other cinemas and historic buildings around town.

🛏 Sleeping

Alexandria continues to suffer from a dearth of midrange hotels. Budget accommodation is well represented, with hotels running the gamut from downright seedy to halfway decent. The selection of places to rest your head then quickly shoots straight into the top-end category with several five-star hotel chains and a handful of historic hotels still hanging on along the seafront.

Quite a few of the budget hotels front at least partly on to the Corniche. One of the pleasures of staying in Alexandria is pushing open the shutters in the morning to get a face full of fresh air off the Mediterranean, but light sleepers may want to consider a room off the Corniche because of the unrelenting din of traffic. At any of Alexandria's budget hotels, it's wise to bring along your own soap, towel and toilet paper, as supplies can be erratic.

The summer months of June to September are Alexandria's high season, when half of Cairo seems to decamp here to escape the heat of the capital. Pre-booking during this period is advised.

Hotel Union
HOTEL $

(Map p318; ☑ 03-480-7312; 5th fl, 164 Al Corniche; s/d LE175/195, with sea view LE200/250; ☎) Book a seafront room and princely views of the Med from the balcony are yours for a pauper's budget. Alexandria's safest, most solid budget option is always bustling with a mix of Egyptian holidaymakers and foreign travellers. The simple rooms are decently maintained and clean, and the staff is a cheerful lot even if the service can be hilariously haphazard.

Triomphe Hotel
HOTEL $

(Map p318; ☑ 03-480-7585; www.triomphehotel. com; 3rd fl, 26 Sharia Al Ghorfa Al Togareyya; d/tr LE200/250, s/d with shared bathroom LE110/160; ☎) The homely Triomphe has a leafy lobby that feels like you've wandered into someone's living room. Spacious rooms cling to shreds of former elegance, with high ceilings and dark-wood furniture, though some are ageing more gracefully than others. It's worth paying extra for the en-suite doubles (which have balconies with side sea views) even if you're travelling solo. The rooms on the main street are much more noisy.

Hotel Crillon
HOTEL $

(Map p318; ☑ 03-480-0330; 3rd fl, 5 Sharia Adib Ishaq; s/d LE162/217, with sea view LE185/246) This old-timer has oodles of character but is rough around the edges. On the plus side, sea-facing rooms boast million-dollar harbour vistas, balconies, high ceilings – and a bizarre hodgepodge of furniture. But all rooms share shabby bathrooms, and if you're offered a room that isn't on the 3rd floor, view before committing – some look quite rundown.

The airy lobby has lovely sea views and a cabinet of stuffed seabirds.

Alex Otel
HOTEL $$

(Alexander the Great Hotel; Map p318; ☑ 012-2560-3476, 03-487-0081; www.facebook.com/alexhotel 2014; 5 Sharia Oskofia; s/d/tr LE500/750/900; ☎) In a quiet spot beside St Katherine School, the Alex might not have grand harbour views, but its squeaky-clean rooms are a breath of fresh air compared to most of Alexandria's hotels. Here you get bright and breezy contemporary style thanks to lashings of white paint, Islamic-design art prints on the walls, new furniture, modern bathrooms and even in-room kettles.

Try to bag room 205 or 200, with balconies overlooking St Katherine Church, and you won't miss the Mediterranean vistas at all. The hotel is near Midan Tahrir (with its big statue of 19th-century Egyptian ruler Mohammed Ali) but can be tricky for taxis to find. Ask for Sharia Sant Katrin. When you're next to the church, you'll spot the hotel signs.

Windsor Palace Hotel
HISTORIC HOTEL $$

(Map p318; ☑ 03-484-0910; www.facebook.com/ paradiseinngroup; 17 Sharia Ash Shohada; s/d US$79/84, with sea view US$89/94, ste from US$139; ☎) This bejewelled Edwardian gem has been keeping a watchful eye on the Med since 1907. It's undergone a much-needed nip and tuck since then, but thankfully the wonderful old elevators and grand lobby were retained, and rooms still boast an old-world, green-and-gold pizazz that wouldn't

LITERARY ALEXANDRIA

Alexandria is better known for its literature and writers than for any bricks-and-mortar monuments, and many a traveller arrives at Misr Train Station (p329) with a copy of novelist Lawrence Durrell's *Alexandria Quartet* in hand. Unlike the Alexandria of ancient days past, the city evoked by Durrell, EM Forster and the Alexandrian-Greek poet Constantine Cavafy can still be seen draped over the buildings of the city's central area.

Born of Greek parents, Cavafy (1863–1933) lived all but a few of his 70 years in Alexandria. In some poems, he resurrects figures from the Ptolemaic era and classical Greece; in others he captures fragments of the city through its routines or chance encounters. He was born into one of the city's wealthiest families, but a reversal of fortune forced him to spend most of his life working as a clerk for the Ministry of Public Works, in an office above the Trianon (p325) cafe.

Cavafy was first introduced to the English-speaking world by EM Forster (1879–1970), the celebrated English novelist who'd already published *A Room with a View* and *Howards End* when he arrived in Alexandria in 1916. Working for the Red Cross, Forster spent three years in the city and, although it failed to find a place in his subsequent novels, he compiled what he referred to as an 'antiguide'. His *Alexandria: A History & Guide* was intended, he explained, as a guide to things not there, based on the premise that 'the sights of Alexandria are in themselves not interesting, but they fascinate when we approach them from the past'.

The guide provided an introduction to the city for Lawrence Durrell (1912–90), who arrived in Egypt 22 years after Forster's departure. Durrell had been evacuated from Greece and resented Alexandria, which he called a 'smashed up broken down shabby Neapolitan town'. But as visitors discover today, first impressions are misleading; between 1941 and 1945 Durrell found great distraction in the slightly unreal air of decadence and promiscuity engendered by the uncertainties of the ongoing desert war, which led to the writing of his most famous work.

Travellers on a literary pilgrimage may want to hunt down the lesser-seen Cavafy Museum (p311), and the Abou El Sid restaurant, which has taken the place of the famous Pastroudis Cafe, a frequent meeting point for the characters of the *Alexandria Quartet*.

be out of place on the *Orient Express*. Bag a seafront room if you can.

Metropole Hotel　　　　　HISTORIC HOTEL $$
(Map p318; ☑03-480-8123; www.facebook.com/paradiseinngroup; 52 Sharia Saad Zaghloul, on Mahattat Ramla; s/d with street view US$74/84, with sea view US$89/94; ☎) The Metropole could once have been called classy but has fallen on hard times. Although it was entirely revamped in the 1990s – including a magnificently tacky lobby with Parthenon-style friezes – there's definite wear and tear beyond its hilarious gilded doors, panelled walls and over-the-top chandeliers in the mammoth rooms. Still, the place has atmosphere in spades.

★**Steigenberger**
Cecil Hotel　　　　　HISTORIC HOTEL $$$
(Map p318; ☑03-487-7173; www.steigenberger.com; 16 Midan Saad Zaghloul; s/d/tr US$137/152/168, s/d with sea view US$152/165; ☎) The historic Cecil Hotel is a true Alexandria legend, though a series of refits over the years has unfortunately erased most of the days-gone-by lustre from when Winston Churchill and writer Lawrence Durrell propped up the famous bar here. Rooms are elegantly attired in red and cream, and seafront ones have sweeping views over the Eastern Harbour.

Monty's Bar (now on the 1st floor) and the grand lobby retain only a fraction of their historic glory, but the creaky old-fashioned elevator still trundles between floors.

Four Seasons Hotel　　　　　HOTEL $$$
(Map p308; ☑03-581-8000; www.fourseasons.com; 399 Al Corniche, San Stefano; r US$220-330, ste from US$370; @☎☒) The much-loved old Casino San Stefano made way for this grand edifice, whose gleaming towers dwarf neighbouring buildings. Inside no expense has been spared: the marble lobby gleams, the army of staff is eager to please, and the rooms – decked out in soft lemon – sport

modern conveniences while reflecting Alexandria's Egyptian, Greek and French heritage. All rooms have balconies.

✕ Eating

One of the great dining pleasures here is tucking into the day's fresh catch in one of the seafood restaurants overlooking the Eastern Harbour. The city's culinary scene has been changed by Syrian refugees who have opened popular shawarma stalls along the Corniche.

Note that many restaurants don't serve alcohol. For a beer with your meal, you'll have to head to one of the luxury hotels or upmarket restaurants.

✕ Central Alexandria

★ Mohammed Ahmed   EGYPTIAN $
(Map p318; ☑ 03-487-3576; 17 Sharia Shakor Pasha, off Sharia Saad Zaghloul; dishes LE2-12; ⊘ noon-midnight; ✐) The perfect lunch stop to scoff *fuul* (fava bean paste) and falafel. Mohammed Ahmed is the undisputed king of spectacularly good and cheap Egyptian standards. Select your *fuul* (we recommend *iskandarani*, mashed up with lots of lime juice and spices), add some falafel, choose a few accompanying salads and let the feasting begin.

There's an English menu to aid your selection. The tahini, *banga* (beetroot) and *torshi* (bright-pink pickled vegetables) are all good choices to add to your meal. Note that the street sign on the corner of Saad Zaghloul calls this Sharia Abdel Fattah El Hadary.

La Veranda   EUROPEAN €
(Map p318; ☑ 03-486-1432; 46 Sharia Saad Zaghloul; mains LE25 60; ⊘ 11am-midnight; ✿) Next door to famous tea room Delices (p325) and run by the same people, La Veranda is a cosy place that specialises in Greek and French cuisine, with steaks, good meatball dishes and *youvetsi* (Greek pasta) on the menu. Dessert is taken care of by the mammoth patisserie selection at Delices (p325). Beer and Egyptian wine are served.

Taverna   EGYPTIAN $
(Map p318; ☑ 03-487-8591; 1 Midan Saad Zaghloul; mains LE12-48; ⊘ noon-4am; ✐) This bustling joint serves some of the best shawarma in town plus excellent hand-thrown sweet or savoury *fiteer* (Egyptian flaky 'pizza'). Can't choose? Order the shawarma *fiteer* for an Egyptian fast-food double-up. Don't

miss watching the *fiteer* chef showing off his craft; he could give any Italian a run for their money with his dough-stretching skills. Eat in or takeaway.

Abou Nasr   EGYPTIAN $
(Map p318; ☑ 03-480-6635; www.facebook.com/abounasser1234; 13 Sharia Al Shohadaa, Mahattet Raml; mains LE6-9; ⊘ 8am-midnight) This unusually tidy place serves good, filling *kushari* (a mix of noodles, rice, black lentils, fried onions and tomato sauce). Don't forget to douse your dish with liberal lashings of vinegar and spicy sauce. There's no sign in English, so look for the gleaming gold bowls.

Awalad Abdou   SANDWICHES $
(Map p312; Sharia Mohafaza; sandwiches LE4-8; ⊘ 24hr) With only minor concessions made to hygiene, this uber-budget place is nonetheless a smashing find, whipping up micro-sandwiches with the scrumptious, meaty filling of your choice. Just point to what looks good and gobble it up while standing at the counter. There's no sign, so look for a small shop with hanging cured meats near Sharia Attareen.

Chez Gaby   ITALIAN $
(Map p318; ☑ 03-487-4404; www.facebook.com/moby.food; 22 Sharia Tariq Al Horreyya; mains LE25-55; ⊘ 1-11.30pm) Visiting this old-fashioned taverna is like stepping back in time. We love the intimate atmosphere, complete with chequered tablecloths, friendly service and a good menu of well prepared pasta, pizza and other Italian classics. Alcohol is served.

★ Abou El Sid   EGYPTIAN $$
(Map p318; ☑ 03-392-9609; 39 Sharia Tariq Al Horreyya; mains LE56-125; ⊘ 1pm-1am) This swish Egyptian restaurant has kept much of the old setting of Pastroudis Cafe, the famous literary haunt, adding the wonderful art of Chant Avenisslan and an excellent menu of Egyptian classics. It includes mezze, stuffed pigeon, a seafood stew and a delicious *molokhiyya* (garlicky leaf soup) with rabbit or chicken. Alcohol is served. Book ahead.

★ Teatro Eskandariya   EGYPTIAN $$
(Map p318; ☑ 03-390-1339; www.facebook.com/Teatro.Eskendria.Official; 25 Sharia Fouad, Mahattet Ramleh; mains LE28-118; ⊘ 9am-1am) Popular with local artists and creatives, the Teatro has it all: a cafe, restaurant, cultural centre, theatre, music venue and art gallery. Set in an alley back from the main street there is a large outdoor terrace with traditional

seating, and several colourful, cosy indoor rooms. Honest simple food and a lively atmosphere.

China House
CHINESE $$

(Map p318; ☑ 012-2248-6661, 03-487-7173; 16 Midan Saad Zaghloul, top fl, Cecil Hotel; mains LE45-120; ☺ 11am-11.30pm; ☑) Need a change from shawarma and kebabs? Atop the Cecil Hotel (p322), this restaurant serves decent Asian flavours complete with lovely service, dangling lanterns and stunning harbour views. The ambience is breezy, and the chicken dumplings and grilled beef with garlic are first-rate. There is a wide selection of sushi, and the banana fritters are a scrumptious treat. Alcohol is served.

L Passage
FOOD HALL $$

(Downtown Mall; Map p312; ☑ 03-486-0066; www.facebook.com/theLPassage; 52 Sharia Fouad, cnr Sharia Tariq Al Horreyya; mains LE45-130; ☺ 7am-1am; ☎) This cosmopolitan food mall in a downtown mansion is very popular with young, middle-class locals. Several cafes serve coffee, cakes and shisha, including Brew and Chew, the Pottery Cafe and the Nutopia, where everything is Nutella-flavoured. Various trendy chain restaurants include the urban-Lebanese Taboon, the Egyptian Man'ousha Street and Mori Sushi. A perfect place for a coffee or good lunch.

Fish Market
SEAFOOD $$$

(Map p312; ☑ 03-480-5119; Al Corniche, next to Sea Scouts Club; mains LE60-300; ☺ noon-1am; ☐) An Alexandria institution for the hoity-toity set, Fish Market's dining room is in a prime position slap on the Med and is one of the city's most popular spots for a seafood splurge. Choose from a dazzling array of fishy mains displayed in the cabinets and dive into the fantastic mezze (served with excellent Lebanese-style bread) while you wait.

✕ Anfushi

For some authentic Alexandrian flavour and atmosphere, head for the simple, good-value streetside restaurants in Anfushi. Sharia Safar Pasha is lined with a dozen places where fires crackle and flame under the grills barbecuing meat and fish. You could chance a table at any of them and probably come away satisfied. Don't hesitate to bring the kids to any of the places we recommend; most are filled with families. All are open well past midnight.

El Sheikh Wafik
DESSERTS $

(Map p312; ☑ 010-6332-8930; 34 Sharia Qasr Ras Al Tin, Bahary; desserts LE7-19; ☺ 10am-4am) This unassuming and breezy corner cafe serves up some of the best traditional desserts in town. You can get the usual ice cream in several flavours, but the real treats are Egyptian classics such as *couscousy* – a yummy mix of couscous, shredded coconut, nuts, raisins and sugar, topped with hot milk – or rice pudding with nuts.

★ Kadoura
SEAFOOD $$

(Map p312; ☑ 03-480-0405; 33 Sharia Bairam At Tonsi; mains LE70-190; ☺ 11.30am-2pm) Pronounced 'Adora', this is one of Alexandria's most authentic fish restaurants, with food served at simple tables in a narrow street. Pick your fish (priced per kilo) from a huge ice-packed selection, usually including sea bass, red and grey mullet, bluefish, sole, squid, crab and prawns. A selection of mezze is served with all orders (don't hope for a menu).

Most fish costs LE70 to LE190 per kg, prawns LE400 per kg. Kadoura has an air-conditioned (though less atmospheric) **branch** (Map p312; ☑ 03-480-0967; 47 Al Corniche; mains LE70-190; ☺ 11.30am-2am) along the Corniche.

★ Greek Club
GREEK $$

(White and Blue Restaurant; Map p312; ☑ 03-480-2690; 63 Sharia Iskandar Al Akbar, top fl, Greek Nautical Club, next to Qaitbey Fort; mains LE40-80; ☺ noon-midnight; ☑) The Greek Club's wide terrace is just the ticket for catching the evening breeze and watching the lights along Alexandria's legendary bay. The moussaka and the souvlaki are both easy menu winners, and the seafood selection (priced by weight) is excellent too. Order your fish Greek-style – oven-baked with lemon, olive oil and oregano. Alcohol is served.

This is one of the best places in the city for a sundowner beer or cocktail. Minimum charge in the restaurant is LE75. Check out the recently opened lounge club on the roof called **Olive Island** (mains LE75-165; ☺ 5pm-12.30am Sat-Wed, to 1am Thu & Fri; ☎).

Abdo Farag Fish
SEAFOOD $$

(Map p312; ☑ 03-481-1047; 7 Souq Al Tabakheen; mains LE45-110; ☺ noon-3am) This local spot is deep in the heart of the souq (p329). Sit outdoors under the awning or inside the air-conditioned dining room to feast on perfectly cooked and seasoned seafood. It's a bit hard to find – the sign is high above street

ALEXANDRIA'S CAFE CULTURE

Alexandria is a cafe town – and we're not talking Starbucks double-decaf-soy-low-fat-vanilla-grande lattes. Ever since the early 1900s, Alexandria's culture has revolved around cafes, where the city's diverse population congregated to live out life's dramas over pastries and a cup of tea or coffee. Famous literary figures met here, chattering and pondering the city they could not quite grasp. Many of these old haunts remain, and even though the food and drink in many aren't up to scratch, they are definitely worth a visit, to experience them as living relics of times past and to catch a glimpse of their grand decor. Here's a run-down of classic java joints where you can get a sip of the old days.

Delices (Map p318; ☑ 03-486-1432; www.delicesgroup.com; 46 Sharia Saad Zaghloul; ⊗ 8am-11pm; 🛜) This old tea room has been in business since 1922 and is *the* place to come for tea and cake. Although much of its original grandeur has been scrubbed away, its high-ceilinged halls still exude a sense of old-world atmosphere. The patisserie here once supplied Egypt's royalty, and the cafe was a favourite haunt of Allied soldiers during WWII. On a hot day, order the speciality Deliccino drink (ice cream and espresso milkshake).

Sofianopoulos Coffee Store (Map p318; ☑ 03-593-0000; www.facebook.com/Sofiano poulo-for-Import-Coffee-Stores-189063451160251; 21 Sharia Saad Zaghloul; ⊗ 8am-10pm) You can smell the coffee from half a block away. This old-fashioned coffee retailer would be in a museum anywhere else in the world. Dominated by huge silver coffee grinders, stacks of glossy beans and the wonderful, faintly herbal aroma of roasted java, it's caffeine heaven and it serves coffee fit for a king.

Trianon (Map p318; ☑ 03-486-0986; 56 Midan Saad Zaghloul; continental breakfast LE48, mains LE35-110; ⊗ 9am-midnight; 🖋) This was a favourite haunt of the Greek poet Cavafy, who worked in offices on the floor above. Stop here to admire the 1930s grandeur of its sensational ornate ceiling and faded but still glorious wall panels. Grab a slice of something from the patisserie selection, order a juice (the coffee here is underwhelming), and soak up the historic atmosphere.

Athineos (Map p318; ☑ 03-486-8131; 21 Midan Saad Zaghloul) Opposite Midan Ramla, this place lives and breathes nostalgia. The cafe part still has some of its original 1940s fittings and pastries that taste like they've been sitting around since then, but most of it has had a painful revamp.

Brazilian Coffeestore (Map p318; ☑ 03-486-5059; www.facebook.com/Brazilian.coffee.stores; 44 Sharia Saad Zaghloul; ⊗ 7.30am-10pm) This coffee store from 1929 has been revamped but retains its old-world atmosphere and makes a wicked espresso.

level. If you do miss it, just ask around; everyone knows it.

Samakmak EGYPTIAN $$
(Map p312; ☑ 03-481-1560; 42 Qasr Ras El Tin, Anfushi; mains LE60-200; ⊗ 1pm-2am) Owned by Zizi Salem, the retired queen of the Alexandrian belly-dancing scene, Samakmak is one step up from the other fish eateries in Anfushi. The fish is as fresh as elsewhere, but customers flock to this place for its specials, including crayfish, marvellous crab *tagen* (a stew cooked in a deep clay pot) and a great spaghetti with clams.

Abu Ashraf SEAFOOD $$
(Map p312; ☑ 010-0139-3333; 28 Sharia Safer Pasha, Bahary; mains LE40-100; ⊗ 10am-midnight) Choose from the day's catch, then take a seat under the awning and watch it being cooked. Sea bass stuffed with garlic and herbs is a speciality, as is the creamy prawn *kishk* (casserole). Price is determined by weight and type of fish, ranging from grey mullet at LE75 per kg to jumbo prawns at LE300 to LE350 per kg.

Hosny Grill GRILL $$
(Map p312; ☑ 03-484-3488; 30 Sharia Safar Pasha, Bahary; mains LE45-90; ⊗ 11am-1am) Hosny Grill is a semi-outdoor place specialising in tasty grilled chicken, kebabs and other meat dishes, all served with the usual triumvirate of vegetables, salad and rice. You'll have to roll out the door after eating here. It's opposite Abu Ashraf restaurant.

Eastern Suburbs

Abo Fares Al Soury
KEBAB $

(Map p308; ☑03-554-5500; 60 Sharia Iskandar Ibrahim, Miami; mains LE25-45; ⊙10am-4am) This excellent restaurant specialises in Syrian-style shawarma, a mouth-watering concoction of spicy grilled lamb or chicken, slathered in garlicky mayonnaise and pickles, rolled up inside roasted *shammy* (pita-like bread). A full menu of mezze and shawarma is available, and seating is indoors or in a garden patio. Taxi drivers should know it. Takeaway available.

Drinking & Nightlife

After dinner it's de rigueur to spend a lazy evening in a city-centre cafe watching the world go by, but those looking for an alcoholic tipple have relatively little choice. Sixty years ago Alexandria was so famous for its watering holes that the 1958 film *Ice Cold in Alex* was based on a stranded WWII ambulance crew dreaming of making it back to Alexandria to sip a beer.

During summer the 20km length of the Corniche from Ras El Tin to Montazah seems to become one great strung-out *ahwa* (coffeehouse). With a few exceptions, these are not the greatest places – they're catering for a passing holiday trade and tend to overcharge. Nevertheless, Alexandria is a great place to get in some quality shisha time.

Solo women should note that many of Alex's backstreet *ahwas* remain the exclusive domain of backgammon-playing men. The majority along the Corniche are women- and family-friendly.

Central Alexandria

★ Cap d'Or
BAR

(Map p318; ☑03-487-5177; 4 Sharia Adib Bek Ishak; mains LE30-60; ⊙10am-3am) The Cap d'Or, just off Sharia Saad Zaghloul, is one of the only surviving typical Alexandrian bars. With beer flowing generously, stained-glass windows, a long marble-topped bar, plenty of ancient memorabilia decorating the walls and crackling tapes of old French *chanson* (a type of traditional folk music) or Egyptian hits, it feels like a throwback to Alexandria's cosmopolitan past.

Bohemian crowds come to drink cold beer, snack on great seafood and just hang out at the bar talking or playing guitar with fellow drinkers.

El Tugareya
COFFEE

(Map p318; Al Corniche; ⊙9am-midnight) Although it may not look like much to the uninitiated (it doesn't even sport a sign), this 90-year-old institution is one of the most important *ahwas* (coffeehouses) in town. It's an informal centre of business and trade (the name roughly translates to 'commerce'), where deals are brokered in time-honoured tradition – over a glass of *shai* (tea) or *ahwa* (coffee).

The cafe is separated into multiple rooms, covering a whole block. The southern side is a male-dominated area dedicated to games and informal socialising, while along the Corniche you're likely to be part of a rambunctious mix of writers, film-makers, students and courting couples filling the hall with a cacophony of animated conversation.

THE THREAT TO ALEXANDRIA'S HERITAGE

Since Alexandria has not much space to expand inland, where it abuts Lake Mariout, it can only grow in length along the coast, or go higher within the city. Sadly since the 2011 revolution many historic buildings have been destroyed to make way for hotels, high-rises and shopping malls. A 2006 law forbids the demolition or alteration of 'any building of significant architectural style related to national history or a historical figure, a building that represents a historical era, or a building that is considered a touristic attraction'. The organisation AlexMed compiled a legal Heritage Preservation List in 2007, but owners seek to remove their properties from the list to sell the land to developers. In recent years many villas and other historic buildings have been knocked down, and everywhere in the city centre there are the open wounds of buildings that have recently been demolished. The seafront Corniche is still more or less intact but the houses right behind it have made way for high-rises at least twice the height of the original buildings.

A group of young Alexandrian volunteers called Description of Alexandria (https://descriptionofalexandria.wordpress.com) is trying to keep an eye on the situation, record and map what is left of the city's heritage, and fight to protect it.

Imperial Cafe & Restaurant
CAFE

(Map p318; ☑ 03-480-6812; www.facebook.com/imperial.cafe.alexandria; 28 Midan Saad Zaghloul; ⊘ 9am-1am; 🛜) This classic cafe has been tastefully refitted to become a chic yet comfortable space with air-conditioning, wi-fi and a list of espresso-based coffees, smoothies and fancy juices. There's a full menu featuring burgers, sandwiches and fajitas. You can also sit out on the sidewalk at an umbrella-covered table. It's a great place to take a break.

Spitfire
BAR

(Map p318; ☑ 012-7728-2791; 7 Sharia L'Ancienne Bourse; ⊘ 2pm-1.30am Mon-Sat) One of the best bars in town, Spitfire is a dimly lit but friendly place with a bit of a rough-and-ready feel, just north of Sharia Saad Zaghloul. Walls are plastered with shipping-line stickers, rock-and-roll memorabilia and photos of drunk regulars. It's a great place for a fun evening out with a mixed clientele of locals, foreign residents and passers through.

Ahwa Sayed Darwish
COFFEE

(Map p318; Sharia Abu Shusha; ⊘ 11am-midnight) Named for the composer of Egypt's national anthem, this tiny and highly enjoyable local coffeehouse, near Sharia Al Nabi Daniel, is set on a quiet and leafy side street around the corner from the Cavafy Museum (p311). The chairs are comfortably padded, and the shisha pipe comes fast and clean. The clientele is exclusively men.

🍸 Anfushi

El Qobesl
JUICE BAR

(Map p312; ☑ 03-486-7860; 51 Al Corniche; ⊘ 24hr) El Qobesi has crowned itself the 'king of mango' – take one sip of the juice here and you will bow down, a loyal peon. Slivers of several ripe mangoes are cajoled nearly whole into a tall, chilled glass to make some of the best mango juice we've ever tried. Open around the clock, and always bustling.

Sit streetside and watch the chaos: locals often pull up for a quick in-car slurp, and we've even seen full microbuses stop by.

Farouk Cafe
COFFEE

(Map p312; ☑ 03-480-3103; Sharia Ismail Sabry) This venerable shisha joint looks like it hasn't changed an iota since opening in 1928. It's a delightfully ramshackle old place, with dusty bronze lanterns outside and charmingly fusty old men arguing and play-ing board games at the tables under huge photos of the former king.

🍸 Eastern Suburbs

★Selsela Cafe
CAFE

(Map p312; Al Corniche, Shatby Beach; ⊘ approx 10am-late) At this fantastic cafe across from the Bibliotheca Alexandrina (p314) you can sip tea and smoke shisha to the sound of waves rolling in, and smell sea air instead of petrol fumes (yay). Directly on the water, it has rustic palm-frond-shaded tables replete with twinkling coloured lights, set on a small curving beach where you can hardly hear the traffic.

It's a great place to relax in the sultry breeze, enjoying the Mediterranean vibe. To find it, look for the modern sculpture with three white needles, directly across the Corniche from the library. Walk past the sculpture towards the sea; the entrance is down the steps to the right.

El Rehany
COFFEE

(Map p308; ☑ 03-590-5521; cnr Al Corniche & Sharia Ismail Fangary, Camp Chesar; ⊘ 9am-midnight) This expansive and breezy Alexandrian classic is reputed to have the best shisha in town, served with a flourish by attentive boys in smart two-toned waistcoats while black-and-white-clad waiters bring tea in silver urns. The decor is eclectically elegant, including lofty ceilings etched with elaborate floral patterns, tables and chairs in Islamic designs, and burgundy tablecloths.

Check out the bizarre assortment of knick-knacks in the glass displays in the back, too. There's no sign in English, so look for the place with green awnings, next to the Premiere Wellness and Fitness Centre.

☆ Entertainment

Alexandria's cultural life has never really recovered from the exodus of Europeans and Jews in the 1940s and '50s, but in recent years things have started to change for the better. Since the opening of the Bibliotheca Alexandrina (p314), which hosts major music festivals, international concerts and performances, the town is again competing with Cairo as Egypt's cultural capital.

The free monthly booklet *Alex Agenda*, available at some hotels, is extremely useful for its extensive list of concerts, theatre events and live gigs throughout Alexandria.

Check the website of Bibliotheca Alexandrina (p314) to see what's happening at the city's most important cultural venue while you're in town. **Teatro Eskandariya** (Map p318; ☑ 03-390-1339; www.facebook.com/Teatro. Eskendria.Official; 25 Sharia Fouad, Mahattet Ramleh; ⊙ 9am-1am) is very active too; check its Facebook page for the current schedule of events.

Alexandria Centre of Arts   PERFORMING ARTS
(Map p318; ☑ 012-7057-8134; 1 Sharia Tariq Al Horreyya; ⊙ 9am-9pm Sat-Thu) This active cultural centre, housed in a whitewashed villa, hosts contemporary arts exhibitions, poetry readings and occasional free concerts in its theatre. There is also an art studio, a library and a cinema on the 1st floor.

Alexandria Opera House   OPERA
(Map p318; ☑ 03-480-0138; www.facebook.com/ AlexandriaOperaHouseOfficial; 22 Sharia Tariq Al Horreyya) The former Sayed Darwish Theatre has been refurbished and now this lovely, frivolous building houses the city's modestly proportioned but splendid opera house.

Jesuit Cultural Center   ARTS CENTRE
(The Garage; Map p308; ☑ 03-542-3553; 298 Sharia Port Said) Very active cultural centre offering contemporary theatre, film screenings, contemporary art exhibitions and music performances, of Egyptian artists and those from around the world. There is a small cafe on the grounds as well as a school for film.

Shopping

Sayed El Safty   ANTIQUES
(Map p312; ☑ 03-392-2972; 63 Sharia Attareen; ⊙ 11am-late) Probably the most interesting antique shop in the city. Well worth a browse with a wide variety of antiques and plenty of good junk.

Hassan Fouad   MARKET $
(Map p312; ☑ 03-485-9213; cnr Sharia Abdul Hamid Badawy & Moursi Gamil Aziz; ⊙ 9.30am-4am) This tiny and incredibly tidy market offers beautifully displayed produce, such as grapes from Lebanon and tasty Egyptian mangoes, and a good selection of imported staples such as digestive biscuits. There's no sign in English; look for the place with artfully stacked fruits and a bright red sign.

Drinkies   DRINKS
(Map p318; ☑ delivery 03-480-6309; Sharia Al Ghorfa Al Tugareya; ⊙ noon-midnight) Takeaway beer is available in the city centre at this aptly named place. It also delivers.

Al Maaref Bookshop   BOOKS
(Map p318; ☑ 03-487-3303; 32 Midan Saad Zaghloul) This centrally located bookshop has a small English-language section that includes titles on Egypt and Alexandria.

❶ Information

DANGERS & ANNOYANCES
The city is generally peaceful and calm, but a terrorist attack on St Mark's Cathedral on Palm Sunday 2017 claimed 18 lives.

EMERGENCY
Tourist Police (Map p318; ☑ 03-485-0507; Midan Saad Zaghloul) Upstairs from the main tourist office.

MEDICAL SERVICES
Al Madina At Tibiya (Alexandria Medical City Hospital; Map p308; ☑ 03-543-2150, 03-543-7402; Sharia Ahmed Shawky, Rushdy; ⊙ 24hr) Well-equipped private hospital.
Central Pharmacy (Map p318; ☑ 03-486-0744; 19 Sharia Ahmed Orabi; ⊙ 9am-10pm) This 100-year-old establishment is worth visiting just for the soaring ceilings and beautiful display cabinets.
German Hospital (Map p308; ☑ 010-6552-1110, 03-584-0757; www.facebook.com/ TheGermanHospital; 56 Sharia Abdel Salaam Aarafa, Glymm; ⊙ 8am-10pm) Near Saba Basha tram stop (line 2) and next to Al Obeedi Hospital. Staffed by highly qualified doctors, and has a day clinic for non-emergency patients.

MONEY
There is no shortage of banks and ATMs in central Alexandria, particularly on Sharia Salah Salem and Sharia Talaat Harb, the city's banking district.

If changing cash, it's simplest to use one of the exchange bureaux on the side streets between Midan Ramla and the Corniche.
American Express (Map p318; ☑ 03-487-4073; www.amexfranchise.com; 15 Midan Saad Zagloul, Al Raml Station; ⊙ 9am-4pm Sun-Thu) Changes cash and travellers cheques, and is also a travel agency.
Travel Choice (Thomas Cook; Map p318; ☑ 03-484-7830; 15 Midan Saad Zaghloul; ⊙ 8.30am-5pm Sat-Thu)

TOURIST OFFICE
Main Tourist Office (Map p318; ☑ 03-485-1556; Midan Saad Zaghloul; ⊙ 8.30am-3pm) Hands out a good brochure (with map) of Alexandria sights and has friendly staff.

SOUQ SHOPPING

Although you won't find the sort of antediluvian bazaars here that you do in Cairo, Alexandria has several souqs that are ideal spots to immerse yourself in some lively market action.

Souq District (Map p312) At the western end of Midan Tahrir, the battered, grand architecture switches scale to something more intimate as you enter the city's main souq district. It's one long, heaving bustle of produce, fish and meat stalls, bakeries, cafes and sundry shops selling every imaginable household item. This is a great area to check out at night.

Sharia Faransa begins with cloth, clothes and dressmaking accessories. The tight weave of covered alleys running off to the west is known as Zinqat As Sittat ('the alley of the women'). Here you'll find buttons, braid, baubles, bangles, beads and much more. Beyond the haberdashery you will find the gold and silver dealers and then the herbalists and spice vendors. A couple of blocks west of Sharia Faransa, Sharia Nokrashi (also known as Al Midan) starts at Midan Nasr and runs for about a kilometre through the heart of Anfushi.

Attareen Antique Market (Map p312; Sharia Attareen; ⏱10am-late) Antique and junk collectors will have a blast diving through the confusion of backstreets and alleys of this antique market. Many items found their way here after the European upper class was forced en masse to make a hasty departure from Egypt following the 1952 revolution.

Souq Ibrahimiyya (Map p308; Sharia Omar Lofty) This is one of our favourite markets for peeking into Egyptian life. Down several tiny, covered side streets near the Sporting Club, it's packed with fresh produce, piles of still-wet seafood and stalls selling poultry and meats, both before and after they've seen the butcher's block. It's best in the morning, when the vendors are most vocal and enthusiastic.

Anfushi Fish Market (Map p312; Qasr Ras El Tin; ⏱approx 6am-noon) In a city that devours more fish than a hungry seal, you'd expect to find a pretty impressive fish market – and Alexandria delivers. Located at the northern tip of Anfushi this market bustles daily with flapping seafood that's literally just been thrown off the boat. Get here early, when it's busiest. Things die down by mid-morning. Women travelling alone should be aware that this can be a high-testosterone zone.

🛈 Getting There & Away

AIR

Burg Al Arab Airport (☎03-459-1484; http://borg-el-arab.airport-authority.com), about 45km southwest of Alexandria, handles all flights in and out of the city. Most services are to/from the Arabian Peninsula and North African destinations.

BUS

The city's main bus station is **Al Moaf Al Gedid Bus Station** (New Garage; Map p308; Moharrem Bey), several kilometres south of Midan Saad Zaghloul. To get there, either catch a microbus (LE2) from Misr Train Station or grab a taxi (LE35) from the city centre.

The main companies operating from Al Moaf Al Gedid are **West & Mid Delta Bus Co** (Map p318; ☎03-480-9685; Midan Saad Zaghloul; ⏱9am-7pm) and **Super Jet** (Map p308; ☎03-546-7999; 374 Tareq El Horreya; ⏱8am-10pm); both have central-city booking offices, though Super Jet's is inconveniently located in Sidi Gaber.

Go Bus services leave from a separate terminal close by Al Moaf Al Gedid. Its ticket booking office (Escort Tourism; Map p318; Sharia Mohammed Talaat Noeman, Mahattet Raml) is near Midan Saad Zaghloul.

SERVEES & MICROBUS

Servees (service taxis) and microbuses for **Aboukir** (Map p312), and servees for **Cairo** (Map p312), depart from outside **Misr Train Station**; all others leave from **Al Moaf Al Gedid Bus Station** (p329) out at Moharrem Bey. Fares cost around LE50 to Cairo or Marsa Matruh. Sample fares to other local destinations include Zagazig (LE25), Tanta (LE15), Mansura (LE15), Rosetta (LE10) and Aboukir (LE6).

TRAIN

There are two train stations in Alexandria. The main terminal is **Misr Train Station** ((Mahattat Misr; ☎03-426-3207; https://enr.gov.eg; Sharia Al Nabi Daniel)), about 1km south of Midan Ramla. **Sidi Gaber Train Station** (Mahattat Sidi Gaber; ☎03-426-3953) serves the eastern suburbs. Trains from Cairo stop at Sidi Gaber first and most locals get off here, but if you're going to the city centre around Midan Saad Zaghloul, make sure you stay on until Misr Train Station.

BUSES FROM ALEXANDRIA

DESTINATION	PRICE	DURATION	TIME (COMPANY)
Cairo	LE50-65	2½-3hr	hourly 5am-11pm (West & Mid Delta; Super Jet); seven/day (Go Bus)
Hurghada	LE115-150	9hr	9am & 6.30pm (West & Mid Delta); 10pm (Super Jet); 8am & midnight (Go Bus)
Ismailia	LE60	5hr	7am & 2.30pm (West & Mid Delta)
Marsa Matruh	LE50	4hr	hourly 6am-10pm (West & Mid Delta); five daily Jun-Sep (Super Jet)
Port Said	LE35	4hr	6am, 11am & 2.30pm (West & Mid Delta)
Sharm El Sheikh	LE130-150	8-10hr	9pm (West & Mid Delta); 11pm (Go Bus)
Siwa	LE75	9hr	8.30am, 11am & 10pm (West & Mid Delta)
Suez	LE60	5hr	7am, 9am, 2.30pm & 5pm (West & Mid Delta)

Most bus services to Marsa Matruh can drop you off in El Alamein (one hour) or Sidi Abdel Rahman; you will have to pay the full Marsa Matruh fare though.

At Misr Train Station, 1st- and 2nd-class tickets to Cairo are sold at the ticket office along platform 1; 2nd- and 3rd-class tickets to destinations other than Cairo are purchased in the front hall.

If you're getting a taxi from the station, it's advisable to bypass the drivers lurking outside the entrance as they're renowned for overcharging new arrivals – instead walk out on to the street and flag one down.

❶ Getting Around

As a visitor to Alexandria, you'll rarely use the buses; the tram is fun but painfully slow. Taxis and microbuses are generally the best options for getting around.

TO/FROM THE AIRPORT

An air-conditioned **airport bus** (Map p318; Midan Saad Zaghloul) leaves from outside the Cecil Hotel (p322) on Midan Saad Zaghloul three hours before all flight departures; confirm the exact bus departure time at the Cecil (one-way LE10, plus LE2 per bag, one hour). You can also catch bus 475 (LE5, one hour) from Misr Train Station (p329).

A taxi to or from the airport should cost between LE130 and LE180.

CAR

The price of using a car-and-driver service can be comparable to the price of hiring a car and saves the headache of negotiating traffic yourself. The tourist office (p328) and most of Alexandria's hotels can usually help with recommending a driver.

If you do fancy striking out on the road yourself, car hire starts from US$50 per day (including 100km). Ensure that you're especially scrupulous with the initial and return inspections to avoid any compensation claims for very minor vehicle damage.

Avis (Map p318; ☏ 010-2803-9400; Midan Saad Zaghloul, Cecil Hotel; ◷ 8am-4pm) has a full range of cars, with drivers available for an additional US$30 to US$50 per day.

MICROBUS

Want to travel like the locals? Hop on a microbus. The most useful are the ones zooming along the Corniche. There are no set stops, so when one passes, wave and shout your destination; if it's heading that way, it will stop to pick you up. It costs anywhere from LE1 to LE2 for a short trip, to LE5 to go all the way to Montazah.

Minibuses to **Sidi Gaber** (Map p318) start at Midan Saad Zaghloul.

MAJOR TRAINS FROM MISR STATION

DESTINATION	PRICE	DURATION	TIMES
Aswan	LE270	17hr	4.45pm
Cairo (direct)	LE70-100	2½hr	7am, 8am, noon, 2pm, 3pm, 4.45pm, 6pm, 7pm, 8pm & 10pm
Cairo (stopping)	LE60	3-3½hr	6am, 8.15am, 10am, 1pm, 3.30pm, 8.10pm & 9.30pm
Luxor	LE160	15hr	4.45pm & 10pm

Ticket prices are for seats in air-con 1st-class.

TAXI

There are no working taxi meters in Alexandria. Locals simply pay the correct amount as they get out of the taxi, but since fares are both unpublished and subjective, this can be a challenge for a visitor to pull off (especially considering many drivers expect visitors to pay higher fares and won't hesitate to aggressively argue the point). Negotiate a price before you get in and try to give the driver the exact amount.

Some sample fares are: Midan Ramla to Misr Train Station, LE10 to LE15; Midan Saad Zaghloul to Fort Qaitbey, LE15; Midan Saad Zaghloul to the Bibliotheca Alexandrina, LE10 to LE15; Steigenberger Cecil Hotel to Montazah, LE35 to LE50.

TRAM

Alexandria's rumbling, clackety old trams are fun to ride, but they can be almost unbearably slow and hence not the best option for getting around.

The central tram station, Mahattat Ramla, is at Midan Ramla; from here lime-yellow-coloured trams go west and blue-coloured ones travel east. Check the city-tram route maps at the stations to find the line you're looking for. The line numbers on each tramcar are in Arabic, but you can tell which line it is by the colour of the sign at the front and then match that to the colour of the line number on the route map. Some trams have two or three carriages, in which case one of them is reserved for women. Fares range from 50pt to LE2.

Tram 14 goes to Misr Train Station; tram 15 goes through Anfushi; trams 1 and 25 go to Sidi Gaber Train Station.

AROUND ALEXANDRIA

Aboukir

🞂046

Aboukir (pronounced abu-eer) shot to fame in 1798 when the British admiral Horatio Nelson sank Napoleon's French fleet in what became known as the Battle of the Nile. Just offshore from Abukir, underwater excavations have revealed the sunken city of legendary Herakleion-Thonis, which was swallowed by the Mediterranean about 1200 years ago.

The beach isn't the cleanest, but local Alexandrians head here in summer for lunch at one of the excellent fish restaurants.

🍴 Eating

⭐ **Zephyrion**   SEAFOOD $$

(📞010-9510-8484;   fish   per   kg   LE75-210; 🕐11am-midnight) This excellent fish taverna (the name is Greek for 'sea breeze') was founded in 1929 and serves first-class fish and seafood on a sweeping blue-and-white terrace overlooking the bay. There is no wine list, but you can bring your own bottle, and it will be uncorked for you without complaint. Beer is available. Everyone along the seafront knows this place.

ℹ Getting There & Away

The easiest way to get to Aboukir is by flagging down an eastbound microbus along Alexandria's Corniche (LE2). It will drop you at a roundabout; the sea is to your left as you face the large mosque beyond the roundabout.

Alternatively, a taxi from Alexandria's city centre should cost around LE90 to LE110 each way.

Rosetta (Ar Rashid)

🞂045 / POP 69,000

Rosetta (also called Ar Rashid) squats on the western branch of the Nile. It was founded in the 9th century, but its heyday was during the 18th and 19th centuries, when it became Egypt's most significant port. British tourists flocked to the town in the 1800s to see charming Ottoman mansions and to stroll through the many citrus groves. Alas, as Alexandria got back on its feet and regained power in the mid-19th century, Rosetta was thrust into near-irrelevance.

Today its backwater appeal strikes a contrast with the modern hustle of nearby Alexandria. The citrus groves have mostly disappeared, but some restored mansions are open to visitors. The unpaved streets are packed with donkeys pulling overloaded carts, and the souq area has an atmosphere of centuries past, with basket-weavers artfully working fronds and blacksmiths hammering away in medieval-looking shopfronts.

There are no hotels in Rosetta, and the tourist police don't allow visitors to stay overnight, so take a day trip from Alexandria.

👁 Sights

Built in the traditional Delta style using small flat bricks painted alternately red and black, Rosetta's Ottoman houses are generally three-storey structures with the upper floor slightly overhanging the lower. At ground level the doorways often feature intricate painted floral designs, while jutting and ornate *mashrabiyya* (lattice) windows decorate the walls. The town prides itself on being the second city in Egypt, after Cairo, for Islamic monuments.

When you arrive in the town square, you will be greeted by the tourist police who will show you around town. You can admire some excellent examples of this local architecture along the main souq, which runs the length of Sharia Port Said from the microbus station and town square.

House of Amasyali   HISTORIC BUILDING
(Sharia Al Anira Feriel; adult/student LE15/10; ⊙9am-5pm) One of the most impressive of all Rosetta's fine buildings, with beautiful lantern lights on the facade and vast expanses of windows with *mashrabiyya* (lattice), which circulate cool breezes around the house. The main reception room upstairs is overlooked by a screened wooden gallery, behind which the women would sit, obscured from view. The gorgeous ceilings are painted in red and blue. It's next door to the House of Abu Shaheen, entry to which is included on the same ticket.

To get here from the central souq, take the second left-hand turn down Sharia Port Said and walk four blocks.

House of Abu Shaheen   HISTORIC BUILDING
(Mill House; off Sharia Al Anira Feriel; adult/student LE15/10; ⊙9am-5pm) The House of Abu Shaheen has a reconstructed mill on the ground floor, featuring enormous wooden beams and planks. You can actually see the gears and teeth rotate, a mechanism which 200 years ago would have been pushed in an endless circle by a draught animal. In the courtyard, the stables roof is supported by granite columns with Graeco-Roman capitals.

It's right next door to the House of Amasyali, entry to which is included on the same ticket.

Rachid Museum   MUSEUM
(Manzil Hussein Arab Killi; adult/student LE40/20; ⊙9am-4pm Sat-Thu, 9am-noon & 2-4pm Fri) Although recently restored, the Rachid Museum just off the main square is a dusty

THE ROSETTA STONE

Now a crowd-pulling exhibit at the British Museum in London, the Rosetta Stone is the most significant find in the history of Egyptology. Unearthed in 1799 by a French soldier doing his duty improving the defences of Fort St Julien near Rosetta, the stone is the lower half of a large, dark granitic stele. It records a decree issued in 196 BC by the priests of Memphis, establishing the religious cult of Ptolemy V and granting the 13-year-old pharaoh status as a deity – in exchange for tax exemptions and other priestly perks. To be understood by Egyptians, Greeks and others living here then, the decree was written in the three scripts current at the time – hieroglyphic, demotic (a cursive form of hieroglyphs) and Greek, a language that European scholars would have read fluently. The trilingual inscription was set up in a temple beside a statue of the pharaoh. At the time of its discovery, much was known about ancient Egypt, but scholars had still not managed to decipher hieroglyphs. It was quickly realised that these three scripts would make it possible to compare identical texts, and therefore to crack the code and recover the lost world of the ancient Egyptians.

When the British defeated Napoleon's army in 1801, they wrote a clause in the surrender document insisting that antiquities be handed to the victors, the Rosetta Stone being foremost among them. The French made a cast and the original was shipped to London, where Englishman Thomas Young established the direction in which the hieroglyphs should be read, and recognised that hieroglyphs enclosed within oval rings (cartouches) were the names of royalty.

But in 1822, before Young devised a system for reading the mysterious script, Frenchman Jean-François Champollion recognised that signs could be alphabetic, syllabic or determinative, and established that the hieroglyphs inscribed on the Rosetta Stone were actually a translation from the Greek, and not the other way around. This allowed him to establish a complete list of signs with their Greek equivalents. His obsessive work not only solved the mystery of Pharaonic script but also contributed significantly to a modern understanding of ancient Egypt.

provincial museum in a very beautiful example of the town's Ottoman houses. The ground floor has a copy of the famous Rosetta Stone and local finds, while the 1st floor illustrates life in these houses. The 2nd floor was the private part of the house with the bedrooms, kitchen and living area.

Fort of Qaitbey   FORT

(adult/student LE40/20; ⊗8am-5pm) About 5km north of Rosetta along the Nile, this fort was built in 1479 to guard the mouth of the Nile 6km further on. It was on this spot that the famous Rosetta Stone was found; we'll wager that this is now the site of the lamest historical exhibit in the world, especially in relation to the importance of the discovery that was made here. A round trip by taxi should cost LE30 to LE40.

The views over the Nile are wonderful, and the fact that this is where this impressive river meets its end into the Mediterranean, makes it a perfect spot for romantics.

❶ Getting There & Away

There are regular microbuses (LE10, one hour) to Rosetta from Al Moaf Al Gedid Bus Station in Alexandria. Rosetta's microbus station is right on the square that leads into the main souq. A private car or a taxi to Rosetta from Alexandria should cost you around LE300 return.

MEDITERRANEAN COAST

El Alamein

◪ 046

This small coastal outpost is famed for the decisive victory won here by the Allies during WWII. More than 80,000 soldiers were killed or wounded in the series of desert battles fought nearby, which helped cement Allied control of North Africa. The thousands of graves in the Commonwealth, German and Italian war cemeteries in the vicinity of the town are a bleak reminder of the losses.

Much cheerier are the fine sands and heavenly water of the nearby beaches. Finding a place to access the sea is easier if you're staying at one of the local resorts, but there are a few places where independent travellers can get in the water.

◉ Sights

War Museum   MUSEUM

(LE50; ⊗9am-4pm Sat-Thu, 9am-noon & 1-4pm Fri) This museum is an excellent introduction to the North African campaigns of WWII, including the Battle of El Alamein. The museum has separate halls dedicated to the four main countries involved in the war: Great Britain, Italy, Germany and Egypt. Another hall contains collections of memorabilia, uniforms, photos and maps. On display outside is a range of tanks and artillery from the battlefield.

The turn-off to the museum is along the main highway; just look for the large tank in the middle of the road.

Commonwealth War Cemetery   CEMETERY

(⊗9am-2.30pm) The Commonwealth War Cemetery is a haunting place where more than 7240 tombstones stand in regimented rows between beautifully tended desert plants. Most of the Commonwealth soldiers who lie here died in the Battle of El Alamein at the end of October 1942 and in the period immediately before that. As you enter, a separate memorial commemorating the Australian contingent is to your right. The cemetery is about 1km east of El Alamein's War Museum.

At the Australian memorial a small plaque with a relief map gives an insightful overview of the key battlefield locations. The cemetery itself was a rear area during the fighting; the front line ran from the Italian memorial and wound its way 65km south to the Qattara Depression.

The cemetery can supposedly be visited outside of regular hours as the police guard outside the gate should have a key, but don't count on it.

German War Memorial   MEMORIAL

About 7km west of El Alamein, what looks like a hermetically sealed sandstone fortress overlooking the sea is actually the German War Memorial. Inside this silent but unmistakable reminder of war lie the tombs of approximately 4000 German servicemen and, in the centre, a memorial obelisk. To reach the memorial, take the marked turn-off from the main highway; the entrance to the memorial is locked, but if you wait for a moment, the keeper will let you in.

From the memorial, there's a panoramic view of the stretch of shore in this area.

THE SIGHTS OF ST MENA

St Mena was an Egyptian soldier in the Roman army who was martyred for refusing to renounce his Christian faith. During the late 4th century the area surrounding St Mena's tomb, on the outskirts of modern-day Burg Al Arab, 45km south-west of Alexandria, became synonymous with miraculous acts. By the 5th century pilgrims were flocking here from as far away as Europe and the area became the bustling city of Martyroupolis – only Jerusalem rivalled it as a place of pilgrimage. After the Arab armies conquered Alexandria in AD 641, Martyroupolis fell into obscurity and many of the churches were destroyed. In the early 20th century, Martyroupolis (now known as Abu Mena) was redis-covered by archaeologists and the modern Monastery of St Mena the Miracle Giver was subsequently founded near its ruins.

Abu Mena Thanks to Bedouin raids and marble pilfering, not much remains of the once-grand Byzantine pilgrimage centre of Martyroupolis, although the outline of its mammoth basilica is still easily traced. A modest wooden chapel has been built over the basilica's altar with the altar stone still in place. A piece of St Mena's body is kept in a cabinet here. From the chapel, a row of stubby column remnants leads to the saint's tomb. Changes in the water table have caused degradation to the excavations, and the site has been placed on Unesco's endangered monuments list. Despite the damage to the site, travellers interested in Egypt's Coptic history will find Abu Mina sheds some light on Egypt's leading role in the early Christian era. The site is along a desert track (accessible by normal vehicles) just to the south of the Monastery of St Mena. If you're unsure of directions, ask at the monastery.

Monastery of St Mena the Miracle Giver (www.stmina-monastery.org) This monas-tery, built in 1959, is a major pilgrimage site for Egyptian Coptic Christians. Aswan gran-ite and marble were used to build the large cathedral. Skilled monk artisans created the interior's resplendent mosaic tile-work dome and the ornate wooden panel iconostasis that graces the interior. Behind the cathedral is the tomb of Pope Kyrillos VI, who found-ed the monastery.

German Memorial Beach   BEACH

Across 2km of desert directly in front of the German War Memorial is the tiny and glorious German Memorial Beach, which is relatively rubbish-free. The sea here is mul-tiple shades of blue, and you'll feel miles away from Alexandria's teeming sands. To get there, ask the keeper at the memorial to open the gate leading to the sand tracks – he might urge you to first get permission from the Coast Guard post, a good walk away.

There's also a road direct to the beach from the Alexandria–Marsa Matruh high-way. It's an unmarked sand track, leading over some low hills to the beach. The turn-off is 150m east of the road to the German War Memorial.

Italian Memorial   MEMORIAL

About 11km west of El Alamein, roughly where the front line between opposing ar-mies ran in WWII, the Italian memorial has a wide path rimmed by flowering shrubs leading up to a tall, slender tower. It's mov-ing to see the simple design inside the tow-er – square white marble slabs covering the walls, engraved only with the names of the dead. The tower is kept locked, but the caretaker will appear and open it up for you soon after you arrive.

At the roadside entrance to the memorial, there is a small one-room **museum** with some interesting maps, artillery, photos and mem-orabilia from the battle. Most of the informa-tion is in Italian only, although there are a couple of translations into English and Arabic.

Before reaching the memorial, you'll notice on the left (south) side of the road what appears to be a large rock milestone. Inscribed on it is the Italian summary of the battle: *'Mancò la fortuna, non il valore'* ('We were short on luck, not on bravery').

⌕ Tours

If you spend time in town, you may field of-fers of desert excursions to visit key battle sites, such as **Ruweisat Ridge**; however, if you want to explore the WWII sites fully, you should consider opting for a specialised tour. Aside from the fact that millions of landmines were planted during the fighting and no one seems to know how many remain, officially you must obtain approval from the Egyptian military to access the battlefields. It's a controlled area, and if you're caught without permission, you risk serious trouble; what's more, if anything goes wrong in the desert, you will not be able to rely on the authorities for assistance.

As well as visiting the battle sites, a specialist tour operator will be able to take you to other areas that played important roles during the fighting. These include the Egyptian Railway workers' building known as the **blockhouse**, which, during the worst of the fighting, served as a hospital where German and Australian doctors worked alongside each other treating the wounded of both sides.

Wilderness Ventures Egypt CULTURAL (www.wilderness-ventures-egypt.com) The highly recommended Wilderness Ventures Egypt runs excellent three-day El Alamein tours, camping at night on the Qattara Depression. Tours take in all the important sites in the area, including the major battlefields of Ruweisat Ridge, Tel El Eissa and Point 29, along with sites such as the blockhouse and the war memorials.

🛏 Sleeping & Eating

It's possible to stay overnight here, or in nearby Sidi Abdel Rahman, but El Alamein is easiest visited as a day trip from Alexandria. The luxury hotels along the coast from here to Sidi Abdel Rahman are an alternative, if you don't mind parting with a wad of cash.

The shop beside the War Museum has a small cafeteria where you can get a good spread of *fuul*, *ta'amiyya* (Egyptian falafel) and salads. Otherwise, head back to the main Alexandria–Marsa Matruh road, where you'll find several restaurants catering to Egyptians, and restaurants in the beach resorts.

❶ Getting There & Away

The easiest option is to organise your own car and driver. A taxi will charge around LE500 to LE600 to take you from Alexandria to the War Museum, ferry you between the cemeteries, make a stop at a beach and bring you back to Alexandria.

Alternatively, catch any of the Marsa Matruh buses or microbuses from Al Moaf Al Gedid Bus Station in Alexandria. You'll be dropped on the main road about 200m down the hill from the War Museum. This is fine to visit the museum, but the war cemeteries are far away from one another.

Sidi Abdel Rahman

📞 046

The gorgeous beaches of Sidi Abdel Rahman are the raison d'être for this growing resort hamlet, and with charter flights between

---

TURNING POINT AT EL ALAMEIN

For a brief period in 1942, the tiny railway station at El Alamein commanded the attention of the entire world. Since 1940 the British had battled the Italians and Germans for control of North Africa, fighting raged back and forth from Tunisia to Egypt as first one side and then the other seized the advantage.

By 1942, Axis units under Field Marshal Erwin Rommel, the celebrated 'Desert Fox', had pushed the Allies back to the last defensible position before Cairo – a line running from El Alamein 65km south-west to the impassable Qattara Depression. The situation appeared hopeless. British staffers burnt their papers to prevent them from falling into enemy hands; the Germans were expected in Alexandria any day; and Mussolini flew to Egypt to prepare for his triumphal entry into Cairo.

In desperate fighting, however, the Allies repulsed the next German thrust by late July. In early September, galvanised by the little-known general Bernard Law Montgomery, the Allies parried a second attack that focused on the famous Alam Al Halfa ridge.

Montgomery gathered his strength for an all-out counteroffensive, which he launched on 23 October 1942. Intense fighting raged for 13 days, with each side suffering appalling losses, until the Axis line at last crumbled. Rommel's routed legions retreated westward, never to return to Egypt. The Desert Fox was recalled to Germany to spare him the disgrace of defeat, but 230,000 of his soldiers eventually surrendered in Tunisia.

Montgomery was knighted and became the most famous British general of the war. In 1946 he was made First Viscount Montgomery of Alamein, a title he used for the rest of his life. Of the battle, Winston Churchill famously said, 'Before Alamein we never had a victory. After Alamein we never had a defeat.'

Europe and nearby El Alamein (23km east), development is likely to continue. Several resorts take prime position on the sparkling waters and white sands of the Mediterranean and are the major draw – though there is little else to see or do here.

◉ Sights

Shaat Al Hanna   BEACH
This gorgeous beach is a real find, with irresistible milky-blue water that's great for swimming. Even out here, conservative dress for women applies. The main free beach is, unfortunately, more rubbish-strewn than it used to be, so if that turns you off, pay LE50 per person for the clean private beach, which has umbrellas and lounge chairs.

Heading west along the Alexandria–Marsa Matruh road, the turn-off for the beach is marked by three rusting yellow signs 1.9km after the 155km to Marsa Matruh milestone. The road is part paved and part sand, but fine for regular cars.

🛏 Sleeping

★ El Alamein Hotel   BOUTIQUE HOTEL $$$
(📞03-468-0140; www.alalameinhotel.com; km 129 on Alexandria–Marsa Matruh rd, inside Marassi Resort; s/d US$330/445; 🅿🛜🏊) This beautiful luxury beach hotel in the middle of the high-end Marassi resort is favoured by wealthy Cairenes. The large, plush rooms have panoramic views over the stunning bay. There are several lovely bars and restaurants; sushi is de rigueur. This is one of the best beaches along this stretch, with white sand and crystal-clear turquoise water.

❶ Getting There & Away

Buses and microbuses to Marsa Matruh from Al Moaf Al Gedid Bus Station in Alexandria can drop you here, but it's quite a trek to the resorts from the road. It's better to arrive by private car or taxi (LE250 to LE300 one way).

Marsa Matruh
📞046 / POP 120,600

During summer, Marsa Matruh provides the real-deal Egyptian resort-town experience. From June to September it can seem like half of the Nile Valley has decamped here for their holidays. The brilliant white sandy beaches are squeezed full of families, and the dusty streets buzz with people well into the wee hours of the morning. Throngs of street stalls sell hot food and souvenirs, and impromptu street musicians bang out rhythmic tunes.

For the rest of the year, Marsa Matruh presses the snooze button and returns to its usual near-comatose state. The city's turquoise water bays lie empty and the only visitors are Bedouins and Siwans stocking up on goods.

Whatever the time of year, few foreign tourists make the trip out here, except to break the journey to Siwa.

◉ Sights

The luminescence of the water along this stretch of coast is marred only by the town's overflowing hotel scene. The beaches on the east side of town, near the bridge over to Rommel's Beach, have calm, shallow water great for small kids, plus palm-frond-shaded cubicles. At any of the town beaches, expect to pay from LE10 to LE30 for a chair and umbrella.

Further away, the water is just as nice, and you can still find a few places where the developers have yet to start pouring cement. During the hot summer months it's advised that women swim in baggy clothing over their bathing suits, unless they can handle being the object of intense harassment and ogling. The exceptions are the private beaches of the top-end hotels, although even here most Egyptian women remain fully dressed and in the shade.

Lido   BEACH
(Map p337) Marsa Matruh's main beach has decent sand and clear water, but during summer you'll have trouble finding space to throw down your towel.

Cleopatra's Beach   BEACH
(Map p338) Possibly the most beautiful piece of coastline in the area, Cleopatra's Beach sits about a 14km drive north-west of Marsa Matruh around the bay's thin tentacle of land. The sea here is an exquisite hue, and the rock formations are worth a look. You can wade to Cleopatra's Bath, a natural pool where legend has imagined the queen and Mark Antony enjoying a dip, but you can't actually swim because of the waves and rocks just offshore.

Shaati Al Gharam   BEACH
(Map p338) At the tip of the strip of land west of Marsa Matruh, you'll find Shaati Al Gharam (Lovers' Beach). The water here is sublime, but the sand is only marginally less

Marsa Matruh

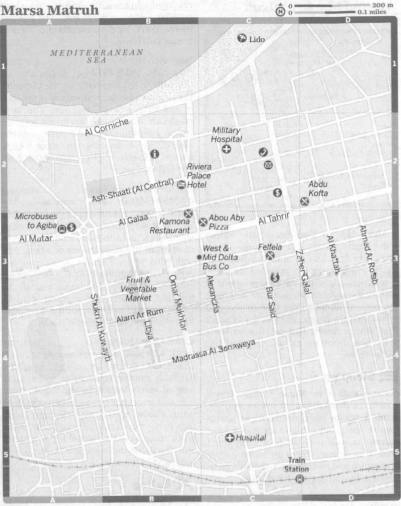

MEDITERRANEAN SEA

Lido

Al Corniche

Military Hospital

Riviera Palace Hotel

Ash-Shaati (Al Central)

Abdu Kofta

Microbuses to Agiba

Al Matar

Al Galaa

Kamona Restaurant

Abou Aby Pizza

Al Tahrir

West & Mid Dolta Bus Co

Felfela

Zaher Galal

Al Khattab

Ahmad Ar Rosb

Fruit & Vegetable Market

Omar Mukhtar

Alexandria

Bur Said

Shukri Al Kuwayti

Alam Ar Rum

Libya

Madrassa Al Sanaweya

Hospital

Train Station

busy than at the main city beaches. In summer, boats (LE5) shuttle back and forth from the Lido beach (p336) across the bay. Taxis charge about LE30 to LE40 each way.

Rommel's Beach
BEACH
(Map p338) Right at the tip of Marsa Matruh's eastern peninsula, this quiet but rocky piece of shore is good for swimming. Just before the beach is the cave system where Colonel Rommel planned the Axis forces' military operations during WWII. The caves are now home to **Rommel's Cave Museum**

(LE40/20; ⊘9am-2pm Sun-Thu, to 8pm in summer).

Agiba Beach
BEACH
Agiba means 'miracle' in Arabic, and Agiba Beach, about 24km west of Marsa Matruh, is just that. It is a small, spectacular cove, accessible only via a path leading down from the clifftop. The water here is a dazzling clear turquoise. It's packed in summer and near empty the rest of the year. Note that it isn't ideal for toddlers, as the waves roll in strongly. **Microbuses** (Map p337; LE2) to Agiba leave from in front of the National Bank of Egypt.

Around Marsa Matruh

Cleopatra's Beach
Shaati Al Gharam
MEDITERRANEAN SEA
Rommel's Cave Museum
Rommel's Beach
Reem Hotel
Negresco Hotel
Lido
See Marsa Matruh Map (p337)
Train Station
Carol's Beau Rivage (7km);
Agiba Beach (16km);
Jaz Almaza Beach Resort (31km)
Marsa Matruh-Siwa Rd
Airport
Bus Station & Microbuses
Alexandria-Marsa Matruh Rd
0 1 km
0 0.5 miles

About 1km to 2km east of the hilltop above Agiba, there's a long expanse of accessible beach with fine sand and deep blue water, which is far less crowded than the cove. Confusingly, this stretch of shore is also known as Agiba Beach. To get here, take the turn-off marked by a blue, white and yellow sign (in Arabic) 3km west of Carol's Beau Rivage resort. This paved road leads to the beachfront; the entrance is gated, but there's no fee.

🛏 Sleeping

Accommodation in Marsa Matruh leaves a lot to be desired. With a few exceptions, hotels generally offer mediocrity at unreasonable rates, but demand for rooms over summer is such that hoteliers really don't need to try harder. Prices are much higher in summer, and rooms need to be booked in advance. In winter many hotels close.

Riviera Palace Hotel   HOTEL $
(Map p337; ☑ 046-493-0472; 2 Sharia Alexandria; s/d LE200/450; ☎) The Riviera Palace has a slightly eclectic and strange lobby, but the rooms are quite large and, despite the obvious wear and tear, good value with crisp white linen on the beds and big bathrooms. It also has a cosy cafe.

Reem Hotel   HOTEL $$
(Map p338; ☑ 046-493-3605; Al Corniche; s/d LE650/850, without air-con LE360/525; ☎) On the plus side, Reem is a hop, skip and jump across the Corniche from the beach. On the negative side, the rooms are straight out of a 1980s how-to-decorate-your-cheap-motel

catalogue and are fairly expensive for what's on offer – but are very clean. The cheaper rooms don't have air-conditioning. Prices are for half board.

Negresco Hotel   HOTEL $$
(Map p338; ☑ 046-493-4491; Al Corniche; s/d LE650/1000; ☎) Slap bang on the Corniche, the Negresco (under restoration at the time of research) is a solid choice. The large rooms are ridiculously overpriced for their sparse furnishings, but all have powerful air-con, great showers (in roomy bathrooms), flat-screen TVs, comfortable beds and little balconies.

Jaz Almaza Beach Resort   RESORT $$$
(☑ 046-436-0000; www.jaz.travel/almaza/hotels/jaz-almaza-beach-resort.aspx;s/dUS$250/300; @☎❄) Serious luxury-resort-seekers should look no further. On a remote stretch of seafront 37km south-east of Marsa Matruh, this resort features a sweep of supreme sand fronting the palm-tree-strewn grounds, fantastic restaurants and all the bells and whistles a sun-worshipper needs. Little ones are well-looked-after here with kids clubs and child-friendly pools.

Carol's Beau Rivage   RESORT $$$
(☑ 011-4252-1444; www.carolsbeaurivage.com; s/d US$220/350; @☎❄) Set around a delightful bay with glowing aquamarine water, 15km west of Marsa Matruh on the Sallum highway, this resort has comfortable rooms done up in a safari theme, with elephant paintings, dark-wood furnishings and cane chairs on the balconies. The overall feel is a bit institutional, but the beach is certainly one of the nicest in the area.

✗ Eating

Marsa Matruh has a few restaurants spread over the town centre, mostly catering to hungry locals. However, its outdoor food market makes it a great town for self-catering. Pick up bread, cheese and fruit, including Siwan dates and olives, for a perfect beach picnic.

Kamona Restaurant   EGYPTIAN $
(Map p337; Sharia Al Galaa; meals LE25-40; ⊙11am-11pm) This simple restaurant does a roaring trade in grilled chicken and kebabs. Follow your nose at the intersection with Sharia Alexandria and you can't miss it.

Felfela   FALAFEL $
(Map p337; Sharia Port Said; meals LE5-30; ⊙noon-midnight; ☑) The best *fuul* and falafel

joint in town, this is the spot vegetarians – or anyone looking to fill up cheaply – should seek out.

Abou Aby Pizza
PIZZA $

(Map p337; Sharia Alexandria; mains from LE18; ⊙ noon-midnight; 🖉) This popular place serves up tasty Western-style pizza. Upstairs seating offers good views onto the street action below.

Abdu Kofta
EGYPTIAN $$

(Map p337; 🖉 012-314-4989; Sharia Al Tahrir; dishes LE10-80, grilled meat per kg LE160; ⊙ 11am-midnight) Locals swear that this is the best restaurant in town. In a clean and cool 1st-floor room, it serves kofta (mincemeat and spices grilled on a skewer) or grilled meat by the weight, served with good mezze and salads.

❶ Information

There are various banks and exchange bureaux on and around Sharia Al Galaa, including **Bank Wataniy** (Map p337; Sharia Al Matar), **Banque Misr** (Map p337; Sharia Al Galaa; ⊙ 9am-2.30pm Sun-Thu) with an ATM, and **CIB Bank** (Map p337; Sharia Port Said; ⊙ 8am-3pm Sun-Thu) with an ATM.

The **tourist office** (Map p337; 🖉 046-493-1841; Sharia Omar Mukhta; ⊙ 8.30am-7pm Jun-Sep, to 2pm Oct-May) is one block off the Corniche. Staff are eager to help despite the lack of information on offer.

❶ Getting There & Away

AIR

EgyptAir has flights on Thursdays and Sundays between Cairo and Marsa Matruh from June to September. Check with the airline as the flights are fully booked well in advance and are often cancelled.

BUS

Marsa Matruh's **bus station** (Sharia Alexandria) is 2km south-east of town. Expect to pay LE15 for a taxi to the town centre. Microbuses (50pt) cruise Sharia Madrassa Al Sanaweya, around where the fruit-and-vegetable market dead-ends, then head to the bus station.

West & Mid Delta Bus Co has hourly services to Alexandria from 7am to 2am (LE55, four hours). During summer it runs buses to Cairo (LE110, five to six hours) at 7.30am, 10.30am, noon, 3.30pm, 4pm, 5pm, 10pm and midnight. In winter, buses leave for Cairo at noon and

3.30pm. For Siwa (LE40, three hours) buses leave at 1.30pm and 4pm.

Note that the West & Mid Delta buses running between Alexandria and Marsa Matruh seem like the oldest fleet in the country, and breakdowns are common.

From June to September, Super Jet runs daily bus services to Alexandria and Cairo from the bus station; its fleet is, in general, better maintained than West & Mid Delta.

Between June and September there's a ticket booking office for **West & Mid Delta Bus Co** (Map p337; 🖉 046-490-5079; Sharia Alexandria) open in the centre of town.

MICROBUSES

The microbus lot is beside the bus station. Microbuses to Siwa, if there are enough passengers, cost LE35; they are much more comfortable and efficient than West & Mid Delta buses on the same route but you may have to wait for an hour or two for them to fill up. Other options include Fl Alamein (LE34), Alexandria (LE34) and Cairo (LE70).

TRAIN

From June to September three sleeper trains (s/d US$60/86; www.wataniasleepingtrains.com) run weekly between Cairo and Marsa Matruh, a journey of seven hours. Trains depart Cairo Monday, Wednesday and Saturday at 11.30pm, arriving in Marsa Matruh at 6.30am. For the return journey, trains leave Marsa Matruh on Sunday, Tuesday and Thursday at 10pm, arriving in Cairo at 5.40am. Reserve in advance.

Between June and September two air-conditioned express trains run daily between Cairo and Marsa Matruh (1st/2nd class LE90/110, seven hours).

Ordinary 2nd/3rd-class trains without aircon run year-round between Marsa Matruh and Alexandria (6½ hours), but these are not recommended – even employees working at the station have described the trains as 'horrible'.

❶ Getting Around

Private taxis or pick-ups can be hired for the day, but you must bargain aggressively, especially in summer. Expect to pay LE100 to LE150, depending on the distance.

A taxi from the bus station to the Corniche costs between LE15 and LE20.

Bikes can be hired from makeshift rental places along Sharia Alexandria during high season for LE15 to LE25 per day.

Suez Canal

Best Places to Eat

➜ Central Perk (p344)

➜ El Borg (p344)

➜ Pizza Pino (p344)

➜ Reda Helmy (p346)

Best Places to Stay

➜ Mercure Forsan Island (p346)

➜ Holiday Hotel (p343)

➜ New Continental (p342)

Why Go?

The Suez Canal, Egypt's glorious triumph of engineering over nature, dominates this region, slicing through the sands of the Isthmus of Suez for 163km, not only severing mainland Egypt from Sinai but also Africa from Asia. The canal was the remarkable achievement of Egypt's belle époque, an era buoyed by grand aspirations and finished by bankruptcy and broken dreams. This period also gave birth to the canalside cities of Port Said and Ismailia. Today their streets remain haunted by this fleeting age of grandeur, their distinctive architecture teetering on picturesque disrepair.

Although the area is often bypassed by all but the most rampant supertanker-spotters, anyone with an interest in Egypt's modern history will enjoy the crumbs of former finery on display. And while the Canal zone may have no vast ruins or mammoth temples, there's a slower pace to life here that will be appreciated by those travelling with time up their sleeve.

When to Go
Port Said

Apr–May Spring's pleasant temperatures are perfect for picnicking beside Lake Timsah in Ismailia.

Aug Escape the frazzling heat with Port Said's cooling canal-side breezes.

Sep Spot flocks of storks as they head south, swooping over the skies across the Canal zone.

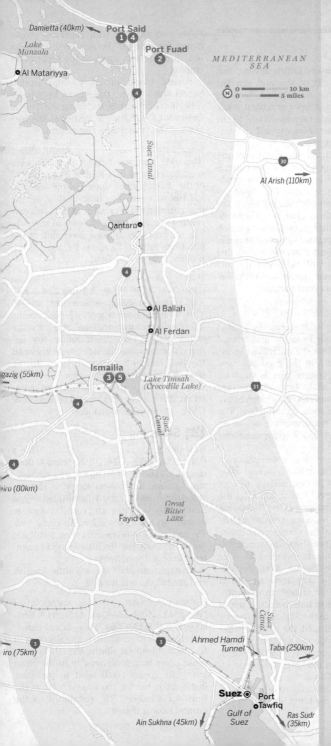

Suez Canal Highlights

1 Port Said
(p342) Exploring the architecture of faded grandeur slowly slipping into genteel dilapidation within this city's waterfront quarter.

2 Port Fuad
(p345) Commuting from Africa to Asia in 15 minutes flat: jump on the ferry from Port Said to sample life on the canal.

3 Ismailia (p345)
Taking a break from Egypt's usual hectic pace among the colonial-era villas.

4 Port Said Boardwalk (p342)
Making peace with your inner supertanker-spotting geek with a canal-side walk.

5 Ismailia Museum (p345)
Admiring this tiny and rarely visited museum that crams more than 4000 objects from Pharaonic and Graeco-Roman times into its dusty displays.

Port Said

☏ 066 / POP 678,564

In its late-19th-century raffish heyday, Port Said was Egypt's city of vice and sin. The boozing seafarers and packed brothels may have long since been scrubbed away, but this louche period is evoked still in the waterfront's muddle of once-grand architecture slowly going to seed.

While the yesteryear allure of the centre is enough to prompt a visit, the main attraction, and the reason for the town's establishment, is the Suez Canal. The raised pedestrian-only boardwalk running along the waterfront provides up-close views over the canal's northern entry point, allowing travellers to admire the passing supertanker traffic up close. The free ferry that crosses the canal to the languid suburb of Port Fuad is the only opportunity for casual visitors to ride the waters of this marvel of construction.

◉ Sights

The historic heart of Port Said is located along the edge of the canal, on and around Sharia Palestine. Here, the waterfront seems infused with a 'back in the good old days' atmosphere; the streets are lined with late-19th-century and early-20th-century buildings replete with rickety wooden balconies, louvred doors and high verandahs. The raised **boardwalk** running all the way along Sharia Palestine affords sweeping views over the canal.

Take a stroll down Sharia Memphis past its decrepit **Woolworth's building** (Map p343) down Sharia Al Gomhuriyya, to spot the archway entrances still announcing the **Bible Society building** and the **Old Canal Shipping Agency building**, and around the streets just north of the Commercial Basin. Along Sharia Palestine there are wonderfully odd colonial remnants, including the once highly fashionable **Simon Arzt department store**. At the very northern end of Sharia Palestine is an empty **stone plinth**. Originally this was to have been the site of what's now known as the **Statue of Liberty**. When funds were denied, the much smaller scale plinth was made and a statue of Ferdinand de Lesseps erected. It stood here until it was torn down in 1956 with the nationalisation of the Suez Canal.

East of here, on Sharia 23rd of July, is the **Italian consulate building**, erected in the 1930s and adorned with engraved propaganda from fascist dictator Benito Mussolini: 'Rome – once again at the heart of an empire'.

Several blocks inland, on and around Sharia Salah Salem, there is an impressive collection of churches, including the **Coptic Orthodox Church of St Bishoi of the Virgin** and the **Franciscan compound**.

Suez Canal House   HISTORIC BUILDING
(Map p343; Commercial Basin) If you've ever seen a picture of Port Said, it was probably of the striking green domes of the Suez Canal House, which was built in time for the inauguration of the canal in 1869. As it's currently fenced off (and not open to the public), the best way to get a good look at the building's famous facade is by hopping on the free ferry to Port Fuad.

Military Museum   MUSEUM
(Map p343; ☏ 066-322-4657; Sharia 23rd of July; adult/student LE30/10; ⊙10am-3pm Sat-Thu) This little museum is worth a peek for its information on the canal and also for some rather bizarre exhibits (including toy soldiers) documenting the 1956 Suez Crisis and the 1967 and 1973 wars with Israel. In the museum gardens you can view a few captured US tanks with the Star of David painted on them, as well as an odd collection of UXOs (unexploded ordnances).

🛏 Sleeping

New Continental   HOTEL $
(Map p343; ☏ 066-322-5024; 30 Sharia Al Gomhuriyya; s/d LE200/305) The friendly management makes this typical Egyptian cheapie stand out from the crowd. Light-filled rooms have teensy balconies and come in a range of sizes, so ask to see a few. All come with TV and an astounding clutter of furniture. We particularly love the hilarious gold palm-tree decor in the hallways.

Management staff speak a little English and are helpful and friendly.

Hotel de la Poste   HISTORIC HOTEL $
(Map p343; ☏ 066-322-4048; 42 Sharia Al Gomhuriyya; s/d LE190/300) This faded classic still manages to maintain a tiny smidgen of its original colonial charm, though to get a sense of its long-gone hey-day in the clean but basic rooms you'll need to put your imagination-hat on. You want a room at the front for a balcony. The restaurant on the ground floor is decent.

Port Said & Port Fuad

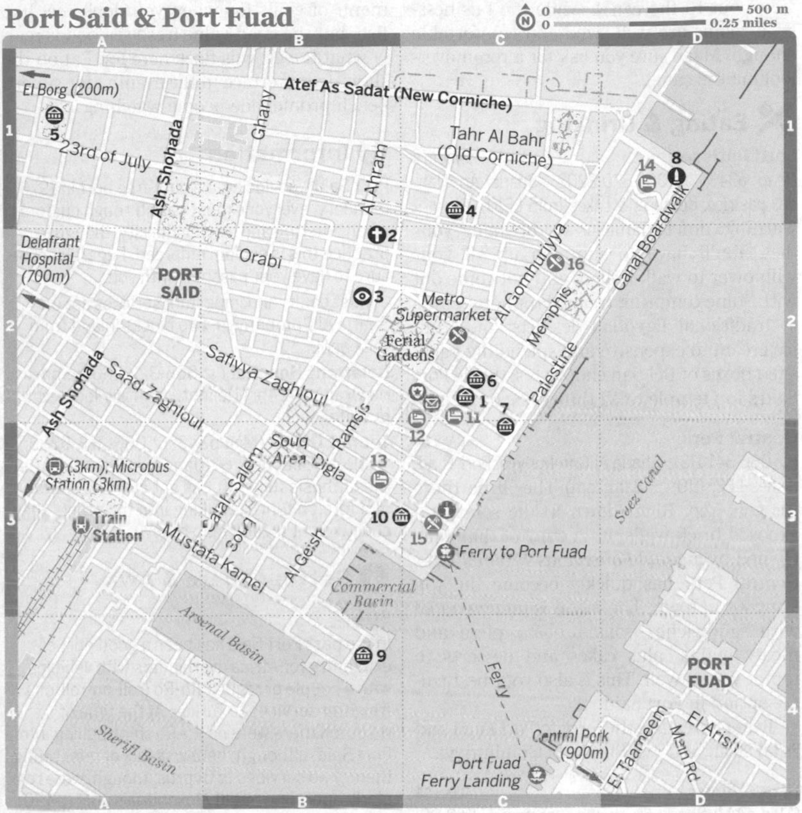

Port Said & Port Fuad

Sights

1 Bible Society Building.......C2
2 Coptic Orthodox Church.......B2
3 Franciscan Compound.......B2
4 Italian Consulate.......C1
5 Military Museum.......A1
6 Old Canal Shipping Agency Building.......C2
7 Simon Arzt Department Store Building.......C3
8 Stone Plinth.......D1
9 Suez Canal House.......B4
10 Woolworth's Building.......B3

Sleeping

11 Holiday Hotel.......C2
12 Hotel de la Poste.......C2
13 New Continental.......B3
14 Resta Port Said Hotel.......D1

Eating

15 Lord Pâtisserie.......C3
16 Pizza Pino.......C2

Holiday Hotel HOTEL $
(Map p343; ☎066-322-0711; Sharia Al Gomhuriyya; s/d LE300/400; wi-fi) The Holiday is a wee step up from Port Said's cheapies, with modern tile-floored rooms decked out in shades of beige and boasting Ikea-style furniture and decent bathrooms. Plenty of company employees from the ships stay here, so the staff is used to foreigners. It loses points for the wi-fi not being free.

Resta Port Said Hotel HOTEL $$$
(Map p343; ☎066-320-0511; www.restahotels.com; off Sharia Palestine; s/d US$120/150; P wi-fi pool) Not as posh as it likes to think it is and ridiculously overpriced, but the Resta is as snazzy as Port Said gets. The pool area has

views out to the canal, while the business-style rooms are well sized and comfortable enough. Make sure you ask for a room over-looking the canal.

🍴 Eating & Drinking

Lord Pâtisserie   SWEETS $
(Map p343; ☎066-320-8202; Sharia An Nah-da; pastries, desserts & cakes from LE10) First a warning: don't blame us for breaking your diet. You'll have to summon up all your willpower to walk in here and not come out with some tempting treats. From croissants to traditional Egyptian desserts, and from ice cream to expensive and splendidly pack-aged boxes of Belgian chocolates, this is Port Said's top temple to all things sugary.

Central Perk   CAFE $$
(☎066-341-1131; Sharia Al Gomhuriyya, Port Fuad; dishes LE25-110; ⊙8am-2am) They'll be there for you. Yep. Right down to the sofas and exposed brick walls, it's a copy of that cafe. Owned by a couple of serious *Friends* fans, Central Perk has quickly become the top hangout in town. The menu is international with sandwiches, salads, pasta, pizza and meaty mains, plus cakes and desserts to tempt you as well. This is also your best cof-fee option in Port Said.

To get here, take the ferry to Port Fuad and head straight down Sharia Al Gomhuriyya.

Pizza Pino   ITALIAN $$
(Map p343; Sharia Al Gomhuriyya; mains LE40-90; ⊙10am-2am) This cosy bistro, with comfy cane chairs and attentive staff, has been Port Said's main pasta and pizza joint for dec-ades. It's comfort food done right, and a qui-et place to relax with a coffee after treading the streets soaking up the old-world ambi-ence. The pasta is better than the pizza.

El Borg   SEAFOOD $$
(☎066-332-3442; Beach Plaza, off Sharia Atef As Sadat; mains LE40-150; ⊙10am-3am) This mas-sive Port Said institution is always buzzing with families on a night out. There's a small menu of grills for when you don't feel like fish, but the good-value fresh seafood is real-ly what the crowds flock here for. Eat on the shore-front terrace in the evening for superb beach promenade people-watching.

ℹ️ Information

Port Said was declared a duty-free port in 1976. In theory, everyone must pass through customs when entering and leaving the city, though in practice this is seldom enforced. Regardless, be sure to have your passport with you.

Most banks and important services are on Sharia Al Gomhuriyya, two blocks inland from the canal.

Delafrant Hospital (☎066-322-2663; Sha-ria Orabi; ⊙24hr) Decent, centrally located hospital.

Tourist Office (Map p343; ☎066-323-5289; 8 Sharia Palestine; ⊙10am-7pm Sat-Thu) After the enthusiastic staff has got over the shock of a foreign tourist walking into the office, they can give out a good map of town.

ℹ️ Getting There & Away

BOAT

In the past Port Said has been a good port of exit/entry for Africa overlanders with vehicles, with a couple of regular Ro-Ro (roll-on-roll-off) freighter services to Turkey. At the time of research there were no Ro-Ro ships pulling into Port Said, although there was talk of reinstating them. Two services to Cyprus, though, were reg-ularly operating out of Alexandria's port (p490). If you have managed to find a Ro-Ro service from Europe or Turkey that arrives in Port Said, make sure to purchase an Egyptian visa in advance as Port Said isn't a tourist entry point and so doesn't issue tourist visas.

BUS & MICROBUS

The **bus station** is about 3km from the town centre at the beginning of the road to Cairo (about LE10 in a taxi). Both **Super Jet** (☎066-372-1779) and **East Delta Travel Co** (☎066-372-9883) operate buses from the station.

The microbus and servees (service taxi) sta-tion is next door to the bus station.

BUSES FROM PORT SAID

DESTINATION	PRICE	DURATION	TIME/COMPANY
Alexandria	LE40	4-5hr	7am, 11am, 2pm, 6pm & 8pm (East Delta); 4.30pm (Super Jet)
Cairo	LE40	4hr	hourly (East Delta); every two hours (Super Jet)
Ismailia	LE20	1-1½hr	hourly 6-11am & 2-6pm (East Delta)
Suez	LE30	2½hr	6am, 10am, 2pm & 4pm (East Delta)

DON'T MISS

CROSSING THE CANAL

Keen to travel across the waters of the Suez Canal but don't have your own yacht? Not best buddies with the captain of a supertanker? Stroll down to the **ferry terminal** (Map p343) at the south-western end of Sharia Palestine in Port Said and hop aboard the free ferry to Port Fuad. Ferries leave about every 10 minutes throughout the day and the quick journey offers panoramic views of all the canal action.

Once deposited in Port Fuad (founded in 1925) head south from the quayside mosque to explore boulevards lined with sprawling French-inspired residences. Although the streets are now mired in litter and many of the villas teeter on the brink of decay, their sloping tiled roofs, lush gardens and wooden balconies hung with colourful washing still invoke the genteel splendour of a bygone era.

TRAIN

Services to Cairo are in creaky, scruffy, slow trains. Expect delays. There are supposedly departures (2nd class/3rd class LE30/15) at 5.30am, 1pm and 5.30pm, though times change regularly and departure delays are very common. Buses are, in general, a quicker and much more comfortable option.

ℹ Getting Around

There are plenty of blue-and white taxis around Port Said. Fares for short trips within the town centre average LE5.

Microbuses run along main arteries such as Sharia Orabi and Sharia Ash Shohada, and cost LE1.50 for a short ride.

Ismailia

📞 064 / POP 366,669

Ismailia was founded by and named after Pasha Ismail, khedive of Egypt in the 1860s while the Suez Canal was being built. The city was also the temporary home of Ferdinand de Lesseps, the director of the Suez Canal Company, who lived here until the canal was completed. Not surprisingly, Ismailia grew in the image of the French masters who had ensconced themselves in Egypt during the colonial era. Today, Ismailia's historic town centre, with its elegant colonial streets, expansive lawns and late-19th-century villas, is one of the most peaceful and picturesque neighbourhoods in the country. The heart of Ismailia and the area most worth exploring is the old European quarter around Sharia Thawra and the central square, Midan Al Gomhuriyya.

◉ Sights

Ismailia Museum   MUSEUM
(Map p346; 📞 02-391-2749; Mohammed Ali Quay; adult/child LE40/20; ⊙8am-4pm, closed for noon prayers Fri) More than 4000 objects from Pharaonic and Graeco-Roman times are housed in this tiny but interesting museum on the eastern edge of town. The collection includes statues, scarabs, stelae and records of the first canal, built between the Bitter Lakes and Bubastis by the Persian ruler Darius. The highlight is a 4th-century mosaic depicting Phaedra sending a love letter to her stepson Hippolytus, while below Dionysus rides a chariot driven by Eros.

Garden of the Stelae   MONUMENT
(Map p346; Mohammed Ali Quay) Just southwest of Ismailia's museum is a garden containing a rather forlorn little sphinx from the time of Ramses II (1279–1213 BC). You need permission from the museum to visit the garden, but you can see the unremarkable statue from the street.

De Lesseps' House   HISTORIC BUILDING
(Map p346; Mohammed Ali Quay; ⊙closed to visitors) Unfortunately, unless you're a guest of the Suez Canal Authority (the house is its private guesthouse), you can only admire the exterior of the one-time residence of the French consul to Egypt from the road outside. Inside the grounds de Lesseps's private carriage has been encased in glass and remains in impeccable condition. The house is located near the corner of Sharia Ahmed Orabi.

🛏 Sleeping

New Palace Hotel   HISTORIC HOTEL $
(Map p346; 📞064-391-8333; Midan Orabi; s/d LE350/450; 🖭) This old-timer hotel is home to clean, simple rooms that have a decent dose of old-fashioned flair. You want one of the front-facing rooms; some have charming touches such as dark furniture and barrel chairs. Interior-facing rooms are far plainer and pokier.

Ismailia

N ⊙
0 ————————— 500 m
0 ————————— 0.25 miles

Tourist Office (1.6km);
Ismailia (🚊) (2.1km)

Train Station
Al Horreyya
Midan Orabi
Thawra (Sultan Hussein)
Saad Zaghloul
Midan Mustafa Kamel
Suez Canal Rd
Mosque
At Tahrir
Midan Al Gomhuriyya
Mohammed Farid
Suez Canal Rd
Al Geish
Farid Nada
Ahmed Orabi
Adly Pasha
Mohammed Ali Quay (The Promenade or Salah Salem)
Sweetwater Canal
Al Montanasihat
Mercure Forsan Island (500m)

YHA Ismailia (1.2km);
Tourist Police (1.3km);
Lake Timsah
Beaches (1.5km)

SUEZ CANAL ISMAILIA

Ismailia

YHA Ismailia   HOSTEL $
(☎ 064-392-2850; Lake Timsah Rd; d/tr LE160/165) This cement block out of town on the shore of the lake doesn't look like much, but its sparkling clean (if institutional) rooms are decent sized and all come with their own bathrooms, so it's a budget steal. The hostel is a LE7 taxi ride from the centre; ask the driver for Beit Shebab.

Note that couples can only stay in the same room here if they are married.

Mercure Forsan Island   RESORT $$$
(☎ 064-391-6316; www.mercure.com; Gezirat Forsan; s/d from €95/110; 🛜🏊) Occupying its own island 1.6km south-east from Ismailia's downtown area, the Mercure's private beach and gardens make it a tranquil haven. The snazzy rooms outfitted with modern bath-

rooms and brightened by colourful textiles are worth splashing out for.

🍴 Eating & Drinking

Pizza Massimo   PIZZA $
(Map p346; ☎ 064-392-3232; Sharia Thawra; pizza LE25-40; ⊙ noon-11pm; 🍴) This little place serves up pretty decent pizza and has fast and friendly service.

Reda Helmy   GRILL $$
(Map p346; ☎ 064-332-0409; Sharia Shabeen El Khom; mains LE35-150; ⊙ 24hr) The top spot in town for *shish tawooq* (marinated chicken grilled on skewers), Egyptian-style liver and pretty much every other kind of meat you can stick on a grill. There are great salads and mezze to mop up all that meat with as well as *tagens* (stew cooked in a deep clay pot).

Cilantro   CAFE
(www.cilantrocafe.net; Rd 6, Armed Forces Beach;
⊘8am-1am; 🔊) The Ismailia branch of
Egypt's home-grown coffee empire has the
best view in town. Drink your latte, cappuccino or juice on the terrace overlooking the
calm blue waters of Lake Timsah. Cilantro also does decent sandwiches and other
snacks. It's 3km east of town on the main
road that runs alongside the canal.

El Mestkawu   COFFEE
(Map p346; Sharia Al Geish; ⊘noon-late) A fabulous shaded verandah cafe where the town's
old-timers gossip, drink coffee and watch
the world go by while smoking a shisha.

ℹ️ Information

There are banks and ATMs scattered throughout
town including Sharia Thawra and Sharia Al
Geish.

Tourist Office (📞064-332-1078; 1st fl, New
Governorate Bldg, Sharia Tugary, Sheikh Zay
eed area; ⊘8.30am-3pm Sat-Thu) About 1.5km
north-east of Midan Orabi.

ℹ️ Getting There & Away

BUS

Ismailia's **bus station** (Sharia Mohammed Sabry) is about 3km north of the old quarter; taxis
to the town centre cost around LE5. From here,
East Delta Travel Co (📞064-332-1513) has
buses to the following destinations:

Alexandria LE45, five hours, twice daily at 7am
and 2.30pm

Cairo LE25, four hours, every 30 minutes
between 6am and 8pm

Dahab LE80, seven to eight hours, daily at
10.30pm

Port Said LE15, one hour, hourly from 6am to
11am and 1pm to 5pm

Sharm El Sheikh LE70, six hours, twice daily at
2pm and 10.30pm

Suez LE15, 1½ hours, hourly from 6.30am to
11.30am and 1.30pm to 6.30pm

TRAIN

Services to Cairo (2nd class LE25, four to
five hours) run at 11am, 2.20pm, 4.15pm and
5.20pm. Three trains daily run to Port Said (2nd
class LE10) at 9.45am, 11.15am and 2.15pm,
while six services head to Suez (2nd class LE7)
at 7am, 8.10am, 10.30am, 1.15pm, 3.15pm
and 6pm.

Departure times should be taken with a pinch
of salt on this line; trains often just leave when
they decide to.

ℹ️ Getting Around

Microbuses ply the main arteries of the city.
Fares cost between LE1.50 and LE2.50. Taxis are
plentiful. Short trips cost LE5 to LE8.

Suez
📞062 / POP 497,000

Poor old Suez; the heavy thumping delivered
during the 1967 and 1973 wars with Israel
wiped out most of its colonial relics, so it
has none of the nostalgic appeal of Port Said
and Ismailia. Instead, a sprawl of grim and
gritty concrete blocks overwhelms much of
the city, with the additional piles of festering
rubbish sprouting along most of the streets
simply compounding the down-and-out
air. There are a few old remnants hanging
on along a couple of streets in Port Tawfiq,
which managed to escape the bombing, but
nothing of note to deserve a stopover. If you
do get stuck here, note that overzealous security measures have made canal-viewing
here a no go; plenty of barbed wire and
bored guards stop any wannabe sightseers
from snapping photos.

🛏️ Sleeping

Preferably, endeavour to avoid spending the
night in Suez.

Hotel Green House   HOTEL $$
(Map p348; 📞062-319-1553, 062-319-1554; green
house_suez@hotmail.com; Sharia Al Geish; s/d from
LE700/1150; @🔊🌊) Because of a complete
lack of competition, Hotel Green House is
still the nicest place to bed down in Suez.
Rooms are desperately dated in dreary
1980s motel style, which would be fine if
the room rate was lower. On a positive note,
you do get a TV and fridge, and (supposedly)
there's wi-fi.

Red Sea Hotel   HOTEL $$
(📞062-319-0190; 13 Sharia Riad, Port Tawfiq; r
from LE966; 🔊) In a quieter location than
most Suez hotels, near the yacht basin, the
Red Sea has rough-around-the-edges rooms
with battered TVs and ugly brown carpets.
Looking on the bright side, there are decent
canal views from your balcony if you get a
room at the back.

🍴 Eating

Koshary Palace   EGYPTIAN $
(Map p348; Sharia Al Geish; mains LE7-15) Clean
and friendly, lots of local flavour and good

Suez

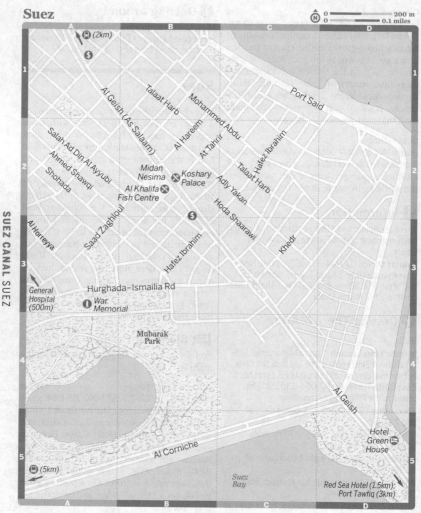

kushari (mix of noodles, rice, black lentils, fried onions and tomato sauce), all in your choice of sizes.

Al Khalifa Fish Centre
SEAFOOD $$
(Map p348; ☎ 062-333-7303; Midan Nesima; mains LE35-90; ⊗ noon-11pm) Tucked away on the edge of Midan Nesima in the congested town centre, this no-frills place sells the day's ocean catch by weight; you can pick out your fish and then wait for it to be grilled.

ⓘ Information

Sharia Al Geish, running through the centre of town, has banks and ATMs.

ⓘ Getting There & Away

BUS & MICROBUS

The **bus station** (Cairo–Suez Rd) is 5km out of town along the road to Cairo. **East Delta Travel Co** (☎ 062-356-4853) operates the following:
Cairo LE25, two hours, every 30 minutes from 6am to 9pm

THE SUEZ CANAL

The Suez Canal represents the culmination of centuries of effort to enhance trade and expand the empires of Egypt by connecting the Red Sea with the Mediterranean Sea, but it was Ferdinand de Lesseps, the French consul to Egypt, who pursued the idea through to its conclusion. In 1854 de Lesseps presented his proposal to the Egyptian khedive Said Pasha, who authorised him to excavate the canal; work began in 1859.

A decade later the canal was completed amid much fanfare. When two small fleets, one originating in Port Said and the other in Suez, met at the new town of Ismailia on 16 November 1869, the Suez Canal was declared open and Africa was officially severed from Asia.

Ownership of the canal remained in French and British hands for the next 86 years until, in the wake of Egyptian independence, President Gamal Abdel Nasser nationalised the Suez in 1956. The two European powers, in conjunction with Israel, invaded Egypt in an attempt to retake the waterway by force. In what came to be known as the 'Suez Crisis', they were forced to retreat in the face of widespread international condemnation.

Today the Suez Canal remains one of the world's most heavily used shipping lanes. With just under 50 ships passing through the Suez each day, and yearly toll revenues amounting to US$50 billion, in August 2014 Egypt's President Sisi launched a plan to further capitalise on the canal's importance. The project to construct a new 35km-long channel running parallel to the original canal (which would be deepened and widened at the same time), effectively turns the canal into a two-lane water highway for part of its length and also allows larger ships to traverse it.

Initially costed at US$4 billion, the new canal project quickly ballooned in costs, with 43,000 workers involved in the construction and a price tag thought to be nearer US$8 billion by the completion date. Nevertheless, the new canal was completed and opened for business with much pomp and ceremony in August 2015.

The project, though, remains controversial. With the new canal in operation, the government hoped to up the number of ship daily crossings to more than 90 daily (doubling the old canal's total) and to bring in revenues of US$13 billion per year by 2023. More than two years on from its inauguration, and both daily crossings and revenues remain static. The Suez Canal remains one of the largest contributors to the Egyptian state coffers and a vital component in the country's economy. Whether the new Suez Canal can safeguard and further boost that position remains to be seen.

SUEZ CANAL SUEZ

Dahab LE75, seven hours, daily at 11am

Ismailia LE15, 1½ hours, every 30 minutes from 6am to 4pm

Port Said LE30, 2½ hours, daily at 7am, 9am, 11am, 12.15pm and 3.30pm

Sharm El Sheikh LE65, six hours, departing 8.30am, 11am, 1.30pm, 3pm, 4.30pm, 5.15pm and 6pm

St Katherine Protectorate LE45, four hours, daily at 2pm

Upper Egypt Bus Co (☎ 062-356-4258) runs buses to Hurghada (LE50 to LE55, four hours) almost hourly between 5am and 11pm, and to Luxor (LE90 to LE100, nine to 10 hours) at 8am, 2pm and 8pm.

The microbus and servees station is beside the bus station. The only place in Sinai they serve is Al Tor (LE25).

TRAIN

Six uncomfortable 2nd-class Cairo-bound trains depart Suez daily (LE15 to LE20, three hours) going only as far as Ain Shams, 10km northeast of central Cairo; the first Cairo-bound train leaves at 5.30am. There are also eight slow trains to Ismailia.

ⓘ Getting Around

Taxis (painted blue) are easy to find almost everywhere. Expect to pay LE10 between the bus station and town, LE15 between the bus station and Port Tawfiq, and LE5 between Suez and Port Tawfiq.

There are regular microbus services along Sharia Al Geish to Port Tawfiq. They will pick up or drop off anywhere along the route. Short journeys cost LE1 to LE2.

Red Sea Coast

Best Places to Eat

➡ Zia Amelia (p356)

➡ Le Garage (p356)

➡ Dolce e Salato (p370)

➡ El Fardous (p367)

Best Places to Stay

➡ La Maison Bleue (p356)

➡ Oberoi Sahl Hasheesh (p360)

➡ Marsa Shagra Village (p369)

➡ Captain's Inn (p355)

➡ Deep South (p369)

Why Go?

The 'Red Sea Riviera' is a place of many different attractions. On the one hand, it is famous (or infamous, depending on your view) for cheap package holidays – overdevelopment has pockmarked the coastline deeply, leaving a trail of mega resorts and half-finished hotels in its wake. Alongside these are some exceptional exclusive resorts secluded from the hustle of the packages. Dig deeper and you will find other, more surprising sides to the region.

Some of the most important sites in Christianity's early evolution lie in the northern Red Sea coast's barren mountains. Venture south of brashly loud and proud Hurghada, and you'll not only find some of Egypt's best diving but also the epic, wild expanse of the Eastern Desert. Criss-crossed by trade routes dating back to the far reaches of prehistory, and scattered with ancient rock art and lonely ruins, this little-visited area is a desert-adventurer's dream.

When to Go
Hurghada

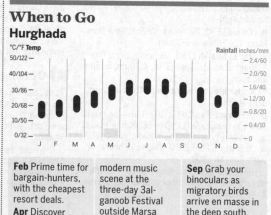

Feb Prime time for bargain-hunters, with the cheapest resort deals.

Apr Discover Egypt's vibrant modern music scene at the three-day 3alganoob Festival outside Marsa Alam.

Sep Grab your binoculars as migratory birds arrive en masse in the deep south.

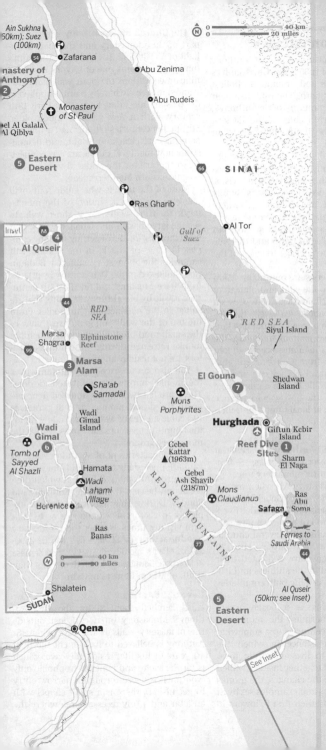

Red Sea Coast Highlights

❶ Hurghada
(p357) Making a diving date with world-class offshore reefs to discover why the Red Sea was catapulted onto the tourism stage.

❷ Monastery of St Anthony
(p352) Reflecting on monasticism's millennia-old roots by visiting this isolated complex and climbing to the hermit's cave.

❸ Marsa Alam
(p367) Flopping down at one of the area's chilled-out eco beach camps.

❹ Al Quseir (p365) Wandering the old town, where the streets are imbued with an evocative haze of yesteryear.

❺ Eastern Desert
(p370) Trekking through wadis and an endless expanse of mountains.

❻ Wadi Gimal
(p371) Exploring remnants of Rome's mighty emerald mines.

❼ El Gouna (p354) Hanging out with some of the Cairo smart set in one of Egypt's best-run resort towns.

Red Sea Monasteries

The Coptic monasteries of St Anthony (p352) and St Paul (p353) are Christianity's oldest monasteries and among the holiest sites in the Coptic faith. The establishment of the religious community of St Anthony's, hidden in the barren cliffs of the Eastern Desert, marks the beginning of the Christian monastic tradition.

If you're at all interested in Egypt's lengthy Christian history, both monasteries make for fascinating and inspiring visits. The surrounding desert scenery is simply breathtaking and, depending on where you're coming from, the Red Sea monasteries are a refreshing change of scene from the hassles and noise of Cairo and the Nile Valley, and from the package tourism of the coastline.

The two monasteries are only about 25km apart, but thanks to the cliffs and plateau of Gebel Al Galala Al Qibliya (which lies between 900m and 1300m above sea level), the distance between them by road is around 85km.

If you don't have your own vehicle, the easiest way to visit the monasteries is to join an organised tour from Cairo or Hurghada (any hotel or travel agency can arrange these). It's also possible to join a pilgrimage group from Cairo – the best way to arrange this is by enquiring at local Coptic churches.

⊙ Sights

★ **Monastery of St Anthony**　MONASTERY
(donation appreciated for guided tours; ⊙4am-5pm) **FREE** This historic monastery traces its origins to the 4th century AD when monks began to settle at the foot of Gebel Al Galala Al Qibliya, where their spiritual leader lived. Today the monastery is a large complex surrounded by high walls with several churches, a bakery and a lush garden. The 120 monks who live here have dedicated their lives to seeking God in the stillness and isolation of the desert, in a life built completely around prayer.

From its beginnings as a loosely organised grouping of hermits, the monastery evolved over a few centuries to a somewhat more communal existence in which the monks continued to live anchoritic lives, but in cells grouped together inside a walled compound. Despite the changes, the monks still follow traditions and examples set by St Anthony, St Paul and their first followers 16 centuries ago.

The **Church of St Anthony** is the oldest part of the monastery and the main highlight of a visit here. It's built over the saint's tomb and contains one of Egypt's most significant collections of Coptic wall paintings. Painted in *secco* (whereby paint is applied to dry plaster), most date back to the early 13th century, with a few possibly much older. Stripped of centuries-old dirt and grime, the paintings are clear and bright, and demonstrate how medieval Coptic art was connected to the arts of the wider Byzantine and Islamic eastern Mediterranean.

Most of the monks who guide tours will take you up onto a section of the monastery's **fortified walls** for a short walk to see the large basket and wooden winch that were the only means of getting into the complex in times of attack. In the 8th and 9th centuries the monastery suffered Bedouin raids, followed in the 11th century by attacks from irate Muslims and, in the 15th century, a revolt by bloodthirsty servants that resulted in the massacre of the monks. From the top of the walls you get a great view of the small mud-brick **citadel** into which the monks retreated during these attacks. Visitors are not usually allowed to enter.

You also get an excellent panorama over the monks' impressive cultivated gardens. These are fed by a spring sourced deep beneath the desert mountains that produces 100 cubic metres of water daily, allowing for the bountiful oasis of shady trees within the monastery grounds.

The monasteries of of St Anthony and St Paul are open daily throughout the year except during Advent and Lent, at which time it can only be visited on Friday, Saturday and Sunday. During Holy Week it's closed completely to visitors. For enquiries or to confirm visiting times, contact the **monastery headquarters** (☑St Anthony's info 02-2590-6025, St Paul's info 02-2590-0218; 26 Al Keneesa Al Morcosia, Downtown), located off Clot Bey, south of Midan Ramses in Cairo.

Cave of St Anthony　CAVE
FREE Perched about 300m above St Anthony's Monastery on a cliff just outside the monastery walls is the cave where St Anthony is believed to have spent the final 40 years of his life. Inside the cave, which is for the svelte and nonclaustrophobic only (you must squeeze through a narrow entry to get inside), there is a small chapel with an altar and a tiny recessed area where the

saint lived – bring a torch (flashlight) along to illuminate the interior.

The climb up the 1158 wooden steps to the cave entrance is hot and steep and takes about half an hour if you're reasonably fit. At the top, as you catch your breath on a small ledge (littered with the graffiti of countless pilgrims), you can admire the wide vistas over the hills and valley below.

★ **Monastery of St Paul**　　　MONASTERY
(donation appreciated for guided tours; ⊙6am-6pm daily, Fri-Sun during Advent & Lent, closed Holy Week) FREE Dating to the 4th century, the Monastery of St Paul began as a grouping of hermitages in the cliffs around the site where Paul had his cell. The complex's heart is the Church of St Paul, which was built in and around the cave where Paul lived. It's cluttered with altars, candles, ostrich eggs (the symbol of the Resurrection) and murals representing saints and biblical stories. The fortress above the church was where the monks retreated during Bedouin raids.

St Paul's monastery is quieter and much more low-key than nearby St Anthony's, and is often bypassed in favour of its larger neighbour. But a visit is well worthwhile and gives a glimpse into the life of silence, prayer and asceticism that has flowered here in the Eastern Desert for almost two millennia. Visitors are welcome and can wander freely around the monastery but taking a guided tour with an English-speaking monk will allow you to access many of the locked areas.

Paul was born into a wealthy family in Alexandria in the mid-3rd century and originally fled to the Eastern Desert to escape Roman persecution. He lived alone in a cave here for more than 90 years, finding bodily sustenance in a nearby spring and palm tree. According to tradition, in AD 343 the then-90-year-old Anthony had a vision of Paul's death and made a difficult trek through the mountains to visit Paul, and then to bury him.

🏃 **Activities**

It is possible to hike between the monasteries of St Paul and St Anthony along a 30km (approximately) trail across the top of the plateau, taking one to two days to do so. Hiking this rugged area, commonly known as 'Devil's Country', is only for the fit and experienced, and should under no circumstance be attempted without a local guide. In 2001 a lone tourist attempting the walk died of thirst after losing his way. Those who have made the hike recommend starting from St Paul's.

🛏 **Sleeping & Eating**

Male pilgrims are allowed to sleep at the Monastery of St Anthony with prior written consent from the monastery's Cairo

---

THE FATHER OF MONASTICISM

Although St Paul is honoured as the earliest Christian hermit, it is St Anthony who is considered the father of monasticism. Anthony was born around AD 251, the son of a provincial landowner from a small Upper Egyptian town near Beni Suef. Orphaned with his sister at the age of 18, he was already more interested in the spiritual than the temporal and soon gave away his share of the inheritance to the poor. After studying with a local holy man, Anthony went into the Eastern Desert, living in a cave and seeking solitude and spiritual salvation. Word of his holiness soon spread and flocks of disciples arrived, seeking to imitate his ascetic existence.

After a brief spell in Alexandria ministering to Christians imprisoned under Emperor Maximinus Daia in the early 4th century, Anthony returned to the desert. Once again, he was pursued by eager followers, though he managed to flee even further into the desert in search of solitude. After he established himself in a cave on a remote mountain, his disciples formed a loose community at its base, and thus was born the first Christian monastery.

The number of Anthony's followers grew rapidly, and within decades of his death, nearly every town in Egypt was surrounded by hermitages. Soon after, the whole Byzantine Empire was alive with monastic fervour, which by the next century had spread throughout Italy and France.

It is ironic that, for all his influence, Anthony spent his life seeking to escape others. When he died at the advanced age of 105, his sole wish for solitude was finally respected and the location of his grave became a closely guarded secret.

headquarters. Accommodation is in a dormitory and guests are expected to attend prayer sessions, respect the atmosphere of the grounds and leave a donation at the time of departure.

Both monasteries have canteens that sell snacks, drinks and simple meals.

❶ Getting There & Away

Zafarana is located 62km south of Ain Sukhna and 150km east of Beni Suef on the Nile. Buses running between Cairo or Suez and Hurghada will drop you at Zafarana, but direct access to the monasteries is limited to private vehicles and to tour buses from Cairo or Hurghada.

To get to **St Anthony's**, start from the main Zafarana junction and follow the road west towards Beni Suef for 37km, where you'll reach the monastery turn-off. From here, it's 17km further south along a good road through the desert to St Anthony's.

The turn-off for **St Paul's** is about 27km south of the Zafarana lighthouse along the road to Hurghada (watch for a small signpost). Once at the turn-off, it's then 10km further along a good tarmac road to the main gate of the monastery, and about 3km further to the monastery itself.

Buses running between Suez and Hurghada can drop you along the main road at the turn-off, from where the only option is hitching. If you do decide to hitch (which isn't the best idea), don't go alone, and be sure you're properly equipped, especially with water, as it's a long, hot, dry and isolated stretch.

El Gouna

📞 065 / POP 15,000

El Gouna is a self-contained holiday town and probably the best-run resort in Egypt. The brainchild of Egyptian billionaire Onsi Sawiris, it is built around lagoons and waterways, ensuring there are plenty of beaches and that many places have views of the water. El Gouna is frequented by Egypt's chichi set and Europeans on package tours. Boasting 16 hotels, an 18-hole golf course, plenty of villas, and boutique shopping, restaurants and bars galore, it's about as far removed from Egypt's usual chaotic hustle as you can get. The only local experience you are likely to have is smoking shisha (albeit on a marina terrace overlooking some mighty swanky yachts). But if you're after a place to laze on a beach and do some diving, then you'll definitely enjoy your time here.

◉ Sights & Activities

El Gouna is a veritable paradise for water sports. A variety of dive operators and resort activity centres offer a laundry list of activities including sailing, ocean kayaking, fishing, parasailing, jet-skiing, windsurfing, kitesurfing and water-skiing. El Gouna is increasingly used by divers as an alternative base to explore the dive sites (p357) around Hurghada.

Bibliotheca Alexandrina
El Gouna CULTURAL CENTRE
(Culturama; 📞 065-358-0023; Kafr El Gouna; LE10; ⊙10am-10pm Sat-Thu) Also known as the Embassy of Knowledge and linked to Alexandria's modern Bibliotheca Alexandrina library, this peaceful oasis is El Gouna's sleepy cultural hub. A multimedia ('culturama') show takes visitors through Egypt's vast history – check the schedule for the various different language screenings – while in the library you can access a huge range of rare books via online links to the Alexandrian library. For those who have forgotten to bring a beach read, take advantage of the fiction lending library.

Emperor Divers DIVING
(📞012-2234-0995; www.emperordivers.com; Abu Tig Marina, Three Corners Ocean View Hotel; up to €66 per day) One of the leaders in scuba diving along this stretch of the Red Sea for the past 25 years, Emperor's Gouna team works out of Abu Tig Marina and offers a full range of services from PADI open-water courses (4 days, €379) to advanced diving courses and outings.

✦ Festivals & Events

El Gouna Film Festival FILM
(http://elgounafilmfestival.com; ⊙Sep-Oct) El Gouna Film Festival, the first of its kind in Egypt, had a successful inaugural run in September 2017. It's a must-visit for cinephiles, and you're guaranteed to spot Egypt's top actors, socialites and award-winning artists.

▭ Sleeping

Advance bookings are the name of the game here. Walk-ins are practically unheard of and booking online, or through a travel agent, will score you a much better deal. Most accommodation is resort-style, and some offer all-inclusive packages. The Abu Tig Marina area has a clutch of smaller, more midrange options.

COPTIC ART 101

Coptic art refers to the distinct Christian art of Egypt. Although it originated from the ancient Egyptian and Greek heritages, it has also been influenced by the Persians, Byzantines and Syrians. In fact, because of its myriad influences, the exact nature of Coptic art can be difficult to define, though it is fortunately easy to identify. Since early Christian artisans were extremely utilitarian in their aims, Coptic art typically manifests itself in daily items such as textiles and religious illustrations. Furthermore, Coptic art has a strong tradition of painting, particularly portraits and wall paintings.

Textiles

The Coptic Church inherited a strong textile-making tradition from the ancient Egyptians, particularly loom- and tapestry-weaving. For the most part, Coptic textiles are made from linen, though there is some evidence of sophisticated silk-weaving as well. In regards to design, Coptic textiles borrow heavily from Greek-Egyptian themes, and include traditional pattern motifs such as cupids, dancing maidens and animals. These are typically incorporated with specific Christian motifs such as fish, grapes and biblical scenes, especially the Immaculate Conception.

Religious Illustrations

Religious illustration originated in ancient Egypt when pharaohs started adorning papyrus texts with liturgies and prayers. Coptic Christians retained this tradition, and early papyrus texts maintained the original Egyptian design of protective illustrations surrounded by elaborate borders and text. Like the Egyptians, Coptic artisans used bright colours for vignettes, and striking black ink for all texts. Later on, however, Coptic illustrations began to take on greater complexity as they started to incorporate religious imagery, landscapes and intricate geometric designs.

Portraits

In comparison to other early Christian movements, the Coptic Church is unique in regard to its abundance of martyrs, saints and ascetics. Since the actions and deeds of these individuals helped to form the foundation of the church, their images were immortalised in portraits, and hung in every chapel and church throughout the land. In these paintings the human figure is usually depicted from the front, with placid, almond-shaped eyes and idealised expressions. Coptic portraits of Jesus Christ are unique in that they usually depict him enthroned by saints and angels as opposed to suffering on the cross.

Wall Paintings

Early Coptic wall paintings were unsophisticated in comparison to later endeavours, primarily because ancient Egyptian temples were being converted into churches. To complete the transformation, Pharaonic reliefs were covered with layers of plaster, and Christian themes were painted on top. As Coptic art developed and prospered, however, wall painting became increasingly complex, particularly following the mastery of dye mixing and gold stencilling. Some of the finest Coptic wall paintings depict spiritual scenes that are awash with vibrant colours and accented with gold.

Coptic Art Today

Long overshadowed by both ancient Egyptian and Islamic themes, Coptic art does not receive much attention in Egypt despite its lengthy history and established tradition. Fortunately, this cultural heritage has been preserved in museums, churches and monasteries throughout Egypt and the world, and the artistic traditions continue to flourish among communities of modern-day Copts.

⭐ **Captain's Inn** HOTEL **$$**
(☑ 065-358-0170; http://captainsinn.elgouna.com; Abu Tig Marina; s/d from US$75/78; 🛜🏊) This friendly hotel is a favourite home-away-from-home for divers and kitesurfers in town for thrills on the water rather than fancy rooms. The location, off the main marina and near to restaurants and the beach, is fantastic; the flower-filled courtyard is a

great place to relax. The rooms – decked out in natty blue and white – are light-filled and comfortable.

Mosaique
HOTEL $$

(☎065-358-0077; http://mosaique.elgouna.com; Abu Tig Marina; s/d from US$81/84; 🛜🌊) We really like Mosaique's bright rooms, with their balconies, comfortable beds and blue-and-white textiles. The location on Abu Tig Marina makes it easy to go out and explore shops and restaurants, although the extremely tempting heated-pool area may put plans for leaving the hotel on hold. A short walk to the beach, this hotel is popular with families and kitesurfers.

Dawar El Omda
RESORT $$

(☎065-358-0063; http://dawarelomda-elgouna.com; Kafr El Gouna; s/d from US$75/79; 🛜🌊) In the heart of downtown El Gouna, this tastefully decorated four-star is adults-only. The hotel, whose name translates as 'the mayor's house', eschews European design in favour of classic Egyptian lines and arches, and has cosy, well-appointed rooms and a convenient lagoon-side location. There's no beach, but shuttles are at the ready to whisk you away to the sands.

★La Maison Bleue
HOTEL $$$

(☎012-8359-1116; www.lamaison-bleue.com; Kite Centre Rd; r US$400; 🅿@🛜🌊) A fantasy constructed out of the imaginary life of a wealthy Levantine. With an eclectic interior that is all grand tiled floors, intricate wooden ceilings and walls graced with a quirky mix of art deco, Minoan and Egyptian art, La Maison Bleue exudes both opulence and decadence. Suites are enormous and supremely comfortable with distinctive early-20th-century styling fit for royalty.

Like at home, you need to spend time at La Maison Bleue to appreciate it best. Service is flawless but not imposing. The restaurant serves some of the best food in the area, with an emphasis on local ingredients and Mediterranean inspiration. There's a sweep of private beach out front, and if a long, hard day on the sand gets too much, the hotel's pool and gloriously sumptuous spa and hammam will soothe your sun-frazzled soul. If you're out to impress your other half with a romantic getaway, you really can't go wrong here.

Sheraton Miramar
RESORT $$$

(☎065-354-5606; www.sheratonmiramarresort.com; s/d from US$110/160; 🅿@🌊) Designed by architect Michael Graves, this mammoth pastel-toned five-star resort is one of the original signature properties of El Gouna. The entire complex is strung along a series of beach-fringed private islands just offshore from town and it's a lovely place to stay if you just want to flop out on the beach.

🍴 Eating

★Zia Amelia
ITALIAN $$

(☎012-2527-1526; www.facebook.com/ziaamelia elgouna; Kafr El Gouna; mains LE115-150; ⊙1-11pm; 🍴🖶) El Gouna's cutest restaurant is rustic done right with a charmingly intimate interior and, weather permitting, an outdoor-dining area shaded by a vine-covered trellis. The menu is home-style Italian with generous portions of lasagne, crisp pizza, homemade pasta and seafood. Leave room for dessert because the tiramisu is decidedly wicked. There's live music most Wednesdays. Booking essential.

★Le Garage
INTERNATIONAL $$

(☎012-2741-2100; www.facebook.com/Le-Garage-Gourmet-Burger-El-Gouna-Egypt-1624447677819893; Abu Tig Marina; mains LE80-150; ⊙4pm-midnight; 🛜🍴) Flying the flag for the gourmet-burger craze in El Gouna, the 20-selection strong range at Le Garage includes a straight-up burger and varieties such as tandoori chicken, blue cheese with walnuts and grapes, and a burger that's topped with truffles and edible gold leaf. There are a couple of decent veggie options, too.

Upstairs
INTERNATIONAL $$

(☎010-2888-8923; www.facebook.com/pg/upstairs.elgouna; Kafr El Gouna; mains LE40-90; 🍴) A fine-dining experience for the carnivore in your life, Upstairs (which confusingly is not upstairs) has a menu packed to the rafters with French-influenced meat dishes. The signature dish is a rather delicious slow-cooked camel in a yellow curry sauce, but there's plenty of steak, chicken, duck, seafood and other delights if you're not feeling adventurous, and vegetarian options too.

ℹ Information

Information on all aspects of a visit to El Gouna, from where to eat and sleep to what's happening on the dates you might be there, can be found at www.elgouna.com.

ℹ Getting There & Away

AIR
Hurghada Airport is 20km south along the main coastal highway.

BUS
Go Bus Co (www.gobus-eg.com) runs up to nine services daily to Cairo (LE115 to LE220, six hours), finishing at its office beside the Ramses Hilton near Cairo's Tahrir Square. Tickets are best booked in advance and online (where you can choose your seat). The ticket office and bus stop in El Gouna is on the main plaza in Kafr El Gouna, opposite the tourist information centre.

To Hurghada, buses leave every 20 minutes between 7am and midnight from a bus stop also on the main plaza. Tickets cost LE15.

TAXI
Taxis run frequently between El Gouna and Hurghada; fares start at LE150. To Hurghada airport, expect to pay US$10 to US$30, depending on who you book with.

ℹ Getting Around
You can get around the El Gouna sprawl in a number of ways, from water and shuttle buses (LE10 for a day token) to tuk-tuks (LE10 per person per ride). There are also private taxis (LE20 within the resort).

Hurghada

🗷 065 / POP 392,540

Plucked from obscurity during the early days of the Red Sea's tourism drive, the fishing village of Hurghada has long since morphed into today's dense band of concrete that marches along the coastline for more than 20km. Still, it's a convenient destination for combining a diving holiday with the Nile Valley sites. Further offshore there is still superb diving aplenty; local NGOs are helping the town clean up its act, and the southern resort area and Sigala's sparklingly modern marina have brought back some of Hurghada's sheen.

Unfortunately, the rampant construction has left the coast blighted by half-finished shells of pleasure palaces never realised, while the coral reefs closest to the shore have been degraded by illegal landfill operations and irresponsible reef use. Hurghada's star has largely lost its lustre with package holiday-makers, while independent travellers prefer to press on to Dahab, El Gouna or further south to Marsa Alam.

Hurghada is split into three main areas. To the north is Ad Dahar, the most 'Egyptian' part of the city, with lively backstreet neighbourhoods and a bustling souq. Separated from Ad Dahar by a sandy mountain called Gebel Al Afish is the congested Sigala area, the heart of the place with shops and restaurants aplenty. South of Sigala is the resort strip, home to megaresorts catering to the package holiday crowd.

◉ Sights & Activities
Although many of Hurghada's beaches are bare and stark, developers have snapped up almost every available spot. Apart from the not-so-appealing **public beach** (Map p360; Sigala; I F10; ☻8am-sunset), the main option for enjoying sand and sea is to head to one of the resorts, which charge non-guests somewhere between LE25 and LE100 for beach access.

★**Hurghada Marina**   WATERFRONT
(Map p360; www.hurghada-marina.com) Hurghada's marina is a pleasant, car-free place to stroll, especially in the evening. When you get tired of staring out to sea or dreaming about owning one of the many huge yachts tied up here, drop by one of the numerous bars or restaurants.

Dive Sites
The reefs close to Hurghada and El Gouna have suffered heavy damage because of unfettered tourism development, so most dive sites are accessed by boat. Shop around for tours through your hotel may not be the best way to book. For any boat trip, take your passport as you'll need to show it at the port.

★**Gota Abu Ramada**   DIVE SITE
(Map p38) A mind-boggling abundance of marine life is on display here, 5km south of the Giftun Islands (p357), making Gota Abu Ramada a popular spot for underwater photographers, snorkellers and night divers. Depth: 3m to 15m. Rating: novice.

Giftun Islands   DIVE SITE
(Map p38) These islands, among the closest to Hurghada, form part of a marine reserve and are surrounded by a number of spectacular reefs teeming with marine life, including Hamda, Banana Reef, Sha'ab Sabrina, Erg Somaya and Sha'ab Torfa. Depth: 5m to 100m. Rating: intermediate to advanced.

Hurghada Coast

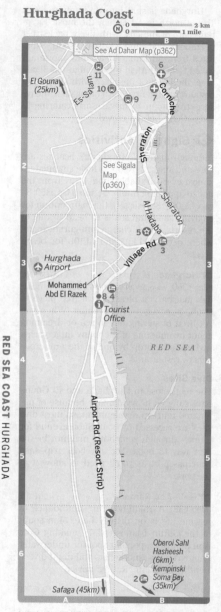

See Ad Dahar Map (p362)

El Gouna
(25km)

See Sigala
Map
(p360)

Hurghada
Airport

Mohammed
Abd El Razek

Tourist
Office

RED SEA

Airport Rd (Resort Strip)

Oberoi Sahl
Hasheesh
(6km);
Kempinski
Soma Bay
(35km)

Safaga (45km)

RED SEA COAST HURGHADA

Hurghada Coast

🏃 Activities, Courses & Tours
1 Jasmin Diving Centre A6

😴 Sleeping
2 Dana Beach Resort............................ B6
3 Hurghada Marriott Beach Resort...... B3
4 Steigenberger Al Dau Beach Hotel.... A3

🎭 Entertainment
5 El Sawy Culture Wheel B3

ℹ️ Information
6 El Salam Hospital................................ B1
7 Naval Hyperbaric & Emergency
   Medical Center.................................. B1

ℹ️ Transport
8 EgyptAir.. A3
9 Go Bus B1
10 Super Jet A1
11 Upper Egypt Bus Co A1

---

site is easily accessible by boat from Hurghada and offers plenty of thrills for divers and snorkellers.

Sha'ab Al Erg DIVE SITE
(Map p38) Ease of access means this is an excellent dive site for beginners, though veteran divers will still enjoy the towering brain corals and fan-encrusted rock formations. Depth: 5m to 15m. Rating: novice.

Shedwan Island DIVE SITE
There is some fabulous diving off this island, which sits in the straits between Hurghada and Sharm. Pilot whales and large pods of dolphins have been seen off the north reef wall.

Siyul Kebira DIVE SITE
(Map p38; Southern Straits of Gubal) The reef's upper section is home to bannerfish, angelfish and snapper. If the current is strong, you can drift along the wall skirting the edges of huge coral outcroppings. Depth: 10m to 30m. Rating: intermediate.

Dive Centres

⭐ **Jasmin Diving Centre** DIVING
(Map p358; ☎ 065-346-0334; www.jasmin-diving.com; Resort Strip, Grand Seas Resort Hostmark; 3-day, 6-dive package €159) This centre, down on the main resort strip, has an excellent reputation and was a founding member of the Hurghada Environmental Protection & Conservation Association (HEPCA).

Umm Qamar DIVE SITE
(Map p38) Umm Qamar, 9km north of the Giftun Islands (p357), is highlighted by three coral towers that are swathed in beautiful soft, purple coral and surrounded by a large range of fish as well as a wreck at 25m. The

Aquanaut Diving Club
DIVING

(Map p360; ☑ 012-2248-0463; www.aquanautclub. com; Hurghada Marina, Sigala; 1-day, 2-dive package €45; ⊙ 9am-4pm) Long-standing Hurghada dive centre, located off Sharia Sheraton.

Subex
DIVING

(Map p362; ☑ 065-354-7593; www.subex.org; Ad Dahar; 6-dive package €170) This reputable Swiss outfit is known for its professionalism, friendliness and attention to detail.

☞ Tours

Tours to almost anywhere in Egypt can be organised from Hurghada. The most popular options are desert jeep safaris (from LE200); visits to either Mons Porphyrites (p370) or Mons Claudianus (p371); full-day excursions to Luxor or to the monasteries of St Paul (p353) and St Anthony (p352); camel treks, quad-bike trips (from LE250) and sunset desert excursions.

Falco Safari
ADVENTURE

(☑ 010-0390-5492; www.falcosafari.com; quad-bike trip from €25, jeep/buggy safari €30/80) This outfit runs dune-buggy and quad-biking excursions, and jeep trips into the desert. Vehicle maintenance and safety are of a high standard. Pick-up and drop-off are available at hotels in the Hurghada or El Gouna areas.

🛏 Sleeping

Prices fluctuate according to the season and state of the tourism industry, but since Egypt's tourism downturn, most Hurghada resorts and hotels have continually slashed prices in an effort to entice travellers back.

Most budget accommodation is located within Ad Dahar and Sigala, but booking a resort in advance usually offers significant reductions on the rack-rate, making many four- and five-star resorts fall into the mid-range category.

★ Luxor Hotel
HOTEL $

(Map p362; ☑ 065-354-2877; www.luxorhotel -eg.com; Sharia Mustafa, Ad Dahar; s/d/tr LE120/200/270; 🔊) This small hotel on top of Ad Dahar's hill is run by friendly Said and has good-sized, clean rooms, all home to drab brown furnishings but with surprisingly good facilities for the price tag, including TV and fridge. If you're solo, upgrade yourself from a single room, as they're a bit poky and dark. Good views from the roof terrace.

White Albatross
HOTEL $

(Map p360; ☑ 065-344-2519; walbatros53@ hotmail.com; Sharia Sheraton, Sigala; s/d/tr LE150/200/250) If you are on a budget and want to be slap in the centre of the Sigala action, this small hotel has cosy, extremely clean and comfortable rooms with little homely touches. Management is not always forthcoming, but if you're happy to fend for yourself, it's fantastic value.

Hurghada Marriott Beach Resort
RESORT $$

(Map p358; ☑ 065-344-4420; www.marriott.com; Resort Strip; r from €80; ℗@🛜🏊) Within walking distance of the resort strip's nightlife and restaurants, the well-kept rooms here are spacious and light-filled, and each comes with a balcony. Some visitors may be disappointed by the small beach area, but if you want full facilities and the freedom to pick and choose where to eat, it's a great choice.

Dana Beach Resort
RESORT $$

(Map p358; ☑ 065-346 0401; www.pickalbatros. com; Resort Strip; r full board from €80; ℗🛜🏊) If you simply want an easygoing beach break, this 841-room megaresort serves up masses of amenities, making it a winner for families. There's a reef just offshore that's great for snorkelling, and the well-tended gardens, four swimming pools and a long strip of sand are prime fodder for kicking back and chilling out.

Steigenberger Al Dau Beach Hotel
RESORT $$

(Map p358; ☑ 065-346 5400; www.steigenberger aldaubeach.com; Resort Strip; r half board from €67; ℗🛜🏊) Large, tastefully decorated rooms, a mind-boggling amount of activities on offer and an absolutely mammoth pool make the Steigenberger a long-running favourite for a family holiday, although service suffers when the resort is busy. The private beach is kept beautifully clean and the manicured gardens offer a shady retreat after a day in the sun.

Roma
HOTEL $$

(Map p360; ☑ 065-344-8140; www.romahotel hurghada.com; Sharia Al Hadaba, Sigala; s/d $50/75; 🛜🏊) This business-style hotel has a glitzy lobby that promises much more than the simple rooms deliver, but everything is kept neat and clean, and the staff are smiley and helpful. The swimming pool and private beach are extra bonuses.

Sigala

RED SEA COAST HURGHADA

Geisum Village
RESORT $$

(Map p362; ☎065-354-6692; Corniche, Ad Dahar; s/d/tr US$15/32/39; @ 🛜 ☀) This stalwart of the Hurghada scene isn't going to win any style awards, but its tidy and bright rooms, decked out in a cream-and-green combo, are popular for a cheap beach break. The centre of the action is the curvaceous swimming pool surrounded by well-tended gardens that run down to a minuscule patch of private beach.

It's popular with Egyptian families up for boisterous fun-in-the-sun, so don't expect a peaceful retreat.

★ Oberoi Sahl Hasheesh
HOTEL $$$

(☎065-344 0777; www.oberoihotels.com; Hurghada–Safaga Coastal rd, Sahl Hasheesh; ste from €140; P 🛜 ☀) Peaceful, exclusive and opulent beyond your imagination, the Oberoi sits a good 30-minute drive south from Hurghada and features palatial suites decorated in minimalist Moorish style. Each comes complete with sunken marble baths, private courtyards – some with pools – and panoramic sea views. Justifiably advertised as the most luxurious destination on the Red Sea, the Oberoi is world-class.

The Oberoi chain prides itself on service and this hotel is no exception, offering a class way beyond anywhere else in Hurghada. Dining options include international and Indian. The spa, off the two-tier pool, offers a range of top-end treatments. The hotel has its own dive centre, with snorkelling and junior dive programmes for kids. The hotel also arranges excursions to Luxor, the Red Sea monasteries and sailing to the Giftun Islands (p357).

Kempinski Soma Bay
RESORT $$$

(☎065-356-1500; www.kempinski.com/somabay; Soma Bay; r full board from €130; P @ 🛜 ☀) Kempinski doesn't do understated and this massive complex is no exception. From the palatial arabesque lobby to the immense beach and huge pool area, this is luxury firing on all five-star cylinders. Be aware that Soma Bay is a good 40km south of Hurghada, so this isn't a place for people who like popping into town.

✕ Eating

For international dining, the Hurghada Marina Promenade has a multitude of choices. For budget eating, Ad Dahar and Sigala have dozens of inexpensive local-style restaurants squirrelled away in the backstreets.

Gad EGYPTIAN $
(Map p360; Sharia Sheraton, Sigala; shawarma LE12-22, mains from LE20, 1kg kofta LE160; ⊙10am-late; P🍴) If you're looking for cheap, filling and tasty Egyptian staples, you can't go wrong with Egypt's favourite fast-food restaurant. The sprawling menu covers soup and salad, falafel and shawarma, *fiteer* (sweet or savoury flaky pizza) and full kebab and kofta meals (sold by the kilo). There's another branch (Map p362; Sharia An Nasr, Ad Dahar; shawarma LE12-22, mains from LE20, 1kg kofta LE160; ⊙10am-late) in Ad Dahar.

El Zahraa Bakery SWEETS $
(Map p360; Sigala; sweets LE2-6; 🍴) Don't blame us if your dentistry bill skyrockets after a visit to this place. El Zahraa's myriad variations of baklava and *kunafa* (vermicelli-like pastry over a vanilla base soaked in syrup) are manna for those inclined to a sweet tooth.

El Halaka EGYPTIAN $
(Map p360; Sharia Shedwan, Sigala; mains LE20-60) This place makes up for its understated location and interior with its fresh seafood (the fish market is close by). Fish is priced by weight, but there are plenty of cheaper grills and seafood dishes on the menu.

Abu Khadigah EGYPTIAN $
(Map p360; Sharia Sheraton, Sigala; mains LE20-60; ⊙noon-10pm) For authentic Egyptian kebabs and other local staples, Abu Khadigah is just the ticket. It's known for its kofta (spiced mincemeat patties grilled on a skewer) and stuffed cabbage leaves.

★ Star Fish SEAFOOD $$
(Map p360; 🖀065-344-3751; www.facebook.com/starfishredsea; Sharia Sheraton, Sigala; mains from LE60; ⊙noon-midnight; P) An extremely popular fish restaurant on the main Sigala drag. You can choose fish from the display, or opt

for prawns (grilled, with pasta, or deep-fried) and an excellent fish soup. Or you could go for the blow-out special of soup, lobster, shrimp, fish fillet, calamari and kofta with rice and salad.

★ White Elephant ASIAN $$
(Map p360; 🖀010-0102-5117; Hurghada Marina Promenade, Sigala; mains LE80-130; ⊙4pm-midnight; 🍴) This is the real deal, Thai food prepared by a Thai chef. So if you want a spicy and zingy Thai feast, let the waiter know you can handle the heat and White Elephant won't scrimp on the spice. *Tom yum* (hot and sour Thai soup) is excellent, as are most dishes with fresh fish from the market.

Moby Dick INTERNATIONAL $$
(Map p360; Sharia Sheraton, Sigala; mains from LE85) People rave about Moby Dick's succulent steaks, but the restaurant also serves pasta and seafood and does a fine line in crispy, fresh salads. And there's the curiosity of camel steak with mushroom or pepper sauce. This is a consistently popular place with a really good vibe and helpful, chatty staff. Drinks are also well-priced.

Nubian Cafe EGYPTIAN $$
(Map p360; Hurghada Marina Promenade, Sigala; mains LE40-120; ⊙noon-10pm; 🍴) In a town where international food rules, it's nice to see a restaurant taking a stand for Egyptian cuisine. The Nubian Cafe does flavoursome *tagens* (stews cooked in a deep clay pot); good mezze, including a scrumptious baba ganoush (purée of grilled aubergine); and meaty grills. There's plenty for vegetarians to sink their teeth into, too.

Shade Bar & Grill INTERNATIONAL $$
(Map p360; Hurghada Marina, Sigala; mains LE80-120) If you're pining for a steak, look no further. Sprawl out on the terrace beanbags and order your red meat fix. For those too lazy to bar-hop, Shade conveniently turns into a popular bar with lively music late at night.

⬤ Drinking & Nightlife

Because of the tourism downturn, Hurghada's lively nightlife has taken a hit lately. Nevertheless, you'll have no problem finding a beer here. There are plenty of bars, cafes and restaurants which all serve alcohol.

★ Caribbean Beach Bar BAR
(Map p360; Sharia Sheraton, Sigala; 🖀) If you're looking to chill with a cocktail right next to the sea, this palm-thatched pontoon over

Ad Dahar

Pharaonic art. It's easy to spot – the facade is decorated with fake *mashrabiyya* (wooden lattice) windows.

Retro
BAR
(Map p360; Sharia Sheraton, Sigala; ⊙noon-late) This relaxed pub dishes up live music every Sunday and Wednesday and plays an eclectic mash of rock, blues and soul at other times. An easy-going vibe, decent bar menu and pool table make it an all-round winner.

Papas HRG
BAR
(Map p360; ☑065-344-4920; Hurghada Marina Promenade, Sigala; ⊙5pm-late) The centre of Hurghada nightlife is this popular Dutch-run bar, which has enough live music, pool table and game action to keep even the dive instructors and expats coming back for more. It's lively and has a great atmosphere most nights, and there's basic food (burgers, pizzas and the like) on offer.

☆ Entertainment

El Sawy Culture Wheel
ARTS CENTRE
(Map p358; ☑010-0167-8274; www.facebook.com/ElSAWYculturewheelHurghada; Hadaba Rd, Dibaj Mall) An offshoot of the Cairo-based cultural and performance space, El Sawy stages music and theatre performances and other events and activities for children and adults.

🔒 Shopping

Ad Dahar Souq
MARKET
(Map p362; off Sharia An Nasr, Ad Dahar; ⊙noon-late) Hurghada's souq is a dusty sprawl of lanes crammed with shops selling silver and copper products, leather, papyrus and shisha pipes. This is the place to put your haggling hat on and snag a bargain. It's best visited at night when the day's heat is done and the alleys are packed with people out for an evening stroll.

ℹ Information

El Salam Hospital (Map p358; ☑065-361-5013, 065-361-5012; www.elsalamhospital.com; Corniche; ⊙24hr) Just north of the Iberotel Arabella.

Naval Hyperbaric & Emergency Medical Center (Map p358; ☑065-344-9150, 065-354-8450; Corniche) Has a hyperbaric chamber. Near Iberotel Arabella.

Tourist Office (Map p358; ☑065-344-4420; Resort Strip; ⊙8am-8pm Sat-Thu, 2-10pm Fri) Small kiosk in the middle of the resort strip.

the water has a laid-back atmosphere made for lounging. Once the sun has set there's often live music or parties. You have to walk through the Bella Vista Hotel to get here.

Waves
CAFE
(Map p360; ☑010-0589-7367; www.facebook.com/waves.cafeshop; Hurghada Marina Promenade, Sigala; ⊙noon-late) The outdoor seating here is prime yacht-watching territory, and the cafe serves up a surprisingly decent cappuccino, good shisha and decently priced cocktails.

El Mashrabia
CAFE
(Map p360; Sharia Sheraton, Sigala; ⊙10.30am-late) This is our favourite pit stop in Hurghada for a juice, *shai* (tea) or shisha. El Mashrabia is slap on Sigala's main road, with shady outdoor seating and a dimly lit cafe decorated in a mishmash of Chinese lanterns and

RESCUING THE RED SEA

The Red Sea's coral and aquatic life has been devastated by huge fleets of pleasure and fishing boats that ply the waters between Hurghada and the many reefs situated within an hour of town. Until recently, there was nothing to stop captains from anchoring to the coral, or snorkellers and divers breaking off a colourful chunk to take home. But thanks to the efforts of the Hurghada Environmental Protection & Conservation Association (HEPCA), the Red Sea's reefs are at last being protected.

Set up in 1992 by 12 of the town's larger, more reputable dive companies, HEPCA's programme to conserve the Red Sea's reefs includes public-awareness campaigns, direct community action and lobbying of the Egyptian government to introduce appropriate laws. Thanks to these efforts, the whole coast south of Suez Governorate is now known as the Red Sea Protectorate. One of the programme's earliest successes was to establish a system of more than 570 mooring buoys at popular dive sites in the region to prevent boat captains dropping anchor on the coral.

While continuing in its efforts to ensure the Red Sea's diving sites are protected, in recent years HEPCA has launched even more ambitious conservation projects. In 2009 the NGO took over responsibility for waste management in the southern Red Sea, a service which had previously been sporadic and unregulated. Now Marsa Alam and its environs have a regular door-to-door rubbish-collection service and a recycling plant. The service was judged such a success that in 2010 it was expanded to include Hurghada as well, and is now seen as a model for solid-waste management in Egypt.

For more information on safe diving practices or if you'd like to get involved with helping HEPCA protect the Red Sea by joining in on one of its beach or reef clean-ups, check the organisation's website (www.hepca.org).

DANGERS & ANNOYANCES

Although Hurghada is a resort town, this is still Egypt; both men and women will garner more respect and receive less hassle if they save their swimwear for the hotel beaches. Women should also note that topless bathing is illegal in Egypt. All visitors should dress modestly when walking around town, especially in the souq area of Ad Dahar.

ⓘ Getting There & Away

AIR

Hurghada Airport (p350), near the resort strip, receives (mostly charter) flights direct from European destinations.

EgyptAir (Map p358; ☏ 065-346-3035; www.egyptair.com; ⊙ 8am-8pm Sat-Thu, from 10am Fri) has several daily flights to Cairo. Prices fluctuate greatly, but tickets can be as low as LE718.

BOAT

The high-speed catamaran ferry service between Hurghada and Sharm El Sheikh is operated by **La Pespes** (Map p360; ☏ 012-1014-2000; www.lapespes.com; Midan Aka, Sharia An Nasr, High Jet Office, Sigala; ⊙ 10am-10pm). Boats leave at 8am on Sunday, Tuesday and Thursday (adult/child US$40/30, 2½ hours) from Hurghada Tourist Port in Sigala. You must be at the port 1½ hours before departure and have your passport on hand for identification.

Tickets can be purchased in advance from the **La Pespes ticket office**. Many travel agents and hotels in Hurghada can also book the tickets for you.

BUS

Hurghada doesn't have a central bus station. Instead, the major companies, including **Upper Egypt Bus Co** (Map p358; ☏ 065-354-7582; off Sharia An Nasr, Ad Dahar), **Super Jet** (Map p358; ☏ 065-355-3499; Sharia An Nasr, Ad Dahar) and **Go Bus** (Map p358; www.gobus-eg.com; Sharia An Nasr, Ad Dahar), all arrive and depart from their own separate stations, which are strung out along Sharia An Nasr in Ad Dahar. Go Bus has a handy **ticket booking office** (Map p360; Sharia Sheraton, Sigala; ⊙ 10am-10pm) in Sigala, but it's easiest to book online, where you can also choose your seat.

Go Bus runs the most comfortable and quickest service to Luxor. Bus schedules change randomly, so check timings when booking.

BUSES FROM HURGHADA

DESTINATION	PRICE	DURATION	TIMES/COMPANY
Al Quseir	LE20	1½hr	1.30am, 5am, 9.30am & 4pm (Upper Egypt)
Alexandria	LE150-230	9hr	2pm, 4.30pm, 10pm (Go Bus), 2.30pm & 11pm (Super Jet)
Aswan	LE90	7hr	12.30am & 10.30pm (Upper Egypt)
Cairo	LE65-295	6-7hr	20 Go Bus, eight Upper Egypt and five Super Jet departures daily
Luxor	LE50-90	4-5hr	8.30am & 5.30pm (Super Jet), 12.30am & 1.30am (Upper Egypt), 8.15am & 3.30pm (Go Bus)
Marsa Alam	LE50	4hr	2am, 5.30am, 8pm (Upper Egypt)
Suez	LE50-60	4-5hr	1am & 2am (Upper Egypt)

🛈 Getting Around

TO/FROM THE AIRPORT
A taxi to downtown Ad Dahar should cost around LE80, but you'll need to bargain hard.

CAR
There are numerous car rental agencies along Sharia Sheraton in Sigala, plus nearby **Avis** (Map p360; ☑ 065-344-7400; www.avis.com; Sharia Al Hadaba; ☻ 8am-1pm & 5-10pm), which runs a reliable and friendly service.

MICROBUS
Microbuses run throughout the day from central Ad Dahar, south along the resort strip, and along Sharia An Nasr and other major routes. Rides cost between LE1 and LE3.

TAXI
Taxis from Ad Dahar to the start of the resort strip (around the Marriott hotel) charge about LE40. Expect to pay LE20 travelling from the bus offices to the centre of Ad Dahar, and between LE30 and LE40 to the resort strip.

Safaga
☑ 065 / POP 43,990

Safaga is a rough-and-ready port town that most people pass through, but if you are a windsurfer or diver, you might want to stop a while to enjoy its turquoise waters and some excellent offshore reefs. However, Safaga's main business is the export of phosphates and acting as a major local terminal for the ferry to Saudi Arabia – during the hajj, thousands of pilgrims from the Nile Valley set off from here on their voyages to Mecca. The centre of town is an unattractive grid of flyblown, dusty streets, but the resort strip at the northern end of the bay has its sleepy charms.

⊙ Sights & Activities

Most people come to Safaga for the diving. It's also a famously windy place, with a fairly steady stream blowing in from the north. Most of the resort hotels have windsurfing centres, plus kitesurfing and other aquatic sports.

Salem Express
DIVE SITE

(Map p38; south Safaga Bay) The *Salem Express* is a stunning yet mournful sight. In 1991 this passenger ferry sank, killing about 1000 pilgrims returning from the hajj. While diving, take a moment to reflect on this watery graveyard. Do not enter the vessel. Depth: 12m to 30m. Rating: intermediate. Access by boat.

Panorama Reef
DIVE SITE

(Map p38; outer Safaga Bay) Panorama Reef is famous for its schooling barracuda, as well as numerous dolphins, eagle rays, grey reef sharks and silvertips, and for its soft and hard corals. Depth: 3m to 40m. Rating: intermediate. Access by boat.

Dive Operators

Orca Dive Club
DIVING

(☑ 065-326-0111; www.orca-diveclub-safaga.com; Resort Strip; 1-day (2 dives) €58, 3-days (6-dives) €164) One of the Red Sea's leading technical diving centres, with its own small hotel on the beach. Orca offers discounts on dive packages booked online.

Mena Dive
DIVING

(☑ 065-326-0060; www.menadive.com; Resort Strip; 1 day (2 dives) €52, 3 days (6 dives) €142) Mena Dive has been the centre of Safaga's diving scene since the 1990s. The dive team here offers everything from beginners' open-water courses to tech dives. It also has all the gear you might need to get out there into the deep.

🛏 Sleeping

There is an assortment of midrange and lower-priced options just north of town, mostly geared towards divers.

Toubia Hotel HOTEL **$**
(📞012-2313-5676; Corniche; s/d LE150/240) Owner Hakim and his welcoming family create a homely atmosphere, but his cement-block hotel looks tired and in need of an update. All 22 basic rooms are kept clean, and there's a simple private beach just outside.

Menaville Resort RESORT **$$**
(📞065-326-0065; www.menaville-resort.com; Resort Strip; s/d half board per week €330/484; 🅿@☒) This low-key four-star resort is popular with European divers. The hotel fronts a wonderful stretch of sand and accommodation is in whitewashed, airy bungalows surrounded by flowers, set around a large pool. It also attracts visitors for its climatotherapy cures for skin diseases such as psoriasis and for arthritis. There's an in-house medical team and treatments include black-sand baths.

Nemo Dive Hotel HOTEL **$$**
(📞010-0364-8708; www.nemodive.com; s/d €25/40; 🅿🤶☒) A well-run, 30-room Dutch-owned hotel across a quiet road from the beach on the edge of town, the Nemo has attentive staff, some neat modern decorative touches and a small, good beach with pool and bar. Rooms are spacious and bright and the rooftop seaview restaurant serves simple international food and cold beers. Perfect for divers. One-week full-board packages available. The hotel offers PADI open-water courses for €287.

🍴 Eating & Drinking

At the northern end of town are several inexpensive restaurants, though nothing worth travelling for. Most visitors prefer to eat in their hotels, and all-inclusive plans are generally available.

Nemo Dive Hotel (p365) dishes up food and music on its beach some weekends. Otherwise, there are a few cafes in town.

Diver's House BAR
(www.facebook.com/diverhouse.safaga; off the Corniche; ☺4pm-2am) The only place to party in Safaga, dispensing cold beers and cocktails, simple food and big cheer. On a good night there's a mix of locals, dive instructors and travellers.

ℹ Getting There & Away

BOAT
There are regular passenger boats from Safaga to Duba (Saudi Arabia), and services to Jeddah (Saudi Arabia) during the hajj.

BUS
The bus station is near the southern end of town. Safaga is located along the main coastal highway, 53km south of Hurghada. There are seven daily buses to Cairo (LE85, seven to eight hours) and regular daily departures to Suez (LE50 to LE65, five to six hours), which also stop in Hurghada (LE20, one hour). There are also a few daily departures to Al Quseir (LE20, one hour), Marsa Alam (LE35 to LE40, three hours) and Shalatein (LE60, seven hours).

Al Quseir

📞065 / POP 49,313
Far removed from the resort clamour of the rest of the Red Sea coast, the historic city of Al Quseir is a muddle of colourful and creaky coral-block architecture dating from the Ottoman era that sadly is bypassed by most tourists. This charmingly sleepy seaside town has a history stretching back to Pharaonic times, when it was the main port for boats heading south to the fabled East African kingdom of Punt. Although little remains from this earliest era, strolling through Al Quseir's photogenic old streets – backed by the battered ramparts of its Ottoman fortress and speckled with the domed tombs of various holy men who died en route to or from Mecca – provides a fascinating glimpse into this region before tourism took over.

History

Throughout Egyptian history, Al Quseir has been an important port, serving as a thriving centre of trade and export between the Nile Valley and the Red Sea and beyond. A Greek historian recorded a fleet of 120 ships exporting pottery, slaves, wine and precious materials and bringing back silk, spices and stone, which were then carried by camel to Qift on the Nile and shipped north to Alexandria and Europe. It has also been a major departure point for pilgrims travelling to Mecca for the hajj. Even during its period of decline, the city remained a major settlement and was sufficiently important for the Ottomans to fortify it during the 16th century. Later the British beat the French for control of Al Quseir and for some time it

Al Quseir

Tourist Police (750m)
Mövenpick Resort El Quseir (7km);
Rocky Valley Beach Camp (10km)

Al Quseir

was an important step on the trade route between India and Britain. The opening of the Suez Canal in 1869 put an end to all this, and the town's decline accelerated, with only a brief burst of prosperity as a phosphate-processing centre in the early decades of the 20th century.

⊙ Sights & Activities

Al Quseir is a lesser-known dive destination. There is a dive shop on the seafront, but most operators are affiliated with hotels.

★ Ottoman Fortress   FORTRESS
(Map p366; Sharia Al Gomhurriyya; LE15; ⊙ 9am-5pm) This small fortress was built in 1571 to provide Ottoman troops with control to the port and therefore passage to Mecca. Modified several times by the French and then by the British, who permanently altered the fortress by firing some 6000 cannonballs upon it during a heated battle in the 19th century, it was used until 1975 by the Egyptian coast guard. A recent renovation has made it the best sight in town.

Much of the original exterior walls remain intact and the interior has been well renovated. Some rooms have interesting information boards documenting the history of Al Quseir, the trade conducted here and the people of the region. The **North Bastion** has a small exhibition about the local Ababda tribe and elsewhere there are displays explaining the trading routes across the desert to the Nile and down the Red Sea, as well as explanations of what was traded. A staircase in the **watchtower** gives wide views of the town and port.

Dive Sites

El Qadim   DIVE SITE
(Map p38) Located 7km north of Al Quseir in a small bay abutted by the Mövenpick Resort (p367), this dive site boasts a complex network of interconnecting caves and canyons. Depth: 5m to 30m. Rating: intermediate. Access from the shore.

El Kaf   DIVE SITE
(Map p38) An easy plunge 10km south of Al Quseir that appeals to divers of all levels, El Kaf is a canyon pitted with small caves and passages, and accented by massive coral boulders and sandy ravines. Depth: 18m to 25m. Rating: novice. Access from the shore.

🛏 Sleeping & Eating

Rocky Valley Beach Camp   CAMPGROUND $$
(☎ 065-333-5247; www.rockyvalleydiverscamp.com; full board dive package per person €50) About 10km north of Al Quseir, this camp is a veritable paradise for shoestringing scuba aficionados. Rocky Valley lures in divers by offering a variety of cheap all-inclusive packages, which include Bedouin-style tents, beachside barbecues, late-night beach parties and some incredible reefs right off the shore. It's a fun place where management works hard to foster a communal atmosphere.

★ Mövenpick Resort El Quseir   RESORT $$$
(☎ 065-335-0410; www.movenpick.com; s/d with half board US$190/220; P@🛜🏊) Al Quseir's best hotel stretches around a coral bay 7km

STROLLING AROUND THE OLD TOWN

Ringed in between Sharia Al Gomhurriyya and the waterfront is Al Quseir's old town. It's a twisting labyrinth of alleyways where progress seems happy to hit the snooze button and local life is snail-paced. Within the squiggle of lanes below the **Ottoman fortress** (p366), wind your way past pastel-washed houses, some still boasting original *mashrabiyya* window screens and in various states of decay, while looking out for hand-painted hajj decorations and quirkily coloured doors.

A few historic buildings to keep an eye out for as you wander:

Old Police Station (Map p366; Sharia Port Said) Originally an Ottoman *diwan* (council chamber), the once grand old police station on Al Quseir's waterfront is now a picturesque but dilapidated shell.

Granary (Map p366) Just behind the old police station is the fortress-like facade of the granary. It dates to the early 19th century and was used to store wheat that was destined for Mecca.

Faran Mosque (Map p366; Sharia Port Said) The minaret was built in 1704.

north of the centre, with the best rooms just above the shore. It offers good European and Egyptian food and the usual five-star facilities, including a nice spa. Among the most laid-back resorts along the coast, it also offers quiet evenings and a refreshing absence of glitz.

Although the resort has expanded, the management has retained its environmentally conscious approach, as evidenced by the fine state of the local coral reef, which has excellent coral and fish to view either by snorkelling or diving. The hotel has extensive grounds and a large pool overlooking the sea. But perhaps the biggest reason to stay here is the bay itself, which has a sand beach and direct access to the sea (good for kids). There is also a house dive centre.

⭐ **El Fardous**   SEAFOOD **$$**
(Map p366; ☑012-8332-4884; Sharia Port Said; mains LE50-150; ⊘noon-10pm) A no-nonsense waterfront restaurant serving the best fish in Al Quseir, El Fardous has half a dozen tables, big windows onto the sea, a big cooler where you choose your fish, calamari or lobster, and some friendly waiters who will advise on what's best. No alcohol, but despite a 'no smoking' sign, the restaurant does serve shisha.

There's air-con for hot days, a TV for cold nights and tables out on the waterside when weather permits eating with your feet in the sand. Locals and Egyptians from elsewhere in the country eat here. Located across the road from the Faran Mosque (p367).

Restaurant Marianne   EGYPTIAN **$$**
(Map p366; ☑065-333-4386; Sharia Port Said; mains LE40-80) A popular local restaurant with friendly service, a great menu featuring seafood as well as all the usual Egyptian favourites, and seating right on the sand.

ⓘ Getting There & Away

The **bus station** is roughly 500m north-west from the old town. Buses run to Cairo (LE100, 10 hours) via Hurghada (LE30, 1½ to two hours), departing at 11am, noon, 9pm and 10.30pm. Buses to Marsa Alam (LE25, two hours) leave at 9am, 2pm, 9pm, 10pm and midnight. The bus continues to Shalatein (LE50).

ⓘ Getting Around

Microbuses go along Sharia Al Gomhuriyya; some also head to the bus and servees stations. Fares are LE1 to LE2, depending on the distance travelled. A taxi from the bus station to the waterfront costs LE10 to LE15.

Marsa Alam

☑065 / POP 6526

In-the-know divers have been heading to Marsa Alam for years, attracted to the seas that offer up some of Egypt's best diving just off the rugged coastline. Despite this, the far-flung destination stayed well off the tourism radar for a long time. While the town itself remains a sleepy, nondescript place, the strip of coast to its north and south has been snapped up by eager developers and is now home to a plethora of resorts and half-built hotels.

RED SEA COAST MARSA ALAM

Despite the construction, Marsa Alam's coastline is still a diving aficionado's dream, and there are some long-standing beach camps here specifically for those who want to spend most of their time underwater. This is also the best base from which to venture into the southern reaches of Egypt's vast Eastern Desert, where gold and emeralds were once mined by the Romans in the barren, mineral-rich mountains just inland.

◉ Sights & Activities

Elphinstone
DIVE SITE

(Map p38) North of Marsa Alam, Elphinstone has steep reef walls covered with soft corals and is washed by strong currents that make it ideal for spotting sharks – seven species reportedly frequent its waters. This is one of the best dives in the region. Depth: 20m to 40m. Rating: advanced.

Sha'ab Sharm
DIVE SITE

(Map p38) Impressive topography and excellent marine life (hammerheads, barracuda, groper and yellowmouth moray eels) mark this large, kidney-shaped offshore reef 30km north-east of Wadi Gimal. Depth: 15m to more than 40m. Rating: advanced.

Hamada
DIVE SITE

(Map p38) Atop an inshore reef 60km north of Berenice (p372) lies the wreck of this 65m-long cargo ship. Lying on its side in just 14m of water, *Hamada* is a fairly easy, extremely picturesque dive site. Depth: 6m to 14m. Rating: novice.

Sataya Reef
DIVE SITE

(Map p38) Horseshoe-shaped Sataya, 50km north of Berenice (p372), is the main reef of the Fury Shoals, and has steep walls leading down to a sandy slope scattered with a great variety of coral heads. Depth: 4m to 40m. Rating: intermediate.

Rocky Island
DIVE SITE

A sandy island east of Berenice (p372), Rocky Island has a range of dive possibilities, including a 25m drop off the east side of the island. Plenty of coral and reef life, including a range of sharks. Rating: advanced.

NOMADS OF THE EASTERN DESERT

Although the desert of the southern Red Sea may seem empty and inhospitable, the area has been home to nomadic Ababda and Besharin tribes for millennia. The Beja, a nomadic tribe of African origin, are thought to be descendants of the Blemmyes, the fierce tribespeople mentioned by classical geographers. Until well into the 20th century, the extent of the territory in which they roamed was almost exactly as described by the Romans, with whom they were constantly at war some 2000 years earlier.

Expert camel herders, the Ababda and Besharin lived a nomadic lifestyle that hardly changed until the waters of Lake Nasser rose and destroyed their traditional grazing lands. While most Besharin, many of whom do not speak Arabic, live in Sudan, most of the Arabic-speaking Ababda are settled in communities in the Nile Valley between Aswan and Luxor. A small number continue to live in their ancestral territory, concentrated in the area from Marsa Alam to Wadi Gimal, as well as on the eastern shores of Lake Nasser.

If you spend time in the region, you'll still likely see traditional Ababda huts, lined inside with thick, handwoven blankets, or hear Ababda music, characterised by rhythmic clapping and drumming and heavy use of the five-stringed lyre-like tamboura. At the centre of Ababda social life is *jibena* – heavily sweetened coffee prepared from fresh-roasted beans in a small earthenware flask heated directly in the coals.

With the rapid expansion of tourism along the southern Red Sea, long-standing Ababda lifestyles have become increasingly threatened. Tourism has begun to replace livestock and camels as the main source of livelihood, and many Ababda men now work as guards or labourers on the resorts springing up around Marsa Alam, while others have started working with travel companies, offering camel safaris to tourists.

There are differing views on the impact of tourism in this region. On one hand, revenue from tourism can play a vital role in the development of the region, particularly through the sale of locally produced crafts or payment for services of a local guide. However, indigenous tourism sometimes becomes exploitative, and visits can take on an unfortunate 'human zoo' quality. If you are considering a visit, ask questions about the nature of your trip and consider the potential positive and negative impact that it may have on the community.

Red Sea Diving Safari   DIVING

(📞02-337-1833, 02-337-9942; www.redsea-div-ingsafari.com; Marsa Shagra; 5-day diving package from €170, 3-5 day open water PADI course €325) Founded by environmentalist and long-time diver Hossam Hassan, who pioneered diving in the Red Sea's deep south, Red Sea Diving Safari has emerged as one of the leading dive operators in the region. Bases at Masrsa Shagra, Marsa Nakari and Wadi Lahami.

🎉 Festivals & Events

⭐ 3alganoob Music Festival   MUSIC

(📞011-1181-2277; http://3alganoob-festival.com; Tondoba Bay; ☉Apr) Egypt's only modern music festival, this three-day feast at Tondoba Bay, 14km south of Marsa Alam, features the country's most interesting independent bands in every genre from electronica to alternative rock. Camping areas are set up for festival-goers, and activities such as yoga, film screenings, diving and even a beach clean-up are organised.

From a single band and an audience of 40 in 2004, the festival has now attracted a devoted following; expect a crowd in the hundreds.

🛏 Sleeping

There are few places to stay in Marsa Alam village itself, but north and south along the coast there's an ever-growing number of all-inclusive resorts and of simpler, diver-oriented camps, many of which practise sustainable tourism.

⭐ Deep South   CAMPGROUND $

(📞010-0748-7608; http://deepsouthredsea.com; hut/chalet per person €20/30, P) 🏊 If you're looking to strip it back to the basics of sun, sea and sand, Deep South offers palm-thatch huts and simple but extravagantly painted chalets, a warm welcome and good food in an exceptionally mellow atmosphere. There are good dive packages too. It's located on a hill across the road from Tondoba Bay, 14km south of Marsa Alam.

Karim Noor, who started and runs Deep South, is originally from Cairo but is committed to the life here. Proceeds from the camp help fund his efforts to preserve the area's natural beauty and to improve life in the region, whether by providing healthcare for the local Ababda people, taking a guest at Deep South to his favourite swimming hole, or running the 3alganoob Music Festival here every April.

WORTH A TRIP

ENCOUNTERING DOLPHINS AT SHA'AB SAMADAI

This lagoon (Samadai Dolphin Sanctuary; LE105) 18km south-east of Marsa Alam is home to three dive sites with a reef system full of interesting coral pinnacles and fish life. What makes Samadai so special, though, is the pod of spinner dolphins (numbering up to 480) that regularly visits the lagoon. As with any wildlife-watching, there is no guarantee that you'll see dolphins on your visit; however, the huge diversity of corals and other sea life makes snorkelling or diving here a wonderful experience.

Samadai is managed by a local conservation NGO, the Hurghada Environmental Protection & Conservation Association (www.hepca.org), which has established a daily cap on visitor numbers to protect the dolphins and introduced an admission fee that goes towards maintaining the conservation of the lagoon.

⭐ Marsa Shagra Village   CAMPGROUND $$$

(📞065-338-0021, Cairo office 02-333-71833; www.redsea-divingsafari.com; Marsa Shagra; s/d full board tent €65/100, royal tent €70/110, hut €75/110, chalet €95/140; P📶) 🏊 This large-scale camp 24km north of Marsa Alam offers a range of accommodation from tents to deluxe chalets, and spectacular snorkelling and diving on the house reef, as well as a full dive centre. Marsa Shagra was one of the first eco-minded places on the Red Sea and, despite the development around it, has stayed true to its sustainable-tourism credentials.

Among this outfit's many initiatives have been successful efforts to create national parks, bringing local Bedouin into tourism as guides and helping conservation groups clean up local beaches.

⭐ Wadi Lahami Village   CAMPGROUND $$$

(📞010-6577-9300, Cairo head office 02-333-71833; www.redsea-divingsafari.com; Wadi Lahami; s/d full board tent €60/90, royal tent €65/110, chalet €80/120; P📶) 🏊 Tucked into a remote mangrove bay 120km south of Marsa Alam, this hideaway is worth the extra effort it takes to get here. Diving is the main activity – the pristine reefs of the Fury Shoals are easily accessed by boat – but the lonely location is perfect for nature-lovers too. Service is as good as at sister camp Marsa Shagra (p369).

Wadi Lahami has a thorough environmental policy and recycles waste and water as well as supporting and promoting sustainable diving practices. It offers simple but spotless and comfortable accommodation in a choice of two-bed tents sharing bathroom facilities or stone chalets with en suite. A superb choice for those seeking beautiful vistas and plenty of tranquillity.

Oasis Resort RESORT $$$
(☑010-0505-2855; www.oasis-marsaalam.de; Marsa Shagra; s/d half board standard €74/122, deluxe €96/158; ☀) Located 24km north of Marsa Alam along the main road, Oasis is smaller than many of the megaresorts along this stretch. Its 49 chalets were built with a nod to traditional architecture and are individually decorated. Rooms here are spacious, airy and comfortable, and all have sea views.

✖ Eating

★ Dolce e Salato ITALIAN $
(☑010-9239-0441; St 68; mains from LE35; ☺2-10pm Mon-Sat; Ⓟ✎) The best Italian food in Marsa Alam, prepared by Mara from Rome. Pizzas are shortcrust, made using extra virgin olive oil, and range from a simple Margherita to pepperoni, mozzarella and tomato. The pastas and salads are equally good, and there are burgers and sandwiches as well. Coffee is Italian-style, as are desserts, including homemade biscuits. Beach delivery available.

Mashrabiya Restaurant EGYPTIAN $$
(☑012-8224-9078; St 68; mains LE40-70; Ⓟ) A friendly, local grill on Marsa Alam's main drag, serving kofta (spiced mincemeat grilled on a skewer), chicken, *kebab hala* (pot-roast meat) and meat *fatta* (meat, rice and bread soaked in a garlicky-vinegary sauce).

❶ Information

Hyperbaric Chamber (☑012-243-3116, 012-2218-7550, 010-9510-0262; http://baromedical-eg.com) Located 24km north of Marsa Alam on the coastal road.

❶ Getting There & Away

AIR

Marsa Alam Airport (☑370 0021) is 67km north of Marsa Alam along the Al Quseir road. There is no public transport, so you'll need a taxi or to arrange a transfer in advance with your hotel.

EgyptAir has flights to Cairo four days per week, from LE1525 one way. The airport is also served by European charter flights.

BUS

Marsa Alam bus station is just past the T-junction along the Edfu road. Buses to Cairo (LE85 to LE90, 10 to 11 hours) via Al Quseir (LE15, two hours) and Hurghada (LE30 to LE35, 3½ to four hours) depart at 1.30pm and 8.30pm, but check beforehand as timetables change frequently.

Eastern Desert

This vast, desolate area, rimmed by the Red Sea Mountains to the east and the Nile Valley in the west, was once criss-crossed by ancient trade routes and dotted with settlements that played vital roles in the development of many of the region's greatest civilisations. Today the Eastern Desert's rugged expanses are filled with fascinating footprints of this history, including rock inscriptions, ancient gold and mineral mines, wells and watchtowers, and religious shrines and buildings. Time spent here is one of the highlights of any visit to the Red Sea coast; it's a world apart from the commercialised coastline.

However, none of the roads crossing the desert can be freely travelled – some are completely closed to foreigners – and all the sites require a guide. As a result, it is strongly advised (in fact necessary) that you explore the Eastern Desert with the aid of an experienced tour operator.

⊙ Sights

Mons Porphyrites RUINS
These ancient Roman porphyry quarries were the only source for the precious white-and-purple crystalline stone associated with imperial grandeur. Porphyry was used in the Temple of Venus in Rome, the imperial palace in Constantinople and for sarcophagi and columns in Egypt. It was transported across the desert along the Via Porphyrites to the Nile and then shipped across

ON THE EMERALD TRAIL

The source of Egypt's famed emerald mines, the southern region of the Eastern Desert is a wild place of white sand wadis and craggy peaks that are rarely visited. Starkly beautiful **Wadi Gimal Protectorate** extends inland for about 85km from its coastal opening south of Marsa Alam and is home to a rich variety of bird life, gazelles and stands of mangrove. The tumbled remains of emerald and gold mines dating from the Pharaonic and Roman eras are scattered throughout the interior. This area provided emeralds that were used across the ancient world and was the exclusive source of the gem for the Roman Empire.

Some major remnants of the Romans' thirst for emeralds have been left in this harshly beautiful desert, including:

Sikait Thought to be the main settlement for the workers of the Roman emerald mines, this site is about 80km south-west of Marsa Alam. The small **Temple of Isis** still stands, while the remnants of other buildings lie strewn across the hillside.

Nugrus The ruins of the actual emerald mines can be seen on the slopes of Nugrus, where the ground is littered with pottery fragments. The smaller ruins of **Geili** and **Appalonia** (both trading points) are nearby.

Karba Matthha The mysterious ruins of what must have once been a substantial villa or complex sit on top of an isolated desert ridge. From here there are incredible panoramas over the sprawling desert tracts.

---

the Roman world. Remains of the quarry town, including encampments, workshops and temples, can still be seen, although not much is standing.

Tours can be easily arranged in Hurghada. Mons Porphyrites is about 40km northwest of Hurghada. A road leading to the site branches off the main road about 20km north of town.

Mons Claudianus   RUINS
This granite quarry/fortress complex was one of the largest Roman settlements in the Eastern Desert. For Roman prisoners, brought to hack granite out of the barren mountains, this was the end of the line: there was no return. You can see the remains of the tiny cells that these unfortunates inhabited. There is also an immense cracked pillar, left where it fell 2000 years ago, and a small temple. Tours can be easily arranged in Hurghada.

There's a signposted turn-off about 40km along the Safaga–Qena road; from there it's another 25km north-west along a track of deteriorated tarmac.

Barrameya   HISTORIC SITE
One of the most impressive rock-inscription collections in the Eastern Desert is at Barrameya, which fringes the Marsa Alam–Edfu road. Here in the smooth, grey rock are hunting scenes with dogs chasing ostriches,

depictions of giraffes and cattle, and hieroglyphic accounts of trade expeditions.

Wadi Hammamat   HISTORIC SITE
The main route between the Nile and Red Sea for thousands of years, Wadi Hammamat runs from Qift, just north of Luxor, to Al Quseir. Inscriptions, remains of old wells and other evidence of the area's long history can be seen along the way. Part of the route is marked on what might be the world's earliest map, drawn up for Ramses IV's quarrymen in 1160 BC, found in Luxor in the 1820s and now in Turin's Museo Egizio.

A collection of rock inscriptions lies along the high, smooth walls of Wadi Hammamat, about halfway along the road between Al Quseir and Qift. This remarkable graffiti dates from Pharaonic times down to Egypt's 20th-century King Farouk. In Graeco-Roman times, watchtowers were built along the trail at short enough intervals for signals to be visible, and many of them are still intact on the barren hilltops on either side of the road.

Sharm El Luli   BEACH
FREE In the middle of the Wadi Gimal Protectorate, 60km south of Marsa Alam, lies a pristine sand beach with azure water and excellent coral and fish viewing. Because it is located inside a national park, Sharm El Luli has no development at all – no hotels, restaurants or shops and no facilities. Most

of the very few visitors come for the day, bring what they need and take everything away when they leave.

Berenice ARCHAEOLOGICAL SITE

Founded in 275 BC by Ptolemy II Philadelphus, Berenice was one of the most important harbours and trading posts on the Red Sea coast from about the 3rd to the 5th century AD. Remnants of the ancient town, including ruins of the Temple of Serapis, are located just south of the present-day village. Excavations are ongoing; between seasons, archaeologists cover the site to aid preservation, so there's not much to see outside the wonderfully clear water.

Berenice is located 150km south of Marsa Alam, which has the nearest airport. Buses (LE50, nine hours) departing from Hurghada, bound for Shalatein, stop in Berenice. You will need to arrange your own transport to get out to the ruins.

The nearest accommodation is just north of Berenice, along the coast around Hamata and Wadi Lahami Village (p370). Outside of these coastal resorts there's little on offer in Berenice in terms of supplies. You can get basic dried food and tins in Berenice, and there may be a cafe open serving the usual coffee and a water pipe.

At the time of writing, security concerns made it difficult to travel south of Wadi Lahami Village.

🐪 Tours

Red Sea Desert Adventures OUTDOORS

(📱 012-2322-4606; Marsa Shagra; per person from €60) This highly recommended safari outfit, created by the late Dutch geologist Karin van Opstal and run by the Ababda tribe trained, offers tailor-made walking, camel and 4WD and quad-bike safaris throughout the Eastern Desert. Tours can be day trips or last several nights. Guides are knowledgeable in the geography, culture and history of this beautiful area.

Tours start at approximately €60 per person, though cost varies depending on the specifications of your uniquely catered tour, the size of your party and the time of year. Red Sea also offers day tours to Shalatein (from €80) and the emerald mines of Wadi Gimal (p371) (from €90 depending on group size). An overnight in the desert with dinner, tent and breakfast costs from €120. Permits for longer expeditions are currently almost impossible to obtain and need at least three months' wait time.

ℹ️ Getting There & Away

Apart from trips to **Mons Claudianus** (p371) and **Mons Porphyrites** (p370), which are easily arranged in Hurghada, the only viable option for accessing the southern Eastern Desert sites is to go through a local tour operator, who can organise permissions and transport arrangements.

Sinai

Includes ➡

Best Places to Eat

Best Places to Stay

Why Go?

Rugged and starkly beautiful, the Sinai Peninsula has managed to capture imaginations throughout the centuries. The region has been coveted for its deep religious significance and its strategic position as a crossroads of empires: prophets and pilgrims, conquerors and exiles have all left their footprints on the sands here.

In recent years security fears have rippled through the region, creating a tourism downturn that is only now beginning to pick up again. For those venturing back, the lure of this region is easily explained. As a springboard to the Red Sea's underwater wonders, Sinai's seaside resorts serve up sun-drenched holiday fun. Head away from the coastal buzz, however, and Sinai's true soul can be found. Here the Bedouin continue to preserve their traditions amid the red-tinged, ragged peaks and endless never-never of sand. On a star-studded night, surrounded by the monstrous silhouettes of mountains, you'll realise why Sinai continues to cast a spell over all who visit.

When to Go
Dahab

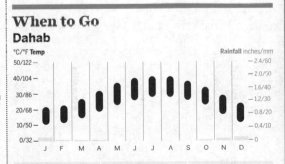

Mar In the desert, spring's colourful flurry of life carpets the sands.

Jun–Aug Air temperatures are scorching, but diving conditions and sea-life spotting are at their peak.

Oct Sneak in some autumn sun along the coast.

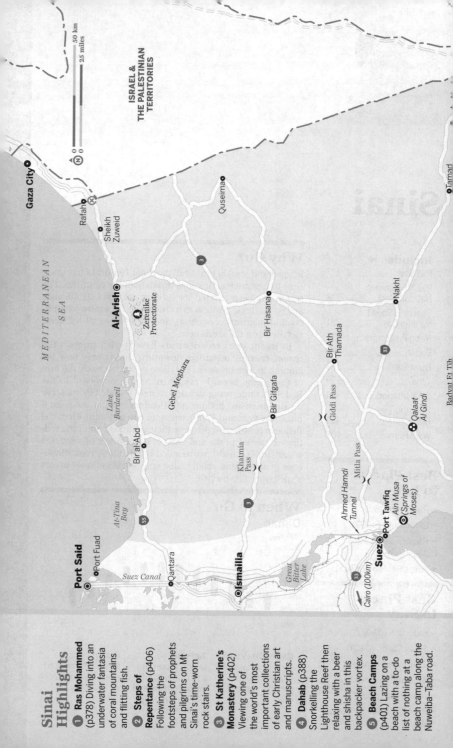

Sinai Highlights

1 Ras Mohammed (p378) Diving into an underwater fantasia of coral mountains and flitting fish.

2 Steps of Repentance (p406) Following the footsteps of prophets and pilgrims on Mt Sinai's time-worn rock stairs.

3 St Katherine's Monastery (p402) Viewing one of the world's most important collections of early Christian art and manuscripts.

4 Dahab (p388) Snorkelling the Lighthouse Reef then relaxing with a beer and shisha in this backpacker vortex.

5 Beach Camps (p401) Lazing on a beach with a to-do list of nothing at a beach camp along the Nuweiba–Taba road.

Sinai

50 km
25 miles

ISRAEL &
THE PALESTINIAN
TERRITORIES

MEDITERRANEAN SEA

Gaza City

Rafah
Sheikh Zuweid

Al-Arish
Zeranike Protectorate

Quseima

Lake Bardaweil

Bir al-Abd

Gebel Meghara

Bir Hasana

3

Port Said
Port Fuad

At-Tina Bay

Qantara

Suez Canal

Ismailia

3

Khatmia Pass

Bir Gifgafa

Bir Ath Thamada

Giddi Pass

Qalaat Al Gindi

Nakhl

33

Badyat Et Tih

Tamad

Great Bitter Lake

Cairo (100km)

33

Ahmed Hamdi Tunnel

Mitla Pass

Suez
Port Tawfiq
Ain Musa (Springs of Moses)

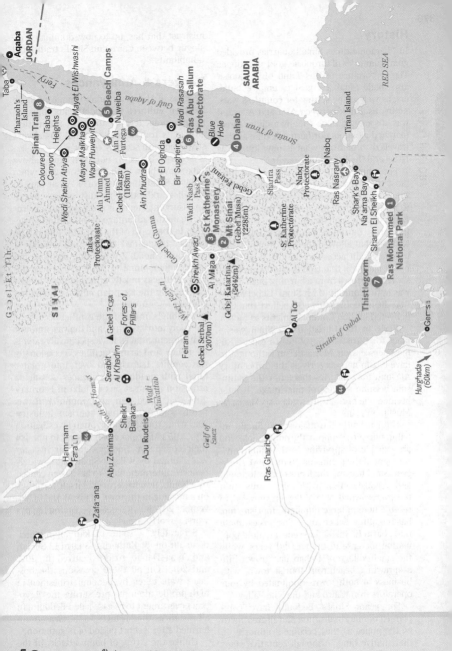

6 Ras Abu Gallum Protectorate (p395)
Discovering this park's raw beauty on a camel-trek with a Bedouin guide.

7 Thistlegorm (p383) Exploring one of the top five wreck-dives in the world.

8 Sinai Trail (p402) Experiencing Sinai's rugged allure on foot through the desert, on Egypt's ultimate trek.

RED SEA

SAUDI ARABIA

JORDAN

Aqaba

Taba

Pharaoh's Island

Taba Heights

Coloured Canyon

8 Sinai Trail

Wadi Sheikh Atiya

Mayat El Wishwashi

5 Beach Camps

Mayat Malkha

Wadi Huwelyit

Ain Al Furtega

Nuweiba

Ain Umm Ahmed

Gebel Barga (1163m)

Ain Khudra

Bir El Oghda

Bir Sugheira

Wadi Rasasah

Wadi Abu Gallum

6 Ras Abu Gallum Protectorate

1 Blue Hole

4 Dahab

Gulf of Aqaba

Straits of Tiran

Tiran Island

Taba Protectorate

Gebel El Gunna

Sheikh Awad

Al Miga

Wadi Nasb Pass

3 St Katherine's Monastery

2 Mt Sinai (Gebel Musa) (2285m)

Gebel Feiruni

Shartira Pass

St Katherine Protectorate

Gebel Katarina (2642m)

Nabq Protectorate

Nabq

Ras Nasrany

Shark's Bay

Na'ama Bay

Sharm El Sheikh

1 Ras Mohammed National Park

7 Thistlegorm

SINAI

Gebel Foga

Forest of Pillars

Serabit Al Khadim

Wadi Mukattab

Feiran

Gebel Serbal (2070m)

Al Tor

Sheikh Barakat

Abu Rudeis

Hammam Fara'un

Abu Zenima

Wadi el-Homur

Gulf of Suez

Straits of Gubal

Ras Gharib

Zafarana

Hurghada (60km)

Gersa

History

In Pharaonic times Sinai's quarries provided great quantities of turquoise, gold and copper. The importance of this 'Land of Turquoise' also made Sinai the goal of empire builders, as well as the setting for countless wars. Acting as a link between Asia and Africa, it was of strategic value – many military forces marched along its northern coastline as they travelled to or from what is now known as Israel and the Palestinian Territories.

For many people, Sinai is first and foremost the 'great and terrible wilderness' of the Bible, across which the Israelites are said to have journeyed in search of the Promised Land, having been delivered from the Egyptian army by the celebrated parting of the Red Sea that allowed the 'Children of Israel' to safely gain access to the dry land of Sinai. It was here that God is said to have first spoken to Moses from a burning bush and it was at the summit of Mt Sinai (Gebel Musa) that the monotheistic faiths believe that God delivered his Ten Commandments to Moses.

Early in the Christian era Sinai was a place for Christian Egyptians to escape Roman persecution. Monasticism is thought to have begun here as early as the 3rd century AD, and for centuries thereafter the peninsula became a place of pilgrimage. It later became one of the routes taken to Mecca by Muslim pilgrims.

Until recently the majority of Sinai's inhabitants were Bedouin, the only people who are capable of surviving in the harsh environment of the peninsula. In the 1990s, however, Sinai became the focus of development and 'reconstruction', with inhabitants from the overcrowded Nile Valley encouraged to resettle here in large numbers. Tourism, too, has brought great changes. Surveys estimate that Sharm El Sheikh has seen a tenfold population increase in the past 20 years, while the small village of Dahab has grown into a sprawling beachfront tourist town, with business in both towns dominated by tour operators from Cairo and the Nile Valley.

For years Sinai's Bedouin have complained of marginalisation and ill-treatment by the police as they become a minority in their native land. Although tentative steps towards more inclusion were made following the 2011 revolution, the upsurge in militant activity in north Sinai has since then pushed the two sides further apart. It remains to be seen if any future government can manage to mend the bridge of mutual mistrust that has, up to now, dominated dialogue between Cairo and Sinai's traditional inhabitants.

Dangers & Annoyances

Because of the peninsula's unique position between cultures and continents, plus its mountainous terrain and – in recent decades – its tourist masses, Sinai has always struggled with security concerns.

Security issues in northern Sinai (above Taba) have been at the fore since 2011 when Wilayet-Sinai (then known as Ansar Bayt Al Maqdis) and other jihadist groups began an insurgency against the Egyptian government, taking advantage of the authority vacuum in the wake of the 2011 revolution. The conflict intensified in the area around Al Arish and Sheikh Zuweid after the downfall of President Morsi in 2013, with an escalation of attacks mostly aimed at government targets, and the Egyptian military launching counter-operations.

Although much of the conflict occurs far from any tourist centre, and the vast amount of insurgent attacks have specifically targeted police and army facilities, occasionally the conflict has rippled over into greater Sinai with deadly consequences. A suicide attack on a tourist bus in Taba in February 2014 that killed four and wounded 16 was firmly aimed at Sinai's tourism industry. And while the official Egyptian investigation into 2015's Metrojet crash has yet to publish their conclusive findings, the air disaster was claimed by Wilayet-Sinai and is widely believed internationally to have been caused by a bomb. In northern Sinai itself, an attack on a mosque in the town of Bir Al Abd in November 2017 left 305 dead, becoming Egypt's worst terrorist attack.

Separately, a spate of kidnapping incidents on the St Katherine–Sharm El Sheikh and Taba–Dahab roads occurred in 2012 and 2013. On all these occasions the hostages were taken by Bedouin tribesmen in high-profile attempts pressuring the Egyptian government to release jailed Bedouin. In all instances the hostages were released unharmed after a short period of negotiation.

Unlike the string of bomb attacks in the mid-2000s which hit the heart of Sinai's tourism industry in Taba, Sharm El Sheikh and Dahab (after which tourism numbers bounced back) quite quickly, the current Sinai crisis continues to affect Sinai's tourist economy severely.

It is impossible to offer anything other than speculation regarding the possibility of future terrorist attacks in Sinai. The majority of travellers to South Sinai enjoy their visit without incident. However, because of security fears over the ongoing conflict in North Sinai, many foreign governments issue cautionary travel advisories for most of South Sinai; most still consider Sharm El Sheikh a safe destination but warn against travelling by air. Travellers should read their embassy's advice for updates on the situation and keep informed of the latest events while making travel plans.

SINAI COAST

A barren coastline of extraordinary beauty, the Sinai Coast has seen some of history's most significant events of the past several millennia played out against its isolated shores. These days the region is more renowned for its superb coral reefs, unique Bedouin culture and sandy beaches. South Sinai is both nirvana for members of the international diving community and a famous package-tourism escape for Europeans after sun, sand and sea.

Ras Sudr

069

Ras Sudr (or simply Sudr) was originally developed as the base town for one of Egypt's largest oil refineries, though its coastline and proximity to Cairo have spurred its transition into a resort area for wealthy Cairene families. The town centre lies just off the main highway, while to the south and north lie a handful of ageing resorts interspersed with holiday villas. With near constant winds, blowing at mostly force five or six, Sudr also enjoys a fine reputation among windsurfers.

Activities

Moon Beach WINDSURFING
(011-1100-8801; www.facebook.com/MoonbeachWindsurfing; Km 98; 7-day windsurfing course incl kit hire UK£150) One of Egypt's most famous windsurfing spots, Moon Beach has a professionally staffed and stocked windsurfing centre as well as a fully licensed school for windsurfers of all levels and ages. The

set-up, with chilled-out beach bar, makes for a friendly and sociable scene. It is a very popular spot for Egyptian windsurfers on weekend breaks from Cairo.

Accommodation can be provided in the beachfront **bungalows** of neighbouring Moon Beach Resort which, although a little dated and worn, are still comfortable. Phone, or contact through their Facebook page, for accommodation and windsurfing packages.

ℹ Getting There & Away

East Delta has a **bus station** along the main road about 500m south of the main junction. Buses to Cairo (LE30, two to three hours) depart at 7.30am, 2pm and 4pm. A taxi from the bus station in Ras Sudr to Moon Beach costs about LE30.

Al Tor

069 / POP 32,877

Al Tor, also known as Tur Sinai, has been a significant port since ancient times, although today it primarily serves as the administrative capital of the South Sinai Governorate. Because of its stiff and constant breezes, Al Tor has been trying in recent years to establish itself as a wind- and kitesurfing destination. For most travellers though, the only reason to make a specific trip here is if you're Sinai-based and need to extend your tourist visa.

Visa extensions and multiple-entry stamps are available at the **Mogamma** (Main Rd), the large administrative building on the main road in the town centre.

◉ Sights

Hammam Musa SPRING
(Moses Pool; LE25) Tradition holds that these hot springs, about 5km from Al Tor, were one of the possible stopping points used by Moses and the Israelites on their journey through Sinai. It's possible to bathe in the springs, and there are some paved walkways, a changing area and a small cafe.

ℹ Getting There & Away

The **bus station** (Main Rd) is along the main road at the northern edge of town, opposite the hospital. Buses depart from 7am onwards throughout the day to Sharm El Sheikh (LE15 to LE25, two hours).

Ras Mohammed National Park

About 20km west of Sharm El Sheikh on the road from Al Tor lies the headland of **Ras Mohammed National Park** (Map p379; €5; ⊙8am-4pm), named by local fishers for a cliff that resembles a man's profile. The waters surrounding the peninsula are considered the jewel in the crown of the Red Sea. The park is visited annually by more than 50,000 visitors, enticed by the prospect of marvelling at some of the world's most spectacular coral-reef ecosystems, including a profusion of coral species and teeming marine life. Most, if not all, of the Red Sea's 1000 species of fish can be seen in the park's waters, including sought-after pelagics, such as hammerheads, manta rays and whale sharks. As well as the park's world-famous Shark and Jolanda Reefs dive sites, snorkelling just off the shore here is truly rewarding. Back on land, Ras Mohammed's landscape of isolated beaches, mangrove forest and mammoth surface cracks (caused by ancient earthquakes) are a harshly barren counterpoint to the bright lights of nearby Sharm.

Ras Mohammed occupies a total of 480 sq km of land and sea, including the desert in and around the ras (headland), Tiran Island, and the shoreline between Sharm El Sheikh harbour and Nabq Protectorate.

◉ Sights & Activities

Those planning to dive in Ras Mohammed need to arrive via boat tour or liveaboard, both of which typically depart from Sharm El Sheikh or Dahab.

If arriving at the park by private car, you can follow the network of (colour-coded) tracks to a variety of wilderness beaches for snorkelling on the offshore reefs – bring your own snorkelling equipment.

Khashaba Beach   BEACH
From Ras Mohammed visitors centre, a pink-signposted track leads to pretty Khashaba Beach, which has a designated camping area (permit necessary) nearby.

Marsa Bareika Beach   BEACH
Yellow arrows point the way to the sandy beaches and calm waters of Marsa Bareika, an excellent spot for snorkelling and safe for children.

Main Beach   BEACH
Aptly named Main Beach gets crowded with day trippers from Sharm El Sheikh, but with its vertical coral walls just offshore, it remains one of the best snorkelling destinations in Ras Mohammed National Park. Follow the blue-arrowed track to get here.

Aqaba Beach   BEACH
A track (with brown arrows) leads to Aqaba Beach. Just offshore is the Eel Garden dive site, named after an eel colony 20m down.

Shark Observatory Clifftop   VIEWPOINT
This clifftop area, near Main Beach, has views over the dive-site area known as the Shark Observatory. Despite the name, you would be very lucky to spot a shark. The view though, spanning both the Straits of Gubal and the Straits of Tiran, is lovely.

Jolanda Bay   BEACH
There's some excellent snorkelling at Jolanda Bay, which is reached by a track marked with red arrows.

WORTH A TRIP

SLEEPING AT RAS MOHAMMED

Early-morning snorkelling in crystal-clear waters, spotting desert foxes loitering around camp under star-strewn night skies: camping in Ras Mohammed is a soul-soothing balm to the stress of everyday life. **Bedawi** (overnight trip half-board per person adult/child LE350/175) is a locally run, sustainable travel company that sets up camp, complete with composting toilet, shower and canvas tents, on a prime slice of Ras Mohammed shore.

If you're not a hard-core camper, lugging your own tent and full equipment around with you, this is the perfect, and hugely comfortable, alternative for sampling Ras Mohammed's stark, visceral beauty at its best – after the day trippers have left. Tasty meals are whipped up by your hosts, there's a communal traditional-style Bedouin tent for lounging in the shade, and there's no generator, so after sunset no noise will cut through the silence.

Reservations (at least a fortnight in advance) are essential. Details and inclusions can be found on the website: www.bedawi.com.

Ras Mohammed National Park

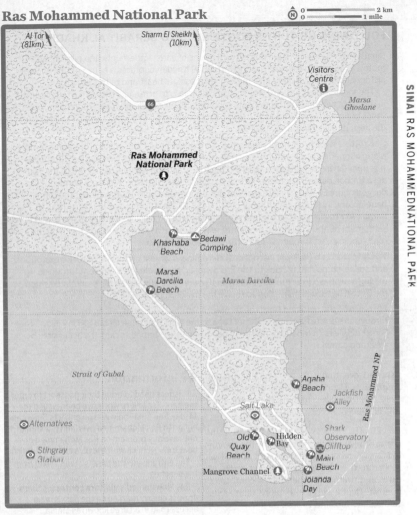

Old Quay Beach
BEACH

Old Quay Beach is perfect for snorkelling; it has a spectacular vertical reef teeming with fish just offshore.

Mangrove Channel
FOREST

Green arrows lead to Ras Mohammed's Mangrove Channel, one of the most northerly mangrove forests in the world. Nearby, you can see huge cracks (one of the largest is 40m long) in the earth's surface, caused by ancient earthquakes. The beach of **Hidden Bay** is also nearby.

Salt Lake
LAKE

(Magic Lake) This stunningly aqua-blue salt lake is about 200m inland from Ras Mohammed's Mangrove Channel and is a popular swimming stop.

Diving

Shark & Jolanda Reefs
DIVE SITE

This two-for-one special off the southern tip of Ras Mohammed is among the most famous dives in the Red Sea and rated one of the top five dives in the world. Strong currents take divers on a thrilling ride along sheer coral walls, through vast schools of

FOLLOWING HISTORY'S FOOTPRINTS TO SERABIT AL KHADIM

Sinai's rugged expanses are dotted with traces of early settlements and pilgrimage routes. A journey to the area around Serabit Al Khadim captures a sense of this ancient history and takes travellers into the rugged, desolate heartland of this region.

The most straightforward way to visit this area is to arrange a trip with a tour operator in Dahab (a two-day 4WD tour costs roughly LE800 per person for a group of six). Advance planning is required as the tour operator will need one week's notice to apply for the permit to visit this area.

Serabit Al Khadim One of Sinai's most impressive sites, this ruined Pharaonic temple is surrounded by ancient turquoise mines and starkly beautiful landscapes. Turquoise was mined here as far back as the Old Kingdom, and the temple, dedicated to the goddess Hathor, dates back to the 12th dynasty. Beside it is a New Kingdom shrine to Sopdu, god of the Eastern Desert. Inscriptions upon the temple court walls list the temple's benefactors, including Hatshepsut (1473–1458 BC) and Tuthmosis III (1479–1425 BC). Serabit Al Khadim can be reached via an unsignposted track just south of the coastal settlement of Abu Zenima or, more interestingly, from a track branching north off the road running east through Wadi Feiran via Wadi Mukattab.

Wadi Mukattab (Valley of Inscriptions) Here Sinai's largest collection of rock inscriptions and stelae, some dating back to the 3rd dynasty, give evidence of ancient turquoise-mining activities. Unfortunately, many of the workings and stelae were damaged when the British unsuccessfully tried to revive the mines in 1901.

Forest of Pillars Inland from the temple of Serabit Al Khadim, a long track heads through the colourful wadis of Gebel Foga to the cliffs that edge Gebel Et Tih Tih and the Forest of Pillars (a mound of naturally occurring tube-shaped rocks). It's accessible by 4WD and camel.

---

fish and eventually to the remains of the *Jolanda,* a Cypriot freighter that sank in 1980. Depth: surface to more than 40m. Rating: advanced. Access: boat.

Ras Za'atir DIVE SITE
(Marsa Bareika) Off the south lip of the mouth of Marsa Bareika, marking the start of the Ras Mohammed wall, Ras Za'atir has a series of caves and overhangs where black coral trees flourish. Depth: surface to more than 40m. Rating: intermediate. Access: boat.

Shark Observatory DIVE SITE
This dive site, underneath the promontory of the same name, takes its name from the fact that whale sharks can occasionally be sighted while diving here. Even if you don't get lucky with your pelagic spotting, this is an interesting wall dive. Depth: surface to more than 40m. Rating: advanced. Access: boat.

Jackfish Alley DIVE SITE
(Ras Mohammed) A comparatively shallow site that is good for a second or third dive, Jackfish Alley has two enormous caves filled with shoaling glassfish. Depth: 6m to 20m. Rating: intermediate. Access: boat.

ℹ Information

All visitors need to bring their passport to enter the park. Travellers who have been issued the 14-day free Sinai-only visa on entry to Sinai cannot go to Ras Mohammed overland but should not have any problem on Ras Mohammed dive-boat trips – check with the dive clubs to confirm.

The entrance to the park is about 20km from the beaches.

Ras Mohammed's **visitors centre** (⊙10am-4pm) is clearly marked on the park's main access road in an area known as Marsa Ghoslane. Maps are usually available here.

ℹ Getting There & Around

There are plenty of half-day bus excursions from Sharm El Sheikh that visit Ras Mohammed's major land-based sights and stop off on the beaches for swimming and snorkelling. Expect to pay around €25.

Dive operators in both Sharm El Sheikh and Dahab offer diving and snorkelling boat excursions in the Ras Mohammed area.

To move around the park, a vehicle is necessary. For conservation reasons, it's forbidden to leave the official tracks.

Sharm El Sheikh & Na'ama Bay

☑ 069 / POP 73,000

The southern coast of the Gulf of Aqaba, between Tiran Island and Ras Mohammed National Park, features some of the world's most amazing underwater scenery. The crystal clear waters and incredible variety of exotic fish darting in and out of the colourful coral reefs have made this a scuba-diving paradise. Purpose-built Sharm El Sheikh occupies a prime position here, devoting itself solely to sun-and-sea holidays offering a family-friendly vibe and resort comforts, with world-class diving thrown in.

That said, Sharm isn't everyone's cup of tea. The relentless sprawl of megahotels along the coastline here has led to pressing issues of sustainability and environmental degradation. Since the downing of Metrojet Flight 9268 in 2015, the legions of European holidaymakers who flock here on all-inclusive tour packages have petered out because of the lack of direct flights from Europe.

Many independent travellers prefer the lower-key and more backpacker-friendly town of Dahab.

◉ Sights

Al Sahaba Mosque
MOSQUE

(Sharia Al Souk, Sharm Old Market) Designed by Fouad Tawfik, Sharm El Sheikh's new mosque fuses Fatimid, Mamluk and Ottoman style elements into its architecture and interior design. Whether it all really gels or just looks like a weird mish-mash is up to the eye of the beholder but there's no denying that this mosque is Sharm's most spectacular piece of architecture.

Diving & Snorkelling

It's something of a tragedy that Sharm's truly exquisite diving has been overshadowed by unfettered tourist development; however, if you're not a resort fan, the offshore dive sites in both Sharm and the adjacent Ras Mohammed National Park are easily accessible by liveaboards, or even on boat trips departing from Dahab.

Snorkelling in the waters around Sharm is excellent. While there are some easily accessed reefs in central Na'ama Bay, it's better to head to the more impressive Gardens or Ras Um Sid reefs.

Most resorts have beach access – either their own stretch of waterfront or by agreement with another resort. Check when booking, as if you've booked a non–seafront

Sharm El Sheikh

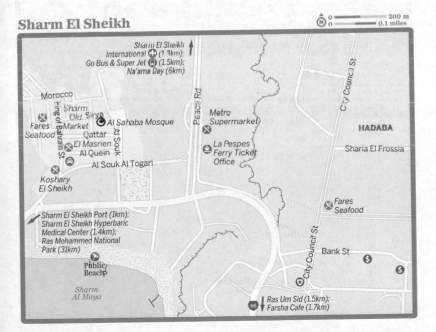

0 — 200 m
0 — 0.1 miles

Sharm El Sheikh International (1.3km); Go Bus & Super Jet (1.5km); Na'ama Bay (6km)

Morocco

Sharm Old Sirya Market

Fares Seafood

Qattar
El Masrien
Al Quein

Al Sahaba Mosque

Al Souk Al Togari

Koshary El Sheikh

Peace Rd

Metro Supermarket

La Pespes Ferry Ticket Office

City Council St

HADABA

Sharia El Frossia

Fares Seafood

Sharm El Sheikh Port (1km); Sharm El Sheikh Hyperbaric Medical Center (1.4km); Ras Mohammed National Park (31km)

Public Beach

Sharm Al Maya

Bank St

City Council St

Ras Um Sid (1.5km); Farsha Cafe (1.7km)

Sharm El Sheikh & Na'ama Bay

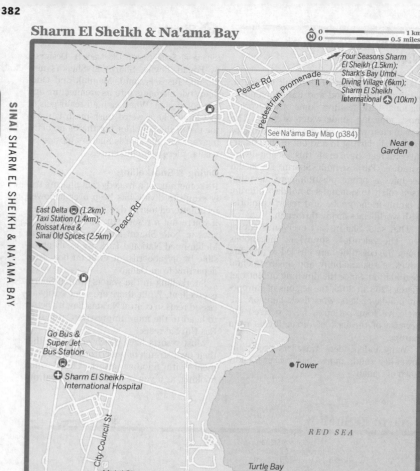

N
0 — 1 km
0 — 0.5 miles

Peace Rd

Pedestrian Promenade

Four Seasons Sharm
El Sheikh (1.5km);
Shark's Bay Umbi
Diving Village (6km);
Sharm El Sheikh
International ✈ (10km)

See Na'ama Bay Map (p384)

Near
Garden

Peace Rd

East Delta 🚌 (1.2km);
Taxi Station (1.4km);
Roissat Area &
Sinai Old Spices (2.5km)

Tower

Go Bus &
Super Jet
Bus Station

✚ Sharm El Sheikh
International Hospital

RED SEA

City Council St

Turtle Bay
Amphoras

Motel St

See Sharm El Sheikh
Map (p381)

HADABA

Sharm Old
Market

Sharia El Frossia

66

RAS
UM SID

Farsha Cafe

Al Fanar ✕

Lighthouse ◎ Ras Um
Sid

hotel (in the Hadaba neighbourhood for example), beaches can be fairly distant (up to 10km) from the hotel itself and can only be accessed via shuttle. Nearly all hotels allow day-access on their beaches.

★**Thistlegorm**　　　　　　DIVE SITE
(Map p38; Sha'ab Ali) One of the top five wreck dives in the world, the *Thistlegorm* is a 129m-long cargo ship built in Sunderland, England, which was sunk during World War II. The ship had been on its way to Alexandria carrying supplies to restock the British army there; its cargo of armaments and vehicles including Bren gun carriers, motorbikes, Bedford trucks and jeeps can all be seen on dives within the wreck. Depth: 17m to 30m. Rating: intermediate to advanced. Access: boat.

★**Thomas Reef**　　　　　　DIVE SITE
(Map p38; Straits of Tiran) The smallest, but easily the most spectacular, of the Tiran reefs, Thomas is home to steeply plunging walls that are lined with soft coral, schooling fish and patrolling sharks. Depth: surface to more than 40m. Rating: advanced. Access: boat.

Jackson Reef　　　　　　DIVE SITE
(Map p38; Straits of Tiran) Home to sharks and large pelagic fish, Jackson Reef is crowned with the remains of a Cypriot freighter, the *Lara*, which ran aground here in 1985. Depth: surface to more than 40m. Rating: intermediate to advanced. Access: boat.

★**Ras Um Sid**　　　　　　DIVE SITE
(Map p38; Map p382) One of the best dive sites in the area, Ras Um Sid features a spectacular gorgonian forest along a dramatic drop-off that hosts a great variety of reef fish. It's opposite Hotel Royal Paradise. Depth: 15m to 40m. Rating: intermediate. Access: shore or boat.

Gardens　　　　　　DIVE SITE
(Map p38; Map p382 btwn Shark's Bay & Na'ama Bay) At the perennially popular Gardens there are actually three sites in one. **Near Garden** (Map p382) is home to a lovely chain of pinnacles; **Middle Garden** features a fringing ridge that gently slopes down to a bed of sandy 'trails'; and **Far Garden** is home to the 'Cathedral', a colourful overhang in deep water. Depth: surface to more than 40m. Rating: intermediate. Access: shore or boat.

★**Dunraven**　　　　　　DIVE SITE
(Map p38) The *Dunraven* sank in 1876 on its way from Bombay to Newcastle. Today the wreck, found at the southeast tip of Sha'ab Mahmud, is encrusted in coral and home to various knick-knacks including china plates, metal steins, and jars of gooseberries and rhubarb, among the detritus. Depth: 15m to 28m. Rating: intermediate to advanced. Access: boat.

🏃 Activities

Almost all travel agencies and large hotels organise jeep or bus trips to St Katherine's Monastery (€55), Ras Mohammed National Park (€25), and to desert attractions such as the Coloured Canyon (€40). Be aware that group sizes are often large.

Camel Dive Club　　　　　　DIVING
(Map p385; ☑069-360-0700; www.cameldive. com; King of Bahrain St, Camel Hotel, Na'ama Bay; PADI discover scuba €80, 1-day 2 dives shore/boat +45/64 snorkelling boat trips €38; ☺8am-6pm) This highly professional and respected club is owned by Sinai diver Hisham Gabr. As well as being a five-Star PADI Instructor Development Centre, it is fully fitted out for wheelchair access and holds a PADI Accessibility Award. When booking, look out for the good-value accommodation-and-dive packages on the website.

Oonas Dive Club　　　　　　DIVING
(Map p385; ☑069-360-0581; www.oonasdiveclub. com; Na'ama Bay Promenade, Oona's Hotel, Na'ama Bay; PADI discover scuba €72, 1-day 2 dives €63, snorkelling boat trips €35; ☺8am-6.30pm) Recommended for its friendly and professional instructors, Oonas offers the full gamut of PADI courses as well as liveaboard packages and fun dives. Many people sign up for the good-value one-week dive and hotel (p384) packages for €320 (three days' diving), €420 (five-days' diving) or €468 (six-days' diving).

Sinai Divers　　　　　　DIVING
(Map p385; ☑069-360-0697; www.sinaidivers. com; Na'ama Bay Promenade; PADI discover scuba €95, 1-day 2 dives €60, 1-day snorkelling boat trips €25; ☺8am-6pm) Based at the Ghazala Beach Hotel, this is one of Sharm El Sheikh's most established dive centres.

Sharm Equestrian　　　　　　HORSE RIDING
(☑010-2739-4572; www.sharmequestrian.com; Nabq Heights; 1-/2hr beach ride €22/38, 4hr desert ride incl dinner €95) This well-run stables offers everything from easy one hour rides

Na'ama Bay

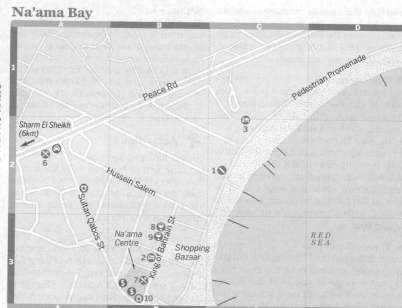

along the beach and half-day desert trails to full multi-day riding holidays within Nabq National Park.

🛏 Sleeping

Sharm El Sheikh and the surrounding area have one of the greatest concentrations of hotels in Egypt, with all-inclusive resorts being the standard rather than the exception. For anyone serious about pinching their pennies, it's wise to continue on to Dahab.

★ **Camel Hotel**　　　　　　HOTEL $$
(Map p385; ☎069-360-0700; www.cameldive. com; King of Bahrain St, Na'ama Bay; s €36-42, d €42-48, tr €56-63; ❈ ⑦ ☎) Attached to the highly reputable dive centre (p383) of the same name, Camel Hotel is the smart choice to stay at if diving is your main agenda. Despite being in the heart of Na'ama Bay the spacious, modern rooms, set around a lovely courtyard pool area, are gloriously quiet (thanks to soundproof windows), so you're guaranteed a good night's sleep.

Oonas Hotel　　　　　　HOTEL $$
(Map p385; ☎069-360-0581; www.oonasdive-club.com; Na'ama Bay Promenade; s/d/tr/ste €45/64/81/90; ❈ ⑦) The good-size rooms at this friendly combo dive centre (p383) and hotel may be a tad plain, but they come with

excellent facilities (kettle, fridge and satellite TV) and balconies. The dive centre here comes highly recommended and accommodation is cheaper if booked as part of a dive package. The beach (shared with the neighbouring resort) is a stone's throw away.

Mövenpick Sharm El Sheikh　RESORT $$
(Map p385; ☎069-360-0081; www.movenpick. com; Peace Rd, Na'ama Bay; s/d/f US$80/90/135; ❈ ⑦ ☎) Dominating Na'ama Bay's northern cliff, this whitewashed hotel terraces majestically down towards the sea like a sultan's palace. Standard rooms are surprisingly bland and could do with a revamp, but the breakfast, views and facilities (five private beaches, spa, pool, dive centre and on-site horse stables) are five-star.

Sinai Old Spices　　　　GUESTHOUSE $$
(☎012-2680-3130; www.sinaioldspices.com; Roissat area; d/q €33/40; ℗ ❈ ⑦ ☎) Behind the terracotta walls, this charming guesthouse serves up quirky style with locally inspired architecture. The five colourful rooms come with kitchenettes, modern bathrooms, and tiny patios. If you're looking for a retreat from Na'ama Bay's bright lights, you're in the right place; it's in a local residential suburb west of the bus station, so it won't suit everyone.

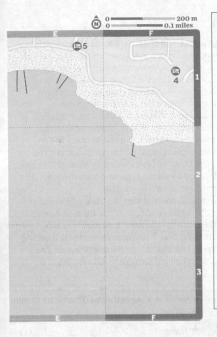

Na'ama Bay

Phone before arriving to arrange a pick-up, or get directions; it's tricky to find.

Shark's Bay Umbi Diving Village HOTEL $$
(☑069-360-0942; www.sharksbay.com; Shark's Bay; s/d cabin €26/40, r €37/50; P🛜) This long-standing Bedouin-owned place is a tumble of chalets flowing down to the beach. Fine beach cabins are spick and span, if a bit of a squeeze, and larger concrete rooms are built into the cliff above. A great option if you're all about diving, don't mind being out of town, and prefer a friendly, local atmosphere to luxurious facilities.

Hilton Sharm El Sheikh Fayrouz Resort RESORT $$$
(Map p385; ☑069-360-0136; www.hilton.com; Peace Rd, Na'ama Bay; s US$80-110, d US$100-139; ❄@🛜🏊) It may pale in comparison to the flash-the-cash ostentation of Sharm's newer megahotels, but this family-friendly resort is a low-key, relaxing place in prime position in the middle of Na'ama Bay's promenade. Set amid well-tended gardens of swaying palms and blooming bougainvillea spilling over trellises, the spacious bungalows here have a jaunty blue-and-white theme, big queen-sized beds and well-maintained facilities.

🍴 Eating

Koshary El Sheikh EGYPTIAN $
(King of Bahrain St, Sharm Old Market, Sharm Al Maya; mains LE7-12; ⊙2pm-late) Egypt's favourite carbohydrate-fuelled feast, *kushari* (mix of noodles, rice, black lentils, fried onions and tomato sauce), is dished up here.

★Fares Seafood SEAFOOD $$
(☑069-366-3076; City Council St, Hadaba; dishes LE40-300; ⊙noon-1am) Always crowded with locals, Fares is a Sharm El Sheikh institution for good-value seafood. Order fish priced by weight or choose from one of the pasta or *tagen* (stew cooked in a deep clay pot) options on the menu. We're pretty partial to the mixed *tagen* of calamari and shrimp. There's another **branch** (☑069-366-4270; Sharm Old Market, Sharm Al Maya; dishes LE40-300; ⊙11am-1am) at Sharm Old Market.

Pomodoro ITALIAN $$
(Map p385; King of Bahrain St, Camel Hotel, Na'ama Bay; pizza & pasta LE79-119, other mains LE109-279; ⊙11am-midnight; 🛜🍴) Hands down the best pizza in Sinai. A great spot for casual dining, Pomodoro has a modern, buzzy, friendly vibe and a menu stuffed with pasta and a fair whack of seafood, but its thin-crust pizzas are the serious winner here. Try the house special pizza with olives, lip-smacking

THE TIRAN ISLANDS HANDOVER

As well as hosting some of Sharm El Sheikh's best dive sites, the Straits of Tiran in the Red Sea are also home to the two small islands of Sanafir and Tiran, uninhabited except for a military base. The islands have been claimed as sovereign territory by both Egypt and Saudi Arabia since the break-up of the Ottoman Empire, but since the 1950s (excluding between 1967 and 1982 when Israel occupied the Sinai Peninsula) both have been under Egyptian administration after an agreement between the two nations.

In April 2016 during a visit to Cairo by Saudi King Salman bin Abdul-Aziz, President Sisi announced that both the Tiran and Sanafir Islands lay within Saudi Arabia's maritime boundaries and Egypt would hand administration back to its neighbour. The announcement resulted in a public backlash with protests against the handover, and the Egyptian court in June 2016 ruling to nullify the transfer. Despite this, in June 2017 President Sisi ratified the handover and officially passed sovereignty over to Saudi Arabia. The decision remains deeply unpopular and controversial with Egyptians.

Those coming to Sharm El Sheikh specifically to dive the famed Straits of Tiran dive sites will be relieved to hear that away from the rights or wrongs of the handover deal, diving in the waters surrounding the islands remains unaffected. A proposed bridge project linking Saudi Arabia and the Sinai, crossing over Tiran Island and the surrounding strait, has so far raised significant environmental concerns the affect on the area's delicate coral reefs. The project has yet to get the green light for construction to begin.

tomato sauce, mozzarella, rocket and generous lashings of Parmesan.

Fairuz   MIDDLE EASTERN $$
(Map p385; King of Bahrain St, Na'ama Bay, Na'ama Centre; mezze LE32-35, mains LE70-160; ☑) This restaurant is a journey through the subtle flavours of the Middle East. Choose the chicken livers (cooked in a garlic and pomegranate molasses sauce) and *makinek* (spicy sausages), pair with *loubieh* (green-bean stew) and okra, and fresh-from-the-oven bread. The mezze set menu (LE130 per person, minimum two people) is the best way to sample a variety of flavours.

El Masrien   EGYPTIAN $$
(King of Bahrain St, Sharm Old Market, Sharm Al Maya; dishes LE8-80; ☺noon-late; ☑) This old-fashioned restaurant, sprawling over both sides of the road, is our top dining spot in Sharm Old Market. There's a huge range of kebabs but also plenty of gutsy flavoured *tagens* and vegetarian dishes from which you can make a cheap, tasty mezze spread. Egyptian holidaymakers flock here in the evening.

Al Fanar   ITALIAN $$
(Map p382; Ras Um Sid; dishes LE40-150; ☺10am-10.30pm) Thanks to a great slice of beach out front (home to one of Sharm's best snorkelling spots), lovely views from the terrace, and decent pasta and pizza on the menu, Al

Fanar is a long-standing Sharm El Sheikh favourite.

★ Rangoli   INDIAN $$$
(Map p385; ☑069-360-0081; Na'ama Bay, Mövenpick Resort; mains LE55-180; ☺6.30-10.30pm; ☑) If you're a fan of the flavours of the subcontinent, don't miss Rangoli: romantically perched within the cliffside tumble of the Mövenpick Resort with the sweep of Na'ama Bay laid out below. Thanks to the Mumbai-born chef, all the dishes here burst with authentic Indian flavour from the punchy black lentil dhal to the clay tandoori specialities.

🍷 Drinking & Nightlife

The main nightlife centre is Na'ama Bay. As well as the shisha cafes and bars strung along King of Bahrain St and Sultan Qabos St, there are hotel beach bars scattered down the Na'ama Bay Promenade. Sharm's newest nightlife hub is **Soho Square** (www. soho-sharm.com; White Knight Bay, near the Savoy Hotel; ☺4pm-1am), which has several bars.

★ Farsha Cafe   CAFE
(Map p382; Sharia El Bahr, Ras Um Sid; ☺11am-late; ☎) All nooks and crannies, floor cushions, Bedouin tents and swinging lamps, Farsha is the kind of place that travellers come to for a coffee and find themselves lingering at four drinks and a shisha pipe later. Great for a lazy day full of lounging or a night of chilled-out music and cocktails.

★ **Camel Roof Bar** BAR
(Map p385; King of Bahrain St, Camel Hotel, Na'ama Bay; ⊙3pm-2.30am; 🛜) Camel is a favourite among dive instructors for its relaxed, casual vibe. This is the optimal place to start off the evening, especially for divers looking to swap stories from down under.

Bus Stop Lounge BAR
(Map p385; King of Bahrain St, Na'ama Bay; ⊙6pm-3am) This bar is known for its good music and up-for-it, fun-loving crowd. There's a pool table for those who don't feel like getting on the dance floor, and happy hour from 8pm to 9pm gets you two-for-one beers and half-price cocktails. Earlier in the evening there's a menu of snack-style meals, while after 10pm the DJ takes to the decks.

Pacha CLUB
(Map p385; 🔲ext 300 069-360-0197; www.pacha sharm.com; King of Bahrain St, Na'ama Bay; tickets presale/at door LE140/180; ⊙11pm-late) The hub of Sharm's nightlife. Watch for advertising around town to find out about upcoming events. Women gain free entry into the club before midnight.

❶ Information

DANGERS & ANNOYANCES
Serious security concerns regarding Sharm El Sheikh's airport were raised in the aftermath of the downing of Russian Metrojet Flight 9268 in October 2015, which disintegrated mid-air shortly after take off from Sharm El Sheikh, killing all 224 aboard. A bomb is widely thought to be the cause of the crash. International direct flights into Sharm El Sheikh were suspended afterwards, and many European countries have yet to lift the suspension. Meanwhile, the Egyptian civil aviation authority has been working with a specialist UK security firm to upgrade the airport's security procedures. It's expected that direct international flights into Sharm will resume when the upgrade is completed and European authorities are satisfied that Sharm's airport security meets international standards.

Sharm El Sheikh town itself, though, is generally considered a safe destination. The town has not been targeted since the July 2005 terrorist bombings at Sharm Old Market and Ghazala Gardens Hotel (which killed 88 and injured more than 200), after which security in and around the town was beefed up considerably, and continues to be so.

EMERGENCY
Tourist Police (Map p385; 🔲069-360-0311, 069-366-0675; Sultan Qabos St, Na'ama Bay; ⊙8am-7pm) In a booth on the main road into downtown Na'ama Bay. There is also another **branch** (🔲069-366-0311; City Council St, Hadaba; ⊙10am-5pm) in Hadaba.

MEDICAL SERVICES
Sharm El Sheikh Hyberbaric Medical Center (🔲069-360-0865, emergency 012-2212-4292; hyper_med _center@sinainet.com.eg; main Sharm Al Maya Rd; ⊙24hr)
Sharm El Sheikh International Hospital (Map p382; 🔲069-366-0318; Peace Rd, Hadaba; ⊙24hr)

MONEY
There are copious ATMs in Na'ama Bay, including several in and around Sharia Sultan Qabos. All the larger hotels also have ATMs in their lobbies. Otherwise, all the major banks have branches in Hadaba.

Sharm hotels, and many businesses, accept British pounds, euros and US dollars as payment as well as Egyptian pounds.

❶ Getting There & Away

AIR
Sharm El Sheikh International Airport is Sinai's major travel hub.

At the time of research only a handful of international airlines had restarted direct flights including TUIfly Belgium (www.tuifly.be) from Brussels, Germania (www.flygermania.com) from Zurich and Royal Jordanian (www.rj.com) from Amman.

For now, to travel to Sharm by air you'll usually have transit through Cairo. Egypt Air (www. egyptair.com) has several flights to and from Cairo per day. Prices fluctuate wildly but fares start from about LE1000.

BOAT
The **La Pespes high-speed catamaran ferry service** (www.lapespes.com; Sharm El Sheikh Marine Port, Sharm Al Maya; adult/child US$40/30; ⊙6pm Sun, Tue & Thu) operates between Sharm El Sheikh and Hurghada three times per week. The journey takes 2½ hours.

Tickets can be bought from the **ticket office** (🔲012-2449-5592, 012-1014-4000; High Jet Office, Peace Rd, Sharm Al Maya; ⊙10am-10pm) near Sharm Old Market.

The ferry sails from Sharm El Sheikh Marine Port. Travellers must be at the port 90 minutes before departure time and have their passport on hand as proof of ID.

BUS
The **East Delta Travel Co bus station** (🔲069-366-0660; Sharia Al Rewaysat) is just off Peace Rd behind the Mobil petrol station. A taxi shouldn't cost more than LE25 into Na'ama Bay, though drivers at the station will try for LE40.

BUS SERVICES FROM SHARM EL SHEIKH

DESTINATION	PRICE	DURATION	TIMES/COMPANY
Alexandria	LE150-260	10hr	9pm (East Delta); 3pm & 11pm (Super Jet); 2pm & 9pm (Go Bus)
Cairo	LE95-240	7hr	9 services daily 7.30am-midnight (East Delta); 6am, 11am, 1pm, 2.30pm, 5.30pm & 11pm (Super Jet); 16 services daily 1.30am-midnight (Go Bus)
Dahab	LE25	1½hr	7am, 8am, 9am, 3pm, 5pm & 9pm (East Delta)
Luxor	LE175	16hr	6pm (East Delta)
Nuweiba	LE50	3½hr	9am (East Delta)
Taba	LE50	4½	9am (East Delta)

As well as the East Delta buses to Dahab, a couple of Go Bus's direct Cairo–Dahab services will pick up passengers from the taxi station. Check with the office for the latest schedule.

The **taxi station** (☑ 069-366-1622; Main Rd), just behind the East Delta station, has ticket offices and is the main bus arrival/departure point for Super Jet and Go Bus (www.go-bus. com) services. Go Bus and Super Jet also have a new **ticket office/station** (Map p382; ☑ 19567; Peace Rd) in Hadaba, near Sharm El Sheikh International Hospital, for passenger pickups and ticket purchasing. A taxi from here to Na'ama Bay shouldn't cost more than LE15.

❶ Getting Around

TO/FROM THE AIRPORT

The airport is 10km north of Na'ama Bay at Ras Nasrany. Taxis wait outside the arrivals hall and quote around LE100 to Na'ama Bay. Prepare to bargain hard. Most travellers prefer to skip the taxi debacle completely and prebook an airport transfer with their hotel.

MICROBUS & TAXI

Blue-and-white microbuses regularly ply the stretch between central Na'ama Bay and Sharm El Sheikh. The fare is LE2, although foreigners are often charged LE5.

Taxis charge a minimum of LE20 between **Sharm Old Market** and **Na'ama Bay** (Map p385). Coming from Na'ama Bay, drivers will often quote LE40. You will need to bargain.

Nabq Protectorate

Thirty-five kilometres north of Sharm El Sheikh, **Nabq** (entry US$5) is the largest coastal protectorate on the Gulf of Aqaba. Named after an oasis that lies within its boundaries, Nabq straddles 600 sq km of land and sea between the Straits of Tiran and Dahab. Less frequently visited than Ras Mohammed National Park further south, Nabq is a good place to see Sinai as it was before the arrival of mass tourism. Within

the park are several hiking trails and snorkelling spots.

There is a **visitors centre** (◔8am-5pm) located off the road leading from Sharm El Sheikh past the airport and Ras Nasrany. Nabq's main attraction is its mangrove forest, which runs along the shoreline at the mouth of Wadi Kid and is the most northerly mangrove stand in the world. Mangrove root systems filter most of the salt from seawater and help to stabilise shorelines, while also providing an important habitat for birds and fish.

Just inland from the mangrove forest are the dunes of Wadi Kid, which are home to one of the Middle East's largest stands of arak bushes (arak twigs were traditionally used by Bedouin to clean teeth). Gazelles, rock hyraxes and Nubian ibexes can be seen in the protectorate, and there are two villages of Bedouin from the Mizena tribe. Offshore, rich reefs are easy to access, although visibility can be poor because of sediment from the mangroves.

You'll need a vehicle to get here, or join an organised tour from Sharm El Sheikh or Dahab.

Dahab

☑ 069 / POP 7494

Low-key, laid-back and low-rise, Dahab is the Middle East's prime beach resort for independent travellers.

The startling transformation from dusty Bedouin outpost to spruced-up tourist village is not without its detractors, who reminisce fondly of the days when beach bums dossed in basic huts by the shore. But for all the starry-eyed memories, there are plenty of pluses that have come with prosperity. Diving is now a much safer and more organised activity thanks to better regulation of operators; the town is cleaner and more family-friendly, offering accommodation choices for everyone rather than just hardened backpackers.

This is the one town in South Sinai where independent travellers are the rule rather than the exception, and Dahab's growth has not destroyed its budget-traveller roots. Reeled in by its mellow ambience, many travellers plan a few nights here and instead stay for weeks.

◉ Sights

Dahab's sights are all underwater. Those who want to simply hit the beach may be a tad disappointed, as central Dahab is a beach town that has managed to thrive without much of a beach – instead the rocky coastline leads straight out on to the reef. In typical make-do Dahab style, the waterfront cafes have solved the where-to-sunbathe conundrum by setting up shaded loungers at the water's edge.

For the golden sands after which Dahab was named, head south to **Dahab Lagoon**, where the luxury resorts are clustered. Most resorts offer beach-use day access starting from LE50, and pedalos and kayaks can be hired. The **Eel Garden** area in Assalah (at the northern end of Dahab's shorefront promenade) has a long, narrow strip of yellow sand.

★ Blue Hole   DIVE SITE
(Map p38) Carved into a reef, 8km north of Dahab, is Egypt's most infamous dive site. The Blue Hole is a gaping sinkhole that drops straight down – some say as deep as 130m. Exploring the deeper depths should be left to experienced technical divers, but there's plenty to discover close to the surface. The outer lip is full of marine life and a reasonable plunge into the hole is somewhat akin to skydiving. Depth: 7m to 27m. Rating: intermediate to advanced. Access: shore.

Advanced divers can enter at the **Bells**, a narrow breach in the reef table that forms a pool close to shore. From here, divers descend through a chimney, exiting at 27m on a ledge that opens to the sea. Swim south along the wall, a saddle in the reef at 7m allows entry to the Blue Hole. As long as divers monitor their depth carefully, they can finish up by swimming across the sinkhole towards shore.

Unfortunately, the site has claimed several lives, mainly thrill-seekers venturing well below the sport-diving limit. The trap is an archway at approximately 65m, which connects the sinkhole to the open ocean. Under-prepared solo divers attempting to find this archway have succumbed to narcosis, missed the archway entirely, lost all sense of direction or simply run out of air. In 2017 these dangers were highlighted yet again when renowned Irish freediving safety diver Stephen Keenan tragically died when rescuing another freediver who had become disorientated.

Canyon   DIVE SITE
(Map p38) One of the area's most popular dives, the Canyon is a long, narrow trench that runs perpendicular to the reef shelf, and is home to prolific hard and soft corals. It's on the north side of Dahab. Depth: 5m to 33m. Rating: intermediate. Access: shore.

Eel Garden   DIVE SITE
(Map p38) Eel Garden takes its name from the countless garden eels that carpet the sea floor. Other highlights include huge coral boulders and dense congregations of barracudas. Located off the Assalah shore. Depth: 5m to 20m. Rating: intermediate. Access: shore.

Lighthouse Reef   DIVE SITE
(Map p390) This sloping reef is home to a bounty of fish life and is Dahab's main night-diving site. More experienced divers can descend to the sandy bottom, where there's a profusion of coral towers. Depth: 5m to 30m. Rating: novice. Access: shore.

Islands   DIVE SITE
(Map p38) This underwater *Alice in Wonderland*-esque site south of Dahab offers an outstanding topography of coral alleyways, amphitheatres, valleys and gulleys. Depth: 5m to 18m. Rating: novice. Access: shore.

Umm Sid   DIVE SITE
(Map p38) An impressive entrance through a wide corridor carved into a steeply sloping reef is a highlight of this dive site 15km south of Dahab. Further down you'll find table corals and two enormous gorgonians. Depth: 5m to 35m. Rating: intermediate to advanced. Access: shore.

Gabr El Bint   DIVE SITE
(Map p38) This dive 25km south of Dahab features a dramatic seascape highlighted by a 60m wall cut by numerous chasms, faults and sandy ravines. If you access the site by land, the journey combines a 4WD trip and a Bedouin-led camel convoy. Depth: 10m to 30m. Rating: intermediate. Access: boat or shore.

Dahab

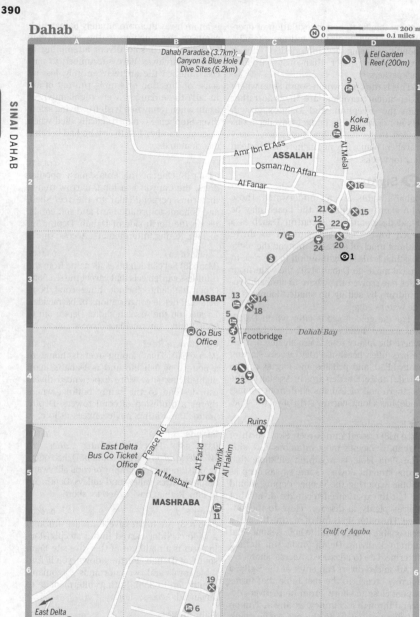

0   200 m
0   0.1 miles

Dahab Paradise (3.7km);
Canyon & Blue Hole
Dive Sites (6.2km)

Eel Garden
Reef (200m)

Koka
Bike

ASSALAH

Amr Ibn El Ass

Osman Ibn Affan

Al Fanar

Al Melal

MASBAT

Go Bus
Office

Footbridge

Dahab Bay

Peace Rd

Ruins

East Delta
Bus Co Ticket
Office

Al Masbat

Al Farid

Tawfik

Al Hakim

MASHRABA

Gulf of Aqaba

East Delta
Travel Co (1.7km);
Dahab City (3km);
Lagoon Area (3km)

Al Mashraba

Happy Kite
(2.1km)

🏃 Activities

Diving & Snorkelling

The best reefs for snorkelling are Lighthouse Reef (p389) and Eel Garden (p389), both in Assalah. You can hire snorkelling gear from all the dive centres and many other places in Masbat for about LE25 to LE40 per day. Keep in mind that some of the reefs have unexpected currents – drownings have occurred in Dahab – so keep your wits about you.

Despite the intimidating reputation of the Canyon (p389) and Blue Hole (p389) dive sites as danger zones for careless divers, the tops of the reefs are teeming with life, making them fine snorkelling destinations when the sea is calm. Most tour companies in town organise half-day Blue Hole snorkelling trips for between LE50 and LE120.

Dive Urge   DIVING
(Map p390; 069-364-0957; www.dive-urge.com; Sharia Al Melal, Assalah; 1 dive €40, PADI discover scuba €85) This five-star PADI centre has commendable environmental credentials: no more than four divers per dive, plus litter clean-ups are a standard part of their daily diving. The centre and adjoining resort are fully wheelchair accessible.

Red Sea Relax Dive Centre   DIVING
(Map p390; 069-364-1309; www.red-sea-relax.com; Waterfront Promenade, Masbat; per shore/night dive from US$21/26, PADI discover scuba US$58) Long-standing five-star PADI centre with an excellent reputation. Highly recommended for PADI learn-to-dive courses. AIDA free-diving courses also available.

Poseidon Divers   DIVING
(Map p390; 069-364-0091; www.poseidondivers.com; Waterfront Promenade, Mashraba; 2 dives €44, half-day try dive €45) Award-winning PADI centre that consistently gets recommended by travellers.

Nesima Dive Centre   DIVING
(Map p390; 069-364-0320; www.nesimaresort.com; Sharia Tawfik Al Hakim, Mashraba, Nesima Resort; 1/2 dives €28/55, PADI discover scuba €90) A reputable club owned by local environmental activist and veteran diver Sherif Ebeid.

Jeep & Camel Safaris

This is one of the best places in Sinai to arrange camel safaris into the dramatic mountains lining the coast, especially the spectacular Ras Abu Gallum Protectorate (p395). Further afield, the desert area around Nuweiba is home to some of the South Sinai coast's most interesting sights, including the Coloured Canyon (p399). Jeep safaris to the canyon from Dahab cost between LE300 and LE500 per person.

Watersports

The lagoon area is Dahab's water-sports centre and a top spot for learning to windsurf and kitesurf.

Happy Kite   WATER SPORTS
(010-6056-1912; www.happy-kite.com; Dahab Lagoon; 6hr beginner courses €280; ⊘8am-6pm) Happy Kite offers kitesurfing lessons, full-day courses and equipment rental.

☞ Tours

All the tour operators in Dahab offer tours to Mt Sinai (p403) and St Katherine's Monastery (p402) for about LE180 to LE250 per person.

Nearly all also offer one-day, whirlwind trips to either Petra in Jordan (US$200) or Jerusalem in Israel and the Palestinian Territories (US$90). Unless you are seriously strapped for time, it's usually best to make your own independent arrangements. If you do decide to take one of these international tours, be aware that most of your time will be spent travelling there and back, with very little time actually spent at the sights.

🛏 Sleeping

The Masbat side of the shore has weathered the tourism downturn much better than Mashraba and is a much livelier area to stay in.

Luxury accommodation is available at the lagoon resort area.

★ El Salam Hotel   HOTEL $
(Map p390; ☎ 069-364-0182; https://elsalamhotel. wordpress.com; Sharia Al Melal, Assalah; s/d/tr US$20/25/35; ❀❢) This friendly hotel is centred on a garden with traditional-style Bedouin tent chill-out area. It offers bright, spacious rooms kitted out with lashings of white and nice little touches such as local appliqué textiles and oriental bedside lamps. If you don't mind being one street back from the shore, it's a great find. Breakfast is US$5 extra.

Christina Beach Palace & Christina Pool   RESORT $
(Map p390; ☎ 069-364-0390; www.christina hotels.com; Sharia Al Mashraba, Mashraba; annexe s/d/tr/q US$14/17/23.50/28, with air-con US$18/21/27.50/32, beach or pool room s/d US$20/25.50, with air-con US$24/29.50; ❀❢☷) You get a lot of bang for your buck at this resort-style hotel with rooms to suit all preferences. Choose either a beach room, with sea views, or a room set around the pool. All have balconies and good facilities, although furnishings are rather beige. Across the road, Christina annexe is a budget option, set amid a leafy garden.

Seven Heaven   HOSTEL $
(Map p390; ☎ 069-365-2752, 012-2785-6002; www. 7heavenhotel.com; Waterfront Promenade, Masbat; dm LE15, r LE80-120, with air-con LE140; ❢) This all-in-one ramshackle place (combining dive shop and tour office) offers one of the best-value shoestringer deals in town. It has a huge range of rooms, which go up in price as you add in extras; the six-bed dorms, which come with air-con and bathroom, are a bargain. Breakfast not included.

Ghazala Hotel   HOTEL $
(Map p390; ☎ 069-364-2414, 010-0117-5869; www. ghazaladahab.com; Waterfront Promenade, Mashraba; s/d/tr €20/25/30; ❀❢) Ghazala's white-domed rooms rim a narrow courtyard set with colourful mosaic tiles. There's a level of spic-and-span cleanliness here that punches well above most of Dahab's budget scene, although we're personally not fans of the numerous 'funny' signs posted around the place. It's located right at the southern end of the shorefront promenade, so may be too quiet for some.

Alaska Camp & Hotel   HOTEL $
(Map p390; ☎ 012-2710-8067, 069-364-1004; www. dahabescape.com; Waterfront Promenade, Masbat; r LE200-250, with air-con LE300-350; ❢) These bright, sparkling-clean, simple rooms with comfortable beds are an easy-on-the-wallet deal. Grab one upstairs for a balcony. The central location means you're just a couple of steps from the promenade bustle. Breakfast not included.

★ Eldorado   BOUTIQUE HOTEL $$
(Map p390; ☎ 069-365-2157, 012-2759-3235; www. eldoradodahab.com; Sharia Al Melal, Assalah; s/d €30/50, with shared bathroom €20/35; ❀❢) This intimate, Italian-owned hotel oozes chic, easygoing beach style. The colourful cabana-type rooms host big beds, painted wood panels and cheerful lemon detailing, plus modern bathrooms and exceptional levels of brushed-up maintenance. Even better, there's a proper patch of sandy beach out front, which is immaculately cared for and comes replete with beckoning sun loungers and shaded seating.

Dahab Paradise   RESORT $$
(☎ 010-0700-4133; www.dahabparadise.com; s/d/ tr €31/38/57; ❀❢☷) This low-key resort, on a sweep of bay along the main road to the Blue Hole, is the perfect getaway. Decorated in warm, earthy tones with accents of antique wood, the charming rooms have a touch of understated beach-chic elegance. If all the peace and serenity gets too much, the bright lights of Dahab are a 10-minute taxi ride away.

Dahab Coach House
GUESTHOUSE **$$**

(Map p390; ☎010-0487-4017; www.dahabcoach house.com; Masbat; s/d €25/30; ❄️🛜) Snaffled just off the waterfront drag, hidden behind tall walls, is one of Dahab's most relaxing guesthouses. Spacious rooms are decked out in neutral tones offset by blue or yellow accent walls. There's a guest-use kitchen and the central courtyard has fat-cushioned cane chairs that beg to be curled up on after a long day of diving. Breakfast not included.

Red Sea Relax
RESORT **$$**

(Map p390; ☎069-365-2604; www.red-sea-relax. com; Waterfront Promenade, Masbat; s/d/tr/f US$38/48/58/78, with shared bathroom dm/d US$6/18; ❄️🛜🏊) A small resort tailor-made for divers. Spacious rooms are wrapped around a glistening pool, and are kitted-out with kettles and TVs. Plus there are free water fill-ups, free kayak use, a beckoning rooftop bar and an excellent dive centre. The dormitory means budgeteers get resort facilities for backpacker costs, while dive centre clients can get their dorm bed for free.

Nesima Resort
RESORT **$$**

(Map p390; ☎069-364-0320; www.nesima-resort.com; Sharia Tawfik Al Hakim, Mashraba; s/d €42/55, seaview r €76; ❄️🛜🏊) A lovely compromise if you want resort living without being isolated from town. Set amid a mature garden of blooming bougainvillea, Nesima's cosy (read: small) brick cottages have domed ceilings and cute terraces. Upgrade to a seaview room, rimming the pool, to sit on your terrace looking out to the Red Sea.

Rates can drop significantly during quiet periods.

🍴 Eating

If you're a dessert fan, keep an eye out for the mobile carts which work the waterfront promenade. In particular, Ali's blue cart roams the length of the pedestrian strip serving up traditional *ruz bi laban* (rice pudding).

Athanor
ITALIAN **$**

(Map p390; Sharia Al Melal, Assalah; dishes LE18-60; ⏲11am-midnight; 🛜📶) Dahab's best thin-crust pizzas are served up here in the shady garden terrace.

King Chicken
FAST FOOD **$**

(Map p390; Sharia Tawfik Al Hakim, Mashraba; mains LE40-60; ⏲11.30am-11pm) Always crowded with locals, here for the quarter chicken and chips, this cheap and cheer-ful little place hits the spot for budget chicken-dinner heaven.

★Ralph's German Bakery
CAFE **$$**

(Map p390; Sharia Al Fanar, Masbat; pastries LE7-25, sandwiches & breakfasts LE35-85; ⏲7am-6pm; 🛜📶) Everybody in Dahab ends up at Ralph's at some point. This is Dahab's top stop for breakfast, brunch, and coffee and croissant breaks, and it does a fine line in quiche and apple strudel as well. People who have the willpower not to add one of the delectable Danish pastries on to their order are doing better than we are.

★Lakhbatita
ITALIAN **$$**

(Map p390; Waterfront Promenade, Mashraba; mains LE65-180; ⏲6-11.30pm; 📶) We adore Lakhbatita's eccentric decoration, friendly service and serene ambience, all of which bring a touch of Italian flair to Dahab. The small menu of homemade pasta dishes, many featuring seafood, is a cut above what's served up elsewhere. Try the mushroom ravioli or the garlic and chilli prawns.

Kitchen
ASIAN **$$**

(Map p390; Waterfront Promenade, Masbat; mains LE50-120; 📶) The pan-Asian menu here offers a choice of Chinese and Thai while the proper sofas at the tables have to be in the running for Dahab's comfiest seating. The Thai curry dishes and the spicy Chinese options are the stand-out dishes, but if you've got a sweet tooth, save room for the fried ice-cream dessert.

Hell's Kitchen
INTERNATIONAL **$$**

(Map p390; ☎010-2292-4824; Sharia Al Melal, Assalah; mains LE85-125; ⏲11am-11pm; 🛜📶) The inventive menu here veers away from Dahab's grilled meat/seafood combos and cherry-picks influences from North African, Asian and Mediterranean cuisines to offer a fusion of global flavours. Great vegetarian and vegan selection on offer, such as sweet-and-sour cauliflower, while carnivores get to tuck into Moroccan-style chicken. It also does a cheaper range of sandwiches.

Ali Baba
INTERNATIONAL **$$**

(Map p390; Waterfront Promenade, Masbat; mains LE87-193; ⏲10am-late; 🛜📶) This place adds flair to its seafood selection with some inspired menu choices. Great service, comfy sofas to lounge on, stylish lanterns and twinkly fairy lights add to the relaxed seaside ambience. All meals come with a mezze selection to start with. Bring your appetite.

Nirvana
INDIAN $$

(Map p390; Waterfront Promenade, Masbat; mains LE60-70; ⊙approx noon-11pm; 🛜📶) A slice of the subcontinent complete with direct beach access and sun-loungers. All mains are served with rice, salad, raita, and pappadams, making for a bit of a feast. We highly recommend the not entirely authentic but still yummy *palak paneer* (spinach and paneer curry).

🍷 Drinking & Nightlife

A hike in restaurant alcohol-licence fees has meant that many of the waterfront restaurants no longer serve alcohol. Don't fret about not being able to have a sunset beer though – many now allow you to bring your own alcohol in, to drink with your meal or have with your shisha. Just check with the staff before sitting down and ordering. A number of new beer shops have conveniently opened up in the waterfront area to supply you with all your BYO needs.

Yalla Bar
BAR

(Map p390; Waterfront Promenade, Masbat; ⊙11am-late; 🛜) This hugely popular waterfront bar-restaurant has a winning formula: plenty of comfy seating, including sunloungers out front, friendly staff, cold beer and a decent list of cocktails to keep the punters happy.

El Mahalawy
JUICE BAR

(Map p390; Sharia Al Fanar, Masbat; ⊙9am-10pm) Just the best little juice shack in Dahab. Get your sugarcane fix, or sup on a freshly squeezed juice or shake in the cubby-hole seating area, bedecked in stripy canvas, or takeaway.

Churchill's
BAR

(Map p390; Waterfront Promenade, Masbat; ⊙11am-11pm; 🛜) Dahab's sports bar has a big-screen TV so fans won't miss their favourite team play, plus there's a breezy rooftop terrace that's perfect for sunset drinks. It's in Hotel Red Sea Relax.

Tota Downtown
BAR

(Map p390; Waterfront Promenade, Mashraba; ⊙10pm-late) Dahab's iconic ship-shaped bar has had a topsy-turvy few years of closures and re-openings but is open once again. If you're after a bit of a bigger night than simply sinking a few beers while watching the sunset, this is the main spot in town for a clubbing vibe.

ℹ️ Information

DANGERS & ANNOYANCES

After the Dahab suicide bombing of April 2006 (which killed 23 people and injured dozens), the government pumped up security within Dahab, and the town hasn't been targeted since. Dahab's location, however, within the greater South Sinai region, does mean that many government travel advisories currently warn against all but essential travel here. Although the potential for a future terrorist attack can never be wholly ruled out, it's important to emphasise that since the 2011 revolution, Dahab has remained one of Egypt's most relaxed destinations and, within the town itself, has experienced no problems.

EMERGENCY

Police (Map p390; ☑069-364-0215, 069-364-0213; Waterfront Promenade, Mashraba; ⊙8am-8pm)

MEDICAL SERVICES

For hospital care, it's best to head to Sharm El Sheikh if possible.

Dr Haikal (☑010-0143-3325; Dahab City) His surgery, near the lagoon, has a hyperbaric chamber.

MONEY

There are stand-alone **ATMs** (Map p390; Waterfront Promenade) scattered along the waterfront.

Banque du Caire (Map p390; Sharia Al Mashraba, Mashraba; ⊙8.30am-2pm Sun-Thu) Has an ATM.

ℹ️ Getting There & Away

BUS

The **East Delta bus station** (☑069-364-1808) is in Dahab City, well southwest of the action. East Delta also has a **ticket office** (Map p390; Peace Rd; ⊙9am-6pm) in Masbat. Buses will pick up passengers from here; double-check when booking. Departure times change frequently so always check a day beforehand.

The **Go Bus office** (Map p390; ☑19567; www.gobus-eg.com; Peace Rd) is conveniently central, just west of Masbat's footbridge.

TAXI

Unfortunately, because of security issues, the local pick-up taxis are no longer allowed to operate outside the Dahab area. Taxis touting for business to Nuweiba (LE200), Sharm El Sheikh airport (LE250) and St Katherine's (LE300 to LE350) are always hanging out at the East Delta bus station. They can also be booked through your hotel or a travel agency in town.

BUS SERVICES FROM DAHAB

DESTINATION	PRICE	DURATION	TIMES/COMPANY
Cairo	LE115-270	9hr	9am, 12.30pm, 3pm, 7.30pm & 10pm (East Delta); 12.30am, 9am, 1.15pm & 9.30pm (Go Bus)
Luxor	LE210	18hr	4pm (East Delta)
Nuweiba	LE30	1hr	10.30am (East Delta)
Sharm El Sheikh	LE25	1½hr	8am, 9am, 10am, 12.30pm, 3pm, 4pm, 5pm, 7pm, 7.30pm, 9.30pm, 10pm, 10.30pm & 11pm (East Delta)
Taba	LE40	2½hr	10.30am (East Delta)

Note that a couple of the Go Bus Cairo-bound services will also drop off passengers in Sharm El Sheikh. Check at the Go Bus office for the current schedule.

ⓘ Getting Around

BICYCLE & MOTORCYCLE
Bicycles are a great way to get around Dahab and can be hired from many hotels and travel agencies in town.
Dahab Cycling Club (Map p390; ☑ 010-1962-4821; www.facebook.com/dahabcclub; Waterfront Promenade, Masbat; bike rental per day/week LE120/560; ⊙10am-10pm) Rents good-quality bikes.
Koka Bike (Map p390; ☑ 012-8012-2815; Sharia Al Melal; scooter/motorcycle per day LE250/450; ⊙11am-8pm) This repair shop also rents out motorcycles and scooters by the day.

TAXI
A variety of variously banged-up pick-ups operate as local taxis. From Masbat to the bus station costs between LE10 and LE15. To get to the Blue Hole independently you can negotiate with any of the pick-up drivers in town (LE100 to LE120 return). Don't forget to arrange a return time.

Travel agencies in Dahab offer camel, jeep and walking excursions to Ras Abu Gallum. Hiking into the reserve by following the path from the Blue Hole (p389) is also popular. The track winds along the shoreline to Ras Abu Gallum village and El Omeyid village (one hour), where it's possible to camp overnight in a hut. Most tour agencies in Dahab offer day trips to Ras Abu Gallum for around LE200 or overnight for LE350 (including return transport to the Blue Hole, lunch and snorkelling gear) or it can easily be hiked independently.

There are several walking trails in the reserve, and Bedouin guides and camels can be hired at either Ras Abu Gallum village or, if coming from the Nuweiba side, through the ranger house at the edge of Wadi Rasasah. Popular destinations within the protectorate include **Bir El Oghda**, a now-deserted Bedouin village, and **Bir Sugheir**, a water source at the edge of the protectorate.

Ras Abu Gallum Protectorate

The starkly beautiful **Ras Abu Gallum Protectorate** covers 400 sq km of coastline between Dahab and Nuweiba, mixing coastal mountains, narrow valleys, sand dunes and fine-gravel beaches with several diving and snorkelling sites. Scientists describe the area as a 'floristic frontier', where Mediterranean conditions are influenced by a tropical climate. With its 165 plant species (including 44 found nowhere else in Sinai) and wealth of mammals and reptiles, this environmentally important area is a fascinating place to visit.

Bedouin of the Mizena tribe live within the protectorate confines, fishing here as they have done for centuries (although this is now regulated by the protectorate).

Nuweiba

☑ 069 / POP 20,000

For a brief period following the Egypt–Israel peace treaty of 1979, a thriving Israeli tourism trade meant Tarabin (Nuweiba's waterfront beach-camp area) could claim rivalry to Dahab as Sinai's hippy beach paradise. Unfortunately, the vagaries of the regional politics over recent decades have meant Israeli travellers, for the most part, shun Sinai. While Sharm boomed and Dahab grew steadily into a low-key resort, Nuweiba was left to go to seed.

Nuweiba these days isn't much of a looker. Stretching over 15km, it lacks a defined centre or cohesive ambience, and functions primarily as a port for the Aqaba-bound ferry to Jordan. Both the port and city areas are litter strewn, fly-blown and have an air

Nuweiba

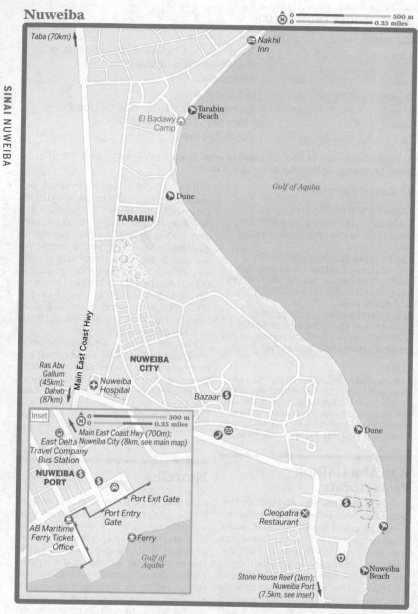

of serious neglect. Tarabin itself has become ever-more ramshackle, which is a shame because with a little sprucing up it could easily be the mellow beach-camp paradise that Dahab was a decade ago.

◉ Sights & Activities

Diving & Snorkelling

The dive sites around Nuweiba tend to be less busy than others along the Gulf of Aqaba and host an impressive variety of marine life. Shallow reefs offshore are reasonable places for snorkelling, but the best spot is **Stone House Reef** just south of town.

Sinker
DIVE SITE

(Map p38) The Sinker is a massive submerged mooring buoy designed for cargo ships, which was sunk by mistake in the mid-1990s. Since then it has developed into a fantastic artificial reef, attracting a host of small, colourful species. The access point is 5km north of Nuweiba. Depth: 6m to 35m. Rating: intermediate. Access: shore.

Ras Mumlach
DIVE SITE

(Map p38) A sloping reef about 30km south of Nuweiba interspersed with enormous boulders and excellent table corals. Depth: 10m to 25m. Rating: intermediate. Access: shore.

Ras Shaitan
DIVE SITE

(Map p38) The highlight of this dive 15km north of Nuweiba is undoubtedly the contoured topography, including narrow valleys, sand-filled depressions and deep chasms. Depth: 10m to 30m. Rating: intermediate. Access: shore.

Jeep & Camel Safaris

The desert around Nuweiba has plenty of lush oases and interesting rock formations to explore. Camps in Tarabin and along the Nuweiba–Taba road (p401) can organise trips to the outlying area. We recommend choosing a local Bedouin guide – not only does it benefit those typically marginalised by tour operators from the Nile Valley, but there have been some instances of travellers lost in the desert without water because their so-called guides didn't know the routes.

Itineraries – and, as a result, prices – are generally custom-designed, but expect to pay from about LE300 to LE400 per person per day for a safari including all food and water.

🛏 Sleeping & Eating

On the northern edge of town, Tarabin is a thin strip of pebbly sand backed by beach camps that stretches along the waterfront for 1.5km. Unfortunately the lack of business in recent years has contributed to a lackadaisical attitude in both beach cleaning and camp repairs. The places we recommend are all in good shape.

Most people staying here eat at their accommodation. All the open beach camps in Tarabin serve meals.

At the port, a cluster of places sell *fuul* (fava bean paste) and *ta'amiyya* (Egyptian falafel) in the area behind the National Bank

of Egypt and before the ticket office for Aqaba ferries.

El Badawy Camp
HUT $

(Map p396; ☑ 010-6525-4115; www.elbadawycamp.dk; Tarabin; hut per person US$5, with air-con US$12, r with air-con US$18) This big well-maintained complex has everything from basic huts with just mattresses to air-con rooms in a concrete row at the back that come with private en suites. The restaurant has a decent menu, and there's plenty of communal palm-thatch shaded areas right on the shore to hang out.

★ Nakhil Inn
BOUTIQUE HOTEL $$

(Map p396; ☑ 069-350-0879; www.nakhil-inn.com; Tarabin; s/d €35/42; ❄ 🛜) The Nakhil is a cosy compromise for those who want hotel comforts without the crowds. The studio-style wooden cabins exude simple beach chic, while guests can go kayaking, diving, or simply unwind while lazing about in one of the hammocks or palm-thatched cabanas along the immaculately kept private beach. The big drawcard is snorkelling the house reef just offshore.

Cleopatra Restaurant
SEAFOOD $$

(Map p396; Nuweiba City; dishes LE20-90; ⏰ noon-11pm) One of the more popular tourist restaurants in Nuweiba City (not that there's much competition), Cleopatra offers up the bounty of the sea along with a few Western fast-food favourites.

🛈 Information

Banks in Nuweiba will not handle Jordanian dinars.

Banque Misr (Map p396; Main Rd, Nuweiba Port; ⏰ 8.30am-2.30pm Sun-Thu) Has an ATM.

Nuweiba Hospital (Map p396; ☑ 069-350-0302; Nuweiba City; ⏰ 24hr) Just off the Main East Coast Hwy to Dahab.

Tourist Police (Map p396; ☑ 06-350-0231; Nuweiba City; ⏰ 8am-2pm Sat-Thu)

🛈 Getting There & Away

BOAT

AB Maritime (www.abmaritime.com.jo) runs two public **ferries** (Map p396) from Nuweiba to Aqaba. The so-called 'fast-ferry' service leaves Nuweiba from Sunday to Friday at (supposedly) 1pm and takes roughly 2½ hours, assuming normal sea conditions. One-way tickets cost US$100. Heading back to Nuweiba, fast ferries depart from Aqaba at 11pm.

The regular ferry, commonly called the 'slow-ferry', leaves Nuweiba at (again, supposedly) noon

THE BEDOUIN OF SINAI

Sinai's rugged tracts are home to desert dwellers, most of whom live in the north of the peninsula. The Bedouin – whose numbers are variously estimated to be between 80,000 and 300,000 – belong to 14 distinct tribes, most with ties to Bedouin in the Negev (Israel), Jordan and northern Saudi Arabia, and each with their own customs and culture. The Sukwarka, who live along the northern coast near Al Arish, is the largest tribe. Others include the Tarabin, who have territory in both northern and southern Sinai; the Tyaha in the centre of the peninsula who, together with the Tarabin, trace their roots to Palestine; and the Haweitat, centred in an area southeast of Suez, and originally from the Hejaz in Saudi Arabia.

The seven Bedouin tribes in southern Sinai are known collectively as the Towara or 'Arabs of Al Tor', the provincial capital. Of these, the first to settle in Sinai were the Aleiqat and the Suwalha, who arrived soon after the Muslim conquest of Egypt. The largest southern tribe is the Mizena, which is concentrated along the coast between Sharm El Sheikh and Nuweiba. Some members of the tiny Jabaliyya tribe, centred in the mountains around St Katherine, are said to be descendants of Macedonians sent by Emperor Justinian to build and protect the monastery in the 6th century.

Thanks to centuries of living in the harsh conditions of Sinai, the Bedouin have developed a sophisticated understanding of their environment. Strict laws and traditions govern the use of precious resources. Water use is closely regulated and vegetation carefully conserved, as revealed in the Bedouin adage 'killing a tree is like killing a soul'. Local life centres on clans and their sheikhs (leaders), and loyalty and hospitality – essential for surviving in the desert – are paramount. Tea is traditionally taken in rounds of three. Traditional tent dwellings are made of woven goat hair, sometimes mixed with sheep's wool. Women's black veils and robes are often elaborately embroidered, with the use of red signifying that they are married, and blue unmarried.

Sinai's original inhabitants have often been left behind in the race to build up the coast, and they are sometimes viewed with distrust because of their ties to tribes in neighbouring countries, and allegations of criminal activity and links to terrorist cells throughout Sinai. Bedouin traditions also tend to come second to the significant economical benefits brought by development in the peninsula – benefits that, according to Bedouin activists, Bedouins have yet to fully experience. Egyptian human rights organisations have also reported ongoing persecution of Bedouin people, including imprisonment without charges, and there have been regular Bedouin demonstrations claiming mistreatment by the police. These concerns, as well as loss of traditional lands, pollution of fishing areas and insensitive tourism, have contributed to the sense of marginalisation and unrest.

Throughout the world – and especially in Egypt – tourism has the power to shape the destinies of communities. Travellers can help limit negative effects by seeking out Bedouin-owned businesses, buying locally, staying informed of prevalent issues and never being afraid to ask questions.

daily and arrives in Aqaba on average about four hours later. One-way tickets cost US$90.

We cannot stress enough how much more comfortable the 'fast-ferry' service is than its sister regular service.

A word of caution: the Nuweiba–Aqaba ferry service (both 'fast' and 'slow' ferries) is renowned for interminable delays. A small sampling of horror stories we have received from travellers includes a monumental 20-hour delay because of heavy thunderstorms and rough seas, as well as a truly epic three-day delay because of severe power outages. While the majority of travellers experience a delay of around two or three hours (a sailing time of 3pm or 4pm is typical), it's best to leave some flexibility in onward Jordanian travel schedules in case of mishaps.

Tickets can be paid in either US dollars or Egyptian pounds. Egyptian departure tax (LE50) is paid at the time of purchase. Tickets can only be purchased on the day of departure, at the **ferry ticket office** (Map p396; ☎ 069-352-0427; Nuweiba Port area; ☺ 9am-3pm) in a small building near the port. Travellers must be at the port two hours before sailing to buy tickets and get through the shambolic departure formalities in the terminal building. Note that during the hajj, boats are booked weeks before departure. For travel during this period – the only exception to the rule – it's necessary to buy tickets as far in advance as possible.

The East Delta bus from Sharm El Sheikh and Dahab can drop passengers directly in front of Nuweiba port. Make sure to ask the driver. To find the ticket office, turn right at the port car park and walk one block to the end of the port wall. The ticket office is the sand-coloured building on the left.

Most nationalities are entitled to receive a free Jordanian visa upon arrival in Aqaba. Passports are handed to the immigration officials once on-board the ferry and collected again once arrived at the immigration building in Aqaba.

BUS

From the **bus station** (Map p396; ☑ 069-352-0371; Nuweiba Port), East Delta Travel Co has buses to Sharm El Sheikh (LE50, three to four hours) via Dahab (LE30, 1½ hours) at 7.30am and 4.30pm. Buses to Taba (LE25, one hour) leave at 9am, noon, and 3pm. The 9am and 3pm Taba services carry on to Cairo but because of security issues, foreign travellers are not allowed to travel on the Taba–Cairo road. Anyone attempting to travel to Cairo this way will be made to get off the bus at either Taba bus station or Taba police checkpoint.

If you're arriving in Nuweiba from Dahab, the East Delta bus stops first directly opposite Nuweiba port, then at the bus station, and after-wards on the highway, at the nearest entrance to the Tarabin beach area.

TAXI & SERVEES

Taxis (Map p396) and a few servees (service taxis) hang out by the port. Unless you get there when the ferry has arrived from Aqaba, you'll have to wait a long time for a servees to fill up.

A taxi to Dahab costs about LE200 and roughly LE100 to the further beach camps on the Nuweiba–Taba road.

ℹ️ Getting Around

Nuweiba taxi drivers are hard bargainers. Expect to pay LE15 for a **taxi** from the port or bus station to Nuweiba City, and to be quoted a rather exorbitant LE40 from the port to Tarabin.

Local taxi driver **Asmail** (☑ 010-0397-0416) is a good contact for port pick-ups and transfers from Nuweiba to Dahab or the beach camps on the Nuweiba–Taba road.

Around Nuweiba

Home to some of Sinai's most interesting, and easily accessible, desert landscapes, the stretch of coastal desert around Nuweiba is prime camel- and jeep-safari territory. Safaris into this area are best arranged from Dahab, Nuweiba or the beach camps strung along the Nuweiba–Taba road.

👁️ Sights

Coloured Canyon   CANYON

This canyon derives its name from the lay-ers of bright, multicoloured stones that re-semble paintings on its steep, narrow walls. It's magnificently beautiful. As the canyon is sheltered from the wind, the silence is one of its most impressive features. It's a favour-ite day trip from both Dahab and Sharm El Sheikh, so unfortunately the ambience can be destroyed somewhat if a couple of large bus tours arrive at the same time.

Mayet El Wishwashi   SPRING

The area around the spring of Mayat El Wishwashi is great for hiking. The actual spring is hidden within a canyon and only has only a trickle of water, except after floods. Nearby is **Mayat Malkha**, a palm grove fed by the spring's waters and set amid colourful sandstone.

Ain Umm Ahmed   OASIS

Picturesque Ain Umm Ahmed is the largest oasis in eastern Sinai, with lots of palms, Bedouin houses and a famous stream that becomes an icy river in the winter months.

Wadi Huweiyit   CANYON

Wadi Huweiyit is an impressive sandstone canyon with lookouts that give panoramic views over to Saudi Arabia.

Gebel Barga   MOUNTAIN

The climb up Gebel Barga is quite tricky but the summit affords stunning views over the mountains of eastern Sinai.

Taba

☑ 069

If you're entering Egypt overland from Isra-el and the Palestinian Territories, the scruffy border town of Taba, loomed over by the monolithic Taba Hotel and backed by barren hills, will be your first taste of Sinai. With its narrow shore lapped by the calm, azure blue waters of the Gulf of Aqaba, this coast-line has been bigged-up by developers as the new Sharm El Sheikh for years, with the self-contained resort-town of Taba Heights purpose built to reel in package tourists. A combination of security worries and a heav-ily destructive flood in 2014 have continued to put the brakes on Taba's dreams of sun-and-fun holidaymaker hordes.

For fully resort-based holidays (for those who don't mind a lack of restaurants and other amenities outside the resort walls), Taba provides good beach-break deals. Though for sand-between-your-toes beach hut bliss, hop a bit further south to the beach camps along the Taba–Nuweiba road.

⊙ Sights

Pharaoh's Island — ISLAND
(Gezirat Fara'un; adult/child LE160/80; ⊙ 9am-5pm) About 7km south of Taba and 250m off the Egyptian coast, this tiny islet in turquoise waters is dominated by the much-restored Castle of Salah Ad Din. The castle was originally a fortress built by the Crusaders in 1115, but was captured and expanded by Saladin in 1170 as a bulwark against feared Crusader penetration south from Palestine.

🛏 Sleeping

Steigenberger Taba Hotel — RESORT $$
(☎ 069-353 0140; www.steigenberger.com; Taba Beach; r from US$80) You can't miss this mammoth resort complex. It towers over Taba's low-rise town. If you've just wandered across the dusty border and want to rest up before moving onward, this is a fine place to relax for a day. Staff are friendly and helpful, classically styled rooms come with all mod-cons and comfy queen-sized beds, and the pool is enormous.

ℹ Information

The town centre is home to a couple of banks, a small hospital and various shops. The Taba Heights resort area lies about 20km south of the main town.

DANGERS & ANNOYANCES
The Taba bus bombing on 16 February 2014 was directly aimed at tourists. In their statement claiming responsibility for the attack, Wilayet-Sinai (formerly known as Ansar Bayt Al Maqdis) militants pledged to continue on a campaign of attacks that directly affect Egypt's economic interests. In the aftermath most foreign governments issued cautionary travel advisories (which have yet to be lifted) for the entire South Sinai area.

The Taba border remains the only reliable crossing between Egypt and Israel and overland travellers continue to cross here, just as a small number of package-tourists are continuing to holiday within the Taba Heights resort. Travellers heading this way should check the latest travel advisories and, more importantly, pay attention to local advice once on the ground.

ℹ Getting There & Away

BOAT
AB Maritime (☑ Aqaba, Jordan +962 3-201 9849, mobile +962 791 017 777; www.abmaritime.com.jo/en/touristic_line; Sharia King Hussein bin Talal, Aqaba, Jordan; ⊙ office 10am-7pm) runs a tourist ferry between Taba and Aqaba. The unfortunate caveat is that it only operates on a return basis and is aimed at group tours. Anyone taking this ferry needs to return to Egypt within eight days. The other restriction is that immigration officials at Taba port only issue the free Sinai-only entry stamp. The most organised work-around is to either have been issued with a multiple-entry stamp at the passport office in either Cairo or Al Tor beforehand or to buy a new Egypt visa online while in Jordan. Full Egypt visas are also available at the Egyptian Consulate in Aqaba. We also know of at least one case where someone returning on this ferry travelled on to Sharm El Sheikh and then obtained a full Egypt visa at the airport before returning to Cairo.

Return ferry tickets (adult/child US$106/66) include Egyptian departure tax but not the Jordanian departure tax of JD10, which you have to pay separately.

The ferry leaves from Taba Marina (just north of the Taba Heights resort area) at 6am daily and arrives in Aqaba at 6.30am. On the return leg, the ferry leaves from Aqaba's Royal Yacht Club port (rather than the public port) at 7.30pm and arrives in Taba at 8pm. Passengers should be at the ports one hour before departure.

Annoyingly, tickets can be difficult for independent travellers to obtain. The easiest option is to get a travel agency in Dahab or Sharm El Sheikh to book the ferry tickets for you.

BUS
Taba's **bus station** (☑ 069-353 0250) is along the main road about 800m south of the border. East Delta Travel Co buses to Nuweiba (LE15, one hour) leave at 6am and 3pm. Both services carry on to Dahab (LE35, 2½ hours) and Sharm El Sheikh (LE50, four hours). There are also two buses daily to Cairo (LE80, six to seven hours) via the Nakhl–Suez road, but foreign travellers are not allowed to travel this route due to security issues. For travellers who've crossed the border from Eilat and want to journey directly to Cairo, the only option is to go via Sharm El Sheikh.

CROSSING TO & FROM ISRAEL
The Taba–Eilat border is open 24 hours daily. Just inside the border you'll find an ATM and foreign-exchange booths.

Egyptian departure tax is LE75. Crossing from Eilat into Egypt, Israeli departure tax is 105NIS. The Taba side of the border technically only issues the free Sinai-only entry stamp, with full

SINAI BEACH CAMPS

The coastline between Nuweiba and Taba is Egypt's last bastion of the traditional beach camp. For years this region's business came from Israelis looking for a closer-to-home Goa. Plenty of the more adventurous are now venturing back but Sinai's security issues continue to keep away the masses who once descended here, while other foreign travellers are still to venture north and discover this tranquil beach-bum haven. Ideal for those who want to seriously veg out, this stretch of shore is all about back-to-basics beach living where lazing in a hammock is still the preferred activity.

We name just a small selection of the beach camps here. There are plenty more for those who want to explore. All the camps recommended have restaurants and can help organise desert treks for guests who tire of slothing out on the sand. Note that breakfast is usually not included in the room rate. For travellers who don't have their own transport and don't want to hire a taxi, the East Delta (p394) buses running between Dahab and Taba can drop people anywhere along this shore.

Sawa Camp (☑ 010-0272-2838; www.sawacamp.com; Mahash area, Nuweiba–Taba rd, 28km north of Nuweiba; s/d hut US$6/8) A wide strip of perfect soft white-sand beach, hammocks on every hut porch, solar-powered showers and a restaurant dishing up delicious meals; Sawa ticks all the boxes for a laid-back, family-friendly travel stop that's great for unwinding. Bedouin owner Salama has got all the little touches right. Simple *hoosha* (palm thatch) huts all have electricity and the communal bathrooms are kept spotless.

Sabah Camp (☑ 012-2222-4957; Bir Sweir area, Nuweiba–Taba road, 36km south of Taba; huts per person from LE60) Speckled with trees and shrubs and fronted by the golden sand of Bir Sweir beach, Sabah is a long-time hit with young hippy Israelis, who come here for serious chill-out time and to doss in basic but well-kept *hoosha* huts just steps from the sea.

Basata (☑ 069-350-0481; www.basata.com; Ras Burgaa area, Nuweiba–Taba road, 42km south of Taba; camp sites per person €12, s/d hut €23/40, 3-person chalets €80) ✿ Its name meaning 'simplicity' in Arabic, Basata is an ecologically minded settlement that uses organically grown produce and recycles its rubbish. Self-catering is the norm – there's a communal kitchen and a shop where cooking ingredients are available to buy – but it does serve dinner for those feeling lazy. The ambience is laid-back and family-friendly with a New Age twist.

Egyptian visas having to be bought in advance either online, or in either Israel or Jordan. If you have time up your sleeve, a full Egyptian visa can usually be purchased here though you'll have to pay an extra fee for a local Taba travel agency to process the visa.

Servees wait by the border for passengers. If business is slack, there may be a long wait for the vehicle to fill up – alternatively, travellers can pay the equivalent of all seven fares and leave immediately. Per-person fares are about LE20 to Nuweiba, LE40 to Dahab and LE60 to Sharm El Sheikh. Bargaining power increases when the bus departure times are approaching.

SINAI INTERIOR

Sinai's rugged interior is populated by barren mountains, wind-sculpted canyons and wadis that burst into life with even the briefest rains. The rocks and desert landscapes turn shades of pink, ochre and velvet-black as the sun rises and falls, and what little vegetation there is appears to grow magically out of the rock. Bedouin still wander through the wilderness, and camels are the best way to travel, with much of the terrain too rocky even for a 4WD. Against this desolate backdrop, some of the most sacred events in recorded human history are said to have taken place, which has consequently immortalised Sinai in the annals of Judaism, Christianity and Islam.

St Katherine Protectorate

☑ 069

The 4350-sq-km **St Katherine Protectorate** was created in 1996 to counteract the detrimental effects of rapidly increasing tourism on St Katherine's Monastery and the adjacent Mt Sinai. In addition to the ar-

DON'T MISS

DESERT HIKING ON THE SINAI TRAIL

Egypt's first long-distance through-hike, the Sinai Trail (www.sinaitrail.org) is a 250km, 12- to 14-day trek traversing from the coast's vast sand plains and narrow canyons into the rugged mountain heartland around St Katherine. Organised by a cooperative of three Bedouin tribes (the Tarabin, Mizena, and Jabaliyya), the Sinai Trail offers a desert experience steeped in local culture.

Although the idea of multi-day desert trek may at first seem a challenge best left to the seriously gung-ho, the Sinai Trail has been designed and is run for anyone with a good level of fitness and a sense of adventure. Most of the trail, utilising age-old Bedouin routes, is straight hiking with small sections of scrambling (which can be avoided if necessary). Local Bedouin – all trained in wilderness first aid – provide guiding services along the entire route, giving this hike a rich cultural component that allows an insight into Sinai's traditional Bedouin life. For the tribes themselves, the trail offers a small but sustainable economy, creating jobs and other tourism opportunities; it's a vital initiative in a region where the Bedouin communities have often been sidelined in Sinai's tourism economy.

The main trail has its trailheads on the coast between Nuweiba and Taba (at Ras Shaitan and Bir Sweir) and at St Katherine's, and can be walked in either direction. If time restraints mean you can't complete the entire trail, sections can be hiked individually, and a network of shorter hikes at various points along the trail is being developed.

The daily hiking costs (per person per day in a group of six/four/two people LE750/850/950) cover everything: guiding fees, food, water and camels (for carrying equipment and packs). The Sinai Trail is committed to paying a fair wage to guides and cameleers.

ea's unique high-altitude desert ecosystem, it protects a wealth of historical sites sacred to the world's three main monotheistic religions.

Rising up out of the desert and jutting above the other peaks surrounding the monastery is the towering 2285m Mt Sinai (Gebel Musa). Tucked into a barren valley at the foot of Mt Sinai is the ancient St Katherine's Monastery. Approximately 3.5km from here is the small town of Al Milga, which is also called Katreen and is known as the 'Meeting Place' by local Jabaliyya Bedouin.

◉ Sights

★ **St Katherine's Monastery** MONASTERY (Illustration p404; ☑ Cairo 02-2482-8513; www. sinaimonastery.com; ⏲ 9-11.30am Mon-Thu & Sat, except religious holidays) FREE This ancient monastery traces its founding to about AD 330, when Byzantine empress Helena had a small chapel and a fortified refuge for local hermits built beside what was believed to be the burning bush from which God spoke to Moses. Today St Katherine's is considered one of the oldest continually functioning monastic communities in the world. If the monastery museum is locked, ask at the Church of the Transfiguration for the key.

The monastery – which, together with the surrounding area, has been declared a

Unesco World Heritage site – is named after St Katherine, the legendary martyr of Alexandria, who was tortured on a spiked wheel and then beheaded for her faith. Tradition holds that her body was transported by angels away from the torture device (which spun out of control and killed the pagan onlookers) and onto the slopes of Egypt's highest mountain peak. The peak, which lies about 6km south of Mt Sinai, subsequently became known as Gebel Katarina. Katherine's body was 'found' about 300 years later by monks from the monastery in a state of perfect preservation.

In the 6th century, Emperor Justinian ordered a fortress to be constructed around the original chapel, together with a basilica and a monastery, to provide a secure home for the monastic community that had grown there, and as a refuge for the Christians of southern Sinai.

Since then the monastery has been visited by pilgrims from throughout the world, many of whom braved extraordinarily difficult and dangerous journeys to reach the remote and isolated site. Today a paved access road has removed the hazards that used to accompany a trip here, and the monastery has become a popular day trip from Sharm El Sheikh and Dahab.

Travellers visiting should remember that this is still a functioning monastery, which necessitates conservative dress – no one with shorts is permitted to enter, and women must cover their shoulders.

➡ **Touring the Monastery**

Inside the walled compound, the ornately decorated 6th-century **Church of the Transfiguration** has a nave flanked by massive marble columns and walls covered in richly gilded icons and paintings. At the church's eastern end, a gilded 17th-century iconostasis separates the nave from the sanctuary and the apse, where St Katherine's remains are interred (off limits to most visitors). High in the apse above the altar is one of the monastery's most stunning artistic treasures, the 6th-century mosaic of the Transfiguration, although it can be difficult to see it past the chandeliers and the iconostasis. To the left of and below the altar is the monastery's holiest area, the Chapel of the Burning Bush, which is off limits to the public.

It's possible to see what is thought to be a descendant of the original **burning bush** in the monastery compound; however, due to visitors snipping cuttings of the bush to take home as blessings, the area surrounding it is now fenced off. Near the burning bush is the Well of Moses, a natural spring that is supposed to give marital happiness to those who drink from it.

Above the Well of Moses, and the main highlight of a monastery visit, is the superb **Monastery Museum** (Sacred Sacristy; LE80), which has been magnificently restored. It has displays (labelled in Arabic and English) of many of the monastery's artistic treasures, including some of the spectacular Byzantine-era icons from its world-famous collection. There are numerous precious chalices, and gold and silver crosses, along with displays of ancient manuscripts. In the lowest room of the museum is the prize exhibit: parchments from the Codex Sinaiticus, the world's oldest near-complete bible.

The monastery's **library**, the second largest in the world, contains a priceless collection of illuminated bibles and ancient manuscripts, including a hand-written copy of the New Testament, and has reopened to the public after three years of restoration.

Just inside the monastery walls you'll find a gift shop selling replicas of icons. In the wider monastery grounds, outside the thick walls, are the guest house and a lovely courtyard area with a cafe (though it was closed during our last visit due to lack of custom). As tourism numbers are down, the narrow lane inside the monastery is pleasantly crowd-free but when tourism picks up again be aware that the monastery can get crammed with tour-bus crowds, particularly on Saturdays and Mondays.

★ **Mt Sinai**   MOUNTAIN
(Gebel Musa; compulsory guide LE175, camel rides one-way LE250) Known locally as Gebel Musa, Mt Sinai is revered by Christians, Muslims and Jews, all of whom believe that God delivered his Ten Commandments to Moses at its summit. The mountain is easy and beautiful to climb, and offers a taste of the magnificence of southern Sinai's high mountain region. For pilgrims, it also offers a moving glimpse into biblical times. All hikers must be accompanied by a local Bedouin guide (hired from the monastery car park).

Nearly all visitors take one of the two well-defined routes up to the summit that have their trailhead at the monastery car park – the camel trail and the Steps of Repentance. Both meet about 300m below the summit at a plateau known as Elijah's Basin. Here, everyone must take a steep series of 750 rocky and uneven steps to the top, where there is a small chapel and mosque (these are kept locked).

Both the climb and the summit offer spectacular views of nearby plunging valleys and of jagged mountain chains rolling off into the distance, and it's usually possible to see the even-higher summit of Gebel Katarina in the distance. Most people on tours from Sharm El Sheikh make the climb in the predawn hours to see the magnificence of the sun rising over the surrounding peaks, and then arrive back at the base before 9am, when St Katherine's Monastery opens for visitors.

An alternative is to walk up for sunset, when there are rarely more than a handful of other hikers on the summit. For this option, travellers must be comfortable making the descent down the camel trail in the dark and make sure they have sturdy shoes and a good torch (flashlight).

Because of the sanctity of the area, the Egyptian National Parks Office has instituted various regulations. Those wanting to spend the night on the mountain are asked to sleep below the summit at the small Elijah's Basin plateau. Here there are several composting toilets and a 500-year-

St Katherine's Monastery

A HISTORY OF THE MONASTERY

4th Century With hermetic communities congregating in the area, a chapel is established around the site of Moses' miraculous ❶ **Burning Bush**.

6th Century In a show of might, Emperor Justinian adds the monastery ❷ **fortifications** and orders the building of the basilica, which is graced by Byzantine art, including the ❸ **Mosaic of the Transfiguration**.

7th Century The prophet Mohammed signs the ❹ **Ahtiname**, a declaration of his protection of the monastery. When the Arab armies conquer Egypt in AD 641, the monastery is left untouched. Despite the era's tumultuous times, monastery abbot St John Klimakos writes his famed ❺ **Ladder of Divine Ascent** treatise, depicted in the Sacred Sacristy.

9th Century Extraordinary happenings surround the monastery when, according to tradition, a monk discovers the body of St Katherine on a mountain summit.

11th Century To escape the wrath of Fatimid caliph Al-Hakim, wily monks build a mosque within the monastery grounds.

15th Century Frequent raids and attacks on the monastery lead the monks to build the ❻ **Ancient Gate** to prevent the ransacking of church treasures and to keep the monastic community safe.

19th Century In 1859 biblical scholar Constantin von Tischendorf borrows 347 pages of the ❼ **Codex Sinaiticus** from the monastery, but fails to get his library books back on time. Greek artisans travel from the island of Tinos in 1871 to help construct the ❽ **bell tower**.

20th Century Renovations inside the monastery reveal 18 more missing parchment leaves from the Codex Sinaiticus, proving that all the secrets hidden within these ancient walls may not yet be revealed.

Fortifications

The formidable walls are 2m thick and 11m high. Justinian sent a Balkan garrison to watch over the newly fortified monastery, and today's local Jabaleyya tribe are said to be their descendents.

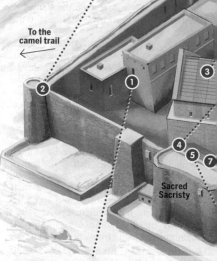

To the camel trail ←

Sacred Sacristy

The Burning Bush

This flourishing bramble (the endemic Sinai shrub *Rubus Sanctus*) was transplanted in the 10th century to its present location. Tradition states that cuttings of the plant refuse to grow outside the monastery walls.

Mosaic of the Transfiguration

avishly made using thousands of pieces
glass, gold, silver and stone tesserae,
is Byzantine mosaic (completed AD 551)
ecreates Christianity's Gospel accounts of
esus' miraculous revelation as the son of God.

Ahtiname

A monastery delegation sought the
protection of Mohammed, and he
signed his guarantee by handprint.
This document on display in the
Sacred Sacrity is only a copy; the
original is in Istanbul.

**Steps of
pentence**

Library

Bell Tower

The nine bells that
hang inside the
tower were a present
from Tsar Alexander
II of Russia. While
these are rung for
Sunday services,
an older semantron
(wooden percussion
instrument) signals
vespers and matins.

❽

**Church of the
Transfiguration**

Codex
Sinaiticus

The world's oldest
near-complete
bible; 347 pages
of the Codex were
taken to Russia in
1859 and sold by
Stalin to the UK in
1933. Remaining
parchments are
displayed in the
manuscript room.

❻

Ancient Gate

Look up at the high
walls and you'll
see a ramshackle
wooden structure.
In times of strife
monks left via
this primitive
lift, lowered to
the ground by a
pulley.

adder of Divine Ascent

his 12th-century icon is one of the
onastery's most valuable. It depicts
bbot St John Klimakos leading
band of monks up the ladder of
alvation to heaven.

old cypress tree, marking the spot where the prophet Elijah is said to have heard the voice of God. Bring sufficient food and water, warm clothes and a sleeping bag. It gets cold and windy, even in summer; in winter light snow is common.

➡ Camel Trail

The start of the camel trail is reached by walking along the northern wall of St Katherine's Monastery past the end of the compound. This is the easier route, and takes about two hours to ascend, moving at a steady pace. The trail is wide, clear and slopes gently as it moves up a series of switchbacks. The only potential difficulty – apart from sometimes fierce winds – are gravelly patches that can be slippery on the descent.

Most people walk up, but it's also possible to hire a camel at the base, just behind the monastery, which travellers can ride to where the camel trail ends at Elijah's Basin. Those who decide to try this should note that it's easier on the anatomy (especially for men) to ride up the mountain, rather than down.

En route are several kiosks selling tea and soft drinks, and near the summit vendors rent out blankets (LE5) to help ward off the chill. For those ascending in the pre-dawn hours to wait for sunrise at the summit, these are a worthy investment to protect against the howling winds (though the blankets do smell like camels).

➡ Steps of Repentance

The other path to the summit from the monastery car park is the taxing 3750 **Steps of Repentance**, which begin outside the southeastern corner of the monastery compound. They were laid by one monk as a form of penance. The steps – 3000 up to Elijah's Basin and then the final 750 to the summit – are made of roughly hewn rock, and are steep and uneven in many places, requiring strong knees and concentration in placing your feet. The stunning mountain scenery along the way, though, makes this path well worth the extra effort, and the lower reaches of the trail afford impressive views of the monastery.

For those who want to try both routes to Mt Sinai's summit, it's easier to take the camel trail on the way up and the steps on the way back down. The steps shouldn't be attempted in the dark, so those heading to the summit for sunset and not staying overnight should go up via the steps and come down the easier camel trail.

➡ Wadi Al Arbain Trail

This alternative route to the summit threads up the neighbouring mountain of Gebel Safsafa and takes in more historic sites. It starts from Wadi Al Arbain behind Al Milga village and passes by the 6th-century Monastery of Forty Martyrs and the Rock of Moses – believed to be the rock which miraculously produced drinking water after Moses struck it with his staff – as well as some hermit cells. This trail connects to the main Mt Sinai trail near Elijah's Basin. To walk this route, you'll need to organise a guide before (LE250) with one of the tour operators in Al Milga.

🏃 Activities

For anyone with a rugged and adventurous bent, this region, lying in the heart of South Sinai's high mountain region, is an ideal trekking destination. It's easy to organise all trekking activities independently at Al Milga.

Trekking

Prices for guided treks and camel treks vary widely depending on itineraries, number of people and operators but range between €20 to €50 per person per day including food, water, a camel for carrying equipment, and guide. You should buy firewood in Al Milga to discourage destruction of the few trees in the mountains. Make sure you bring water-purification tablets, unless you trust the mountain springs. You'll also need comfortable walking boots, a hat and sunglasses, sunblock, a warm jacket, a good sleeping bag and toilet paper. Keep in mind that it can get very cold at night – frost and even snow are common in winter. Treks range from half a day to a week or more, and can be done either on camel or on foot. Even if you decide to walk, you'll need at least one camel for your food and luggage. Whoever you go with, be sure to register with the police prior to leaving. For detailed information on trekking in this area, check out www.discoversinai.net and www.st-katherine.net.

One of the most common circuits goes to the **Galt Al Azraq** (Blue Pools), with its crystal-clear icy waters, and travels through some of Sinai's most dramatically beautiful scenery of high passes and lush wadis. The trail takes four to five days to and from Al Milga.

Other destinations include **Sheikh Awad**, home to a sheikh's tomb and Bedouin settlement; the **Nugra Waterfall**, a difficult-to-reach, rain-fed cascade about 20m high, which is reached through a winding canyon

DESERT SERENITY AT AL KARM ECOLODGE

In a remote wadi, this Bedouin-owned **ecolodge** (☑010-0132-4693; www.facebook.com/Al-Karm-Mountains-Ecolodge; Sheikh Awaad; r with shared bathroom incl half/full board per person LE100/120) is the perfect spot to sample the tranquillity and rugged beauty of southern Sinai. It deserves kudos for its environmental efforts: solar-powered showers; composting toilets; and beautifully designed, simple stone and palm-trunk rooms decorated with local textiles, which blend into the scenery. Due to the lodge's remote location, advanced reservations are essential.

Lit only by the flicker of candlelight by night, this is a truly unique spot that is worth the effort to get here. There is plenty of good trekking that can be arranged by the lodge. Due to the fact that minimal English is spoken, it is easiest to get a native Arabic speaker – such as the Mountain Tours Office in Al Milga – to help you make your booking. It can also arrange transport to the lodge by either 4WD or by guided trek. If coming by car, the lodge is only accessible by 4WD. The turn-off is signposted 'Garaba Valley' about 20km from St Katherine on the Wadi Feiran road.

called Wadi Nugra; and **Naqb Al Faria**, a camel path with rock inscriptions.

A shorter trip is the hike to the top of **Gebel Katarina**, Egypt's highest peak at 2642m. It takes about five hours to reach the summit along a straightforward but taxing trail. The views from the top are breathtaking, and the panorama can even include the mountains of Saudi Arabia on a clear day. The **Blue Valley**, given its name after a Belgian artist painted the rocks here blue some years ago, is another popular day trip.

Trekking Operators

Mountain Tours Office　　　OUTDOORS
(☑069-347-0457; www.sheikhmousa.com; El Malga Bedouin Camp, Al Milga) The main hub for trekking activities in the St Katherine region, this office (part of El Malga Bedouin Camp) can organise anything from a short afternoon stroll to a multiday itinerary. It can also arrange yoga and meditation retreats, rock climbing and 4WD tours. Depending on numbers and itineraries, treks cost €35 to €50 per person per day.

Wilderness Ventures Egypt　　OUTDOORS
(☑012-8282-7182; www.wilderness-ventures-egypt.com) Working closely with local Jabaliyya Bedouin, this highly recommended company organises a variety of treks and activities inside St Katherine Protectorate, with a strong focus on Bedouin culture and local history. Of particular note, it organises hikes in the nearby Wadi Itlah gardens that include a slap-up lunch in one of the gardens and fascinating astronomy sessions.

🛏 Sleeping

El Malga Bedouin Camp　　　HOSTEL **$**
(Sheikh Mousa Camp; ☑010-0641-3575; www.sheikhmousa.com; Al Milga; dm/s/d LE30/125/180, s/d with shared bathroom LE75/120; 🛜) Owned by the affable Sheikh Mousa and run by on-the-ball Salah, this is by far the best-run camp in town. The en-suite rooms are large and comfortable, while the small, basic rooms and dorms share excellent bathroom facilities with hot water. There's a shaded, cushion-strewn terrace to chill out on and good meals are dished up by the kitchen.

Desert Fox Camp　　　　HOSTEL **$**
(☑010-9473-2417; www.sinaidesertfox.com; Main Rd, Al Milga; s/d with shared bathroom LE50/100, camping per person LE25) This slightly ramshackle and friendly set-up offers very basic rooms amid grounds with plenty of shaded seating areas for chilling out after a long trek, or for tucking into a hearty meal whipped up by the kitchen. It can organise trekking (around LE400 per person per day for two people) and myriad activities in the area.

Monastery Guesthouse　　GUESTHOUSE **$$**
(☑069-347-0353; www.sinaimonastery.com; St Katherine's Monastery; s/d US$35/60; ❄) This guesthouse right next to St Katherine's Monastery offers well-kept rooms surrounding a pleasant courtyard where a cafe offers filling and tasty meals. Make sure to ask for a mountain-view rather than a courtyard-view room. Note that the guesthouse was temporarily closed during our last visit so make sure to phone ahead to check it's open and to make a reservation.

SINAI WADI FEIRAN

✗ Eating

Al Milga has a bakery opposite the mosque, a couple of simple restaurants and several well-stocked supermarkets for buying supplies before hitting the trails. Most tourists take their meals at their camp or hotel. For much-needed fresh juices and hot drinks after a Mt Sinai hike, there's a friendly cafe in the car park at the monastery entrance.

ℹ Information

The **St Katherine Protectorate Office** (☏ 069-347-0032), located near the entrance to Al Milga, is where you pay your entrance to St Katherine Protectorate. It sometimes has informative booklets to four 'interpretive trails' established in the area, including one for Mt Sinai. These booklets take you through each trail, explaining flora and fauna as well as sites of historical and religious significance.

Banque Misr (⊙10am-1pm & 5-8pm Sat-Thu) Beside the petrol station; has an ATM and also changes US dollars and euro.

Police (☏069-347-0046; Al Milga; ⊙8am-5pm) Beside the St Katherine Protectorate Office.

DANGERS & ANNOYANCES

In April 2017 there was a gun attack on a police checkpoint in the St Katherine Protectorate area, which resulted in the death of one policeman. This was the first incident since the spate of tourist kidnappings in 2012 and 2013 along the St Katherine–Sharm El Sheikh road. The police presence around the St Katherine area remains high with several security checkpoints along the road. Many governments issue cautionary travel advisories for this area and tour buses are sometimes made to travel by convoy between St Katherine and the coastal resorts.

ℹ Getting There & Away

The **bus station** (☏069-347-0250) is just off the main road in Al Milga, behind the mosque. East Delta Travel Co runs one daily bus to Cairo (LE90, seven hours) at 6am via Wadi Feiran and Suez.

There is no public bus service between St Katherine and the Sinai coast but local transport initiative Bedouin Bus (www.bedouinbus.com; LE50 per person) runs a twice-weekly bus service from Al Milga to Nuweiba. The bus leaves every Wednesday and Sunday at 8am from in front of the bakery (opposite the mosque) on Al Milga's main street. This bus also used to have a service to Dahab, but because of the tourism downturn this has been cancelled for now. For current information on the bus, check with Salah at **El Malga Bedouin Camp** (p407).

Taxis charge around LE300 to LE350 to either Dahab or Sharm El Sheikh.

Taxis and pick-ups usually wait at the monastery car park for people coming down from Mt Sinai in the morning, and then again around noon when the monastery's visiting hours end. A lift to the village costs LE10 to LE15.

Wadi Feiran

This long valley serves as the main drainage route for the entire high mountain region into the Gulf of Suez. Sinai's largest oasis, it is lush and very beautiful, containing more than 12,000 date palms, as well as Bedouin communities representing all of Sinai's tribes. Stone walls surround the palms, and the rocky mountains on each side of the wadi have subtly different colours that stand out at sunrise and sunset, making the landscape even more dramatic.

Feiran also has biblical significance – it is believed to be the Rephidim mentioned in the Old Testament where the Israelites defeated their enemies. Because of this it later became the first Christian stronghold in Sinai. An extensively rebuilt early Christian convent remains from this time, but you need permission from St Katherine's Monastery if you want to visit.

The valley is an ideal spot from which to trek into the surrounding mountains.

The Bedouin Flower Garden (well signposted along the main road) is an ad-hoc campground and restaurant.

◉ Sights

Gebel Serbal MOUNTAIN
(Mt Serbal) To the south of Wadi Feiran, the 2070m Gebel Serbal (believed by early Christians to have been the real Mt Sinai) is a challenging six-hour hike to the summit along a track known as **Sikket Ar Reshshah**. Those who persevere are rewarded with fantastic panoramic views. You must be accompanied by a Bedouin guide for all hikes, which can be arranged either in Al Milga (at St Katherine) or at the Bedouin Flower Garden in Wadi Feiran itself.

ℹ Getting There & Away

The daily Cairo–St Katherine bus passes through Wadi Feiran and can pick up passengers as it trundles by.

Understand
Egypt

Egypt Today

Egypt was long seen as the land of eternity, where nothing ever changed. That image has been shattered by political events since 2011, but some things remain: Egypt's location, its huge population and its control of the Suez Canal ensure that it is still a major player in the region. Even with the turmoil following the downfall of two presidents in as many years, it still enjoys great prestige in diplomacy, the arts and as a moderate Islamic country.

Best on Film

The Square (2013) A documentary that looks at the turmoil in Egypt from 2011–13. It won three Emmys and was nominated for an Oscar.

The Yacoubian Building (2006) Blockbuster Egyptian movie adapted from Alaa Al Aswany's novel, portraying the stories of the residents of one block of flats in downtown Cairo.

In Search of Oil and Sand (2012) Egyptian historian Mahmoud Sabet's brilliant documentary uses home-movie footage to show the downfall of King Farouk.

Best in Print

Taxi (Khaled Alkhamissi; 2006) Best-selling novel, and now also play, of 58 fictional monologues of Cairo taxi drivers.

The City Always Wins (Omar Robert Hamilton; 2017) Dazzling first novel set in Cairo during the 2011 uprising.

The Cairo Trilogy (Naguib Mahfouz; 1956–57) By the Nobel prizewinner, this epic trilogy tells the story of three generations of a Cairene family in the early 20th century.

The Yacoubian Building (Alaa Al Aswany; 2007) Best-selling exposé of Egyptian society during the 1990s.

After Mubarak

When interim president Adly Mansour made way for the newly elected President Sisi in June 2014, it was the first time an incumbent Egyptian president had ever relinquished power. Sisi's rule so far, though, has struggled to address Egypt's political and economic instability. There have been grand gestures – most notable being an extra channel for the Suez Canal, pushed through quickly and at vast expense – and even grander statements, including building a new capital city. But behind the headlines, the old problems fester. Mass poverty, poor education and healthcare, growing sectarian conflict and economic turmoil are all, to some degree, interconnected, and none of them can be resolved easily. Steps in 2016 to devalue the Egyptian pound and slash subsidies to secure a US$12 billion loan from the IMF and stimulate the economy have, in the short term, resulted in sky-rocketing prices that have hit the poorest segments of Egyptian society the hardest.

The role of the armed forces, one of the taboo subjects under Mubarak, has become one of the main bones of contention in postrevolution Egypt. But with a former defence minister and field marshal as president, the independence and power of the armed forces remains unchallenged as yet. The continuing crackdown on journalists and political opponents, rights campaigners and other elements of civil society also seriously hampers efforts to address Egypt's problems. For as long as the regime refuses to consider the sort of independent, open government that is needed to address the country's problems, the situation will likely continue to deteriorate.

Pressing Problems

Modern Egypt is bursting at the seams. While presidents and promises have come and gone, the problems they allowed to grow remain: a booming population, notably high unemployment and a basket-case economy. Once home to the all-powerful pharaohs, the country has largely been reduced to dependency on the US, Gulf States, the EU and, most recently, to the IMF.

The list of woes continues and includes torture and ill-treatment of prisoners in detention, described by Amnesty International as 'systematic'; the issue of child labour, particularly within the lucrative national cotton industry (UNICEF reports more than one million children are believed to work in this industry alone); regularly reported cases of 'administrative detention' of individuals without trial, including many pro-democracy activists, which has brought criticism from both local media and international human-rights organisations; continuing restrictions on women under personal-status laws, which, for example, deny the freedom to travel without permission, now compounded by a growing problem of sexual harassment; rampant inflation, leading to food shortages within the poorest communities; and constant environmental threats, with polluted waterways, overpopulation, unregulated emissions, a looming water crisis and soil salinity being of serious concern. Most obvious for the visitor is a crisis in tourism: the crowds that used to throng the temples and tombs now stay on the Red Sea beaches, or at home.

Eternally Egypt

Even in postrevolutionary Egypt, some things have remained unchanged, such as lingering over coffee in one of Alexandria's cosmopolitan cafes or sipping a calming glass of *shai* (tea) after a frenzied shopping episode in Cairo's Khan Al Khalili. Magnificent monuments are everywhere – the pointed perfection of the Pyramids and the majestic tombs and temples of Luxor are some of the wonders that generations of visitors have admired during their city sojourns, jaunts up and down the Nile and expeditions through spectacularly stark desert landscapes.

One thing that can be said with certainty is this: just as the monuments that tell the story of the country's glorious past remain, so too do the special talents that have always singled out the Egyptians – their ability to laugh and to improvise. Whether in the suffocating density of Cairo's city streets or the harsh elements of the open desert, they remain an incredibly resilient people who find humour and optimism in the most unlikely of circumstances. While your travels in Egypt might not always be easygoing or hassle-free, they'll certainly be eye-opening.

POPULATION: **95.7 MILLION**

ANNUAL POPULATION GROWTH RATE: **2.4%**

AVERAGE ANNUAL INCOME: **US$6700**

UNEMPLOYMENT: **12%**

if Egypt were 100 people

63 would be 15-64 years old
32 would be under 14 years old
5 would be over 64 years old

belief systems
(% of population)

90 Muslim
9 Coptic
1 Other

population per sq km

EGYPT   UK   USA

= 30 people

History

The history of Egypt is as rich as the land, as varied as the landscape and as long as the Nile, longer than most in the world. As recent events continue to show, it can also be as lively as the character of its people. While much of Europe was still wrapped in animal skins and wielding clubs, ancient Egyptians enjoyed a sophisticated life, dedicated to maintaining order in the universe and to making the most of their one great commodity, the Nile.

The Nile

The Nation's Gift

The Greek historian Herodotus observed that Egypt was the gift of the Nile, and although it might now be a cliché, it also happens to be true. The ancient Egyptians called it simply *iteru*, the river. Without the Nile, Egypt as we know it would not exist.

The exact history is obscure, but many thousands of years ago the climate of North Africa changed dramatically. Patterns of rainfall also changed and Egypt, formerly a rich savannah, became increasingly dry. The social consequences were dramatic. People in this part of Africa lived as nomads, hunting, gathering and moving across the region with the seasons. But when their pastures turned to desert, there was only one place for them to go: the Nile.

Rainfall in east and central Africa ensured that the Nile in Egypt rose each summer; this happened some time towards the end of June in Aswan. The waters would reach their height around the Cairo area in September. In most years this surge of water flooded the valley and left the countryside hidden. As the rains eased, the river level started to drop and water drained off the land, leaving behind a layer of rich silt washed down from the hills of Africa.

The best source for accurate plans of the Theban tombs can be found in Nicholas Reeves and Richard H Wilkinson's *The Complete Valley of the Kings*, or online at Kent Weeks's Theban Mapping Project (www.theban mappingproject. com).

TIMELINE	c 250,000 BC	c 3100 BC	2650–2323 BC
	Earliest human traces in Egypt. The valley savannah provides ample food for hunter-gatherers until climate change turns lush countryside to desert and forces settlement along the fertile Nile.	Legend credits a pharaoh named Narmer with uniting the people between the Mediterranean and the First Cataract at Aswan. Memphis becomes capital of a united Upper Egypt and Lower Egypt.	This period of great pyramid building at Giza and Saqqara suggests that for part of each year, presumably when the Nile flooded, a substantial workforce was available for civic projects.

Egyptians learned that if they planted seed on this fertile land, they could grow a good crop. As more people settled along the valley, it became more important to make the best use of the annual floodwater, or there would not be enough food for the following year. A social order evolved to organise the workforce to make the most of this 'gift', an order that had farmers at the bottom, bureaucrats and governors in the middle and, at the top of this pyramid, the pharaoh.

Egyptian legend credited all this social development to the good king Osiris, who, so the story went, taught Egyptians how to farm, how to make the best use of the Nile and how to live a good, civil life. The myth harks back to an idealised past, but also ties in with what we know of the emergence of kingship: one of the earliest attributions of kingship, the predynastic Scorpion Macehead, found in Hierakonpolis around 3000 BC, shows an irrigation ritual. This suggests that even right back in early times, making use of the river's gift was a key part of the role of the leader.

Source Stories

The rise of the Nile was a matter of continual wonder for ancient Egyptians, as it remained right up to the 19th century, when European explorers settled the question of the source. There is no evidence that ancient Egyptians knew where this lifeline came from. In the absence of facts, they made up stories.

One of the least convincing of all Egyptian myths concerning the rise of the Nile places the river's source in Aswan, beneath the First Cataract. From the cataract, the river was said to flow north to the Mediterranean and south into Africa.

The river's life-giving force was revered in many ways, most obviously as a god, Hapy. He was an unusual deity in that, contrary to the slim outline of most gods, Hapy was most often portrayed as a pot-bellied man with hanging breasts and a headdress of papyrus. Hapy was celebrated at a feast each year when the Nile rose. In later images he was often shown tying papyrus and lotus plants together, a reminder that the Nile bound together the north and south of the country.

But the most enduring and endearing of all Egyptian myths concerning the river is devoted to the figure of Isis, the mourning wife. Wherever the river originated, the annual rising of the Nile was explained as being tears shed by the mother goddess at the loss of the good king Osiris.

Matters of Fact

Wherever it came from, the Nile was the beginning and end for most Egyptians. They were born beside it and had their first postnatal bath in its waters. It sustained them throughout their lives, made possible

Ancient Egypt: The Great Discoveries by Nicholas Reeves is a chronology of 200 years of marvellous finds, from the Rosetta Stone (1799) to the Valley of the Golden Mummies (1999).

The Modern History of Egypt by PJ Vatiokis is the best one-volume history of the 19th and 20th centuries. John Romer's *A History of Ancient Egypt* is as long and surprising and fascinating as its subject.

2125–1650 BC	1650–1550 BC	1550–1186 BC	1352–1336 BC
Thebes emerges as capital of Upper Egypt and as the pre-eminent seat of religious power. When the Theban ruler Montuhotep II establishes the Middle Kingdom, Thebes becomes its capital.	The Hyksos – western Asian tribes who settled in northern Egypt – control the valley, ushering in the Second Intermediate Period, a time of great technological and social innovation.	Ahmose, prince of Thebes, defeats the Hyksos c 1532 BC and begins a period of expansion into Nubia and Palestine. Over the next two centuries, his successors expand the empire.	Akhenaten establishes monotheism at his new capital, Akhetaten. After his death around 1335 BC, his heir, Tutankhamun, returns the capital to Thebes again and power is restored to the priests of Amun.

the vegetables in the fields, the chickens, cows, ducks and fish on their plates, and filled their drinking vessels when they were thirsty. When it was very hot or at the end of a day's work, it was the Nile that provided relief, a place to bathe. Later, when they died, if they had the funds, their body would be taken along the river to the cult centre at Abydos. And it was water from the Nile that the embalmers used when they prepared the body for burial. But burial was a moment of total separation from this life source for, if you were lucky, you were buried away from the damp, where the dry sands and rocks of the desert would preserve your remains throughout eternity.

Not everything about the river was generous – it also brought dangers in many forms: the crocodile, the sudden flood that washed away helpless children and brought the house down on your head, the diseases that thrived in water, and the creatures (among them the mosquito) that carried them. The river also dictated the rhythm of life and everything started with the beginning of the inundation: New Year fell as the waters rose. This was a time of celebration and also, for some, of relaxation. As the land was covered with water and a boat was needed to travel from one village to the next, farmers found time to catch up on long-neglected chores, fixing tools and working on their houses. This was also the period of the corvée, the labour system by which it is thought many civic projects were built, among them the pyramids, the canal cut through from the Nile to the Red Sea and, in the 19th century, the Suez Canal.

The river also brought the taxman, for it was on the level of flood that the level of the annual tax was set. The formula was simple. Bureaucrats watched the rise of the river on Elephantine Island, where a gauge had been cut along the side of the rock. Each year's flood was recorded at its height. If the water rose to the level of 14 cubits, there would be enough food to go around. If it rose to 16, there would be an abundance – and abundance meant higher taxation. And if there were, say, only eight cubits, then it was time to prepare for the worst because famine would come and many would follow Osiris to the land of spirits beyond the valley.

Old Habits

Even when the old gods were long dead, and roads and railways ran alongside the river, the Nile exerted its magic and its power. In the 18th and 19th centuries it was the way in which foreigners uncovered the mysteries of the past, sailing upriver when the winds blew from the north, and finding themselves face to face with unimaginable splendour. Even then, Egyptians clung to their habits and their dependence on the river. In the 1830s the British Orientalist Edward Lane recorded that 17 June was still called the Night of the Drop. 'It is believed', he wrote, 'that

1294–1279 BC	1279–1213 BC	1184–1153 BC	1070 BC
Seti I restores the empire and initiates a period of neoconservatism: his temple at Abydos copies Old Kingdom styles. He then constructs the finest tomb in the Valley of the Kings.	Seti's son, Ramses II, constructs more buildings than any other pharaoh. He makes Avaris, his home town, the centre of Egyptian trade, but adds to the glory of Thebes.	Ramses III provides a stable moment in an unstable century, controlling the Libyans, defeating the 'Sea People' and suppressing internal dissent. After his death, power slips from the throne.	By the time of his death, Ramses XI has lost control of much of southern Egypt and central authority has disappeared. The New Kingdom grown old.

a miraculous drop then falls into the Nile; and causes it to rise.' Lane also recorded the custom of creating a figure of a girl, the 'Bride of the Nile', out of mud, which was then washed away as the river rose, an echo of an ancient ceremony in which effigies – and perhaps also young women – were sacrificed to the rising river.

Some 100 years later, in 1934, the Egyptologist Margaret Murray spent a mid-September night in a Coptic village, celebrating the night of the high Nile, giving thanks 'to the Ruler of the river, no longer Osiris, but Christ; and as of old they pray for a blessing upon their children and their homes'. (*The Splendour that was Egypt*, 1963, p.233)

This kind of spiritual bond with the river was broken when dams and barrages stopped the annual flood. But Egyptians, whether they live along the river or in one of the new satellite cities in the desert, remain as dependent on the Nile as ever. Now, instead of praying to the 'Ruler of the river', they put their faith in engineers, who, like kings of old, help them make the most of the water; and in politicians, who are currently renegotiating water-sharing agreements with Nile-basin neighbours. Wherever they pin their hopes, they know that, as ever, their existence depends on water flowing past Aswan on its way to the Mediterranean.

Coptic Egypt by Christian Cannuyer tells the story from the earliest preachings by Mark the Evangelist in 1st century AD Alexandria to 21st century Christianity in Egypt.

Christian Egypt

In the Beginning

Coptic tradition states that Christianity arrived in Egypt in AD 45 in the form of St Mark. According to this tradition, St Mark, originally from Cyrene in modern-day Libya, was in Alexandria when his sandal broke. He took it to a cobbler, Ananias, who hurt his hand while working on the sandal and shouted 'O One God', at which St Mark recognised his

---

MARTYRS & HEROES

Alexandria's history is scarred by fights between devotees of different religions, as St Mark discovered to his cost: the man who brought Christianity to Egypt was executed for speaking out against the worship of the city's pagan god Serapis. Many decrees came from Rome that litigated against Christians, the worst coming from Emperor Diocletian. The persecution was so extreme and cost so many lives (some Coptic historians have estimated 144,000) that the Coptic Church calendar, the Era of Martyrs, begins with the year of Diocletian's accession, AD 284. But change was not far away.

In AD 293 Diocletian found himself sharing power with Constantine. In 312, just as Constantine went into battle against his opponents, he had a vision of a cross blazing in the sky, on which was written 'In This Conquer'. When he emerged victorious, becoming ruler of the empire, Constantine converted to Christianity and, in 324, made Christianity the imperial religion.

945–715 BC	663 BC	610–595 BC	525 BC
Libyan settlers become increasingly powerful in the Delta, eventually taking power as the 22nd and 23rd dynasties, but the Egyptian Nile is divided among a series of princes.	Ashurbanipal, King of the Assyrians, attacks Egypt, sacks Thebes and loots the Temple of Amun. Devastated Egypt is ruled by Libyan princes from Sais in the Delta.	Late Period pharaoh Necho encourages foreign trade by strengthening ties (and his navy) in the Mediterranean, cutting a canal to the Red Sea and sending an expedition to sail around Africa.	The Persian king Cambyses makes Egypt part of his empire and rules as pharaoh, launching an attack against Nubia and then on Siwa, in which his army disappears into the desert.

The Penguin Guide to Ancient Egypt by William J Murnane is one of the best overall books on the lifestyle and monuments of the Pharaonic period, with illustrations and descriptions of major temples and tombs.

first convert to the new religion. While there is no way to prove the story, there is no denying the basic truth that Christianity arrived early in Egypt, direct from Palestine.

At the height of their power, ancient Egyptians had exported their religions – Amun of Thebes was known and feared throughout the Mediterranean. And even in times of weakness, the cult of the goddess Isis spread throughout the Roman Empire. But Egyptians were also open to foreign religious ideas. The Persians did little to impose their gods on the country when they sacked Thebes in the 6th century BC and made Egypt part of their empire. Two centuries later, Alexander the Great viewed things differently, at least in the north of the country: while he built shrines to Amun at Karnak and was happy to be welcomed as pharaoh by the priests at Memphis, he also encouraged Greeks and Jews to bring their gods to his new city. Alexandria, under the Macedonian's successors, the Ptolemies, became a centre for multiculturalism, where people of many different beliefs and religions lived and worshipped side by side.

The Early Church

Egypt's Coptic Christians absorbed much from both the form and the content of the ancient pagan religion. It is impossible to make direct parallels, but the rise of the cult of Mary appears to have been influenced by the popularity of Isis: both were said to have conceived through divine intervention. According to the late Coptic musicologist Dr Ragheb Moftah, the way in which the Coptic liturgy was performed seems to have evolved from ancient rites and in it, even today, we can hear an echo of ancient Egypt's rituals. Even the physical structure of Coptic churches echoes the layout of earlier pagan temples in the use of three different sacred spaces, the innermost one containing the altar reserved for priests. This is hidden from the rest of the congregation by the iconostasis, with its images of saints, just as ancient priests were hidden behind walls decorated with gods and pharaohs.

The Complete Pyramids: Solving the Ancient Mysteries by Mark Lehner and Richard H Wilkinson is a readable reference to the famous threesome of Giza and the other 70-plus triangular-sided funerary monuments besides.

The early need to hold hidden prayer, the desire to follow Jesus's example of retreat from the world, the increasing difficulty of reconciling spiritual values with the demands and temptations of urban life, and perhaps also the memory of pagan hermits, led some Christians to leave the Nile Valley and seek spiritual purity in the desert. The man credited with being the first is St Paul, born in Alexandria in AD 228. He fled to the Eastern Desert to escape the persecutions around 250. The desert life obviously suited him for he is said to have survived there for almost a century, dying around 343. Although there are 5th-century accounts of the man, there is still some controversy as to whether St Paul existed. There is no such problem with the man he is said to have inspired.

521–486 BC	c 450 BC	331 BC	323 BC
Persian king Darius I appeases Egyptians by building temples and promoting trade, completing Necho's canal to the Red Sea.	The Greek historian Herodotus visits Egypt and calls it 'the gift of the Nile'.	Alexander invades Egypt and visits the capital, Memphis, and the oracle at Siwa. He lays out a city, Alexandria, that will become the pivot of Hellenic culture in the Mediterranean.	On Alexander's death in Babylon, his general Ptolemy is given control of Egypt. Alexander's body is buried in Alexandria, where Ptolemy builds the Museion and Library and perhaps also the Pharos.

ST ANTHONY: CREATOR OF MONASTICISM

St Anthony was said to be son of wealthy landowners, but found himself orphaned at an early age. As an adult, he sold his inheritance, gave the proceeds to the poor and retreated to the desert near St Paul. Other Christians soon followed, inspired by his example and perhaps also to escape persecution. The hermit moved further up into the hills, hiding alone in a cave, while leaving his followers to a life of collective retreat – the first monastery – in the valley below.

There may have been earlier religious communities in the desert, especially one in Palestine, but St Anthony is credited with creating this new way of living, one that sought salvation through retreat. It was left to St Pachomius, born around AD 285, to order the life of these hermits into what we would now recognise as monasteries, which has proved to be one of the most important movements in Christianity.

Egypt's Christians played a decisive role in the evolution of the young religion. In a series of meetings with Christians from across the empire, Copts argued over the nature of divinity, the duties of a Christian, the correct way to pray and many other aspects of religious life. In one matter in particular, Copts found themselves isolated. Many Christians argued that, as Jesus was born, there must have been a time when he was not divine and part of God. The Coptic clergy, particularly one Athanasius, argued that this idea of a dual nature was a throwback to polytheism. The crunch came in 325 at a council in Nicea, organised by the emperor, at which the Alexandrians triumphed: the Nicene Creed stated unequivocally that Father and Son are one. With this success, Alexandria confirmed its status as the centre of Mediterranean culture.

Death of the Old Gods

In 391 AD Emperor Theodosius issued an edict that banned people from visiting pagan temples, but also even looking at pagan statues. While the edict was ignored in some places, it was taken seriously in Alexandria, where the Temple of Serapis still stood in the city centre. The golden statue of the god remained in his sanctuary, adored by the faithful, until the Christian patriarch of Alexandria stirred a crowd and led them in an attack on the temple: the god was toppled from his plinth – proving false the prophets who foresaw doom should he be damaged – and then dragged through the streets and burned. The crowd is also believed to have set fire to the temple library, which had contained one of the largest collections of scrolls in the world since the Alexandrian 'mother library' had been burned during an attack by Julius Caesar. The patriarch then built a church over the ruins.

Ramses: The Son of Light by Christian Jacq is the first of a five-volume popular hagiography of the famous pharaoh. The prose is simplistic, but Jacq is an Egyptologist and so the basics are accurate.

c 310–250 BC	255 BC	246–221 BC	196 BC
With access to a library of 700,000 written works, Alexandrian scholars calculate the earth's circumference, discover it circles the sun and compile the definitive edition of Homer's poems.	The Greek astronomer Eratosthenes of Cyrene (Libya) settles in Alexandria, from where he makes the first accurate calculation of the world's circumference.	Ptolemy III Euergetes I begins a building program that includes the Serapeum in Alexandria and the Temple of Horus at Edfu. His successor continues his work.	A block of granodiorite stone is carved with a decree in three scripts: hieroglyph, demotic and Greek. Later it will be uncovered in the town of Rosetta and provide the key for deciphering the ancient language.

The site of Luxor Temple has been a place of worship for the last 3500 years and remains one today: the Mosque of Abu Al Haggag is situated high above the great court.

Constantine had moved his capital to the city of Byzantium, renamed Constantinople (now Istanbul), in 330 and from that moment power seeped from Alexandria. More than a century later, in 451, the Egyptians were officially sidelined at the Council of Chalcedon. Refusing to accept that Jesus was one person but had two natures, which again seemed a revival of polytheism, the Egyptians split with the rest of Christianity, their patriarch was excommunicated and soon after Alexandria was sacked.

Yet in spite of the religious split, Egypt was still part of the Byzantine Empire, ruled by a foreign governor, and its fortunes were tied to the empire. This caused ever-greater tension, which peaked in the reign of Emperor Justinian (528–565). Alexandrians stoned the emperor's governor, who retaliated by sending his army to punish the people. In 629 a messenger travelled to the emperor in Byzantium from Arabia. He had been sent by a man named Mohammed to reveal a new religion, Islam. The messenger was murdered on the way. Ten years later, Arab armies invaded Egypt.

After Byzantium

Under their brilliant general Amr Ibn Al As, the Arabs swept through a badly defended and ill-prepared Egypt, defeated the Byzantine army near Babylon and found the gates of Alexandria opened to them without a fight.

Amr didn't force Egyptians to convert to the new religion, but did levy a tax on nonbelievers and showed preference to those who did convert. Slowly, inevitably, the population turned, although how fast is open to dispute. Eventually, however, some monasteries emptied and Coptic writing and language, the last version of the language of the pharaohs, stopped being spoken in public. Christian communities remained strongest in the new capital, Cairo, and in the valley south as far as the ancient capital, Thebes (Luxor). Increasingly, Christians also fell back on the monasteries. In places such as Wadi Natrun and studded along the Nile Valley, monastic communities hid behind their high walls, preserving the old language, the old traditions and, in their libraries, some of the old wisdom.

By the middle of the 19th century, even the monasteries were under threat and European travellers sailing up the Nile were shocked to discover monks swimming naked up to their boats to beg for food and money. The decline continued until the 20th century. By then, only around 10% of Egyptians were Christians and the great monasteries were at their lowest ebb. Ironically, Christianity responded to these threats by enjoying something of a revival. Modernising influences in the early 20th century sparked a cultural renewal that breathed new life into, among other things, the long-defunct tradition of icon painting. Islamist violence

170–116 BC	48 BC	30 BC	AD 45
Ptolemy VIII Euergetes II's reign is characterised by violence and brutality, but also by the opening of the Edfu Temple and by building at Philae and Kom Ombo.	The fire that Julius Caesar lit to destroy the fleet in Alexandria harbour spreads through the city and burns down the Great Library.	After Antony and Cleopatra are defeated at Actium, Ptolemaic rule ends and Roman rule starts, with Egypt initially the personal property of the Octarian (the future emperor Augustus Caesar).	According to Coptic tradition, St Mark arrives in Alexandria this year and converts an Alexandrian cobbler. Christianity is certainly established in Egypt by the end of the century.

aimed at Copts in the 1980s and 1990s had the effect of significantly increasing the number of monks. At St Anthony's Monastery numbers rose from 24 in 1960 to 69 in 1986, and in St Bishoi from 12 to 115.

The election of a Muslim Brotherhood–led government in 2012, in the wake of the downfall of President Mubarak, did nothing to ease tensions and Copts continued to find themselves targeted with impunity. Many wealthier Copts chose to emigrate to the US, Canada or Australia. Also in 2012, the popular Coptic Pope Shenouda III died. He was succeeded by His Holiness Pope Tawadros II, the 118th Patriarch of Alexandria.

The new pope stood alongside the Sheikh of Al Azhar and Field Marshal Sisi to announce the overthrow of the Muslim Brotherhood government in 2013. But in spite of their continued support for Sisi, Copts face ongoing persecution and a lack of security. In 2017 there were bomb attacks against churches on Palm Sunday, and at least 28 died when a gunman fired at a busload of pilgrims near Minya.

The sixth Fatimid caliph, El Hakim, was notorious for his unusual behaviour: convinced that a woman's place was in the home, he banned the manufacture of women's shoes.

The Coming of the Arabs

Around 628 AD a man called Mohammed, the leader of a newly united Arab force, wrote to some of the most powerful men in the world, including the Byzantine Emperor Heraclius, inviting them to convert to his new religion. The emperor, who had never heard of Islam and who regarded the people of Arabia as nothing more than a mild irritant on the edge of his mighty empire, declined. By the time of Heraclius's death in 641, Arab armies had conquered much of the Byzantine Empire, including Syria and most of Egypt, and were camped outside the walls of the Egyptian capital, Alexandria.

FOREIGN INVADERS

The story of ancient Egypt is the story of Egypt's relationships with its neighbours, for its wealth attracted some, and its strategic location on the Mediterranean and Red Seas, and on the trade routes between Africa and Asia, attracted others. When it was strong, it controlled the gold of Nubia and the trade route across the Levant – not for nothing was the image of Ramses II crushing the Hittites at Kadesh splashed across so many temple walls. When Egypt was weak, it caught the attention of the power of the moment. In 663 BC the Assyrian leader Ashurbanipal sacked Thebes. A century later the Persians were in control of the Nile. In 331 BC Alexander the Great moved against the Egyptians and incorporated them into his Hellenic empire. In 30 BC Octavian, the future Roman emperor Augustus Caesar, annexed the country as his own property. Arab armies stormed through in the 7th century AD just as Ottoman ones did in the 16th century, and Egypt remained officially a part of the Ottoman Empire until 1919.

c 271	391	451	640
St Anthony is said to retreat to a cave in the Eastern Desert. He soon attracts others, whom he organises into a loose community, Christianity's first monks.	Byzantine Emperor Theodosius makes paganism a treasonable offence and Alexandria's Temple of Serapis burns.	At the Council of Chalcedon, Egyptian Christians refuse to accept that Jesus Christ had two natures, human and divine, and the Coptic Church separates from the rest of Christianity.	An Arab army under Amr Ibn Al As sweeps through Egypt and establishes a base at the Roman fort of Babylon (now part of Cairo). The following year, Amr captures the Byzantine capital, Alexandria.

The Victorious

Egyptians were used to foreign invaders but had never before experienced any like the Arabs, who came with religious as well as political intentions. After Alexandria fell, the Arab general Amr wrote to his leader, the Caliph Omar, to say that he had captured a city of 4000 palaces, 4000 baths, 400 theatres and 12,000 sellers of green vegetables. Omar, perhaps sensing danger in such sophistication, ordered his army to create a new Muslim capital. The site chosen was beside the Roman fort of Babylon, at the place where the Nile fanned out into the delta. Initially a tented camp known as Al Fustat, Arabic for 'the tents', it soon grew into one of the region's key cities, until it was eclipsed by newer neighbouring settlements – the 8th-century Abbassid city Al Askar, the 9th-century Tulunid city Al Katai and, finally, the 10th-century Fatimid city Al Qahira, Arabic for 'victorious' and the origin of the word Cairo.

Zayni Barakat by Gamal Al Ghitani is full of intrigue, backstabbing and general Machiavellian goings-on in the twilight of Mamluk-era Cairo.

Sunni or Shiite?

The shift of Egypt's capitals was matched by instability in the Arab empire, whose power centre moved from Mecca to Damascus and then Baghdad. This also reflected the shifting nature of the caliphate, the leadership of Islam, divided between the Sunni and the Shiite factions. The earlier Arab dynasties were Sunni. The Fatimids, who conquered Egypt in the 10th century and created the city of Al Qahira, were Shiite. At the centre of their new city was a mosque, Al Azhar, whose sheikh became the country's main authority on religious matters. But Saladin (Salah Ad Din), who took power in Egypt in 1171 and created the Ayyubid dynasty, was a Sunni. From then on, and ever since, the sheikhs of Al Azhar have taught Sunni orthodoxy. The majority of Egyptians today are Sunni.

The Mamluks

One of the last rulers of Saladin's Ayyubid dynasty, a man named Sultan As Salih, brought the innovation of a permanent Turkic slave-soldier class. Most sultans relied on friends and relatives to provide a measure of security. As Salih was so despised by all that he thought it wise to provide his own protection and did so by purchasing a large number of slaves from the land between the Urals and the Caspian. These men were freed on arrival in Egypt – their name, Mamluks, means 'owned' or 'slave' – and formed into a warrior class, which came to rule Egypt.

Mamluks owed their allegiance not to a blood line but to their original owner, the emir. New purchases maintained the groups. There was no system of hereditary lineage; instead it was rule by the strongest. Rare was the sultan who died of old age. Natural-born soldiers, Mamluks fought a series of successful campaigns that gave Egypt control of all of Palestine and Syria, the Hejaz and much of North Africa, the largest

Many of the tales recounted each night by Sheherazade in *The Thousand and One Nights* are set in Mamluk-era Egypt, particularly in Cairo, referred to as 'Mother of the World'.

832	868	969	996
The caliph Al Mamun, son of Haroun Ar Rashid, arrives to suppress a Coptic uprising. He also forces a way into the Pyramid of Cheops, although no treasure is recorded as being found.	Ahmed ibn Tulun, the son of a Turkish Mamluk, took control of Egypt, creating a new dynasty (Tulunid) and a new capital, Al Qatai, in Cairo, of which only his mosque survives.	The Shiite general Jawhar lays the foundations for a new palace-city, Al Qahira (Cairo), and founds a new university-mosque, Al Azhar. Two years later the Fatimid caliph, Al Muizz, settles here from Tunis.	Fatimid caliph Al Hakim ushers in one of the least tolerant of all regimes, forbidding women to leave their houses, discriminating against Christians and Jews, banning the sale of grapes and having all dogs in Cairo killed.

FEATURE: QAITBEY

The contradictions in the Mamluk constitution are typified in the figure of Sultan Qaitbey, who ruled between 1468 and 1496. Bought as a slave-boy by one sultan, he witnessed the brief reigns of nine others before clawing his way to power. As sultan he rapaciously taxed all his subjects and dealt out vicious punishments with his own hands, once tearing out the eyes and tongue of a court chemist who had failed to transform lead into gold. Yet Qaitbey marked his ruthless reign with some of Cairo's most beautiful monuments, notably his madrassa and tomb in the Northern Cemetery.

Islamic empire of the late Middle Ages. Because they were forbidden to bequeath their wealth, Mamluks built on a grand scale, endowing Cairo with exquisite mosques, schools and tombs. During their 267-year reign (1250–1517), the city became the intellectual and cultural centre of the Islamic world.

The funding for the Mamluks' great buildings came from trade. A canal existed that connected the Red Sea with the Nile at Cairo, and thus the Mediterranean, forming a vital link in the busy commercial route between Europe and India and east Asia. In the 14th and 15th centuries, the Mamluks worked with the Venetians to control east–west trade and both grew fabulously rich from it.

The end of these fabled days came about for two reasons at the beginning of the 16th century: Vasco da Gama's discovery of the sea route around the Cape of Good Hope freed European merchants from the heavy taxes charged by Cairo; and the Ottoman Turks emerged as a mighty new force, looking to unify the Muslim world. In 1516 the Mamluks, under the command of their penultimate sultan Al Ghouri, were obliged to meet the Turkish threat. The battle, which took place at Aleppo in Syria, resulted in complete defeat for the Mamluks. In January of the following year the Turkish sultan Selim I entered Cairo, and although the Mamluks remained in power in Egypt, they never again enjoyed their former prominence or autonomy.

> Favoured punishments employed by the Mamluks included *al tawsit*, in which the victim was cut in half at the belly, and *al khazuq* (impaling).

Modern Times

Napoleon & Description de l'Égypte

When Napoleon and his musket-armed forces blew apart the scimitar-wielding Mamluk cavalry at the Battle of the Pyramids in 1798, which he claimed he was doing with the approval of the Ottoman sultan, he dragged Egypt into the age of geopolitics. Napoleon professed a desire to revive Egypt's glory, free it from the yoke of tyranny and educate its masses, but there was also the significant matter of striking a blow at

1171	1249	1250	1260
Saladin, a Kurdish Sunni, seizes power and establishes the Ayyubid dynasty. In 1176 he begins work on a citadel in Cairo, home to the city's rulers for the next seven centuries.	The start of the Fifth Crusade, directed against Egypt and led by Louis IX. The following year, the French king was taken captive by the Egyptians and ransomed for a huge sum.	Mamluk slave warriors, most of Turkish or Kurdish origin, seize control of Egypt. Although their rule is often harsh and anarchic, they build some of Cairo's most impressive and beautiful monuments.	The Mamluk Baybars becomes sultan. He moves against the last Crusaders in the Holy Land, capturing their Syrian stronghold of Krak des Chevaliers in 1271.

At the Battle of
the Pyramids,
Napoleon's forces
took just 45
minutes to rout
the Mamluk army,
killing 1000 for
the loss of 29 of
their own men.

Britain. Napoleon found a way to strike at British interests by capturing Egypt, and in the process taking control of the quickest route between Europe and Britain's fast-growing empire in the East.

Napoleon's forces weren't always successful. In 1798 a British fleet under Admiral Nelson had been criss-crossing the Mediterranean trying to find the French force and, on 1 August, they found them at anchor in Aboukir Bay, off the coast of Alexandria. Only three French warships survived the ensuing Battle of the Nile. Encouraged by the British, the Ottoman sultan sent an army that was trounced by the French, which put paid to any pretence that the French were in Egypt with the complicity of Constantinople. Despite these setbacks, the French still maintained rule.

During Napoleon's time in the newly conquered Egypt, he established a French-style government, revamped the tax system, brought in Africa's first printing press, implemented public-works projects and introduced new crops and a new system of weights and measures. He also brought 167 scholars and artists, whom he commissioned to make a complete study of Egypt's monuments, crafts, arts, flora and fauna, and of its society and people. The resulting work was published as the 24-volume *Description de l'Egypte*, which did much to stimulate the study of Egyptian antiquities.

However, relations between the occupied and occupier deteriorated rapidly and there were regular uprisings against the French in Cairo. When the British landed an army, also at Aboukir, in 1801, the French agreed to an armistice and departed.

The Albanian Kings

The French departure left Egypt politically unstable, a situation that was soon exploited by a lieutenant in an Albanian contingent of the Ottoman army, named Mohammed Ali. Within five years of the French evacuation, he had fought and conspired his way to become pasha (governor) of Egypt. Although he was nominally the vassal of Constantinople, like so many governors before him he soon realised that the country could be his own.

The sultan in Constantinople was too weak to resist this challenge to his power. And once he had defeated a British force of 5000 men, the only threat to Mohammed Ali could come from the Mamluk beys (leaders). Any danger here was swiftly and viciously dealt with. On 1 March 1811, Mohammed Ali invited some 470 Mamluk beys to the Citadel to feast his son's imminent departure for Mecca. When the feasting was over the Mamluks mounted their lavishly decorated horses and were led in procession down the narrow, high-sided defile below what is now the Police Museum. As they approached the Bab Al Azab, the great gates were swung closed and gunfire rained down from above. After the

1468	1517	1798	1805
Mamluk sultan Qaitbey begins a 27-year reign that brings stability to the country. Qaitbey constructs a tomb complex in Cairo and a fort in Alexandria.	Turkish sultan Selim I takes Cairo, executes the last Mamluk sultan and makes Egypt a Turkish province. For almost 300 years it will be ruled, however weakly, from Istanbul.	Napoleon invades, bringing a group of scholars who produce the first full description of Egypt's antiquities. The British force the French out but the French – and European – fascination with ancient Egypt lives on.	An Albanian mercenary, Mohammed Ali, exploits the power vacuum left by the French to seize power and establish a new 'Egyptian' dynasty; his modernisation program transforms the country.

fusillades, Mohammed Ali's soldiers waded in with swords and axes to finish the job. Legend relates that only one Mamluk escaped alive, leaping over the wall on his horse.

Mohammed Ali's reign is pivotal in the history of Egypt. Having watched the old Mamluk army flounder against superior European weapons and tactics, he recognised the need to modernise his new army, as well as his new country. Under his uncompromising rule, Egypt abandoned its medieval-style feudalism and looked to Europe for innovation. In his long reign (he died in 1848), Mohammed Ali modernised the army, built a navy, built roads, cut a new canal linking Alexandria with the Nile, introduced public education, improved irrigation, built a barrage across the Nile and began planting Egypt's fields with the valuable cash crop, cotton. His heirs continued the work, implementing reforms and social projects, foremost of which were the building of Africa's first railway, opening factories and starting a telegraph and postal system. Egypt's fledgling cotton industry boomed as production in the USA was disrupted by civil war, and revenues were directed into ever-grander schemes. Grandest of all was the Suez Canal, which opened in 1869 to great fanfare and an audience that included European royalty, including Empress Eugenie of France.

Khedive Ismail, Mohammed Ali's grandson, had taken on more debt than even Egypt's booming economy could handle and European politicians and banks were quick to exploit his growing weakness. Six years after opening the canal, Ismail was forced to sell his controlling share to the British government, and soon after that, bankruptcy and British pressure forced him to abdicate. This sort of foreign involvement in Egyptian affairs created great resentment, especially among a group of officers in the Egyptian army, who moved against the new khedive. In 1882, under the pretext of restoring order, the British fleet bombarded Alexandria, and British soldiers defeated a nationalist Egyptian army.

The Veiled Protectorate

The British had no desire to make Egypt a colony: their main reason for involvement was to ensure the safety of the Suez Canal. So they allowed the heirs of Mohammed Ali to remain on the throne, while the real power was concentrated in the hands of the British agent Sir Evelyn Baring. By appointing British 'advisors' to Egyptian ministries and himself advising the khedive, Baring operated what became known as the veiled protectorate, colonisation by another name.

British desire to ensure the safety of their passage to India coloured Egyptian policy for the next few decades. For instance, it became increasingly obvious that controlling Egypt meant controlling the Nile and therefore an Egyptian force was sent to protect that interest in Sudan.

Famed as an American icon, the monument now known as the Statue of Liberty was originally intended to stand at the mouth of the Suez Canal.

The opera *Aida* was originally commissioned for the opening ceremony of the Suez Canal, but Verdi was late delivering. *Rigoletto* was performed in 1869 and *Aida* first performed on Christmas Eve, 1871, two years after the opening.

1833	1856	1859	1869
Mohammed Ali's new army moves through the Levant and crushes the Ottoman army at Konya. Constantinople is exposed, but the European powers force the Egyptians to withdraw.	Africa's first railway, between Tanta and Cairo, is built by British engineer Robert Stephenson. The line, extended to Suez in 1858, carries Europeans heading east until the opening of the Suez Canal.	Ferdinand de Lesseps, a French engineer, sees work begin on his project to build a canal between the Mediterranean and Red Seas, making it the quickest way from Europe to the East. The canal takes 10 years to complete.	Khedive Ismail, Mohammed Ali's grandson, opens the Suez Canal. The British, who had preferred a railway, soon take control of the waterway as the quickest route to their Eastern empire.

As a young Egyptian officer during WWII, Anwar Sadat was imprisoned by the British for conspiring with German spies.

When they came up against the Islamist uprising of the Mahdi, and following the death of General Charles Gordon in Khartoum in 1885, British troops became involved on the middle Nile.

Under the 'veiled protectorate' the Suez Canal was secured, Egypt's finances bolstered, the bureaucracy and infrastructure improved, and there were some social advances. But the situation became ever more frustrating for Egyptians with the outbreak of WWI, when Turkey's alliance with Germany allowed Britain to make Egypt an official protectorate.

The Egyptians' desire for self-determination was strengthened by the Allies' use of the country as a barracks during a war that most Egyptians regarded as having nothing to do with them. Popular national sentiments were articulated by riots in 1919 and, more eloquently, by the likes of Saad Zaghloul, the most brilliant of an emerging breed of young Egyptian politicians, who said of the British, 'I have no quarrel with them personally but I want to see an independent Egypt'. The British allowed the formation of a nationalist political party, called the Wafd (Delegation), and granted Egypt its sovereignty, but this was seen as an empty gesture. King Fuad enjoyed little popularity among his people and the British still kept a tight rein on the administration.

The British and their Allies came to Egypt in greater numbers following the outbreak of WWII. The war wasn't all bad news for the Egyptians – certainly not for shopkeepers and businessmen who saw thousands of Allied soldiers pouring into the towns and cities with money to burn on 48-hour leave from the desert. But there was a vocal element who saw the Germans as potential liberators. Students held rallies in support of Rommel, and a small cabal of Egyptian officers, including future presidents Nasser and Sadat, plotted to aid the German general's advance on their city.

Rommel pushed the Allied forces back almost to Alexandria, which had the British hurriedly burning documents in such quantities that the skies over Cairo turned dark with the ash, but the Germans did not break through. Instead, the British maintained a military and political presence in Egypt until a day of flames almost seven years after the war.

Two centuries of the adventures and interests of foreigners in Egypt, up to the 1956 Suez crisis, are evoked in Lonely Planet writer Anthony Sattin's *Lifting the Veil*.

Independent Egypt

Emerging from the Ashes

After years of demonstrations, strikes and riots against foreign rule, an Anglo-Egyptian showdown over a police station in the Suez Canal zone provided the spark that ignited the capital. On 26 January 1952, shops and businesses owned or frequented by foreigners in Cairo were torched by mobs and many landmarks of 70 years of British rule were reduced to charred ruins within a day.

1879	1882	1902	1914
Having bankrupted the country, running up debts of more than £100 million, Khedive Ismail is forced to abdicate but not before selling his shares in the Suez Canal to Britain.	British troops invade to suppress nationalist elements in the army. Although they officially restore power to the khedive, Britain effectively rules Egypt in what becomes the 'veiled protectorate'.	Inauguration of the Aswan Dam and the Asyut Barrage, which help control the Nile flood. The Egyptian Museum is also opened on what is now Cairo's Midan Tahrir.	When Turkey sides with Germany in the war, Britain moves to make Egypt an official British protectorate. A new ruler, Hussein Kamel, takes the title of Sultan of Egypt.

While the smoke cleared, the sense of agitation remained, not just against the British but also against the monarchy that most Egyptians regarded as too easily influenced by the British. King Farouk assumed the monarchy would survive the turmoil because it could count on the support of the Egyptian army. But a faction within the officer corps, known as the Free Officers, had long been planning a coup. On 20 July 1952, the leader of the Free Officers, Colonel Gamal Abdel Nasser, heard that a new minister of war knew of the group and had planned their arrest. Two nights later, army units loyal to the Free Officers moved on key posts in the capital and by the following morning the monarchy had fallen. King Farouk, descendant of the Albanian Mohammed Ali, departed from Alexandria harbour on the royal yacht on 26 July 1952, leaving Egypt to be ruled by Egyptians for the first time since the pharaohs.

Colonel Nasser became president after the 1956 elections. With the aim of returning some of Egypt's wealth to its much-exploited peasantry, but also in an echo of the events of Russia in 1917, the country's landowners were dispossessed and many of their assets nationalised. Nasser also moved against the country's huge foreign community, and although he did not force them to emigrate, his new measures persuaded many to sell up and ship out.

In the year of his inauguration, Nasser successfully faced down Britain and France in a confrontation over the Suez Canal, which was mostly owned by British and French investors. On 26 July, the fourth anniversary of King Farouk's departure, Nasser announced that he had nationalised the Suez Canal to finance the building of a great dam that would control the flooding of the Nile and boost Egyptian agriculture. When a combined British, French and Israeli invasion force, sent to take possession of the canal, was forced into an undignified retreat after the UN and US applied pressure, Nasser emerged from the conflict a hero of the developing world. He was seen as a sort of Robin Hood and Ramses rolled into one, and the man who had finally and publicly shaken off the colonial yoke.

Neighbours & Friends

Nasser's show of strength in 1956 led to many years of drum-beating and antagonism between Egypt and its Arab friends on one side, and their unwelcome neighbour Israel on the other.

Relations with Israel had been hostile ever since its founding in 1948. Egypt had sent soldiers to fight alongside Palestinians against the newly proclaimed Jewish state and ended up on the losing side. Although Nasser privately acknowledged that the Arabs would probably lose another war against Israel, for public consumption he gave rabble-rousing speeches about liberating Palestine. But he was a skilled orator and by

Cairo: The City Victorious by Max Rodenbeck is the most authoritative and entertaining read on the convoluted and picturesque 1000-year history of the Egyptian capital.

HISTORY INDEPENDENT EGYPT

1922	1922	1936	1942
Britain grants Egypt independence, but reserves the right to defend Egypt, its interests in Sudan and, most importantly, the Suez Canal, where Britain continues to maintain a large military presence.	Howard Carter discovers the tomb of Tutankhamun. The first great Egyptological discovery in the age of mass media, the tomb contains more than 3000 objects and takes 10 years to excavate.	The Anglo-Egyptian treaty commits British troops to confine themselves to the Suez Canal and to leave Egypt within 20 years.	The German Field Marshal Rommel pushes his tanks corps across the Libyan coast and into Egypt, causing panic in Cairo. His adversary, British General Montgomery, pushes him back from El Alamein to Tunisia.

early 1967 the mood engendered throughout the Arab world by these speeches was beginning to catch up with him. Soon other Arab leaders started to accuse him of cowardice and of hiding behind the UN troops stationed in Sinai since the Suez Crisis. Nasser responded by ordering the peacekeepers out and blockading the Straits of Tiran, effectively closing the southern Israeli port of Eilat. He gave Israel reassurances that he wasn't going to attack but meanwhile massed his forces east of Suez. In June, Israel struck first, launching a surprise attack that destroyed the Egyptian air force before it was airborne and following up with a ground assault.

When the shooting stopped six days later, Israel controlled all of the Sinai Peninsula and had closed the Suez Canal (which didn't reopen for another eight years). A humiliated Nasser offered to resign, but in a spontaneous outpouring of support, the Egyptian people wouldn't accept this move and he remained in office. However, it was to be for only another three years; in November 1970 the president died of a heart attack.

Anwar Sadat, another of the Free Officers and Egypt's next president, instigated a reversal of foreign policy. Nasser had looked to the Soviet Union for inspiration, but Sadat looked to the US, swapping socialist principles for capitalist opportunism. Having kept a low profile for a decade and a half, the wealthy resurfaced and were joined by a large, new, moneyed middle class who grew rich on the back of Sadat's much-touted *al infitah* (open-door policy). Sadat also believed that to revitalise Egypt's economy he would have to deal with Israel.

In November 1977, a time when Arab leaders still refused to talk publicly to Israel, Sadat travelled to Jerusalem to negotiate a peace treaty with Israel. The following year, he and the Israeli premier signed the Camp David Accords, in which Israel agreed to withdraw from Sinai in return for Egyptian recognition of Israel's right to exist. There was shock in the Arab world, where Sadat's rejection of Nasser's pan-Arabist principles was seen as a betrayal. As a result, Egypt lost much prestige among the Arabs, who moved the HQ of the Arab League out of Cairo, and Sadat lost his life. On 6 October 1981, at a parade commemorating the 1973 war, one of his soldiers, a member of an Islamist group, broke from the marching ranks and sprayed the presidential stand with gunfire. Sadat was killed instantly.

> Both Egypt and Israel were able to claim victory in the October 1973 war. The Egyptians boast of having broken the Israeli hold on Sinai while the Israelis were fighting their way towards Cairo when the UN imposed a ceasefire. This sense of victory helped make the Camp David peace talks possible.

Mubarak & the Rise of the Islamist Movement

Sadat was succeeded by Hosni Mubarak, a former air force chief of staff and vice president. Less flamboyant than Sadat and less charismatic than Nasser, Mubarak was regarded as unimaginative and indecisive, but managed to carry out a balancing act on several fronts, abroad and at home. To the irritation of more hard-line states such as Syria and Libya,

1952	1956	1967	1970
Anti-British sentiment leads to many foreign buildings in Cairo being burned. By the summer, Nasser and his fellow Free Officers have overthrown King Farouk and established the Republic of Egypt.	President Nasser nationalises the Suez Canal. British, French and Israeli forces attack the canal zone, but are forced to retreat.	Egypt, Syria and Jordan are defeated by Israel in the Six Day War. Egypt loses control of the Sinai Peninsula and Nasser resigns, but he is returned to power by popular demand.	Fifty-two-year-old Gamal Abdel Nasser, Egyptian president since 1956, dies of a heart attack and is replaced by his fellow revolutionary Anwar Sadat.

Mubarak rehabilitated Egypt in the eyes of the Arab world without abandoning the treaty with Israel. At the same time, he managed to keep the lid on the Islamist extremists at home. In the early 1990s the lid blew off.

Theories abound regarding the rise of fundamentalist Islamist groups in Egypt. Some believe it had more to do with harsh socio-economic conditions, despite the use of religion by Islamist groups. More than 30 years after the revolution, government promises had failed to keep up with the population explosion and a generation of youths was living in squalid, overcrowded housing, without jobs and many feeling little or no hope for the future. With a political system that allowed little chance to voice legitimate opposition, many felt the only hope lay with Islamist parties such as the Muslim Brotherhood and their calls for change. They were denied recognition by the state as a legal political entity, and in the 1980s and 1990s the Islamists turned to force. There were frequent attempts on the life of the president and his ministers, and clashes with the security forces. The matter escalated from a domestic issue to a matter of international concern when Islamists began to target one of the state's most vulnerable and valuable sources of income: tourists.

Several groups of foreign tourists were shot at, bombed or otherwise assaulted throughout the 1990s, including the 1997 fire-bomb attack on a tour bus outside the Egyptian Museum in Cairo, followed a few weeks later by the killing of holidaymakers at the Temple of Hatshepsut in Luxor by members of the Gama'a Al Islamiyya (Islamic Group), a Muslim Brotherhood splinter group.

The brutality of the massacre and its success at deterring foreign visitors destroyed grassroots support for militants, and the Muslim Brotherhood declared a ceasefire the following year. Things were relatively quiet until October 2004, when bombs at Taba, on the border with Israel, and the nearby Ras Shaytan camp, killed 34 and signalled the start of an unsettled 12 months.

First Elections

In 2005 President Mubarak bowed to growing international pressure to bring the country's political system in line with Western-style democracy, and proposed a constitutional amendment (subsequently approved by parliament and ratified at a national referendum) that aimed to introduce direct and competitive presidential elections. While some pundits saw this as a step in the right direction, others suspected it was a sham, particularly as popular opposition groups such as the Muslim Brotherhood were still banned and other independent candidates were required to have the backing of at least 65 members of the lower house of parliament. As the lower house was dominated by the National Democratic Party (NDP), the possibility of real change was slight. When the Kifaya!

1971	1973	1981	1988
The Aswan High Dam is completed. Eleven years in the making, it extends Lake Nasser to some 510km and Egypt's farmland by 30%. Around 50,000 Nubians and many monuments are relocated.	In October, Egyptian forces attack and cross Israeli defences along the Suez Canal. Although the Egyptians are repulsed and Israel threatens Cairo, the war is seen as an Egyptian success.	President Sadat is assassinated, an event precipitated by his having signed the Camp David peace accord with Israel in 1978. He is replaced by Vice President Hosni Mubarak.	Naguib Mahfouz becomes the first Arab to win the Nobel Prize for Literature. His nomination is the cause of great national pride.

(Enough!) coalition of opposition groups protested at these restrictions, security forces cracked down. Ayman Nour, the leader of the popular Ghad (Tomorrow) party, was jailed on forgery charges. Local human rights organisations questioned the validity of the charges and expressed concern for Nour's safety, while the US released a statement declaring it was 'deeply troubled' by the conviction.

At this stage the banned Muslim Brotherhood began holding its own rallies and there were two isolated terrorist incidents in Cairo aimed at foreign tourists, both carried out by members of the same pro-Islamist family. Soon afterwards, three bombs at the popular beach resort of Sharm El Sheikh claimed the lives of 88 people, most of them Egyptian. Various groups claimed responsibility, tourism took an immediate hit and Egyptians braced themselves for the possibility of further terrorist incursions and domestic unrest.

In 2005 Mubarak won the country's first multicandidate presidential election with 89% of the vote, after a turnout of just 23% of the 32 million registered voters. There were many reports from observers, such as the Egyptian Organization for Human Rights (EOHR), of disorganisation, intimidation and abusive security forces at the polls, and opposition parties and candidates (including Ayman Nour) alleged the vote was unfair and the result invalid. Still, other observers noted the process was a great improvement on previous elections.

In subsequent parliamentary elections in November 2005, Muslim Brotherhood independents won 88 seats in the 444-seat national parliament (six times the number they had previously held), making the Brotherhood a major player on the national political scene despite its officially illegal status.

Egypt Moving Forward

On 11 February 2011 President Mubarak resigned as president. The most obvious reason for his departure, 30 years into his presidency, was the hundreds of thousands of people who had been demonstrating for months, most notably in an 18-day occupation of Cairo's Midan Tahrir. Mubarak's loss of support among the Egyptian military and the US may have been equally significant. Economic problems, particularly a rise in food prices, and the prospect of Gamal Mubarak succeeding his ailing father were among many reasons for the loss of popularity. The huge popular reaction to the death of Khaled Said – killed in Alexandria by security forces in the summer of 2010 – was an indication of how desperate many Egyptians had become in the last years of Mubarak's rule.

The euphoria that followed Mubarak's departure was heightened by the fact that security forces had not fired on protestors. The army was seen as the protector of the revolution and people in Tahrir chanted 'the

1997	2011	2012	2013
Sixty-two foreign tourists and Egyptians are gunned down at the Temple of Hatshepsut in Luxor, an event that sparks a security crackdown and a tourism crisis.	Mubarak resigns as president after mass protests against his regime throughout the country, most notably in Cairo's Midan Tahrir. He is replaced by a ruling council of his former generals.	The Muslim Brotherhood emerges from Egypt's first democratic parliamentary elections with 235 of the 508 seats. The biggest surprise is the 121 seats won by the extreme Islamist Salafi party, Nour.	The Brotherhood's Mohammed Morsi is overthrown after only a year as president, following mass demonstrations across the country.

people, the army, one hand'. Mubarak's old generals, including former minister for defence and head of armed forces Field Marshal Tantawi, took power and formed a ruling council.

The Supreme Council of the Armed Forces (SCAF) presented itself as an honest broker to usher the country towards democracy, but before elections were held, ensured autonomy for the armed forces by passing a decree that future governments will not be able to select the head of the armed forces or intervene in the military's internal or economic affairs.

Egypt's first open presidential and parliamentary elections in 2012 confirmed the rise of the Muslim Brotherhood and Salafist parties. The Brotherhood's Mohammed Morsi became Egypt's first democratically elected president. The euphoria that greeted his election soon faded after he pushed through a pro-Islamist constitution, granted himself unlimited powers, put himself beyond the law and suppressed public protests. By the summer of 2013 Egypt's economic crisis had created huge queues at petrol stations and daily power cuts to homes and business. Millions took to the streets to demand his resignation. When that failed, the army stepped in.

Morsi's defence minister, Abdel Fattah Al Sisi, who was behind the regime change, insisted he had no desire for power. But in spring 2014, with an interim government in place, Sisi resigned from the army, with the rank of field marshal, and announced his candidacy. Only one person opposed him, left-wing politician Hamdeen Sabahi. Sisi won around 96% of the votes. But although he had called for 40 million Egyptians, some 75% of the electorate, to turn out to vote, more than half of them abstained. Although he could claim to have the backing of more Egyptians than Morsi ever had, Sisi's position was weakened by the low turnout. Not that this has stopped him from increasing his grip on power.

President Sisi presented himself as the popular choice and was seen among the people soon after his election, at hospital bedsides, cycling in the streets. But he soon became seen as yet another authoritarian leader. Within a couple of years, he had established a more repressive regime than his predecessors, passing laws that make it almost impossible for there to be a popular uprising against him and outlawing civil rights groups among others. But at the same time, he has failed to defeat the Islamist insurgency in Sinai – bomb attacks against Copts in Tanta and Alexandria in spring 2017 and the attack on the Al Rawda Mosque in northern Sinai which killed over 300 people in December 2017, were proof of that.

2013	2014	2015	2017
Protest sit-ins outside the Rabaa Al Adaweya and Al Nahda mosques in Cairo are broken up by security forces. Casualty figures are disputed but at least 900 protesters die that day (Amnesty International figures).	In June, Field Marshal Abdel Fatah Al Sisi is sworn in as president after a landslide victory in an election where less than half of the electorate turned out to vote.	In August, Sisi opens a 22-mile Suez Canal extension at a cost of US$8.4 billion.	In June, Sisi ratifies an agreement to give two uninhabited Red Sea islands to Saudi Arabia, in spite of widespread protests and legal challenges.

Ancient Egypt & the Pharaohs

Despite its rather clichéd image, there is so much more to ancient Egypt than temples, tombs and Tutankhamun. As the world's first nation-state, predating the civilisations of Greece and Rome by several millennia, Egypt was responsible for some of the great achievements in human history – it was one of the places where writing was invented in 3200 BC, the first stone monuments were erected and an entire culture set in place, which remained largely unchanged for thousands of years.

Eternal Life

All of Egypt's achievements were made possible by the Nile River, which brought life to this virtually rainless land. In contrast to the vast barren 'red land' of desert, which the Egyptians called *deshret,* the narrow river banks were known as *kemet* (black land), a reference to the rich silt deposited by the river's annual floods. Abundant harvests grown in this red earth were then gathered as taxes by a highly organised bureaucracy working on behalf of the pharaoh. They used this wealth to run the administration and to fund ambitious building projects designed to enhance royal status.

The Greeks were so impressed with the ancient culture that they regarded Egypt as the 'cradle of civilisation', and even the occupying Romans adopted the country's ancient gods and traditions.

The survival of these pyramids, temples and tombs often give the misleading impression that Egyptians were a morbid bunch obsessed with religion and death. In fact it seems they, or at least the elite, loved life so much that they went to enormous lengths to ensure the fun continued forever.

This longing for eternity suffused almost every aspect of ancient Egyptian life and gave the culture its incredible coherence and conservatism. Egyptians believed they had to appease their gods so they would take care of them. The pharaoh, who ruled by divine approval, ensured order in a world of chaos and was the intermediary between the people and the gods. Absolute monarchy was therefore integral to Egyptian culture.

Although successive invaders took over Egypt from the end of the New Kingdom (around 1069 BC), Egypt's indigenous culture was so deeply rooted that they could not escape its influence. Libyans, Nubians and Persians all came to adopt traditional Egyptian ways, and their kings and emperors continued to build temples to the Egyptian gods, and to proclaim their divine birth on the temple walls. It was only at the end of the 4th century AD, when the Roman Empire adopted Christianity, that this ancient Egyptian belief system finally collapsed: their gods were taken from them, their temples were closed and all knowledge of the 'pagan' hieroglyphs that transmitted their culture was lost, until it was recovered in the 19th century.

The Great Monuments

Ancient Egyptians built a stunning array of monumental buildings along the Nile. They had very little wood, so they mainly used sun-baked mudbrick for their houses, fortresses and palaces. Of these, very little remains today. For their tombs and temples, however, they used quarried sandstone, limestone or granite, which in many cases have really withstood the test of time.

Temples

Many gods had their own cult centres, but they were also worshipped at various temples throughout Egypt. Built on sites considered sacred, existing temples were added to by successive pharaohs to demonstrate their piety. This is best seen at the enormous complex of Karnak, the culmination of 2000 years of reconstruction.

Surrounded by huge enclosure walls of mudbrick, the stone temples within were regarded as houses of the gods where daily rituals were performed on behalf of the pharaoh. As the intermediary between gods and humans, the pharaoh was high priest of every temple, although in practice these powers were delegated to each temple's high priest.

As well as temples to house the gods (cult temples), there were also funerary (mortuary) temples where each pharaoh was worshipped after death. Eventually sited away from their tombs for security reasons, the best examples are on Luxor's West Bank, where pharaohs buried in the Valley of the Kings had huge funerary temples built closer to the river. These include Ramses III's temple at Medinat Habu, Amenhotep III's once vast temple marked by the Colossi of Memnon and the best known example built by Hatshepsut into the cliffs of Deir Al Bahri.

Pyramids

Initially, tombs were created to differentiate the burials of the elite from the majority, whose bodies were placed directly into the desert sand.

By around 3100 BC the mound of sand heaped over a grave was replaced by a more permanent structure of mudbrick, whose characteristic bench-shape is known as a mastaba, after the Arabic word for bench.

As stone replaced mudbrick, the addition of further levels to increase height created the pyramid, the first built at Saqqara for King Zoser. Its stepped sides soon evolved into the familiar smooth-sided structure, with the Pyramids of Giza the most famous examples.

Pyramids are generally surrounded by the mastaba tombs of officials wanting burial close to their pharaoh in order to share in an afterlife, which was still the prerogative of royalty.

Rock-Cut Tombs

When the power of the monarchy broke down at the end of the Old Kingdom, the afterlife became increasingly accessible to those outside the royal family, and as officials became more independent they began to opt for burial in their home towns.

With little room for grand superstructures along many of the narrow stretches beside the Nile, an alternative type of tomb developed, cut tunnelfashion into the cliffs that border the river. Most were built on the west bank, the traditional place of burial where the sun was seen to sink down into the underworld each evening. These simple rock-cut tombs consisting of a single chamber gradually developed into more elaborate structures complete with an open courtyard, offering a chapel and entrance facade carved out of the rock, with a shaft leading down into a burial chamber.

The most impressive rock-cut tombs were those built for the kings of the New Kingdom (1550–1069 BC), who relocated the royal burial ground south to the religious capital Thebes (modern Luxor), to a remote desert valley on the west bank, now known as the Valley of the Kings. There is evidence suggesting the first tomb (KV 39) here may have been built by Amenhotep I. The tomb of his successor Tuthmosis I was built by royal architect Ineni, whose biographical inscription states that he supervised

The funerary texts in the tombs gave the deceased all the knowledge that would be needed to reach the afterlife: knowledge of the power of those in the underworld, knowledge of the hidden forces, knowledge of each hour and each god, knowledge of the gates the deceased must pass through and knowledge of how the powerful enemies could be destroyed.

The worldly goods buried with the mummies for use in the afterlife give valuable details about everyday life and how it was lived, be it in the bustling, cosmopolitan capital Memphis or in the small rural settlements scattered along the banks of the Nile.

its construction alone, 'with no one seeing, no one hearing'. In a radical departure from tradition, the offering chapels that were once part of the tomb's layout were now replaced by funerary (mortuary) temples built some distance away to preserve the tomb's secret location.

The tombs themselves were designed with a long corridor descending to a network of chambers decorated with scenes to help the deceased reach the next world. Many of these were extracts from the Book of the Dead, the modern term for ancient funerary works including the Book of Amduat (literally, 'that which is in the underworld'), the Book of Gates and the Litany of Ra. These describe the sun god's nightly journey through the darkness of the underworld, the realm of Osiris, with each hour of the night regarded as a separate region guarded by demigods. In order for Ra and the dead souls who accompanied him to pass through on their way to rebirth at dawn, it was essential that they knew the demi gods' names in order to get past them.

Pharaonic Who's Who

Egypt's Pharaonic history is based on the regnal years of each pharaoh, a word derived from *per-aa,* meaning palace. Among the many hundreds of pharaohs who ruled Egypt over a 3000-year period, the following are some of the names found most frequently around the ancient sites:

Narmer (Menes; c 3100 BC) The first king to unite Lower and Upper Egypt. Narmer from south (Upper) Egypt is portrayed as victorious on the famous Narmer Palette in the Egyptian Museum. He is perhaps to be identified with the semi-mythical King Menes, founder of Egypt's ancient capital city Memphis.

Zoser (Djoser; c 2667–2648 BC) As second king of the 3rd dynasty, Zoser was buried in Egypt's first pyramid, the world's oldest monumental stone building, designed by the architect Imhotep. Zoser's statue in the foyer of the Egyptian Museum shows a long-haired king with a slight moustache.

Sneferu (c 2613–2589 BC) The first king of the 4th dynasty, and held in the highest esteem by later generations, Sneferu was Egypt's greatest pyramid builder. He was responsible for four such structures, and his final resting place, the Red (Northern) Pyramid at Dahshur, was Egypt's first true pyramid and a model for the more famous pyramids at Giza.

Khufu (Cheops; c 2589–2566 BC) As Sneferu's son and successor, Khufu was the second king of the 4th dynasty. Best known for Egypt's largest pyramid, the Great Pyramid at Giza, his only surviving likeness is Egypt's smallest royal sculpture, a 7.5cm-high figurine in the Egyptian Museum.

Khafre (Khephren, Chephren; c 2558–2532 BC) Khafre was a younger son of Khufu who succeeded his half-brother to become fourth king of the 4th dynasty. He built the second of Giza's famous pyramids and is best known as the model for the face of the Great Sphinx.

Menkaure (Mycerinus; c 2532–2503 BC) As the son of Khafre and fifth king of the 4th dynasty, Menkaure built the smallest of Giza's three huge pyramids. He is also well represented by a series of superb sculptures in the Egyptian Museum.

Amenhotep I (c 1525–1504 BC) As second king of the 18th dynasty, Amenhotep I ruled for a time with his mother Ahmose-Nofretari. They founded the village of Deir Al Medina for the workers who built the tombs in the Valley of the Kings, and Amenhotep I may have been the first king to be buried there.

Hatshepsut (c 1473–1458 BC) As the most famous of Egypt's female pharaohs, Hatshepsut took power at the death of her brother-husband Tuthmosis II and initially ruled jointly with her nephew-stepson Tuthmosis III.

Tuthmosis III (c 1479–1425 BC) As sixth king of the 18th dynasty, Tuthmosis III (the Napoleon of ancient Egypt) expanded Egypt's empire with a series of foreign campaigns into Syria. He built extensively at Karnak, added a chapel at Deir Al Bahri and his tomb was the first in the Valley of the Kings to be decorated.

Amenhotep III (c 1390–1352 BC) As ninth king of the 18th dynasty, Amenhotep

III's reign marks the zenith of Egypt's culture and power. He is the creator of Luxor Temple and the largest ever funerary temple marked by the Colossi of Memnon, and his many innovations, including Aten worship, are usually credited to his son Amenhotep IV (later 'Akhenaten').

Akhenaten (Amenhotep IV; c 1352–1336 BC) Changing his name from Amenhotep to distance himself from the state god Amun, Akhenaten relocated the royal capital to Amarna with his wife Nefertiti. While many still regard him as a monotheist and benign revolutionary, the evidence suggests he was a dictator whose reforms were political rather than religious.

Nefertiti (c 1338–1336 BC (?)) Famous for her painted bust in Berlin, Nefertiti ruled with her husband Akhenaten, and while the identity of his successor remains controversial, it may have been Nefertiti herself, using the throne name 'Smenkhkare'.

Tutankhamun (c 1336–1327 BC) As the 11th king of the 18th dynasty, Tutankhamun's fame is based on the great quantities of treasure discovered in his tomb in 1922. The son of Akhenaten by one of Akhenaten's sisters, Tutankhamun reopened the traditional temples and restored Egypt's fortunes after the disastrous reign of his father.

Horemheb (c 1323–1295 BC) As a military general, Horemheb restored Egypt's empire under Tutankhamun and after the brief reign of Ay, eventually became king himself, marrying Nefertiti's sister Mutnodjmet. His tomb at Saqqara was abandoned in favour of a royal burial in a superbly decorated tomb in the Valley of the Kings.

Seti I (c 1294–1279 BC) The second king of the 19th dynasty, Seti I continued to consolidate Egypt's empire with foreign campaigns. Best known for building Karnak's Hypostyle Hall, a superb temple at Abydos and a huge tomb in the Valley of the Kings.

Ramses II (c 1279–1213 BC) As son and successor of Seti I, Ramses II fought the Hittites at the Battle of Kadesh and built temples including Abu Simbel and the Ramesseum, once adorned with the statue that inspired poet PB Shelley's 'Ozymandias'.

Ramses III (c 1184–1153 BC) As second king of the 20th dynasty, Ramses III was the last of the warrior kings, repelling several attempted invasions portrayed in scenes at his funerary temple Medinat Habu.

Taharka (690–664 BC) As fourth king of the 25th dynasty, Taharka was one of Egypt's Nubian pharaohs and his daughter Amenirdis II was high priestess at Karnak, where Taharka undertook building work. A fine sculpted head of the king is in Aswan's Nubian Museum, and he was buried in a pyramid at Nuri in southern Nubia.

Alexander the Great (331–323 BC) Alexander invaded Egypt in 331 BC, founded Alexandria, visited Amun's temple at Siwa Oasis to confirm his divinity, and after his untimely death in Babylon in 323 BC, his mummy was eventually buried in Alexandria.

Ptolemy I (323–283 BC) As Alexander's general and rumoured half-brother, Ptolemy seized Egypt at Alexander's death and established the Ptolemaic line of pharaohs. Ruling in traditional style for 300 years, they made Alexandria the greatest capital of the ancient world.

Cleopatra VII (51–30 BC) As the 19th ruler of the Ptolemaic dynasty, Cleopatra VII ruled with her brothers Ptolemy XIII and then Ptolemy XIV before taking power herself. A brilliant politician who restored Egypt's former glories, she married Julius Caesar then Mark Antony, whose defeat at Actium in 31 BC led to the couple's suicide.

Thirty royal dynasties ruled over a 3000-year period, now divided into the Old, Middle and New Kingdoms separated by intermittent periods of unrest (Intermediate periods) when the country split into north (Lower Egypt) and south (Upper Egypt).

The vast quantities of food and drink offered in temples and tombs were duplicated on surrounding walls to ensure a constant supply for eternity. The offerings are shown piled up in layers, sometimes appearing to float in the air if the artist took this practice too far.

CHRONOLOGY OF THE PHARAOHS

EARLY DYNASTIC PERIOD

1st Dynasty	**3100–2890 BC**
Narmer (Menes)	c 3100 BC
2nd Dynasty	**2890–2686 BC**

OLD KINGDOM

3rd Dynasty	**2686–2613 BC**
Zoser	2667–2648 BC
Sekhemket	2648–2640 BC
4th Dynasty	**2613–2494 BC**
Sneferu	2613–2589 BC
Khufu (Cheops)	2589–2566 BC
Djedefra	2566–2558 BC
Khafre (Chephren)	2558–2532 BC
Menkaure (Mycerinus)	2532–2503 BC
Shepseskaf	2503–2498 BC
5th Dynasty	**2494–2345 BC**
Userkaf	2494–2487 BC
Sahure	2487–2475 BC
Neferirkare	2475–2455 BC
Shepseskare	2455–2448 BC
Raneferef	2448–2445 BC
Nyuserra	2445–2421 BC
Unas	2375–2345 BC
6th Dynasty	**2345–2181 BC**
Teti	2345–2323 BC
Pepi I	2321–2287 BC
Pepi II	2278–2184 BC
7th–8th Dynasties	**2181–2125 BC**

FIRST INTERMEDIATE PERIOD

9th–10th Dynasties	**2160–2025 BC**

MIDDLE KINGDOM

11th Dynasty	**2055–1985 BC**
Montuhotep II	2055–2004 BC
Montuhotep III	2004–1992 BC
12th Dynasty	**1985–1795 BC**
Amenemhat I	1985–1955 BC
Sesostris I	1965–1920 BC
Amenemhat II	1922–1878 BC
Sesostris II	1880–1874 BC
Sesostris III	1874–1855 BC
Amenemhat III	1855–1808 BC
Amenemhat IV	1808–1799 BC
13th–14th Dynasties	**1795–1650 BC**

SECOND INTERMEDIATE PERIOD	
15th–17th Dynasties	**1650–1550 BC**
NEW KINGDOM	
18th Dynasty	**1550–1290 BC**
Ahmose	1550–1525 BC
Amenhotep I	1525–1504 BC
Tuthmosis I	1504–1492 BC
Tuthmosis II	1492–1479 BC
Tuthmosis III	1479–1425 BC
Hatshepsut	1473–1458 BC
Amenhotep II	1427–1400 BC
Tuthmosis IV	1400–1390 BC
Amenhotep III	1390–1352 BC
Akhenaten	1352–1336 BC
Tutankhamun	1336–1327 BC
Horemheb	1323–1295 BC
19th Dynasty	**1295–1186 BC**
Ramses I	1295–1294 BC
Seti I	1294–1279 BC
Ramses II	1279–1213 BC
Seti II	1200–1194 BC
20th Dynasty	**1186–1069 BC**
Ramses III	1184–1153 BC
THIRD INTERMEDIATE PERIOD	
21st Dynasty	**1069–945 BC**
Psusennes I	1039–991 BC
22nd–23rd Dynasties	**945–712 BC**
24th–26th Dynasties	**727–525 BC**
LATE PERIOD	
27th Dynasty	**525–404 BC**
Cambyses	525–522 BC
Darius	521–486 BC
28th–31st Dynasties	**404–332 BC**
GRAECO-ROMAN PERIOD	
Macedonian and Ptolemaic	**332–30 BC**
Alexander the Great	332–323 BC
Ptolemy I	305–282 BC
Ptolemy III	246–222 BC
Ptolemy VIII	170–163 and 145–116 BC
Cleopatra VII	51–30 BC
Roman	**30–313 BC**
Augustus	30 BC–AD 14
Hadrian	117–138
Diocletian	284–305

The texts for the afterlife give various visions of paradise, from joining the sun god Ra in his journey across the sky, to joining Osiris in the underworld or rising up to become one of the Imperishable Stars, the variety of final destinations reflecting the ancient Egyptians' multi faceted belief system.

Gods & Goddesses

Initially representing aspects of the natural world, Egypt's gods and goddesses grew more complex through time. As they began to blend together and adopt each other's characteristics, they started to become difficult to identify, although their distinctive headgear and clothing can provide clues as to who they are. The following brief descriptions should help travellers spot at least a few of the many hundreds who appear on monuments and in museums.

Amun The local god of Thebes (Luxor) who became the state god of the New Kingdom Egypt. Originally he may have been associated with the power of the wind, and he was a creator god. Later he became closely associated with the fertility god Min and combined with the sun god to create Amun-Ra, king of the gods. He is generally portrayed seated on a throne with a double-plumed crown and sometimes the horns of his sacred ram to accentuate his procreative vigour.

Anubis The funerary god who deals with burial and afterlife. Anubis is the god of mummification, the patron of embalmers and guardian of cemeteries is generally depicted as a black jackal or a jackal-headed man.

Apophis The huge snake embodying darkness and chaos was the enemy of the sun god Ra. It tried to destroy him every night during his journey through the underworld, to prevent him reaching the dawn. Seth speared the serpent, and the blood stain that was left explained the red sky at sunset and sunrise.

Aten The solar disc whose rays end in outstretched hands was worshipped as a god during the 18th dynasty, and became chief deity under the reign of Akhenaten.

Atum Creator god of Heliopolis who rose from the primeval waters and ejaculated (or sneezed, depending on the myth) to create gods and humans. He was also the god who would destroy everything at the end of times. Generally depicted as a man wearing the double crown, but sometimes also with the head of a ram or a scarab, Atum represented the setting sun.

Bastet Cat goddess whose cult centre was Bubastis; ferocious when defending her father Ra the sun god, she was often shown as a friendly deity, a symbol of motherhood, personified by the domestic cat.

Bes A household deity, Bes was a grotesque yet benign dwarf god fond of music and dancing; he kept evil from the home and protected women in childbirth by waving his knives and sticking out his tongue.

Geb God of the earth associated with vegetation and fertility, he is generally depicted as a green man lying beneath his sister-wife Nut, the sky goddess, supported by their father Shu, god of air. He is the father of Osiris, Isis, Seth and Nephtys.

Hapy God of the Nile flood and the plump embodiment of fertility shown as an androgynous figure with sagging breasts and a swollen belly, sometimes shown with a clump of papyrus on his head.

Hathor Goddess of love, sexuality and pleasure represented as a cow or a woman with a crown of horns and sun disc in her guise as the sun god's daughter. Patron of music and dancing whose principle cult centre was at Dendara, she was known as 'she of the beautiful hair' and 'lady of drunkenness'. She was the wife of Horus.

Horus Falcon god of the sky and son of Isis and Osiris, he avenged his father to rule on earth and was personified by the ruling pharaoh. He can appear as a falcon or a man with a falcon's head, and his eye *(wedjat)* was a powerful amulet. Horus, the husband of Hathor, was closely associated with kingship and is often seen hovering as a falcon over the pharaoh's head.

Isis Goddess of magic and protector of her brother-husband Osiris and their son Horus. She represented the ideal wife, made the first mummy of Osiris' body and was a protector of the dead. As symbolic mother of the pharaoh she appears as a woman with a throne-shaped crown, or sometimes has Hathor's cow horns. She is often seen suckling the infant Horus.

Khepri God of the rising sun represented by the scarab beetle, whose habit of rolling balls of dirt was likened to the sun's journey across the sky.

Khnum Ram-headed god who created life on a potter's wheel; he also controlled the waters of the Nile flood from his cave at Elephantine and his cult centre was Esna.

Khons Young god of the moon and son of Amun and Mut. He is generally depicted in human form wearing a crescent moon crown and the 'sidelock of youth' hairstyle.

Maat Goddess of cosmic order, truth and justice, depicted as a woman wearing an ostrich feather on her head, or sometimes by the feather alone.

Mut Amun's consort and one of the symbolic mothers of the king; her name means both 'mother' and 'vulture' and she is generally shown as a woman with a vulture headdress.

Nekhbet Vulture goddess of Upper Egypt worshipped at Al Kab; she often appears with her sister-goddess Wadjet the cobra, protecting the pharaoh.

Nut Sky goddess usually portrayed as a woman whose star-spangled body arches across tomb and temple ceilings. She swallows the sun each evening to give birth to it each morning.

Osiris God of death, fertility and resurrection whose main cult centre was at Abydos. As the first mummy created, he was magically revived by Isis to produce their son Horus, who took over the earthly kingship, while Osiris became ruler of the underworld and symbol of eternal life. He represented good, while his brother Seth represented evil.

Ptah Creator god of Memphis who brought the world into being by his thoughts and spoken words. He is patron of craftsmen, wears a tight-fitting robe and a skullcap, and usually clutches a tall sceptre (resembling a 1950s microphone).

Ra The supreme deity in the Egyptian pantheon, the sun god is generally shown as a man with a falcon's head topped by a sun disc, although he can take many forms (eg Aten, Khepri) and other gods merge with him to enhance their powers (eg Amun Ra, Ra-Atum). In his underworld aspect he can be shown with a ram's head. Ra travelled through the skies in a boat, sinking down into the underworld each night before re-emerging at dawn to bring light.

Sekhmet Lioness goddess of Memphis whose name means 'the powerful one'. As a daughter of sun god Ra she was capable of great destruction and was the bringer of pestilence, her priests functioned as doctors, and her statues were erected to protect Egypt from the plague.

Seth God of chaos and confusion personified by a mythological, composite animal. In pre-Dynastic times the king was revered as the incarnation of both Horus and Seth. However, during the Old Kingdom, the myth arose that after murdering his brother Osiris he was defeated by Horus, and from then on he was regarded as evil, too dangerous to be depicted on temple walls, even as a hieroglyph.

Sobek Crocodile god representing Pharaonic might, he was worshipped at Kom Ombo and Fayyum. Both sites had sacred lakes with crocodiles.

Taweret Hippopotamus goddess who often appears upright to scare evil from the home and protect women in childbirth.

Thoth God of knowledge and writing, and patron of scribes. He is portrayed as an ibis or baboon, or most frequently as an ibis-headed man holding a scribe's palette, and his cult centre was at Hermopolis. He was closely identified with the moon, and was considered the guardian of the deceased in the underworld.

The earliest monumental hieroglyphs were found in 2017 on a rock outside El Kaba and they date from 3250 BC. The last hieroglyphic inscription was carved on a temple wall in Philae on 24 August AD 394.

ANCIENT EGYPT & THE PHARAOHS GODS & GODDESSES

The Egyptian calendar was based on the annual cycle of the Nile, with three seasons – *akhet* (inundation), *peret* (spring planting) and *shemu* (summer harvest). As the flood waters receded by October, farmers planted their crops in the silt left behind, using irrigation canals to water their crops until harvest in April.

Art in Life & Death

Ancient Egyptian art is instantly recognisable, its distinctive style remaining largely unchanged for more than three millennia. With its basic characteristics already in place at the beginning of the Pharaonic Period (c 3100 BC), the motif of the king smiting his enemies on the Narmer Palette was still used in Roman times.

The Purpose of Art

Despite being described in modern terms as 'works of art', the reasons for the production of art in ancient Egypt are still very much misunderstood. Egyptian art was primarily functional, and closely linked to religion and ideology. All ancient Egyptian art was part of a unified system of representation; there was no tradition of an individual artistic expression. To represent an object in art was to make it eternal, to give it permanence. There was also a standard repertoire of funerary scenes, from the colourful images that adorn the walls of tombs to the highly detailed vignettes illuminating funerary texts. Each image, whether carved on stone or painted on papyrus, was designed to serve and protect the deceased on their journey into the afterlife.

The majority of artefacts were produced for religious and funerary purposes and, despite their breathtaking beauty, would have been hidden away from the public gaze, either within a temple's dark interior or, like Tut's mask, buried in a tomb with the dead. This only makes the objects – and those who made them – even more remarkable. Artists regarded the things they made as pieces of equipment to do a job rather than works of art to be displayed and admired.

HOW TO WRAP A MUMMY

Mummification was used by many ancient cultures, but the Egyptians were the masters of this highly complex procedure, which they refined over thousands of years.

At first bodies were simply buried in the desert away from cultivation. The hot, dry conditions and aridity of the sand allowed body fluids to drain away while preserving the skin, hair and nails intact.

As society developed, those who would once have been buried in a hole in the ground demanded tombs befitting their status. But as the bodies were no longer in direct contact with the sand, they rapidly decomposed. An alternative means of preservation was therefore required. After a long process of experimentation, and a good deal of trial and error, the Egyptians seem to have finally cracked it around 2600 BC when they started to remove the internal organs, where putrefaction begins.

All the organs were removed except the kidneys, which were hard to reach, and the heart, considered to be the source of intelligence. The brain was generally removed by inserting a metal probe up the nose and whisking until it had liquefied sufficiently to be drained down the nose. All the rest – lungs, liver, stomach and intestines – were removed through an opening cut in the left flank. Then the body and its separate organs were covered with natron salt (a combination of sodium carbonate and sodium bicarbonate) and left to dry out for 40 days, after which they were washed, purified and anointed with a range of oils, spices and resins. All were then wrapped in layers of linen, with the appropriate amulets set in place over the various parts of the body as priests recited the necessary incantations.

With each of the internal organs placed inside its own burial container (one of four Canopic jars), the wrapped body with its funerary mask was placed inside its coffin. It was then ready for the funeral procession to the tomb, where the vital Opening of the Mouth ceremony reanimated the soul and restored its senses. The essential offerings of food and drink then sustained the soul of the deceased that resided within the mummy as it was finally laid to rest inside the tomb.

The Egyptians believed it was essential that the things they portrayed had every relevant feature shown as clearly as possible. Then when they were magically reanimated through the correct rituals they would be able to function as effectively as possible, protecting and sustaining the unseen spirits of both the gods and the dead.

Figures needed a clear outline, with a profile of nose and mouth to let them breathe, and the eye shown whole as if seen from the front, to allow the figure to see. This explains why eyes were often painted on the sides of coffins to allow the dead to see out and why hieroglyphs such as snakes or enemy figures were sometimes shown in two halves to prevent them causing damage when re-activated.

> The ancient Egyptians' secret to a contented life is summed up by the words of one of their poems: 'it is good to drink beer with happy hearts, when one is clothed in clean robes'.

Art & Nature

While working within very restrictive conventions, the ancient artists still managed to capture a feeling of vitality. Inspired by the natural world around them, they selected images to reflect the concept of life and rebirth, as embodied by the scarab beetles and tilapia fish thought capable of self-generation. Since images were also believed able to transmit the life force they contained, fluttering birds, gambolling cattle and the speeding quarry of huntsmen were all favourite motifs. The life-giving properties of plants are also much in evidence, with wheat, grapes, onions and figs stacked side by side with the flowers the Egyptians loved so much. Particularly common are the lotus (water lily) and papyrus, the heraldic symbols of Upper and Lower Egypt often shown entwined to symbolise a kingdom united.

The Meaning of Colour

Egypt was represented politically by the White Crown of Upper Egypt and the Red Crown of Lower Egypt, fitted together in the dual crown to represent the unification of the two lands.

The country was also represented by the colours red and black, the red desert wastes of *deshret* contrasting with the fertile black land of *kemet*. For Egyptians, black was the colour of life, and black was the colour of choice to represent Osiris, the god of fertility and resurrection, in contrast to the redness associated with his brother Seth, god of chaos. Sometimes Osiris is also shown with green skin, the colour of vegetation and new life. Some of his fellow gods are blue to echo the ethereal blue of the sky, and the golden yellow of the sun is regularly employed for its protective qualities.

Human figures were initially represented with different-coloured skin tones, the red-brown of men contrasting with the paler, yellowed tones of women, and although this has been interpreted as indicating that men spent most of the time working outdoors whereas women led a more sheltered existence, changes in artistic convention meant everyone was eventually shown with the same red-brown skin tone.

Romancing the Stone

Sculptors worked in a variety of different mediums, with stone often chosen for its colour – white limestone and alabaster (calcite), golden sandstone, green schist (slate), brown quartzite and both black and red granite. Smaller items could be made of red or yellow jasper; orange carnelian or blue lapis lazuli; metals such as copper, gold or silver; or less-costly materials such as wood or highly glazed blue faience pottery.

All these materials were used to produce a wide range of statuary for temples and tombs, from 20m-high stone colossi to gold figurines a few centimetres tall. Amulets and jewellery were another means of ensuring the security of the dead. While their beauty would enhance the appearance of the living, each piece was also carefully designed as a protective talisman or a means of communicating status. Even when creating such small-scale masterpieces, the same principles employed in larger-scale works of art applied, and little of the work that the ancient craftsmen produced was either accidental or frivolous.

Texts for the Afterlife

Initially, the afterlife was restricted to royalty and the texts meant to guide the pharaohs towards eternity were inscribed on the walls of their burial chambers. Since the rulers of the Old Kingdom were buried in pyramids, the accompanying funerary writings are known as the **Pyramid Texts**.

In the hope of sharing in the royal afterlife, Old Kingdom officials built their tombs close to the pyramids until the pharaohs lost power at the end of the Old Kingdom. No longer reliant on the pharaoh's favour, the officials began to use the royal funerary texts for themselves. Inscribed on their coffins, they are known as **Coffin Texts** – a Middle Kingdom version of the earlier Pyramid Texts, adapted for nonroyal use.

This 'democratisation' of the afterlife evolved even further when the Coffin Texts were literally brought out in paperback, inscribed on papyrus and made available to the masses during the New Kingdom. It's now referred to by the modern term the **Book of the Dead**, but he Egyptians knew this as the Book of Coming Forth by Day. There are sections entitled 'Spell for not dying a second time', 'Spell not to rot and not to do work in the land of the dead' and 'Spell for not having your magic taken away'. These spells and instructions acted as a kind of guidebook to the afterlife, with some of the texts accompanied by maps, and images of some of the gods and demons that would be encountered en route together with the correct way to address them.

Royal vs Commoner Tomb Decoration

The New Kingdom royal tombs in the Valley of the Kings are decorated with highly formal scenes showing the pharaoh in the company of the gods and all the forces of darkness defeated. Since the pharaoh was always pharaoh, even in death, there was no room for the informality and scenes of daily life that can be found in the tombs of lesser mortals.

THE HUNTING SCENE

In one of the most common nonroyal tomb scenes, the tomb owner is seen hunting on the river. On a basic level one can see this as the deceased enjoying a day out boating with his family. However, the scene is far more complex than it first appears. The tomb owner, shown in a central position in the prime of life, strikes a formal pose as he restores order amid the chaos of nature all around him. In his task he is supported by the female members of his family, from his small daughter to the wife standing serenely beside him. Dressed far too impractically for a hunting trip on the river, his wife wears an outfit more in keeping with a priestess of Hathor, goddess of love and sensual pleasure. Yet Hathor is also the protector of the dead and capable of great violence as defender of her father, the sun god Ra, in his eternal struggle against the chaotic forces of darkness.

Some versions of this riverside hunting scene also feature a cat. Often described as a kind of 'retriever' (who ever heard of a retriever cat?), the cat is one of the creatures who was believed to defend the sun god on his nightly journey through the underworld. Similarly, the river's teeming fish were regarded as pilots for the sun god's boat and were themselves potent symbols of rebirth. Even the abundant lotus flowers are significant, since the lotus, whose petals open each morning, is the flower that symbolised rebirth. Once the coded meaning of ancient Egyptian art is understood, such previously silent images almost scream out the idea of 'life'.

MAGIC SIGNS

The small figures of humans, animals, birds and symbols that populate the script were believed to infuse each scene with divine power. In fact certain signs were considered so potent they were shown in two halves to prevent them causing havoc should they magically reanimate.

Yet the ancient Egyptians also liked a joke, and their language was often onomatopoeic – for example, the word for cat was 'miw' after the noise it makes, and the word for wine was 'irp', after the noise made by those who drank it.

The nonroyal tombs show a much more relaxed, almost eclectic nature of scenes, which feature everything from eating and drinking to dancing and hairdressing. But here again, these apparently random scenes of daily life carry the same message found throughout Egyptian art – the eternal continuity of life and the triumph of order over chaos. As the pharaoh is shown smiting the enemy and restoring peace to the land, his subjects contribute to this continual battle of opposites in which order must always triumph for life to continue.

A common tomb scene is the banquet at which guests enjoy generous quantities of food and drink. Although no doubt reflecting some of the pleasures the deceased had enjoyed in life, the food portrayed was also meant to sustain their souls, as would the accompanying scenes of bountiful harvests which would ensure supplies never ran out. Even the music and dance performed at these banquets indicate much more than a party in full swing – the lively proceedings were another way of reviving the deceased by awakening their senses.

The culmination of this idea can be found in the all-important Opening of the Mouth ceremony, performed by the deceased's heir (either the next king or the eldest son). The ceremony was designed to reanimate the ka (soul), which could then go on to enjoy eternal life once all its senses had been restored. Noise and movement were believed to reactivate hearing and sight, while the sense of smell was restored with incense and flowers. The essential offerings of food and drink sustained the soul that resided within the mummy as it was finally laid to rest inside the tomb.

Hieroglyphs

Hieroglyphs, meaning 'sacred carvings' in Greek, are the pictorial script used by the ancient Egyptians. It is generally agreed that writing was invented in Sumer, Mesopotamia. Egyptian hieroglyphs differ greatly from Mesopotamian cuneiform, but some suggest that the Egyptians took the concept of writing from the Sumerians, but developed their own script. Others believe that the Egyptians developed the world's first script. For 3500 years it remained fairly unchanged, only written by a very small literary elite, while the spoken language underwent huge changes.

The Privilege of Writing

It is very possible that the overall literacy rate in ancient Egypt was less than 1% of the entire population, but the impact of hieroglyphs on Egyptian culture cannot be overestimated, as they provided the means by which the state took shape. They were used by a civil service of scribes working on the king's behalf to collect taxes and organise vast workforces.

During the Old Kingdom, literary works included funerary texts, letters, hymns and poems; by the early Middle Kingdom, narrative Egyptian literature was created by the growing intellectual class of scribes.

THE WISE SCRIBE

A huge civil service of scribes worked on the pharaoh's behalf to record taxes and organise workers. Taught to read and write in the schools attached to temples where written texts were stored and studied, the great majority of scribes were male. However, some women are also shown with documents and literacy would have been necessary to undertake roles they are known to have held, including overseer, steward, teacher, doctor, high priestess, vizier and even pharaoh on at least six occasions.

Within a few centuries, day-to-day transactions were undertaken in a shorthand version of hieroglyphs known as hieratic, whereas hieroglyphs remained the perfect medium for monumental inscriptions. Covering every available tomb and temple surface, hieroglyphs were regarded as 'the words of Thoth', the ibis-headed god of writing and patron deity of scribes, who, like the scribes, is often shown holding a reed pen and ink palette.

Reading Hieroglyphs

Hieroglyphs may at first appear deceptively simple, but they are best understood if divided into three categories – logograms (ideograms), determinatives and phonograms. Logograms represent the thing they depict (eg the sun sign meaning 'sun'), while determinatives are simply placed at the ends of words to reinforce their meaning (eg the sun sign in the verb 'to shine'). Phonograms are less straightforward and represent either one, two or three consonants.

The 26 signs usually described in simple terms as 'the hieroglyphic alphabet' are the single consonant signs (eg the owl pronounced 'm', the zig-zag water sign 'n'). Another 100 or so signs are biconsonantal (eg the bowl sign read as 'nb'), and a further 50 are triconsonantal signs (eg 'nfr' meaning good, perfect or beautiful). There are no actual vowels as such.

It can be a bit tricky to read ancient Egyptian texts. Scribes usually wrote hieroglyphs from right to left, and in columns which needed to be read from top to bottom. But sometimes they wrote from left to right. To complicate matters further, no punctuation was used. The direction human figures or animals face is usually a pointer to the way one should read the text.

What's in a Name?

The majority of hieroglyphic inscriptions are endless repetitions of the names and titles of the pharaohs and gods, surrounded by protective symbols. Names were of tremendous importance to the Egyptians and as vital to an individual's existence as their ka, and it was sincerely believed that 'to speak the name of the dead is to make them live'.

Royal names were also followed by epithets such as 'life, prosperity, health', comparable to the way in which the name of the Prophet Mohammed is always followed by the phrase 'peace be upon him'. For further protection, royal names were written inside a rectangular fortress wall known as a *serekh,* which later developed into the more familiar oval-shaped cartouche (the French word for cartridge).

Although each pharaoh had five names, cartouches were used to enclose the two most important ones: the 'prenomen' or 'King of Upper and Lower Egypt' name assumed at the coronation and written with a bee and a sedge plant; and the 'nomen' or 'Son of Ra' name, which was given at birth and written with a goose and a sun sign.

As an example, Amenhotep III is known by his nomen or Son of Ra name 'Amun-hotep' (meaning Amun is content), although his prenomen or King of Upper and Lower Egypt name was Neb-maat-Re (meaning

As well as a priests and priestesses, temples employed their own scribes, butchers, gardeners, florists, perfume-makers, musicians and dancers, many of whom worked on a part-time basis.

Ra, lord of truth). His grandson had the most famous of all Egyptian names, Tut-ankh-amun, which literally translates as 'the living image of Amun', yet he had originally been named Tut-ankh-aten, meaning 'the living image of the Aten' – a change in name that reflects the shifting politics of the time.

The loss of one's name meant permanent obliteration from history, and those unfortunate enough to incur official censure included commoners and pharaohs alike. At times it even happened to the gods themselves, a fate which befell the state god Amun during the reign of the 'heretic' pharaoh Akhenaten, who in turn suffered the same fate together with his god Aten when Amun was later restored.

In order to prevent this kind of obliteration, names were sometimes carved so deeply into the rock it is possible to place an outstretched hand right inside each hieroglyph, as is the case of Ramses III's name and titles at his funerary temple of Medinat Habu.

Gods were incorporated into the names of ordinary people, and as well as Amunhotep there was Rahotep (the sun god Ra is content) and Ptahhotep (the creator god Ptah is content). By changing 'hotep' (meaning 'content') to 'mose' (meaning 'born of'), the names Amenmose, Ramose and Ptahmose meant that these men were 'born of' these gods.

In similar fashion, goddesses featured in women's names. Hathor, goddess of love, beauty and pleasure, was a particular favourite, with names such as Sithathor (daughter of Hathor). Standard male names could also be feminised by the simple addition of 't', so Nefer (good, beautiful or perfect) becomes Nefert, which could be further embellished with the addition of a verb, as in the case of the famous name Nefertiti (goodness/beauty/perfection has come).

Others were known by their place of origin, such as Panehesy (the Nubian), or could be named after flora and fauna – Miwt (cat), Debet (hippopotamus) and Seshen (lotus), which is still in use today as the name Susan.

Everyday Living

With ancient Egypt's history focused on its royals, the part played by the rest of the ancient population is frequently ignored. The great emphasis on written history also excludes the 99% of the ancient population who were unable to write, and it can often seem as if the only people who lived in ancient Egypt were pharaohs, priests and scribes.

The silent majority are often dismissed as little more than illiterate peasants, although these were the very people who built the monuments and produced the wealth on which the culture was based.

Fortunately Egypt's climate, at least, is democratic, and has preserved the remains of people throughout society, from the mummies of the wealthy in their grand tombs to the remains of the poorest individuals buried in hollows in the sand.

Domestic Life

In Egypt's dry climate, houses were traditionally built of mudbrick, whether they were the narrow back-to-back homes of workers or the sprawling palaces of the royals. The main differences were the number of rooms and the quality of fixtures and fittings. The villas of the wealthy often incorporated walled gardens with stone drainage systems for small pools, and some even had en-suite bathroom facilities – look out for the limestone toilet seat found at Amarna and now hanging in the Egyptian Museum in Cairo.

Just like the mudbrick houses in rural Egypt today, ancient homes were warm in winter and cool in summer. Small, high-set windows re-

THE LADY OF THE HOUSE

The home was very much the female domain. The most common title for women of all social classes was *nebet per* (lady of the house), emphasising their control over most aspects of domestic life. Although there is little evidence of marriage ceremonies, monogamy was standard practice for the majority, with divorce and remarriage relatively common and initiated by either sex. With the same legal rights as men, women were responsible for running the home, and although there were male launderers, cleaners and cooks, it was mainly women who cared for the children, cleaned the house, made clothing and prepared food in small open-air kitchens adjoining the home.

duced the sun's heat but allowed breezes to blow through, and stairs gave access to the flat roof where the family could relax or sleep.

While homes were often whitewashed on the outside to deflect the heat, interiors were usually painted in bright colours, the walls and floors of wealthier homes further enhanced with gilding and inlaid tiles. Although the furniture of most homes would have been quite sparse – little more than a mudbrick bench, a couple of stools and a few sleeping mats – the wealthy could afford beautiful furniture, including inlaid chairs and footstools, storage chests, beds with linen sheets and feather-stuffed cushions. Most homes also had small shrines for household deities and busts of family ancestors, and a small raised area seems to have been reserved for women in childbirth.

The staple food was bread, produced in many varieties, including the dense calorie-laden loaves mass-produced for those working on government building schemes. Onions, leeks, garlic and pulses were eaten in great quantities along with dates, figs, pomegranates and grapes. Grapes were also used, along with honey, as sweeteners. Spices, herbs, nuts and seeds were added to food, along with oil extracted from native plants and imported almonds and olives. Although cows provided milk for drinking and making butter and cheese, meat was only eaten regularly by the wealthy and by priests allowed to eat temple offerings once the gods had been satisfied. This was mostly beef, although sheep, goats and pigs were also eaten, as were game and wild fowl. Fish was generally dried and salted and, because of its importance in workers' diets, a fish-processing plant existed at the pyramid builders' settlement at Giza.

Although the wealthy enjoyed wine (with the best produced in the vineyards of the Delta and western oases, or imported from Syria), the standard beverage was a rather soupy barley beer, which was drunk throughout society by everyone, including children.

At Work

The majority of ancient Egyptians were farmers, whose lives were based around the annual cycle of the Nile. Agriculture was so fundamental to life in both this world and the next that it was one of the dominant themes in tomb scenes. The standard repertoire of ploughing, sowing and reaping is often interspersed with officials checking field boundaries or calculating the grain to be paid as tax in this pre-coinage economy. The officials are often accompanied by scribes busily recording all transactions, with hieroglyphs now known to have been first developed c 3250 BC as a means of recording produce.

Closely related to the scribe's profession were the artists and sculptors who produced the stunning artefacts synonymous with ancient Egypt. From colossal statues to delicate jewellery, all were fashioned using simple tools and natural materials.

Building stone was hewn by teams of labourers supplemented by prisoners, with granite obtained from Aswan, sandstone from Gebel Silsila, alabaster from Hatnub near Amarna and limestone from Tura near modern Cairo. Gold came from mines in the Eastern Desert and Nubia, and both copper and turquoise were mined in the Sinai. With such precious commodities being transported large distances, trade routes and border areas were patrolled by guards, police (known as *medjay*) and the army, when not out on campaign.

Men also plied their trade as potters, carpenters, builders, metalworkers, jewellers, weavers, fishermen and butchers, with many of these professions handed down from father to son: this is especially well portrayed in the tomb scenes of Rekhmire. There were also itinerant workers such as barbers, dancers and midwives, and those employed for their skills as magicians. Men worked alongside women as servants in wealthy homes, performing standard household duties, and thousands of people were employed in the temples, which formed the heart of every settlement as a combination of town hall, college, library and medical centre.

Laundry marks were found on ancient garments; male launderers were employed by the wealthy, and even a few ancient laundry lists have survived, listing the types of garments they had to wash in the course of their work.

Clothing & Jewellery

Personal appearance was clearly important to the Egyptians, with wigs, jewellery, cosmetics and perfumes worn by men and women alike. Garments were generally linen, made from the flax plant before the introduction of cotton in Ptolemaic times. Status was reflected in the fineness and quantity of the linen, but as it was expensive, surviving clothes show frequent patching and darning.

The most common garment was the loincloth, worn like underpants beneath other clothes. Men also wore a linen kilt, sometimes pleated, and both men and women wore the bag-tunic made from a rectangle of linen folded in half and sewn up each side. The most common female garments were dresses, most wrapped sari-like around the body, although there were also V-neck designs cut to shape, and detachable sleeves for easy cleaning.

Linen leggings have also been found, as well as socks with a gap between the toes for wearing with sandals made of vegetable fibre or leather. Plain headscarves were worn to protect the head from the sun or during messy work; the striped nemes (headcloth) was only worn by the pharaoh, who also had numerous crowns and diadems for ceremonial occasions.

Jewellery was worn by men and women throughout society for both aesthetic and magical purposes. It was made of various materials, from gold to glazed pottery, and included collars, necklaces, hair ornaments, bracelets, anklets, belts, earrings and finger rings.

Hairstyles

Wigs and hair extensions were popular, at least from c 3400 BC, as was the use of henna (*Lawsonia inermis*) as a hair dye. Many people shaved or cropped their hair for cleanliness and to prevent head lice (which have been found in the hair of pharaohs). The clergy had to shave their heads for ritual purity and children's heads were partially shaved to leave only a side lock of hair as a symbol of youth.

Pharaonic Glossary

akh	usually translated as 'transfigured spirit', produced when the *ka* (soul) and *ba* (spirit) united after the deceased was judged worthy enough to enter the afterlife
Ammut	composite monster of the underworld who was part crocodile, part lion and part hippo, and ate the hearts of the unworthy dead; her name means 'The Devourer'
ba	usually translated as 'spirit', which appeared after death as a human-headed bird, able to fly to and from the tomb and into the afterlife
Book of the Dead	modern term for the collection of ancient funerary texts designed to guide the dead through the afterlife, developed at the beginning of the New Kingdom and partly based on the earlier Pyramid Texts and Coffin Texts
Canopic jars	containers usually made of limestone or calcite to store the preserved entrails (stomach, liver, lungs and intestines) of mummified individuals
cartouche	the protective oval shape (the name derived from the French word for cartridge), which surrounded the names of kings, queens and occasionally gods
cenotaph	a memorial structure set up in memory of a deceased king or queen, separate from their tomb or funerary temple
Coffin Texts	funerary texts developed from the earlier Pyramid Texts, which were then written on coffins during the Middle Kingdom
coregency	a period of joint rule by two pharaohs, usually father and son
cult temple	the standard religious building(s) designed to house the spirits of the gods and accessible only to the priesthood, usually located on the Nile's east bank
deshret	'red land', referring to barren desert
djed pillar	the symbolic backbone of Osiris, bestowing strength and stability and often worn as an amulet
false door	the means by which the soul of the deceased could enter and leave the world of the living to accept funerary offerings brought to their tomb
funerary (mortuary) temple	the religious structures where the souls of dead pharaohs were commemorated and sustained with offerings, usually built on the Nile's west bank
Heb-Sed festival	the jubilee ceremony of royal renewal and rejuvenation, which pharaohs usually celebrated after 30 years' rule
Heb-Sed race	part of the Heb-Sed festival when pharaohs undertook physical feats such as running to demonstrate their prowess and fitness to rule
hieratic	ancient shorthand version of hieroglyphs used for day-to-day transactions by scribes
hieroglyphs	Greek for 'sacred carvings', referring to ancient Egypt's formal picture writing used mainly for tomb and temple walls
hypostyle hall	imposing section of temple characterised by densely packed monumental columns
ka	Usually translated as 'soul', this was a person's 'double', which was created with them at birth and which lived on after death, sustained by offerings left by the living
kemet	'black land', referring to the fertile areas along the Nile's banks
king lists	chronological lists of each king's names kept as a means of recording history
lotus (water lily)	the heraldic plant of Upper (southern) Egypt
mammisi	the Birth House attached to certain Late Period and Graeco-Roman temples and associated with the goddesses Isis and Hathor
mastaba	Arabic word for bench, used to describe the mudbrick tomb structures built over subterranean burial chambers and from which pyramids developed

name	an essential part of each individual given at birth, and spoken after their death to allow them to live again in the afterlife
naos	sanctuary containing the god's statue, generally located in the centre of ancient temples
natron	mixture of sodium carbonate and sodium bicarbonate used to dry out the body during mummification and used by the living to clean linen, teeth and skin
nemes	the yellow-and-blue striped headcloth worn by pharaohs, the most famous example found on Tutankhamun's golden death mask
nomarch	local governor of each of Egypt's 42 nomes
nome	Greek term for Egypt's 42 provinces – 22 in Upper Egypt and later 20 added in Lower Egypt
obelisk	monolithic stone pillar tapering to a pyramidal top that was often gilded to reflect sunlight around temples and usually set in pairs
Opening of the Mouth ceremony	the culmination of the funeral, performed on the mummy of the deceased by their heir or funerary priest using spells and implements to restore their senses
Opet festival	annual celebration held at Luxor Temple to restore the powers of the pharaoh at a secret meeting with the god Amun
papyrus	the heraldic plant of Lower (northern) Egypt whose reedlike stem was sliced and layered to create paperlike sheets for writing
pharaoh	term for an Egyptian king derived from the ancient Egyptian word for palace, per-aa
pylon	monumental gateway with sloping sides forming the entrance to temples
Pyramid Texts	funerary texts inscribed on the walls of late Old Kingdom pyramids and restricted to royalty
sacred animals	living creatures thought to represent certain gods – eg the crocodile (identified with Sobek), the cat (identified with Bastet) – and often mummified at death
sarcophagus	derived from the Greek for 'flesh eating' and referring to the large stone coffins used to house the mummy and its wooden coffin(s)
scarab	the sacred dung beetle believed to propel the sun's disc through the sky in the same way the beetle pushes a ball of dung across the floor
serapeum	vast network of underground catacombs at Saqqara in which the Apis bulls were buried, later associated with the Ptolemaic god Serapis
serdab	from the Arabic word for cellar, a small room in a mastaba tomb containing a statue of the deceased to which offerings were presented
shabti (or ushabti)	small servant figurines placed in burials designed to undertake any manual work in the afterlife on behalf of the deceased
shadow	an essential part of each individual, the shadow was believed to offer protection, based on the importance of shade in an extremely hot climate
sidelock of youth	characteristic hairstyle of children and certain priests in which the head is shaved and a single lock of hair allowed to grow
solar barque	the boat in which the sun god Ra sailed through the heavens, with actual examples buried close to certain pyramids for use by the spirits of the pharaohs
Uraeus	an image of the cobra goddess Wadjet worn at the brow of royalty to symbolically protect them by spitting fire into the eyes of their enemies
Weighing of the Heart (The Judgement of Osiris)	the heart of the deceased was weighed against the feather of Maat with Osiris as judge; if light and free of sin they were allowed to spend eternity as an *akh,* but if their heart was heavy with sin it was eaten by Ammut and they were damned forever

The Egyptian People

A badge worn by a Cairene woman soon after President Mubarak stepped down read 'Egyptian and proud'. Understanding what it means to be Egyptian has never been easier, nor more difficult, because there are now so many possibilities. But one characteristic that still links the majority of Egyptians, from the university professor in Alexandria to the shoeshine boy in Luxor, is an immense pride in simply being Egyptian, pride in their extraordinary history and in some of their recent achievements.

Sense of Community

It's hard sometimes for outsiders to see where the Egyptians' sense of pride comes from, given the pervasive poverty, low literacy levels, high unemployment, housing shortages, infrastructure failings and myriad other pitfalls that face the country. But aiding each Egyptian in the daily struggle is every other Egyptian, and indeed there is a real sense that everybody's in it together. Large extended families and close-knit neighbourhoods act as social support groups, strangers fall easily into conversation with each other, and whatever goes wrong, somebody always knows someone somewhere who can help fix it.

Comforters

For Egyptians, religion cushions life's blows and permeates every aspect of life. But for many, the Muslim Brotherhood's brand of Islam was too strident: Egyptians love enjoying themselves too much to welcome an authoritarian, politicised version of Islam. But religion is always there in the background. Ask after someone's health and the answer, from a Christian or a Muslim, is *Alhamdulallah* (Fine. Praise to God). Arrange to meet tomorrow and it's *Inshallah* (God willing). Then, if your appointee fails to turn up, God obviously didn't mean it to be.

And when all else fails – and it so often fails – there's humour. Egyptians are renowned for it. Jokes and wisecracks are the parlance of life. Comedy is the staple of the local cinema industry and the backbone of TV scheduling. The stock character is the little guy who through wit and a sharp tongue always manages to prick pomposity and triumph over the odds. Laughter lubricates the wheels of social exchange and one of the most enjoyable aspects of travelling in Egypt is how much can be negotiated with a smile.

Lifestyle

The people of the south – anywhere south of Minya and down as far as Aswan – are known as Saidis (pronounced sai-eed-ees). They tend to be more traditional than people of the north.

There's no simple definition of Egyptian society. There are obviously unfathomable differences between someone living off their land in the Nile Delta and someone working in Cairo. But even among the latter, there are extremes of experience. On the one hand there's religious conservatism, where women wear the long, black, all-concealing *abaya* and men wear the gownlike *galabeya*. In traditional circles, cousins marry cousins; going to Alexandria constitutes the trip of a lifetime; and all is 'God's will'. On the other hand, there are sections of society whose members order out from McDonald's; whose daughters wear slinky black numbers and flirt outrageously; who think nothing of regular trips to the US; and who never set foot in a mosque until the day they're laid out in one. The bulk of the Egyptian populace falls somewhere between these two extremes.

A City Story

The typical urban family is among the 11 million Cairenes who live in 'informal housing' (slums), in a six-floor breeze-block apartment building with cracking walls and dodgy plumbing in an overcrowded suburb. They are probably not technically poor – only 18% of Cairenes live below the poverty line. If they're lucky they may own a small car; otherwise, the husband will fight for a handhold on one of the city's sardine-can buses. He may well be a university graduate (about 40,000 people graduate each year), although a degree no longer guarantees a job – graduate unemployment has shot up in the past decade. He may also be one of the million-plus paper-pushing civil servants, earning a pittance to while away each day in an undemanding job. This at least allows him to slip away from work early each afternoon to borrow his cousin's taxi for a few hours to bring in some much-needed supplementary cash. His wife remains at home cooking, looking after the three or more children, and swapping visits with his mother, her mother and various other family members.

The Country Scene

Life in rural Egypt is undergoing a transformation. Just over half the country's population lives there, creating some of the most densely populated agricultural land in the world. What little land remains is divided into small plots (averaging just 0.6 hectares), which don't even support a medium-sized family. Just under one-third of Egyptians make their living off the land. Returns are small – agriculture accounts for just 14% of Egypt's GDP – which explains why so many live below the poverty line. The small size of plots prevents mechanisation and improved yields. As a result, farmers increasingly rely on animal husbandry or look for other ways of surviving. The farmer you see working his field may spend his afternoons working as a labourer or selling cigarettes from a homemade kiosk to make ends meet.

The countryside remains the repository of traditional culture and values. Large families are still the norm, particularly in Upper Egypt, and extended families still live together. High rates of female illiteracy are standard. Though all of this is gradually changing.

BACKHAND ECONOMY

Baksheesh means tip, but it's more than just a reward for services rendered. Salaries and wages in Egypt are much lower than in Western countries (the average monthly wage across the country is LE4000), so baksheesh is an essential means of supplementing income. Even Egyptians have to constantly dole out the baksheesh – to park their cars, receive mail and ensure they get fresh produce at the grocers.

For travellers not used to tipping, demands for baksheesh for pointing out the obvious in museums can be quite irritating. But services such as opening a door, delivering room service or carrying your bags warrant baksheesh. This may only be a few Egyptian pounds, but will always be welcome.

We suggest carrying lots of small change with you (trust us – you'll need it!) and also to keep it separate from bigger bills. And remember, there is only one immutable rule and that is that you can never give too much.

Sport

Egypt is football obsessed. The country hosts the Egyptian Premier League, which is regarded as one of the top 20 most competitive leagues in the world. The two most popular clubs are Ahly and Zamalek; both are located in Cairo and both inspire fervent loyalty in their fans. The Egyptian national team hasn't qualified for the FIFA World Cup since 1990 (and its 2009 loss to Algeria in a qualifier match sparked passionate protests and riots in Egypt and abroad). But it has won the African Nations Cup seven times, including a run of three victories in 2006, 2008 and 2010.

Egypt has a strong national team of swimmers and tennis players. Their female athletes were the 2016 world squash champions and in the same year a weightlifter became the first Egyptian female to win an Olympic medal.

Multiple Identities

Most Egyptians will proudly tell you that they are descendants of the ancient Egyptians and there seems to be some truth in that. The country was invaded by Libyans, Persians, Greeks, Romans and, most significantly, the 4000 Arab horsemen who invaded in AD 640. In the centuries since then, there was significant Arab migration and intermarriage with the indigenous population. The Mamluks, rulers of Egypt between the 13th and 16th centuries, were of Turkish and Circassian origins, and then there were the Ottoman Turks, rulers and occupiers from 1517 until the latter years of the 18th century. And yet recent DNA studies have shown that 68% of the indigenous population is originally from North Africa.

Desert Tribes

Besides the Egyptians of the Nile Valley, there is a handful of separate indigenous groups with ancient roots. The ancestors of Egypt's Bedouins are believed to have migrated from the Arabian Peninsula, before settling the Western and Eastern Deserts and Sinai. But their nomadic way of life is under threat as the interests of the rest of the country increasingly intrude on their once-isolated domains.

In the Western Desert, particularly in and around Siwa Oasis, are a small number of Berbers who have retained much of their own identity. They are quite easily distinguished from other Egyptians by the dress of the women, who usually don the *meliyya* (head-to-toe garment with slits for the eyes). Although many speak Arabic, they have preserved their own native tongues.

People of the South

In the south, the tall, dark-skinned Nubians originate from Nubia, the region between Aswan in southern Egypt and Khartoum in Sudan. Their homeland almost completely disappeared in the 1970s when the High

---

SILENT COMMUNICATION IN EGYPT

Egyptians have a range of nonverbal ways to get a point across – and if you know some of them, you'll be much less likely to get offended, run over or neglected in a restaurant.

First, 'no' is often communicated with a simple upward nod or a brusque *tsk* sound – which can seem a bit rude if you're not expecting it. But if you use it casually to touts on the street, they're more likely to leave you alone.

Another signal that can be misinterpreted by foreigners is a loud hissing sound. That guy might be trying to get your attention so you don't get trampled by his donkey cart coming down the narrow lane. But he might also be insulting you by implying you are a prostitute.

But the most essential gesture to learn is the one for asking for the bill at a restaurant. Make eye contact with your waiter, hold out your hand palm up, then make a quick chopping motion across it with the side of your other hand, as if to say 'Cut me off'. Works like a charm.

Dam created Lake Nasser. Some of Egypt's Nubians emigrated to Cairo, but the majority were resettled in towns and villages between Edfu and Aswan. Their cultural identity has survived, however; whether in the way they decorate their homes or play their music, Nubians are recognisably distinct from other Egyptians.

Religion

Some 90% of Egypt's population is Muslim. Islam prevails in Egyptian life at a low-key, almost unconscious level, and yet almost all men heed the amplified call of the *muezzin* (mosque official) each Friday noon, when the crowds from the mosques block streets and footpaths. The vast majority of the 10% of Egypt that isn't Muslim is Coptic Christian. The two communities have a mixed history, with periodic flare-ups. One of the most inspiring images of the 2011 Tahrir protests was the sight of Muslims protecting Christians while they prayed, and vice versa. The current government, like its Muslim Brotherhood predecessor, has been criticised for inciting violence towards Copts and for not offering sufficient support and security to communities and churches.

Islam

Islam, the predominant religion of Egypt, shares its roots with Judaism and Christianity. Adam, Abraham (Ibrahim), Noah and Moses are all prophets in Islam; Jesus is recognised as a prophet, but not the son of God. Muslim teachings correspond closely to the Torah (the foundation book of Judaism) and the Christian Gospels. The essence of Islam is the Quran, which Muslims believe is the last and truest message from God, delivered by the Archangel Gabriel to the Prophet Mohammed.

The Life of Mohammed

Islam was founded in the early 7th century by Mohammed, who was born around AD 570 in Mecca. Mohammed is said to have received his first divine message at about the age of 40. The revelations continued for the rest of his life and were transcribed to become the holy Quran. To this day not one dot of the Quran has been changed, making it, Muslims believe, the direct word of God.

Mohammed started preaching in 613, three years after the first revelation, but could only attract a few dozen followers. Having attacked the ways of Meccan life, especially the worship of a wealth of idols, he made many enemies. In 622 he and his followers retreated to Medina, an oasis town some 360km from Mecca. This Hijira, or migration, marks the start of the Muslim calendar.

Mohammed died in 632 but the new religion continued its rapid spread, reaching all of Arabia by 634 and Egypt in 642.

Pillars of Islam

Islam means 'submission' and this principle is visible in the daily life of Muslims. The faith is expressed by observance of the five 'pillars of Islam', which oblige Muslims to publicly declare that 'there is no god but God, and Mohammed is His Prophet'; pray five times a day: at sunrise, noon, mid-afternoon, sunset and night; give zakat (alms) for the propagation of Islam and to help the needy; fast during daylight hours during the month of Ramadan; and complete the hajj (the pilgrimage to Mecca).

The first pillar is accomplished through prayer, which is the second pillar and an essential part of the daily life of a believer. Five times a day the *muezzins* sing out the call to prayer through speakers on top of the minarets. It is perfectly permissible to pray at home or elsewhere; only the noon prayer on Friday is meant to be conducted in the mosque.

One of the most influential Islamic authorities in Egypt is the Grand Sheikh of Al Azhar, a position appointed by the Egyptian president and currently held by Sheikh Ahmed Al Tayeb. It is his role to define the official Egyptian Islamic line on any particular matter from organ donations to heavy-metal music.

Women typically pray at home; when they go to the mosque, there is a separate section for them.

The fourth pillar, sawm (fasting), is done during the ninth month of the Muslim calendar, Ramadan, when all believers fast during the day. Pious Muslims do not allow anything to pass their lips in daylight hours. Although many Muslims do not follow the injunctions to the letter, most conform to some extent. The impact of the fasting is often lessened by a shift in waking hours (aided by the cancellation of daylight saving time in Egypt when necessary), and people tend to sleep late if they can, or nap in the afternoon. They then live much of their social life until sunrise.

Far from being a month of austerity, Ramadan is a joyous time, with great camaraderie among fellow fasters. The evening meal during Ramadan, called *iftar* (breaking the fast), is always a celebration. In some parts of town, tables are laid out in the street as charitable acts by the wealthy to provide food for the less fortunate. Evenings are imbued with a party atmosphere and there's plenty of street entertainment, often through until sunrise.

Christianity

The majority of Egyptian Christians are known as Copts. The term is the Western form of the Arabic *qibt*, derived from the Greek *aegyptios* (Egyptian), which in turn comes from the ancient Egyptian language.

Although Christianity did not become the official religion of Egypt until the 4th century, Egypt was one of the first countries to embrace the new faith. St Mark, companion of the apostles Paul and Peter, is said to have begun preaching Christianity in Egypt around AD 45. From the closure of the pagan temples to the arrival of Islam, Christianity was the predominant religion in Egypt.

The Monophysite Controversy

Egyptian Christians split from the Orthodox Church of the Eastern (or Byzantine) Empire, of which Egypt was then a part, after the main body of the church described Christ as both human and divine. Dioscurus, the patriarch of Alexandria, refused to accept this description, and embraced the theory that Christ is totally absorbed by his divinity and that it is blasphemous to consider him human.

The Coptic Church is ruled by a patriarch (presently Pope Shenouda III), other members of the religious hierarchy and an ecclesiastical council of laypeople. It has a long history of monasticism and in fact the first Christian monks, St Anthony and St Pachomius, were Copts.

The Coptic language, which has its origins in Egyptian hieroglyphs and ancient Greek, is still used in religious ceremonies, sometimes in conjunction with Arabic for the benefit of the congregation. Today the Coptic language is based on the Greek alphabet with an additional seven characters taken from hieroglyphs.

The Coptic Church was influential in shaping the rituals of the early Christian Church. Some, including the hidden altar and use of incense, were adapted from existing pagan practices.

The Copts

The Copts have long provided something of an educated elite in Egypt, filling many important government and bureaucratic posts. They're perceived as being an economically powerful minority, and a good number of Copts are wealthy and influential.

With that said, there are also a lot of Copts at the very bottom of the heap: the *zabbalin*, the garbage-pickers of Cairo, who sort through much of the city's rubbish, have always been Copts.

The Copts have suffered as a result of recent upheavals. Many churches and Coptic homes and businesses have been destroyed in the past few years and, faced with a lack of protection, many Copts have chosen to emigrate.

Other Denominations

Other Christian denominations are represented in Egypt, each by a few thousand adherents. In total there are about one million members of other Christian groups. Among Catholics, apart from Roman Catholics of the Latin rite, the whole gamut of the fragmented Middle Eastern rites is represented, including the Armenian, Syrian, Chaldean, Maronite and Melkite rites; some of these communities have been boosted by the recent arrival of refugees from elsewhere in the region. The Anglican communion comes under the Episcopal Church in Jerusalem. The Armenian Apostolic Church has around 10,000 members, and the Greek Orthodox Church is based in Alexandria.

Women in Egypt

Some of the biggest misunderstandings between Egyptians and Westerners occur over the issue of women. Half-truths and stereotypes exist on both sides: many Westerners assume all Egyptian women are repressed, while many Egyptians see Western women as sex-obsessed and immoral.

For many Egyptians of both sexes, the role of a woman is as defined as ever: she is the mother and the matron of the household while the man is the provider. But there are thousands of middle- and upper-middle-class professional women in Egypt who, like their counterparts in the West, now juggle work and family responsibilities. There are also female members of the Egyptian cabinet, and in 2017 the first female governor was appointed. Among the working classes, where adherence to tradition is theoretically strongest, it's certainly the ideal for women to concentrate on home and family, but economic reality means that millions of women are forced to work at the same time as being responsible for all domestic chores.

The issue of sex is big, naturally. Premarital sex (or any sex outside marriage) is taboo in Egypt. But marriage is an expensive business, so men must often put it off until well into their 30s. This leads to a frustration that can often seem palpable in the streets. For women the issue is potentially far more serious. Women are typically expected to be virgins when they marry and a family's reputation can still rest on this point. Thus the social restrictions placed on young women are meant to protect them for marriage.

This has long had the effect of dampening discussions of sexual abuse and harassment. But in 2008 a woman for the first time sued a man who had attacked her in the street, and the perpetrator was sentenced to jail. Women were targeted by gangs during some of the protests in Tahrir Square and there were many incidents of harassment and rape. In June 2014 newly elected President Sisi pushed the issue into the limelight when he went to visit a rape victim in hospital to apologise on behalf of the nation.

As with so many aspects of Egyptian life since the revolution, the role of women is in flux. The 2014 constitution states the right of all women to access education and also to hold government posts – several female ministers sit in government at present, including a female National Security Advisor. But although Sisi declared 2017 the Year of Egyptian Women, a survey that year showed that 87% of Egyptian men think a woman's place is still in the home (*Egypt Independent*, 8 May 2017).

Women in Egypt received the vote in 1956. Six years later, Hakmet Abu Zeid became the first woman in the Egyptian cabinet.

On their return from a women's suffrage conference in Rome in 1923, pioneer Arab feminists Huda Sharawi and Saiza Nabarawi threw away their *abayas* at Ramses Station in Cairo. Many in the crowd of women who had come to welcome them home followed suit.

The Arts

While Egyptian culture has not had much impact in the West, many Egyptian actors and musicians are revered cultural icons throughout the Arab world. The 2011 revolution spawned a cultural outpouring like no other, and several visual artists have been successful in the global art market. Egypt's cultural identity and the right of all Egyptians to be active participants in the cultural process is one of the big achievements of the 2011 revolution.

Literature

Naguib Mahfouz, who won a Nobel Prize for his work, was for many years just about the only Egyptian writer frequently read in the West. Things are changing, however. In the last decade several writers have tried to define a new Egyptian novelistic style, striving for a fresh language and approach, and many of these are now being translated into English.

Naguib Mahfouz

Awarded the Nobel Prize for Literature in 1988, Naguib Mahfouz was one of the most important 20th-century writers of Arabic literature. Born in 1911 in Cairo's Islamic quarter, Mahfouz began writing when he was 17 and published over 50 novels and 350 short stories, as well as movie scripts, plays and journalism. His first efforts were influenced by the European greats, but over the course of his career he developed a voice that was uniquely Egyptian, and drew its inspiration from the talk in the coffee houses and the dialect of Cairo's streets. In 1994 he was the victim of a knife attack that left him partially paralysed. The attack was a response to a book Mahfouz had written, which was a thinly disguised allegory of the life of the great religious leaders including Prophet Mohammed. Mahfouz died in 2006 after falling and sustaining a head injury.

Beyond Mahfouz

Mahfouz came out of a strong literary tradition. Other respected writers working at the time included Taha Hussein, a blind author and intellectual who spent much of his life in trouble with whichever regime happened to be in power; the Alexandrian playwright Tawfiq Al Hakim; and Yusuf Idris, a writer of powerful short stories.

Egypt's female writers have also enjoyed international success. Feminist and activist Nawal El Saadawi's fictional work *Woman at Point Zero* has been translated into 28 languages. An outspoken critic on behalf of women, she is marginalised at home – her nonfiction book *The Hidden Face of Eve,* which criticises the role of women in the Arab world, is banned in Egypt. Those interested in learning more about her fascinating and inspirational life should read her autobiography *Walking Through Fire,* which was published in 2002.

Born in Cairo, Ahdaf Soueif writes in English as well as Arabic, but most of her work has yet to appear in Arabic. Her most successful novel, *The Map of Love,* set in Egypt, was short-listed for the Booker prize, and her other novels are *Aisha, Sandpiper* and *In the Eye of the Sun*. In early 2012 she published her memoir: *Cairo: My City, Our Revolution*.

Egyptian Classics

➡ *Beer in the Snooker Club* (1964) by Waguih Ghali is a fantastic novel of youthful angst set against a backdrop of 1950s revolutionary Egypt and literary London. It's the Egyptian *Catcher in the Rye*.

➡ *The Cairo Trilogy* by Naguib Mahfouz is usually considered Mahfouz's masterpiece; this generational saga of family life is rich in colour and detail, and has earned comparisons with Dickens and Zola.

➡ *Love in Exile* and *Sunset Oasis* by Bahaa Taher, one of the most respected living writers in the Arab world, have both won awards.

➡ *The Harafish* (1977) by Naguib Mahfouz would be our desert-island choice if we were allowed only one work by Mahfouz. This is written in an episodic, almost folkloric style that owes much to the tradition of *The Thousand and One Nights*.

➡ *Proud Beggars* (1955), *The Jokers* (1964) and *The Colours of Infamy* (1999) by Albert Cossery were all recently translated and published following the author's death in 2008. His novels were written in French, and have a cult following among Egyptophiles.

➡ *Zayni Barakat* (1974) by Gamal Al Ghitani is a drama set in Cairo during the waning years of the Mamluk era. It was made into an extremely successful local TV drama in the early 1000s.

Contemporary Egyptian Novels

As well known globally as Naguib Mahfouz, contemporary dentist-turned-novelist Alaa Al Aswany writes about Egyptians, poverty and class differences. His 2002 blockbuster *The Yacoubian Building* is a bleak but compelling snapshot of contemporary Cairo seen through the stories of the occupants of a Downtown building. The world's biggest-selling novel in Arabic, it is remarkable for the way it depicts Egypt towards

I Loved You for Your Voice by Selim Nassib is a delightful historical novel based on the romantic obsession of the Egyptian poet and lyricist Ahmad Rami for singer Umm Kulthum. He writes despairing poems that become lyrics she sings. Their relationship is never consummated, and as she becomes famous, he becomes increasingly pathetic.

A NEW GENERATION OF AUTHORS

Mansoura Ez Eldin This journalist, activist and writer was a voice of the 2011 revolution and her novel *Maryam's Maze* is considered a masterpiece of imagination and literary form.

Khaled Al Khamissi His wonderful novel *Taxi* (2006) consists of essays of the conversations with Cairene taxi drivers, highlighting the Egyptian passion and sense of humour. His second novel is called *Noah's Ark*.

Muhammad Aladdin This young novelist and activist is very much part of the new literary scene in Cairo, and his second novel, *The Gospel According to Adam* (2006), set in Midan Tahrir, examines a society that has lost all certainties. *A Well-Trained Stray* was published in Arabic in 2014.

Ahmed Alaidy The author of *Being Abbas el Abd* (2003) writes with profound cynicism and humour about the despair of Egypt's youth.

Ibrahim Abdel Meguid *No One Sleeps in Alexandria* (1999) is an antidote to the mythical Alexandria of Lawrence Durrell. The first book in a trilogy, it portrays the city in the same period as the Quartet but as viewed by two poor Egyptians. His latest novel, the last in the trilogy, is *Clouds over Alexandria*.

Miral Al Tahawy *The Tent* (1998) is a bleak but beautiful tale of the slow descent into madness of a crippled Bedouin girl.

Nael El Toukhy His novel *Women of the Karentina* (2013) describes an imaginary underworld in Alexandria, containing a rich mix of humour and misery.

the end of Mubarak's rule and for introducing archetypes that hadn't previously been captured in Arabic literature. Al Aswany's subsequent writing – *Chicago*, *Friendly Fire* and *The Automobile Club of Egypt* have not lived up to the earlier promise.

Salwa Bakr tackles taboo subjects such as sexual prejudice and social inequality. Her work includes the novels *The Golden Chariot* and the excellent *The Man from Bashmour*.

Youssef Rakha's work is firmly rooted in Cairo. His award-winning *The Book of the Sultan's Seal* tells of a search for identity and also happens to be a great read. In *Crocodiles* he weaves a story around the events of 2011.

One of the most promising of a very vibrant new generation of writers is Mansoura Ez Eldin, whose novel *Maryam's Maze* is the wonderfully written story of a woman trying to find her way in the confusion all around her. *Beyond Paradise* (2009) is also rewarding. Other younger writers to look out for include Amina Zaydan (*Red Wine*), Hamdi Abu Golayyel (*A Dog with No Tail*) and Miral Al Tahawy (*Blue Aubergine*).

Egypt in Western Novels

➡ *The Alexandria Quartet* (1962) by Lawrence Durrell is perhaps essential reading, but to visit Alexandria looking for the city of the *Quartet* is a bit like heading to London hoping to run into Mary Poppins.

➡ *Baby Love* (1997) by Louisa Young is a smart, hip novel that shimmies between Shepherd's Bush in London and the West Bank of Luxor, as a former belly dancer, now single mother, skirts romance and a violent past.

➡ *City of Gold* (1992) by Len Deighton is a thriller set in wartime Cairo, elevated by solid research. The period detail is fantastic and brings the city to life.

➡ *Death on the Nile* (1937) by Agatha Christie draws on Christie's experiences of a winter in Upper Egypt. An absolute must if you're booked on a cruise.

➡ Although the well-known film of the same name bears little resemblance to the novel, Michael Ondaatje's *The English Patient* (1992) – a story of love, desert and destiny in WWII – remains a beautifully written, poetic novel.

➡ Egypt during the war serves as the setting for the trials and traumas of a despicable bunch of expats in *The Levant Trilogy* (1980) by Olivia Manning. It has some fabulous descriptions of life in Cairo during WWII, and was filmed by the BBC as *Fortunes of War* starring Kenneth Branagh and Emma Thompson.

➡ A section that is set on a Nile cruise is only a small part of John Fowles's brilliant novel *Daniel Martin* (1977), but his descriptions are razor sharp.

➡ *Moon Tiger* (1987) by Penelope Lively is an award-winning romance, very moving in parts, with events that occurred in Cairo during WWII at its heart.

➡ *The Photographer's Wife* (1996) by Robert Sole is one of three historical romances by this French journalist set in late-19th-century Egypt. They're slow-going but worth it for the fine period detail and emotive stories.

The father-and-son team of screenwriter Wahis Hamed and director Marwan Hamed adapted Alaa Al Aswany's best-selling *The Yacoubian Building* for the screen. The budget of more than US$3 million was the largest ever seen in Egypt. The film was released to great acclaim in 2006.

Cinema

In the halcyon years of the 1940s and '50s, Cairo's film studios turned out more than 100 movies annually, filling cinemas throughout the Arab world with charming musicals that are still classics of regional cinema. Until the 1980s Cairo remained a major player in the film industry, but currently only about 20 films are made each year. The chief reason for the decline, according to the producers, was excessive government taxation and restrictive censorship. Asked what sort of things are censored, one film industry figure replied, 'Sex, politics, religion – that's all'. However, at least one Cairo film critic has suggested that another reason for the demise of local film is that so much of what is made is of poor quality.

NEW EGYPTIAN CINEMA

Several Egyptian films have won international awards in recent years, although some are banned in Egypt for being critical of the new regime.

➡ Jehane Noujaim's *The Square* was shortlisted for the Best Documentary Award at the 2014 Oscars.

➡ Mohamed Khan, who has made a comeback with *Fatat El Masnaa* (Factory Girl; 2013), a film about women seeking independence in a society that place great restrictions on them.

➡ In *Harag W' Marag* (Chaos, Order; 2012) Mohamed Khan's daughter Nadine Khan tells a story of two tough youths vying for a girl in a poor but lively and exotic-looking Cairo neighbourhood.

➡ *Rags and Tatters* (2013) by Ahmad Abdalla, another brilliant award-winning film, is an honest take on the Egyptian revolution, and unusual, as it is for the most part silent.

➡ *Villa 69* (2013), director Ayten Amin's debut film, shows how Hussein (Khaled Abul-Naga), a solitary man in his 50s who lives alone in a beautiful but dilapidated villa, is forced to deal with reality when his sister and her grandson come to stay.

➡ *Coming Forth By Day* (2012), the debut feature film by writer-director Hala Lotfy, shows a small family being worn down by the indignities of everyday life: sickness, money problems, rejection, restlessness, frustration.

➡ *The Nile Hilton Incident* (2017) is a thriller about a policeman on the make who is called in to investigate a murder in pre-2011 Cairo.

The ingredients of the typical Egyptian film are shallow plot lines, farcical slapstick humour, over-the-top acting and perhaps a little belly dancing.

One Egyptian director who consistently stood apart from the mainstream was Youssef Chahine (1926–2008). He directed over 35 films, has been called Egypt's Fellini and was honoured at Cannes in 1997 with a lifetime achievement award. His later and more well-known works are 1999's *Al Akhar* (The Other), 1997's *Al Masir* (Destiny) and 1994's *Al Muhagir* (The Emigrant). Others to look out for are *Al Widaa Bonaparte* (Adieu Bonaparte), a historical drama about the French occupation, and *Iskandariyya Ley?* (Alexandria Why?), an autobiographical meditation on the city of Chahine's birth.

Since the 2011 revolution a new wave of filmmakers has entered the Egyptian cinema scene and are taking Egyptian cinema into exciting and uncharted territory. Jehane Noujaim won an Oscar nomination and three Emmys for *The Square* (2013), which looks at events in Tahrir from 2011–13. In early 2014 Zawya, a new cinema in downtown Cairo, opened, showing art-house movies and work by young Egyptian filmmakers.

The trilogy of *The Mummy* (1999), *The Mummy Returns* (2001) and *The Scorpion King* (2002) was written by Stephen Sommers. The films feature fabulous art direction and far-fetched plots set in ancient and early-20th-century Egypt.

Music

Forty years after her death, the 'Star of the Orient', Umm Kulthum, still provokes huge emotion in Egypt. But the new kids on the block are making a loud noise. The latest sound heard in Cairo is *mahraganat,* created by artists from some of the poorest suburbs and slums, who are shouting about their disenchantment with their situation.

Classical

Classical Arabic music peaked in the 1940s and '50s. These were the golden days of a rushing tide of nationalism and then, later, of Nasser's rule when Cairo was the virile heart of the Arab-speaking world. Its singers were icons and, through radio, their impassioned words captured and inflamed the spirits of listeners from Algiers to Baghdad.

Chief among them was Umm Kulthum, the most famous Arab singer of the 20th century. Her protracted love songs and *qasa'id* (long poems) were the very expression of the Arab world's collective identity. Egypt's love affair with Umm Kulthum was such that on the afternoon of the first Thursday of each month, streets would become deserted as the whole country sat beside a radio to listen to her regular live-broadcast performances. She had her male counterparts in Abdel Halim Hafez and Farid Al Attrache, but they never attracted anything like the devotion accorded 'As Sitt' (the Lady). She retired after a concert in 1972. When she died three years later, millions of grieving Egyptians poured onto the streets of Cairo. The Umm Kulthum Museum opened in Cairo in 2002.

Popular

Ahmed Adawiyya did for Arabic music what punk did to popular music in the West. Throwing out traditional melodies and melodramas, his backstreet, streetwise and, to some, politically subversive songs captured the spirit of the times and dominated popular culture throughout the 1970s. He set the blueprint for a new kind of music known as *al jeel* (the generation), characterised by a clattering, hand-clapping rhythm overlaid with synthesised twirling and a catchy, repetitive vocal. This evolved into a more Western-style pop, helmed by Amr Diab, who is often described as the Arab world's Ricky Martin.

Adawiyya's legacy also spawned something called *shaabi* (from the word for popular), much cruder than *al jeel,* and often with satirical or politically provocative lyrics. The acceptable face of *shaabi* is TV-friendly Hakim, whose albums regularly sell around the million mark. In 2010 *shaabi* singer Mohamed Mounir brought out a song *Ezay?* (How?), that was banned for being too political; he brought it out again with the backdrop of the people in Midan Tahrir during the 2011 revolution.

The uprisings of the revolutionary youth in Cairo and elsewhere was fuelled by rap and hip-hop music, the so-called *shebabi* (youth) music. The sound of Cairo now is *mahraganat,* a relentless mix of drumbeats and auto-tuned rap that started in Cairo's slums but has been likened to grime music. The artists often record at home, and spread their music via the internet. Diesel, AKA Mohamed Saber, is one of *mahraganat's* most innovative artists, while Sadat, AKA Al Sadat Abdelaziz, is its biggest star. The music expresses the reality of young people, using their slang

SOUNDTRACK OF THE REVOLUTION

The following songs and bands formed part of the soundtrack of the 2011 revolution. Some are available internationally; all are on YouTube.

➤ *Irhal* (Leave) by Ramy Essam – This song made Ramy Essam one of the stars of the revolution; he sang it on stage on 11 February, when it was announced that Mubarak had gone.

➤ *Eid Fi Eid* (Hand in Hand) by The Arabian Knightz – One of the first Egyptian rap bands to release music about the revolution, they filmed a video for their track in Midan Tahrir.

➤ *Rebel* by The Arabian Knightz, featuring Lauryn Hill – This track was recorded during the first days of the revolution.

➤ *Thawra* by Rayess Bek – Lebanese band sings about and for the revolution with a background of the slogan '*as shab yurid thawra*' ('the people want revolution') chanted in Midan Tahrir.

➤ *Sout El Hurriya* (Voice of Freedom) by Amir Eid, Hany Adel, Hawary and Sherif – The YouTube clip shows the song sung by people in Midan Tahrir.

CONTEMPORARY EGYPTIAN ARTISTS

Chant Avedissian (www.chantavedissian.com) Armenian-Egyptian artist whose stencils of iconic celebrities from the past have become very much in demand with Middle Eastern art collectors.

Youssef Nabil (www.youssefnabil.com) Egyptian artist living in New York who makes hand-coloured gelatin silver prints of photographs of Egyptian and international celebrities.

Ghada Amer (www.ghadaamer.com) Egyptian artist who embroiders on abstract canvases that deal with female sexuality and eroticism.

Wael Shawky One of the most powerful and poignant voices coming out of Egypt, Shawky reinterprets faith, myth and history through video installations.

to express their struggle. They sing about revolution, drugs and sexual harassment, and mainly perform live in street weddings.

Visual Arts

Egypt's visual arts scene was as depressed as the country until 2011, when it was transformed by the uprising against the Mubarak regime. The artist and musician Ahmed Bassiouny, killed on the third day of the uprising against Mubarak, had his work shown posthumously at the 2011 Venice Biennale. With the downfall of the president, the art scene entered a period of chaotic freedom that saw many other Egyptian artists enjoy international acclaim.

Until the rise of Sisi, graffiti artists made the streets their canvas, as a way of taking ownership of public space. In post-revolution Cairo, street art is forbidden. Ganzeer, possibly Egypt's most famous street artist and who created some of the strongest and most politically engaged images, now lives and works in the US. Many others have also moved abroad.

And yet the visual arts scene continues to flourish, helped in part by the support of contemporary art spaces such as Townhouse Gallery and Mashrabia Gallery in Cairo.

Belly Dancing

Tomb paintings in Egypt prove that the tradition of formalised dancing goes back as far as the pharaohs. During medieval times the *ghawazee* (cast of dancers), travelled with storytellers and poets and performed publicly. In the 19th century the Muslim authorities were outraged that Muslim women were performing for 'infidel' men on their Grand Tour, and dancers were banished from Cairo to Esna. Belly dancing began to gain credibility and popularity in Egypt with the advent of cinema, which imbued belly dancing with glamour and made household names of a handful of dancers: in the 1990s, Fifi Abdou danced her way to become one of the most famous people in the country.

Since the early 1990s Islamist conservatives have patrolled weddings in poor areas of Cairo and forcibly prevented women from dancing or singing, cutting off a vital source of income for lower-echelon performers. At the same time, a number of high-profile entertainers donned the veil and retired, denouncing their former profession as sinful. Now few Egyptian belly dancers perform in public, and their place has been taken by foreigners mainly dancing for tourists. The future for Egyptian belly dancing looks uncertain.

One of Egypt's most famous belly dancers, Soheir El Babli, renounced show business and started wearing a veil in 1993, setting off a wave of religiously motivated resignations among the country's belly-dance artists.

Egyptian Cuisine

Compared to the highly regarded regional cuisines of Lebanon, Turkey and Iran, Egyptian food is more like fresh, honest peasant fare. Pulses are served stewed (for breakfast, lunch or dinner), as a soup or fried in patties as ta'amiyya (Egyptian falafel). Egyptians love lamb kebabs, grilled chicken, pigeon and kofta (spiced mincemeat patties grilled on a skewer), while fish comes from the Mediterranean and Red Seas, and the Nile.

Staples & Specialities

Egyptian meals typically centre on stews and vegetables. Street food is what most Egyptians can afford, and they happily wait in line at the best *kushari* (mix of noodles, rice, black lentils, fried onions and tomato sauce) and *ta'amiyya* stalls. Egyptian specialities include the love-it-or-hate-it *molokhiyya* (garlicky leaf soup), *hamam* (pigeon) and *mahshi* (stuffed vegetables). Egyptians have a serious sweet tooth and no meal is complete without dessert. *Mahallabiye* (milk custard with pine nuts and almonds) and *ruz bi laban* (rice pudding) are the most popular.

Omm ali is said to have been introduced into Egypt by Miss O'Malley, an Irish mistress of Khedive Ismail; another tradition has it that the dish was prepared to mark the murder of Omm Ali (Mother of Ali), wife of a 13th-century sultan of Egypt, by her rival.

Mezze

Largely vegetable-based and always bursting with colour and flavour, mezze (a selection of hot and cold starters) aren't strictly Egyptian, as many standards hail from the Levant or Turkey. But they have been customised here in a more limited and economical form. They're the perfect start to any meal, and it's usually acceptable for diners to order an entire meal from the mezze list and forego the mains.

Bread

A'aish (bread) is the most important staple of the national diet. *A'aish baladi*, the traditional bread, is made from a combination of plain and wholemeal flour with sufficient leavening to form a pocket and soft crust, and cooked over an open flame. Locals use it in lieu of cutlery to scoop up dips and rip it into pieces to wrap around morsels of meat. *A'aish shammy*, a bigger version made with plain white flour only, is the usual wrapping for *ta'amiyya*. In the countryside the women bake a round leavened bread with three handles – the same shape in which the ancient

---

TRAVEL YOUR TASTEBUDS

Fatta Rice and bread soaked in a garlicky-vinegary sauce with lamb or chicken and then oven cooked in a *tagen* (clay pot). It's very heavy – after eating retire to a chaise longue.

Mahshi kurumb These rice- and meat-stuffed cabbage leaves are decadently delightful when correctly cooked with plenty of dill and *samna* (clarified butter).

Molokhiyya A slightly slippery but delicious soup made from jute leaves, served with rabbit (or chicken) and plenty of garlic.

Hamam mahshi Roast pigeon stuffed with *fireek* (green wheat) and rice. This dish is served at all traditional restaurants and can be fiddly to eat; beware the plentiful little bones.

A TABLE OF MEZZE

Hummus A paste of mashed chickpeas with lemon, garlic and tahini

Tahini A paste of sesame seeds with oil, garlic and lemon, served with pita bread or grilled fish

Baba ganoush A purée of grilled aubergines with garlic and oil

Wara ainab Vine leaves stuffed with rice, herbs and meat, cooked in a broth

Bessara Cold broad-bean purée

Kibbeh Fried patty of bulgur wheat stuffed with minced lamb and pine nuts

Sambusas Cheese- or meat-filled mini pies

Torshi Crunchy pickled cucumbers, carrots and turnips

Egyptians made bread. Bakeries also sell a sweetish white Western-style roll, called *kaiser*, often served in restaurants or hotels for breakfast.

Salads
Simplicity is the key to Egyptian salads, which are eaten as a mezze or an accompaniment to a meat or fish main. The standard *salata baladi* of chopped tomatoes, cucumber, onion and pepper sometimes gets a kick from peppery rocket. The Middle East's delicious and healthy signature salad, tabbouleh (bulgur wheat, parsley and tomato, with a sprinkling of sesame seeds, lemon and garlic), is also common. Seasonal vegetables, such as beetroot or carrots, are often boiled and served cold with a tangy oil-and-lemon dressing.

Vegetables & Soups
The archetypal Egyptian veg is *molokhiyya*, a leafy green of the jute plant, which was known to be part of the pharaohs' diet. It has a similar sticky texture to okra, and Egyptians prepare it as a slimy and surprisingly sexy soup with a bright, nourishing flavour. Traditionally served as an accompaniment or sauce to rabbit or chicken and served with rice, it inspires an almost religious devotion among locals. The most popular soup is *shurbat ads* (lentil soup), made with red split lentils and served with cumin and wedges of lemon. *Fuul nabed* (broad-bean soup) is also common.

Meats
Kofta and kebab are two of the most popular meat dishes in Egypt. Kofta, spiced minced lamb or beef peppered with spices and shaped into balls, is skewered and grilled. It is the signature element of the Egyptian favourite *daood basha,* meatballs cooked with pine nuts and tomato sauce in a *tagen* (clay pot). Kebab is skewered and flame-grilled chunks of meat, normally lamb (the chicken equivalent is called *shish tawooq*). The meat usually comes on a bed of *baqdounis* (parsley), and you eat it with bread, salad and tahini.

Firekh (chicken) roasted on a spit is common, and in restaurants is typically ordered by the half. *Hamam* (pigeon) is also extremely popular, and is eaten stuffed and roasted, grilled or as a *tagen* stew with onions, tomatoes and rice.

Fish & Seafood
When in Alexandria, along the Red Sea and in Sinai, you'll undoubtedly join the locals in falling hook, line and sinker for the marvellous array of fresh seafood on offer. Local favourites are *kalamaari* (squid),

Books for Cooks

Egyptian Cooking: A Practical Guide by Samia Abdennour

The New Book of Middle Eastern Food by Claudia Roden

Apricots on the Nile: A Memoir with Recipes by Colette Rossant

Cairo Kitchen Cookbook by Suzanne Zeidy

Ancient Egyptians believed that when Osiris was chopped into pieces by his brother Seth, his wife Isis found the pieces strewn all over Egypt. She found all but one: his penis had been swallowed by a catfish. Even today some Egyptians are reluctant to eat catfish.

balti (fish that are about 15cm long, flattish and grey with a light belly), and the larger, tastier *bouri* (mullet). You'll also commonly find sea bass, seabream, red mullet, bluefish, sole and *subeit* or *gambari* (shrimp) on restaurant menus. The Red Sea is famous for its spiny lobsters, while the tilapia from Lake Nasser is a delight. The most popular ways to cook fish are to grill them over coals or fry them in olive oil.

Copts are very fond of *fesikh,* sun-dried, salted and fermented grey mullet, traditionally eaten during the Sham An Nessim festival, a spring celebration that goes back to ancient times. The shops selling *fesikh* are recognisable by the smell; the flavour is an acquired taste.

Desserts & Sweets

The prince of local puds is *mahallabiye,* made using rice flour, milk, sugar and rose or orange water, and topped with chopped pistachios and almonds. Almost as popular are *ruz bi laban* (rice pudding) and *omm ali* (layers of flaky pastry with nuts and raisins, soaked in cream and milk, and baked in the oven).

Best of all are the pastries, including *kunafa,* a vermicelli-like pastry soaked in syrup, or rolled and stuffed with nuts. The most famous of all pastries is baklava, made from delicate filo drenched in syrup. Variations on baklava are flavoured with fresh nuts or stuffed with wickedly rich *ishta* (clotted cream).

Drinks

Arabic *shai* (tea), closely followed by *ahwa* (coffee), both drunk black, are Egypt's favourite drinks. Delicious seasonal fresh juices are cheap and readily available too. Many Egyptians don't drink alcohol in accordance with Islamic traditions, but locally brewed beer is served in higher-end and tourist-orientated restaurants. Drinking on the street is taboo, as is public drunkenness.

Tea & Coffee

Drinking *shai* (tea) is the signature pastime of the country, and it is seen as strange and decidedly antisocial not to sip the tannin-laden beverage at regular intervals throughout the day. *Shai* usually comes as a strong brew of local leaves, ground fine and left in the bottom of the glass, or served 'English'-style, as a teabag plonked in a cup or glass of hot water. It is usually served sweet; to moderate this, order it *sukar khafif* – with 'a little sugar'. If you don't want any sugar, ask for *min ghayr sukar.* Far

---

FAST FOOD, EGYPTIAN STYLE

Once you've sampled the joys of the traditional Egyptian fast food you'll be hooked. These are the staples:

Fuul The national dish, often eaten for breakfast, is an unassuming peasant dish of slow-cooked fava beans with garlic, parsley, olive oil, lemon, salt, black pepper and cumin.

Ta'amiyya (Egyptian variant of falafel) Ground broad beans and spices rolled into patties and deep fried.

Shawarma Strips of lamb or chicken sliced from a vertical spit, sizzled on a hot plate with chopped tomatoes and garnish, and then stuffed into *shammy* bread.

Kushari A vegetarian's best friend: noodles, rice, black lentils, chickpeas and fried onions, with a tangy tomato sauce. Many *kushari* shops also sell *makaroneh bi-lahm,* a baked pasta-and-lamb casserole.

Fiteer The Egyptian pizza has a thin, flaky pastry base, and is topped with salty haloumi and olives, or comes sweet with jam, coconut and raisins.

more refreshing is *shai* served with mint leaves: ask for *shai bi-na'na*. In winter locals love to drink sweet *shai bi-haleeb* (tea with milk).

Arabic *ahwa* (coffee), traditionally served in coffeehouses, is a thick and powerful Turkish-style brew that's served in small cups and drunk in a couple of short sips. As with tea, you have to specify how much sugar you want: *ahwa mazboot* is a moderate amount of sugar, *ahwa saada* is without sugar, and *ahwa ziyada* (extra sweet) will likely make your teeth fall out on contact. Traditionally you can tell your future from the coffee mud left at the bottom. In hotels and Western-style restaurants you are more likely to be served instant coffee (always called *neskafe*), although upmarket places increasingly serve Italian-style espressos and cappuccinos.

Traditional Coffeehouses

The coffeehouse, known as *ahwa* (the Arabic word for coffee is now synonymous with the place in which it's drunk), is one of the great Egyptian social institutions. Traditionally *ahwas* have been all-male preserves, but it's now common to see young, mixed-sex groups of Egyptians in *ahwas*, especially in Cairo and Alexandria. The *ahwa* is a relaxed and unfussy place where regulars go every day to sip a glass of tea, meet friends, talk about politics or wind down for the night.

A feature of coffeehouses from Alexandria to Aswan, shisha is a pastime that's as addictive as it is magical. Most people opt for tobacco soaked in apple juice *(tuffah)* but in trendier places it's also possible to order strawberry, melon, cherry or mixed-fruit flavours. A decorated glass pipe filled with water will be brought, hot coals will be placed in it to get it started and you will be given a disposable plastic mouthpiece to slip over the pipe's stem. The only secret to a good smoke is to take a puff every now and again to keep the coals hot. Bliss!

Of course, it's worth mentioning that even though the smoke from shisha is filtered through water and tastes nothing like the tobacco from cigarettes, it's smoke nevertheless, and the nicotine hit you'll get is far more intense.

Beer & Wine

For beer in Egypt just say 'Stella' – though not to be confused with the Belgian lager, it's light and perfectly drinkable. It now has sister brews in crisp, lower alcohol Sakara Gold and the dangerous Sakara King (10%). Most locals just stick to the unfussy basic brew – it's the cheapest (around LE15 for a half-litre retail) and, as long as it's cold, it tastes fine.

Over the past decade the quality and choice of wine in Egypt has improved significantly. For the better wines, such as the Château des Rêves cabernet sauvignon, the grapes are imported from Lebanon. The Gianaclis whites are serviceable. These wines retail between LE70 and LE270 per bottle. Imported wines are both harder to find and significantly more expensive.

Other Drinks

Over the hot summer months many *ahwa*-goers opt for cooler drinks such as chilled, crimson-hued *karkadai*, a wonderfully refreshing drink boiled up from hibiscus leaves and famous for 'strengthening the blood' (lowering blood pressure). It's also served hot in winter. Another refresher is fresh *limoon* (lemon juice), sometimes blended with mint (*bi-na'na*). In winter many prefer *sahlab*, a thick warm drink made with the starch from the orchid tuber, milk and chopped nuts; *helba*, a fenugreek tea; or *yansoon*, a digestive aniseed drink.

Juice stands are recognisable by the hanging bags of netted fruit (and carrots) that adorn their facades and are an absolute godsend on a hot

EGYPTIAN CUISINE DRINKS

The New Book of Middle Eastern Food (1968) by Egyptian-born Claudia Roden brought the cuisines of the region to the attention of Western cooks. It's still an essential reference, now updated and expanded, as fascinating for its cultural insights as for its great recipes.

day. Standard *asiir* (juices) include *moz* (banana), *guafa* (guava), *limoon*, *manga* (mango), *bortuaan* (orange), *rumman* (pomegranate; say *min ghayr sukar* to avoid sugar overload), *farawla* (strawberry) and *qasab* (sugar cane). A glass costs between LE5 and LE15 depending on the fruit used and where you drink it.

Water
Egyptians say that once you drink water from the Nile, you will always come back. Once you drink water from the tap, however, you might not feel like going anywhere – the stuff can be toxic. The exception is in Cairo, where, if you have a hardier constitution, you can usually drink it without injury – most locals do, even if it tastes heavily of chlorine.

When & Where to Eat
Unfortunately for visitors, the best food in Egypt is invariably in private homes. If you are lucky enough to be invited to share a home-cooked meal, take up the offer (bring a box of sweets for the hostess). On these occasions you will most likely be stuffed to the point of bursting – the minute you look close to cleaning your plate, you will be showered with more food, which no amount of protesting can stop.

In restaurants stick with Egyptian standards and you'll be well fed, if not dazzled by variety. The only place we'd recommend trying other regional cuisines is Cairo, as well as the tourist zones of Luxor, Sharm El Sheikh and Dahab. In Alexandria follow locals' lead and dine out in the seafood restaurants – they're some of the best in the region.

Egyptians usually dine at a later hour than in the West; it's usual to see diners arrive at a restaurant at 10pm or even later in the cities, particularly in summer. They also dine in large family groups, smoke like chimneys and linger over their meals.

Unless it's a special occasion, the main meal of the day is usually lunch for standard restaurant and cafe business hours. At night, Egyptians typically eat lighter or grab snacks. Portion sizes can be enormous at any time, so order with restraint – wasting food is not appreciated.

DIY Egyptian Food

....

Food of Egypt (www.foodofegypt. com)

....

Food in Egypt (www.foodby country.com)

....

Egyptian Food Study Guide (http://quatr.us/ egypt/food/egypt food.htm)

Vegetarians & Vegans
Though it's usual for Egyptians to eat lots of vegetables, the concept of voluntary vegetarianism is quite foreign. Observant Copts follow a vegan diet much of the year (hence the popularity of *kushari*), but more standard Egyptian logic is, 'Why wouldn't you eat meat if you can afford it?'

Fortunately, it's not difficult to order vegetable-based dishes. You can eat loads of mezze and salads, *fuul*, *ta'amiyya*, the occasional omelette, or oven-baked vegetable *tagens* with okra and eggplant. When in doubt, you can always order a stack of pita bread and a bowl of hummus. If you do eat fish, note that fresh seafood is nearly always available in tourist towns and along the coasts.

The main cause of inadvertent meat eating is meat stock, which is often used to make otherwise vegetarian *tagens* and soups. Your hosts or waiter may not even consider such stock to be meat, so they will reassure you that the dish is vegetarian.

RAMADAN NIGHTS
Ramadan is the Muslim holy month of fasting from sunrise to dusk, but it is also a month of feasting and eating well at night. *Iftar*, the evening meal prepared to break the fast, is a special feast calling for substantial soups, chicken and meat dishes, and other delicacies. It's often enjoyed communally in the street or in large, specially erected tents. Like other celebrations it is also accompanied by a flurry of baking of sweet pastries.

DOS & DON'TS

➡ Remember to always remove your shoes before sitting down on a rug or carpet to eat or drink tea.

➡ Avoid putting your left hand into a communal dish if you're eating Egyptian style – your left hand is used for, well, wiping yourself in the absence of toilet paper.

➡ If you need to blow your nose in a restaurant, leave the dining area and go outside or to the toilet.

➡ Make sure you refrain from eating, drinking or smoking in public during the daytime in the holy month of Ramadan (international hotels are an exception to this rule).

➡ Always sit at the dinner table next to a person of the same sex unless your host or hostess suggests otherwise.

Habits & Customs

Egyptians eat a standard three meals a day. For most people breakfast consists of bread and cheese, maybe olives or a fried egg at home, or a *fuul* (fava bean paste) sandwich on the run to work. Lunch is the day's main meal, taken from 2pm onwards, but more likely around 3pm or 4pm when dad's home from work and the kids are back from school. Whatever is served, the women of the house (usually the mother) will probably have spent most of the morning in the kitchen preparing it, it'll be hot and there'll probably be plenty to go around. What's left over is usually served up again later in the evening as supper.

Environment

Egypt's extremities, its deserts and Red Sea coral reefs are rich in wildlife. But else-where, environmental issues are increasingly acute. The narrow strip of fertile land be-tween the desert and river faces threats from overpopulation, pollution, a reduced share of the Nile water, salinisation of the land and rising ground-water levels caused by the building of the High Dam in Aswan.

The Land

Egypt has four of the world's five officially identified types of sand dunes, including the *seif* (sword) dunes, so named because they resemble the blades of curved Arab swords.

The Nile Valley is home to most Egyptians, with some 90% of the population confined to the narrow strip of fertile land bordering the great river. To the south the river is hemmed in by mountains and the agricultural plain is narrow, but as the river flows north the land becomes flatter and the valley widens to between 20km and 30km.

To the east of the valley is the Eastern Desert (this is also known as the Arabian Desert), a barren plateau bounded on its eastern edge by a high ridge of mountains that rises to more than 2000m and extends for about 800km. To the west is the Western Desert (also known as the Libyan Desert), which officially comprises two-thirds of the land surface of Egypt. If you ignore the political boundaries on the map, the Western Desert stretches right across the top of North Africa under its better-known and highly evocative name, the Sahara (Arabic for 'desert').

Cairo also demarcates Egyptian geography as it lies roughly at the point where the Nile splits into several tributaries and the valley becomes a 200km-wide delta. Burdened with the task of providing for the entire country, this Delta region ranks among the world's most intensely cultivated lands.

To the east, across the Suez Canal, is the triangular wedge of Sinai. It's a geological extension of the Eastern Desert; the terrain here slopes from the high mountain ridges, which include Mt Sinai and Gebel Katarina (the highest mountain in Egypt at 2642m) in the south, to desert coastal plains and lagoons in the north.

Wildlife

Egypt is about 94% desert – such a figure conjures up images of vast, barren wastelands where nothing can live. However, there are plenty of desert regions where fragile ecosystems have adapted over millennia to extremely hostile conditions.

Animals

Egypt is home to about 100 species of mammals, though you'd be lucky to see anything other than camels, donkeys, horses and buffalo. Egypt's deserts were once sanctuaries for an amazing variety of larger mammals, such as the leopard, cheetah, oryx, aardwolf, striped hyena and caracal, but all of these have been brought to the brink of extinction through hunting. Creatures such as the sand cat, the fennec fox and the Nubian ibex are rarely sighted, and Egyptian cheetahs and leopards have most likely been wiped out already.

There were three types of gazelle in Egypt: the Arabian, dorcas and white. Unfortunately, Arabian gazelles are thought to be extinct, and there are only individual sightings of dorcas and white gazelles, though herds were common features of the desert landscape only 35 years ago.

The zorilla, a kind of weasel, lives in the Gebel Elba region. In Sinai you may see the rock hyrax, a small creature about the size of a large rabbit, which lives in large groups and is extremely sociable.

Less loveable are the 34 species of snake in Egypt. The best known is the cobra, which featured prominently on the headdress of the ancient pharaohs. Another well-known species is the horned viper, a thickset snake that has horns over its eyes. There are also plenty of scorpions, although they're largely nocturnal and rarely seen. Be careful if you're lifting up stones as they like to burrow into cool spots.

The Egyptian tortoise, native to the Mediterranean coastal desert, is one of the world's smallest tortoises; most males are less than 9cm long.

Birds

About 430 bird species have been sighted in Egypt, of which about one-third actually breed there. Most of the others are passage migrants or winter visitors. Each year an estimated one to two million large birds migrate via certain routes from Europe to Africa through Egypt. Most large birds, including flamingos, storks, cranes, herons and all large birds of prey, are protected under Egyptian law.

The most ubiquitous birds are the house sparrow and the hooded crow, while the most distinctive is the hoopoe. This cinnamon-toned bird has a head shaped like a hammer and extends its crest in a dramatic fashion when it's excited. Hoopoes are often seen hunting for insects in gardens in central Cairo, though they're more common in the countryside.

Plants

The lotus that symbolises ancient Egypt can be found, albeit rarely, in the Delta area; the papyrus reed, depicted in ancient art in vast swamps where the pharaohs hunted hippos, has disappeared from its natural habitats. Except for one clump found in 1968 in Wadi Natrun, papyrus is now found only in botanical gardens.

More than 100 varieties of grass thrive in areas where there is water, and the date palm can be seen in virtually every cultivable area. Along with tamarisk and acacia, the imported jacaranda and poinciana (red and orange flowers) have come to mark Egyptian summers with their vivid colours.

Environmental Issues

Cairo is one of the world's most polluted cities. Air in the capital contains 76 micrograms per cubic metre, as opposed to 9 in New York and 15 in London (according to the World Health Organization). The consequences of this, according to a startling feature article by Ursula Lindsey published in *Cairo* magazine, is that as many as 20,000 Cairenes die each year of pollution-related disease and that close to half a million contract pollution-related respiratory diseases.

The biggest culprits for the air pollution are the industrial plants, particularly those burning the heavy, low-quality mazut in generating plants. The increase of cement and steel factories, often established by Western countries in Egypt over the past two decades, is highly polluting, and has ruined the health of workers and nearby residents. A second factor is the desert storms, as most of Egypt is desert. The growing number of vehicles adds to the problem. Some estimates place over two million cars in the greater Cairo area, and it's clear that this number is increasing every year. Most are poorly maintained diesel-run Fiats and Peugeots that spew out dangerous fumes; very few run on unleaded petrol.

ENVIRONMENT ENVIRONMENTAL ISSUES

RESPONSIBLE TRAVEL

Tourism is vital to the Egyptian economy, and with fewer visitors the country is hitting rock bottom. At the same time, millions of visitors each year can't help but add to the ecological and environmental overload. As long as outsiders have been stumbling upon or searching for the wonders of ancient Egypt, they have also been crawling all over them, chipping bits off or leaving their own contributions engraved in the stones. Needless to say, this is not sustainable.

Mass tourism threatens to destroy the very monuments that visitors come to see. In the recent past, at sites such as the Valley of the Kings, thousands of visitors a day mill about in cramped tombs designed for one occupant. The deterioration of the painted wall reliefs alarms archaeologists, whose calls for limits on the number of visitors have largely fallen on deaf ears.

Even the Pyramids, which have so far survived 4500 years, are suffering. Cracks have begun to appear in inner chambers and, in cases such as these, authorities have been forced to limit visitors and to close the great structures periodically to give them some rest and recuperation. It is likely only a matter of time before similar measures are enforced elsewhere.

In the meantime it's up to the traveller to be aware of these serious concerns. Don't be tempted to baksheesh guards so you can use your flash in tombs. Don't clamber over toppled pillars and statues. Don't touch painted reliefs. It's all just common sense.

Though factories are officially required to undertake environmental-impact assessments and the government lays out a system of incentives and penalties designed to encourage industrial polluters to clean up their acts, few have done so and little is being done to prosecute offenders. Laws designed to ensure emission levels of vehicles are tested don't appear to be regularly enforced. Organisations such as the US Agency for International Development (USAID) have tried to turn the situation around by funding initiatives such as the Cairo Air Improvement project, costing several hundreds of millions of US dollars.

The seriousness of the situation is particularly apparent each spring and autumn, when the infamous 'black cloud' appears over the city. A dense layer of smog that is variously blamed on thermal inversion, rice-straw burning in the Delta, automobile exhaust, burning rubbish and industrial pollution, it is a vivid reminder of an increasingly serious environmental problem.

Impact of Tourism

The HEPCA (Hurghada Environmental Protection & Conservation Association; www.hepca.com) website has information on the efforts to conserve the Red Sea's reefs through public awareness campaigns, direct community action and lobbying.

Ill-planned tourism development remains one of the biggest threats to Egypt's environment, particularly along the Red Sea coast and in Sinai. Following decades of frenzied development along the Red Sea coast, damaged coral reefs now run along most of its length. In Sinai the coastline near Sharm El Sheikh was the site of a building boom for many years: the downturn in tourism since 2011 has left half-finished resorts defacing the seafront. Whether the businesspeople investing here will make good on their promises to protect the reefs around the area remains to be seen.

Since the opening of the Nile bridge in Luxor (previously there was only a ferry) many more tourists visit the west bank monuments, causing much damage in the fragile tombs. Several villages built over the tombs have been bulldozed as part of the project to make Luxor the largest open-air museum in the world. Large residential areas in Luxor have also been demolished to clear areas around historical sites, despite protests from some locals and organisations.

Fortunately, there have been some positive developments. A National Parks office has opened in Hurghada and is hoping to rein in some of the more grandiose development plans in the Marsa Alam area. New 'green' guidelines for running hotels are being trialled under a joint US–Egyptian Red Sea Sustainable Tourism Initiative (RSSTI). Recommendations focus on energy use, water conservation, and the handling and disposal of waste, including simple measures such as installing foot-pedal taps at sinks, which make it harder to leave water running.

Finally, Egypt has an increasing number of high-profile ecolodges. It started with the fabulous Basata in Sinai and Adrère Amellal at Siwa, and they appear to have inspired a few others towards environmentally responsible tourism.

Natural Selections: A Year of Egypt's Wildlife, written and illustrated by Richard Hoath and published by the American University in Cairo Press, is a passionate account of the birds, mammals, insects and marine creatures that make Egypt their home.

ENVIRONMENT NATIONAL PARKS

National Parks

Egypt currently has 29 'Protected Areas' in a bid to preserve the incredible biodiversity in the country, which ranges from river islands and underwater coral reefs to desert ecosystems. However, just what 'protected area' means varies wildly. Take, for instance, the Nile Islands Protected Area, which runs all the way from Cairo to Aswan: nobody is clear which islands are included and most are inhabited and cultivated without restriction. Other sites are closed to the public while some, such as Egypt's oldest national park, Ras Mohammed National Park in the Red Sea, are popular tourist destinations that have received international plaudits for their eco smarts. Even hunting is allowed in some of the protectorates if you have the right permit from Egyptian environmental authorities.

The problem, as always, is a lack of funding. The Egyptian Environmental Affairs Agency (EEAA) has neither the high-level support nor the resources needed to provide effective management of the protectorates. Some help has arrived through foreign donors and assistance: the Italians at Wadi Rayyan; the EU at St Katherine; and USAID at the Red Sea coast and islands.

NOTABLE NATIONAL PARKS

Egypt has a number of notable national parks:

Lake Qarun (p153) Scenic lake important for wintering water birds.

Nabq Protectorate (p388) Southern Sinai coastal strip with the most northerly mangrove swamp in the world.

Ras Mohammed National Park (p378) Spectacular reefs with sheer cliffs of coral, a haven for migrating white storks in autumn.

Wadi Gimal Protectorate (p371) Eastern desert protected area with spectacular scenery.

St Katherine Protectorate (p402) Mountains rich in plant and animal life including Nubian ibex and rock hyrax.

Wadi Rayyan Protected Area (p153) Uninhabited Saharan lake with endangered wildlife.

White Desert National Park (p286) White chalk monoliths, fossils and rock formations.

High Dam Effect

The Aswan High Dam and its sibling, Lake Nasser, have been a mixed blessing. They allowed more irrigation for farming, but stopped the rich deposits of silt that were left after the annual flood and fertilised the land. This has led to a serious degradation of Egypt's soil and has made agriculture in Egypt entirely dependent on fertilisers. The annual inundations also flushed away the salts from the soil. But now that there is no annual flood, the biggest problem facing farmers is the high salinity of the soil.

Soil erosion has also become a major problem, particularly in the Delta region. The Nile has so little outflow, and deposits so little silt, that the Mediterranean is now gradually eating away the coastline. This also threatens the thriving fishing industry in the Delta lagoons. And, as the rich nutrients of the Nile no longer reach the sea, fish stocks there have been seriously reduced.

Another potentially catastrophic consequence of the dam and lake appears to be the rise in ground-water levels. With the water table higher, and salt levels raised, the sandstone blocks of many Egyptian monuments are being eaten away.

Survival Guide

Safe Travel

Social Unrest

A 2014 protest law has made it more difficult for crowds to gather. This was explained by the current regime as intended to deter Muslim Brotherhood supporters from gathering in large numbers, as they had been doing on a regular basis. It has also made it more difficult for any other group to gather en masse to protest. But that doesn't mean that everything is quiet, and a quick look through the Egyptian daily press reveals a long list of continuing flashpoints and protests: there were wide-scale protests in spring 2017 against the government's plan to hand Egyptian Red Sea islands to Saudi Arabia. Most flashpoints are far from tourist sites, so it should not intrude on a holiday to Egypt. But in the current climate, it pays to be more than usually aware.

Terrorism

There has been a significant rise in terror attacks in Egypt since the downfall of President Morsi in 2013. Almost all have been aimed at security and government targets, with the majority occurring in the North Sinai where Wilayat-Sinai (formerly Ansar Bayt Al Maqdis) and other jihadi groups are fighting against Egyptian military forces. North Sinai (above Taba) remains a no-travel region, while cautionary travel advisories remain in place for most of the South Sinai and parts of the Western Desert.

There have been no conclusive reports or definitive statements on either the downing of a Russian airliner over the Sinai in 2015 or the EgyptAir crash over the Mediterranean in 2016. The Sinai crash, though, was claimed by Wilayat-Sinai and is widely believed to have been caused by a bomb. Since then Egypt has begun upgrading its airport security systems, bringing in a British aviation security consultancy.

Most recently there has been sporadic militant activity. Explosions in Coptic churches in Tanta and Alexandria in April 2017 (Palm Sunday) killed at least 44 people while 30 people died in a gun attack on Christian pilgrims near Minya in May 2017. Daesh has claimed responsibility for both. In response, President Sisi announced a three-month state of emergency. In November 2017 militants attacked the Al Rawda Mosque in Bir Al Abd in northern Sinai, killing 305 and injuring over 100. No group came forward to claim the attack in the immediate aftermath.

Unsurprisingly, there is a heavy security presence throughout the country, including at tourist sites.

GOVERNMENT TRAVEL ADVICE

Many government websites offer travel advisories that have up-to-date information on current hot spots. It should be remembered, however, that these are often overly cautious.

Australian Department of Foreign Affairs (www.smarttraveller.gov.au)

British Foreign Office (www.fco.gov.uk)

Canadian Department of Foreign Affairs (www.dfait-maeci.gc.ca)

US State Department (www.travel.state.gov)

Theft & Crime

In spite of all the media attention, crime in Egypt is still significantly less prevalent than in many Western countries. You can usually leave your camera with the guard at the entrance to a tomb, or your bag with the concierge of a hotel, without worrying whether it will be there, and intact, when you get back. Locals have too much to lose by stealing in a country

KEEPING SAFE & AVOIDING TROUBLE

Some dos...

➡ Be vigilant in cities, keeping clear of large public gatherings.

➡ Cooperate politely with security checks in hotel foyers and at road checkpoints.

➡ Keep up-to-date with news in English-language newspapers – they are online if you cannot find a hard copy.

➡ Check the latest travel warnings online through your country's state department or foreign ministry.

➡ Consult your embassy/consulate on arrival if there have been recent public order issues. Some countries operate a register to ensure you receive notifications if trouble is expected.

➡ Be aware of the specific risks to women travellers (p474).

➡ Keep your passport and wallet in a safe place.

➡ Recognise that some taxi drivers, cafe owners and even hoteliers might try to charge you more than locals. Hotels, like museums, often have different rates for locals (this applies to international chains as much as budget hostels). Often this is something you have to accept.

Some don'ts...

➡ Don't lose a sense of proportion – the chances of running into trouble are very slim.

➡ Don't get involved: if you see political protests or civil unrest, move away as fast as possible.

➡ Don't strike up conversations of a stridently political nature with people you don't know.

➡ Avoid driving outside towns and cities at night: the majority of road incidents in Egypt happen after dark.

➡ Don't photograph military installations. Some other buildings are also prohibited, including the old Aswan Dam. You can be arrested for doing so, however innocent you might be.

---

where thieving from guests is particularly frowned upon. Punishments are harsh and, with unemployment so high, the chance of losing one's job is something most Egyptians will not risk. But that doesn't mean that you should not take normal street-smart precautions.

More common theft, such as items stolen from locked hotel rooms and even from safes, continues, so secure your belongings in a locked suitcase.

Generally, though, unwary visitors are parted from their money through scams, and these are something that you really do have to watch out for.

➡ Most Cairo taxis now have up-to-date meters, but in some places the old meters, with their fares in piastres, are still in use. Be sure that the meter is working, or that you know how much you will pay at the end. Otherwise, leave and look for another taxi.

➡ Shop-owners and hawkers will sometimes claim that an item is locally crafted. Some are. But many things you will be offered in souqs and in shops around antiquity sites are mass-produced, some imported from China.

➡ Most visitors to Egypt's sites are offered something that looks old. *Antika* is the word, with its suggestion of antiquity. Most things

openly for sale are no older than the time it took for them to be covered in dust, or faded by the sun (months, perhaps, occasionally years). If you were to buy an actual antiquity and try to take it home, however innocently, you would be smuggling, a crime which can carry a prison sentence with hard labour, and a huge fine.

➡ In taxis and elsewhere, you might be told a hard-luck story, which may involve a relative in hospital needing funds for drugs or an operation, or to buy materials to study or food to eat. You must decide for yourself whether it is better to give something, in case it is true (which it sometimes is), or turn away.

Women Travellers

Lots of women travel solo in Egypt, and most have a great time in the country. Travelling alone as a female, though, is unfathomable to many Egyptians, so expect a lot of attention. Some of this is welcome; as a lone female you're more likely than a single male or travelling couple to be befriended by families and local women and garner invites to people's houses. Unfortunately though, you're more likely to encounter some unwelcome attention as well.

Egypt has a bad reputation for sexual harassment. In a 2013 UN survey, a staggering 99.3% of Egyptian women stated that they had been subjected to some form of harassment. For the most part, this presents as wearying amounts of cat-calling, declarations of love, leering or being followed down the street, and minor groping in crowds or closed-in spaces such as buses or taxis. This can all put something of a dampener on your travels.

Attitudes are slowly changing. Sexual harassment was made a criminal offence in Egypt in June 2014; in September 2014 Cairo University took the initiative to officially adopt an anti-sexual-harassment policy on campus. Both these unprecedented steps are a huge leap forward in recognising a problem that has been brushed under the carpet for years. In saying that, Egypt has a long road to travel in tackling its harassment issues head on.

Top Tips

➜ Expect copious questions about your marital status and number of children. Egyptians are highly family-orientated and talking about family is a normal conversation starter, particularly with strangers. If you're single and childless, expect countless queries about why this is. Sometimes, to preserve your sanity, it's easier to make up a cover-story about your 'husband' and 'children' back home.

➜ Use the women-only carriages on the Cairo metro. Not only are they less crowded than the other carriages, but they're also a great opportunity to meet local women.

➜ Stock up on tampons and other female sanitary products before travelling. Even in the main centres they can be difficult to source.

➜ Trust your instincts. If you enter a hotel or restaurant and feel the atmosphere is leery, you're probably right. Don't grin and bear it. Just walk straight out.

➜ Carry a scarf to cover your head inside mosques.

➜ Sunglasses help deflect attention.

➜ Get older: after your mid-30s, the hassle diminishes.

Adopting the Right Attitude

It's easier said than done, but ignoring most verbal harassment is usually the best policy. If you respond to every one, you'll wear yourself out, and public shaming seldom gets satisfying results. Very few harassers will persist following or cat-calling for more than a few metres if you act as if you haven't noticed them.

Walk and act confidently; persistent harassers tend to latch onto those who look like they don't know what they're doing.

Most importantly, don't presume that every man who wants to strike up a conversation is out to get you. Egyptians tend to be gregarious, naturally hospitable and extremely open to talking to strangers. As the majority of Egyptians who work in tourism are male, you'll miss out on some great local interactions if you're too scared to talk to them.

Appropriate Dress

Egypt is a highly conservative country, so this is not the place to be breaking out your hot pants and strappy tank tops. You will stick out less like a sore thumb if you dress modestly, covering shoulders, cleavage and knees. T-shirts (with a sleeve that covers upper arms), long pants and long skirts not only aid to deflect unwanted attention but also help in encouraging interactions with local women, some of whom wouldn't approach travellers wearing skimpier attire.

Bikinis and swimsuits are best left to the private beaches of hotels. On public beaches and in the desert hot springs wear a t-shirt and shorts over your swimsuit at the least.

Public Spaces to be Wary of

➡ Never sit in the front passenger seat of taxis, servees or microbuses. On all public transport, try to sit next to another woman.

➡ Don't go to baladi (local bars) unaccompanied.

➡ Some coffeehouses are strictly men-only affairs. Check out the scene before sitting down.

➡ Avoid city buses at peak times; the crowds make them prime groping zones.

➡ The evenings of Eid Al Fitr (the holiday at the end of Ramadan) seem to be an excuse for groups of young men to roam the streets harassing women. If you're in Luxor, Cairo or Alexandria at this time, it can be best to stay off the street after nightfall.

➡ Avoid crowds where testosterone is high: street protests, post-football match celebrations and the like.

Persistent Harassment

For serious encounters and any incidences of physical contact, don't be afraid to create a scene. Saying 'haraam aleik!' or 'ayb aleik!' (both mean 'shame on you!') or the simpler 'imshi!' ('go away!') is usually enough to stop most harassers. Don't hesitate to ask for help. Most Egyptians are hugely ashamed of the harassment problem their country has. While, because of embarrassment, many won't intercept as they see harassment occurring, bystanders will usually jump to your aid if prompted.

Also, report any harassment to HarassMap (www.harassmap.org). This NGO does excellent work in breaking the stereotypes that surround sexual harassment in Egypt by documenting the extent of incidents throughout the country.

What to do in an Emergency

For help, counselling and legal advice if you have been seriously attacked, you can contact the Egyptian women's rights organisations El Nadeem Center for Victims of Violence and Torture (010-0666-2404; info@elnadeem.org) or Nazra for Feminist Studies (010-1191-0917; info@nazra.org).

HarassMap (www.harassmap.org) is also an excellent resource for advice.

DECIPHERING CAT-CALLS

For many female travellers being cat-called in Egypt can be particularly unnerving if you can't understand what is being said. Once you know what the wannabe Lotharios are actually muttering as you walk past, you may find it more cringeworthy than scary. Egypt's most common cat-calls are:

Muza Hugely popular slang term for a curvaceous, pretty female. You're being compared to a *muz* (banana) for your curves.

Asal (honey) Exactly the same as in English.

Sarokh (rocket) In young male street-slang this means 'this girl is rocket', a compliment to your exceptional beauty.

Ishta (cream) Going out of fashion but still occasionally heard; describing a good-looking female.

Mahallabiye In a country of sweet-tooths, it's not surprising that the popular dessert of *mahallabiye* (milk custard with pine nuts and almonds) has become a slang word for a pretty woman.

Gazelle Although you may be feel slightly put out at being compared to a small desert-dwelling mammal of the antelope family, Egyptians consider gazelles their most beautiful native animal and being called one is supposed to be complimentary.

Directory A–Z

Accommodation

Egypt offers visitors the full spectrum of accommodation: hotels, resorts, pensions, B&Bs, youth hostels, cruise boats and even a few camping grounds and ecolodges.

In Cairo, Alexandria, Luxor and Aswan, there are options for all budgets, from budget to super-luxury.

Elsewhere along the Nile options are more limited, with fairly bare-bones operations that mostly cater to Egyptian travellers.

In the oases budget options range from decent to very good and backpacker-friendly.

The Red Sea coast and Sharm El Sheikh are largely dedicated to package tourism. Resorts here typically offer all-inclusive rates that cover most drinks and some activities, though some also offer half- or full-board options (two or three meals). Booking well in advance can yield major discounts, as can booking at the last minute.

Rates

Rates at all hotels are negotiable in off-peak seasons, generally March to September (November to January on the Mediterranean coast) and especially during the middle of the week. Some last-minute booking websites sometimes have lower rates for top-end hotels.

Many hotels will take US dollars or euros in payment, and some higher-end places even insist on it, though officially taking payment in currencies other than Egyptian pound is illegal. Lower-end hotels are usually cash only, though it's not a given that all upmarket hotels accept credit cards.

Most top-end chains and a few midrange hotels in Egypt offer nonsmoking rooms, though you can't always count on one being available.

Seasons

Rates often go up by around 10% during the two big feasts (Eid Al Fitr and Eid Al Adha) and New Year (20 December to 5 January).

On the Mediterranean coast, prices may go up by 50% or more in the summer season (approximately 1 July to 15 September).

Camping

Officially, camping is allowed at only a few places around Egypt, at a couple of camping grounds and at a few hotels. These facilities are extremely basic.

With the current security situation, we advise against camping wild. If you really want to camp in national parks such as the White Desert, you must go with an approved operator who has permission from Egyptian security services.

Hostels

Egypt has several hostels recognised by Hostelling International, where having a HI card will earn you a discount.

There are also a number of independent operations offering dorm beds and small private rooms.

Hostels tend to be noisy and often a bit grimy. In a few there are rooms for mixed couples or families but on the whole the sexes are segregated. Most of the time you'll be better off staying at a budget hotel instead.

Brace yourself for heavy sales pressure for guided tours, especially in Cairo.

SLEEPING PRICE RANGES

The following price ranges refer to a double room in high season (November to February). Unless stated otherwise breakfast and taxes are included.

$ less than LE540 (US$30)

$$ LE540–1800 (US$30–100)

$$$ more than LE1800 (US$100)

Hotels

BUDGET

At the low end, there's little consistency in standards. You can spend as little as LE50 a night for a clean single room with hot water, or LE150 or more for a dirty room without a shower. Generally, rates include a basic breakfast, usually a couple of pieces of bread, a wedge of processed cheese, a serving of jam, and tea or coffee.

Competition among budget hotels in cities such as Cairo and Luxor is fierce, which keeps standards reasonably high and developing all the time. At this point, most rooms have private bathrooms, but some older hotels still have shared bathrooms only. Air-con is also an option, sometimes for an extra LE20 to LE50. Places catering to backpackers often have welcoming lounges with satellite TV, internet access and backgammon boards.

Some hotels will tell you they have hot water when they don't. Turn the tap on and check, or look for an electric water heater when checking the bathroom. If there's no plug in your bathroom sink, try using the lid of a mineral-water bottle – it often fits well enough.

Some budget establishments economise on sheets and will change linens only on request. Toilet paper is usually supplied, but you'll often need to bring your own soap and shampoo.

MIDRANGE

Midrange options are surprisingly limited, particularly in Cairo and Alexandria, where investment is channelled into top-end accommodation. Moreover, many hotels in this category coast on package-tour bookings. As a result, you could wind up paying more for TV and air-con, in grungy surrounds.

BOOK YOUR STAY ONLINE

For more accommodation reviews by Lonely Planet authors, check out http://lonelyplanet.com/hotels/egypt. You'll find independent reviews, as well as recommendations on the best places to stay. Best of all, you can book online.

Even if you typically travel in this price bracket, consider budget operations as well – some will be dramatically nicer for half the price. Alternatively, look for online deals on top-end hotels.

TOP END

Most international luxury and business chains are represented, and amenities are (for the most part) up to international standards.

Independent luxury hotels can be hit-and-miss, especially at the entry level of this price bracket, so you may want to inspect your room in person before committing any money. Most luxury lodging can be booked at a discount in advance, particularly in low season and these days while few tourists visit Egypt.

Beware taxes: quoted rates often don't include them, and they can be as high as 24%.

Activities

For many visitors, getting around the sites is all the activity they want. But Egypt has so much more to offer, from sailing the Nile and taking a fishing safari on Lake Nasser, to windsurfing and diving in the Red Sea.

Customs Regulations

➡ Duty-free allowances on arrival: 1L alcohol, 1L perfume, and either 200 cigarettes, 25 cigars or 200g tobacco.

➡ Up to 48 hours after arrival, you can purchase another 3L alcohol plus up to US$200 in other duty-free articles at dedicated Egypt Free shops at the airport, in Cairo and at official tax-free shops in Hurghada, Sharm El Sheikh and elsewhere. (Touts in tourist areas may ask you to use your allotment to buy alcohol for them.)

➡ Customs Declaration Form D is occasionally required for electronics, jewellery and cash.

➡ Prohibited and restricted articles include tools for espionage as well as books, pamphlets, films and photos that are 'subversive or constituting a national risk or incompatible with the public interest'. This needs to be taken seriously.

Discount Cards

International Student Identity Card (ISIC) Gives discounts on museum and site entry fees. Some travellers have also been able to get the discount with HI cards and Eurail cards.

Egyptian Student Travel Services (Map p58; ☑02-2531-0330; www.isicegypt.net; 23 Sharia Al Manial, Roda Island; ⊗9am-4pm Sat-Thu) Head here to get an ISIC in Cairo. You'll need a university ID card, a photocopy of your passport and one passport photo. Cards can also be bought online. Beware counterfeit operations in Downtown Cairo.

Electricity

Increasingly unreliable since 2011; everywhere in Egypt, including the centre of Cairo, suffers regular, usually daily, outages.

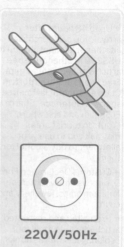

220V/50Hz

Embassies & Consulates

Embassies are in Cairo.

Australian Embassy (Map p58; ☎02-2770-6600; www.egypt. embassy.gov.au; 11th fl, World Trade Centre, 1191 Corniche El Nil; ☺8am-4.15pm Sun-Wed, to 1.30pm Thu)

Canadian Embassy (☎02-2461-2200; www.canadainter national.gc.ca/egypt-egypte; 18th fl, South Tower, Nile City Towers, 2005 Corniche El Nil;

☺8am-4.30pm Sun-Wed, to 1.30pm Thu)

Dutch Embassy (Map p94; ☎02-2739-5500; http://egypt. nlembassy.org; 18 Sharia Hassan Sabry, Zamalek; ☺8am-5pm Sun-Thu)

French Embassy (Map p92; ☎02-3567-3200; www. ambafrance-eg.org; 29 Sharia Charles de Gaulle, Giza; ☺9.30am-5pm Sun-Thu)

German Embassy (Map p94; ☎02-2728-2000; www.kairo. diplo.de; 2 Sharia Berlin, off Sharia Hassan Sabry, Zamalek; ☺8am-3pm Sun-Thu)

Irish Embassy (Map p94; ☎02-2728-7100; www.dfa. ie/irish-embassy/egypt; 18 Sharia Hassan Sabry, Zamalek; ☺9am-3pm Sun-Thu)

Israeli Embassy (Map p92; ☎02-2359-7304; http://embas sies.gov.il; 6 Sharia Ibn Malek, Giza; ☺9am-4pm Sun-Thu)

Italian Embassy (Map p92; ☎02-2794-3194; www.ambil cairo.esteri.it; 15 Sharia Abd Al Rahman Fahmy, Garden City; ☺9am-3.30pm Sun-Thu)

Jordanian Embassy (Map p92; ☎02-3749-9912, 02-3748-5566; 6 Sharia Gohainy, Doqqi; ☺9am-3pm Mon-Thu)

Lebanese Embassy (Map p94; ☎02-2738-2823; 22 Sharia Mansour Mohammed, Zamalek; ☺9.30am-12pm Sat-Thu)

New Zealand Embassy (Map p58; ☎02-2461-6000; www. mfat.govt.nz; Level 8, North Tower, Nile City Towers, 2005 Corniche El Nil; ☺9am-3pm Sun-Thu)

Saudi Arabian Embassy (Map p92; ☎02-3762-5000; http:// embassies.mofa.gov.sa; 2 Sharia Al Yaman, Giza; ☺9am-4pm Sun-Thu)

South Sudanese Embassy (☎02-2358-6513; www.erss egypt.com; 53 Sharia El Nadi, Maadi; ☺9am-3pm Sun-Thu)

Spanish Embassy (Map p94; ☎02-2735-6462; www.exteri ores.gob.es; 41 Sharia Ismail Mohammed, Zamalek; ☺8am-3.30pm Sun-Thu)

Sudanese Embassy (☎02-3748-5648; 3 Sharia Ahmed Ali Al Shatouri, Doqqi; ☺9am-4pm Sun-Thu)

Turkish Embassy (Map p58; ☎02-2797-8410; http://cairo. emb.mfa.gov.tr; 25 Sharia Falaki, Mounira; ☺9am-1pm & 1.30-5.30pm Sun-Thu)

UK Embassy (Map p92; ☎02-2791-6000; www.ukinegypt.fco. gov.uk; 7 Sharia Ahmed Ragheb, Garden City; ☺8am-3.30pm Sun-Wed, to 2pm Thu)

US Embassy (Map p92; ☎02-2797-3300; https://eg.us embassy.gov; 5 Sharia Tawfiq Diab, Garden City; ☺9am-4pm Sun-Thu)

Food

Many midrange and top-end restaurants do not quote taxes (10%) in the menu prices and will also add 12% for 'service'. This is typically used to cover waitstaff salaries and is not strictly a bonus, so an additional cash tip paid directly to your server is nice.

Overall, tipping is appreciated in budget places, advisable in midrange establishments and essential in all top-end restaurants.

Note that most budget restaurants do not serve alcohol.

Health

Travel insurance is highly recommended, particularly coverage with emergency evacuation services, as road accidents and the like are quite common. Also see your doctor and dentist before travelling. Consider registering with the International Association for Medical Assistance to Travellers (www. iamat.org) for a list of reputable doctors.

The best healthcare in Egypt is private and you may be asked if you have insurance before being admitted for treatment.

Before You Go

No vaccines are required for Egypt, but check the status of standard injections (diphtheria, tetanus, pertussis, polio, measles, mumps and rubella), as boosters in adulthood are now recommended for many. In addition, consider the following:

Hepatitis A and B Administered together or separately, at least two weeks before travel.

Rabies Only if you'll be in remote areas near animals.

Typhoid At least two weeks before travel.

Yellow fever Required if you're coming from or travelling to certain countries in southern Africa, including Sudan.

In Egypt

Hygiene standards are low. Always wash your hands thoroughly before and after eating, and choose restaurants with a high turnover.

Private and university hospitals have excellent standards, but it's patchier elsewhere. Dental care is variable. Be prepared to pay upfront for all medical and dental treatment.

You may need to provide medicine and sterile dressings from a pharmacy. Nursing care may be rudimentary, as this is something families and friends are expected to provide.

For minor illnesses, consult a pharmacist first. They are well trained, speak English and can dispense all kinds of medication.

SPECIFIC HEALTH RISKS

Heat exhaustion This is common, given the shadeless settings of most archaeological sites, as well as a lack of sanitary restrooms, which might lead you to drink less water than is required. Symptoms include headache, dizziness and tiredness and can progress to vomiting if untreated. Drink liquids (ideally sports drinks or water with rehydrating salts) before you're thirsty and wear a hat to keep off the sun. Treat yourself to an air-con hotel if necessary.

Heatstroke A much more serious condition, caused by a breakdown in the body's heat-regulating mechanism, that can cause death if untreated. This leads to irrational behaviour, a cessation of sweating and loss of consciousness. Rapid cooling with ice and water, plus intravenous fluid replacement, is required.

Insect bites and stings More annoying than toxic, but look out for sandflies on Mediterranean beaches, and mosquitoes. All bites are at risk of infection, so it's better to avoid them in the first place, with a DEET-based repellent.

Rift Valley fever A rare haemorrhagic fever spread through blood, including from infected animals. It causes a flulike illness with fever, joint pains and occasionally more serious complications. Complete recovery is possible.

Schistosomiasis (bilharzia) An infection of the bowel and bladder caused by a freshwater fluke. It can be contracted through the skin. Avoid all stagnant water, canals and slow-running rivers. Symptoms include a transient fever and rash and, in advanced cases, blood in the stool or in the urine. A blood test can detect antibodies if you have been exposed, and treatment is quick and easy.

Travellers' diarrhoea This and other mild food poisoning are virtually unavoidable, as food hygiene standards are not high. The best cure is rest, fluids (best with oral rehydration salts, sold as Rehydran in Egypt) and a cool environment. Antinal pills, a widely available stomach disinfectant, can also help. If symptoms persist more than 72 hours or are accompanied by fever, see a doctor as you might have dysentery.

Tuberculosis TB is common in Egypt, though nowhere near as rampant as in sub-Saharan Africa. The respiratory infection is spread through close contact and occasionally through milk or milk products. Risk is high only for people in teaching positions or health care.

Typhoid Spread through contaminated food or water and marked by fever or a pink rash on the abdomen.

Yellow fever Mosquito-borne and extremely rare in Egypt. If you need a vaccination for onward travel to Sudan, you can obtain it at the medical clinic in Terminal 1 of Cairo airport, or at the Giza governorate building (next to the Giza Court by the train station). It costs approximately LE100.

THE GREATEST THREAT

The greatest threat to you on your journey in Egypt will be to your intestines. Many people visiting the country suffer from some sort of intestinal trouble and for a variety of reasons, from unfamiliar diet and lack of hygiene to contaminated food and water. The amount of food offered, usually considerably more than one eats at home, can also threaten your intestinal happiness. Eat moderately, at least at the start of your trip. Always use bottled water, for drinking and for brushing your teeth. Wash your hands before eating. And make sure you drink enough water during the day.

TAP WATER

In Cairo tap water is heavily chlorinated and relatively drinkable, but elsewhere it

TRAVEL HEALTH WEBSITES

Check these government sites before your trip for advice and news of possible outbreaks or seasonal concerns.

Australia www.dfat.gov.au/travel

Canada www.travel health.gc.ca

UK www.dh.gov.uk and http://nathnac.net

USA www.cdc.gov/travel

PRACTICALITIES

Checkpoints Security checkpoints are common on highways outside Cairo. Always carry your passport with you.

Newspapers The best English-language newspaper is the *Daily News Egypt* (www.dailynewsegypt.com). The leading government paper *Al Ahram* (http://english.ahram.org.eg) is also available online in English.

Magazines The monthly *Egypt Today* (www.egypttoday.com) covers social and economic issues.

Radio BBC World Service is on the Middle East shortwave schedule, broadcasting from Cyprus. See www.bbc.co.uk/worldservice for details. In Cairo, European program 95.4FM/557AM runs news in English at 7.30am, 2.30pm and 8pm. Nile Radio 104.2FM (104.2kHz) has English-language pop music.

Smoking Common in Egypt, including in restaurants and bars. Nonsmoking facilities are rare. Shisha (hookah or water pipe) is a common social pastime. It delivers substantially more nicotine than you might be used to.

TV If your hotel room has satellite TV, you'll have access to a range of English-language TV news. The most commonly available are CNN, BBC World and Al Jazeera English.

Weights & Measures Egypt uses the metric system.

is generally unsafe to drink. Bottled water is cheap and readily available in even the smallest towns, but consider using iodine or a Steripen to reduce the use of plastic bottles, especially if you're on a longer trip.

Insurance

Travel insurance to cover theft, loss and medical problems is a good idea. Some policies exclude 'dangerous activities', which can include scuba diving, motorcycling and trekking.

Insure yourself to the gills if you're driving. Road conditions are hazardous. For the same reason, check that the policy covers ambulances and an emergency flight home.

Worldwide travel insurance is available at www.lonelyplanet.com/bookings. You can buy, extend and claim online any time, even if you're already on the road.

Internet Access

Free wi-fi is widely available in hotels throughout Egypt, though it's not always fast and often doesn't reach all the guest rooms. Many cafes in Cairo, and tourist centres such as Luxor and Dahab, also have free wi-fi.

Internet cafes are common, if not rampant; rates are usually between LE5 and LE10 per hour.

Mobile USB Wi-Fi

Both of Egypt's two main internet and mobile phone service providers, Vodafone Egypt (www.vodafone.com.eg) and Etisalat (www.etisalat.eg), offer mobile dongles (USB adapters) for your laptop, allowing internet access anywhere with mobile phone coverage. Vodafone charges LE200 for the USB stick and has a range of data price plans starting at LE80 for 1.25GB for one month. Bring your passport when purchasing.

Language Courses

Studying Arabic in Egypt is popular because the dialect is understood throughout the Arab world, and classes are plentiful and inexpensive. You're entitled to a student visa only if enrolled at an accredited university such as the American University in Cairo (AUC), so bear in mind the need for extending your tourist visa.

Alexandria

Qortoba Institute for Arabic Studies (Map p308; ☎010-0209-3065, 03-556-2959; www.qortoba.net; cnr Muhammad Nabeel Hamdy & Khalid Bin Waleed, Miami; ⊙7am-11pm) Offers modern standard and colloquial Arabic courses, private tuition and online courses for everyone from absolute beginners to experienced speakers. The institute can also arrange accommodation nearby in good-value student apartments.

Cairo

Arabic Language Institute (ALI; www.aucegypt.edu; AUC, New Cairo Campus, New Cairo) For college students or postgrads, this department of the American University in Cairo is the strongest Arabic language learning option, but the New Cairo campus – where ALI is based – is isolated.

International House (International Language Institute (ILI); Map p58; ☎3346-3087; www.arabicegypt.com; 4 Sharia Mahmoud Azmy, Mohandiseen; 2-week course from US$190) This is the largest school in Cairo, so it's able to offer the biggest range of levels. Two-week and four-week courses in both Egyptian-colloquial and Modern-standard Arabic with possibility to study both concurrently. Excellent Egyptian-colloquial textbooks. Also has online courses.

Kalimat (Map p58; ☎3761-8136; www.kalimategypt.com; 22 Sharia Mohammed Mahmoud Shaaban, Mohandiseen; 4-week course from US$260) Small language school with four-week courses in both Modern-standard Arabic and Egyptian-colloquial.

Luxor

Hotel Sheherazade (Map p186; 010-0611-5939; www.hotelsheherazade.com; Gezira Al Bayrat; €285) Bespoke Arabic courses for beginner and basic levels, run by teachers trained by and using course books from DEAC (Department for Teaching Contemporary Arabic, Institut Français). The price includes accommodation at Hotel Sheherazade, 40 hours of tuition, airport transfers and three sightseeing tours around Luxor.

Legal Matters

Foreign travellers are subject to Egyptian laws and get no special consideration. If you are arrested, you have the right to telephone your embassy immediately.

Bribes Egypt is notoriously corrupt, but don't assume this means you can pay your way through. You may encounter an official who'd like to exploit the awkward situation you're in, and of course, your bribe only perpetuates the system.

Drugs Drug use can be penalised by hanging, and you'll get no exemption just because you're a tourist. That said, you will no doubt be offered at least hashish during your travels, especially in backpacker-friendly zones. We highly recommend you don't accept the offer.

Political activity Post-revolution, police are particularly suspicious of 'foreign agitators' or anyone who could be perceived as such, including journalists and people working for NGOs. Both writers and foreign students have been detained on charges of abetting violence. Some have been tortured and at least one killed. It's best to avoid political affiliation of any kind, and avoid taking photos of government buildings and other sensitive areas.

LGBTQI+ Travellers

Egypt is a conservative society that increasingly condemns homosexuality. Although homosexuality is technically not a crime in Egypt, homosexual acts in public are, and gay men have been prosecuted using debauchery and public morals laws with prison terms of up to 17 years. In late 2017 the Egyptian government launched a large crack-down on the LGBT community, arresting 57 people in a series of raids.

The situation for the local LGBT community remains very tense, and although there is a small and very underground gay scene in Cairo and Alexandria, tapping into it as a foreigner can be tricky and is risky. Solo male gay travellers should not use gay dating apps while here as the police are known to target app users.

As long as common sense discretion is used and public displays of affection are avoided – the same goes for heterosexual couples – foreign gay or lesbian couples should have no issues. Most midrange and top-end accommodation will have no problem with a same-sex couple requesting a double bed (though you may notice a raised eyebrow from some staff), but it's advisable to steer clear of the very budget end of the accommodation market, particularly in non-touristy towns.

Single gay men should exercise caution if propositioned by an Egyptian man as, although rare, there have been reports of set-ups targeting foreign gay males

---

RAMADAN: WHAT TO EXPECT

Travelling in Egypt during the month of Ramadan, when observant Muslims abstain from all food and drink (including water) during daylight hours, presents some challenges. It also affords visitors a unique insight into local culture – provided you can stay up late enough to enjoy it.

Most restaurants that serve Egyptians are closed during the day, and the only reliable place to eat is in hotels – the same goes for finding alcohol of any kind. Don't plan on taking desert tours, as guides will not want to venture far. Shop-owners get cranky as the day wears on, and tend to shut by 2.30pm or so, so do your bargaining early. Avoid taking taxis close to sundown, as everyone wants to get home to their families.

Once night falls and everyone has nibbled on the customary dates, Egyptians regain their energy. Restaurants reopen and lay out a lavish fast-breaking feast called *iftar* (reserve ahead at high-end places). The streets are decked with glowing lanterns and thronged with families. The goal is to stay up – or at least catnap and get up again – for the *sohour*, another big meal just before dawn. In Cairo and Alexandria, there's a whole circuit of *sohour* scenes, from the funkiest *fuul* vendors trotting out their best spreads to chic waterside pavilions with DJs – think after-party, but with food.

The best way to cope is to keep sightseeing expectations low, don't eat in front of Muslims and take a long nap in the afternoon. Then put on your stretchy pants and accept any invitation to join the feast.

for theft. Gay male travellers should also be aware that signals in Egypt can be ambiguous; Egyptian men routinely hold hands, link arms and kiss each other on the cheek in greeting.

Lesbian travellers are unlikely to encounter any problems in the country. For the majority of Egyptians, lesbianism is unfathomable and most would declare that there is no such thing as an Egyptian lesbian.

Maps

Nelles Verlag has one of the most complete general maps of Egypt (scale 1:2,500,000), including a map of the Nile Valley (scale 1:750,000) and a good enlargement of central Cairo. You can find it and a number of other good maps at the **AUC bookshop** (Map p62; ✆2797-5929; www. aucpress.com; Sharia Sheikh Rihan, Downtown; ◷10am-6pm Sat-Thu; MSadat) in Cairo; elsewhere in Egypt, selection dwindles.

Freytag & Berndt's Egypt road map (scale 1:800,000) has good coverage of the road network, with motorway and duel carriageways labelled with both route numbers and distance markers in kilometres. It also has city maps in an attached booklet: Alexandria and Aswan at 1:15,000, and Cairo and Sharm El Sheikh at 1:10,000.

Money

Currency

There is a severe shortage of small change, which is invaluable for tips, taxi fares and more. Withdraw odd amounts from ATMs to avoid a stack of unwieldy LE200 notes, hoard small bills and always try to break big bills at fancier establishments.

The currency is the Egyptian pound (LE), *guinay* in Arabic, divided into 100 piastres (pt). Coins of 5pt, 10pt and 25pt are basically extinct; 50pt notes and coins are also on their way out. LE1 coins are the most commonly used small change, while LE5, LE10, LE20, LE50, LE100 and LE200 notes are commonly used.

The government freed the exchange rate in 2016, which led to the Egyptian pound losing half its value against hard currencies, but since then it has been fairly stable. There is no real black-market exchange.

Some tour operators and hotels insist on US dollars or euros, even though this is technically illegal. It's a good idea to travel with a small stash of hard currency, though increasingly you can pay by credit card.

Produce markets and some other venues sometimes write prices in piastres: LE3.50 as 350pt, for example.

ATMs

Cash machines are common, although in some places (in Middle Egypt and the oases, for instance) you might have to look harder to find one. Then you'll be stuck if there's a technical problem, so load up before going somewhere remote. Some ATMs won't let you withdraw more than LE2000. All Banque du Caire ATMs allow larger withdrawals.

Banque Misr, Banque du Caire, CIB, Egyptian American Bank and HSBC have the most reliable ATMs.

Credit Cards

All major cards are accepted in midrange and high-end establishments. In remote areas they remain useless. You may be charged a percentage of the sale in fees (anywhere between 3% and 10%).

Retain receipts to check later against your statements as there have been cases of shop owners adding extra zeros.

Visa and Mastercard can be used for cash advances at Banque Misr and the National Bank of Egypt, as well as at Travel Choice Egypt offices.

Money Changers

Money can be officially changed at Amex and Travel Choice Egypt (formerly Thomas Cook) offices, as well as at commercial banks, foreign exchange (forex) bureaux and some hotels. Rates no longer vary, though some places may charge commission.

US dollars, euros and British pounds are the easiest to change (and change back at the end of your stay). Inspect the bills you're given, and don't accept any badly defaced, shabby or torn notes because you'll have difficulty offloading them later.

TIPPING IN EGYPT

Always keep small change as baksheesh is expected everywhere. When in doubt, tip.

Cafes Leave LE5 to LE10.

Guards at tourist sites LE5 to LE20.

Metered taxis Round off the fare or offer around 5% extra, depending on the ride.

Mosque attendant Leave LE5 to LE10 for shoe covers, more if you climb a minaret or have some guiding.

Restaurants For good service leave 10%; in smart places leave 15%.

Opening Hours

The weekend is Friday and Saturday; some businesses close Sunday. During Ramadan, offices, museums and tourist sites keep shorter hours.

Banks 8.30am to 2.30pm Sunday to Thursday

Bars and clubs Early evening until 3am, often later (particularly in Cairo)

Cafes 7am to 1am

Government offices 8am to 2pm Sunday to Thursday; tourist offices are generally open longer

Post offices 8.30am to 2pm Saturday to Thursday

Private offices 10am to 2pm and 4pm to 9pm Saturday to Thursday

Restaurants Noon to midnight

Shops 9am– to 1pm and 5pm and 10pm June to September, 10am and 6pm October to May; in Cairo shops generally open 10am and 11pm

Photography

Egyptians on the whole, and Egyptian women in particular, are relatively camera-shy, so you should always ask before taking pictures.

➡ Photos are theoretically prohibited inside ancient tombs, though guards often encourage camera use in exchange for tips.

➡ You can buy a permit to photograph at some sites. This should be paid for at the ticket office. Costs vary.

➡ To combat the glare of sun, a UV filter is recommended.

➡ A standard daylight filter helps keep dust off your lens. Also pack compressed air and cleaning cloths.

➡ Avoid taking photos of anything that could be considered of military or other strategic importance. Taking photos out of bus windows especially provokes suspicion.

➡ Lonely Planet's *Travel Photography*, by Richard I'Anson, provides excellent advice on gear and taking photos on the road.

Post

In recent years Egypt Post has improved and is reasonably reliable as long as you post from a main post office in a major centre. The express service (EMS) is downright speedy. Egypt's post offices have yellow and green signs.

Parcels

➡ Usually only the main post office in a city will handle parcels; bring them unsealed so the contents can be inspected for customs. Clerks usually have cartons and tape on hand.

➡ Many shops provide shipping of goods for a relatively small fee.

➡ Parcel surface mail to the US, Australia or Europe costs roughly LE150 for the first kilogram, and LE40 for each thereafter.

Poste Restante

The poste restante service functions well and is generally free. If the clerk can't find your mail, ask them to check under Mr, Ms or Mrs in addition to your first and last names.

Public Holidays

Businesses and government offices also close on major Islamic holidays.

MAJOR ISLAMIC HOLIDAYS

The Islamic calendar is based on the lunar year, approximately 11 days shorter than the Gregorian calendar, so holidays shift through the seasons. Principal religious holidays in Egypt can cause changes to bus schedules and business openings.

Moulid An Nabi The birthday of the Prophet Mohammed, and children receive gifts.

Eid Al Fitr (Feast of Fast-Breaking) The end of Ramadan, essentially a three-day feast.

Eid Al Adha (Feast of the Sacrifice) Commemorates Ibrahim's (Abraham's) sacrifice, and families that can afford it buy a sheep to slaughter. The holiday lasts four days, though many businesses reopen by the third day. Many families go out of town, so if you want to travel at this time, book your tickets well in advance.

Ras As Sana (New Year's Day) A national day off, but only a low key celebration.

Dates for Ramadan and Eid Al Fitr are approximate, as they rely on the sighting of the new moon.

HOLIDAY	2018	2019	2020	2021
Ramadan begins	16 May	6 May	24 Apr	12 Apr
Eid Al Fitr	15 Jun	5 June	24 May	12 May
Eid Al Adha	22 Aug	12 Aug	31 Jul	19 Jul
New Year begins	12 Sep	31 Aug	20 Aug	9 Aug
Moulid An Nabi	20 Nov	10 Nov	29 Oct	18 Oct

SCAMS & HUSTLES

Many Egyptians will greet you in the street and offer you tea and other hospitality, all out of genuine kindness. But in tourist hot spots, 'Hello, my friend' can be double-speak for 'This way, sucker'. Next thing you know, you're drinking tea with your new friend...in a perfume shop.

The smoothest operators don't reveal their motives immediately. A kindly professor wants to show you a good restaurant; a mosque *muezzin* starts by showing off his skills; or a bystander warns you not to get caught up in a (fictitious) demonstration ahead. They adapt tactics rapidly. They've taken up the 'Don't you remember me?' or 'I work in your hotel' line used in many other African countries, for instance.

It's all pretty harmless, and many are genuinely friendly and interesting to talk to. But it can be wearing to be treated like a walking wallet. Everyone works out a strategy to short-circuit a pitch for when a smile and a quick stride fails. Claiming not to speak English, on the other hand, usually backfires, as polyglot touts can perform in nearly any language.

Aside from the hustling, there are touts who lie and misinform to divert travellers to hotels for which they get a commission.

If you do get stung, or feel you might crack at the next 'Excuse me, where are you from?', take a deep breath and put it in perspective: Cairene traders so completely fleeced the king of Mali, who arrived in the 14th century with a vast amount of gold, on pilgrimage to Mecca, that he had to borrow money to get home. Today's touts aren't picking on you because you look like a soft target – they're doing it because it's their job. Your angry tirade won't halt centuries of sales tradition. But it could offend an honest Egyptian who just wants to help.

New Year's Day (1 January) Official national holiday, but many businesses stay open.

Coptic Christmas (7 January) Most government offices and all Coptic businesses close.

January 25 Revolution Day

Sham An Nessim (March/April) On the first Monday after Coptic Easter, this tradition with Pharaonic roots is celebrated by all Egyptians, with family picnics. Few businesses close, however.

Sinai Liberation Day (25 April) Celebrating Israel's return of the peninsula in 1982.

May Day (1 May) Labour Day

Revolution Day (23 July) Date of the 1952 coup, when the Free Officers seized power from the monarchy.

Armed Forces Day (6 October) Celebrates Egyptian successes during the 1973 war with Israel, with some military pomp.

Safe Travel

The incidence of crime, violent or otherwise, in Egypt is negligible compared with many Western countries, and you're generally safe walking around day or night. There has been a spike in petty crime since 2011, though it is statistically still quite rare for tourists to become involved and is easily avoided.

Since 2011 bag and wallet snatchings have been on the rise, usually as drive-bys on mopeds, though very occasionally at knife- or gunpoint. Don't let this deter you: you're still more likely to lose your wallet in Barcelona – and more likely to have your lost wallet returned to you in Cairo. To be safe, carry your bag across your body or at least on the side away from the street, and keep it looped around a chair leg in restaurants. Don't walk on empty streets past 1am or 2am. Be aware of your surroundings when you take your wallet out, and don't go to an ATM alone at night.

Minefields

There are still unexploded landmines left over from WWII, around El Alamein and elsewhere along the Mediterranean and Red Sea coasts. There are usually danger signs and the areas ought to be closed off. If in doubt, consult a local.

Shopping

The best shopping in Egypt is usually done away from the tourist zones. Encouraged by the government ban on some imports, shop owners are increasingly commissioning stylish home items from traditional artisans, with some beautiful results. Look out for traditional Siwan, Bedouin and Nubian handicrafts such as embroidery.

The undisputed shopping capital is Cairo's medieval souq, **Khan Al Khalili** (Map p77; off Sharia Al Azhar & Al Gamaliyya, Islamic Cairo), which is just as much a tourist circus as it is one of the Middle East's most storied markets. There are some treasures to be had, assuming you have the time (and the patience), but beware trying to leave Egypt with an antique or antiquity in your bag. Increasingly, fixed-price shops elsewhere in Cairo stock familiar Egyptian crafts, often with better quality than you'd find in the souq.

Appliqué & Fabric

Embroidered cloth in intricate patterns and scenes is available as pillow cases, bedspreads and wall hangings. Stitches should be small and barely visible. Printed fabric used for tents is inexpensive when sold by the meter (about LE20) and a bit more if worked into a tablecloth.

Gold & Silver

A gold cartouche with a name in hieroglyphics is a popular gift, as is a silver pendant with a name in Arabic. Gold and silver are sold by weight. Check the international market price before you buy, then add in a bit extra for work.

Inlay

Wood boxes and other items are inlaid with mother of pearl and bone in intricate patterns. Surfaces should be smooth and not gummed with glue. An inlaid backgammon set, with pieces, should cost about LE300.

Muski Glass

This bubble-shot glass in blue, green and brown is made from recycled bottles and fashioned into cups and other home items. It's extremely fragile, so pack it well.

Papyrus

Papyrus dealers are as ubiquitous as perfume shops, and this Egyptian invention makes an easy-to-carry souvenir. True papyrus is heavy and difficult to tear; it should not feel delicate, and veins should be visible when it is held up to the light. Good artwork should be hand-painted, not stamped. A small painting on faux papyrus (made from banana leaves or paper printed in China) can go for just LE10; a good-quality piece can easily be 10 times as much.

THE ART OF BARGAINING

Haggling is part of everyday life. It's essentially a kind of scaled pricing: it can be a discount for people who have more time than money, but if your time is too valuable to discuss a transaction over tea, then you're expected to pay more. Your relative affluence of course factors into the calculations as well.

Shopping this way can seem like a hassle, but it can be fun (as long as it's considered a game, not a fight). The basic procedure:

➡ Shop around and check fixed-price stores to get an idea of the upper limit.

➡ Decide how much you would be happy to pay.

➡ Express a casual interest and ask the vendor the price.

From here, it's up to your own style. The steeliest hagglers start with well below half the starting price, pointing out flaws or quoting a competitor's price. A properly theatrical salesman will respond with indignant shouting or a wounded cry, but it's all bluster. We know one shopper who closed deals in less than five minutes by citing her intense gastrointestinal distress – although unfortunately this was not bluster on her part.

A gentler tactic is to start out just a bit lower than the price you had in mind, or suggest other items in the shop that might be thrown in to sweeten the deal. Resist the vendor's attempts to provoke guilt – he will never sell below cost. If you reach an impasse, relax and drink the tea that's perpetually on offer – or simply walk out, which might close the deal in your favour.

You're never under any obligation to buy – but you should never initiate bargaining on an item you don't actually want, and you shouldn't back out of an agreed-upon price. The 'best' price isn't necessarily the cheapest – it's the one that both you and the seller are happy with. Remember that LE5 or LE10 makes virtually no difference in your budget, and years from now, you won't remember what you paid – but you will have your souvenir of Egypt, and a good story of how you got it.

Perfume

You can't escape Egypt without visiting an essential-oils dealer. Most are less than essential, being diluted with vegetable oil. Be sceptical if a salesman drips more than a tiny drop on your arm and then rubs furiously. And watch when your bottles are packed up – make sure they're filled from the stock you sampled. Lotus (sawsan) and jasmine (full) are the most distinctively Egyptian scents.

Spices

Spices are a good buy, particularly kuzbara (coriander), kamoon (cumin), shatta (chilli), filfil iswid (black pepper) and karkadai (hibiscus). Buy whole spices, never ground, for freshness, and skip the 'saffron' – it's really safflower and tastes of little more than dust. The shops that sell these items (attareen) also deal in henna, soaps and herbal treatments. The best are neighbourhood dealers, not in tourist zones.

Telephone

Egypt Country Code	📞20
International Access Code From Egypt	📞00
Directory Assistance	📞140 or 📞141

When calling an Egyptian number from outside Egypt, leave off the area code's initial zero.

Mobile Phones

Egypt's GSM network (on the 900MHz/1800MHz band) has thorough coverage, at least in urban areas. SIM cards from any of the three carriers (Vodafone, the largest; Mobinil; Etisalat) cost LE15. You can buy them as well as top-up cards from most kiosks, where you may be asked to show your passport. For pay-as-you-go data service (about LE5 per day or LE50 per month), register at a company phone shop.

Time

Egypt is two hours ahead of GMT/UTC.

Egypt does observe Daylight Saving Time, but the clocks are turned back an hour during Ramadan, if it falls in the summer, to cut the day short for observers.

Toilets

➡ Few official public toilets exist, but it's acceptable to use one in a restaurant or hotel even if you're not a customer.

➡ Toilet paper is seldom in stalls – an attendant may provide it as you enter, for a tip.

➡ Do not flush paper – deposit it in the bin next to the toilet.

➡ Many toilets have an integrated bidet tube, which unfortunately can get quite mucky. The knob for the bidet is usually to the right of the toilet tank – open it very slowly to gauge the pressure.

➡ Some toilets are of the 'squat' variety – use the hose (and bucket, if provided) to 'flush' and to wash your hands.

➡ In cities it's a good idea to make a mental note of all Western-style fast-food joints and five-star hotels, as these are where you'll find the most sanitary facilities.

➡ When you're trekking in the desert or camping on a beach, either pack out your toilet paper or burn it. Do not bury it – it will eventually be revealed by the wind.

Tourist Information

The Egyptian Tourist Authority (www.egypt.travel) has offices throughout the country and its website has magazine-type features, news and a huge range of resources and links. Individual office staff members may be helpful, but often they're just doling out rather dated maps and brochures. The smaller towns and oases tend to have better offices than the big cities. In short, don't rely on these tourist offices, but don't rule them out either.

The State Information Service (www.sis.gov.eg) website provides information on everything from geography to the economy.

Travellers with Disabilities

Although there are an estimated 10 million Egyptians with special needs, the country is not well equipped for travellers with mobility constraints. Ramps are few, public facilities don't necessarily have lifts, curbs are high (except in Alexandria, which has wheelchair-friendly sidewalks) and traffic is lethal. Gaining entrance to some of the ancient sites – such as the Pyramids of Giza or the tombs on the West Bank near Luxor – is all but impossible because of narrow entrances and steep stairs.

Despite all this, there is no reason why intrepid travellers with disabilities shouldn't visit Egypt. In general you'll find locals willing to assist with any difficulties. Anyone with a wheelchair can take advantage of the large hatchback Peugeot 504s that are often used as taxis (though they're rarer in Cairo now). One of these, together with a driver, can be hired for the day. Chances are the driver will be happy to help you in and out of the vehicle. For getting

---

MOBILE PHONE NUMBERS IN EGYPT

All mobile phone numbers have had 11 digits, beginning with 01, since October 2011, although you may still see old-format numbers in print. Use this table to determine the extra digit:

OLD PREFIX	NEW PREFIX
📞010	📞0100
📞011	📞0111
📞012	📞0122
📞014	📞0114
📞016	📞0106
📞📞017	📞0127
📞018	📞0128
📞019	📞0109

around the country, most places can be reached via comfortable internal flights. In June 2017 the transport minister announced a new initiative making wheelchairs available at some railway and metro stations.

Opportunities for travel will improve as the new initiative by Helm (www.helm egypt.org) expands: called Entaleq (https://entaleq. helmegypt.org/en) at the time of writing, it provides an online database and phone app of 500 hotels, restaurants and other facilities and activities that are accessible.

The following businesses in Egypt make a special effort:

El Nakhil Hotel (Map p186; ☑012-2382-1007, 095-231-3922; www.elnakhil.com; Al Gozira; s/d/tr €25/35/45; ❄🛜) Nestled in a palm grove, the Nakhil or 'Palm Tree' is on the edge of Al Gezira on Luxor's west bank. This resort-style hotel has three rooms that can cater for disabled guests.

Flats in Luxor (☑010-0356-4540; www.flatsinluxor.co.uk; per night from US$50; ❄🌐🛜) Has been working with Helm to make two of their flats accessible to people with disabilities.

Camel Hotel (Map p385; ☑069-360-0700; www.cameldive.com; King of Bahrain St, Na'ama Bay; s €36-42, d €42-48, tr €56-63; ❄🛜🏊) Specific poolside accommodation and other facilities for divers with disabilities.

Egypt for All (☑012-2657-7774; www.egyptforall.com) Agency specialised in making travel arrangements for mobility-impaired visitors, from day trips to complete Egypt tours.

Visas

Visas are required for all foreigners visiting Egypt, excepting nationals of certain Arab countries. About 40 nationalities, including citizens of Australia, Canada, the EU, Japan and the US, can purchase a visa online (www.egyptvisa.com) in advance;

otherwise, visas are available on arrival.

➡ Tourist visas cost US$25 and are valid for 30 days.

➡ The visa can be purchased in US dollars, euros or British pounds.

➡ If you want more time or a multiple-entry visa, apply in advance or get an extension with multiple-entry once in Egypt.

➡ Visa extensions used to be routine, but are now subject to scrutiny, especially after repeat extensions. Be polite and say you need more time to appreciate the wonders of Egypt.

➡ There is a 14-day grace period for extension applications, with a LE100 late fee. If you leave during this time, you must pay an LE135 fine at the airport

➡ On arrival at Cairo and Egypt's other international airports, visa stickers are sold at a row of bank booths

in every arrivals terminal. Purchase the visa sticker at the booth and then present it along with your arrival form and passport at the immigration desks.

➡ If you are entering Egypt through Sinai (at Sharm El Sheikh Airport or at Taba), and are not leaving the South Sinai area (between Sharm El Sheikh and Taba, including St Katherine's Monastery but not Ras Mohammed National Park), you do not require a visa and can be issued with a free Sinai-only entry stamp, good for a 15-day stay.

➡ If you are arriving by ferry from Jordan into Nuweiba, visas are available at Nuweiba port. You can also apply in advance online or at the Egyptian Consulate in Aqaba.

➡ Entering from Eilat in Israel, through the Taba land border, the free Sinai-only entry stamp is normally issued. Full Egyptian visas

---

VISA EXTENSIONS: WHERE TO GO

Wherever you apply for a visa extension, you'll need one photo and two copies each of your passport's data page and the visa page. The fee depends on where you apply, but it's no more than LE15. Re-entry visa stamps (allowing you multiple re-entries) can be purchased at the same time and cost around LE61.

Alexandria (Map p318; ☑03-482-7873; 2nd fl, 25 Sharia Talaat Harb; ⊙8.30am-2pm Mon-Thu, from 10am Fri, 9am-11am Sat & Sun) Go to counter eight on the 2nd floor.

Aswan (Map p241; ☑097-231-2238; 1st fl, Police Bldg, Corniche An Nil; ⊙8am-2pm & 6-8pm Sun-Thu)

Cairo, Agouza (Map p94; ☑3338-4226; El Shorta Tower, Sharia Nawal; ⊙8am-1.30pm Sat-Wed) For Giza addresses only: go to window 4, 2nd floor.

Cairo, Downtown (Passport Office; Map p62; Mogamma Bldg, Midan Tahrir; ⊙8am-1.30pm Sat-Wed) Head to the 1st floor, get a form from the hallway table manned by police officers, have your form signed at window 12, then get stamps from window 43 and file all back at window 12; next-day pickup is at window 38.

Luxor (Map p186; ☑095-238-0885; Sharia Khaled Ibn Al Walid; ⊙8am-2pm Sat-Thu)

Minya (Map p166; ☑086-236-4193; 2nd fl, above main post office, off Sharia Corniche An Nil; ⊙8.30am-2pm Sat-Thu)

are available but you will have to pay an extra US$10 fee for a local Taba travel agency to guarantee the visa. The process can be long-winded. Alternatively, apply online in advance, or at the Egyptian Embassy in Tel Aviv or the consulate in Eilat.

➡ If you have entered at Taba or Sharm El Sheikh and have been issued the free Sinai-only entry stamp but decide that you'd like to travel onward into the rest of Egypt, you can purchase Egyptian tourist visas at Sharm El Sheikh Airport. You can also pay a fee for a travel agent in Sharm El Sheikh to go to the airport and purchase it for you.

Volunteering

An online search will reveal many opportunities to volunteer both formally and informally in Egypt. In the current political climate, it is important to ensure that the organisation you volunteer for is licensed and that you have entered the country on the correct visa. If you enjoy animals, **ACE** (Animal Care in Egypt; ☎095-928-0727; www. ace-egypt.org.uk; at the start of Sharia Al Habil, near traffic police; by donation; ☺8am-noon & 1-5pm) is usually looking for help.

Work

Many foreign firms operate in Egypt and hire foreigners, but you must typically be hired before arriving in the country, to have your work visa arranged properly. Consult *Cairo: The Practical Guide* (AUC Press), edited by Claire E Francy and Lesley Lababidi, for possible avenues.

Bars & Hotels

In Sharm El Sheikh and other Red Sea resorts, travellers can often find short-term work as bartenders or hotel workers. Masseurs and others with spa skills are also in demand. Most of this work is under the table and is often short-term, due to employers' tax concerns.

Diving

If you are a dive master or diving instructor you can find work in Egypt's resorts fairly easily. Owners also look for language and social skills.

Teaching English

The best-paying schools require at least a Certificate in English Language Teaching to Adults (CELTA), but there are other, more informal outlets as well. Cairo's ILI is one of the better schools, and offers CELTA training as well.

Transport

GETTING THERE & AWAY

Entering the Country

If you are entering or leaving Egypt as a tourist through the international airports, procedures are typically speedy, no questions asked. By land or sea, the process is similar, though it is usually slower and more chaotic.

If you are crossing a land border with your own vehicle or arriving on your own boat, prepare for a lengthy spell with immigration and customs officials.

E-visas can now be purchased before arrival from the official government site www.egyptvisa.com.

Passport

➡ Your passport must be valid for at least eight months from your date of entry.

➡ Israeli stamps in your passport (and Israeli passports, for that matter) present no problem, unlike in some other Middle Eastern countries.

Air

Egypt is well connected to the region and the rest of the world by air.

Airports & Airlines

Cairo International Airport (flight info phoning from landline ☑0900 77777, flight info phoning from mobile ☑27777; www.cairo-airport.com; ☎) Egypt's main entry point, served by most international carriers.

Burg Al Arab Airport (☑03-459-1484; http://borg-el-arab.airport-authority.com) Alexandria's airport mostly receives flights from Middle Eastern and North African cities.

Hurghada Airport (Map p358; ☑065-346-2722; Main Hwy) Receives mainly charter international flights.

Luxor Airport (☑095-232-4455) Has very few international direct flights; EgyptAir flies direct from London Heathrow.

Marsa Alam Airport (☑065-370-0029; www.portghalib.com/airport; 60km north of Marsa Alam) Served by a handful of charter flights from European destinations.

Sharm El Sheikh International Airport (Map p38; ☑069-362-3304; www.sharm-el-sheikh.airport-authority.com; Peace Rd) Historically an excellent Egypt entry point for travellers looking for low-cost fares, and served by a number of European budget airlines. Since the 2015 Metrojet Flight 9268 disaster, most direct international services have been suspended. Improved security arrangements should change this situation.

EgyptAir (www.egyptair.com.eg) is the national carrier and a member of Star Alliance. Ticket prices are usually exceptionally good value. No alcohol is served on flights. Its international fleet is in good shape and air marshals are present on every flight. The 2016 hijacking incident (when an EgyptAir flight was re-routed to Cyprus, with all hostages eventually released unharmed) and the crash of EgyptAir Flight 804 en route from Paris to Cairo (which resulted in the deaths of all 66 passengers and crew) have brought the company's safety and security record into question.

Land

Israel & the Palestinian Territories

RAFAH

The border crossing to the Gaza Strip opens only intermittently. Foreign travellers cannot cross at this border.

TABA

The Taba border is the main entry/exit point between Egypt and Israel. Technically, only the free Sinai-only entry stamp is issued here and full Egyptian visas have to be bought in advance. In reality, a full Egyptian visa can be purchased here after paying an extra fee to a local Taba travel agency. The introduction of Egypt e-visas in late 2017 means it's much easier to buy one online beforehand. Departure tax from Israel is 101NIS. Departure tax from Egypt is LE75. Entry procedures can be slightly shambolic on the Egyptian side.

Libya

The Amsaad border crossing is officially open, but because of the security situation, travel to Libya is not recommended.

Sudan

The two land border crossings between Egypt and Sudan reopened in 2014 and a number of Sudanese bus companies now operate Aswan–Wadi Halfa–Khartoum services. The Argeen crossing, on the west bank, is rarely used. The Qustul border crossing, on the east bank, is the most commonly used.

From Aswan, buses drive to Abu Simbel and cross Lake Nasser on a vehicle ferry (one hour) to Qustul, from where it's a short drive (15 minutes) to the border. Be prepared for plenty of hurry-up-and-wait; travellers who have used this route in both directions report long waits (up to five hours) and chaotic proceedings on both the Egyptian and Sudanese side of the border. After all border for-

PORT TAX

All Egyptian international ferries charge LE50 port tax per person on top of the ticket price.

malities are finalised the bus carries on to Wadi Halfa and then onwards to Khartoum.

If travelling to Sudan, you need to purchase your Sudanese visa beforehand in either Cairo or Aswan. Travelling north from Sudan into Egypt, Egyptian visas are issued at the border. Egyptian departure tax is LE50.

Sea

Europe

With no passenger ferries to Europe operating out of Egyptian ports, African-overlanders with vehicles only have the option of Ro-Ro (roll-on, roll-off) freighter services.

At the time of research, both Grimaldi (www.grimaldi.napoli.it) and Van Uden Shipping (www.vanudenshipping.com) were operating a weekly Ro-Ro service to Limassol in Cyprus from Alexandria's port.

The freighter service situation changes rapidly. In Egypt one of the best in-country contacts for up-to-date information on operating Ro-Ro services is **Kadmar** (☑066-334-4016; www.kadmar.com), which can also help you organise reservations on ships.

Jordan

AB Maritime (www.abmaritime.com.jo) runs both a daily fast and slow passenger ferry connecting Nuweiba in Egypt and Aqaba in Jordan. The service is noted for its delays. Both Egyptian and Jordanian visas are available on arrival.

Saudi Arabia

Ferries run from Hurghada in Egypt to Duba in Saudi Arabia, though they follow erratic schedules, which fluctuate according to work and hajj (pilgrimage) seasons. There is also a service from Safaga. Note that tourist visas are not available for Saudi Arabia, though there is an elusive tourist transit visa,

which you must apply for well in advance.

Sudan

The Nile River Valley Transport Corporation operates twice-weekly from Aswan to Wadi Halfa. Tickets (1st/2nd class LE350/250) can be bought a week ahead either in **Cairo** (☑02-2575-9058, 02-2578-9256; Ramses Train Station, Downtown) or **Aswan** (Map p241; ☑097-578-9256, 011-2709-2709, 097-244-0384; ⊗8am-2pm Sat-Thu). You must show a valid Sudanese visa in your passport.

The trip is slow, taking up to 24 hours; tea, soft drinks and snacks are available. Boarding is usually announced for 10am, but it's a good idea to arrive at about 8.30am to clear customs and get a decent seat. The ferry might not leave until sometime in the afternoon, depending on how much there is to load. Some Sudanese immigration formalities are carried out on the boat, including checking yellow-fever certificates. The return trip departs from Wadi Halfa on Wednesday.

Tours

The majority of visitors see Egypt on an organised tour. The schedules on such trips are usually fairly tight, leaving little room to explore on your own. However, a tour often comes with excellent guides, and a group can insulate you from some of the day-to-day hassle and sales pressure that independent travellers receive.

Abercrombie & Kent (www.abercrombiekent.co.uk) First-class packages, including on the Sanctuary Nile cruisers.

Bestway Tours & Safaris (www.bestway.com) Small-group tours, often combining Egypt with neighbouring countries.

Djed Travel (www.djedegypt.com) An independent Dutch-Egyptian outfit which offers tailor-made tours. They also own **Sofra Restaurant & Café** (Map p186; ☎095-235-9752; www.sofra.com.eg; 90 Sharia Mohammed Farid) in Luxor and several dahabiyyas on the Nile.

Kuoni (www.kuoni.co.uk) One of the bigger tour operators.

Intrepid Travel (www.intrepid travel.com) Emphasis on responsible tourism.

On the Go (www.egyptonthego.com) PADI diving-course holidays.

Wind, Sand & Stars (www.windsandstars.co.uk) A Sinai specialist with desert excursions and retreats.

GETTING AROUND

Air

EgyptAir is the main domestic carrier. Nile Air also flies between Cairo and the main centres, though it has fewer services. Fares for both

airlines can be surprisingly cheap. Domestic one-way fares on EgyptAir start from LE650.

For the best prices when booking domestic flights using EgyptAir's website, always change your home location (at the top of the webpage) to Egypt. Prices will then show up in Egyptian pounds, and they are often half what the same flight costs when using the website with a home location outside of Egypt.

Bicycle

Cycle tourism is rare because of long distances plus intense heat. Winter can be manageable, but even in spring and autumn it's necessary to make an early-morning start and finish by early afternoon. And yet... President Sisi is keen to encourage two-wheel transport and has been seen pedalling his way around the capital (once, at least).

Carry a full kit, as spares are hard to come by, although in a pinch Egyptians are excellent 'bush mechanics'.

The Cairo-based club Cycle Egypt (www.cycle-egypt.com), and its very active Facebook group, is a good starting point for making local contacts and getting advice on shops and gear.

Boat

No trip to Egypt is complete without a trip down the Nile River. There are plenty of cruise ships plying between Aswan and Luxor, ranging from midrange to five-star luxury experiences. The main centre for organising and beginning multiday felucca (Egyptian sailing boat) trips is Aswan.

La Pespes (www.lapespes.com) runs a high-speed catamaran ferry service three times per week between Sharm El Sheikh and Hurghada.

Domestic Flights

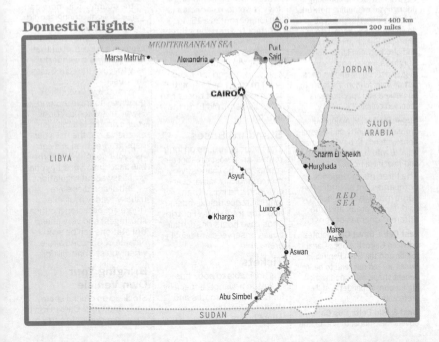

CLIMATE CHANGE & TRAVEL

Every form of transport that relies on carbon-based fuel generates CO_2, the main cause of human-induced climate change. Modern travel is dependent on aeroplanes, which might use less fuel per kilometre per person than most cars but travel much greater distances. The altitude at which aircraft emit gases (including CO_2) and particles also contributes to their climate change impact. Many websites offer 'carbon calculators' that allow people to estimate the carbon emissions generated by their journey and, for those who wish to do so, to offset the impact of the greenhouse gases emitted with contributions to portfolios of climate-friendly initiatives throughout the world. Lonely Planet offsets the carbon footprint of all staff and author travel.

Bus

You can get to most cities, towns and villages in Egypt on a bus, at a very reasonable price. For many long-distance routes beyond the Nile Valley, it's the best option, and sometimes the only one. Buses aren't necessarily fast though, and if you're going to or from Cairo, you'll lose at least an hour just in city traffic. Delays are common, especially later in the day as schedules get backed up.

Companies

Go Bus (www.gobus-eg.com) Egypt's newest bus company operates an expanding network of routes in northern Egypt, down the Red Sea coast, to Sharm El Sheikh and Dahab, and also between Luxor and Hurghada. Ticket prices vary hugely depending on bus class but all have air-con. Tickets can be booked and specific seats reserved online.

Super Jet Serves major routes around the country and internationally; tends to be efficient and reliable with comfortable seats and freezing air-con.

The three major regional companies are all under the same management, but cover different areas and offer different degrees of service:

East Delta Travel Co Operates between Cairo, the Suez Canal region and the Sinai Peninsula. Buses are old but tend to be in decent shape with good working air-con; Super Jet is still preferable.

West & Mid Delta Bus Co Covers Alexandria, the Delta, the Mediterranean Coast and Siwa. Buses, especially to Marsa Matruh and beyond, were showing substantially worse service, with chronic breakdowns, at the time of research.

Upper Egypt Bus Co Fairly serviceable buses cover most of the Western Desert oases and the Nile Valley, though for the latter destinations, the train is preferable.

Deluxe Buses

Air-con 'deluxe' buses connect main destinations throughout the country. Most have a strict no-smoking rule; some buses on long routes have toilets, though they're seldom very clean. On longer routes a 15- to 20-minute stop every three hours or so is the norm.

Videos are usually shown, often at top volume – earplugs are a good idea if you want to sleep, as is an extra layer, as overnight buses can often be very cold from the air-con.

Standard Buses

The cheapest buses on long routes, and most on shorter routes, can be markedly more uncomfortable, overcrowded and noisy than long-distance deluxe buses, and stop frequently. For trips under two hours or so, minibuses or servees are usually preferable.

Tickets

It is advisable to book bus tickets in advance, especially for Cairo–Sinai routes and Western Desert services where buses run infrequently. Hang on to your ticket until you get off as inspectors almost always board to check fares. You should always carry your passport as buses are often stopped at military checkpoints for random identity checks. This is particularly common on the bus between Aswan and Abu Simbel, and on all Sinai buses.

Car & Motorcycle

Proceed with caution. Driving in Cairo is a crazy affair, and although it's slightly less nerve-racking in other parts of the country, it is more dangerous. Night driving should be completely avoided. That being said, some intrepid readers have reported that self-driving is a wonderful way to leave the tour buses in the dust.

A motorcycle would be a good way to travel around Egypt, but you must bring your own, the red tape is extensive and the risks perhaps greater than in a car. Ask your country's automobile association and Egyptian embassy about regulations.

Petrol and diesel are usually readily available (there are occasional critical shortages) and very cheap. But stations can be scarce outside of Cairo. As a rule, when you see one, fill up.

Bringing Your Own Vehicle

Stock up on crucial spare parts and tyres. Cars in Egypt are also required to carry a fire extinguisher. Registration papers, liability insurance and an International Driving Permit, in addition to your domestic driving licence, are required.

Get multiple copies of a *carnet de passage en douane*. The *carnet* should also list any expensive spare parts you're carrying with you.

At the Egyptian border you'll be issued with a licence of the same duration as your visa. You can renew the licence, but you'll have to pay a varying fee each time. The customs charge is approximately US$200, plus another US$50 for number-plate insurance.

Driving Licence

An International Driving Permit is required to drive in Egypt, and you risk a heavy fine if you're caught without one. Likewise, ensure that you always have all car registration papers with you while driving.

Hire

Finding a cheap deal with local agencies is virtually impossible – it's advisable to make arrangements via the web before you arrive. Using international agencies is usually recommended. Read insurance terms carefully to see whether lower-quality roads are ruled out.

Road Rules

Driving is on the right-hand side. The speed limit outside towns is usually 70km/h to 90km/h, and 100km/h on major highways.

For traffic violations, the police will confiscate your driving licence and you must go to the traffic headquarters in the area to get it back.

Tolls are charged on the Cairo–Alexandria Desert Hwy, the Cairo–Fayoum road and the tunnel under the Suez Canal. Checkpoints are frequent. Be ready with identity papers and licence.

In cities, whoever is in front has the right of way,

even if it's only a matter of inches. In the countryside, keep an eye out for people and livestock wandering into the road.

Be aware of the risk of carjacking, particularly along the valley roads and at night.

If you have an accident, get to the nearest police station as quickly as possible and report what happened.

Note that because of security issues, foreign travellers are not allowed to use the Suez–Taba road, which runs across the middle of the Sinai Peninsula. You have to instead use the southern Sinai coastal route via Al Tor and Sharm El Sheikh.

Hitching

Hitching is never entirely safe in any country in the world, and it is certainly not recommended in Egypt. Travellers who decide to hitch should understand that they are taking a small but potentially serious risk. Those who do choose to hitch will be safer if they travel in pairs and let someone know where they are planning to go. Women should never hitch on their own in Egypt, as it's generally assumed that only prostitutes would do such a thing.

Local Transport

City Buses

Several of the biggest Egyptian cities have bus systems. Practically speaking, you might use them only in Cairo and Alexandria. They're not particularly visitor-friendly, as numbers are displayed only in Arabic numerals, the routes are unpublished and the buses themselves are often overcrowded to the point of record-breaking.

There's no orderly queue to board – in fact, quite the opposite – and the bus rarely rolls to a complete stop, whether you're getting on or off. If you do make it on, at some point a conductor will

manage to squeeze his way through to sell you your ticket.

Metro

Cairo is the only city in Egypt with a metro system.

Microbus

The microbus (pronounced 'meekrobas'), often also called a micro or a minibus, is a (usually Toyota) van with seats for 14 passengers. Privately owned and usually unmarked, they run along most of the same routes as buses and are a bit cheaper. They also stop anywhere along the route on request, and will pick up riders along the way if there's a free seat. There are certain parts of the country (the lower Nile valley, for instance) where foreigners are currently not allowed to use microbuses between towns.

Pick-up

Toyota and Chevrolet pick-up trucks cover some routes between smaller towns and villages off the main roads, especially where passengers might have cargo. A dozen or so people squeeze into the rear of the truck (covered or uncovered), often with goods squeezed in on the floor.

Covered pick-up trucks are also sometimes used within towns, similar to microbuses. This is especially so in some of the oases, on Luxor's west bank and in smaller places along the Nile. There are a couple of ways you can indicate to the driver that you want to get out: if you are lucky enough to have a seat, pound on the floor with your foot. Alternatively, ask one of the front passengers to hammer on the window behind the driver; or, last, use the buzzer that you'll occasionally find rigged up.

Servees

The servees (service taxi) is the predecessor to the microbus (minivan) and runs on the same principle: buy a seat, wait for the car to fill and you're off. These big Peugeot 504 station wagons, with seats for seven passengers, are now less common than the vans and are being phased out. As with microbuses, you might find them near bus and train stations, and you're welcome to buy extra seats for more space or just to speed along the departure.

Taxi

Even the smallest cities in Egypt have taxis. They're inexpensive and efficient, even if in some cities the cars themselves have seen better days.

Fares In Cairo metered taxis are taking over, but everywhere else, locals know the accepted price and pay it without (much) negotiation. Check with locals for taxi rates, as fares change as petrol prices rise.

Hailing Just step to the roadside, raise your hand and one will likely come screeching to a halt. Tell the driver where you're headed before getting in – he may decline the fare if there's bad traffic or it's too far.

Negotiating For short fares, setting a price beforehand backfires, as it reveals you don't know the system. But for long distances – from the airport to the city centre, for instance – you should agree on a price before getting in. And confirm it, as some drivers tend to try to change the deal on arrival.

Paying In unmetered taxis, avoid getting trapped in an argument by getting out first, then handing money through the window. If a driver suspects you don't know the correct fare, you'll get an aghast 'How could you possibly pay me so little?' look, if not a full-on argument. Don't be drawn in if you're sure of your position, but do remember that LE5 makes a far greater difference to your driver than it does to you.

Sharing You may be welcomed into a cab with a passenger, or your cab may stop to pick up others. If you're a man and don't mind sharing, sit in the front seat and leave the back free for others (it's considered a bit forward for women to sit in the front seat).

Tram

Cairo and Alexandria are the only two cities in the country with tram systems. While Alexandria still has a fairly extensive network, Cairo now only has a handful of lines.

Tuk-tuk

These clever scooters-with-seats, ubiquitous in Thailand and India, have arrived in Egypt. Locals call them *tok-tok* (turns out the onomatopoeia of their tiny engines works in Arabic too), and they're especially popular in small towns. They're typically the same price or cheaper than taxis (LE15, say, for a 15-minute ride), with a pounding *shaabi* (music of the working class) soundtrack for free. (Tuk-tuks are popular with young – sometimes too young! – drivers who like to customise their wheels with mega-speakers and other bling.) It's a good idea to negotiate a price before getting in.

Tours

Even if you haven't planned ahead with a full package tour, you can still leave the planning and transport to others for a few days of your trip. The most typical organised tour is a Nile cruise or felucca trip or a Western Desert safari. Most short tours are usually best planned with local agencies on-site, though there are some reliable Cairo-based agencies who can arrange your trip.

Egypt Panorama Tours (02-2359-0200; www.eptours.com; 6 Road 81, Ma'adi; private guides per day from US$60; 9am-5pm Sun-Thu) Just south of Ma'adi metro

THE MAN BEHIND THE WHEEL

Egyptian taxis are a blessing and a curse. They're remarkably convenient and affordable, but outside of Cairo, where reliable meters have yet to be introduced, they can be a frequent source of unpleasantness when it comes to paying the fare. Passengers frequently feel that they've been taken advantage of (which they often have), while drivers may be genuinely (as opposed to just theatrically) aggrieved by what they see as underpayment.

Bear in mind, driving a cab is far from lucrative. Average earnings after fuel has been paid for are rarely more than LE20 per hour. Many drivers don't own their car and have to hand over part of their earnings as 'rent'.

Which isn't to say that the next time you flag a taxi for a 10-block hop and the driver declares '10 pounds', you should smile and say 'OK'. But it might make it easier to see that it was probably worth his while trying. And if you talk to him and listen to his stories, you will likely get entertainment or enlightenment, as well as a ride, for the money.

station, this is one of the best-established agencies in town. It organises private guides, group day-tours of Cairo sights and longer itineraries as well as bookings for Nile and Lake Nasser cruises. It's also good for four- and five-star hotel deals.

Misr Travel (Map p62; 02-2396-4012, 02-3903-1977; www.misrtravel.net; 1 Sharia Talaat Harb, Downtown; 10am-6pm) The official Egyptian government travel agency, which also has offices in most of the luxury hotels.

International Travel Bureau of Egypt (Map p92; 02-3760-1370; www.facebook.com/itbe2016; apt 97, Orman Tower, 48 Sharia Al Giza, Doqqi; 9am-5pm) Reliable small travel agency, catering mostly to high-end clients looking for tailor-made tours.

Train

Egypt's British-founded rail system comprises more than 5000km of track connecting almost every major city and town (but not Sinai). The system is antiquated, cars are often grubby and battered, and there have been some major accidents recently, including a crash near Alexandria in August 2017 that left at least 41 dead and 179 injured. Aside from on two main routes (Cairo–Alexandria, and Cairo–Aswan, both of which have modern rolling stock), you have to be fond of trains to prefer them to a deluxe bus. But for destinations near Cairo, trains win because they don't get stuck in traffic.

For specific schedules, consult the Egyptian Railways (https://enr.gov.eg)

website, where you can also purchase tickets.

Classes

1st (darga ula) Preferable if you're going any distance. Air-con (takyeef), padded seats, relatively clean toilet, tea and snack service from a trolley.

2nd (darga tanya) Seats are battered vinyl. Skip air-con if it's an option – it often doesn't work well. Toilets aren't well kept.

3rd (darga talta) Grimy bench seats, glacial pace and crowds, but lots of activity and vendors. Be prepared for attention – you'll probably be the most exciting thing on the train.

Sleepers

Route The private company **Watania Sleeping Trains** (Map p119; 02-3748-9488; www.wataniasleepingtrains.com; Ramses Train Station, Midan Ramses, Downtown Cairo; 9am-8pm), also now known as Ernst, runs daily sleeper services from Cairo to Luxor and Aswan.

Tickets Reasonably priced, usually including two meals. Reservations must be made before 6pm the day of departure, but should really be done at least a few days ahead.

Compartments Spanish or German-built two-bed sleepers: seats convert to a bed, and an upper bunk folds down. Clean linen, pillows and blankets, plus a small basin with running water. Beds are a bit short. Middle compartments, away from doors, are quieter. Shared toilets are generally clean and have toilet paper. Air-con can get chilly at night.

Meals Serviceable airline-style dinners and breakfasts are served in the compartments. A steward serves drinks (some-

times including alcohol), and there's a club car.

Alexandria

The best trains on the Cairo–Alexandria route are speedy 'Special' trains. Almost all of them go direct, or with just one stop, in 2½ hours. 'Spanish' trains make more stops. Both have 1st class with air-con.

Marsa Matruh

For the summer holiday season, Watania runs a night sleeping-car train from Cairo to this Mediterranean resort town, three days a week from mid-June to mid-September.

Nile Delta

The rail system is most extensive in the agricultural region north of Cairo, as it was built to bring cotton to market. If you're headed anywhere in this area, train is ideal for speed and scenery, though the 1st-class services run only four or five times a day.

Other Upper Egypt Services

Day trains Security rules come and go, but at the time of writing tourists could ride all-day trains south of Cairo. The best is number 980, the express departing Cairo at 8am; it's an enjoyable 10½ hours to Luxor and 14 to Aswan, with views of lush plantations and villages along the way.

Night trains (nonsleepers) There are four-to-five night services to Luxor and Aswan daily. Seats recline, are comfortable enough to get a decent sleep in, and are far cheaper than the Watania Sleeper Train. The day trains, though, are much more scenic.

Language

Arabic is the official language of Egypt. Note that there are significant differences between the MSA (Modern Standard Arabic) – the official lingua franca of the Arab world, used in schools, administration and the media – and the colloquial language, ie the everyday spoken variety of a particular region. Of all the Arabic dialects, Egyptian Arabic (provided in this chapter) is probably the most familiar to all Arabic speakers, thanks to the popularity of Egyptian television and cinema.

Read our coloured pronunciation guides as if they were English and you'll be understood. Note that a is pronounced as in 'act', aa as in the 'a' in 'father', ai as in 'aisle', aw as in 'law', ay as in 'say', e as in 'bet', ee as in 'see', i as in 'hit', o as in 'pot', oo as in 'zoo', u as in 'put', gh is a guttural sound (like the Parisian French 'r'), r is rolled, kh is pronounced as the 'ch' in the Scottish *loch* and zh as the 's' in 'pleasure'. The apostrophe (') indicates the glottal stop (like the pause in the middle of 'uh-oh'). The stressed syllables are indicated with italics.

BASICS

Hello.	أهلا.	*ah·lan*
Goodbye.	مع السلامة.	*ma'* sa·*la*·ma
Yes./No.	لأ./أيوة.	*ai·wa/la'*
Please.	لو سماحت	law sa·*maht* (m)
	لو سمحتي	law sa·*mah*·tee (f)
Thank you.	شكرًا.	*shu*·kran
Excuse me.	عن إزنك.	*'an 'iz*·nak (m)
	عن إزنك.	*'an 'iz*·nik (f)

WANT MORE?

For in-depth language information and handy phrases, check out Lonely Planet's *Egyptian Arabic Phrasebook*. You'll find it at **shop.lonelyplanet.com**, or you can buy Lonely Planet's iPhone phrasebooks at the Apple App Store.

Sorry.	متأسف.	*mu·ta·'as·if* (m)
	متأسفة.	*mu·ta·'a·si·fa* (f)
How are you?		
	إزيّك؟/إزيّك؟	*iz·ay·ak/iz·ay·ik* (m/f)
Fine, thanks. And you?		
	كويّس./كويّسة	*kway·is/kway·is·a* (m/f)
	الحمدللّه؟	*il·am·du·li·lah*
What's your name?		
	إسمك أيه؟	*is·mak ay* (m)
	إسمك أيه؟	*is·mik ay* (f)
My name is ...		
	... إسمي	*is·mee* ...
Do you speak English?		
	بتتكلم/بتتكلمي	*bi·tit·ka·lim/bi·tit·ka·lim·ee*
	إنجليزي؟	*in·gi·lee·zee* (m/f)
I don't understand.		
	مش فاهم.	*mish fa·him* (m)
	مش فهمة.	*mish fah·ma* (f)
Can I take a photo?		
	ممكن أصوّر؟	*mum*·kin a·*saw*·ar

ACCOMMODATION

Where's a ...?	فين ...؟	*fayn* ...
campsite	المخيّم	il·mu·*khay*·am
guesthouse	البنسيون	il·ban·see·*yon*
hotel	الفندق	il·*fun*·du'
youth hostel	بيت شباب	bayt sha·*bab*
Do you have a ... room?	عندك/عندك	*'an*·dak/*'an*·dik
	أوضة ...؟	*o*·da ... (m/f)
single	لواحد	li·*wa*·hid
double	للإتنين	lil·it·*nayn*
twin	بسريرين	bi·si·ree·*rayn*
How much is it per ...?	بكم ...؟	bi kam ...
night	الليلة	il·*lay*·la
person	الشخس	i·*shakhs*

Can I get another (blanket)?
عايز/عايزة (بطنية) 'a·iz/'ai·za (ba·ta·nee·ya)
تنية من ta·nya min
.فضلك/فضلك fad·lak/fad·lik (m/f)

The (air conditioning) doesn't work.
(التكييف) مش شغال .(i·tak·yeef) mish sha·ghal

DIRECTIONS

Where's the ...? فين ...؟ fayn ...

bank البنك il·bank

market السوق is·soo'

post office البسطة il·bus·ta

Can you show me (on the map)?
ممكن تورّيني mum·kin ti·wa·ree·nee
على (الخريطة)؟ ('al il·kha·ree·ta)

What's the address?
العنوان أيه؟ il·'un·wan ay

Could you please write it down?
ممكن تكتبه؟ mum·kin tik·ti·booh (m)
ممكن تكتبه؟ mum·kin tik·ti·beeh (f)

How far is it?
كم كيلو من هنا؟ kam kee·lu min hi·na

How do I get there?
أروح إزّاي؟ a·ruh i·zay

Turn left.
.حود شمال haw·id shi·mal

Turn right.
.حود يمين haw·id yi·meen

It's ... ... هو hu·wa ... (m)
... هي hi·ya ... (f)

behind ... ... ورا wa·ra ...

in front of ... ... قدام 'u·dam ...

near to ... ... قريب من 'u·ray·ib min ...

next to ... ... جمب gamb ...

on the على 'a·lal
corner الناصية nas·ya

opposite ... ... قصاد 'u·saad ...

straight على طول 'a·la tool
ahead

EATING & DRINKING

Can you ممكن mum·kin
recommend تقترحلي/ tik·ti·rah·lee/
a ...? تقترحيلي ...؟ tik·ti·ra·hee·lee ... (m/f)

bar بار baar

cafe قهوة 'ah·wa

restaurant مطعم ma·ta'·am

I'd like a table (for four), please.
عايز/عايزة تربيزة 'a·iz/'ai·za ta·ra·bay·za
(لأربع من) (li·ar·ba') min
.فضلك/فضلك fad·lak/fad·lik (m/f)

QUESTION WORDS

When? إمتى؟

Where? فين؟

Who? مين؟ m

Why? ليه؟ lay

498

sparkline

LANGUAGE DIRECTIONS

What would you recommend?
تقترح أيه؟ tik·tar·ah ey

What's the local speciality?
الأطباق المحلية أيه؟ il at·baa' il ma·ha·lee·ya ay

Do you have vegetarian food?
عندك/عندك 'an·dak/'an·dik
أكل ناتي؟ akl na·ba·tee (m/f)

I'd like (the) عايز/عايزة 'a·iz/'ai·za
..., please. من ... ... min
.فضلك/فضلك fad·lak/fad·lik (m/f)

bill الحساب il·hi·sab

drink list لستة lis·tat
مشروبات mash·roo·bat

menu المنيو il men yu

that dish التبق ده il·ta·ba' da

Could you ممكن تعمل mum·kin ta'·mil
prepare a أكل من akl min
meal without ...? غير ...؟ ghayr ...

butter زبدة zib·da

eggs بيض bayd

meat شربة لحمة shor·bit lah·ma
stock

I'm allergic عندي 'an·dee
to ... حساسية لـ ha·sa·see·ya li ...

dairy produce الألبان al·ban

nuts مكسّرات mi·ka·sa·raat

seafood أسماك البحر as·mak il·bahr

coffee ... قهوة ... 'ah·wa ...

tea ... شاي ... shay ...

with milk مع لبن ma·'a la·ban

without بدون سكّر bi·doon su·kar
sugar

bottle/glass إزازة/كباية i·za·zit/ku·bay·it
of beer بيرة bee·ra

(orange) عصير 'as·eer
juice (برتقان) (bur·tu·'aan)

soft drink حاجة ساقعة ha·ga sa·'a

(mineral) ميّة ma·ya
water (معدنية) (ma·'da·nee·ya)

... wine ... نبيذ ni·beet ...

red أحمر ah·mar

	شمبانيا	sham·ban·ya
te	أبيض	ab·yad

EMERGENCIES

Help!	إلحقني!	il·ha'·nee
Go away!	إمشي!	im·shee

Call ...!	إتصل ب ...!	i·tas·al bi ...
a doctor	دكتور	duk·toor (m)
	دكتورة	duk·too·ra (f)
the police	البوليس	il·bu·lees

I'm lost.

أنا تايه. a·na tay·ih (m)
أنا تهت. a·na tuht (f)

Where are the toilets?

فين التواليت؟ fayn i·tu·wa·leet

I'm sick.

أنا عيّان. a·na ay·an (m)
أنا عيّانة. a·na ay·an·a (f)

It hurts here.

بيوجعني هنا bi·yiw·ga'·nee hi·na

I'm allergic to (antibiotics).

عندي حساسية 'an·dee ha·sa·see·ya
(من (مضاد حيوي). min (mu·daad ha·ya·wee)

SHOPPING & SERVICES

Where's a ...?	فين ...؟	fayn ...
department store	محل	ma·hal
grocery store	بقّال	ba·'al
newsagency	بايع جرايد	bay·aa' ga·ray·id
souvenir shop	محل تذكارات	ma·hal i·tiz·ka·raat
supermarket	سوبرماركت	soo·bir·mar·kit

I'm looking for ...

أنا بدوّر على ... a·na ba·daw·ar 'a·la ...

SIGNS

Entrance	مدخل
Exit	خروج
Open	مفتوح
Closed	مغلق
Information	إستعلامات
Prohibited	ممنوع
Toilets	دورة الميّة
Men	رجال
Women	سيّدات

Can I look at it?

ممكن أشوفه؟ mum·kin a·shoo·fuh (m)
ممكن أشوفها؟ mum·kin a·shoof·ha (f)

Do you have any others?

فيه تاني؟ fee ta·nee

It's faulty.

مش شغّال. mish sha·ghal

How much is it?

بكم؟ bi·kam

Can you write down the price?

ممكن تكتب/تكتبي mum·kin tik·tib/tik·ti·bee
الثمن؟ i·ta·man (m/f)

That's too expensive.

ده غالي قوي. da gha·lee 'aw·ee

What's your lowest price?

الاحسن سعر كم؟ il·ah·san si'r kam

There's a mistake in the bill.

فيه غلطة في الحساب. fee ghal·ta fil his·ab

Where's ...?	فين ...؟	fayn ...
a foreign exchange office	صرّاف	sa·raaf
an ATM	بنك شخصي	bank shakh·see

What's the exchange rate?

نسبة التحويل كم؟ nis·bit i·tah·weel kam

Where's the local internet cafe?

فين كفاي إنترنت؟ fayn ka·fay in·ter·net

How much is it per hour?

الساعة بكم؟ i·sa·'a bi·kam

Where's the nearest public phone?

فين الاقرب تليفون؟ fayn il a'·rab ti·li·fon

I'd like to buy a phonecard.

عايز/عايزة أشتري 'a·iz/'ai·za ash·ti·ri
كرت تليفون. kart ti·li·fon (m/f)

TIME & DATES

What time is it?

الساعة كم؟ is·sa·'a kam

It's (one) o'clock.

الساعة (واحدة). is·sa·'a (wa·hi·da)

It's (two) o'clock.

الساعة (إثنين). is·sa·'a (it·nayn)

Half past (two).

الساعة (إثنين) و نص. is·sa·'a (it·nayn) wi nus

At what time ...?

إمتى ...؟ im·ta ...

yesterday ...	إمبارح ...	im·ba·rih ...
tomorrow ...	بكرة ...	buk·ra ...
morning	الصبح	is·subh
afternoon	الظهر	ba'd·duhr
evening	بالليل	bi·layl

Monday	يوم الإثنين	yom il-it-*nayn*
Tuesday	يوم الثلاث	yom it-ta-*lat*
Wednesday	يوم الأربع	yom il-*ar*-ba'
Thursday	يوم الخميس	yom il-kha-*mees*
Friday	يوم الجمعة	yom il-*gu*-ma'
Saturday	يوم السبت	yom is-*sabt*
Sunday	يوم الحد	yom il-*had*

TRANSPORT

Is this the ... to (Aswan)?	إلى ... أسوان(؟)	... *i*-la (as-*waan*)
boat	دي المركب	dee il-*mar*-kib
bus	ده الأوتوبيس	da il-o-to-*bees*
plane	دي الطيّارة	dee i-ta-*yaa*-ra
train	ده القطر	da il-*atr*

What time's the ... bus?	أتوبيس ... الساعة كم؟	... o-to-*bees* i-*sa*-'a kam
first	الأول	il aw-il
last	الأخر	il á-khir
next	الثاني	i-ta-nee

One ... ticket (to Luxor), please.	تذكرة ... (للقصر)/من فضلك/فضلك	taz-*ka*-rit ... (li-*lu*'-sor) min fad-lak/ fad-lik (m/t)
one-way	ذهاب	zi-*hab*
return	عودة	'aw-da

How long does the trip take?
الرحلة هي كم ساعة؟ *ir*-ri-hla hee-ya kam sa-'a

Is it a direct route?
الطريق مباشر؟ it-taa-*ree*' mu-ba-shir

What station/stop is this?
المحطة دي إسمها/ il-ma-*ha*-ta di is-*ma*-ha/
الموقف ده إسمه إيه؟ il-*maw*-lf da is-*muh* ay

Please tell me when we get to (Minya).
من فضلك/فضلك min fad-lak/fad-lik
/ممكن تقولي mum-kin ti-'ul-ee/
تقوليلي لمّا ti-'ul-ee-lee la-ma
نوصل (المنيا)؟ nuw-sil (il-*min*-ya) (m/f)

How much is it to ...?
بكم إلى ...؟ bi-*kam* i-la ...

Please take me to ...
عايز/عايزة أروح ... 'a-iz/'ai-za a-ruh ...
من فضلك/فضلك. min fad-lak/fad-lik (m/f)

Please ...	... من فضلك / ... من فضلك	... min fad-lak ... (m) / ... min fad-lik ... (f)
stop here	وقّف هنا	wa-'if hi-na
wait here	إستنّى هنا	is-*ta*-na hi-na

NUMBERS

1	١	واحد	wa-hid
2	٢	إثنين	it-nayn
3	٣	ثلاثة	ta-la-ta
4	٤	أربعة	ar-ba'
5	٥	خمسة	kham-sa
6	٦	ستة	si-ta
7	٧	سبعة	sa-ba-'a
8	٨	ثمانية	ta-man-ya
9	٩	تسعة	ti-sa'-a
10	١٠	عشرة	'a-sha-ra
20	٢٠	عشرين	'ish-reen
30	٣٠	ثلائين	ta-laa-teen
40	٤٠	عربين	ar-ba-'een
50	٥٠	خمسين	kham-seen
60	٦٠	ستين	si-teen
70	٧٠	سبعين	sa-ba-'een
00	٨٠	نمين	ta-ma-neen
90	٩٠	تسعين	ti-sa-'een
100	١٠٠	مئة	mee-ya
1000	١٠٠٠	ألف	alf

Note that Arabic numerals, unlike letters, are read from left to right.

I'd like to hire a ...	عايز ... / عايرة ...	'a-iz a-'ag-ar ... (m) / 'ai-za a-'ag-ar ... (f)
4WD	جيب	zheeb
car	عربية	'a ra bee ya
with a driver	مع سواق	ma' sa-wa'
with air conditioning	بتكييف	bi-tak-*yeef*

How much for ... hire?	بكم لإجار ...؟	bi-*kam* li-'ig-aar ...
daily	يومي	yom-ee
weekly	أسبوعي	us-boo'-ee

Is this the road to (the Red Sea)?
ده الطريق da i-taa-*ree*'
للبحر الأحمر(؟) (lil-*bahr* il-ah-mar)

I need a mechanic.
محتاج/محتاجة mih-tag/mih-ta-ga
ميكانيكي. mi-ka-nee-kee (m/f)

I've run out of petrol.
البنزين خلص. il-ben-*zeen* khi-lis

I have a flat tyre.
الكاوتش نائم. il-ka-*witsh* nay-im

ARABIC ALPHABET

Arabic is written from right to left. The form of each letter changes depending on whether it's at the start, in the middle or at the end of a word or whether it stands alone.

Word-Final	Word-Medial	Word-Initial	Alone	Letter
ـا	ـا	ا	ا	alef'
ـب	ـبـ	بـ	ب	'ba
ـت	ـتـ	تـ	ت	'ta
ـث	ـثـ	ثـ	ث	'tha
ـج	ـجـ	جـ	ج	jeem
ـح	ـحـ	حـ	ح	'ha
ـخ	ـخـ	خـ	خ	'kha
ـد	ـد	د	د	daal
ـذ	ـذ	ذ	ذ	dhaal
ـر	ـر	ر	ر	'ra
ـز	ـز	ز	ز	'za
ـس	ـسـ	سـ	س	seen
ـش	ـشـ	شـ	ش	sheen
ـص	ـصـ	صـ	ص	saad
ـض	ـضـ	ضـ	ض	daad
ـط	ـطـ	طـ	ط	'ta
ـظ	ـظـ	ظـ	ظ	'dha
ـع	ـعـ	عـ	ع	ain'
ـغ	ـغـ	غـ	غ	ghain
ـف	ـفـ	فـ	ف	'fa
ـق	ـقـ	قـ	ق	kuf
ـك	ـكـ	كـ	ك	kaf
ـل	ـلـ	لـ	ل	lam
ـم	ـمـ	مـ	م	mim
ـن	ـنـ	نـ	ن	nun
ـه	ـهـ	هـ	ه	'ha
ـو	ـو	و	و	waw
ـي	ـيـ	يـ	ي	'ya
	ء			hamza
ـأ	ـىٔ ـؤ	أ	أ	a
ـأ	ـىٔ ـؤ	أ	أ	u
ـا	ـىٔ ـؤ	ا	ا	i
ـأ	ـىٔ ـؤ	أ	أ	' (glottal stop)
ـا	ـا	آ	آ	aa
ـو	ـؤ	أو	أو	oo
ـي	ـيـ	إي	إي	ee
ـوَ	ـوَ	أوَ	أوَ	aw
ـي	ـيـ	أي	أي	ay

GLOSSARY

(m) indicates masculine gender, (f) feminine gender and (pl) plural

abd – servant of

abeyya – woman's garment

abu – father, saint

ahwa – coffee, coffeehouse

ain – well, spring

al-jeel – a type of music characterised by a hand-clapping rhythm overlaid with a catchy vocal; literally 'the generation'

ba'al – grocer

bab – gate or door

baksheesh – alms, tip

baladi – local, rural

beit – house

bey – leader; term of respect

bir – spring, well

burg – tower

bustan – walled garden

calèche – horse-drawn carriage

caravanserai – merchants' inn; also called khan

centrale – telephone office

dahabiyya – houseboat

darb – track, street

deir – monastery, convent

domina – dominoes

eid – Islamic feast

emir – Islamic ruler, military commander or governor; literally 'prince'

fellaheen – (singular: fellah) peasant farmers or agricultural workers who make up the majority of Egypt's population; 'fellah' literally means ploughman or tiller of the soil

galabiyya – man's full-length robe

gebel – mountain

gezira – island

guinay – pound (currency)

hajj – pilgrimage to Mecca; all Muslims should make the journey at least once in their lifetime

hammam – bathhouse

hantour – horse-drawn carriage

Hejira – Islamic calendar; Mohammed's flight from Mecca to Medina in AD 622

ibn – son of

iconostasis – screen with doors and icons set in tiers, used in Eastern Christian churches

iftar – breaking the fast after sundown during the month of Ramadan

kershef – building material made of large chunks of salt mixed with rock and plastered in local clay

khamsin – a dry, hot wind from the Western Desert

khan – another name for a caravanserai

khanqah – Sufi monastery

khedive – Egyptian viceroy under Ottoman suzerainty

khwaga – foreigner

kuttab – Quranic school

madrassa – school, especially one associated with a mosque

mahattat – station

mammisi – birthhouse

maristan – hospital

mashrabiyya – ornate carved wooden panel or screen; a feature of Islamic architecture

mastaba – mudbrick structure in the shape of a bench above tombs, from which later pyramids developed; Arabic word for 'bench'

matar – airport

midan – town or city square

mihrab – niche in the wall of a mosque that indicates the direction of Mecca

minbar – pulpit in a mosque

Misr – Egypt (also means 'Cairo')

moulid – saints' festival

muezzin – mosque official who calls the faithful to prayer

mugzzabin – Sufi followers who participate in zikrs

muqarnas – stalactite-like decorative device forming tiers and made of stone or wood; used on arches and vaults

oud – a type of lute

piastre – Egyptian currency; one Egyptian pound consists of 100 piastres

qasr – castle or palace

Ramadan – the ninth month of the lunar Islamic calendar during which Muslims fast from sunrise to sunset

ras – headland

sabil – public drinking fountain

sandale – modified felucca

servees – service taxi

shaabi – popular music of the working class

sharia – road or street

sharm – bay

sheesha – water pipe

souq – market

speos – rock-cut tomb or chapel

Sufi – follower of any Islamic mystical order that emphasises dancing, chanting and trances to attain unity with God

tahtib – male dance performed with wooden staves

tarboosh – the hat known elsewhere as a fez

towla – backgammon

umm – mother of

wadi – desert watercourse, dry except in the rainy season

waha – oasis

wikala – another name for a caravanserai

zikr – long sessions of dancing, chanting and trances usually carried out by Sufi mugzzabin to achieve unity with God

Behind the Scenes

SEND US YOUR FEEDBACK

We love to hear from travellers – your comments keep us on our toes and help make our books better. Our well-travelled team reads every word on what you loved or loathed about this book. Although we cannot reply individually to your submissions, we always guarantee that your feedback goes straight to the appropriate authors, in time for the next edition. Each person who sends us information is thanked in the next edition – the most useful submissions are rewarded with a selection of digital PDF chapters.

Visit **lonelyplanet.com/contact** to submit your updates and suggestions or to ask for help. Our award-winning website also features inspirational travel stories, news and discussions.

Note: We may edit, reproduce and incorporate your comments in Lonely Planet products such as guidebooks, websites and digital products, so let us know if you don't want your comments reproduced or your name acknowledged. For a copy of our privacy policy visit lonelyplanet.com/privacy.

OUR READERS

Many thanks to the travellers who used the last edition and wrote to us with helpful hints, useful advice and interesting anecdotes: Alyssa Bivins, Melanie Etherton, Jascha de Ridder, Helen Ryan, Laura Watson and Simon Williams.

WRITER THANKS

Jessica Lee

Among the vast number of people who gave me handy tips, helped with information and dealt with weird and obscure queries, these folk especially deserve a huge *shukran*: Salama Abd Rabbo, Sameh Tawfek, Salah, Asmail, Hisham, Wadia, Ben, Aisha and Mohammed. Also, a big thanks to fellow writer Anthony and to fellow Egypt travellers Chris, Lou and Nat.

Anthony Sattin

Many people have helped create this book by providing assistance, information, tips for things to see and even directions when I took a wrong turn. Among them are: H.E. Khaled El- Enani and the staff at the Ministry of Antiquities; Mrs. Rasha Azaizi and staff at the Ministry of Tourism; Bahaa Gaber, Cecilia Udden, Mounir Neamatalla, Amr Khalil, Ghada Shahbender, Ahmed Shandawili, Selim Shawer, Wael Abed, Abdallah Baghi, Peter Wirth, Badr Abdalmoghny, Mohsen Abdelmonem, Galal, Zeina Aboukheir, Eleonore Kamir, Enrique Cansino, Mamdouh Sayed Khalifa.

ACKNOWLEDGEMENTS

Climate map data adapted from Peel MC, Finlayson BL & McMahon TA (2007) 'Updated World Map of the Köppen-Geiger Climate Classification', Hydrology and Earth System Sciences, 11, 1633-44.

Illustrations pp126–7, pp196–7 and pp404–5 by Javier Zarracina.

Cover photograph: Hieroglyphs on a mummy, Egyptian Museum, Cairo, Jon Arnold/AWL ©.

THIS BOOK

This 13th edition of Lonely Planet's *Egypt* guidebook was researched and written by Jessica Lee and Anthony Sattin. Dr Joann Fletcher co-authored the Ancient Egypt & Pharaohs chapter and other Pharaonic Egypt content. The previous edition was also written by Anthony Sattin and Jessica Lee. This guidebook was produced by the following:

Destination Editor
Lauren Keith

Product Editors Shona Gray, Elizabeth Jones

Senior Cartographer
Valentina Kremenchutskaya

Book Designer Jessica Rose

Assisting Editors Carly Hall, Jennifer Hattam, Gabby Innes, Chris Pitts, Alison Ridgway, Amanda Williamson

Assisting Cartographer
James Leversha

Cover Researcher
Naomi Parker

Thanks to Karima Hassan Ragab, Kate James, Susan Paterson, Kirsten Rawlings, Jessica Ryan, Vicky Smith

Index

Map Legend

Sights
- Beach
- Bird Sanctuary
- Buddhist
- Castle/Palace
- Christian
- Confucian
- Hindu
- Islamic
- Jain
- Jewish
- Monument
- Museum/Gallery/Historic Building
- Ruin
- Shinto
- Sikh
- Taoist
- Winery/Vineyard
- Zoo/Wildlife Sanctuary
- Other Sight

Activities, Courses & Tours
- Bodysurfing
- Diving
- Canoeing/Kayaking
- Course/Tour
- Sento Hot Baths/Onsen
- Skiing
- Snorkelling
- Surfing
- Swimming/Pool
- Walking
- Windsurfing
- Other Activity

Sleeping
- Sleeping
- Camping
- Hut/Shelter

Eating
- Eating

Drinking & Nightlife
- Drinking & Nightlife
- Cafe

Entertainment
- Entertainment

Shopping
- Shopping

Information
- Bank
- Embassy/Consulate
- Hospital/Medical
- Internet
- Police
- Post Office
- Telephone
- Toilet
- Tourist Information
- Other Information

Geographic
- Beach
- Gate
- Hut/Shelter
- Lighthouse
- Lookout
- Mountain/Volcano
- Oasis
- Park
- Pass
- Picnic Area
- Waterfall

Population
- Capital (National)
- Capital (State/Province)
- City/Large Town
- Town/Village

Transport
- Airport
- Border crossing
- Bus
- Cable car/Funicular
- Cycling
- Ferry
- Metro station
- Monorail
- Parking
- Petrol station
- Subway station
- Taxi
- Train station/Railway
- Tram
- Underground station
- Other Transport

Routes
- Tollway
- Freeway
- Primary
- Secondary
- Tertiary
- Lane
- Unsealed road
- Road under construction
- Plaza/Mall
- Steps
- Tunnel
- Pedestrian overpass
- Walking Tour
- Walking Tour detour
- Path/Walking Trail

Boundaries
- International
- State/Province
- Disputed
- Regional/Suburb
- Marine Park
- Cliff
- Wall

Hydrography
- River, Creek
- Intermittent River
- Canal
- Water
- Dry/Salt/Intermittent Lake
- Reef

Areas
- Airport/Runway
- Beach/Desert
- Cemetery (Christian)
- Cemetery (Other)
- Glacier
- Mudflat
- Park/Forest
- Sight (Building)
- Sportsground
- Swamp/Mangrove

Note: Not all symbols displayed above appear on the maps in this book

OUR STORY

A beat-up old car, a few dollars in the pocket and a sense of adventure. In 1972 that's all Tony and Maureen Wheeler needed for the trip of a lifetime – across Europe and Asia overland to Australia. It took several months, and at the end – broke but inspired – they sat at their kitchen table writing and stapling together their first travel guide, *Across Asia on the Cheap*. Within a week they'd sold 1500 copies. Lonely Planet was born.

Today, Lonely Planet has offices in Franklin, London, Melbourne, Oakland, Dublin, Beijing and Delhi, with more than 600 staff and writers. We share Tony's belief that 'a great guidebook should do three things: inform, educate and amuse'.

OUR WRITERS

Jessica Lee

Cairo, Cairo Outskirts & the Delta, Sinai, Suez Canal

In 2011 Jessica swapped a career as an adventure-tour leader for travel writing and since then her travels for Lonely Planet have taken her across Africa, the Middle East and Asia. She has lived in the Middle East since 2007 and tweets @jessofarabia. Jess has contributed to Lonely Planet's *Egypt*, *Turkey*, *Cyprus*, *Morocco*, *Marrakesh*, *Middle East*, *Europe*, *Africa*, *Cambodia* and *Vietnam* guidebooks and her travel writing has appeared in *Wanderlust* magazine, the *Daily Telegraph*, the *Independent*, *BBC Travel* and lonelyplanet.com.

Anthony Sattin

Alexandria & the Mediterranean Coast, Luxor, Northern Nile Valley, Red Sea Coast, Siwa Oasis & the Western Desert, Southern Nile Valley

Anthony has been travelling around the Middle East for several decades and has lived in Cairo, as well as other cities in the region. His highly acclaimed books include *Lifting the Veil*, *A Winter on the Nile* and *The Gates of Africa*. His latest, *Young Lawrence*, looks at the five years TE Lawrence spent in the Middle East leading up to 1914. He happily spends several months each year along the Nile and is still looking for a plot where he can tread mud-bricks and build himself a house. He tweets about Egypt and travel @anthonysattin. Anthony also wrote the Plan, Understand and Survive chapters.

Contributing Writer

Professor Joann Fletcher contributed to the Ancient Egypt & Pharaohs chapter and several boxed texts. She has a PhD in Egyptology and is a research and teaching fellow at the University of York, where she teaches Egyptian archaeology and undertakes scientific research on everything from mummification to ancient perfumes. Joann regularly appears on TV, has contributed to the BBC History website and has written several books.

31901063576575

Published by Lonely Planet Global Limited
CRN 554153
13th edition – July 2018
ISBN 978 1 78657 573 9
© Lonely Planet 2018 Photographs © as indicated 2018
10 9 8 7 6 5 4 3 2 1
Printed in China